T0339572

Stress in Policing

Stress in policing remains a serious concern for individual officers, their families, their organizations and society at large. As an editor of the Psychological and Behavioural Aspects of Risk series, Ronald J. Burke brings together the latest research findings and intervention strategies, shown to be effective, by an international group of experts.

The contributors comprise of a group of high-profile researchers and writers who are experts in their respective fields. This edited collection addresses such issues as:

- The increased risk of international terrorism
- racial profiling
- police culture
- police integrity
- police suicide
- inadequate police training.

The work of police officers exposes them to sources of stress that increase several risks in terms of their psychological and physical health, their family relationships, physical injuries, emotional trauma and ambiguity about their roles in society. Shift work and undercover work add additional burdens to officers and their families. Police work also places risks on the communities in which officers serve, in terms of officers being inadequately trained to deal with mentally ill citizens.

Ronald J. Burke is Emeritus Professor of Organization Studies at Schulich School of Business, York University, Canada. He was Director of the PhD Program and Dean for Research. He was Founding Editor of the *Canadian Journal of Administrative Sciences* and has served on a number of editorial boards. He has published over 500 journal articles and edited or co-edited many books.

Psychological and Behavioural Aspects of Risk
Series editors: Cary L. Cooper and Ronald J. Burke

Risk management is an ongoing concern for modern organizations in terms of their finance, their people, their assets, their projects and their reputation. The majority of the processes and systems adopted are either very financially oriented or fundamentally mechanistic; often better suited to codifying and recording risk, rather than understanding and working with it. Risk is fundamentally a human construct; how we perceive and manage it is dictated by our attitude, behaviour and the environment or culture within which we work. Organizations that seek to mitigate, manage, transfer or exploit risk need to understand the psychological factors that dictate the response and behaviours of their employees, their high-flyers, their customers and their stakeholders.

This series, edited by two of the most influential writers and researchers on organizational behaviour and human psychology, explores the psychological and behavioural aspects of risk; the factors that:

- define our attitudes and response to risk
- important in understanding and managing 'risk managers'
- dictate risky behaviour in individuals at all levels.

Human Frailties
Wrong Choices on the Drive to Success
Edited by Ronald J. Burke, Suzy Fox and Cary L. Cooper

Creating Healthy Workplaces
Stress Reduction, Improved Well-being, and Organizational Effectiveness
Edited by Caroline Biron, Ronald J. Burke and Cary L. Cooper

Mental Illness in the Workplace
Psychological Disability Management
Henry G. Harder, Shannon Wagner and Josh Rash

Coping, Personality and the Workplace
Responding to Psychological Crisis and Critical Events
Edited by Alexander-Stamatios Antoniou and Cary L. Cooper

Stress in Policing
Sources, consequences and interventions
Edited by Ronald J. Burke

Stress in Policing

Sources, consequences and
interventions

Edited by Ronald J. Burke

Routledge
Taylor & Francis Group

LONDON AND NEW YORK

First published 2017 by Routledge

2 Park Square, Milton Park, Abingdon, Oxfordshire OX14 4RN

52 Vanderbilt Avenue, New York, NY 10017

Routledge is an imprint of the Taylor & Francis Group, an informa business

First issued in paperback 2019

British Library Cataloguing in Publication Data
A catalogue record for this book is available from the British Library

Library of Congress Cataloging in Publication Data
A catalog record for this book has been requested

ISBN: 978-1-4724-6163-6 (hbk)
ISBN: 978-0-367-88080-4 (pbk)

Typeset in Bembo
by Swales & Willis Ltd, Exeter, Devon, UK

Contents

Illustrations

Contributors

Amanda Allisey is a Senior Lecturer in the Deakin Business School and a collaborator of the Work Health and Well-being unit in the Deakin School of Population Health. She received her PhD in Organizational Behavior in 2012 and also holds undergraduate and postgraduate degrees in Psychology from Monash University. She specializes in translating research into best practice, with a particular emphasis on the development of effective leadership practices and designing healthy workplaces. She currently teaches People Management and Leadership in the MBA program. As an applied researcher, she has managed large projects focused on employee health and well-being. Her current focus is intervention projects that aim to enhance the well-being of workers through the development of positive organizational practices. She brings considerable expertise in job stress, positive mental health and well-being, organizational behavior, management education and leadership development as well as critical skills in developing, implementing and evaluating organizational interventions.

Mark H. Anshel is Professor Emeritus at Middle Tennessee State University in Murfreesboro, Tennessee (USA). Dr Anshel received a Bachelor of Science degree in education from Illinois State University, a Master of Arts degree from McGill University (Montreal) and a PhD from Florida State University in Performance Psychology. Dr Anshel has written 140 research articles, 22 of which concern coping with stress, published in scientific journals, and numerous books and book chapters in the areas of exercise psychology, coping with stress and sport psychology. His books include *Applied Health Fitness Psychology, Applied Exercise Psychology: A Practitioner's Guide to Improving Client Health and Fitness* (2006), and *Sport Psychology: From Theory to Practice* (5th edn). Dr Anshel has worked as a consultant for the Murfreesboro Police Department for six years in the areas of wellness and stress management. More recently, Dr Anshel has developed, validated (in several journal publications) and authored research articles and book chapters on the Disconnected Values Model.

Briana Barocas, PhD, is a Research Associate Professor at New York University's Silver School of Social Work and the Director of Research at New York University's Center on Violence and Recovery. Her interests in trauma, resiliency and recovery have led to research on first responders, individuals and families affected by domestic violence, and survivors of 9/11. She is committed to developing and researching programs and services that better the lives of individuals, families and communities. Her research has been supported by the National Institute of Justice, the National Science Foundation, the Department of Homeland Security and the Department of Defense.

Amanda Biggs is a Lecturer within the School of Applied Psychology at Griffith University, Australia. Amanda's research interests encompass the management of psychological and physical health at work including work engagement, stress, bullying healthy lifestyle behaviors and positive organizational cultures.

Paula Brough is a Professor of Organizational Psychology in the School of Applied Psychology, Griffith University, Australia. Paula's research focuses on occupational stress, coping, the psychological health of high-risk workers (e.g. emergency service workers), work–life balance and the effective measurement of psychological constructs. Paula has published over 80 books, journal articles and book chapters, and is the Chief Investigator for numerous national and international research grants.

Ronald J. Burke is Professor Emeritus of Organization Studies, Schulich School of Business, York University in Toronto. A Canadian, he received his PhD from the University of Michigan in Organizational Psychology. He is the editor or co-editor of 47 books, with five more due out within the next year, and he has published over 500 articles and book chapters and presented over 500 papers at academic conferences in several countries. Burke is a Fellow of the Canadian Psychological Association. The founding Editor of the *Canadian Journal of Administrative Sciences*, he has served on the editorial boards of over 20 journals. His current research interests include work and health, the sandwich generation, human frailties in the workplace and women in management. He has participated in numerous management development courses and consulted with both private- and public-sector organizations on human resource management issues

Satoris S. Culbertson is an Associate Professor in the management department in the College of Business Administration at Kansas State University. She received her BS degree in psychology and public relations from the University of Central Missouri, her MS degree in industrial and organizational (I/O) psychology from Missouri State University and her PhD in I/O psychology from Texas A&M University. Prior to joining Kansas State University, she worked as a consultant in the Chicago branch of a global leadership solutions consulting firm. Her main research interests include work–family issues, the employment interview, performance appraisal and feedback, and judgment and decision-making – areas in which she has authored and co-authored numerous journal articles and chapters in edited volumes.

Melchor D. de Guzman is a Professor of Criminal Justice and Criminology at Georgia Gwinnett College. He has a PhD in criminal justice from the University of Cincinnati. His research includes civilian reviews, community policing, police behaviour and policed organizations/management, social media, and terrorism. Prior to joining the academy, he served in the legislative and executive branches of the Philippine government. He is the lead editor of two books and is currently revising the book, *Police Community Relations and the Administration of Justice* with Ronald D. Hunter and Thomas Barker.

Danielle Emery, MPA, is the Director of Programs at New York University's Center on Violence and Recovery, where she coordinates programming and education related to the Center's research, including conferences, training and community outreach. Her research and policy interests focus on the intersection of restorative justice with the criminal justice system, how alternative interventions can be used to reduce and prevent involvement with the criminal justice system, and how to help individuals, families and communities heal.

Charlotte Gill is Assistant Professor of Criminology, Law and Society and Deputy Director of the Center for Evidence-based Crime Policy at George Mason University. She holds degrees in criminology and law from the Universities of Pennsylvania and Cambridge and has over ten years' experience in applied experimental and quasi-experimental research. Her research interests include community-based crime prevention, community policing, place-based criminology, programme evaluation and research synthesis. Dr Gill is co-editor of the Campbell Collaboration Crime and Justice Group and a board member of the American Society of Criminology's division of Experimental Criminology. In 2012, she received the Academy of Experimental Criminology's Outstanding Young Scholar Award.

Christopher J. Harris is an Associate Professor in the School of Criminology and Justice Studies at the University of Massachusetts, Lowell, and received his PhD in Criminal Justice from the University of Albany, State University of New York. His research interests are primarily in police accountability and public perceptions of police, as well as evaluation research on police initiatives. He is the author of *Pathways of Police Misconduct* (2010) from Carolina Academic Press and his scholarship has appeared in *Crime and Delinquency, Criminal Justice and Behavior, Police Quarterly*, and other academic journals.

Kimberly D. Hassell (PhD University of Nebraska-Omaha, Crimnal Justice) is Associate Professor of Criminal Justice at the University of Wisconsin-Milwaukee. Her research interests include police organizational behaviour, police decision-making, police–community relations and women in policing. Her research has focused on studies of police behaviour, involving issues such as organizational culture, police–community relations, complaints of police misconduct, workplace climate, promotional issues, and protest policing. Dr Hassell is currently a Research Partner on BJA projects with the Milwaukee and Madison Police Departments. Her published works include *Women and Policing in America* (with Carol Archbold and Dorothy Schulz), *Police Organizational Cultures and Patrol Practices*, and journal articles in *Policing: An International Journal of Police Strategies and Management, Police Quarterly, Crime and Delinquency, Journal of Criminal Justice* and others. Dr Hassell currently serves on the editorial team of, *Advisory Boards for Policing: An International Journal of Police Strategies and Management and Police Quarterly*.

Jonathan Houdmont is Assistant Professor of Occupational Health Psychology at the University of Nottingham (UK), where he is director of the Masters degree and Professional Doctorate in Workplace Health and Well-being. Jonathan's research focus is on the assessment of relations between pychosocial work conditions, health and operational effectiveness in high-stress occupational groups, with a particular focus on policing. He has conducted a series of police stress studies on behalf of English forces and the Police Federation of England and Wales. This organization has commissioned him to undertake a comprehensive police stress study involving all 124,00 police officers of the Constable, Sergeant, and Inspector ranks across England and Wales in 2016–17.

Ann H. Huffman is an Associate Professor of Psychology and Management at Northern Arizona University. Ann received her PhD in Industrial–Organizational Psychology from Texas A&M University in 2004. Prior to Texas A&M University, Ann worked as a principal investigator with the Walter Reed Army Research Institute – Europe. Her primary research interests include the work–life interface, high-stress occupations (e.g. police, military), diversity in the workplace and environmental sustainability issues. Her co-edited book, *Green Organizations: Driving Change with I-O Psychology*, was the recipient of the Organizations and the Natural Environment Division of the Academy of Management Book Award. In addition, her work has appeared in a variety of journals and as chapters in edited books.

Chandler B. Imhof is a student progressing toward a BS degree in Psychology at Kansas State University. He has attended the Kansas Law Enforcement Training Center, where he received his full-time certification as a law enforcement officer in the State of Kansas. Chandler has subsequently been employed as a full-time police officer and as a part-time deputy while attending college. After graduation in spring of 2016, Chandler expects to seek admission into an I/O Psychology or Criminal Justice/Criminology graduate program, where he hopes to conduct research respective to law enforcement organizations.

Michael J. Kyle is a doctoral student in the Department of Criminology and Criminal Justice at Southern Illinois University, Carbondale. Prior to beginning his doctoral studies, Michael served as a law enforcement officer in both Missouri and Kansas. His research interests include policing, police leadership and ethics, and police legitimacy.

Tony D. LaMontagne leads the Work, Health and Well-being Unit in the Population Health Strategic Research center at Deakin University in Melbourne, Australia. His broad research interest is in developing the scientific and public understanding of work as a social determinant of health, and translating this research into policy and practice to improve workplace and worker health. Currently, the Unit's primary focus is on work and mental health, combining a range of etiologic and intervention research projects. Specific areas of interest include workplace metal health, improving job quality and psychosocial working conditions, and evaluating government policy interventions. His unit has worked extensively with police forces in Australia.

Kim Loyens studied Criminology and Public Administration at the University of KU Leuven (Belgium). She holds a PhD in Criminology. For her doctoral study at the KU Leuven, she conducted ethnographic research on ethical decision-making in the Belgian labor inspection and federal police. She currently works at the Utrecht School of Government (Netherlands) as an Assistant Professor and is Senior Affiliated Researcher at the Leuven Institute of Criminology (Belgium). Her research interests include conflicting values at the frontline, whistleblowing and human exploitation investigations. She has published in several journals, including *Administration and Society, Innovation, Journal of Business Ethics, Policing* and *Police Practice and Research*.

Angela Martin is an Associate Professor of Management at the Tasmanian School of Business and Economics, University of Tasmania, Australia. Her research is broadly focused on the psychological aspects of work and organizations, including employee health and well-being. In particular, her work aims to better understand managers' attitudes and capabilities for the effective management of mental health issues in the workplace and the initiation, implementation and success of occupational health interventions.

Rollin McCraty, PhD, is Director of Research of the HeartMath Research Center at the Institute of HeartMath. He is also a Professor at Florida Atlantic University. A psychophysiologist, Dr McCraty's research interests include the physiology of emotion, with a focus on the mechanisms by which emotions influence cognitive processes, behavior and health. Findings from this research have been applied to the development of tools and technologies to optimize individual and organizational health, performance and resilience. He has acted as Principal Investigator (PI) in numerous research studies examining the effects of self-regulation training on heart–brain interactions and on autonomic, cardiovascular, hormonal and immune system function. He has also served as PI in a number of studies to determine the outcomes on interventions and heart-rhythm feedback in diverse organizational and educational settings, as well as in various clinical populations.

Sarah J. McLean is the Associate Director and Director of Research and Technical Assistance at the John F. Finn Institute for Public Safety, Inc. (USA). She holds a PhD in criminal justice from the University of Albany. Dr McLean's scholarship has appeared in *Police Quarterly*, *Criminal Justice Policy Review*, *Criminal Justice Studies* and other academic journals. Her research has been funded by the National Institute of Justice, the Bureau of Justice Assistance, and other state and local sponsors.

Laurence Miller, PhD, is a clinical, forensic, and police psychologist based in Boca Raton, Florida. He provides clinical services and operational assistance to several South Florida law enforcement agencies, and provides consultative services to local, regional, national and international police organizations. He is a psychological examiner for the Palm Beach County Court and serves as an independent expert witness in civil and criminal cases involving competency, insanity, personal injury, disability and police psychology. He is also an Adjunct Professor at Florida Atlantic University and conducts continuing education and training programs around the USA. He is the author of over 400 print and online publications, including two widely used textbooks: *Practical Police Psychology* and *Criminal Psychology*. He writes the 'Practical Police Psychology' column on the PoliceOne.com website and is a frequent presenter at law enforcement and psychology conferences.

Allison J. Milner received her PhD in 2010 and is currently a Senior Research fellow at the School of Health and Social Development, Deakin University, Australia. Her current areas of research interest include the influence of employee characteristics, quality of work, job stress and unemployment as determinants of mental health and suicidality. Her work ranges across a number of externally funded etiological and intervention projects and she has successfully obtained funding from external sources for this work. She works with key policy stakeholders to promote research on the link between work and suicide, and is the co-chair for an international panel of researchers aiming to promote workplace suicide prevention. Greater attention to suicides occurring among working people is necessary, considering that the majority of deaths in Australia occur in the employed population. In her Fellowship, she is investigating whether access to lethal means modifies the risk of suicide in high-risk occupations. This information holds the potential to influence suicide prevention practice in the employed population.

Maura J. Mills is an Assistant Professor of I/O Psychology at Hofstra University, New York, as well as an Adjunct Assistant Professor at the Frank G. Zarb School of Business at Hofstra University. She received her BA degrees in Psychology and English/ Corporate Communications from Massachusetts College of Liberal Arts, and her MS and PhD degrees in I/O Psychology from Kansas State University. Prior to joining Hofstra University, she worked as an associate consultant for an external management-consulting firm in New York. Her primary research interests include the work–family/ work–life interface, gender in the workplace and positive organizational behavior. She has authored and co-authored various journal articles and book chapters on these topics, as well as editing a recent volume on gender and the work–family experience.

Michael Nila honed his leadership skills for 29 years while serving his nation in the policing profession, retiring as a Police Commander with the Aurora, IL Police Department. He served in many law enforcement capacities and led the department's re-engineering from a traditional agency to a community-policing department, His vast experience has made him a trainer of choice; a valued and sought-after speaker. Michael has trained and certified thousands of employees, executives and trainers for organizations worldwide, such as the US Department of Justice, the Chicago Police Department, the Los Angeles Police Department, the New York City Police Department, the United Nations and Fortune 500 companies

Andrew J. Noblet is a Professor in Organizational Behavior in the Deakin Graduate School of Business, Australia. His research interests are in the areas of occupational stress, organizational fairness, leader–member relationships, and organizational health and development. Much of his recent work has focused on planning, implementing and evaluating strategies aimed at enhancing the health of workers and the environments in which they work. He has considerable experience in designing and implementing occupational health interventions and has worked with a variety of occupational groups (professional footballers, middle managers, community heath personnel, secondary school teachers and police officers). His work has appeared in international journals and at leading management conferences in the US, Europe and South East Asia.

Karen Oehme is the Director of the Institute for Family Violence Studies at Florida State University's (FSU) College of Social Work and an FSU Distinguished University Scholar. The Institute houses several large, multi-disciplinary projects on family violence including the Law Enforcement Families Partnership and the Medical Professionals Partnership. She builds online training and resource sites for criminal justice agencies, child protective agencies, social service providers, medical professionals and judges throughout the US to help reduce and prevent family violence. She has provided technical assistance to the Office on Violence Against Women at the Department of Justice and has authored numerous articles on domestic violence-related issues. She is a member of the Florida Attorney General's Domestic Violence Fatality Review Committee and has also served on the Florida's Model Policy on Officer-Involved Domestic Violence Committee and on the Florida Supreme Court's Standing Committee on Diversity and Fairness.

Kathryn M. Page is an Honorary Fellow in the School of Population Health Strategic Research Centre, Deakin University, Australia. Her research interests include the design, implementation and evaluation of interventions for increasing employee well-being and preventing job stress. Kathryn has considerable experience in conducting applied workplace mental health research in the police sector, including interventions to improve psychosocial working conditions and leadership behavior. Specific interventions she has developed and/or applied include positive mental health promotion, a systems approach to job stress prevention and integrated approaches to workplace mental health. Kathryn is also a practicing organizational psychologist and consults extensively with industry on leadership and workplace mental health issues. Kathryn was awarded the Andre Bussing Award for Outstanding Early Career Achievement by the European Academy of Occupational Health Psychology in 2009.

Douglas Paton is Professor of Psychology at Charles Darwin University, Australia. He is a Research Fellow at the Joint Centre for Disaster Research (NZ), a Technical Advisor on risk communication to the World Health Organization, a member of the IRDR Risk Interpretation and Action Committee, and an advisor on community resilience to the Australian Red Cross. He researches all hazards and cross-cultural aspects of disaster risk reduction, residence and recovery and has worked with emergency and protective services agencies in the UK, the USA, Australia and Taiwan. He is Editor of the *International Journal of Mass Emergencies and Disasters* and sits on the Editorial Boards of the *International Journal of Disaster Risk Reduction*, *Disasters*, and the *International Journal of Psychology*.

George T. Patterson is Associate Professor at the Silberman School of social Work, Hunter College, City University of New York. He is a police social worker and New York State certified police instructor. He has provided stress management training to recruits and police officers in numerous law enforcement organizations. He also conducts research in the area of law enforcement, stress and coping. His recent meta-analysis of stress management interventions was published in the *Journal of Experimental Criminology*. In addition, his written testimony on stress management interventions was included in the May 2015 'Final Report of the Task force on 21st Century Policing', established by President Barack Obama.

Stephanie Grace Prost is a Doctoral Candidate and MSW at the Florida State University College of Social Work and received her MSW from FSU in 2008. As a former forensic social worker, she has focused her research on several intersecting areas of social work and criminal justice. These include corrections, law enforcement and juvenile justice. Previously contracted with the Florida Department of Juvenile Justice, she seeks to understand the causes, correlates and consequences of crime for individuals, families and communities. She also examines multiple aspects of the correctional system, namely health care. Her recent research is focused on hospice and palliative end-of-life care in prisons. Specifically, she is exploring the quality of life of inmates with chronic and terminal illness in state prisons and the use of inmate volunteers as caregivers for inmates at the end-of-life stage.

Nicola Reavley is Senior Research Fellow and NHMRC Career Development Fellow in the Melbourne School of Population and Global Health at the University of Melbourne. Her research focuses on improving public knowledge and beliefs about mental health problems, reducing stigma and discrimination and improving support for those with mental disorders. Nicola has led a number of projects that aim to assist organizations to better manage mental health issues, including the development of guidelines for implementation of a strategy for the prevention of mental health problems and for supporting employees returning to work after an episode of anxiety or depression.

Joseph A. Schafer is Professor and Chair in the Department of Criminology and Criminal Justice at Southern Illinois University, Carbondale. His research focuses on policing, organizational change, leadership, citizen perceptions of police, the diffusion of innovation, critical incident response and futures research in policing.

Irina Tchernitskaia is a Business Psychologist, an Organizational Psychology Registrar and Research Fellow at Deakin University, Australia. She completed her Masters of Organizational and Industrial Psychology in 2012, with this project focusing on teams in the workplace. She has experience in coaching, psychological health program design, psychological assessment, group facilitation, leadership and organizational development with police officers. She is particularly passionate about promoting mental health and well-being and, in turn, organizational effectiveness.

John M. Violanti is a Full Research Professor in the Department of Epidemiology and Environmental Health, School of Public Health and Health Professions, University at Buffalo and a member of the University at Buffalo graduate faculty. He was formerly a full Professor at the Rochester Institute of Technology Department of Criminal Justice. He is a police veteran, serving with the New York State Police for 23 years as a trooper, criminal investigator, and, later, as a coordinator of the Psychological Assistance Program (EAP) for the State Police. Dr Violanti has been involved in the design, implementation and analysis of police stress and health studies over the past 25 years. Recent projects include a longitudinal study on psychological stress and cardiovascular disease in police officers and the impact of shift work on police health outcomes, which was funded by the National Institute of Occupational Safety and Health. Dr Violanti has authored over 100 peer-reviewed articles on police stress and PTSD (post-traumatic stress disorder), police mortality and suicide. He has also written and edited 18 books on the topics of police stress, psychological trauma, resilience and suicide.

Robert E. Worden is the Director of the John F. Finn Institute for public Safety, Inc., and Associate Professor of Criminal Justice at the University of Albany, State University of New York. He holds a PhD in political science from the University of North Carolina at Chapel Hill. Professor Worden's interests revolve around questions concerning the accountability and responsiveness of criminal justice institutions to the public. His scholarship has appeared in *Justice Quarterly*, *Criminology*, *Law and Society Review* and other academic journals, and his research has been funded by the National Institute of Justice, the Bureau of Justice Assistance, the New York State Division of Criminal Justice Services, and other sponsors. Professor Worden served on the National Research Council's Committee to Review Research on Police Policies and Practices, whose report, 'Fairness and Effectiveness in Policing: The Evidence', was published by the National Academies Press in 2004.

Acknowledgements

I have been involved in police research earlier in my career and decided about a year ago to develop this collection for Gower as part of our Psychological and Behavioral Aspects of Risk series. I did not realize at that time how police and policing would jump into national debates in several countries. I thank our international writers and researchers for their excellent contributions. I appreciate the support of Gower and their fine staff. And to Carla D'Agostino here in Toronto; thanks for all your invaluable help and for being so nice while offering it. You saved my bacon more than once. My participation was supported in part by York University.

Ronald J. Burke
Toronto

Acknowledgements

Part 1

Introduction

Part I

Introduction

1 Stress in policing

An overview[1]

Ronald J. Burke

> It probably won't be a bullet that strikes an officer down, but the effects of chronic stress.
> Sergeant Robin Klein, Long Beach California Police Department

Police forces are organizations staffed by men and women, sworn officers and civilians, who provide police services to their communities. Some officers perform heroically: the first responder to a possible child drowning, Officer Vinilla King, found the three-year-old unconscious and not breathing. She performed CPR and mouth-to-mouth resuscitation, bringing the child back to life; Officer Jesse Kidder refused to shoot a man wanted for the killing of his best friend and his fiancé, though the suspect kept asking the offer to shoot him; and Police officer Clifford Peterson was honored for saving the life of a man intending to commit suicide by jumping off a bridge in Toronto on December 2013. There are also "bad guys" out there: Shannon Miles, on August 28, 2015, approached an unsuspecting officer filling up his police car at a gas station and shot and killed him (*Toronto Star*, 2015). Miles had a lengthy criminal record. The two had never met. The shooting was termed an assassination by some.

While most police officers and civilian employees perform admirably, there are others, hopefully a small number, who do not. Individuals with "human frailties" exist in all organizations. A 30-year veteran of the Peel Regional Police Force, just outside Toronto, Craig Wattier, has recently been charged with child pornography (Gilllis and Deschamps, 2015). Our intention in this collection is not to "trash" police officers and police forces. Police officers, unlike employees of most other organizations, have unique powers invested in them and carry weapons. Our hope is to reduce risk to police officers and the citizens they serve by identifying areas of concern and suggesting possible remedies to address them.

This opening chapter, of necessity being broad and wide-ranging in identifying risks to both officers and their forces and citizens in their communities, reviews issues related to sources of stress in policing, consequences of stress, and potential interventions to reduce the prevalence and negative impacts of police stress.

Waters and Ussery (2007) briefly reviewed the history of police stress research including causes, symptoms, and potentially useful interventions consistent with the theme of this collection. Here is a sample of some of their conclusions.

- The incidence of police stress continues to escalate and affect officers and their families.
- There was a reluctance of officers to use available services due to the values of the police culture.

- The physical health of officers seemed to deteriorate over time.
- Officers do face stressful events.
- There was high rate of domestic violence in police families, stress-related and control-related.
- There was high divorce rate in police families.
- Police families worry about dangers facing police officers.
- Police officers have a high rate of suicide.

The picture, almost a decade later, has not improved.

Risks to police officers, police organizations, citizens, and communities

Yes there are "bad people" out there. A man with a penchant for hate crimes and bullying others, Norman Radditz, shot and killed Daniel Woodall (aged 35 and a married father of two young children), one of a small group of officers who had come to arrest him (Wittmeier and Pruden, 2015). A second officer was wounded and survived. Raddatz was found dead, a suicide, in the basement of his house, which was demolished by a fire he may have set.

There are risks that police officers face: being shot and killed, being physically assaulted, being hurt or killed in a car crash, and being charged with an assault or a complaint. There are also risks to citizens: being physically assaulted, being shot or killed, being charged with a crime based on fabricated evidence, being harassed as a result of racial profiling, and being given a ticket to fill a quota. New York City paid almost $6 million in July 2015 to the family of Eric Garner, who died from strangulation by police officers while being arrested.

A small number of police officers engage in misconduct, typically in their early career stages. Thus early identification of such risks is important. Police managers then need to have better information (quality and quantity) and make better use of this information. This involves more police monitoring of officers, early identification of performance problems and concerns, and addressing these via training, coaching, and discipline. These will be challenging since most police officers, while working, are not directly observed and there is a gap between "street cops" and "management cops."

Worden *et al.* (2014) focus on risk assessment and risk management of police misconduct. Police misconduct includes excessive use of force, illegal search and seizures, bias in police stops (racial profiling), sexual harassment, lying on the witness stand, theft, and other unprofessional misconduct. They conclude, however, that the tools used to determine risks of misconduct fall short, as they use limited information of questionable value and the models using these tools need improvement. Police managers need to improve the quality and quantity of data they use and make better use of these data.

Public opinion and satisfaction with law enforcement

The public generally holds positive views about the police and police forces. Toronto's retiring Police Chief, Bill Blair, left office in the spring of 2015 with a high Toronto citizen approval rating. Sixty-one percent of Torontonians in a recent survey approved of his performance (Rider, 2015).

Trust and confidence in police organizations

Trust and confidence in the police encourage greater citizen involvement in determining the nature of police services provided to one's community, in making police organizations more accountable and responsive to their communities, and in increasing citizen compliance and cooperation with police officers and with laws (Jackson and Bradford, 2010).

Trust in police organizations is diminished when police investigate police, and no officers are found "guilty" (Hays and Long, 2014). Even when juries investigate the police, they get treated differently from the average citizen. Waddington (2010) writes that standards for convicting a police officer for an offense are higher than those used for other cases. He suggests that juries realize that policing is a "dirty business and one that sometimes leaves stains on one's hands." In too many cases, investigative journalists end up reporting what really happened. Polling data in Canada have shown significant declines in public trust in the police over the past decade. Police organizations need the support and cooperation of citizens if they are to function effectively. This means creating a positive image in the eyes of the public. This requires always treating citizens with respect, regardless of the situation.

In addition, police officers being investigated for wrongdoing, similar to employees in other occupations, are put on paid suspension. One Ontario officer was paid almost $350,000 over three years before retiring. He thanked his force for the opportunity he was given to travel, take courses, play golf, and sit at home during this time (Ferreira, 2015a). The citizens of Ontario pay $13,000 a day to suspended police officers (Ferreira, 2015b); one officer receiving over $600,000 while under suspension. The vast majority of officers will return to their jobs.

The police culture

Police organizations are paramilitary organizations; they have a "macho" culture, in which spending time with other officers following a shift is common. Authority and power are vested in police officers as representatives of their governments; they have guns, tasers, batons, handcuffs, radios, back-up help, and uniforms. They take charge, give orders, and limit citizen freedoms; they can stop and search, and make arrests. But police learn quickly that many citizens dislike their police symbols and behaviors. Police officers divide their world in to "us" and "them"(everyone else) and believe that only other officers can understand them. There is also a stigma attached to admitting difficulties and problems and seeking help. In addition, there is often conflict in the police sub-culture between the official norms and values of policing and actual police behavior, a tension between "street cops" and "management cops" (Reuss-Ianni, 1983; Skolnick and Fyfe, 1996).

Toch (2008: 61) describes police organizations as having "hyper-bureaucratic military organizational attributes – those of formal rank, formal authority and a chain of unquestioned and unquestioning command." Police organizations are described as militaristic and overly bureaucratic (rank-based authority, command and control, top-down decision-making, formal rules and procedures, and army-style uniforms). Police culture embodies the following characteristics: solidarity, authoritarianism, suspicion, conservatism, cynicism, and bias. These cultural values can contribute to policing problems such as excessive use of force, racism, sexism, corruption, and inefficiencies.

Van Maanen (1978) found that officers grouped citizens into three categories: "suspicious persons"—people likely to or who may have already committed a crime;

"assholes"—people who disrespect the police or insult them; and "know nothings"—people who ask police for assistance. Loftus (2010), using ethnographic research in a UK police force, found that long-held views on the nature of police occupational culture were still prevalent. He attributed this continuity to the fact that basic processes and fundamentals of the police role have not changed.

Police cynicism

Police work has been associated with high levels of officer cynicism. Niederhoffer (1967), in his pioneering study of New York City police officers, placed a lot of emphasis on levels of cynicism among police officers. Increases in levels of police cynicism have been linked with officer perceptions of the ineffectiveness of the criminal justice system, poor management in their forces, boredom on the job, disappointment with the quality of their work experiences, excessive amounts of paperwork, the influence of their colleagues, the police culture and forging bonds of unity and solidarity, being cut off from the public ("he/us versus them" mentality), and the lack of relevant training.

Hickman *et al.* (2004), in a study of 499 Philadelphia police officers, found that cynicism increased with years of police service, and officers scoring higher on cynicism also had more departmental disciplinary charges.

Police violence

Former US tennis star, James Blake, who is black, was thrown to the ground and handcuffed by a white police officer, James Frascatore, on Wednesday September 9, while standing in front of his New York City (NYC) hotel. Mayor deBlazio and Police Commissioner Bill Bratton apologized to Blake for the incident of mistaken identity. Frascatore has had multiple complaints raised against him in the past, including being sued four times for excessive use of force. Frascatore is now on desk duty. In a different case, a financial settlement was reached with the family of Walter Scott, who was shot by a white police officer in North Charleston, South Carolina (*Toronto Star*, 2015b). Scott was unarmed. The city agreed to pay the family $6.5million. The officer, Michael Slager, was charged with murder in June 2015. Two Louisiana police officers, Derrick Stafford and Norris Greenhouse, have been charged with murder in the shooting death of an autistic child on November 7, 2015 while attempting to arrest the boy's father (Kunzleman, 2015).

A white Chicago police officer, Jason Van dyke, was charged with the murder of a 17-year-old black male, Laquan Mcdonald. McDonald was shot 16 times (Babwin and Keyser, 2015). Unnamed officers provided written reports of the shooting that were different from what was shown on the video. Protests broke out in Chicago when a video of the shooting was released. Van Dyke was previously charged with 18 civilian complaints over his 14 years on the force, several for the use of excessive force. One person he had arrested was later awarded $350,000 in damages (Babwin, 2015a). The Mayor of Chicago, Rahm Emanuel, fired his Police superintendent, Gary McCarthy, on December 1 despite saying he was doing a good job in reducing levels of crime (Babwin, 2015b). Citizen protests following the release of long-suppressed videos of this shooting made McCarthy a "distraction." Emanuel created a task force on police accountability, due to report back to him in March 2016, as well as authorizing the greater use of body cameras.

A Chicago police officer shot and killed an emotionally disturbed young man, as well as an innocent woman bystander, on December 26, 2015; both victims were black.

Police acknowledged that the shooting of the second person was an accident (a mistake). The race of the officer firing the shots was not made public. Mayor Emanuel indicated on December 27 that all Chicago officers would now be trained on how to deal with a person having mental health problems – a little late unfortunately (Tarm, 2015).

Lerch and Mieczkowski (2009) reviewed the literature on violent police behavior. We do not know the frequency of "police brutality" and "police violence". It seems however that police violence and brutality are relatively rare. Female officers are less likely to engage in violent behavior. Younger black citizens in the US are more likely to be targets of police violence, as are males more generally. Force is more likely to be used when citizens disrespect officers or when a minor offence escalates.

Kop and Euwema (2001), in a sample of Dutch police officers, reported that those indicating higher levels of occupational stress engaged in more use of force. Ingram *et al.* (2014)—based on data from 766 patrol officers and 146 patrol sergeants—found that the way sergeants viewed the use of lethal force policies, and the views of top management and their levels of support for them, influenced patrol officers' views of these policies.

Lerch and Mieczkowski (2009) offer suggestions for reducing levels of violent police behavior. These include the creation of civilian police review boards, the introduction of community-based policing, the use of early warning systems to collect and monitor citizen complaints as well as fellow-officer complaints (typically from supervisors), the hiring of more female officers, police leadership actively opposing police violence by taking this concern seriously, disciplining "guilty" officers with penalties, and the use of training sessions. De-escalating rather than escalating seems to make more sense. The *Globe and Mail* (2014) suggests: (1) disarming some police officers, as they do in the UK (most UK police do not carry guns); (2) putting body cameras on police (most cases of police misconduct arise from someone videotaping them); and (3) offering police training on how to not use force, on ways to resolve conflicts, and on how to calm people down in potentially volatile situations. Ninety-eight percent of police officers in Scotland do not carry guns. Scottish police officers have shot only two people in the past ten years.

Intimate partner violence

Several studies have shown an association between police officer stress and authoritarianism/control spillover, and intimate partner violence (IPV) within law enforcement families (Anderson and Lo, 2011; Johnson *et al.*, 2005; Sheehan, 2000; D'Angelo, 2000). Intimate partner violence is abusive behavior of one partner that physically injures the partner or creates the fear of possible physical injury; it is undertaken to gain or maintain power and control of the other partner.

Oehme *et al.* (2012), in a sample of 853 law enforcement officers (76 percent male), examined the prevalence of domestic violence, PTSD (post-traumatic stress disorder), and hazardous/dependent alcohol use, and focused on the relationship between them. Almost 29 percent reported being physically violent with an intimate partner or family member; 18 percent reported PTSD symptoms; 15 percent were hazardous drinkers; and 8 percent had drinking habits suggesting alcohol dependence (thus 23 percent were problem drinkers). Both PTSD and alcohol use were significantly correlated with physical violence. Police organizations need to emphasize education and training that deals with alcohol use, PTSD, and domestic violence (Oehme *et al.*, 2011).

Increasing militarization of police forces

Police forces in many parts of the world are now looking more like armed forces. Several Canadian police forces have added armored vehicles and retired military combat vehicles to their crime-fighting arsenals. There is an increasing militarization of police forces, with many getting access to unused military equipment. Thus police community disturbances end up looking more like war zones. The *Toronto Star* (2014), citing a *Washington Post* story, reported the following: A town in Georgia, population 32,000, spent $227,000 on armored personnel carriers, and a second even smaller Georgia town, population 8000, spent $5,400 on 27 M4 assault rifles.

Stressors in police work—the research literature

Stress exists in all jobs, varying in sources or types as well as magnitudes, and the experience of moderate levels of stress can actually improve performance. It is unrealistic to think we can eliminate the experience of stress, but high levels of prolonged stress are harmful. Police work has been shown to have negative impacts on officers, their families, and their organizations (see, for example, Waters and Ussery, 2007). Police stresses have been grouped into *organizational* (e.g. the paramilitary structure, autocratic managers, excessive paperwork) and *operational* (e.g. interacting with citizens, potential of fear, and danger, boredom).

Houdmont *et al.* (2012) assessed the prevalence of organizational psychosocial hazards (OPH) in a sample of 1,729 police officers in the UK. Seven psychosocial work hazards were considered: demands, control, managerial support, peer support, relationships, risk, and change, using an instrument developed by the British government. Scores on these seven dimensions were significantly and positively correlated. In addition, scores on these seven dimensions were significantly correlated with a one-item measure of work stress, the average correlation being 0.41 ($p < 0.001$). Forty-six percent of respondents said their jobs were very or extremely stressful. Scores on all seven dimensions fell below the government target level: the eightieth percentile compared to benchmark data; this was better than average but still needed improvement. The Health and Safety Executive (HSE) in the UK developed the Management Standards for Work Related Stress in 2004.

Gershon *et al.* (2009), using data from 1,072 officers in a large US department, examined the relationship of four work stressors (exposure to critical incidents, workplace discrimination, uncooperative co-workers, job dissatisfaction) with various work and health outcomes. Work stress was positively associated with depression and intimate partner abuse. Use of negative and avoidant coping was associated with higher levels of work stress and negative well-being outcomes (e.g. psychosomatic symptoms, depression, anxiety, and post-traumatic stress symptoms), physical symptoms (back pain, migraines, chronic insomnia), and behaviors (alcohol use, family conflict, aggressive behaviors, spouse abuse).

Biggam *et al.* (1997) studied self-perceived occupational stress and distress in a sample of 699 Scottish police officers. Both organizational and occupational stressors were considered. Outcomes included measures of anxiety, depression, somatic complaints, and social dysfunction. Higher levels of stress were associated with organizational not operational factors. The former included staff shortages, inadequate resources, time pressures, work overload, and lack of communication. Women reported higher levels of operational stress than did men, but there were no sex differences in levels of organizational stressors. Constables reported higher levels of stress in operational factors than did sergeants and inspectors. Officers in urban areas reported higher levels of organizational stressors than did officers working in rural areas. Officers working in urban areas reported higher levels of psychological distress (e.g. anxiety, depression). Officers working in rural areas also indicated fewer sick days, as did officers of higher organizational ranks. Levels of organizational and operational stress factors were significantly and positively correlated with a composite measure of the four psychological distress indicators.

Long work hours

In the US, over a million sworn police officers currently work shifts that seriously disrupt their schedules. Police officers also work large amounts of overtime. Officers working patrol, and detectives, can work double shifts (of 16 hours) and sometimes work 24 hours straight. Long work hours and associated fatigue increase health risks, poor sleep quality, and morbidity. Family and social living are also affected. Long work hours have been associated with increased levels of domestic violence in police families. Police fatigue also increases the risks of vehicle crashes and poor decision-making by officers. Driving while fatigued is similar to driving while drunk.

Vila and Moore (2008), directly acknowledging difficulties in changing police behavior, offer some fatigue management strategies. Police management and police officers share an interest in reducing the causes and consequences of long work hours and officer fatigue. Common interests include effectively managing human resources, managing risk to officers and communities, and officer health. It is vital that police forces develop work-hour policies and practices. Police education should address the value of managing fatigue and work hours. Officers should also monitor the quality of their sleep. Officers' families should learn about fatigue and its effects. It is also useful to involve police officers in reducing the prevalence of drowsy driving by citizens.

Dealing with the mentally ill

Wells and Schafer (2006) studied police officer responses to the mentally ill (*n*=125) and concluded that dispositions for the mentally ill did not match the outcomes they desired, that the police training they received was insufficient, but that a recently instituted training course they participated in gave them more confidence in dealing with the mentally ill. Half the participants did not know what to do with the mentally ill.

Eighteen-year-old Sammy Yatin was shot nine times by Toronto police officers while alone on a streetcar in July 2013. Yatim was in obvious psychological distress. Following the shooting death of Sammy Yatim, former Canadian Supreme Court Justice, Frank Iacobucci, following a year-long inquiry, submitted 84 recommendations in his report to the Toronto Police Services board, the group overseeing the Toronto Police Services. Among his recommendations were improved training to defuse conflict situations; the increased use of mobile crisis intervention teams; the requirement for all newly hired constables to undergo a mandatory "mental health first aid" course; the inclusion of the de-escalation of conflict as a factor in promotion decisions; the use of community involvement or involvement in mental health services as a factor in preferential hiring; pairing an officer with a mental health "expert" in mobile crisis response teams; having people with mental illness help in police training; setting a goal of no deaths; the use of body cameras; early identification of and intervention in potential bad behavior of constables; and support for the use of tasers in a very limited number of circumstances (Gillis, 2014).

The Toronto force has adopted 79 of the 84 recommendations aimed at zero deaths. It is too soon to tell whether this goal will be achieved (Gillis, 2015a).

Dealing with citizen disturbances and riots

There are several examples of poor judgment and unacceptable police behaviors in the handling of civil disturbances (Wilder *et al.*, 2014). These include the excessive use of force, the use of aggressive police tactics, the overwhelming show of force, the presence of military armaments, the lack of training on how officers should respond, the wearing of riot gear, the throwing of tear gas, and (as an example of context) the real fear raised in officers by an actual large and boisterous gathering of people, some of whom may commit criminal acts (e.g. breaking windows, looting). Armored SWAT vehicles and heavily armed tactical officers angered protesters after the Michael Brown shooting in Ferguson, Missouri, on August 9, 2014. Instead, officers should wear normal outfits, delay the use of aggressive tactics, and lessen militaristic approaches. Law enforcement officials should immediately join with community leaders in urging calm and holding meetings where members of the public can air their complaints.

Dealing with natural disasters

Police officers are often among first responders when national disasters, such as 9/11, the Oklahoma City bombing, forest fires, and hurricanes happen. West *et al.* (2008) assessed depression and PTSD among New Orleans police officers following Hurricane Katrina. Data were obtained from 912 officers, with 227 (26 percent), reporting depression symptoms, and 170 (19 percent) reporting PTSD symptoms. Risk factors of PTSD included recovery of bodies, injury to a family member, crowd control, and assault. Risk factors for depression included limited family contact, home damage, injury to a family member, assault, and isolation from other police officers. McCanlies *et al.*(2014) studied police officers in New Orleans (84 males and 30 females), following Hurricane Katrina and found that PTSD symptoms were lower among officers with positive psychological factors (resilience, life satisfaction, gratitude).

Undercover police work

Undercover police infiltrate criminal and terrorist organizations to collect evidence on potential and ongoing criminal activities. Undercover operations can be of short or long duration, in some cases years. Undercover officers assume another identity and develop relationships they will eventually betray. There are risks in every undercover operation, some more serious than others. Undercover officers are more likely to shoot someone or be shot than are routine patrol officers. Undercover work is demanding—physically, intellectually, and emotionally. Undercover officers become isolated from their department, have to pretend they are on board with criminal activities, risk being robbed or killed, risk being shot by other police officers, find it hard to transition back to a "normal life" after an undercover assignment ends, find it hard to return to being their former selves, and sometimes become the person they pretended to be. Lowe *et al.* (2008) compared three groups of police officers (current undercover officers, former undercover officers, and officers without undercover experience) on 54 psychological, behavioral, and emotion clinical symptoms. Former undercover officers indicated significantly higher frequencies on 15 clinical symptoms, while current undercover officers indicated significantly fewer clinical symptoms than the two other groups of officers. Lowe *et al.* attributed these findings to issues of adjustment and readjustment by former undercover officers and denial of symptoms by current undercover officers.

Some officers go not only undercover, but under the sheets. Scotland Yard settled legal claims brought by seven women against male undercover officers who formed sexual relationships with them while infiltrating protest movements (*Toronto Star*, 2015c). Scotland Yard said that such behavior was "totally unacceptable" and they have disbanded these units. Two undercover officers had fathered children with two women. It was not clear whether a financial settlement was involved or what happened to these police officers.

Post-traumatic stress disorder

Police officers may deal with a number of potentially traumatic events, including the death of fellow officers, shooting incidents, dealing with the injury and death of citizens, and the abuse, injury and death of children. These events can have long-lasting repercussions. Four Royal Canadian Mounted Police officers were shot and killed by James Roszko on March 3, 2005 near Mayerthorpe in British Columbia. Ten years later, these killings still affect their colleagues (Pruden, 2015).

Police officers are often first responders in crisis situations. Robbers and Jenkins (2005) studied PTSD in police first responders to the crash site following the 9/11 terrorist attack on the Pentagon. Police officers arrived on the scene about 90 minutes after the attack. Robbers and Jenkins collected data from 76 of the initial 78 first responding police officers two years after the attack. More than a third of these officers exhibited higher levels of PTSD, and officers spending more time at the Pentagon crash site reported higher levels of PTSD.

Police suicide

Taber (2014) cites two RCMP suicides within one week. In the Ontario Provincial Police force, from January 1989 to March 2012, 23 Ontario Provincial Police officers killed themselves. Taber quotes a psychiatrist who said that more police officers are killed by suicide than by felons, and Violanti (2007), a long-time researcher of policing, termed police suicide an epidemic. Police suicides have been shown to be associated with relationship problems, alcohol and substance abuse, personal legal difficulties, a negative image of policing, and inconsistencies in the criminal justice system. As intervention strategies, Clark *et al.* (2012) advocate the use of peer-support groups, stressing that seeking help is a measure of strength rather than weakness. They also advise the following: training officers should use healthy constructive coping mechanisms rather than avoidance and destructive coping behaviors and strategies; they should increase officer understanding of the symptoms and risk factors in law enforcement officer suicide, so they might recognize them when they see them; police chiefs should develop and distribute a recommended protocol following a completed police officer suicide; desired funeral practices should set a tone that might encourage officers to consider seeking help; police departments should compile a psychological autopsy and submit it to a central clearing house to increase understanding of police suicide and potential prevention and intervention initiatives.

Chae and Boyle (2013) reviewed prevalence, risk and protective factors in police suicide based on the best available empirically sound research. They found that five aspects of policing increased the risk of suicidal ideation: organizational stressors, critical incident trauma, shift work, relationship problems, and alcohol use and abuse. Preventative factors that mediated stressors and increased officer resilience included the social support of peers, significant others and family members, peer counseling, and use of active coping styles by officers while at work.

Alcohol abuse

Lindsay (2008) raises the question of whether we should be concerned about the alcohol consumption of police officers. Consider a sample of research findings: Obst *et al.* (2001) followed a group of police cadets ($n = 177$) through academy training (six months) then through one year after the training. The risk of harm from alcohol increased throughout this period, thus introducing recruits to an alcohol consumption culture.

Davey *et al.* (2001), in a sample of 749 Australian police officers, studied the prevalence of alcohol consumption and factors contributing to individuals' drinking. Thirty-seven percent of these officers were at risk of harm from excessive alcohol consumption. Officers indicated drinking at celebrations and socializing with other officers as factors in their drinking. However, stress at work emerged as the best predictor of alcohol consumption: officers drank alcohol to reduce stress.

Davey *et al.* (2000), in a sample of 4,191 Australian police officers, found that although their drinking frequency was similar to national statistics, police officers drank greater quantities of alcohol. The 18–25- year-old group had the highest frequency of drinking. Twenty-five percent of officers drank while on duty. Thirty percent fell in the "at risk of harmful consumption" category. Intervention programs and education are clearly needed in the police workplace.

Are there performance costs from these behaviors?

One would expect that alcohol abuse, negative feeling states such as depression, and PTSD would influence levels of police officer job performance. Fox *et al.* (2012) collected data from 150 officers in an urban area in order to study the prevalence of PTSD, depression, alcohol abuse, perceived supports and barriers to using mental health services, and how these factors affected productivity loss. Officers with mental health conditions had higher productivity loss at an annual cost of $4,489 per officer.

Police corruption

An Ontario Court Judge concluded that a Durham (Ontario) officer committed several criminal offenses while on duty in 2013 (Gallant, 2015). James Ebdon was caught on video threatening to beat a man up and plant cocaine on him. He also told the victim that the next time they saw each other, "yes sir no sir, three bags full, whatever the f—k you want, can I suck your c—k sir, can I do a backflip." Ebdon is still with the force. The Durham force said that Ebdon was disciplined for discreditable conduct but would not disclose his penalty.

RCMP records indicated a record number of police officers being disciplined for lying under oath, drunk driving, having sex in cruisers with other officers, sexual harassment, and sharing porn on RCMP computers. Between 2012 and 2013, 104 cases were examined, compared with an average of 88 cases (still a large number) in the preceding 13 years (Brown, 2014). Punishment included a reprimand and a few days off the job, rising to a high of 10 days. The force has 24,667 members, with less than 1 percent being disciplined. It is important to hold police officers to a higher standard because of the oath they take, their power, and the fact that they carry guns.

A female police officer with the Windsor Ontario Force was dismissed from the force for smuggling large quantities of liquor from the US into Canada (*Toronto Star*, 2015d). She was charged in 2010, and was paid about $400,000 for doing no work until late 2015, when her dismissal was upheld. In another instance, eight Quebec police officers were suspended in October 2015 pending charges of paying for sex with prostitutes and/or forcing Aboriginal women to have sex with them (Woods, 2015)

Lee *et al.* (2013), using data from 1,962 front-line officers and 518 supervisors from 26 police agencies, considered both individual-level variables (rank, whether working on patrol, total service length, etc.) and departmental-/organizational-level variables (strength of discipline, presence of a deviant sub-culture, willingness to report fellow officers' misconduct, etc.) as predictors of front-line officers' views on corruption. The results showed that front-line officers' attitudes towards corruption were highly influenced by their supervisors' attitudes and behaviors and the presence of a deviant sub-culture. Citizen oversight, department training and monitoring, supervision, discipline, and legal liability are now used to control police corruption. The effects of external controls, however, have been limited, placing more emphasis on internal controls through management, culture, and discipline.

Some troubling signs

The *Toronto Star*, Canada's most widely circulated daily newspaper, on four straight days, published articles on police officers in Ontario under the title "Breaking Badge" by McLean and Poisson (2015a, 2015b, 2015c, 2015d). The first article referred to hundreds of officers (with detailed descriptions of some) engaging in dishonest and criminal behavior. The second article reported that officers who were found guilty received light punishment and remained with their forces. The third article reported that more than 60 officers have been disciplined for drunk driving since 2010, again receiving little punishment and still remaining with their forces. The fourth and final article provided examples of officers abusing their authority in various ways (interfering with an investigation of a friend, using confidential databases to obtain information on ex-lovers, using police resources to harm people they dislike, and using their badges to get free tickets to sporting events).

What does a police officer need to do to get fired?

Poisson and McLean (2015) reported the following: An officer with the Peel Ontario force (just outside of Toronto), Perry MacVicar, responsible for training, sat in his police car with a female dispatcher being trained. MacVicar asked her which sexual acts she liked, told her that a female dispatcher previously had shown him her breasts, asked if he could fondle her breasts (she refused), then showed her pictures of his erect penis on his cell phone. A year later he showed naked pictures of himself to another women being trained, got her phone number, and continued to harass her until she told him to stop. He is still with the force, having been demoted for six months.

Police watch dogs or police lap dogs?

Davies (2015) notes that although Superior Court justices acknowledge wrongdoing by officers, the Office of the Independent Police Review Director (OIPRD) fails to do so.

The OIPRD substantiated fewer than 13 percent of 3,200 complaints made by the public against the police in one year (most were filed by minorities). He concludes that little police accountability exists.

Career advancement in policing

Career development for police officers is reflected in promotion and advancement. Police organizations are the terrain in which careers develop, with individuals having both opportunities and constraints. Police organizations also have some unique qualities. Most officers, typically 75 percent, are in constable ranks, reflecting a steeply graded hierarchy. Promotions are both slow and rare, with a 15- year period at the rank of constable being common. Police forces have low job turnover, relatively high pay for one's educational credentials, high job security, low rates of transfer across forces, and low rates of transfer of skills to other types of work. New recruits are also more highly educated today and have expectations of faster promotions.

Career stage

Cooper (1982) described changes in police feelings and beliefs as they moved from being newcomers to veterans. While some officers held positive views about police work and their jobs throughout their careers, many did not, instead becoming cynical. Most fell between these two extremes, with "never promoted" officers being a concern. Cooper divided his sample into six career stages: less than one year, one to two years, three to seven years, and nine years or more as a constable, sergeants and staff sergeants in patrol and traffic, and sergeants and staff sergeants in CID. The first stage (first year) involved "breaking in." Individuals faced "reality shock," learned from more experienced officers, and developed an early awareness of criteria for promotion. In the second stage, "settling in," officers had more experience, conflicts about their roles increased, and promotions were now seen as more "political." In the third stage, "making it," the cost and toll of police work had increased and constables became more interested in promotion; they tried to understand promotion criteria, which involved more weight being given to "visibility." In the next stage, officers who had been promoted, and those who had not, began to view their concerns differently. Those officers who were continually passed over still did their jobs but became resigned, outside of work interests becoming more important. As they aged (to between 45 and 50), doing their jobs became more difficult. They became bitter, blaming the system for not seeing their talent and the contributions they had made. Those promoted now had to address new challenges, such as developing "newcomers." Over time, police officers became hardened, less trusting of the public and others, and more willing to help and support other officers. Family problems increased over time. Job demands increased, some finding these stimulating, others debilitating.

Cooper (1982) offers five areas of intervention in addressing career-stage issues:

1   Recruitment and training: applicants should receive a more realistic view of their jobs by talking with more experienced officers and though more realistic training activities and cases in recruitment training sessions.
2   Feedback and supervision: more contact with supervisors and more feedback on their work performance. This requires special effort, given that supervisors typically have limited direct observation of constables.

3   Promotion and assignment information: greater use of peer information, and information about passed-over constables, will provide information on what constables need to do to improve their future chances of promotion.
4   Training of supervisors in employee coaching and development.
5   Better understanding of plateaued officers in sessions on leadership: how keeping these officers challenged, feeling valued, and respected, will reduce the prospect of them becoming cynical, alienated, and dissatisfied. Other potential actions could involve lateral transfers, the use of flatter structures such as team policing, including content on the career plateau and its prevention in management development sessions, and making career counseling available at all career stages.

Women in policing: gender issues

Policing has traditionally been seen as being male dominated, having a "macho" culture, and valuing masculine traits such as aggression and physical strength (Rabe-Hemp, 2008). Although more women are now in policing, they still face obstacles in their work and careers. These include being socially isolated, facing negative attitudes from their male colleagues (Metcalfe and Dick, 2002), and sexual harassment from both colleagues and citizens. Fewer than 20 percent of police officers are women, with significantly fewer women in senior police management roles (Garcia, 2003). And although police forces in some countries have tried to increase the numbers of women in police work, these initiatives have not been very successful (Silvestri, 2003). Women report a lack of equal opportunity, discrimination and sexual harassment (Somvadee and Morash, 2008). Brown and Woolfenden (2011), noting that female officers take more sick days and in some cases maternity leave, see possible the implications of these as factors in available deployment days.

Public attitudes towards women police officers seem ambivalent. The public generally believes that female officers are as effective as male officers (Breci, 1997) particularly in incidents of child abuse, family disturbances, rape incidents, and spousal abuse (Kennedy and Homant, 1983). Kennedy and Homant (1983) for example, in a sample of 103 physically abused women, found that the latter rated the help they received from female officers as more highly valued. Male police offers seem less accepting of their female colleagues (Martin and Jurik, 1996). Many male officers prefer men as partners and back up. Women are often referred to in derogatory terms (Prokos and Padavic, 2002) and are not respected as "real officers" (Remington 1983). Women report great stress as a result of their male colleagues' behavior (Wexler and Logan, 1983). Carlson *et al.* (2011) studied male and female officer preferences for the sex of individuals providing back up in a study of 114 officers (87 of them men). Both male and female officers preferred males for back up, more so for males and females partnered with female officers. Females with female partners expressed the strongest preferences for male back up.

Stress and work–family issues

Jackson and Maslach (1982) found that police officer burnout had negative effects on their families. Police officer burnout increased levels of anger within families, decreased the amount of time spent with family members, lessened interest in family matters, and reduced marital satisfaction. They reported that reported that police officers' level of emotional exhaustion was associated with higher levels of job dissatisfaction, depersonalization, and marital distress.

Howard *et al.* (2004), in a sample of 1,219 police officers, found that work–family conflict was negatively related to several facets of job satisfaction (pay, supervision, promotion, co-workers) while family–work conflict was not as negatively related to these job satisfaction facets.

Factors that influence work and family issues in policing include shiftwork (and the resulting sleep disturbance problems), working undercover and absences from the family, and the effects of critical incidents and line of duty deaths. These factors result in police officers overprotecting their families, alcoholism, increased levels of domestic violence, and police suicide. Interventions targeted at the work–family interface include family therapy, professional counseling, accessing an Employee Assistance Program, and peer counseling.

Policing in a more diverse community

The *National Post* (2015) published a story that originally appeared a day or so earlier in the Associated Press, indicating that a US Justice Department investigation found widespread racial bias in the Ferguson, Mo. Police department (use of excessive force, issuing petty citations, routine traffic stops, etc.). Ferguson officials will meet with Justice Department representatives to develop ways to improve race relations in the department. Since the report was released, the Police Chief, Thomas Jackson, and two police officers have resigned (probably with full pensions), a senior administrator has been fired, and two other senior level administrators have resigned. E-mails sent by white officers referred to US President Barack Obama as a monkey, and a picture of bare-breasted African women was referred to as Mrs Obama's high school reunion (Salter, 2015). More than one year after the shooting of Michael Brown in Ferguson, demonstrations are still being held in several US cities to protest the shooting of an unarmed black man by a white police officer.

Police forces in Canada need to do considerably more to gain the trust of our native and aboriginal communities (Carlson, 2014). They have been criticized for their lack of interest and slow response to the deaths of, and missing, aboriginal women, and their treatment of native youth. In Canada, 1,181 aboriginal women and girls have been either murdered or are missing. Recently, the RCMP Commissioner told a gathering of First Nations leaders on December 9, that there are "racists"" on his force and he wants to get rid of them (Talaga, 2015). The head of the Ontario Provincial Police, Vince Hawkes, later said that there were also racists in his force (Talaga and Smith, 2015).

Police force diversity

There is sometimes tension between white and minority police officers. For example, white officers in Cleveland are suing their force, claiming that white officers receive greater punishments for wrongdoing than black officers (Gustafson, 2013).

Gould (1997) studied the effects of a two-day culture diversity session on 151 cadets and post-academy police officers. The evaluation included a questionnaire, completion of the MMPI (Minnesota Multi-Phasic Personality test), and being interviewed. Older, more experienced officers were more resistant to course objectives and cultural diversity training in general. MMPI scores on anger and cynicism were negatively correlated with respondents' attitudes towards their careers. More experienced officers showed higher levels of both anger and cynicism.

Gould offers five implications for future culture diversity training efforts: culture diversity should begin early in an officer's career; should be reinforced; should allow experienced officers opportunities to vent their frustrations about the training; should include experienced officers and senior executives together; and should explore cultural differences rather than blame police–community conflict on officers.

The "politics" of policing

For better and for worse, politics rears its head in the provision of police services. This is clear in the city of Toronto, in which I live. Officers in the Toronto Police Services belong to a strong union, which raises issues with senior police administrators, elected officials, and citizens. The Police Association serves to protect its members. Toronto has an eight-member Civilian Review Board, appointed by city and provincial leaders, and there have been tension and disagreements between some of these board members and senior police leadership. Obvious tension developed between the police union and NYC Mayor deBlasio following the assassination of two police officers on December 20, 2014. Police officers turned their back on the Mayor as he was speaking at a press conference on this tragedy. A police union asked the Mayor to not attend the funerals of the slain officers (Sherwell, 2014)—Mayor de Blasio had earlier supported demonstrations following the chokehold death of Eric Garner, at which some people shouted "death to cops."

Effective police chief leadership styles

Police organizations operate in a complex environment; many large city forces have billion-dollar budgets and thousands of employees. They now incorporate advanced technologies, have to deal with new types of crimes, and face budget cuts and higher citizen demands for accountability. To address these challenges, effective leadership is vital.

Traditionally, police leadership has been authoritarian—command and control—with little input from subordinates. However, there has been a trend toward more participative and shared leadership more recently. Several factors account for this shift. Subordinates prefer and respond more effectively to a more shared style of leadership. They do not respond well to autocratic leaders, and greater use of community policing calls for more shared leadership. Research has shown that police chiefs use various leadership styles, and their leadership styles may be generic, and similar, across leaders in general.

Bass (1985) distinguishes between transactional, transformational, and laissez-faire approaches to leading. Transactional leaders use contingent rewards based on job performance to achieve agreed-upon goals and rewards, monitor job performance to meet expectations, and prevent shortfalls; they take action only when performance problems occur. In transformational leadership, the leader utilizes emotions, showing trust and confidence in the subordinate to increase their motivations. Transformational leaders inspire subordinates by bonding with them emotionally, developing one-to-one relationships with staff, providing individualized consideration and mentoring, intellectually stimulating staff to question the way things are being done and offer new ideas, and use charisma to increase subordinates liking, respect, and identification with the leader. Laissez-faire leaders are passive and reactive, responding only when problems occur. Transformational leaders are more likely to achieve "performance beyond expectations," whereas transactional leaders are likely to achieve performance that "meets expectations." Laissez-faire leaders, a form of non-leadership, would fail to deliver acceptable job performance (Bass, 1985).

Sarver and Miller (2014) had 161 police chiefs in Texas complete a measure of transformational and transactional leadership, a measure of five personality factors (neuroticism, extraversion, openness, agreeableness, conscientiousness), and a background characteristics survey. Police chiefs fell equally into three leadership styles: transformational, transactional, and passive/avoidant. Transformational police chiefs received fewer formal and informal complaints from both civilians and fellow officers than did leaders having the other two leadership styles. Transformational police chiefs also scored higher on extra effort, effectiveness, and satisfaction than did passive/avoidant police chiefs, with transactional leaders scoring higher on both extra effort and effectiveness than passive/avoidant police chiefs. Transformational police chiefs scored higher on extraversion, openness, and conscientiousness than either transactional leaders (who scored lower on extraversion and openness) or avoidant/passive leaders (who scored lower on extraversion, openness and conscientiousness). None of the background characteristics of police chiefs predicted their leadership styles. However, Cockroft (2014) argues that transformational leadership would be a tough sell in police organizations.

Community policing—boon or burden?

The limitations of military and bureaucratic structures and governance models may have given impetus to the emergence and popularity (at least in rhetoric) of community policing. The concept of community policing has been widely endorsed by the policing community, with many police forces attempting to implement the concept. In addition, an increasing number of citizens claim to know what community policing is as well, and to embrace it. Community policing involves an increase in police and community interaction, a focus on "quality-of-life" concerns of citizens, demilitarizing the police force, increasing neighborhood patrols, problem-oriented and problem-solving police work, and ways of making policing more efficient and effective (Oliver and Bartgis, 1998). Potential benefits of community policing include improved police–community relationships, strengthened community resources for dealing with issues, changes in police attitudes and behaviors (more positive relationships), communities having more favorable views on the potential reduction in crime, and actual decreases in levels of crime. Barriers to community policing that have been identified include the fact that it is difficult to implement, police officers' attitudes and lack of training, community members who are unclear of their roles, and the police culture.

Community policing requires new attitudes and behaviors by police officers. Efforts to implement community policing have, however, produced very mixed results (Terpstra, 2009). There are a number of reasons for this. First, the concept of community policing itself is not well defined. Second, police forces face pressure to undertake their central task of fighting crime, thus reducing time and resources available for community policing. Third, increasing pressure for police accountability, and the need to decrease the costs of policing as the crime rate continues to fall, has now focused on measureable targets. Thus, community policing initiatives that do not directly contribute to meeting these targets are given a lower priority. Fourth, the image of community policing as "soft" is increasingly at odds with an emphasis on "law and order" and "punishment" in the larger community. Finally, given the gap between the views of "street cops" and "police administrators," if street cops do not buy in community policing efforts will fall short.

Increasing police efficiency—again searching for new models

There is now an increasing emphasis on police efficiency. Taxpaying citizens want accountability for costs, particularly as crime rates fall and incomes of police officers become public (e.g. excessive increases over time). A poll of 2,596 Ontario residents found that 53 percent would prefer spending their tax dollars on social services (transit, education, affordable housing, etc.) than on policing (Gillis, 2015b). Only 23 percent said they would spend more money on policing.

Some police departments make use of efficiency measures in evaluating the performance and promotability of officers. Technological advances such as computerization of police-related statistics have also increased pressure on the police for greater efficiency. However, some of these demands for efficiency may go against standards of police culture. In addition, some citizens are likely to be unhappy when newspapers publish the name of the officer handing out the highest number of parking violation tickets, as well as the streets incurring the most parking violation tickets.

In 2010, the British government unilaterally reduced police budgets in England and Wales by 20 percent, reducing police costs by $4.6 billion (Doolittle, 2014) The government did not tell police forces how to do this, but just to do it. Some forces have outsourced particular functions (e.g. HR, procurement, fleet and facilities maintenance, etc.). Other forces have combined back-office administrative functions with less routine patrolling and more use of volunteers. Other aspects of police work (e.g. holding a radar gun to catch speeders) are done by volunteers; unpaid civilians also walk police dogs, unlock police stations in the early morning, and perform garden maintenance on police properties. Other forces, and perhaps most, now focus on core police functions. It is also illegal in the UK for police officers to belong to a union, making it easier for such radical changes to be implemented.

Wexler (2010) noted that 51 percent of departments in his survey reported budget reductions, with most expecting further cuts as well. Some forces have made substantial reductions in staffing levels, with officers now spending less time on patrols. In addition, Phillips (2013), based on a national sample of police supervisors, found considerable support for the use of volunteers in policing.

The Toronto Police Services Board paid consulting firm KPMG $200,000 for a study on transforming Toronto policing and cutting costs, the report being kept secret from the taxpayers who funded it (Pagliaro and Powell, 2015). The report recommended cutting platoon sizes, reducing middle management, increasing civilian positions, closing all 17 police divisions and replacing them with store-front operations, and having more officers in the community. These recommendations would be a difficult sell to police force organizations. The Mayor of Toronto indicated that he would like to make this document public. The report was made public on December 10, 2015. Predictably, the Police Association dismissed the report as containing nothing new; they argued that it was based on flawed analyses, but agreed that there was room for improvement and stated that they would discuss the report with the Police Board. Toronto Mayor John Tory says that this report could lead to change; only time will tell.

Toronto will be spending over $1B on policing in 2016, with Canada spending $14B on policing. Increases in police budgets have outpaced inflation, a trend that cannot continue. There is little evidence that larger police budgets improve public security. Instead bold evidence-based approaches to policing need to be implemented (Kempa and Waller, 2015).

Matching demand for police services with resources

Richbell *et al.* (1998) describe the benefits of applying the Ottawa shift system in Sheffield, UK. The Ottawa system matches demand for policing (crime rates throughout a day, week or year) with changing the number of officers accordingly, using flexible working practices such as overlapping shifts, alternative shift patterns, more part-time police officers, and more civilians to undertake clerical and administrative work. Officers who have worked these new arrangements voted favorably to introduce it. Focus group and questionnaire results showed highly favorable responses to these new arrangements, officers voting (by 82 percent) to retain the new system. Officers indicated improvements in their health and well-being under the new shift arrangement, along with improvements in the quality of their life outside work, and better service to the public. Performance indicators showed reduced sick days and overtime, more arrests, and drops in reported crime.

Reducing police stress

Improving police officer resilience

Oliver and Meier (2009) evaluated the benefits of stress management education of police officers working in small forces in rural areas, using a longitudinal design with a matched control group of officers. Six hundred and sixty-four officers received training, with 132 officers serving as matched controls. Outcome variables included levels of anxiety, self-reported stress levels, and behaviors (e.g. sick days taken, complaints against the officer, etc.). Trained instructors delivered an eight-hour course addressing stress awareness training (definitions of stress and signs and symptoms of stress, stress in policing, stress in rural policing—four hours; and stress management training, diet, exercise, stress reduction techniques, critical incident stress debriefing—4 hours. Levels of perceived stress decreased following the training, as did anxiety levels, but the effects of the training diminished over time, suggesting a need for continuing education.

McCraty and Atkinson (2012) evaluated the effects of Coherence Advantage Resilience and performance enhancement training with a group of police officers from California. The program assessed values, emotional well-being, stress coping and interpersonal skills, work performance, workplace effectiveness and climate, family relationships, and physiological responses following acute stressors. The program of resilience building training increased officers' ability to identify and regulate their responses to stressors, both at work and outside of work. They showed lower levels of stress, fewer negative emotions, and greater peacefulness and vitality compared to officers not receiving the training program. Family relationships, communication and collaboration within their work units, and improved job performance also occurred.

Improving coping behavior

Here are some things we know about the experience of stressful events: events seen as extreme or unusual and potentially threatening will be stressful; failure to successfully cope with short-term stress will produce long-term chronic stress and burnout; and sources of stress that are chronic will reduce well-being, motivation, and performance. Anshel (2000) concluded that the teaching and monitoring of police officers' coping skills is not given enough attention in police training and officers' on-the-job supervision. Ineffective coping is associated with negative psychological and physical well-being outcomes such as stress, burnout, job dissatisfaction, work–family problems, and intention to quit the profession. Anshel offers a model of more effective coping, including an officers' detection of stressful events, the appraisal of these events, use of approach or avoidance coping processes, and cognitive and behavioral coping approaches

Employee Assistance Programs

Employee Assistance Programs (EAPs) tend to be under-utilized in police forces, as officers mistrust them and question whose needs they serve—the organization's or their employees. EAP providers/employees have a dual responsibility to the organization and the individual. All information is considered confidential. Participation in EAPs is not mandatory. EAPs have been shown to be cost effective; every dollar spent on EAPs gets a return on investment of several dollars through reducing absenteeism, reducing job-related accidents, cutting medical costs, lost productivity, reduced turnover, fewer terminations, increased staff morale, and lower disability costs. Unfortunately, officers believe that confidentiality will not be maintained and that sensitive information will be made public, thus damaging careers. The macho nature of police cultures also discourages officers from seeking help and disparages those that do.

Organizational interventions

Amaranto, Steinberg, Castellana and Mitchell (2002) describe two interventions undertaken by the Newark Police Department to deal with potential mental health concerns of officers. One was an educational program, and the second was an awareness hotline that would provide officers with immediate mental health referrals and services. The educational program was viewed positively by participants and senior management and increased use of the phone hotline was observed.

Improving police officer training

Lumb and Breazeale (2002) describe a pilot program to train police supervisors in recognizing and identifying potential problem behaviors of their officer staff and other force employees. It involved employing proactive intervention technology, using coaching and counseling, and covering various ways to help distressed employees identify more constructive behaviors. The training program involved 12 training days, with participants given reading assignments, participating in in-session role plays of coaching skills, and completing a number of self-assessment instruments.

Ruff (2012) highlights the benefits of police officer training in intimate partner violence in response to domestic dispute calls in a sample of Canadian police officers. This particular training program was delivered in sessions spread over a two-day time period. Following the training, officers spent significantly more time with parties and collected more evidence from victims (arresting more of the accused), and more cases were presented to crown prosecutors. The training resulted in better information being collected by officers and more help being provided to victims.

Herringon and Pope (2014) evaluated a training program to improve police officer ability to respond effectively and safely to incidents involving a person with a mental illness (the Mental Health Intervention Team—MHIT). One hundred and eleven officers from three commands were trained. The program had four objectives: to reduce injury to police officers and people with mental illness, to increase police awareness of mental health issues of citizens and how best to deal with these, to reduce unnecessary time spent transporting people with mental illness to care facilities, and to promote increasing inter-agency cooperation in response to incidents involving persons with mental illness. The training program increased police officer confidence in handling mental health incidents, reduced police involvement in transporting people with mental illness, and made the transfer to mental health care services smoother. Difficulties with inter-agency cooperation still were present however.

Scrutiny and surveillance of police officers

Police officers are now also under greater scrutiny, surveillance, and accountability (Walker and Archbold, 2014). Police officer actions can be videotaped by observers, by video recorders in their police cars or on their persons, by cameras on buildings, and in jail cells. Body cameras and video systems are increasingly being used for law enforcement in North America, the UK, and Europe. This "evidence" can work in favor or against officers' credibility and actions, however. Use of these tools has revealed incidents of officer misconduct and has also exonerated officers, given the behavior of the suspect.

Jennings *et al.* (2014), in a sample of 95 Orlando police offers, found positive views on the use of body cameras. They would be comfortable wearing them, saw potential benefits in improving their own behaviors, citizen behaviors, and behaviors of other officers. However, these results should be treated with caution, given the size of the sample and the low officer response rate.

Implications for police organizations

Every organization faces challenges in maintaining or improving its' performance; police organizations are no exception. The following challenges seem relevant today:

1 There is a need for police organizations to monitor and improve the well-being of police officers and their families.
2 There is a need for police forces to be more reflective of the communities they serve.
3 There is a need for police organizations to better integrate and utilize the skills and talents of women and minority officers.
4 There is a need to demilitarize police forces.
5 There is a need for police forces to be more accountable to the communities they serve.
6 There is a need for greater civilian oversight of police organizations. Legitimate concerns are raised when the police "police" the police.
7 There is a need to improve relations, respect, and trust between police organizations and the communities they serve. While community policing may be a step in this direction, implementing community policing has proven to be very difficult.
8 There is a need for police organizations to become more efficient and effective (e.g. reducing costs, improving training, more use of civilians, increasing leadership effectiveness).
9 There is a need for more police training in dealing with the mentally ill, reducing conflict, and problem solving.
10 There is a need to adopt new models of management and innovative policing practices and strategies

11 There is a need for more research on today's police services involving police officers in ongoing internal research, in some cases in partnership with external researchers (Donnely, 2013).

12 There is a need for police forces to terminate "rogue officers," and police officers under investigation for misconduct should not receive pay.

Note

1 Preparation of this chapter was supported in part by York University. Cobi Wolpin helped to identify relevant literature. Carla D'Agostino assisted in the preparation of the manuscript. When this collection was being planned, it seemed to fit well with our series on Psychological and Behavioral Aspects of Risk in Organizations. At that point, no one would have predicted the extent to which policing has moved into the national debate in several countries. It has been a trying year for police forces, which now have to address longstanding issues.

References

Amaranto, E., Steinberg, J., Castellano, C., and Mitchell, R. (2002) Police stress interventions. *Brief Treatment and Crisis Intervention*, 3, 47–53.

Anderson, A. S. and Lo, C. C. (2011) Intimate partner violence with law enforcement families. *Journal of Interpersonal Violence*, 26, 1176–1193.

Anshel, M. H. (2000) A conceptual model and implications for coping with stressful events in police work. *Criminal Justice and Behavior*, 27, 375–400.

Babwin, D. (2015a) "Don't kill our children", protesters tell police. *Toronto Star*, November 26, A21.

Babwin, D. (2015b) Chicago mayor fires police superintendent. *Toronto Star*, December 2, A12.

Babwin, D. and Keyser, J. (2015) Protests erupt in Chicago: Video released of white cop, now charged with murder, shooting black teen 16 times. *Toronto Star*, November 25, A4.

Bass, B. M. (1985) *Leadership and Performance beyond Expectations*. New York: Free Press.

Biggam, F. H., Power, K. G., Macdonald, R. R., Carcary, W. B., and Moodie, E. (1997) Self-perceived occupational stress/distress in a Scottish police force. *Work and Stress*, 11, 118–133.

Breci, M. G. (1997) Female officers on patrol: Public perceptions in the 1990s. *Journal of Criminal Justice*, 20, 153–165.

Brown, J. and Woolfenden, S. (2011) Implications of the changing gender ratio amongst warranted police officers. *Policing*, 5, 356–364.

Brown, L. (2014) RCMP officers disciplined in record numbers. *Toronto Star*, June 27, A1, A4.

Carlson, K. B. (2014) Police work to build trust with First Nations. *Globe and Mail*, October 4. A3.

Carlson, P. E., Nored, L. S., and Downey, R. A. (2011) Officer preferences for male backup: The influence of gender and police partnering. *Journal of Police and Criminal Psychology*, 26, 4–10.

Chae, M. H. and Boyle, D.J. (2013) Police suicide: Prevalence, risk, and protective factors. *Policing: An International Journal of Police Strategies and Management*, 36, 91–118.

Clark, D. W., White, E. K., and Violanti, J. M. (2012) Law enforcement suicide: Current knowledge and future directions. *The Police Chief*, 79, 48–51.

Cockcroft, T. (2014) Police culture and transformational leadership: Outlining the contours of a troubled relationship. *Policing*, 8, 50–13.

Cooper, W. H. (1982) Police officers over career stages. *Canadian Police College Journal*, 6, 93–112.

D'Angelo, J. (2000) Addicted to violence: The cycle of domestic abuse committed by police officers. In D. C. Sheehan (ed.), *Domestic Violence by Police Officers*. Washington, D.C.: U.S. Government Printing Office, pp. 149–161.

Davey, J., Obst, P., and Sheehan, M. (2000) Developing a profile of alcohol consumption patterns of police officers in a large scale sample of an Australian police service, *European Addiction Research*, 6, 205–212.

Davey, J. D., Obst, P. l., and Sheehan, M. C. (2001) It goes with the job: Officers insights into stress and the culture of alcohol consumption within the policing occupation. *Drugs: Education, Prevention and Policy*, 8, 141–149.

Davies, D. T. (2015) Police watchdog a sham. *Toronto Star*, November 6, A14.

Donnelly, D. (2013) The police officer as social scientist: Some reflections. *Police Journal*, 36, 53–65.

Doolittle, R. (2014) A thin blue line. *Globe and Mail*, December 6, M1M6.

Ferreira, V. (2015a) Officer: Paid suspension was "dream come true." *National Post*, July 15, A1, A2.

Ferreira, V. (2015b) Suspended police cost Ontario $13K a day. *National Post*, September 1, A1, Ay.

Fox, J., Desai, M. M., Britten, K., Lucas G., Luneau R., and Rosenthal, M. S. (2012) Mental-health conditions, barriers to care, and productivity loss among officers in an urban police department, *Connecticut Medicine*, 76, 525–531.

Gallant, J. (2015) Judge calls incident report a "work of fiction." *Toronto Star*, September 13, A1, A2.

Garcia, V. (2003) Difference in the police department: Women, policing, and "doing gender." *Journal of Contemporary Criminal Justice*, 19, 130–144.

Gershon, R., Barocas, B., Canton, A. S., Li, X., and Vlahov, D, (2009) Mental, physical, and behavioral outcomes associated with perceived work stress in police officers. *Criminal Justice and Behavior*, 36, 275–289.

Gillis, W. (2014) High hopes for use-of-force study: Experts seek improved training for officers, more de-escalation. *Toronto Star*, July 24, GT1, GT5.

Gillis, W. (2015a) More training, less-lethal force and "zero deaths." *Toronto Star*, September 16, A1, A2.

Gillis, W. (2015b) Support low for a police budget boost, poll finds. *Toronto Star*, November 12, GT1, GT4.

Gillis, W. and Deschamps, T. (2015) Cop makes bail in child porn case. *Toronto Star*, August 21, GT1, G2.

Globe and Mail (2014) Police and guns: How not to use deadly force, November 29, F9.

Gould, L. A. (1997) Can an old dog be taught new tricks? Teaching cultural diversity to police officers. *Policing: An International Journal of Police Strategies and Management*, 20, 339–356.

Gustafson, J. (2013) Diversity in municipal police agencies: A national examination of minority hiring and promotion. *Policing: An International Journal of Police Strategies and Management*, 36, 719–736.

Hays, T. and Long, C. (2014) NYPD officer cleared in chokehold death. *Toronto Star*, December 4, A18.

Herrington, V. and Pope, R. (2014) The impact of police training in mental health: An example from Australia. *Policing and Society*, 24, 501–522.

Hickman, M. J., Piquero, M. L., and Piquero, A. R. (2004) The validity of Niederhoffer's cynicism scale. *Journal of Criminal Justice*, 22, 1–13.

Houdmont, J., Kerr, R., and Randall, R. (2012) Organizational psychosocial hazard exposure in UK policing. *Policing: An International Journal of Police Strategies and Management*, 35, 182–197.

Howard, W. G., Donofrio, H. H., and Bales, J. S. (2004) Inter-domain work-family, family-work conflict and police work satisfaction. *Policing: An International Journal of Police Strategies and Management*, 27, 380–395.

Ingram, J. R., Weidner, R. R., Paoline, E. A., & Terrill, W. (2014) Supervisory influences on officer's perceptions of lethal force policy: a multilevel analysis. Policing: An International Journal of Police Strategies and Management, 37, 355-372.

Jackson, J., and Bradford, B. (2010) What is trust and confidence in the police? *Policing*, 4, 241–248.

Jackson, S.E. and Maslach, C. (1982) After-effects of job-related stress: Families as victims. *Journal of Occupational Behavior*, 3, 63–77.

Jennings, W. G., Fridell, L. A., and Lynch, M. D. (2014)Cops and cameras: Officer perceptions of the use of body-worn cameras in law enforcement. *Journal of Criminal Justice*, 42, 549–556.

Johnson, L. B., Todd, M., and Subramanian, G. (2005) Violence in police families: Work-spillover. *Journal of Family Violence*, 20, 3–12.

Kempa, M. and Waller, I. (2015) Massive police budges don't improve safety for the public. *Toronto Star*, November 12, A23.

Kennedy, D. B., and Homant, R. J. (1983) Attitudes of abused women toward male and female police officers. *Criminal Justice Behavior*, 10, 391–405.

Kop, N. and Euwena, M. C. (2001) Occupational stress and the use of force by Dutch police officers. *Criminal Justice and Behavior*, 28, 631–652.

Kunzleman, M. (2015) Louisiana cops charged in autistic boy's killing. *Toronto Star*, November 10, A11.

Lee, H., Lim, H., Moore, D. D., and Kim, J. (2013) How police organizational structure correlates with frontline officers attitudes toward corruption: A multi-level model. *Police Practice and Research*, 14, 386–401.

Lerch, K. M. and Mieczkowski, T. (2009) Violent police behavior: Past, present, and future research directions. *Aggression and Violent Behavior*, 10, 552–568

Lindsay, V. (2008) Police officers and their alcohol consumption: Should we be concerned? *Police Quarterly*, 11, 74–87.

Loftus, B. (2010) Police occupational culture: Classic themes, altered times. *Policing and Society*, 20, 1–20.

Lowe, K. C., Vinson, J., Tolsma, J., and Kaufmann, G. (2008) Symptoms of undercover police officers: A comparison of officers currently, formerly and without undercover experience. *International Journal of Stress Management*, 15, 136–152.

Lumb, R. C. and Breazeale, R. (2002) Police officer attitudes and community policing implementation: Developing strategies for durable organizational change. *Policing and Society*, 13, 91–106.

McCanlies, E. C., Mnatsakonova, A., Andrew, M. E., Burchfiel, C. M., and Violanti, J. M. (2014) Positive psychological factors are associated with lower PTSD symptoms among police officers: Post Hurricane Katrina. *Stress and Health*, 30, 405–415.

McCraty, R. and Atkinson, M. (2012) Resilience training program reduces physiological and psychological stress in police officers. *Global Advances in Health and Medicine*, 1, 44–66.

McLean, J. and Poisson, J.(2015a) Breaking badge. *Toronto Star*, September 18, A1, A7

McLean, J. and Poisson, J (2015b) Does the punishment fit the crime? *Toronto Star*, September 19, A1, A18.

McLean, J. and Poisson, J. (2001c) Drunk and disorderly. *Toronto Star*, September 20, A1, A7.

McLean, J. and Poisson, J. (2001d) Abuse of authority. *TorontoStar*, September 21, A1, A8.

Martin, S. E. and Jurik, N. C. (1996) *Doing justice, Doing Gender: Women in Law and Criminal Justice Occupations*. Thousand Oaks, C.A.: Sage Publications.

Metcalfe, B. and Dick, G. (2002) Is the force still with her? Gender and commitment in the police. *Women in Management Review*, 17, 392–403.

National Post (2014) Demilitarizing the police. December 3, A12.

National Post (2015) Racial bias found in Ferguson police. March 4, A9.

Niederhoffer, A. (1967) *Behind the Shield*. New York: Anchor.

Obst, P., Davey, J., and Sheehan, M. (2001) Does joining the police drive you to drink? A longitudinal study of the drinking habits of police recruits. *Drugs: Education, Prevention and Policy*, 8, 347–357.

Oehme, K., Donnelly, E., and Martin, A. (2012) Alcohol abuse, PTSD, and officer-committed domestic violence. *Policing: A Journal of Policy and Practice*, 6, 418–430.

Oehme, K., Siebert, D. C., Siebert, C. F., Stern, N., Valentine, C., and Donnelly, E. (2011) Protecting lives, careers, and public confidence: Florida's efforts to prevent officer-involved domestic violence. *Family Court Review*, 49, 84–106.

Oliver, W. M. and Bartgis, E. (1998) Community policing: A conceptual framework. *Policing: An International Journal of Police Strategies and Management*, 21, 490–509.

Oliver, W. M. and Meier, C. (2009) Considering the efficacy of stress management education on small-town and rural police. *Applied Psychology in Criminal Justice*, 5, 1–23.

Pagliaro, J. and Powell, B. (2015) Report urging radical police reform buried: Board paid $200K for study on future of Toronto force, but kept its contents secret. *Toronto Star*, November 7, A1, A18.

Phillips, S. W. (2013) Using volunteers in policing: A force field analysis of American supervisors. *Police Journal*, 86, 289–306.

Poisson, J. and McLean, J. (2015) Disciplinary records reveal more cops behaving badly. *Toronto Star*, November 30, A1, A10.

Prokos, A. and Padavic, I. (2002) "There outta be a law against bitches": Masculinity lessons in police academy training. *Gender Work and Organization*, 9, 439–459.

Pruden, J. G. (2015) Mayerthorpe's long shadow. *National Post*, March 2, A3.

Rabe-Hemp, C. (2008) Survival in an "all boys club": Policewomen and their fight for acceptance. *Policing: An International Journal of Police Strategies and Management*, 31, 251–270.

Remmington, P. W. (1983) Women in the police: Integration or separation? *Qualitative Sociology*, 6, 118–135.

Reuss-Ianni, E. and Ianni, F. (1983) Street cops and management cops: The two cultures in policing. In M. Punch (ed.), *Control in Police Organizations*. Cambridge, M.A.: MIT Press. pp, 251–274.

Richbell, S., Simpson, M., Sykes, G. M. H., and Meegan, S. (1998) Policing with the Ottawa shift system: A British experience. *Policing: An International Journal of Police Strategies and Management*, 21, 384–396.

Rider, D. (2015) Blair leaving with high appraisal survey finds. *Toronto Star*, January 27, GT4.

Robbers, M. L. P. and Jenkins, J. M. (2005) Symptomatology of post-traumatic stress disorder among first responders to the Pentagon on 9/11: A preliminary analysis of Arlington County police first responders. *Police Practice and Research*, 6, 235–246.

Ruff, L. (2012) Does training matter? Exploring police officer response to domestic dispute calls before and after training on intimate partner violence. *Police Journal*, 85, 285–300.

Salter, J. (2015) Ferguson officials forced to tackle police's racial bias. *Toronto Star*, March 7, A13.

Sarver, M. B. and Miller, H. (2014) Police chief leadership: Styles and effectiveness. *Policing: An International Journal of Police Strategies and Management*, 37, 126–143.

Sheehan, D. C. (2000) *Domestic Partner Violence by Police Officers*. Washington, D. C.: U.S. Government Printing Office.

Sherwell, P. (2014) NY police snub mayor after killings: Feel betrayed. *National Post*, December 22, A10.

Silvestri, M. (2003) *Women in Charge: Policing, Gender and Leadership*. Wilson: Devon.

Skolnick, J. H. and Fyfe, J. J. (1996) *Above the Law: Police and the Excessive Use of Force*. New York: Free Press.

Somvadee, C. and Morash, M. (2008) Dynamics of sexual harassment for policewomen working alongside men. *Policing: An International Journal of Police Strategies and Management*, 31, 485–498.

Taber, J. (2014) RCMP suicide stirs treatment debate: Death of Mountie who smoked medical marijuana for PTSD highlights lack of stragtegties for dealing with trauma in first responders. *Globe and Mail*, October 11, A3.

Talaga, T. (2015) "Racists" are in RCMP, commissioner tells AFN Chiefs. *Toronto Star*, December 10, A10.

Talaga, T. and Smith, J. (2015) OPP admits "past issues" with racism among ranks. *Toronto Star*, December 17, A1, A6.

Tarm, M. (2015) Chicago residents in shock after police "accidently shoot woman, agitated teen." *Toronto Star*, December 28, A8.

Terpstra, J. (2009) Community policing in practice: Ambitions and realization. *Policing*, 4, 64–72.

Toch, H. (2008) Police officers as change agents in police reform. *Policing and Society*, 18, 60–71.

Toronto Star (2014) America's spendthrift police. November 1, WD8.

Toronto Star (2015a) Sherriff's deputy shot deal near Houston. August 30, A12.

Toronto Star (2015b) $6.5M settlement reached with family. October 9, A13.

Toronto Star (2015c) U.K. police apologize for undercover officers' "abusive" behaviors. November 21, A25.

Toronto Star (2015d) Police officer's dismissal for smuggling alcohol upheld. November 25, A6.

Van Maanen, J. (1978) The asshole. In P. K. Manning and J. van Maanen (eds.), *Policing: A View from the Street*. Santa Monica, C.A.: Goodyear Publishing, pp. 221–238.

Vila, B. and Moore, J. M. (2008) Police long work hours: Causes, consequences and alternatives. In R. J. Burke and C. L. Cooper (eds.), *The Long Work Hours Culture: Causes, Consequences and Choices*. Bingley: Emerald Publishing, pp. 183–201.

Violanti, J. M. (2007) *Police Suicide: Epidemic in Blue*. Springfield, I.L.: Charles Thomas.

Waddington, P. A. J. (2010) *Police corruption. Policing*, 4, 313–314.

Walker, S. E. and Archbold, C. A. (2014) The New World of Police Accountability. Thousand Oaks, C.A.: Sage Publications.

Waters, J. A. and Ussery, W. (2007) Police stress: History, contributing factors, symptoms, and interventions. *Policing: An International Journal of Police Strategies and Management*, 30, 169–188.

Wells, W. and Schafer, J. A. (2006) Officer perceptions of police responses to persons with a mental illness. *Policing: An International Journal of Police Strategies and Management*, 29, 578–601.

West, C., Bernard, B., Mueller, C., Kitt, M., Driscoll, R., and Tak, S. (2008) Mental health outcomes in police personnel after Hurricane Katrina. *Journal of Occupational and Environmental Medicine*, 50, 698–695.

Wexler, C. (2010) Survey reveals extent of police budget cuts. Washington, D.C.: Police Executive Research Forum.

Wexler, J. G. and Logan, D. D. (1983) Sources of stress among women police officers. *Journal of Police Science and Administration*, 11, 46–53.

Wilder, D., Christoff, C., and Nash, J. (2014) Ferguson doomed to repeat mistakes of other U.S. riots. *Globe and Mail*, August 18, A13.

Wittmeier, B. and Pruden, J. G. (2015) Edmonton suspect "didn't care about law." *National Post*, June 10, A1, A6.

Woods, A. (2015) Cops accused of sex assault. *Toronto Star*, October 24, A14.

Worden, R. E., Harris, C., and McLean, S. J. (2014) Risk assessment and risk management in policing. *Policing: An International Journal of Police Strategies and Management*, 37, 239–258.

2 Community-oriented policing

Implications for officer well-being

Charlotte Gill

Introduction

Community-oriented policing (COP) is a law enforcement philosophy that partners police and citizens in identifying and responding to crime problems. The approach, which became popular between the 1970s and early 1990s, has been highly influential in police departments around the world and has enjoyed significant financial investment and support from governments, including a dedicated federal office in the United States. A substantial body of research and evaluation has documented the implementation of COP and its impact on crime and other community-related outcomes, such as perceptions of disorder, fear of crime, and satisfaction with and trust in the police. There is some, but considerably less, research on COP from the perspective of the police organization—the impact of the reorientation of police departments toward citizen collaboration on culture, management, and the day-to-day activities of police officers. The nature of the relationship between COP and associated organizational change on officer well-being, morale, and safety is a particularly important issue. Police departments cannot expect their officers to effectively engage communities if they themselves feel disillusioned, unsupported, and/or afraid.

This challenge has become increasingly relevant in recent times as the police face a second "crisis of legitimacy." The first "crisis," in the 1960s and 1970s, centered on the perception that "nothing worked" to reduce crime and that the criminal justice system as a whole was out of touch with citizens. But even as we have moved away from the "nothing works" era, the second decade of the twenty-first century has brought new questions and scrutiny about the authority and legitimacy of the police and how they interact with citizens, especially the most vulnerable among them—in particular, young men and women of color and individuals with mental health challenges and cognitive deficits. In response to this crisis, in late 2014 President Obama convened a task force on twenty-first century policing to identify strategies for rebuilding community trust in the police, while maintaining crime control effectiveness. The report of the task force (President's Task Force on 21st Century Policing, 2015) clearly highlights the connection between officer well-being and community safety, recognizing the need for police agencies to promote wellness and stress reduction at all levels of the agency at the same time as improving community relations. However, there is little guidance in the scholarly literature about how to connect and jointly pursue these two goals.

In this chapter I explore the history and impact of COP, and consider the advantages and disadvantages of COP from the perspective of both the organizational structure and culture of the police agency and the well-being and experiences of individual officers. I conclude with some ideas about how the next generation of COP efforts can better support the officers, supervisors, and command staff who participate in them.

Community-oriented policing: overview and history

Community-oriented policing (COP) is a law enforcement philosophy centered on the "co-production" of public safety by police organizations and citizens. The underlying assumption of COP is that the police are not limited to their traditional law enforcement powers and should work in collaboration with community members to define, prioritize, and address crime problems (Weisburd and McElroy, 1988).

The COP philosophy emphasizes three key elements (Office of Community Oriented Policing Services, 2014; Skogan, 2006b). The first is community partnerships. Police are expected to draw upon the expertise of local citizens in identifying and solving problems. "Community" is broadly defined here, and includes community groups, businesses, government agencies and departments, service providers and the media as well as individuals (Office of Community Oriented Policing Services, 2014). The second element is problem-solving. Police should engage in systematic problem analysis and response in collaboration with the community and focus on understanding the root causes of crime problems within the community, rather than reacting to individual crimes as and when they occur. However, COP is distinct from problem-oriented policing, which may or may not involve the community (Goldstein, 1990; Weisburd *et al.*, 2010). The third and final hallmark of COP is organizational transformation. This element is key to distinguishing COP as a philosophy rather than a policing program or strategy. COP requires full organizational commitment to the approach and a philosophical shift in leadership, structure, information-sharing, and other factors. The purpose of this organizational transformation is primarily to allow for the delegation of decision-making and problem-solving to line officers who directly interact with community members (G. W. Cordner, 1999; Office of Community Oriented Policing Services, 2014; Trojanowicz *et al.*, 1998; Weisburd *et al.*, 2003), as well as marking an expanded mandate for the police organization that prioritizes creativity and community empowerment as well as law enforcement and control (Trojanowicz and Bucqueroux, 1994). Thus, problem-solving in collaboration with the community represents the "tactical" element of COP, conducted against the backdrop of a community-oriented organizational culture (G. W. Cordner, 1999).

COP is a popular philosophy in police departments in the United States and around the world, and has been widely used for several decades (Mastrofski *et al.*, 2007; and, for example, Skolnick and Bayley, 1988). Its popularity increased rapidly between the 1970s and early 1990s, following decades of dissatisfaction with the traditional or "standard model" of law enforcement (e.g. Weisburd and Eck, 2004). The standard model emphasized reactive responses to crime rather than proactive problem-solving and a focus on short-term outcomes and targets rather than longer-term priorities such as police effectiveness, legitimacy, or relationships with the community; it rarely required the police to collaborate with citizens or external agencies.

In the United States in particular, but also in other parts of the world (see, for example, Brody (1976) in the United Kingdom), the 1970s were characterized by rising crime rates, a lack of public support for a criminal justice system that was viewed as being "out of touch" with communities, and disillusionment about the effectiveness of a broad range of criminal justice and rehabilitative practices (Martinson, 1974; President's Commission on Law Enforcement and Administration of Justice, 1967). This period coincided with emerging interest in rigorous research on crime and justice issues, including randomized controlled trials (Farrington, 1983, 2003; Farrington, Ohlin, and Wilson, 1986; Weisburd, Petrosino, and Mason, 1993). In policing, several high-profile studies suggested that two key elements of the standard model—random preventive patrol and rapid response to emergency calls—had little impact on crime rates (e.g. Kelling *et al.*, 1974; Spelman and Brown, 1984; see also Weisburd and Braga, 2006). Just as the Martinson (1974) report on the effectiveness of rehabilitation programs led to the overarching conclusion that "nothing works," these studies in their historical context raised questions about the effectiveness of the police in general. By the early 1990s, some scholars believed that the police could not do anything to prevent crime (Bayley, 1994; Goldstein, 1990; Gottfredson and Hirschi, 1990).

However, this crisis of confidence in policing also paved the way for innovation (e.g. Morabito, 2010). While the ideas underpinning COP in the United States can be traced back to the early twentieth century (Skolnick and Bayley, 1988), it was during this period of unrest that scholars and COP advocates envisaged the use of community-oriented approaches as a radical departure from the traditional practices associated with a lack of police effectiveness. Observational studies of police agencies had begun to highlight the fact that police work most often involved community-oriented approaches such as providing services, keeping order, providing reassurance, and resolving conflict rather than "crime fighting," even though the latter had typically been emphasized as the primary focus of policing (Kelling and Moore, 1988; Reiss, 1971; Skogan and Frydl, 2004; Skogan and Hartnett, 1997; Weisburd and Braga, 2006). Given that the effectiveness of reactive patrol strategies and rapid response had been called into question, COP provided an opportunity to reorient police operations toward strengthening relationships with the community rather than emergency call-driven response (Skolnick and Bayley, 1988). Furthermore, by placing the community as central to the police function, COP offered police agencies a chance to reconnect with disillusioned citizens (Scheider *et al.*, 2009).

In 1994, the Office of Community Oriented Policing Services (COPS Office) was created as a branch of the United States Department of Justice under the Violent Crime Control and Law Enforcement Act, with a budget of almost $150 million to encourage agencies to implement COP and hire COP officers.[1] To date, the COPS Office has provided over $14 billion[2] in funding to a majority of police agencies in the United States (Scheider *et al.*, 2009). This significant investment has undoubtedly contributed to the extensive use of COP by police departments across the country (Skogan, 2006b; Skogan and Frydl, 2004; Weisburd and Eck, 2004; J. Zhao *et al.*, 1999). In a 1997 survey by the Police Foundation, 85 percent of all responding departments reported that they had either adopted COP or planned to adopt it, and 100 percent of departments serving municipalities with populations of 100,000 or more reported using COP (see also Hickman and Reaves, 2001; Mastrofski *et al.*, 2007; Skogan, 2004).

During the recent economic downturn in the United States, the proportion of police departments—particularly small departments—employing full-time COP officers declined somewhat (e.g. Reaves, 2010). The events of September 11, 2001 may also have impacted the use of COP in the U.S., especially in larger municipalities, as police officers were reassigned to more security-based duties (Fridell, 2004). However, it is likely that COP will continue to remain a key component of police agencies' toolkits and may even see a resurgence in interest, given increasing recognition of its potential for addressing some of the most pressing issues facing law enforcement today. For example, the recent report of the President's Task Force on 21st Century Policing highlights COP as a means to increase trust and collaboration between police departments and citizens (President's Task Force on 21st Century Policing, 2015), and there is growing interest in the role of COP in efforts to prevent terrorism and counter the development of violent extremism in communities

(International Association of Chiefs of Police, 2014). The most recent Law Enforcement Management and Administrative Statistics (LEMAS) survey, conducted in 2013, indicates that there was a significant increase in the number of police departments including a COP component in their mission statements over the past decade (Reaves, 2015).

The effectiveness of community-oriented policing

Despite the significant investment in and use of community-oriented policing across the United States, the evidence base for its effectiveness is mixed. On the one hand, studies indicate that the impact of COP on crime reduction is limited. On the other, program evaluations have identified that COP can be effective for other non-crime outcomes, such as citizen satisfaction with the police and perceptions of legitimacy.

As the history of the development of COP suggests, crime control was not originally envisaged as the primary outcome of increased police-community engagement (Skogan, 2006b). In fact, one of the driving forces behind COP was the need to identify new priorities for the police because their effectiveness as crime control agents had been called into question. COP places citizen reassurance and relationship-building, order maintenance, and problem-solving ahead of law enforcement as policing's "core function" (Mastrofski *et al.*, 1995) and it was not adopted by police departments as a crime reduction strategy (Skogan, 2006b). The question of whether COP might be effective in reducing crime likely arose in the context of the "crime control" focus of the federal government and the criminal justice system in general during the 1980s and 1990s (Klockars, 1985; Skogan, 2006b).

The lack of a clear connection between COP and crime control may explain why several reviews of the available research offer limited support for the argument that COP is an effective crime reduction tool. Sherman & Eck (2006) highlight a number of commonly-used elements of COP, including neighborhood watch, community meetings, police storefronts, and providing information about local crime to citizens, that have little to no effect on crime (see also Skogan and Frydl, 2004; Weisburd and Eck, 2004). Weisburd and Eck (2004) also note a surprising lack of rigorous research studies evaluating COP, which is at odds with the proliferation of programs over the previous two decades. Gill *et al.* (2014), in a systematic review of 65 studies involving at least a non-equivalent comparison group, find a small but non-significant effect of COP on crime in neighborhoods, and no evidence that it reduces citizens' fear of crime.

However, the emphasis of COP on alternatives to crime fighting, such as addressing disorder and building trust and relationships between police and the community, and its potential for enhancing police legitimacy, suggest that its impact on other non-crime outcomes may be more promising (Mastrofski *et al.*, 1995; Sherman and Eck 2006). Indeed, Gill *et al.* (2014) find a moderate, statistically significant increase in citizens' ratings of satisfaction with the police following the implementation of COP, compared to areas receiving traditional law enforcement. COP also showed promising benefits for citizen perceptions of police legitimacy and reduced disorder across the studies they reviewed.

Furthermore, Gill *et al.* (2014) propose that these benefits could translate into an indirect impact of COP on crime prevention in the long term (although they caution that none of the studies they reviewed had a sufficiently long follow-up period to assess this proposition). Citizens who trust the police and accept their authority to enforce the law are more likely to comply with this authority (Sunshine and Tyler, 2003; Tyler, 1990,

2004; Tyler and Huo, 2002), suggesting that citizens' perceptions of police legitimacy and effectiveness may impact crime rates in neighborhoods or smaller units of geography. Higginson and Mazerolle (2014) find support for this suggestion in a systematic review of procedurally just policing, which was associated with a notable reduction in crime in the target areas. Several studies find that citizens' perceptions of police effectiveness and behavior are related to levels of collective efficacy (e.g. Sampson *et al.*, 1997) in neighborhoods (e.g. Jackson and Sunshine, 2007; Kochel, 2012; Wells *et al.*, 2006), which may themselves be associated with lower crime rates (e.g. Weisburd *et al.*, 2012). Scheider *et al.* (2009) suggest that combining COP with other police strategies and tactics that have been proven to reduce crime may be the most effective way of enhancing both trust and collaboration between police and citizens and crime prevention (see also Weisburd *et al.*, 2015).

While the evidence-base shows that COP clearly has some beneficial effects for the community, it has been criticized for its lack of effectiveness for crime control. The primary challenge of COP is the lack of clear guidance on how it should be implemented by police agencies. Trojanowicz *et al.* (1998) state that COP is a philosophy or guiding framework for policing more generally, and *not* simply another police tactic or program. However, the organizational transformation element of COP has received much less attention than the community engagement or problem-solving aspects. Implementing COP depends heavily on the organizational characteristics and commitment of the specific agency and the nature and needs of the community it serves (Chappell, 2009; Morabito, 2010; Weisburd and McElroy, 1988). Thus, there are no specific criteria for implementation. Maguire and Katz (2002) note that COP is so broadly defined that individual police agencies must engage in an "interpretive process" to define it, make sense of it, and enact it at the local level. Unsurprisingly, this impacts police leaders' abilities to garner resources and support for "doing" COP (Mastrofski *et al.*, 2007).

Adding to the confusion around COP is the fact that so many different strategies and tactics have been used by agencies as evidence of COP implementation. They range from problem-oriented policing and multi-agency partnerships to foot patrol, neighborhood watch, and newsletters (Gianakis and Davis III, 1998; Gill *et al.*, 2014; Mastrofski *et al.*, 2007; Skogan, 2006a; Weisburd and Eck, 2004). In fact, Maguire and Mastrofski (2000) identified over 70 different variables that could measure the extent to which an agency engaged in COP. This heterogeneity in strategies makes COP appear vague and challenging (Mastrofski *et al.*, 2007). Many of the strategies employed have not been rigorously tested, or have variable effects on crime prevention (Eck and Rosenbaum, 1994; Skogan and Frydl, 2004; Weisburd and Eck, 2004). Weisburd and Eck (2004) propose that the variable effects across these different strategies end up canceling each other out, explaining COP's lackluster impact on crime.

The high-level support and funding for COP, even as its implementation and effectiveness were unclear, may have further undermined support within police departments for the approach. Even in the early days of COP, scholars warned of the risk of COP being "oversold" to both communities and police themselves. Skolnick and Bayley (1988, p. 2) note that this risk was greater because COP is both highly popular and difficult to define, leaving it vulnerable to becoming simply a buzzword. They state that "[t]he inevitable result of this overselling will be disillusionment and deepening cynicism about the prospects of meaningful police reform." Over 20 years later, Stone and Travis (2011) confirmed that some police departments felt that the "transformative" power of COP had not lived up to expectations.

The role of community-oriented policing in individual and organizational well-being

COP is clearly effective for important community-related outcomes, but the lack of consistent implementation and attention to the organizational change it involves leaves it open to criticism. In particular, the well-being of officers and the organization itself could be harmed by poorly managed organizational change, haphazard practices, and lack of support. "Well-being" is defined broadly here and includes job satisfaction, performance, and clarity of role and philosophy as well as physical and mental health. Less attention has been paid in the literature to the impact of COP on well-being; however, it is an important and complex issue. Individual officers' attitudes are among the most important predictors of successful implementation of COP and organizational change (Allen, 2002). Job satisfaction can also impact officers' perceptions of community support, which may in turn impact how officers interact with the community (e.g. Yim and Schafer, 2009). On the other hand, the improvement in community attitudes toward police, including greater satisfaction and legitimacy, associated with COP could positively impact officer well-being and safety. From the police perspective, is COP helpful or harmful?

Does COP undermine officer well-being?

Organizational change—and officer receptivity to that change—is crucial to the successful implementation of COP (Lurigio and Skogan, 1994; Redlinger, 1994; Williams, 2003). COP is not simply about seeking traditional forms of cooperation between the police and citizens (which is not a new concept). It requires increased citizen participation, reorienting the patrol force, decentralizing authority, and increasing accountability to the community (Skolnick and Bayley, 1988).

However, change in organizations can be traumatic, and organizations typically resist it (e.g. Trojanowicz and Bucqueroux, 1994). Major changes in the organizational culture can be highly threatening to officers. Sparrow (1988) notes that cultural change often involves addressing what is wrong with the current system and challenging its fundamental goals. For many officers this may also represent a lack of support from the organization—an indication that they have not been doing their jobs well. This can reduce morale and support for the leadership.

If innovations in police practice are poorly defined, inconsistently implemented, and not clearly communicated through all levels of the organization, supervisors may not support the new approach and line officers may become confused and disillusioned. Turnover among the command staff, common in many agencies, can add to negative perceptions of newer strategies like COP if they are seen as "faddish" (see also Wilson, 2005). Longer-serving officers will have seen multiple initiatives come and go, and may resist new approaches that they see as connected to an unpopular chief (e.g. Trojanowicz and Bucqueroux, 1994). Allen (2002) found that supervisors simply gave officers non-COP-related tasks if they did not support the approach, while line officers simply went through the motions of COP rather than actively implementing it if their supervisors or commanders did not champion the process. If COP is not seen as a priority or "standard operating procedure," officers will end up being pulled back and forth into other competing roles. This creates role confusion for the officers and potentially destabilizes relationships with the community (e.g. Zhao *et al.*, 1995).

Skolnick and Bayley (1988) also suggest that placing citizens on an equal footing with police when it comes to defining, prioritizing, and responding to problems in their communities is at odds with the traditional idea that police are the experts who know best how to enforce the law and protect citizens. This represents a threat to their autonomy (see also Skogan and Hartnett, 1997). Some police officers and leaders may also perceive COP as a barrier to their ability to more aggressive law enforcement action when it is necessary, as such action could undermine the relationships built up with the community through COP. As Skolnick and Bayley (1988, p. 76) put it, "[c]an the police put on a velvet glove and keep their iron hand in shape?" Command staff face the pressure of balancing organizational changes that increasingly prioritize COP with the need to maintain the integrity of the reactive patrol force, who will always be an important component of a well-functioning police agency (see also Moore and Trojanowicz, 1988).

For individual officers, organizational change generates a number of stressors. Participation in COP brings the expectation of taking on new responsibilities, for which they may not be trained (see p.000) or do not receive sufficient guidance. COP officers working alongside non-COP officers may experience tension when traditional and community-oriented approaches do not align. It is well established that increased responsibility and workload, as well as role and job ambiguity, are stressful to employees (e.g. Lord, 1996). According to Shane (2010), the organizational context of police work is a greater source of stress to officers than occupational factors. In the specific context of COP implementation, a lack of recognition by the public, police administration, and other non-supportive officers; lack of participation in decision-making; supervision challenges; and a lack of autonomy and feedback can all affect officer stress (Lord, 1996; Morash *et al.*, 2006; Zhao *et al.*, 2002).

An organizational shift toward COP requires a fundamental change in the meaning of the police role. The traditional "command and control" model of policing is often at odds with the decentralized, community-oriented model. However, it remains the case that in most agencies, officers are still hired, trained, and evaluated according to the traditional model. COP changes the expectations of the job and brings pressure to deliver new, different, and often more challenging outcomes. Police are expected to view the community as equal partners in problem-solving, which rejects the "thin blue line" philosophy that can lead officers to view citizens with suspicion. For many officers, this is not the role they signed up for (e.g. Haarr, 2001; Trojanowicz and Bucqueroux, 1994).

The lack of alignment between training and COP goals is a significant challenge for officers. For example, the content of many training academy curricula still emphasizes what Skolnick and Bayley (1988) describe as machismo, athletic training and using force rather than engaging with citizens in difficult situations (see also Rahr and Rice, 2015). Police have traditionally been trained to deal with crime, but not the community. As agencies move toward community-oriented goals, officers may therefore be ill equipped to change along with the organization. Alternatively, officers who are naturally skilled at engaging the community may find that their efforts are not supported by colleagues and supervisors who also lack training in and understanding of COP.

Bradford and Pynes (1999) found, in a review of the curricula of 22 police academies, that less than 3 percent of instructional time was spent in cognitive and decision-making domains—skills that would be crucial to supporting the more creative problem-solving focus of COP—while the remaining time was spent in task-oriented activities. In a U.S. police training academy I visited informally in October 2015, COP and problem solving comprised a single day of the 20-week academy curriculum.[3] Practical, group-based work around problem-solving made up only a couple of hours of that day and there was no input from the community itself (the latter point is by no means unique to this particular academy).

Furthermore, the current structure of police academies not only provides minimal emphasis on COP, but also (consciously or unconsciously) reinforces the traditional model. Grieco (2014) asked recruits from two police academies to rate the relevance of various policing skills at the beginning and end of their training and found that officer safety and survival skills were rated most important at both time points, while COP was rated least relevant. In one of the academies, recruits rated COP as significantly less relevant at the end of the academy than at the beginning, and other survey findings indicated increased cynicism among recruits toward police–community relations.

Even if community engagement is successfully taught in the academy, officers may forget their initial training once they are out in the field, especially if their field training officers do not support the COP philosophy. Haarr (2001) found that the recruits she surveyed viewed COP and problem-solving more favorably at the end of the academy compared to the beginning, in contrast with Grieco's (2014) findings; however, those positive attitudes had disappeared by the end of field training.

The lack of emphasis on COP in the academy and field training may be reflective of what Rahr and Rice (2015) describe as the "warrior vs. guardian" culture of policing. They claim that, beginning as early as the 1960s, but especially since 9/11, the police have increasingly distanced themselves from the people, and the idea of the police officer as a "community guardian" has been replaced with "the urban warrior, trained for battle and equipped with the accoutrements and weaponry of modern warfare." Even as police agencies have paid lip service to COP and boosted their COP units with federal funds, the "thin blue line" has widened. The selection and training of officers remains rooted in the "warrior" mentality, with the primary emphasis on self-preservation in the face of the perceived enemy (Garcia *et al.*, 2004; see also Skolnick and Bayley, 1988).

I do not suggest (and nor do Rahr and Rice (2015)) that officer safety should not be a paramount consideration. Legal procedure, firearm use, pursuit driving, and restraint techniques will always be necessary skills, regardless of the agency's policing philosophy. However, if COP-relevant skills such as problem-solving, community engagement, and communication are not given equal emphasis police will likely be conflicted about the concept of treating community members as partners rather than threats. This not only hinders the effectiveness of COP, but also places additional strain on police officers as they struggle to balance competing expectations or shy away from creative problem-solving because of a lack of skill or support.

Beyond the academy, COP also changes and expands the day-to-day activities of the police beyond their traditional tasks (Frank *et al.*, 1997; Pelfrey Jr., 2004; Smith *et al.*, 2001). Lurigio and Skogan (1994) found that officers involved in the Chicago Alternative Policing Strategy program viewed their new problem-solving role favorably but also worried that the initiative would increase their workload and reduce their autonomy. They also expressed cynicism about the potential impact of strategies such as foot patrol on police–community relations.

At the individual level, Trojanowicz and Bucqueroux (1994, p. 119) suggest that the broader range of activities required of COP officers does not necessarily cause them to "burn out" faster than regular beat officers. On the contrary, COP can provide a number of benefits, including the "satisfaction of a job well done" and the ability to spend more time working on a particular assignment rather than being called away to other incidents frequently. However, COP does create its own stressors for individual officers, including pressure to deliver on promises to community members, which can be challenging when multiple partners need to be involved in developing a response, and being accountable to a broader range of internal and external stakeholders. These more routine occupational stressors can be more significant for officers than even the stress associated with involvement in critical or dangerous incidents (Liberman *et al.*, 2002; Zhao *et al.*, 2002).

In addition to the mismatch between training priorities and COP practice, there is also incongruence between performance evaluation and COP (e.g. Melekian, 2012). Performance evaluation in many agencies has not caught up to the move toward COP and still rewards adherence to the traditional model. Furthermore, assessments necessarily rely on easily quantifiable measures. The number of reports written, arrests made, calls responded to, field interviews conducted, and so on, are much more readily identifiable (Trojanowicz and Bucqueroux, 1994). Data on community-related outcomes such as problems identified and solved, increased community satisfaction and engagement, and other longer-term or qualitative changes, are much more challenging to gather and analyze.

However, when community-related performance measures are not prioritized it is difficult for COP officers to know if they are doing a good job (Trojanowicz and Bucqueroux, 1994). During informal conversations I have had with police officers—even in agencies where COP is generally valued by management—several have told me that they found the *wrong kind* of performance indicators to be a greater source of stress than not being evaluated at all. They were afraid of being penalized if they did anything that their supervisors perceived as too creative or outside the box. Skolnick and Bayley (1988, p. 61) suggest that the incongruence of performance measures harms the organization as well as individual officers by "[exaggerating] the ambiguity of police performance, and, by implication, of measures of evaluation and reward," thus undermining organizational change.

Related to the challenges of performance evaluation is the issue of accountability, to the extent that performance measures should reflect the agency's commitment to its values. Increased public accountability under the COP model can be demanding on the agency, with leadership potentially "afraid to open the floodgates to unfair criticism" (Skolnick and Bayley, 1988, p. 12). Traditionally, agencies have tended to focus on changing individual officers' behavior rather than changing the organization, which is key to COP. The latter requires more transparency and opening the agency up to scrutiny from the community (see also Gianakis and Davis III, 1998). For the individual officer, increased accountability to and scrutiny by the public can be extremely stressful and may lead officers to perceive that they are not supported by the community, thus deepening the divide (Garcia *et al.*, 2004; Lord, 1996).

Police middle managers play a highly significant role in police reform and innovation but they are often overlooked by researchers (Fridell *et al.*, 2011; Kelling and Bratton, 1993; Redlinger, 1994). This is a serious oversight given that, in their role as translators of organizational values and strategies from the command level to the front line, they are essentially the "gatekeepers of innovation." Middle managers who do not support the philosophy of COP or feel disillusioned with the practice can sabotage organizational change (e.g. Rosenbaum *et al.*, 1994).

COP presents a number of specific challenges to middle managers and first-line supervisors. As with line officers, COP changes their normal expectations and duties (Trojanowicz and Bucqueroux, 1994). They experience the same uncertainty about their own performance appraisals, while also having to keep track of the changing expectations for the officers they manage. Furthermore, COP changes the nature of management from a controlling to a supportive orientation (Mastrofski *et al.*, 1998). At the very least this is a change to the status quo, and at worst supervisors who are used to doing business under the traditional model may perceive it as a threat. These managers may subsequently "double down" on reinforcing that model, either deliberately or unconsciously. Engel (2001) notes that supervisors in organizations experiencing change in priorities and strategies, staff turnover, and rapid innovation may resort to traditional roles such as controlling subordinate behavior by enforcing established rules as a way of finding stability among organizational change. At the individual level, first-line supervisors also absorb the stress of organizational change from both their managers and their subordinates. Lord (1996) found that sergeants trying to implement COP with little guidance or support from the organization experienced considerable job dissatisfaction and other stressors, and felt that they lacked social supports.

The decentralization of authority inherent in COP necessarily comes with a loss of power for supervisors. Some middle managers have expressed reservations about the empowerment of the lowest-ranking (and perhaps less experienced) officers (Vito *et al.*, 2005). Trojanowicz and Bucqueroux (1994) suggest that middle managers may also be less supportive of COP because they are fearful of tying their careers to a "fad" that will go away with the current police chief. While this is less likely now that the idea of COP is more mainstream than it was when Trojanowicz and Bucqueroux (1994) were writing, it remains the case that the upper ranks of some organizations are still populated by the "old guard," and the wrong alliance could be fatal to the promotion hopes of a middle manager (see also Weisburd *et al.*, 2003).

The promise of community-oriented policing for the police

While the growth of COP presents clear challenges to the well-being of police officers, there are also a number of potential advantages to an increased focus on COP. In particular, COP may increase officer job satisfaction when implemented well (Trojanowicz and Bucqueroux, 1994). Skolnick and Bayley (1988) suggest that COP professionalizes police by broadening their skill set, and provides more ways for the police to view their role as valuable. Research also links increased job satisfaction to better performance, as officers work harder to maintain their satisfaction (Greene, 1989; Pelfrey Jr., 2004; Zhao *et al.*, 1999). The positive impact of COP on citizen satisfaction with police may reflect this improved performance (Gill *et al.*, 2014). Increased job satisfaction could also help to increase the status of the profession and enrich the careers of individual officers.

There is little evidence that involvement in or commitment to COP improves job satisfaction directly (Ford *et al.*, 2003; Lurigio and Skogan, 1994; Rosenbaum *et al.*, 1994). However, autonomy is a key source of job satisfaction (Greene, 1989; Johnson, 2012; Pelfrey Jr., 2004; Zhao *et al.*, 1999), and the COP model offers increased autonomy to line officers in particular. The traditional model of policing focuses on controlling officers, sometimes to the detriment of them being able to do what is needed to improve outcomes in communities (Kelling and Bratton, 1993; Mastrofski *et al.*, 1998). On the other hand, COP should afford considerably more discretion to officers on the street, allowing them to think creatively about how to solve problems and take more control over outcomes (Lurigio and Skogan, 1994; Rosenbaum *et al.*, 1994). Increased task variety, which COP and problem-solving may offer more of than traditional police work, is also associated with higher job satisfaction (Pelfrey Jr., 2004). Further, Rosenbaum *et al.* (1994) found in a study comparing COP and non-COP officers that feelings of autonomy, improved problem-solving skills, and task identity (the feeling that one's work leads to a completed task) spread throughout the organization when COP was implemented. This suggests that an organizational orientation toward COP could have benefits beyond just those officers tasked with implementing it.

Related to the impact of autonomy, several studies find that the participatory management aspect of COP (i.e. the empowerment of line officers in decision-making) improves officer satisfaction and performance. Wycoff and Skogan (1993) found that when officers believed that participatory management was being practiced, their performance improved. Similarly Adams *et al.* (2002) found that the same perception improved job satisfaction and positive impressions of COP. Involvement in COP activities has even been linked to improved health outcomes for individual officers. For example, Wycoff and Skogan (1993) found that participation in COP was associated with fewer sick days, disciplinary actions, and tardiness.

These advantages come with some caveats. First, officers must feel supported by the organization in their COP and problem-solving efforts in order to reap the benefits of improved job satisfaction and performance. Ford *et al.* (2003) note that officers' commitment to the organization as a whole is more strongly related to job satisfaction than commitment to COP, and is an important antecedent to engaging in COP practices (see also Jaramillo *et al.*, 2005). This requires clear communication by the organizational command that COP is valued and discretion at the street level is encouraged. Organizational instability, and the "role conflict" that officers and their first-line supervisors may experience as a result (such as whether to be authoritarian or exercise discretion), can significantly undermine job satisfaction (e.g. Johnson, 2012).

Second, not all officers will experience the same benefits as a result of COP. Halsted *et al.* (2000) find that service-oriented sheriff's deputies were more likely to be satisfied with their jobs, whereas crime control-oriented deputies tended to derive satisfaction from the quality of the supervision they received. Consequently, crime control-oriented officers may not benefit in the same way from having increased autonomy. Similarly, Greene (1989) finds that officers who are primarily concerned with the security of the job are resistant to community collaboration, while positively-motivated officers are likely to embrace it. However, Yim and Schafer (2009) also note that low job satisfaction can also result in police perceiving that the community views them unfavorably. Thus, for COP to be most effective it appears that strong organizational support and supervision is crucial for both COP and non-COP officers.

COP improves citizen perceptions of police legitimacy and police–community relations (Gill et al., 2014). Several studies have found that COP officers have more positive views toward the public, most likely because COP gives them the opportunity to work collaboratively with local residents (McElroy *et al.*, 1990). In traditional models, police usually encounter the public "at their worst"—not only people who are suspected of committing a crime, but also distressed victims, people suffering from a mental health crisis, and other challenging situations. COP involves meeting the public in lower-stress and more positive circumstances,[4] at times when citizens want to engage with police and are seeking support and reassurance, and reduces anonymity on both sides (Skolnick and Bayley, 1988; see also Trojanowicz and Bucqueroux, 1994). In addition, relationship-building with key social institutions such as schools and places of worship can indirectly increase community support and perceptions of legitimacy when citizens see the community leaders they trust working positively with police (Meares, 2002).

On the public's side, Sadd and Grinc (1996) also found that residents who work collaboratively with the police were more realistic about what the police could achieve in terms of crime control and problem-solving, allowing all parties to manage their expectations effectively. Skolnick and Bayley (1988) add that COP offers an opportunity to develop grassroots support for the police in communities and build consensus about how order should be maintained. This develops what they describe as "moral support" for policing (p. 71), which in turn can make being a police officer more satisfying and personally rewarding.

While some officers may dislike the reduction in anonymity that comes with increased collaboration with the community, Trojanowicz and Bucqueroux (1994) argue that this could also be beneficial in terms of improving officer safety. Residents who regularly collaborate with their local police officers, and even know them by name, are likely to value rather than resent their presence in the neighborhood. Similarly, Skolnick and Bayley (1988) note that when the police and community are on the same page, both under- and over-enforcement are avoided. Under-enforcement may increase fear in the community, causing citizens to withdraw and lower collective efficacy (Sampson *et al.*, 1997; Weisburd *et al.*, 2015). However, over-enforcement may reduce trust in the police and even create hostility. The recent protests in the United States against police-involved shootings, particularly in communities of color, highlight the dangers of over-enforcement to both community relations and the personal safety and mental health of police and citizens alike. The development of a shared understanding between the police and community could reduce the risk of harm to both groups.

Conclusions and recommendations

Community-oriented policing provides important benefits for communities, such as increased satisfaction with police and improved perceptions of legitimacy. However, the impact of COP on police organizations and individual officers has received less attention. This chapter demonstrates that COP, when done well, has the potential to improve officer well-being in a number of domains, including job satisfaction and performance, safety, and perceived support from the community. However, it has also created a number of challenges. COP has not been consistently implemented in police agencies, training and performance evaluation have not kept up with the pace of innovation, and too little attention has been paid to managing the impact of organizational change on the police. These problems can increase stress, role confusion, and disillusionment among line officers and supervisors alike.

This chapter concludes with some recommendations for overcoming these challenges, so that police organizations are better able to realize the internal benefits of COP. These recommendations are organized into five action areas: prioritizing values-based policing and performance management; developing a strategy for managing change; re-evaluating academy and field training; focusing on first-line supervisors; and developing a research agenda for COP and officer well-being.

Prioritize values-based policing and performance management

Melekian (2012) describes "values-based policing," the integration of COP principles with the administrative processes of the department, as the key to organizational transformation. While Melekian's (2012) work focuses primarily on the transmission of values through the discipline process, this idea has broader relevance for police management. It is not enough to simply reorient the overall goals and values of the organization toward COP principles. Police agencies must consider how these new values will be disseminated throughout the organization, and how officers and supervisors will be supported and rewarded for conforming to them.

Performance evaluation is the key mechanism by which police leaders communicate their commitment to certain organizational values as well as providing encouragement and motivation for line officers to absorb them (e.g. DeJong *et al.*, 2001). As discussed above, COP-related performance evaluation indicators are much more challenging to incorporate into these evaluations because they are less easily quantifiable. However, even the older literature on COP includes a number of suggestions for appropriate measures. For example, Trojanowicz and Bucqueroux (1994) offer a long list of COP activities that reflect officer performance and which can be quantified, including crime and disorder rates in the officer's target areas, number and type of contact with external agencies, community meetings and personal contacts, information gathering, and documentation of successful projects (see also Skolnick and Bayley, 1988).

In my own informal conversations with COP officers, I have learned that the increased use of social media and other forms of electronic communication has provided new opportunities for incorporating this type of feedback. For example, one agency has started to incorporate the emails it frequently receives from local citizens giving feedback (both positive and negative) about their encounters with the police into the performance reviews and personnel files of specific officers.

At the departmental level, the values, objectives, and practices of COP can be reinforced through organizational processes such as Compstat—as long as a balance is struck between the traditional top-down management approach of Compstat and the decentralized model of COP (Willis *et al.*, 2010b). Compstat can be used to reorient organizational performance management toward COP rather than traditional policing goals by including systematic reporting of community problems, encouraging citizen involvement in identifying and solving problems, and using crime data to prioritize the policing service in an equitable way (Willis, 2010; Willis *et al.*, 2010a). Recent calls for a fundamental reorientation of the police role from "apprehension agent" to "sentinel" (Nagin *et al.*, 2015)—i.e. from reactive, arrest-focused patrol to guardianship and proactive problem-solving—may eventually drive reform in this area.

Develop a strategy for managing change

Organizational change must be carefully managed (Sparrow, 1988). Staff turnover—particularly at the command level—can be a threat to this process. Police chiefs must show a long-term commitment to change, rather than giving the impression of simply "messing with" structures and practices, in order to avoid the negative impacts of organizational change on officer well-being described above. A lack of attention to the organizational change component of COP may partly explain some of the implementation challenges in the evaluation literature (Maguire, 1997).

The organizational structure is also a key influencer of individual behavior (e.g. Williams, 2003), so well-managed change also increases the likelihood that COP will be implemented consistently on the ground. Ford *et al.* (2003) suggest that police leadership must seek individual officers' support for COP strategies when trying to implement organizational change (see also Goldstein, 1987). This can be achieved through training, performance management (as above), targeted recruitment of service-oriented officers, and clearly communicating agency values through a mission statement (Chappell, 2009; Williams, 2003). Lumb and Breazeale (2002) propose incorporating change models (e.g. Prochaska and DiClemente, 1983) to manage individual officers' receptivity to organizational transformation through skills and behavioral coaching, and providing tailored training and supervision that reflects the officer's current stage of change.

Well-managed organizational change should maximize the benefits of COP for officers. Wycoff and Skogan (1993) found that officers were more satisfied with both COP and their jobs in general when COP was institutionalized throughout the department rather than practiced only in specialized units (see also Williams, 2003). In turn, increased job satisfaction, together with support from supervisors and command staff, could improve police performance and further enhance community satisfaction with the service.

Re-evaluate academy and field training

Training of police officers in COP practices is extremely important for developing buy-in and support for the approach, as well as communicating to the officers that their community-related efforts are valued (Trojanowicz and Bucqueroux, 1994). A challenge to this approach is overcoming the mindset that physical and tactical training should be the primary focus of the academy while still teaching these important skills. However, these two goals are not incompatible. As Rahr and Rice (2015, p. 5) point out:

> the officer's intellect and social dexterity are often the most effective officer safety tools. For the sake of safety, voluntary compliance should be the primary goal in resolving conflict, with physical control reserved for those who present an immediate threat and cannot be managed any other way.

Academy training must equip officers with the tools they need to engage in COP, such as problem-solving and communication strategies, rather than simply focusing on the philosophy of COP. This not only develops the skill set of officers, but also more closely reflects traditional police training, which is procedural rather than belief-based. Training is less effective at changing attitudes and motivations. "Normalizing" COP in this way may help to improve officer buy-in and commitment (Mastrofski, 1999; Palmiotto *et al.*, 2000; Paoline III *et al.*, 2000). However, training should also reinforce what Palmiotto *et al.* (2000) describe as the "territorial and relational aspects of the officer's stake in the community," that is, encouraging and supporting officers to take ownership of a space and the citizens within it. Agencies must also recognize that not all officers are well-suited to community-oriented work and should seek to understand what attracted new recruits to police work in the first place in order to support their individual development and place them appropriately within the organization (Greene, 1989).

Furthermore, this commitment to training officers in community-oriented values and practices cannot stop at the end of the academy. Field training for both new and seasoned officers is crucial, as studies have shown that positive attitudes to COP fade over time as officers become more experienced (Grieco, 2014; Haarr, 2001). Field training officers (FTOs) who guide new recruits through their first few months on the job play a key, but often ignored, role in the diffusion of values-based policing. If FTOs do not support COP, then even the most committed recruits will struggle to put it into practice

(Peak and Glensor, 1996). FTO support for COP can be encouraged through the FTO's own performance evaluation process (Lewis *et al.*, 2013).

Focus on first-line supervisors

The lack of research on the role of first-line supervisors and middle management in policing in general is striking (Fridell *et al.*, 2011). As discussed above (p.000), middle management plays a crucial role in the diffusion of innovation and cultural values throughout an agency, which in turn can impact both the implementation and effectiveness of COP and officer well-being at all levels of the organization. Kelling & Bratton (1993) suggest that police organizations can enhance the role of middle managers by involving them in planning innovation and avoiding organizational threats to individual goals in the middle ranks. Agency leadership is crucial to these efforts. The police chief must promote a strong vision of the organizational culture and values so that expectations for managers are clear (see also Skolnick and Bayley, 1988). Related to this, managers need to feel supported by their command and have their contributions recognized so that they are able to succeed. Thus, leaders need to ensure that resources and communication, as well as the vision, flow down the hierarchy. Kelling and Bratton (1993) also note that in order to allow supervisors to be truly autonomous and creative in their community-oriented work, the organization must be willing to tolerate failure (see also Trojanowicz and Bucqueroux, 1994).

Develop a research agenda for COP and officer well-being

More research on the impact of COP on officer well-being would help to further our understanding of both COP effectiveness and implementation, as well as reducing the harmful effects of police stress. This issue has received much less attention than the relationship between police and citizens; yet it is equally important. We cannot expect the police to be able to treat citizens with respect when they are struggling to deal with the impact of stress, mental or physical health problems, disillusionment with their work, or a lack of support from their agencies (whether real or perceived). Much of the literature that examines the impact of COP on police officers is old and dates from a period when COP was new and innovative. It would be enlightening to revisit those questions again now that the approach is more "institutionalized" (Oliver, 2000), yet still implemented with a wide degree of variation and commitment across police agencies. In particular, how has the recent national attention to police use of force and problems with police–community relations impacted officer well-being, and what role can COP play in addressing the effects of these events? And how does COP impact officers in smaller, suburban or rural agencies where good relationships with the community are typically better established, regardless of overt organizational commitment to community policing (Weisheit *et al.*, 1994)? New studies should also pay more attention to the issue of selection bias in COP research. Both Schafer (2002) and Lurigio and Rosenbaum (1994) have noted that the majority of studies examining the effect of COP on officers were conducted in agencies where COP was implemented as a specialized function rather than a general strategy, meaning that COP officers likely self-selected.

In conclusion, future research and practice should focus on how COP implementation and officer well-being can be better integrated in order to maximize both community engagement and the performance, retention, and protection of officers. The President's Task Force on 21st Century Policing (2015) is clear that both of these goals are equally important to restoring the public's trust in the police. However, in our quest to improve police–community relations and citizen perceptions of police legitimacy, we cannot ignore internal legitimacy (Melekian, 2012). The police will be most effective at engaging the community when they feel respected and supported within their own organizations.

Notes

1 www.cops.usdoj.gov/Default.asp?Item=2754, accessed November 13, 2015.
2 www.cops.usdoj.gov/Default.asp?Item=35, accessed November 13, 2015.
3 As a caveat, I note that was not present to see whether community-oriented values were reinforced during other aspects of the training.
4 However, Parks *et al.* (2006) caution that COP specialists they studied often chose to engage only with citizens with whom they expected to have a positive interaction and whose problems were relatively simple, rather than citizens with the greatest need.

References

Adams, R. E., Rohe, W. M., and Arcury, T. A. (2002). Implementing community-oriented policing: Organizational change and street officer attitudes. *Crime & Delinquency*, *48*(3), 399–430.

Allen, R. Y. W. (2002). Assessing the impediments to organizational change: A view of community policing. *Journal of Criminal Justice*, *30*(6), 511–517.

Bayley, D. H. (1994). *Police for the future*. New York, NY: Oxford University Press.

Bradford, D. and Pynes, J. E. (1999). Police academy training: Why hasn't it kept up with practice? *Police Quarterly*, *2*(3), 283–301.

Brody, S. R. (1976). *The effectiveness of sentencing: A review of the literature* (No. HORS 35). London, UK: HMSO.

Chappell, A. T. (2009). The philosophical versus actual adoption of community policing: A case study. *Criminal Justice Review*, *34*(1), 5–28.

Cordner, G. W. (1999). Elements of community policing. In L. K. Gaines and G. W. Cordner (eds.), *Policing perspectives: An anthology* (pp. 137–149). Los Angeles, CA: Roxbury.

DeJong, C., Mastrofski, S. D., and Parks, R. B. (2001). Patrol officers and problem solving: An application of expectancy theory. *Justice Quarterly*, *18*(1), 31–61.

Eck, J. E. and Rosenbaum, D. P. (1994). The new police order: Effectiveness, equity, and efficiency in community policing. In D. P. Rosenbaum (ed.), *The challenge of community policing: Testing the promises* (pp. 3–23). Thousand Oaks, CA: Sage.

Engel, R. S. (2001). Supervisory styles of patrol sergeants and lieutenants. *Journal of Criminal Justice*, *29*(4), 341–355.

Farrington, D. P. (1983). Randomized experiments on crime and justice. *Crime and Justice*, *4*, 257–308.

Farrington, D. P. (2003). A short history of randomized experiments in criminology: A meager feast. *Evaluation Review*, *27*(3), 218–227.

Farrington, D. P., Ohlin, L. E., and Wilson, J. Q. (1986). *Understanding and controlling crime: Toward a new research strategy*. New York, NY: Springer.

Ford, J. K., Weissbein, D. A., and Plamondon, K. E. (2003). Distinguishing organizational from strategy commitment: Linking officers' commitment to community policing to job behaviors and satisfaction. *Justice Quarterly*, *20*(1), 159–185.

Frank, J., Brandl, S. G., and Watkins, R. C. (1997). The content of community policing: A comparison of the daily activities of community and "beat" officers. *Policing: An International Journal of Police Strategies & Management*, *20*(4), 716–728.

Fridell, L. A. (2004). The results of three national surveys on community policing. In L. A. Fridell and M. A. Wycoff (eds.), *Community policing: The past, present, and future* (pp. 39–58). Washington, DC: Police Executive Research Forum/Annie E. Casey Foundation.

Fridell, L. A., Maskaly, J., Cordner, G., Mastrofski, S. D., Rosenbaum, D., Lanterman, J., and Donner, C. (2011). *The longitudinal study of first line supervisors*. National Police Research Platform.

Garcia, L., Nesbary, D. K., and Gu, J. (2004). Perceptual variations of stressors among police officers during an era of decreasing crime. *Journal of Contemporary Criminal Justice, 20*(1), 33–50.

Gianakis, G. A. and Davis III, G. J. (1998). Reinventing or repackaging public services? The case of community-oriented policing. *Public Administration Review, 58*(6), 485.

Gill, C., Weisburd, D., Telep, C. W., Vitter, Z., and Bennett, T. (2014). Community-oriented policing to reduce crime, disorder and fear and increase satisfaction and legitimacy among citizens: A systematic review. *Journal of Experimental Criminology, 10*(4), 399–428.

Goldstein, H. (1987). Toward community-oriented policing: Potential, basic requirements, and threshold questions. *Crime & Delinquency, 33*(1), 6–30.

Goldstein, H. (1990). *Problem-oriented policing*. New York, NY: McGraw-Hill.

Gottfredson, M. R. and Hirschi, T. (1990). *A general theory of crime*. Stanford, CA: Stanford University Press.

Greene, J. R. (1989). Police officer job satisfaction and community perceptions: Implications for community-oriented policing. *Journal of Research in Crime and Delinquency, 26*(2), 168–183.

Grieco, J. (2014). Police recruits: Attitudes toward the use of research over the course of academy training. In. San Francisco, CA: American Society of Criminology.

Haarr, R. N. (2001). The making of a community policing officer: The impact of basic training and occupational socialization on police recruits. *Police Quarterly, 4*(4), 402–433.

Halsted, A. J., Bromley, M. L. and Cochran, J. K. (2000). The effects of work orientations on job satisfaction among sheriffs' deputies practicing community-oriented policing. *Policing: An International Journal of Police Strategies & Management, 23*(1), 82–104.

Hickman, M. J. and Reaves, B. A. (2001). *Community policing in local police departments, 1997 and 1999*. Washington, DC: U.S. Dept. of Justice, Office of Justice Programs, Bureau of Justice Statistics.

Higginson, A. and Mazerolle, L. (2014). Legitimacy policing of places: The impact on crime and disorder. *Journal of Experimental Criminology, 10*(4), 429–457.

International Association of Chiefs of Police (2014). *Using community policing to counter violent extremism: Five key principles for law enforcement*. Washington, DC: U.S. Department of Justice, Office of Community Oriented Policing Services.

Jackson, J. and Sunshine, J. (2007). Public confidence in policing: A neo-Durkheimian perspective. *British Journal of Criminology, 47*(2), 214–233.

Jaramillo, F., Nixon, R., and Sams, D. (2005). The effect of law enforcement stress on organizational commitment. *Policing: An International Journal of Police Strategies & Management, 28*(2), 321–336.

Johnson, R. R. (2012). Police officer job satisfaction: A multidimensional analysis. *Police Quarterly, 15*(2), 157–176.

Kelling, G. L. and Moore, M. H. (1988). From political to reform to community: The evolving strategy of police. In J. R. Greene and S. D. Mastrofski (eds.), *Community policing: Rhetoric or reality* (pp. 3–26). New York, NY: Praeger.

Kelling, G. L. and Bratton, W. J. (1993). *Implementing community policing: The administrative problem*. Washington, DC: U.S. Department of Justice, National Institute of Justice.

Kelling, G. L., Pate, A. M., Dieckman, D., and Brown, C. E. (1974). *The Kansas City Preventive Patrol Experiment: A summary report*. Washington, DC: The Police Foundation.

Klockars, C. B. (1985). Order maintenance, the quality of urban life, and police: A different line of argument. In W. A. Geller (ed.), *Police leadership in America: Crisis and opportunity* (pp. 309–321). Westport, CT: Praeger.

Kochel, T. R. (2012). Can police legitimacy promote collective efficacy? *Justice Quarterly, 29*(3), 384–419.

Lewis, S., Rosenberg, H., and Sigler, R. T. (2013). Acceptance of community policing among police officers and police administrators. *Policing: An International Journal of Police Strategies & Management, 22*(4), 567–588.

Liberman, A. M., Best, S. R., Metzler, T. J., Fagan, J. A., Weiss, D. S., and Marmar, C. R. (2002). Routine occupational stress and psychological distress in police. *Policing: An International Journal of Police Strategies & Management*, *25*(2), 421–441.

Lord, V. B. (1996). An impact of community policing: Reported stressors, social support, and strain among police officers in a changing police department. *Journal of Criminal Justice*, *24*(6), 503–522.

Lumb, R. C. and Breazeale, R. (2002). Police officer attitudes and community policing implementation: Developing strategies for durable organizational change. *Policing & Society*, *13*(1), 91–106.

Lurigio, A. J. and Rosenbaum, D. P. (1994). The impact of community policing on police personnel: A review of the literature. In D. P. Rosenbaum (ed.), *The challenge of community policing: Testing the promises* (pp. 147–163). Thousand Oaks, CA: Sage.

Lurigio, A. J. and Skogan, W. G. (1994). Winning the hearts and minds of police officers: An assessment of staff perceptions of community policing in Chicago. *Crime & Delinquency*, *40*(3), 315–330.

Maguire, E. R. (1997). Structural change in large municipal police organizations during the community policing era. *Justice Quarterly*, *14*(3), 547–576.

Maguire, E. R. and Mastrofski, S. D. (2000). Patterns of community policing in the United States. *Police Quarterly*, *3*(1), 4–45.

Maguire, E. R. and Katz, C. M. (2002). Community policing, loose coupling, and sensemaking in American police agencies. *Justice Quarterly*, *19*(3), 503–536.

Martinson, R. (1974). What works?–Questions and answers about prison reform. *The Public Interest*, *35*, 22–54.

Mastrofski, S. D. (1999). *Policing for people*. Washington, DC: Police Foundation.

Mastrofski, S. D., Worden, R. E., and Snipes, J. B. (1995). Law enforcement in a time of community policing. *Criminology*, *33*(4), 539–563.

Mastrofski, S. D., Parks, R. B., and Worden, R. E. (1998). *Community policing in action: Lessons from an observational study*. Washington, DC: U.S. Department of Justice, National Institute of Justice.

Mastrofski, S. D., Willis, J. J., and Kochel, T. R. (2007). The challenges of implementing community policing in the United States. *Policing*, *1*(2), 223–234.

McElroy, J., Cosgrove, C. A., and Sadd, S. (1990). *CPOP: The research. An evaluative study of the New York City Community Patrol Officer Program*. New York, NY: Vera Institute of Justice.

Meares, T. L. (2002). Praying for community policing. *California Law Review*, *90*(5), 1593–1634.

Melekian, B. K. (2012). *Values-based discipline: The key to organizational transformation within law enforcement agencies* (PhD thesis). School of Policy, Planning, Development, Los Angeles, CA: University of Southern California.

Moore, M. H. and Trojanowicz, R. C. (1988). *Corporate strategies for policing*. Washington, DC: U.S. Department of Justice, National Institute of Justice.

Morabito, M. S. (2010). Understanding community policing as an innovation: Patterns of adoption. *Crime & Delinquency*, *56*(4), 564–587.

Morash, M., Haarr, R., and Kwak, D.-H. (2006). Multilevel influences on police stress. *Journal of Contemporary Criminal Justice*, *22*(1), 26–43.

Nagin, D. S., Solow, R. M., and Lum, C. (2015). Deterrence, criminal opportunities, and police. *Criminology*, *53*(1), 74–100.

Office of Community Oriented Policing Services. (2014). *Community policing defined*. Washington, DC: U.S. Department of Justice, Office of Community Oriented Policing Services.

Oliver, W. M. (2000). The third generation of community policing: Moving through innovation, diffusion, and institutionalization. *Police Quarterly*, *3*(4), 367–388.

Palmiotto, M. J., Birzer, M. L., and Unnithan, N. P. (2000). Training in community policing: A suggested curriculum. *Policing: An International Journal of Police Strategies & Management*, *23*(1), 8–21.

Paoline III, E. A., Myers, S. M., and Worden, R. E. (2000). Police culture, individualism, and community policing: Evidence from two police departments. *Justice Quarterly*, *17*(3), 575–605.

Parks, R. B., Mastrofski, S. D., DeJong, C., and Gray, M. K. (2006). How officers spend their time with the community. *Justice Quarterly, 16*(3), 483–518.

Peak, K. J. and Glensor, R. W. (1996). *Community policing and problem solving: Strategies and practices.* Upper Saddle River, NJ: Prentice-Hall.

Pelfrey Jr., W. V. (2004). The inchoate nature of community policing: Differences between community policing and traditional police officers. *Justice Quarterly, 21*(3), 579–601.

President's Commission on Law Enforcement and Administration of Justice. (1967). *The challenge of crime in a free society.* Washington, DC: United States Government Printing Office.

President's Task Force on 21st Century Policing. (2015). *Final report of the President's Task Force on 21st Century Policing.* Washington, DC: U.S. Department of Justice, Office of Community Oriented Policing Services.

Prochaska, J. O. and DiClemente, C. C. (1983). Stages and processes of self-change of smoking: Toward an integrative model of change. *Journal of Consulting and Clinical Psychology, 51*(3), 390–395.

Rahr, S. and Rice, S. K. (2015). *From warriors to guardians: Recommitting American police culture to democratic ideals.* Washington, DC: U.S. Department of Justice, National Institute of Justice.

Reaves, B. A. (2010). *Local police departments, 2007.* Washington, DC: U.S. Department of Justice, Office of Justice Programs, Bureau of Justice Statistics.

Reaves, B. A. (2015). *Local police departments, 2013: Personnel, policies, and practices* (No. NCJ 248677). Washington, DC: U.S. Department of Justice, Office of Justice Programs, Bureau of Justice Assistance.

Redlinger, L. J. (1994). Community policing and changes in the organizational structure. *Journal of Contemporary Criminal Justice, 10*(1), 36–58.

Reiss, A. J. (1971). *The police and the public.* New Haven, CT: Yale University Press.

Rosenbaum, D. P., Yeh, S., and Wilkinson, D. L. (1994). Impact of community policing on police personnel: A quasi-experimental test. *Crime & Delinquency, 40*(3), 331–353.

Sadd, S. and Grinc, R. M. (1996). *Implementation challenges in community policing: Innovative neighborhood-oriented policing in eight cities.* Washington, DC: U.S. Department of Justice, Office of Justice Programs, National Institute of Justice.

Sampson, R. J., Raudenbush, S. W., and Earls, F. (1997). Neighborhoods and violent crime: A multilevel study of collective efficacy. *Science, 277*(5328), 918–924.

Schafer, J. A. (2002). "I'm not against it in theory." Global and specific community policing attitudes. *Policing: An International Journal of Police Strategies & Management, 25*(4), 669–686.

Scheider, M. C., Chapman, R., and Schapiro, A. (2009). Towards the unification of policing innovations under community policing. *Policing: An International Journal of Police Strategies & Management, 32*(4), 694–718.

Shane, J. M. (2010). Organizational stressors and police performance. *Journal of Criminal Justice, 38*(4), 807–818.

Sherman, L. W. and Eck, J. E. (2006). Policing for crime prevention. In L. W. Sherman, D. P. Farrington, B. C. Welsh, and D. L. MacKenzie (eds.), *Evidence-based crime prevention* (pp. 295–329). New York, NY: Routledge.

Skogan, W. G. (2004). Community policing: Common impediments to success. In L. A. Fridell and M. A. Wycoff (eds.), *Community policing: The past, present, and future* (pp. 159–168). Washington, DC: The Annie E. Casey Foundation; the Police Executive Research Forum.

Skogan, W. G. (2006a). *Policing and community in Chicago: A tale of three cities.* New York, NY: Oxford University Press.

Skogan, W. G. (2006b). The promise of community policing. In D. Weisburd and A. A. Braga (eds.), *Police innovation: Contrasting perspectives.* New York, NY: Cambridge University Press.

Skogan, W. G. and Hartnett, S. M. (1997). *Community policing, Chicago style.* New York, NY: Oxford University Press.

Skogan, W. G. and Frydl, K. (eds.) (2004). *Fairness and effectiveness in policing: The evidence.* Washington, DC: National Academies Press.

Skolnick, J. H. and Bayley, D. H. (1988). *Community policing: Issues and practices around the world*. Washington, DC: U.S. Department of Justice, National Institute of Justice.

Smith, B. W., Novak, K. J. and Frank, J. (2001). Community policing and the work routines of street-level officers. *Criminal Justice Review*, *26*(1), 17–37.

Sparrow, M. K. (1988). *Implementing community policing*. Washington, DC: U.S. Department of Justice, National Institute of Justice.

Spelman, W. and Brown, D. K. (1984). *Calling the police: Citizen reporting of serious crime*. Washington, DC: Police Executive Research Forum.

Stone, C. and Travis, J. (2011). *Toward a new professionalism in policing*. Washington, DC: U.S. Department of Justice, Office of Justice Programs, National Institute of Justice.

Sunshine, J. and Tyler, T. R. (2003). The role of procedural justice and legitimacy in shaping public support for policing. *Law & Society Review*, *37*(3), 513–548.

Trojanowicz, R. C. and Bucqueroux, B. (1994). *Community policing: How to get started*. Cincinnati, OH: Anderson.

Trojanowicz, R. C., Kappeler, V. E., Gaines, L. K., and Bucqueroux, B. (1998). *Community policing: A contemporary perspective* (2nd edn). Cincinnati, OH: Anderson.

Tyler, T. R. (1990). *Why people obey the law: Procedural justice, legitimacy, and compliance*. New Haven, CT: Yale University Press.

Tyler, T. R. (2004). Enhancing police legitimacy. *Annals of the American Academy of Political and Social Science*, *593*(1), 84–99.

Tyler, T. R. and Huo, Y. (2002). *Trust in the law: Encouraging public cooperation with the police and courts*. New York, NY: Russell Sage Foundation.

Vito, G. F., Walsh, W. F., and Kunselman, J. (2005). Community policing: The middle manager's perspective. *Police Quarterly*, *8*(4), 490–511.

Weisburd, D. and McElroy, J. (1988). Enacting the CPO role: Findings from the New York City pilot program in community policing. In J. R. Greene and S. D. Mastrofski (eds.), *Community policing: Rhetoric or reality*. New York, NY: Praeger.

Weisburd, D. and Eck, J. E. (2004). What can police do to reduce crime, disorder, and fear? *Annals of the American Academy of Political and Social Science*, *593*(1), 42–65.

Weisburd, D. and Braga, A. A. (2006). Understanding police innovation. In D. Weisburd and A. A. Braga (eds.), *Police innovation: Contrasting perspectives*. New York, NY: Cambridge University Press.

Weisburd, D., Petrosino, A., and Mason, G. (1993). Design sensitivity in criminal justice experiments. *Crime and Justice*, *17*, 337–379.

Weisburd, D., Groff, E. R., and Yang, S.-M. (2012). *The criminology of place: Street segments and our understanding of the crime problem*. New York, NY: Oxford University Press.

Weisburd, D., Davis, M., and Gill, C. (2015). Increasing collective efficacy and social capital at crime hot spots: New crime control tools for police. *Policing*, *9*(3), 265–274.

Weisburd, D., Mastrofski, S. D., McNally, A. M., Greenspan, R., and Willis, J. J. (2003). Reforming to preserve: Compstat and strategic problem solving in American policing. *Criminology & Public Policy*, *2*(3), 421–456.

Weisburd, D., Telep, C. W., Hinkle, J. C., and Eck, J. E. (2010). Is problem-oriented policing effective in reducing crime and disorder? *Criminology & Public Policy*, *9*(1), 139–172.

Weisheit, R. A., Wells, L. E., and Falcone, D. N. (1994). Community policing in small town and rural America. *Crime & Delinquency*, *40*(4), 549–567.

Wells, W., Schafer, J. A., Varano, S. P., and Bynum, T. S. (2006). Neighborhood residents' production of order: The effects of collective efficacy on responses to neighborhood problems. *Crime & Delinquency*, *52*(4), 523–550.

Williams, E. J. (2003). Structuring in community policing: Institutionalizing innovative change. *Police Practice and Research*, *4*(2), 119–129.

Willis, J. J. (2010). Enhancing police legitimacy by integrating Compstat and community policing. *Policing: An International Journal of Police Strategies & Management*, *34*(4), 654–673.

Willis, J. J., Mastrofski, S. D., and Kochel, T. R. (2010a). Recommendations for integrating Compstat and community policing. *Policing*, *4*(2), 182–193.

Willis, J. J., Mastrofski, S. D., and Kochel, T. R. (2010b). The co-implementation of Compstat and community policing. *Journal of Criminal Justice*, *38*(5), 969–980.

Wilson, J. M. (2005). *Determinants of community policing: An open systems model of implementation.* Washington, DC: U.S. Department of Justice, National Institute of Justice.

Wycoff, M. A. and Skogan, W. G. (1993). *Community policing in Madison: Quality from the inside out. An evaluation of implementation and impact.* Washington, DC: U.S. Department of Justice, National Institute of Justice.

Yim, Y. and Schafer, B. D. (2009). Police and their perceived image: How community influence officers' job satisfaction. *Police Practice and Research: An International Journal*, *10*(1), 17–29.

Zhao, J., Thurman, Q. C., and Lovrich, N. P. (1995). Community-oriented policing across the U.S.: Facilitators and impediments to implementation. *American Journal of Police*, *14*(1), 11–28.

Zhao, J., Lovrich, N. P., and Thurman, Q. (1999). The status of community policing in American cities: Facilitators and impediments revisited. *Policing: An International Journal of Police Strategies & Management*, *22*(1), 74–92.

Zhao, J., Thurman, Q., and He, N. (1999). Sources of job satisfaction among police officers: A test of demographic and work environment models. *Justice Quarterly*, *16*(1), 153–173.

Zhao, J. S., He, N. and Lovrich, N. (2002). Predicting five dimensions of police officer stress: Looking more deeply into organizational settings for sources of police stress. *Police Quarterly*, *5*(1), 43–62.

Part 2

Sources of police stress

3 Stressors in police work and their consequences

Jonathan Houdmont

Introduction

It is widely acknowledged that policing is a stressful occupation. In recent years, numerous studies have sought to identify and quantify the sources and consequences of stress in policing; these have generated insights into dynamic relations between work characteristics on the one hand and officers' health, well-being, and operational effectiveness on the other. This research has produced a knowledge base that might effectively inform interventions, policies, and procedures to reduce stress in policing. The objective of the current chapter is to provide an illustrative overview of the contemporary science on the causes and consequences of police stress, with a view to providing an evidence-based platform for action on tackling this problem. Some of the evidence cited comes from my own research; over the last decade I have been privileged to assess the prevalence, causes, and consequences of stress among officers within several U.K. police forces. This review, however, is not exclusively focused on the U.K. situation; a diverse literature has been drawn upon to ensure a broad perspective on the issue that will be of interest to an international readership.

As shall be demonstrated, studies have repeatedly shown that it is the organizational aspects of policing work, rather than the operational, that officers report as being the primary occupational source of stress and most strongly linked to negative outcomes. In other words, it is aspects of job *context* as opposed to *content* that appear to be the most problematic for police officers. Accordingly, this chapter has its focus on organizational stressors, those "niggling aspects of the work environment that pervade police organizations because of the structural arrangements and social life inside the organization" (Shane, 2010, p. 815).

Stress can manifest in numerous ways. Its consequences may center on the individual and take the form of psychological or physical health impairment or engagement in health-risk behaviors. Further, stress may generate outcomes that "harm" the employing organization's health by dint of impairment to operational effectiveness. The police stress literature has examined a wide range of individual and organizational health consequences. In order to provide a concise snapshot of the consequences of organizational stressor exposure in policing, this chapter addresses two key indices of individual health that have been the focus of a considerable amount of contemporary police stress research: psychological distress and burnout.

Finally, this review is focused almost exclusively on the scientific literature published from 2010 onwards. This restriction serves two purposes. First, it helps to hone the pool of relevant studies. Police stress research has flourished in recent years, producing a mass of literature; by dint of word count limitations, it is not feasible to provide a comprehensive historical account of the relevant literature in a chapter such as this. Second, a focus on the contemporary literature recognizes the fast pace of change in policing, working life, and the social, economic, and political contexts in which policing and organizational life occur. In this way the restriction serves the overarching aim of the review to provide a summary of the scientific knowledge base that is relevant to policing in the second decade of the twenty-first century.

Theoretical framework and terminology

This chapter takes a transactional theoretical perspective that conceptualizes work-related stress as a process comprising three elements: antecedent factors, namely exposure to psychosocial hazards (also referred to herein as *stressors*); cognitive perceptual processes that give rise to the emotional experience of stress; and correlates of that experience, both individual (e.g. psychological and physical health outcomes and health-risk behaviors) and organizational (e.g. absence, organizational commitment and morale, and performance) (Cox and Griffiths, 2010). Within this theoretical framework, psychosocial hazards are defined as "those aspects of work design and the organisation and management of work, and their social and organisational contexts, which have the potential for causing psychological, social or physical harm" (Cox *et al.*, 2000, p. 14).

The strength of transactional theory lies in its account of the dynamic relationship between the individual and the work environment, and the experience of stress within this relationship as a mediator between psychosocial hazard exposure and negative outcomes. Importantly, transactional theory accommodates subjective experience; the emphasis is upon the individual's appraisal of the environment, taking into consideration available coping resources. Indeed, the word 'transaction' implies that "stress is neither in the environmental input nor in the person, but reflects the conjunction of a person with certain motives and beliefs with an environment whose characteristics pose harm, threats or challenges depending on these personal characteristics" (Lazarus, 1990, p. 3).

Organizational and operational stressors

Given the nature of police work, it might reasonably be assumed that the key stressors experienced by officers are likely to be operational in nature, concerning potentially dangerous situations, such as tackling an offender, or those that have the potential to trigger symptoms of trauma, such as responding to a fatal accident or dealing with a child abuse inquiry. However, there is evidence to suggest that organizational, as opposed to operational, stressors may be of particular import in the police stress process.

The prominence of organizational stressors over operational ones has been illustrated in a number of contemporary studies. For instance, Violanti *et al.* (2015) found that administrative practices and lack of organizational support, but not danger, were associated with hopelessness (after controlling for age, sex, and race/ethnicity) among a sample of 378 officers of the Buffalo, New York, Police Department, leading the authors to conclude that "hopelessness emerges within the social, milieu and structure of the police organization and not in the danger of policing" (ibid. p. 8). In the same way, research involving 1,072 officers of the Baltimore Police Department found that organizational stressors were more strongly associated with stress than were critical incidents, owing to the possibility of:

officers expecting that line-of-duty critical incidents will occur but not expecting to be treated unfairly by their department. It may be seen as a betrayal of the trust that officers place in their leadership; in high-risk jobs such as policing, trust in senior leadership might be especially important.

(Gershon *et al.*, 2009, p. 284)

Similar results have been found in other U.S. police stress studies (Shane, 2010, 2011).

These contemporary findings from the U.S. on the prominence of organizational stressors over operational ones are mirrored in the results of studies conducted in other national contexts including Canada (Della-Rosa, 2014), India (Suresh *et al.*, 2013), and Italy (Garbarino *et al.*, 2011).

Taxonomies of police stressors

Several researchers have developed police stressor taxonomies—lists of stressors commonly experienced in the occupation—some of which have been translated into stressor-exposure assessment questionnaires. Instruments of this type can assist researchers in drawing comparisons between studies, while in the practice setting they can be advantageous because occupational health and human resource services that are able to efficiently assess officers' stressor exposures, and possess knowledge on which stressors are linked to specific negative outcomes, are well placed to develop and implement appropriate support and intervention packages involving the reduction or (where possible) elimination of exposure to particular stressors.

Examples of such measurement instruments include the Police Stressors and Felt Stress Inventory (Brown and Campbell, 1990), Situational Stress Inventory (Gudjonsson and Adlam, 1985), Police Stress Survey (Spielberger *et al.*, 1981), Police Daily Hassles Scale (Hart *et al.*, 1993), Police Stress Scale (Beehr *et al.*, 1995), Police Stress Questionnaire (Biggam *et al.*, 1997), Operational and Organizational Police Stress Questionnaires (McCreary and Thompson, 2006), Law Enforcement Officer Stress Survey (Van Hasselt *et al.*, 2008), Work Environment Index (Liberman *et al.*, 2002), Confidential Police Survey (Stevens, 2008), and the Work and Wellbeing Assessment for Police (Juniper *et al.*, 2010).

Organizational stressor exposures assessed via these instruments have consistently demonstrated associations with negative outcomes. For example, in a study involving 119 U.S. police officers in their first year of service, Wang *et al.* (2010) found that work stress measured via the Work Environment Index (Liberman *et al.*, 2002) accounted for 3 percent of the variance in depression symptoms while, notably, critical incident exposure failed to contribute to the model. Similarly, Maran *et al.* (2015) applied the Operational and Organizational Police Stress Questionnaires (McCreary and Thompson, 2006) to a sample of 617 Italian police officers. Interestingly, exposure to organizational stressors was significantly greater than exposure to operational stressors, with female officers in general and male patrol officers reporting the highest levels of organizational stressor exposure, lending further support to the contention that it is these daily hassles rather than operational duties that present the greatest stress-related challenge in policing.

Measures of organizational psychosocial hazard exposure differ in the extent to which they examine exposure to common generic stressors, police-specific stressors, and role-specific stressors. These are important distinctions because there is evidence to suggest that each may contribute separately to the generation of stress-related outcomes. For instance, in a cross-sectional study of police custody officers ($N = 930$) drawn from 39 forces across

England and Wales, Houdmont and Randall (2014) explored the contribution of a set of generic stressors, assessed via the 25-item version of the Management Standards Indicator Tool (Edwards and Webster, 2012), and a set of stressors specific to the role of the custody officer (Houdmont, 2013a), to explain psychological health. In regression analyses with emotional exhaustion as the criterion variable, after controlling for age, gender, and years in policing, generic stressors accounted for 29 percent of the variance ($p<0.001$), while role-specific stressors accounted for a further 5 percent ($p<0.001$). With psychological distress as the criterion variable, generic stressors similarly accounted for 25 percent of the variance ($p<0.001$). Interestingly, role-specific stressors accounted for only a further 1 percent ($p<0.01$), suggesting that stressors specific to custody work have greater implications for emotional exhaustion than for psychological distress. Role-related variance in the types of stressors to which officers are exposed has often been neglected in the literature; studies such as that described above suggest that the efficacy of interventions to reduce stress-related problems might be enhanced by knowledge of the contribution of role-specific stressors to health and operational effectiveness.

Brief mention is due here of the Management Standards Indicator Tool (MSIT) that was used in the study described above (Houdmont and Randall, 2014) to assess generic stressor exposures. The MSIT was developed by the U.K. Health and Safety Executive—the governmental body with responsibility for regulating and enforcing workplace health and safety—to assist organizations to fulfill their duty (under European Union legislation) to undertake psychosocial risk assessment. It is a freely available[1] measure of exposure to seven dimensions of the psychosocial work environment that, if not properly managed, can lead to harm. In recent times, the MSIT has attracted the attention of police stress researchers, with UK policing reference values having been published (Houdmont et al., 2012), and studies conducted concerning associations between MSIT scores and indices of psychological health (Houdmont et al., 2013) and intention to quit (Allisey, Noblet, LaMontagne, & Houdmont, 2014).

Stressor exposure and psychological distress

The concept of psychological distress is widely used in occupational health research. Though not an illness per se, it is typified by common symptoms of anxiety and depression, irritability, declining intellectual capacity, and tiredness. Given the obvious relevance of these factors to work performance, the concept has been explored extensively in police stress research in a variety of national contexts including Australia (Balmer et al., 2013; Biggs et al., 2014; Tuckey et al., 2010), Canada (Marchand and Durand, 2011), Finland (Leino et al., 2011), Italy (Maran et al., 2015), Pakistan (Naz and Gavin, 2013), Sweden (Arnetz et al., 2013), the U.K. (Houdmont, 2014a–c, 2015; Houdmont et al., 2013; Naz and Gavin, 2013), and the U.S. (Adams and Buck, 2010).

Most studies have measured psychological distress via the 12-item version of the General Health Questionnaire (GHQ-12: Goldberg and Williams, 1988). In addition to permitting comparisons between studies, a key attribute of the GHQ-12 is that it allows researchers to differentiate between likely cases of minor psychiatric disorder and noncases. Drawing on data from the British Household Panel Survey and utilizing a threshold identified as the most accurate for identifying likely cases of minor psychiatric morbidity in the general U.K. working population (Goldberg et al., 1997; Hardy et al., 1999), Murphy and Lloyd (2007) reported a psychiatric morbidity prevalence rate of 19.5 percent for adults in England. This rate appears to be at odds with that found among police officers in the U.K. For instance, a study of 870 officers drawn from four departments of an English county force produced a 51 percent prevalence rate (Houdmont, 2015), while other studies, including a nationwide survey of 747 police custody officers (Houdmont, 2014b) and a survey of public protection unit officers within an English county force (Houdmont, 2014c), produced a rate of 42 percent and 58 percent respectively.

Research from other national contexts indicates that the prevalence of psychological distress among police officers may differ considerably from that found in the U.K. For example, a study involving 986 Finnish officers that applied the GHQ-12 and the same clinical-equivalence threshold as described above found a prevalence rate of just 17 percent (Leino *et al.*, 2011). Vuorensyrjä and Mälkiä (2011) suggest that the low prevalence of psychological health problems among Finnish police officers might be explained in terms of Finland's strong social cohesiveness and sense of fairness, in addition to heavy investment in a comprehensive social security system, resulting in a "lesser than average need for traditional law enforcement" (ibid. p. 383).

Organizational psychosocial hazard exposure may have implications for psychological distress, with several studies reporting cross-sectional associations. Houdmont *et al.* (2013) considered relations between four psychosocial work dimensions—demands, control, relationships, role—and psychological distress assessed via the GHQ-12. Based on a sample of 1,741 officers drawn from a U.K. police force, analyses showed correlations of moderate strength (from $r = 0.35$, $p < 0.001$ for control to $r = 0.42$, $p < 0.001$ for demands) between each of the four dimensions and psychological distress, indicating that as psychosocial hazard exposures rose, so too did psychological distress. Together, the four psychosocial hazard dimensions accounted for one-third of the variance in psychological distress (adjusted $R^2 = 0.33$). Similar findings involving a range of psychosocial hazards and psychological distress measured via the GHQ-12 have been found among police officers in India (Karunanidhi and Chitra, 2013).

Notable for its longitudinal design, an Australian study examined associations between psychological distress (GHQ-12) and a novel organizational stressor—negative workplace behavior (Tuckey *et al.*, 2010). This was defined as actions and practices directed at employees in the workplace that are unwanted and have the potential to cause discomfort. Interestingly, at Time 1, 39 percent of officers reported some level of exposure to negative workplace behavior in the previous 12 months. Past exposure to negative workplace behavior (i.e. exposure at Time 1) was weakly linked to psychological distress at the 12 month follow-up (Time 2) ($r = 0.13$, $p < 0.05$), while current exposure (Time 2) was moderately correlated with psychological distress measured concurrently ($r = 0.23$, $p < 0.001$). After controlling for the possible influence of age, rank, and GHQ caseness at Time 1, current exposure to negative workplace behavior (Time 2) was associated with an elevated risk of GHQ caseness (OR, 1.76; 95 percent CI, 1.13–2.62). It is notable that a significant effect occurred even after controlling for psychological distress at baseline, thereby lending strong support for the premise that being targeted by negative behavior in the workplace is detrimental to psychological health. The findings further highlight the role of non-traditional stressors in the etiology of psychological health problems, leading the authors to conclude that it is now

> timely and vital to go beyond the study of job strain to examine more specific occupational stressors that may function as independent risk factors for . . . psychological health problems. By identifying new specific risks, hazard identification can be initiated and hazard control can be implemented via specific workplace interventions.
>
> (Tuckey *et al.*, 2010, p. 378)

Studies that have used alternative measurement instruments to the GHQ-12 for the assessment of psychological distress have likewise illustrated patterns of relations with psychosocial hazard exposures. Allisey *et al.* (2012) applied the Kessler Psychological Distress Scale (Kessler *et al.*, 2002) to the assessment of psychological distress among 897 Australian police officers. Results showed that the core components of the influential Effort–Reward Imbalance model (Siegrist, 1996)—high effort, low reward, and a high level of personal commitment (over-commitment)—explained a significant portion of the variance in psychological distress. Using a measure of psychological distress developed by Caplan *et al.* (1980), Adams and Buck (2010) examined an interesting category of organizational stressor, "internal social stressors," defined as experiences of disrespectful, rude, or condescending behaviors from co-workers, and found a strong positive correlation with psychological distress ($r=0.57$, $p<0.01$) in a sample of 190 U.S. police officers. The authors concluded that the results highlight the need for primary prevention activities that seek to identify and eliminate the root causes of internal social stressors, including "role conflict, role ambiguity, and situational constraints as well as a combination of high work demands and low control, which are all likely to lead to social stressors" (Adams and Buck, 2010, p. 1038). Most recently, Maran *et al.* (2015) applied a single-item measure of psychological distress—the Distress Thermometer (Roth *et al.*, 1998)—in a study of 617 Italian police officers. The Distress Thermometer requires respondents to indicate their general level of distress over the preceding two weeks on a ten-point scale of 0 (not distressed) to 10 (extremely distressed), with a score of 5 or more usually taken to indicate the presence of distress. Results showed that among front-line police officers, female unit managers, non-commissioned officers, and patrol police officers exceeded the cut-off score. Moreover, strong correlations ($r\geq0.5$) between organizational stressor exposure and psychological distress were evident for male and female unit managers, male and female officers, and male patrol officers.

In sum, studies that have described the epidemiology of psychological distress among police officers indicate that there is considerable variation across national boundaries in terms of prevalence. Contemporary evidence from the U.K. suggests that the situation there is particularly acute. Further research could usefully explore whether the U.K. situation is unique or reflective of a broader international picture of mental health in policing. The extant research base indicates that psychological distress is linked to exposure to various organizational stressors, suggesting that activities targeted on the reduction or elimination of such exposures are warranted to help reduce the burden of psychological distress among police officers.

Stressor exposure and burnout

Burnout can be considered as "a unique response to continuous and prolonged exposure to occupational stress" (Basinska *et al.*, 2014, p. 668). A great deal of police stress research has considered the prevalence of burnout among officers and its association with organizational psychosocial hazards. This research has been conducted in a range of national contexts, including Australia (Hall *et al.*, 2010), Canada (Rajaratnam *et al.*, 2011), Finland (Vuorensyrjä and Mälkiä, 2011), Italy (Garbarino *et al.*, 2013), Poland (Basinska *et al.*, 2014), Turkey (Kula and Sahin, 2015), the U.K. (Houdmont, 2012, 2013a–b, 2014a–c, 2015; Houdmont *et al.*, 2013), and the U.S. (Adams and Buck, 2010; Gershon *et al.*, 2009; Rajaratnam *et al.*, 2011; Schaible and Gecas, 2010). Most researchers have utilized the Maslach Burnout Inventory (MBI) (Maslach *et al.*, 1996), which conceptualizes burnout as:

A psychological syndrome of emotional exhaustion, depersonalization, and reduced personal accomplishment that can occur among individuals who work with other people in some capacity. Emotional exhaustion refers to feelings of being emotionally overextended and depleted of one's emotional resources. Depersonalization refers to a negative, callous, or excessively detached response to other people, who are usually the recipients of one's services or care. Reduced personal accomplishment refers to a decline in one's feelings of competence and successful achievement in one's work.

(Maslach, 1993, pp. 20–21)

Burnout is an important correlate of psychosocial hazard exposure in policing for several reasons. First, the police stress literature has often conceptualized burnout as a consequence of prolonged exposure to stressful working conditions (Vuorensyrjä and Mälkiä, 2011). Second, there is evidence to suggest that among non-policing samples, occupational burnout is associated with a decline in three dimensions of cognitive functioning: executive functions, attention, and memory (Deligkaris *et al.*, 2014), suggesting that burnout might be detrimental not only to the well-being of officers but also their operational effectiveness. Third, Portuguese research has shown that, together, the depersonalization and personal accomplishment dimensions of burnout account for almost one-quarter of the variance in physical aggression, anger, and aggressivity demonstrated by police officers (Queirós *et al.*, 2013). Consistent with this, Dutch research identified significant relationships between the burnout of police officers and a positive attitude toward the use of force, the self-reported use of force, and the independently observed use of force (Kop and Euwema, 2001; Kop *et al.*, 1999). Finally, the emotional exhaustion and depersonalization burnout dimensions have been shown to provide a mediating pathway between emotional dissonance and in-role job performance (i.e. core required outcomes and behaviors) among Dutch police officers (Bakker and Heuven, 2006).

The prevalence of burnout in policing typically exceeds that found in normative samples. A high degree of burnout on each of the three MBI dimensions is reflected in scores in the upper third of the normative distribution (Maslach *et al.*, 1996). On the basis of this threshold the prevalence of high emotional exhaustion in U.K. police officers is notably and consistently high. For instance, data collected in 2015 among officers of four departments within an English county police force ($N=870$) showed a 72 percent prevalence rate for high emotional exhaustion (Houdmont, 2015), with little variation across departments (range: 67–76 percent), while a contemporaneous study of officers employed in the Public Protection Unit of a separate English force ($N=356$) produced a slightly lower rate of 58 percent (Houdmont, 2014c). Overall, the prevalence of high emotional exhaustion appears to be relatively consistent across policing in England and Wales. A 2014 nationwide survey of police custody officers ($N=747$) produced a prevalence rate of 61 percent (Houdmont, 2014b). Similarly, a force-wide survey of officers ($N=1,288$) conducted in the same year within an English county force found a prevalence rate of 74 percent (Houdmont, 2014a). Interestingly, this figure represented a rise on a rate of 61 percent in 2013 and 48 percent in 2012 within the same force (Houdmont, 2012, 2013b). These whole-force studies show an upward trajectory in the prevalence of emotional exhaustion over time that, notably, coincides with cuts to policing budgets imposed by the U.K. government following the 2010 general election, which brought to power a coalition government with an austerity agenda that involved unprecedented cuts to police budgets.

Contemporary policing studies have repeatedly shown patterns of association between organizational stressors and burnout, particularly the emotional exhaustion dimension.

For example, in an English study involving data contributed by 870 officers of four depart-ments within a county police force, strong associations were identified between a series of organizational stressors and emotional exhaustion (Houdmont, 2015). For instance, 58 percent of officers that reported low job demands were identified as presenting with high emotional exhaustion, relative to 91 percent of those that reported high job demands. At the request of the commissioning body, the questionnaire included an item exploring whether or not the officer was in their current role by choice. A total of 15 percent of respondents indicated that they were not in their current role by choice (ranging from 7–24 percent across the four assessed departments). Interestingly, 87 percent of officers who reported that they were not in their current role by choice reported high emotional exhaustion, relative to 68 percent of those who stated that they were. An item that exam-ined whether or not the respondent felt fully qualified for their role produced very similar findings. Though in an era of budget cuts it might sometimes be necessary to place offic-ers in roles without their consent, and there may be an associated lag in the provision of necessary training, these findings suggest that where possible, officers ought to be given a choice in their selection of role and that the provision of such choice might mitigate symptoms of emotional exhaustion.

Several studies beyond the U.K. have similarly examined the emotional exhaustion dimension of burnout in relation to organizational stressor exposures. For example, McCarty and Skogan (2013) found that lack of social support from co-workers and super-visors and perceptions of unfairness were statistically significant predictors of emotional exhaustion among a large sample of 2,078 officers drawn from 12 law enforcement agen-cies across the United States. Similarly, Hall *et al.* (2010) found that emotional exhaus-tion was strongly linked to workload ($r=0.53$, $p<0.01$) and unpaid overtime ($r=0.28$, $p<0.01$) among 257 Australian police officers. In South Africa, Louw and Viviers (2010) found moderate strength correlations between emotional exhaustion (measured via the Shirom-Melamed burnout measure, Shirom, 2003) and job demands ($r=0.39$, $p<0.01$), uncertainty ($r=0.41$, $p<0.01$), and work overload ($r=0.41$, $p<0.01$) in a sample of 505 police officers.

A small group of studies has assessed all three of the burnout dimensions in relation to psychosocial hazard exposures (Houdmont, 2013a; Schaible and Gecas, 2010). For instance, Houdmont (2013a) conducted an exploratory study concerning custody-specific stressors and burnout in a sample of 76 police custody officers with a view to the findings informing the design of a subsequent nationwide study. Among a set of 26 stressors that were reported as problematic by ≥50 percent of respondents, correlations of ≥0.4 were found between a series of organizational stressors and emotional exhaustion, including noise ($r=0.44$, $p<0.01$), intense pace of work ($r=0.42$, $p<0.01$), staffing arrangements that fail to take into account the number of available cells ($r=0.47$, $p<0.01$), understaffing ($r=0.53$, $p<0.01$), inadequate facilities for storage of personal items ($r=0.59$, $p<0.01$), difficulties with task prioritization ($r=0.59$, $p<0.01$), and glare caused by fluorescent lighting ($r=0.41$, $p<0.01$). In combination, and after controlling for the possible influ-ence of age, gender, and departmental tenure, the set of organizational stressors that was significantly correlated with emotional exhaustion accounted for 34 percent of the vari-ance (adjusted) in the criterion variable. For depersonalization, a set of two organizational stressors similarly correlated at ≥ 0.4, including lack of consultation on the introduction of new procedures and technology ($r=0.42$, $p<0.01$) and failure of arresting officers to follow custody suite rules ($r=0.41$, $p<0.01$). In combination, the set of organizational stressors that was significantly correlated with depersonalization accounted for 30 percent of the variance (adjusted) in the criterion variable. Finally, for personal achievement, just one organizational stressor produced a correlation of ≥ 0.4, understaffing ($r = 0.43$, $p < 0.01$). The set of organizational stressors that was significantly correlated with personal achievement accounted for just 5 percent of the variance (adjusted) in the criterion variable, notably far less than was the case for the other two burnout dimensions.

For the sake of brevity in questionnaire length, some studies have applied a subset of MBI items. For instance, Gershon *et al.* (2009) assessed burnout using three MBI items among a sample of 1,072 officers of the Baltimore (U.S.) Police Department. In univariate analyses, burnout was linked to perceived stress (OR, 5.82; 95 percent CI, 4.45–7.63), though after controlling for demographic and coping characteristics in multivariate analyses the relationship failed to reach statistical significance. It is interesting to note that coping characteristics may be influential in determining the impact of certain stressor exposures.

Several studies have demonstrated linkages between burnout and phenomena that may have implications for officers' health and operational effectiveness. For example, using the Oldenburg Burnout Inventory (Demerouti *et al.*, 2003, 2010), Basinska *et al.* (2014) found that acute fatigue at work explained 66 percent of the variance in the exhaustion burnout dimension and 29 percent of the variance in the disengagement dimension. Similarly, Rajaratnam *et al.* (2011) found that officers who reported a sleep disorder were more likely to report emotional exhaustion (OR, 2.85; 95 percent CI, 2.16–3.77) as measured via the MBI.

Taken together, the results of studies that have described the contemporary epidemiology of burnout among police officers indicate a prevalence rate considerably higher than that found in normative data. Data for England and Wales indicate a dramatic rise in burnout that appears to coincide with an unprecedented reduction of 17,000 police officers and 22,000 support staff in a four-year period (Police Federation of England and Wales, 2015). The extant evidence base indicates that burnout is linked to exposure to various organizational stressors and has consequences for both individual and organizational health. Activities targeted on the reduction or elimination of potentially harmful exposures ought to prove effective in helping to protect psychological health among police officers and, by extension, promote their operational effectiveness.

Limitations of the knowledge base

The police-specific literature on relations between psychosocial work conditions and health is extensive, broadly consistent in terms of the magnitude and direction of findings, and increasingly international in scope. One of the strengths of the empirical knowledge base is that many studies have involved large and representative samples. However, the knowledge base has been generated primarily through the application of a cross-sectional research design that involves the collection of data on all variables under investigation at a single point in time, usually via self-report questionnaire. The limitations of the cross-sectional design are such that it is not possible to establish patterns of causation between variables; rather, it is possible only to provide information on the co-occurrence of variables (Taris and Kompier, 2003). Moreover, the cross-sectional design is unable to establish the stability of relationships between variables over time. The limitations of cross-sectional research can make it difficult to convince those with decision-making authority within policing organizations of the need to take action in response to cross-sectional study findings.

These limitations can largely be overcome through the application of a longitudinal research design in which all variables are measured at two or more points over an extended time period. This design allows for the establishment of three key conditions that are required for a causal inference to be drawn, namely that (1) the causal variable precedes the outcome variable in time (temporal order), (2) there is a statistically significant relationship between the predictor variable and outcome variable, and (3) a theoretical interpretation of the relationship should be possible (Taris and Kompier, 2003). However, securing the agreement of policing organizations for longitudinal studies can be extremely difficult. Such studies require a long-term commitment on the part of a host organization and are likely to be more expensive than cross-sectional studies owing to the additional requirements for data analysis and preparation of reports. Longitudinal studies can also be difficult to conduct in policing contexts due to challenges in capturing data from a cohort of officers at multiple points in time. High geographical mobility can make it difficult to track officers as they move across jurisdictions, and frequent rotations between roles can result in officers moving out of departments from which sampling occurred. A similar situation can occur when officers opt out of providing information such as a unique identifier that is required to match questionnaires.

These challenges highlight the need for vigorous project marketing activities prior to data collection that emphasize anonymity in responses, the benefits of participation, commitment of senior leaders to the project and, where appropriate, the independence of the researcher. The production of high-quality longitudinal research will be crucial to engendering a sector-wide focus on the stress problem in policing; the research community must engage further with policing organizations to make such studies a reality.

Addressing the problem

The studies reviewed in this chapter present a consistent picture of linkages between organizational stressors and psychological health. The evidence is extensive and incontrovertible; it may be argued that having established the nature and extent of links between the causes and consequences of police stress, researchers should now turn their attention to the development and implementation of interventions to tackle the problem. Though it is not the purpose of this chapter to review intervention options, brief mention of a possible overarching strategy is useful here.

Given the evidence to implicate organizational psychosocial hazard exposures in the stress process, it would seem appropriate for interventions to focus on exposure reduction. So-called primary, or organizational-level, interventions "aim to reduce the frequency or intensity of stressor exposure derived from organizational sources" (Biggs *et al.*, 2014, p. 45). Though not easy to implement in complex policing organizations, there is emerging evidence to suggest that these can be effective. One such example involved a leadership development intervention that aimed to support senior officers of an Australian police force in developing effective leadership styles and behaviors (Biggs *et al.*, 2014). The intervention comprised three components: a 360 degree review process involving intervention participants, their immediate supervisors, and their direct subordinates; a series of workshops conducted over five days that provided training for participants on leadership styles and behaviors, in addition to practical resources to enhance their leadership skills; and individual coaching for participants, based on the earlier review process. The intervention was significantly associated with higher levels of work-culture support, strategic alignment, work engagement, and job satisfaction among subordinates of intervention participants at follow-up seven months post intervention. However, no significant effects were found for job demands, supportive leadership, turnover intentions, or psychological strain, suggesting that though this form of intervention appears to hold promise, further research is required to refine training for policing leaders on the management of stress.

Though primary interventions clearly have the potential to help reduce psychosocial risk, they are not necessarily straightforward to implement in complex policing organizations. As Lucas *et al.* (2012) observed, the

> potential benefit of work-based [primary] approaches also must be balanced against the practical capacities of organisations to identify work stressors, and to develop and easily implement work-based interventions. Such approaches may be more disruptive to complex work environments than individual-based [secondary] training programs that can be relatively easily implemented.
>
> (Lucas *et al.* 2012, p. 1442)

Lucas and colleagues further suggest that though worker-based [secondary] interventions—such as training to bolster coping skills—may be less effective as a means by which to reduce stress in police officers, they may be "more practical than a work-based intervention that attempts to reduce high levels of stress associated with insufficient police personnel, which is likely a less easily adjusted characteristic of the workplace" (ibid.). Indeed, there is some evidence to indicate that secondary interventions might have an important role to play alongside primary interventions. For example, Gershon *et al.*, (2009) found that 71 percent of officers who employed avoidant coping strategies also reported high stress, relative to 41 percent of those who employed cognitive coping strategies. Moreover, the use of avoidant coping strategies was ineffective and led to higher levels of anxiety and burnout. Results such as these suggest that training on effective coping might constitute one effective secondary-level intervention.

Researchers have long argued that stress management is most effective when a comprehensive approach is adopted that recognizes the role of interventions at all three levels: primary, secondary, and tertiary (Giga *et al.*, 2003). Policing organizations do not represent an exception in this regard. Going forward, police stress researchers have a valuable practical contribution to make in the design and evaluation of interventions at all three levels in policing environments and the dissemination of study findings to the academic and practitioner communities.

Conclusion

Many stressors in police work, particularly those of an organizational nature, are modifiable and amenable to change. Thus, it is not unreasonable for the conclusion to the narrative laid out in this chapter to be a positive one. If the protection and promotion of officers' health is to be a priority, then the targeted modification of organizational stressors linked to stress-related outcomes should likewise be a priority activity. The evidence indicates that the amelioration of stressor exposures would result in benefits to officers, their families and employing organizations and, by extension, the communities they serve.

Note

1 www.hse.gov.uk/stress/standards/pdfs/indicatortool.pdf.

References

Adams, G. and Buck, J. (2010). Social stressors and strain among police officers: It's not just the bad guys. *Criminal Justice and Behavior, 37*, 1030–1040.

Allisey, A., Rodwell, J., and Noblet, A. (2012). Personality and the effort-reward imbalance model of stress: Individual differences in reward sensitivity. *Work & Stress, 26*, 230–251.

Allisey, A., Noblet, A., LaMontagne, A., and Houdmont, J. (2014). Testing a model of officer turnover intentions: The mediating effects of job stress and job satisfaction. *Criminal Justice and Behavior, 41*, 751–771.

Arnetz, B., Arbie, E., Backman, L., Lynch, A., and Lublin, A. (2013). Assessment of a prevention program for work-related stress among urban police oficers. *International Archives of Occupational and Environmental Health, 86*, 79–88.

Bakker, A. and Heuven, E. (2006). Emotional dissonance, burnout, and in-role performance among nurses and police officers. *International Journal of Stress Management, 13*, 423–440.

Balmer, G. M., Pooley, J., and Cohen, L. (2013). Psychological resilience of Western Australian police officers: Relationship between resilience, coping style, psychological functioning and demographics. *Police Practice and Research: An International Journal, 15*, 270–282.

Basinska, B. A., Wiciak, I., and Daderman, A. M. (2014). Fatigue and burnout in police officers: The mediating role of emotions. *Policing: An International Journal of Police Strategies and Management, 37*, 665–680.

Beehr, T. A., Johnson, L. B., and Nieva, R. (1995). Occupational stress: Coping of police and their spouses. *Journal of Organizational Behavior, 16*, 3–25.

Biggam, F. H., Power, K. G., MacDonald, R. R., Carcary, W. N., and Moodie, E. (1997). Self-perceived occupational stress and distress in a Scottish police force. *Work & Stress, 11*, 118–133.

Biggs, A., Brough, P., and Barbour, J. (2014). Enhancing work-related attitudes and work engagement: A quasi-experimental study of the impact of an organizational intervention. *International Journal of Stress Management, 21*, 43–68.

Brown, J. M. and Campbell, E. A. (1990). Sources of occupational stress in the police. *Work & Stress, 4*, 305–318.

Caplan, R. D., Cobb, S., French, F. R. P., Van Harrison, R., and Pinneau, S. R. (1980). *Job Demands and Worker Health*. Ann Arbor: University of Michigan, Institute for Social Research.

Cox, T., Griffiths, A., and Rial Gonzalez, E. (2000). *Research on Work-Related Stress*. Luxembourg: Office for Official Publications of the European Communities.

Cox, T. and Griffiths, A. (2010). Work-related stress: A theoretical perspective. In S. Leka, and J. Houdmont (eds.), *Occupational Health Psychology* (pp. 31–56). Oxford: Wiley-Blackwell.

Della-Rosa, I. (2014). *Stress and Coping in Law Enforcement*. Unpublished Masters Dissertation. University of British Columbia.

Deligkaris, P., Panagopoulou, E., Montgomery, A., and Masoura, E. (2014). Job burnout and cognitive functioning: A systematic review. *Work & Stress, 28*, 107123.

Demerouti, E., Bakker, A. B., Vardakou, I., and Kantas, A. (2003). The convergent validity of two burnout instruments. A multitrait – multimethod analysis. *European Journal of Psychological Assessment, 19*, 12–23.

Demerouti, E., Mostert, K., and Bakker, A. B. (2010). Burnout and work engagement: A thorough investigation of the independency of both constructs. *Journal of Occupational Health Psychology, 15*, 209–222.

Edwards, J. and Webster, S. (2012). Psychosocial risk assessment: Measurement invariance of the UK Health and Safety Executive's Management Standards Indicator Tool across public and private sector organizations. *Work & Stress, 26*, 130–142.

Garbarino, S., Cuomo, G., Chiorri, C., and Magnavita, N. (2013). Association of work-related stress with mental health problems in a special police force unit. *BMJ Open*, e002791.

Garbarino, S., Magnavita, N., Elovainio, M., Heponiemi, T., Ciprani, F., Cuomo, G., and Bergamaschi, A. (2011). Police job strain during routine activities and a major event. *Occupational Medicine, 61*, 395–399.

Gershon, R., Barocas, B., Canotn, A., Li, X., and Vlahov, D. (2009). Mental, physical, and behavioral outcomes associated with perceived work stress in police officers. *Criminal Justice and Behavior, 36*, 275–289.

Giga, S., Cooper, C., and Faragher, B. (2003). The development of a framework for a comprehensive approach to stress management interventions at work. *International Journal of Stress Management, 10*, 280–296.

Goldberg, D., Gater, R., Sartorius, N., Ustun, T., Piccinelli, M., and Gureje, O. (1997). The validity of two versions of the GHQ in the WHO study of mental illness in general health care. *Psychological Medicine, 27*, 191–197.

Goldberg, D. and Williams, P.A. (1988). *User's Guide to the General Health Questionnaire.* Windsor, Canada: NFER-Nelson.

Gudjonsson, G. H. and Adlam, K. (1985). Occupational stressors among British police officers. *Police Journal, 58*, 73–85.

Hall, G., Dollard, M., Tuckey, M., Winefield, A. and Thompson, B. (2010). Job demands, work-family conflict, and emotional exhaustion in police officers: A longitudinal test of competing theories. *Journal of Occupational and Organizational Psychology, 83*, 237–250.

Hardy, G. E., Shapiro, D. A., Haynes, C. E., and Rick, J. E. (1999). Validation of the General Health Questionnire-12 using a sample of employees from the healthcare services. *Psychological Assessment, 11*, 159–165.

Hart, P. M., Wearing, A. J., and Headey, B. (1993). Assessing police work experiences: Development of the police daily hassles and uplifts scales. *Journal of Criminal Justice, 21*, 553–572.

Houdmont, J. (2012). *2012 Whole-force Psychosocial Risk Assessment: West Midlands Police.* Research report for West Midlands Police Federation.

Houdmont, J. (2013a). UK police custody officers' psychosocial hazard exposures and burnout. *Policing: An International Journal of Police Strategies and Management, 36*, 620–635.

Houdmont, J. (2013b). *2013 Whole-force Psychosocial Risk Assessment: West Midlands Police.* Research report for West Midlands Police Federation.

Houdmont, J., Randall, R., Kerr, R. and Addley, K. (2013). Psychosocial risk assessment in organizations: Concurrent validity of the brief version of the Management Standards Indicator Tool. *Work & Stress, 27*, 403–412.

Houdmont, J. (2014a). *2014 Whole-force Psychosocial Risk Assessment: West Midlands Police.* Research report for West Midlands Police Federation.

Houdmont, J. (2014b). *Custody Officers' Stress-related Working Conditions: Relations with Health and Organisational Effectiveness.* Research report for the Sergeants' Central Committee of the Police Federation of England and Wales.

Houdmont, J. (2014c). *Psychosocial Risk Assessment: Public Protection Unit.* Research report for West Midlands Police Federation.

Houdmont, J. (2015). *Psychosocial Risk Assessment: Public Protection Unit, Response, CID, & SODAIT.* Research report for Devon and Cornwall Police Federation.

Houdmont, J., Kerr, R., and Randall, R. (2012). Organisational psychosocial hazard exposures in UK policing: Management Standards Indicator Tool reference values. *Policing: An international journal of police strategies and management, 35*, 182–197.

Houdmont, J. and Randall, R. (2014). Which work stressors predict employee outcomes for police custody officers? An examination of generic and occupation-specific characteristics. In N. Andreou, A. Jain, D. Hollis, J. Hassard, and K. Teoh. *Proceedings of the 11th European Academy of Occupational Health Psychology Conference.* Paper presented at the 11th Conference of the European Academy of Occupational Health Psychology, London, England (pp. 50–51). Nottingham, U.K.: European Academy of Occupational Health Psychology.

Houdmont, J., Randall, R., Kerr, R., and Addley, K. (2013). Psychosocial risk assessment in organizations: Concurrent validity of the brief version of the Management Standards Indicator Tool. *Work & Stress, 27*, 403–412.

Juniper, B., White, N., and Bellamy, P. (2010). A new approach to evaluating the well-being of police. *Occupational Medicine, 60*, 560–565.

Karunanidhi, S. and Chitra, T. (2013). Influence of select psychosocial factors on the psychological well-being of policewomen. *International Research Journal of Social Sciences*, *2*, 5–14.

Kessler, R. C., Andrews, G., Colpe, L. J., Hiripi, E. E., Mroczek, D. K., Normand, S. L., Walters, E. E., and Zaslavsky, A. M. (2002). Short screening scales to monitor population prevalences and trends in non-specific psychological distress. *Psychological Medicine*, *32*, 959–976.

Kop, N. and Euwema, M. (2001). Occupational stress and violence in Dutch policing. *Criminal Justice and Behavior*, *28*, 631–652.

Kop, N., Euwema, M., and Schaufeli, W. B. (1999). Burnout, job stress and violent behaviour among Dutch police officers. *Work & Stress*, *13*, 326–340.

Kula, S. and Sahin, I. (2015). The impacts of occupational stress on the work-related burnout levels of Turkish National Police members. *International Journal of Public Policy*, *11*, 169–185.

Lazarus, R. (1990). Theory-based stress management, *Psychological Inquiry*, *1*, 3–13.

Leino, T., Selin, R., Summala, H., and Virtanen, M. (2011). Violence and psychological distress among police officers and security guards. *Occupational Medicine*, *61*, 400–406.

Liberman, A. M., Best, S. R., Metzler, T. J., Fagan, J. A., Weiss, D. S., and Marmar, C. R. (2002). Routine occupational stress and psychological distress in police. *Policing: An International Journal of Police Strategies and Management*, *25*, 421–439.

Louw, G. and Viviers, A. (2010). An evaluation of a psychosocial stress and coping model in the police work context. *South African Journal of Industrial Psychology*, *36*, 1–11.

Lucas, T., Weidner, N., and Janisse, J. (2012). Where does work stress come from? A generalizability analysis of stress in police officers. *Psychology and Health*, *27*, 1426–1447.

Maran, D. A, Varetto, A., Zedda, M., and Ieraci, V. (2015). Occupational stress, anxiety and coping strategies in police officers. *Occupational Medicine*, *65*, 466–473.

Marchand, A. and Durand, P. (2011). Psychological distress, depression, and burnout: Similar contributions of the job demand-control and job demand-control-support models? *Journal of Occupational and Environmental Medicine*, *53*, 185–189.

Maslach, C. (1993). Burnout: A multidimensional perspective. In W. Schaufeli, C. Maslach, and M. Tadeusz (eds.), *Professional Burnout, Recent Developments in Theory and Research* (pp. 19–32). Philadelphia, P.A.: Taylor & Francis.

Maslach, C., Jackson, S. E. and Leiter, M. P. (eds), (1996). *The Maslach Burnout Inventory: Test Manual, 3rd ed.*, Mountain View, C.A.: CPP Inc.

McCarty, W. and Skogan, W. (2013). Job-related burnout among civilian and sworn police personnel. *Police Quarterly*, *16*, 66–84.

McCreary, D. R. and Thompson, M. M. (2006). Development of two reliable and valid measures of stressors in policing: The operational and organizational police stress questionnaires. *International Journal of Stress Management*, *13*, 494–518.

Murphy, H. and Lloyd, K. (2007). Civil conflict in Northern Ireland and the prevalence of psychiatric disturbance across the United Kingdom: A population study using the British Household Panel Survey and the Northern Ireland Household Panel Survey. *International Journal of Social Psychiatry*, *53*, 397–407.

Naz, S. and Gavin, H. (2013). Correlates of resilience in police officers from England and Pakistan: A cross-national study. *Pakistan Journal of Criminology*, *5*, 215–234.

Police Federation of England and Wales (2015). *Parliamentary Letter*. Retrieved September 2, 2015, from www.polfed.org/campaigning/Cuts_Have_Consequences_Letter.aspx.

Queirós, C., Kaiseler, M., and da Silva, A. L. (2013). Burnout as a predictor of aggressivity among police officers. *European Journal of Policing Studies*, *1*, 110–135.

Rajaratnam, S. (2011). Sleep disorders, health, and safety in police officers. *Journal of the American Medical Association*, *306*, 2567–2578.

Roth, A. J., Kornblith, A. B., Batel-Copel, L., Peabody, E., Scher, H.I., and Holland, J.C. (1998). Rapid screening for psychologic distress in men with prostate carcinoma: A pilot study. *Cancer*, *82*, 1904–1908.

Schaible, L. and Gecas, V. (2010). The impact of emotional labor and value dissonance on burnout among police officers. *Police Quarterly*, *13*, 316–341.

Shane, J. (2010). Organizational stressors and police performance. *Journal of Criminal Justice, 38*, 807–818.

Shane, J. (2011). Daily work experiences and police performance. *Police Practice and Research, 14*, 17–34.

Shirom, A. (2003). Job-related burnout. In J. C. Quick and L. E. Tetrick (eds.), *Handbook of Occupational Health Psychology* (pp. 245–265). Washington, D.C.: American Psychological Association.

Siegrist, J. (1996). Adverse health effects of high effort-low reward conditions at work. *Journal of Occupational Health Psychology, 1*, 27–43.

Spielberger, C. D., Westberry, L. G., Grier, K. S., and Greenfield, G. (1981). The police stress survey: Sources of stress in law enforcement. *Human Resources Institute Monograph Series Three: No. 6.*

Stevens, D. J. (2008). *Police Officer Stress: Sources and Solutions.* Upper Saddle River, N.J.: Pearson/ Prentice Hall Press.

Suresh, R. S., Anantharaman, R. N., Angusamy, A., and Ganesan, J. (2013). Sources of job stress in police work in a developing country. *International Journal of Business and Management, 8*, 102–110.

Taris, T. and Kompier, M. (2003). Challenges in longitudinal designs in occupational health psychology. *Scandinavian Journal of Work, Environment, and Health, 29*, 1–4.

Tuckey, M., Dollard, M., Saebel, J., and Berry, N. (2010). Negative workplace behavior: Temporal associations with cardiovascular outcomes and psychological health problems in Australian police. *Stress and Health, 26*, 327–381.

Van Hasselt, V. B., Sheehan D. C., Malcolm, A. S., Sellers, A. H., Baker, M. T., and Couwels, J. (2008). The Law Enforcement Officer Stress Survey (LEOSS): Evaluation of psychometric properties. *Behavior Modification, 32*, 133–151.

Violanti, J., Andrew, M., Mnatsakanova, A., Hartley, T., Fekedulegn, D., and Burchfiel, C. (2015). Correlates of hopelessness in the high suicide risk police population. *Police Practice and Research*, (ahead of print).

Vuorensyrjä, M. and Mälkiä, M. (2011). Nonlinearity of the effects of police stressors on police officer burnout. *Policing: An International Journal of Police Strategies and Management, 34*, 382–402.

Wang, Z., Inslicht, S., Metzler, T., Henn-Haase, C., McCaslin, S., Tong, H., Neylan, T., and Marmar, C. (2010). A prospective study of predictors of depression symptoms in police. *Psychiatry Research, 175*, 211–216.

4 Balancing the badge

Work–family challenges within policing and recommended supports and interventions

Satoris S. Culbertson, Ann H. Huffman, Maura J. Mills, and Chandler B. Imhof

Law enforcement has been called one of the most stressful occupations (Anshel *et al.*, 1997). Police officers are at greater risk of experiencing moderate amounts of stress and, subsequently, poorer general well-being (Mumford *et al.*, 2015). Being faced with dangers and atypical schedules creates emotional distress on officers. This distress does not remain at work, however, and is not confined to the officer. Emotional baggage is carried over from work to one's home life, spilling over from one domain to the other. Furthermore, the emotions associated with and resulting from a stressful day on the job can cross over from one person to another. As such, the stressors associated with police work are not limited exclusively to officers, but are a concern for officers' loved ones as well.

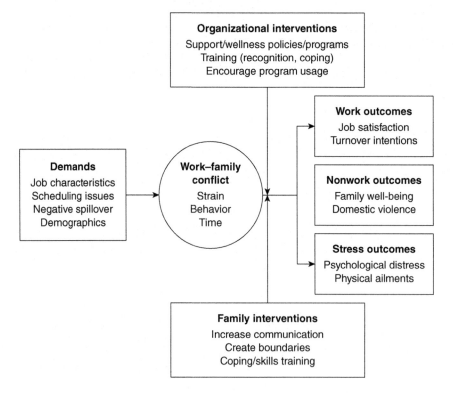

Figure 4.1 Policing Work–Family Stress and Intervention Model

In the present chapter, we will explore issues related to the conflict that officers experience between their work and family lives. We present information on the demands that are inherent in policing that impact the conflict that officers experience, including characteristics of the job itself, demographic considerations, and negative emotional spillover from work to home. In addition, we examine the outcomes associated with this conflict, to include work outcomes (e.g. lower job satisfaction, higher turnover intentions, etc.), non-work outcomes (e.g. diminished family well-being, greater domestic violence, etc.), and stress outcomes for the officer and his/her family (e.g. increased psychological distress and burnout). Lastly, we present organizational and family interventions that can help officers manage work–family conflict. Figure 4.1 summarizes the focus of the current chapter.

Work–family conflict

Work–family conflict occurs when demands in the work domain interfere with responsibilities in the family domain (Greenhaus and Beutell, 1985). Work–family conflict is rooted in role theory (Kahn *et al.*, 1964), which proposes that organizations (e.g. work or family) may be viewed as a role system where the relationships between people are maintained by expectations that have been developed by each role (Kahn *et al.*, 1964). In the case of work–family conflict, the two key roles are as "family member" and as "employee." Roles are helpful for individuals and organizations, as they clarify what behaviors are expected. Yet when expectations between roles differ, work–family conflict may surface. Due to the nature of policing (e.g. shift work, high-stress environment, etc.), it would not be unreasonable to expect that police officers would experience conflict between their work and home lives. In the following section, we will first describe key characteristics of work–family conflict and then discuss how this conflict can affect police officers and policing agencies.

Characteristics of work–family conflict

Work–family researchers have come to the general consensus that work–family conflict has several key characteristics. First, work–family conflict can be bidirectional, such that work can interfere with family (work-to-family conflict), and family can interfere with work (family-to-work conflict) (Frone *et al.*, 1992). For example, officers may experience work-to-family conflict when they have to work late hours, which interferes with being able to be home in time for family dinner. On the other hand, officers could experience family-to-work conflict when they arrive late to work due to struggles with getting children ready for school. Understanding where the source of conflict originates (work or home) is important because it helps pinpoint where to target efforts when attempting to decrease the conflict. Furthermore, understanding the direction of conflict is important because it provides insight into which domain is potentially suffering due to the conflict. In the case of the example of family-to-work conflict cited above, understanding that the stressor is originating in the family domain can help the officers develop strategies specific to the family to help alleviate the initial stressor. For example, an officer could adjust his/her morning schedule, for example, to allow some padding in time in order to ensure that for all mornings (typical mornings and mornings when the kids are more of a challenge), getting to work on time is not an issue. Conversely, understanding that family responsibilities could make the officer late to work on some mornings, s/he could put into place some strategies in the domain that is being affected (in this case the work domain). For this specific example, the officer could ask a co-worker to be "on call" for those select mornings to help out when extreme family demands surface. Another related reason why it is important to distinguish the source of conflict is that it provides insight into what domain will be most negatively affected. If an officer has demands at home, some support may be needed in the work domain to assist in dealing with the stressors that are spilling over into the workplace. Later in the chapter, we will be discussing different organizational and family interventions that can assist officers in managing their work–family conflict.

The second key characteristic of work–family conflict is that it can take on three different forms; time-based, strain-based, and behavior-based (Greenhaus and Buetell, 1985). Time-based conflict describes the situation when there is a temporal element to the conflict. The examples that were presented earlier (i.e. working late and missing family dinner, and struggling with kids and getting to work late) are examples of time-based conflict. Strain-based conflict, on the other hand, occurs when the psychological demands in one domain interfere with normal responsibilities and relationships in the other domain. For example, an officer could have just experienced a traumatic event at work. Strain-based conflict occurs when this traumatic event negatively affects functioning at home (e.g. an inability to concentrate, a failure to communicate with family, mental exhaustion, etc.). It should be noted that strain-based conflict need not originate from an extreme event (trauma), but can also occur as a result of more subtle work stressors (e.g. conflict with a co-worker, an unreasonable boss, job dissatisfaction, etc.). Finally, conflict can be behavior-based, such that work–family conflict occurs when behavior that is more appropriate or effective in one domain spills into the other domain. For example, an officer has worked a shift in which s/he has to display strong authority and be very directive. Once the shift is over, s/he goes home and continues to display this behavior. Whereas it was functional in the work domain, it may not be ideal in the family domain, thereby potentially creating conflict.

In summary, work–family conflict has several different layers; it is bidirectional and it can take on different forms. The importance of these layers becomes more evident as we discuss the antecedents of, and outcomes related to, work–family conflict. In the following section, we explore these issues in the context of policing.

Policing demands and work–family conflict

There has been much research on the consequences of work–family conflict. The consequences are far reaching because the construct crosses life domains and affects both work and family well-being. We propose that the job-demand resource model (JD-R) (Bakker and Demerouti, 2007; Demerouti *et al.*, 2001) is a helpful framework to understand why work–family conflict is related to work, non-work, and stress-related outcomes, especially for police officers whose jobs can have high demands.

The JD-R theory is grounded in two job stress models, the demand-control model (Karasek, 1979) and the effort-reward imbalance model (Siegrist, 1996). These two models both propose that job strain and related outcomes derive from a depletion of job resources. The JD-R model builds on these propositions and is based on two key assumptions. First, occupational stress can be partly understood in terms of the prevalence and extent of job demands and job resources. Key to this assumption is that resources are important, not only to deal with job demands, but to contribute to basic workplace functioning (Hackman and Oldham, 1980; Hobfoll, 1989). Second, jobs with chronic high demands lead to depletion of energy and related negative outcomes. Resources, on the other hand, have motivational potential, and can lead to positive work outcomes such as engagement and performance. The interaction between demands and resources is key to understanding healthy workplace functioning.

The JD-R model provides a context for understanding why and under what conditions work–family conflict is related to negative outcomes. Work–family conflict is related to both determinants: demands and resources. When police officers experience work–family conflict, they are usually experiencing demands that originate in the work domain. For example, a police officer could experience work–family conflict due to the long hours spent at work. The higher the demands, the greater likelihood of work–family conflict that would result in negative outcomes. Yet, if the police officer had some type of resource (e.g. access to resilience training or a supportive network of colleagues) then there would be a decreased likelihood of the resultant negative outcome.

In the following section we will discuss key demands and outcomes that are related to work–family conflict for police officers. We first discuss characteristics of and demands inherent in police work that are likely to lead to work–family conflict. We follow this with demographic considerations that could influence the experience of work–family conflict. We then discuss work, non-work, and stress outcomes, by first providing an overview of key outcomes related to the general population for each and then discussing key outcomes related specifically to policing.

Job characteristics and demands

When considering work–family conflict and its associated stress impact, there must be a consideration of policing's unique job characteristics and demands. As noted earlier, policing is widely recognized as one of the more stressful professions. The physical strain and constant threat of danger associated with the work, as well as the psychological and emotional toll taken by witnessing disturbing scenes and investigating often heinous acts, makes policing a particularly treacherous job, both physically and mentally (Dowling *et al.*, 2006; Harpold and Feemster, 2002; Howard *et al.*, 2004; Miller, 2008). Beyond this, police officers also frequently incur stress from the responsibility of caring for others. Whether arresting or providing medical assistance, the officer is accountable for the general well-being of individuals encountered while on duty, which leads to an extra layer of stress for the officer (Bull *et al.*, 1983). It is no wonder then, that in a survey of over 1,000 officers, Gershon *et al.* (2009) found that work stress was significantly associated with reports of depression.

Even three decades ago, Nordlicht (1979) suggested that stress factors that are fairly unique to law enforcement were likely to have detrimental impacts on family functioning (e.g. via poor communication, inability to express oneself, relational problems with children, alcoholism). Although Nordlicht made these claims from a theoretical versus an empirical perspective, they have since been supported empirically in other research. For instance, Hall and colleagues (Hall *et al.*, 2010) found reciprocal effects between job demands, emotional exhaustion, and officers' work–family conflict in a sample of Australian officers. More recently, Griffin (2012) found that such job-related stress was significantly positively related to officers' emotional exhaustion and depersonalization, as well as work–family conflict overall.

Further evidence has likewise found that such psychological strain and emotional exhaustion are not only detrimental in and of themselves, but are also associated with officer burnout from the job (Burke, 1993; Jackson and Maslach, 1982; Loo, 2004). In this way, work–family relations are further compromised via the spillover of negative emotions from work to home and the associated compromised functioning across domains (Maslach and Jackson, 1979; Maslach *et al.*, 2001).

Compounding the effects of such emotional stressors is the fact that policing is a job high in emotional labor, such that officers are often expected to withhold or curtail their true emotions on the job in favor of maintaining a professional front (Wharton, 1999). In such cases, it is not hard to imagine that officers engage in such emotional management either by internalizing their emotions, creating further psychological distress, and/or by letting those negative emotions spill over into the home domain. Exacerbating this is the fact that policing is such a publicly visible profession, so officers also fall victim to social and administrative scrutiny of their actions, or lack thereof, which can increase the stress associated with work–family conflict (Reiser and Geiger, 1984).

Schedule challenges

Beyond the characteristics of work tasks, however, are the overall time and scheduling challenges presented by a policing career. By virtue of the fact that policing is public service work that is not only proactive but also reactive in the face of unpredictable incidents, the job is characterized by its necessary 24/7 staffing. Arguably more so than any other job characteristic, this one is likely to present the greatest, most frequent, and most frustrating work–family challenges. A continually staffed organization requires employees to work shiftwork, often broken into three shifts (for example, 6 a.m.–2 p.m., 2 p.m.–10 p.m., and 10 p.m.–6 a.m.) and spanning weekdays as well as weekends and holidays. The challenges of such non-standard work schedules have been well established, including work–family conflict (Akanni, 2011; Grosswald, 2003; Willis *et al.*, 2008). This includes both time-based conflict, such that working such shifts compromises employees' abilities to attend various life and family events (Fenwick and Tausig, 2001) and limits participation in the day-to-day goings on of home life (La Valle *et al.*, 2002), and strain-based conflict, such that fatigued persons are at a higher risk of moodiness and stress (Øyane *et al.*, 2013).

Going further, although the nature of shiftwork itself is problematic in terms of establishing work–family balance, a more nuanced but related concern is that of the rotating shift schedule. In rotating shifts, an employee's hours change periodically—sometimes daily—from days to evenings to nights, as well as having inconsistent days of the week off from work (Barthe *et al.*, 2011; Perrucci *et al.*, 2007). Although some researchers (Albertson *et al.*, 2008) have suggested that night and evening shifts may be more detrimental to work–family balance than rotating shifts, others (Rosiello and Mills, 2015) have suggested that the unpredictability of rotating shifts is likely to make them more of a hindrance to family planning. This is true both in terms of scheduling quality family time (e.g. outings), as well as managing day-to-day non-optional commitments such as childcare and housework. With the burden for such responsibilities then falling disproportionately upon the officer's spouse, marital satisfaction and perceptions of an equal partnership can also be negatively impacted, as indicated by Brunner (1976) who found work scheduling to be a chief complaint of officers' spouses.

The implications of such shift (and, to a greater extent, rotating) schedules further extend to compromise officers' physical and mental health in various ways, including insomnia/fatigue (Lindsey, 2007), gastrointestinal disorders (Costa, 1996; Fenwick and Tausig, 2001), and cardiovascular disorders (Fenwick and Tausig, 2001), among other more drastic but less conclusive findings regarding cancer (World Health Organization,

2007) and long-term brain damage (Zhang *et al.*, 2014). Such health issues, besides being detrimental in and of themselves, can also further compromise the quality of family time. From an organizational perspective, compromised sleep health has been found to lead to poorer agility, decreased reaction time, compromised safety-related behaviors, and over-all lessened performance on the job (Costa, 1996; Fenwick and Tausig, 2001; Lindsey, 2007). These findings are particularly relevant for critical safety jobs such as policing, in which momentary decision making, reaction time, and accuracy can all mean the differ-ence between life and death in a variety of on-the-job incidents.

Demographic considerations

There are undoubtedly individual difference characteristics across officers that determine the degree to which their work–family balance will suffer in light of the job. For instance, Burke (1988) found that work–family conflict was more likely when officers were mar-ried, exhibited Type A personality characteristics, had limited opportunities for social support, or worked within a negative environment. With the policing profession becom-ing increasingly diverse in recent decades (He *et al.*, 2005), it is necessary to consider how such a shift may present differential work–family conflict considerations for officers dependent upon their demographic affiliations (e.g. race, gender, etc.).

From a race perspective, Toch (2002) suggested that African-American police offic-ers might be more likely to experience higher stress than Caucasian officers. Dulaney (1996) suggested that this might be at least partly attributed to historically turbulent relations between police forces and African-American civilians, thereby creating a conundrum of allegiance for individuals who identify with both of these groups. This is arguably even more likely to be the case in recent years, as the zeitgeist has shifted to highlight violent exchanges between (often Caucasian) police officers and African-American males, including the highly publicized cases of Michael Brown and Eric Garner, among others (Pinto *et al.*, 2014). It is not difficult to imagine how the stress brought on by these seemingly competing allegiances, as well as any addition har-assment or discrimination that African-American officers may experience from either group as a result, can compromise officers' emotional well-being and consequently spill over into the home domain.

Another demographic identifier likely to play a role in how officers experience work–family conflict is that of officer gender. A substantial part of why this is likely to be the case is rooted in the fact that policing is well-recognized as a gendered profession with a very masculine and workplace culture (Haas and Hwang, 2007). Such stereotypically masculine characteristics embodied in policing include assertiveness, aggression, competi-tiveness, tenacity, physicality, and emotional detachment (Martin and Jurik, 2007). By virtue of the unbalanced gender ratio in policing, increased stress (Kurtz, 2012) and har-assment (Somvadee and Morash, 2008) – including sexual harassment – are not unlikely hazards for female officers to encounter. This can then spill over to negatively impact the home domain, not just on an overarching level, but also on a more specific marital level as in the case of extensive sexual harassment.

Such spillover is further illuminated in Huffman *et al.*'s (2015) Masculine Occupations Gender Role Model, a cyclical model identifying gendered occupations as influencing organizational culture, which in turn impacts work–family conflict (exacerbated for women in "male" roles) and, finally, work and family outcomes such as increased stress and compromised job attitudes. This model, together with other supporting research (e.g. Cook and Minnotte, 2008), suggests that in gendered occupations, employees who are in the minority gender (here, women) are more likely to experience greater work–family conflict than are employees in the majority gender. This can be attributed to the aforementioned harassment, in addition to differential job demands (real or perceived) and promotion opportunities (Schulz, 2004), in professions in which minority gendered employees feel as though they must "prove themselves." In fairness, it should be noted that although this tends to be the most consistent finding, there are also instances that have evidenced otherwise. For instance, Griffin (2012) found that although stress was positively related to work–family conflict for both male and female officers, officers of both genders reported similar stress levels overall. Nevertheless, male officers reported fewer family responsibilities than female officers, reinforcing the differentiation by gender in terms of actual home workload as opposed to mere perceptions of balance/conflict.

Consequences of work–family conflict in policing

Thus far we have described factors that can lead to work-family conflict in policing. As discussed earlier, the JD-R Model (Bakker and Demerouti, 2007; Demerouti *et al.*, 2001) proposes that jobs with high demands lead to depletion of energy and related negative outcomes. This relationship is illustrated in the first two factors (demands, work–family conflict) in the Policing Work–Family Stress and Intervention Model (see Figure 4.1). In the following section, we will discuss the consequences that arise from the work–family conflict. Specifically, we examine how work–family conflict can lead to three broad categories of outcomes; work, non-work, and stress outcomes.

Work outcomes

Whereas there are many work outcomes that are influenced by work–family conflict (e.g. organizational commitment, job performance, career success, etc.), two of the strongest work outcomes of work–family conflict are job satisfaction and intentions to quit (Allen *et al.*, 2000). Job satisfaction is "a positive (or negative) evaluative judgment one makes about one's job or job situation" (Weiss, 2002, p. 175), and has been found to be consistently related to both organizational and employee outcomes (Judge and Kammeyer-Mueller, 2012). In terms of the impact of work–family conflict on job satisfaction for police officers in particular, Burke (1988) collected data from 828 officers and found that officer work–family conflict was associated with important work attitudes such as compromised job satisfaction, and more frequently reported negative feelings, burnout, and intentions to quit. Similarly, Brunetto *et al.* (2010) found that work–family conflict was related to job satisfaction in a sample of Australian police officers. Similarly, Howard *et al.* (2004) found a negative correlation between work–family conflict and job satisfaction in a sample of full-time sworn officers.

Whereas job satisfaction is a more general work-related outcome, intentions to quit are more specific to a job behavior, that is, leaving one's job. Interestingly, there is less research that examines the relationship between work–family conflict and turnover intentions in the police force. In one of the few studies that examined turnover intentions, Burke (1994) found that increased work–family conflict was related to intentions to leave the job. This relationship was also found in other policing studies (e.g. Martinussen *et al.*, 2007).

Non-work outcomes

Although police organizations are interested in work outcomes, they are also interested in non-work outcomes because of the effects they have on their employees, and the indirect effects on the organization. Three of the most commonly identified non-work outcomes related to work–family conflict are life satisfaction, marital satisfaction, and family satisfaction (Allen *et al.*, 2000). Within non-work outcomes, much research in the police domain has been on the effect that policing has on family life. It appears that the stressors associated with police work can spill over into family life and have detrimental effects on the family. Research has shown that there are many different facets of family well-being that can be affected by the stresses of policing. For example, research by Karaffa *et al.* (2014) supports the negative impact police work has on marital relationships. Specifically, spouses highlighted work–family conflict and finances as two primary concerns and sources of distress. It should also be noted that specific jobs within police work can increase the likelihood of negative work–family consequences. Farkas (1986), for example, found that those who engage in undercover work reported frequently experiencing negative clinical symptoms, including marital/relationship problems.

Work–family conflict can affect general family stressors, yet it becomes much more problematic when marital difficulties transform into domestic violence. Although there is much research on domestic violence and policing, there is very little research that directly links work–family conflict as a contributing mechanism in this relationship. In the case of domestic violence, there are many studies that examine the relationship between work stress and domestic violence. For example, Johnson *et al.* (2005) researched police officers and found that domestic violence is an effect of violence exposure, which is commonly found in police work. Furthermore, this process was mediated by factors such as burnout, authoritarian spillover, alcohol use, and spouse violence. Along these lines, Anderson and Lo (2011) conducted a study regarding the effect of work–related stress on domestic violence. They argued that police officers deal with substantial work stress, which leads to interpersonal violence. They contend that this relationship between work stress and violence is a result of spillover authoritarian attitudes and negative emotions that law enforcement officers experience. Similarly, Neidig, Russell, and Seng (1992) found that the more hours police officers worked, the more the likelihood of domestic violence increased. Finally, Gershon *et al.* (2009) surveyed over 1,000 police officers from a large, urban police department and found that work stress was significantly related to intimate partner abuse. It should be noted that in all of these studies, there was a work stressor (e.g. work hours) that was related to domestic violence, suggesting a work–family link, but work–family conflict was not specifically tested.

Stress outcomes

In the general population, stress-related consequences of work–family conflict include psychological strain, physical symptoms, depression, and burnout (Allen *et al.*, 2000). Research suggests that these work–family consequences are similar for police officers. Interestingly, researchers are more likely to examine stress outcomes and work–family conflict in the context of different types of conflict (e.g. time-based, strain-based, etc.) compared to other outcomes. For example, Janzen *et al.* (2007) found that strain-based work–family conflict (but not time-based conflict) was related to psychological distress for police officers. Similarly, Lambert *et al.* (2010) found that strain- and behavior-based work–family conflict (but not time-based conflict) was related to job burnout in a sample of police officers. The stressors not only impact the officers though, as family members also often face emotional, psychological, and social consequences (Miller, 2007). Thus, in general, findings provide evidence that work–family conflict, especially strain-based work–family conflict, is detrimental to employee well-being.

Policies and practices to manage work–family challenges

Clearly, work–family conflict is a likely reality for law enforcement personnel, and the effects can be quite problematic for both officers and the policing agency. In this final section, we discuss interventions within organizations and those within the family domain that can help officers more effectively manage their conflict and alleviate the problems associated with it. In the Policing Work–Family Stress and Intervention model (see Figure 4.1), interventions are considered moderators of the work–family/conflict-outcomes relationship. Based on JD-R theory (Bakker and Demerouti, 2007; Demerouti *et al.*, 2001), we propose that these interventions can decrease the negative outcomes associated with work–family conflict. We understand that work–family conflict is not always avoidable (e.g. the police officer has to work late or will be exposed to a traumatic event), yet we argue that through family and organizational interventions the negative effects of work–family conflict can be managed.

Organizational interventions

Given that police officers are at greater risk of experiencing moderate amounts of stress and, subsequently, poorer general well-being, there is a tremendous need in support services and policy to address alcohol abuse, physical and emotional wellness for officers and families, work scheduling, and officer activity while at work (Mumford *et al.*, 2015). The first area in which organizations can positively impact officers' work–family experiences involves the availability and encouraged usage of support and wellness programs and policies. Youngcourt and Huffman (2005) found that the availability of family-friendly policies was negatively associated with work–family conflict, and that, consequently, such policies moderated the positive relationship between stress and work–family conflict. However, simply having programs available is not sufficient, as many officers do not take advantage of formal programs (Youngcourt and Huffman, 2005). In addition to making programs and services available, supervisors should encourage their usage (Fredriksen-Goldsen and Scharlach, 2001; Secret and Sprang, 2001).

In addition to specific policies that can be in place, special volunteers and crisis support teams should be available for officers as needed. There is evidence that police officers and their families tend to rely most on friends and family for social support, rather than seek professional treatment (Karaffa *et al.*, 2014). However, support from organizations is clearly important. As evidence of its importance, Young *et al.* (2008) conducted a study on the usefulness of on-call mental health volunteers who provided assistance to officers and victims. Over 74 percent of the officers indicated the volunteers provided services that were beneficial and 95 percent believed they helped the victims. The importance of social support from fellow officers cannot be understated. Work–family conflict and family–work conflict are negatively associated with social support, particularly within an organization. Furthermore, increasing support by implementing policies and programs may save organizations money by preventing greater levels of turnover (Sachau *et al.*, 2012).

Another way in which organizations can lessen officer work–family conflict and its deleterious effects is through supervisor awareness training. Supervisors can be trained to recognize problems that an officer may be facing. By training supervisors to recognize signs of stress in an officer, whether originating from the workplace or one's home, potential problems can be addressed before they become overly detrimental to the officer and his/her work and family. For example, supervisors can be trained to become situationally aware of domestic violence (Miller, 2007).

Training can also be targeted towards the officers, and directed at coping skills and strategies for alleviating stress in general, and work–family conflict specifically. This could include, for example, a focus on time management skills to help officers better manage their responsibilities and thereby help alleviate time-based conflicts. Emotion regulation and anger management training could also be used to address strain-based conflict. At the most extreme end, this training can focus on the necessary skills to prevent domestic violence (Miller, 2007). Lastly, behaviors and skills training may be useful to address behavior-based conflict. For example, Borum and Philpot (1993) suggest that officers learn to differentiate between behaviors and skills that help them succeed at work and skills that are more compatible for interactions with their families. They note that learning about balancing skills such as power, control, and dominance may alleviate some tension between the officer and his/her partner.

In addition, it is important that departments do not remain silent when work–family issues escalate to violence. Miller (2007) notes that there has been broad speculation that domestic violence among law enforcement often goes unreported due to the negative consequences it will have on the officer and department as a whole. Rather than remaining silent, departments should aggressively investigate reports of domestic violence when an officer is involved, and deal with it swiftly depending on the findings. In the event that violence has occurred, it may be appropriate to provide training, therapy, a change in job status, or separation from the department. By demonstrating clear workplace repercussions for domestic violence, departments might increase the likelihood that officers will seek and use support programs, and work–family conflict and its deleterious effects might be effectively minimized.

It is worth noting that law enforcement agencies may want to pay particular attention to support provided to officers in undercover work. Undercover officers frequently report experiencing marital/relationship problems, as well as mental health issues even after finishing their assignments (Farkas, 1986). Not surprisingly, according to Arter (2005), undercover officers experience greater levels of stress than fellow patrol officers. Furthermore, Love et al. (2008) found that former undercover officers experience higher frequencies of negative clinical symptoms than current undercover officers. Although, as suggested, this may be partially due to the denial of symptoms or compensatory support mechanisms received while serving in an undercover position.

Family interventions

Officers and their families can also engage in activities to lessen negative consequences for themselves and their loved ones. For example, Borum and Philpot (1993) noted that the survival of relationships, particularly of those serving in law enforcement, is dependent in large part on effective communication. They noted that officers often tend to feel that their work, and the nature thereof, is a reason for limiting rather than increasing communication with one's spouse. Police officers are burdened daily with the stressors the job elicits and tend to compartmentalize it to prevent strain on their family. This is not healthy, however, and instead couples need to openly communicate about aspects of the job, including psychological and emotional stressors. Whether this is done through couples therapy with the help of a professional or done on their own, increasing the quality and quantity of the couple's communication is key to lessening stress resulting from work–family conflict.

Beyond increasing communication, it is also recommended that law enforcement families identify themselves as a separate entity outside of the job itself. Along these lines, Borum and Philpot (1993) specifically recommend that officers and their families create family boundaries separate from the department, essentially creating an "us/them" dichotomy. The intent in doing so is to establish solidarity, allowing the family to perceive themselves as their own functional unit or team.

Children within law enforcement families often face emotional, psychological, and social consequences (Miller, 2007). As such, it is important for officers and their spouses to take additional steps to ensure that their children are emotionally secure. Miller (2007) recommended children waking approximately 30 minutes earlier a few days per week to spend time with their parents. Furthermore, phone calls to the child while the parent is at work might be beneficial to both the child and the parent, and further strengthen their bonds and reduce any anxiety that the child might have as a result of his/her parent working odd hours in an unsafe environment.

Education and understanding are also key for the successful handling of work–family issues. Families should be educated on how they can better provide support and facilitate better coping mechanisms for the officer in his/her choice of career (Woody, 2006). It is important to note that one's family need not be limited to spouse and children: One's extended family should also be made aware of the struggles an officer may experience and how best to support him/her. Indeed, a good understanding of the job may help explain Amin's (2011) finding that having a parent who also served in law enforcement appears to be related to reduced stress. That is, coming from a "police family" is related to a greater ability to manage one's stress. However, since not all officers have a police lineage whereby family members will be able to easily relate to the job, it is important for the officer to educate his/her family members about the various challenges inherent in the job. In fact, talking about and sharing some of the positive events that happen at work with one's family can facilitate enhanced work–family relations (Culbertson *et al.*, 2012).

Effective, constructive coping is essential for police officers and their families. For example, He *et al.* (2005) reported that destructive coping, including drinking and smoking, had strong links with increased work–family conflict and stress. Furthermore, Halbesleben (2010) collected data from 621 police officers and their spouses/live-in partners and found that spousal social support was positively related to the use of active coping and negatively related to avoidant coping. Active coping involves attempts to regain control of one's situation in order to minimize stress. Avoidant coping, conversely, involves attempts to escape the situation that is causing the stress. In general, active coping tends to result in positive psychological outcomes while avoidant coping is related to negative outcomes (Aspinwall and Taylor, 1992; Ingledew *et al.*, 1997).

Conclusion

In this chapter we have introduced the Policing Work–Family Stress and Intervention Model and have discussed and justified its component parts. This model provides a framework that includes key predictors of work–family conflict among police officers, the related outcomes of such conflict, and, finally, interventions to help manage and mitigate the conflict. The model is rooted in the reality that policing is stressful, not only for the law enforcement personnel themselves but also for their loved ones. Many aspects of the job wreak havoc on the home front, which can lead to deleterious outcomes for the family and the agency alike. We have attempted to elucidate these issues here, and provide interventions that can be undertaken by the policing organization as well as those that can be adopted by the individual officer and his/her family in order to lessen the negative outcomes associated with policing work–family conflict. Through open communication, active coping, and ample support from supervisors, colleagues, and family, the officer and his/her family should be better able to manage the competing demands that are placed on him/her within both work and home domains.

References

Akanni, A. (2011). *Shiftwork, job satisfaction and family life: An empirical study among nurses in Osun State Nigeria.* Lambert Academic Publishing.

Albertson, K., Rafnsdottir, G., Grimsmo, A., Tomas-son, K., and Kauppinen, K. (2008). Workhours and work–life balance. *SJWEH Supplements, 5*, 14–21.

Allen, T. D., Herst, D. E., Bruck, C. S., and Sutton, M. (2000). Consequences associated with work-to-family conflict: A review and agenda for future research. *Journal of Occupational Health Psychology, 5*(2), 278.

Amin, S. (2011). *Family relations and its influence on officers' current levels of job stress.* Unpublished doctoral dissertation. Alliant International University.

Anderson, A. S., and Lo, C. C. (2011). Intimate partner violence within law enforcement families. *Journal of Interpersonal Violence, 26*(6), 1176–1193.

Anshel, M. H., Robertson, M., and Caputi, P. (1997). Sources of acute stress and their appraisals and reappraisals among Australian police as a function of previous experience. *Journal of Occupational and Organizational Psychology, 70*(4), 337–356.

Arter, M. L. (2005). Undercover and under stress: The impact of undercover assignments on police officers. Unpublished doctoral dissertation. Indiana Unversity of Pennsylvania.

Aspinwall, L. G., and Taylor, S. E. (1992). Modeling cognitive adaptation: A longitudinal investigation of the impact of individual differences and coping on college adjustment and performance. *Journal of Personality and Social Psychology, 63*, 989–1003.

Bakker, A. B., and Demerouti, E. (2007). The job demands–resources model: State of the art. *Journal of Managerial Psychology, 22*, 309–328.

Barthe, B., Messing, K., and Abbas, L. (2011). Strategies used by women workers to reconcile family responsibilities with atypical work schedules in the service sector. *Work, 40*, S47–S58.

Borum, R. and Philpot, C. (1993). Therapy with law enforcement couples: Clinical management of the "high-risk lifestyle." *American Journal of Family Therapy, 21*(2), 122–135.

Brunetto, Y., Farr-Wharton, R., Ramsay, S., and Shacklock, K. (2010). Supervisor relationships and perceptions of work—family conflict. *Asia Pacific Journal of Human Resources, 48*(2), 212–232.

Brunner, G. D., International Association of Chiefs of Police, & United States of America. (1976). Law Enforcement work schedules – Officers' Reactions. *Police Chief, 43*(1), 30–31.

Bull, R., Bustin, B., Evans, P., and Gahagan, D. (1983). *Psychology for police officers.* New York, NY: John Wiley & Sons.

Burke, R. J. (1988). Some antecedents and consequences of work–family conflict. *Journal of Social Behavior & Personality, 3*(4), 287–302.

Burke, R. J. (1993). Work–family stress, conflict, coping and burnout in police officers. *Stress Medicine, 9*, 171–180.

Burke, R. J. (1994). Stressful events, work–family conflict, coping, psychological burnout, and well-being among police officers. *Psychological Reports, 75*(2), 787–800.

Cook, A. and Minnotte, K. (2008). Occupational and industry sex segregation and the work–family interface. *Sex Roles, 59,* 800-813.

Costa, G. (1996). The impact of shift and night work on health. *Applied Ergonomics, 27,* 9–16.

Culbertson, S. S., Mills, M. J., and Fullagar, C. J. (2012). Work engagement and work– family facilitation: Making homes happier through positive affective spillover. *Human Relations, 65,* 1155–1177.

Demerouti, E., Bakker, A. B., Nachreiner, F., and Schaufeli, W. B. (2001). The job demands–resources model of burnout. *Journal of Applied Psychology, 86,* 499–512.

Dowling, F. G., Moynihan, G., Genet, B., and Lewis, J. (2006). A peer-based assistance program for officers with the New York City police department: Report of the effects of Sept. 11, 2001. *The American Journal of Psychiatry, 163*(1), 151–153.

Dulaney, W. M. (1996). *Black police in America.* Bloomington, IN: Indiana University Press.

Farkas, N. S. (1986). Stress in undercover policing. In J. T. Reese and H. A. Goldstein (eds.), *Psychological services for law enforcement* (pp. 433–440). Washington, DC: US Government Printing Office.

Fenwick, R. and Tausig, M. (2001). Scheduling stress: Family and health outcomes of shift work and schedule control. *American Behavioral Scientist, 44,* 1179–1198.

Fredriksen-Goldsen, K. and Scharlach, A. (2001). *Families and work: New directions in the 21st century.* New York, NY: Oxford University Press.

Frone, M. R., Russell, M., and Cooper, M. L. (1992). Prevalence of work–family conflict: Are work and family boundaries asymmetrically permeable? *Journal of Organizational Behavior, 13,* 723–729.

Gershon, R. R., Barocas, B., Canton, A. N., Li, X., and Vlahov, D. (2009). Mental, physical, and behavioral outcomes associated with perceived work stress in police officers. *Criminal Justice and Behavior, 36*(3), 275–289.

Greenhaus, J. H. and Beutell, N. J. (1985). Sources of conflict between work and family roles. *Academy of Management Review, 10,* 76–88.

Griffin, J. D. (2012). *Are we protecting those who protect us? Stress and law enforcement in the 21st century.* Unpublished doctoral dissertation. University of Delaware.

Grosswald, B. (2003). Shift work and negative work-to-family spillover. *Journal of Sociology and Social Welfare, 30,* 31–56.

Haas, L. and Hwang, C. P. (2007). Gender and organizational culture. *Gender and Society, 21,* 52–79.

Hackman, J. R. and Oldham, G. R. (1980) *Work redesign.* Reading, MA: Addison-Wesley.

Halbesleben, J. R. B. (2010). Spousal support and coping among married coworkers: Merging the transaction stress and conservation of resources models. *International Journal of Stress Management, 17,* 384–406.

Hall, G. B., Dollard, M. F., Tuckey, M. R., Winefield, A. H., and Thompson, B. M. (2010). Job demands, work–family conflict, and emotional exhaustion in police officers: A longitudinal test of competing theories. *Journal of Occupational and Organizational Psychology, 83,* 237–250.

Harpold, M. and Feemster, J. (2002). Negative influences of police stress. *FBI Law Enforcement Bulletin, 70,* 1–7.

He, N., Zhao, J., and Ren, L. (2005). Do race and gender matter in police stress? A preliminary assessment of the interactive effects. *Journal of Criminal Justice, 33,* 535–547.

Hobfoll, S. E. (1989). Conservation of resources: A new attempt at conceptualizing stress. *American Psychologist, 44*(3), 513–524.

Howard, W. G., Boles, J. S., and Heather, H. D. (2004). Inter-domain work-family, family-work conflict and police work satisfaction. *Policing, 27,* 380–395.

Howard, W. G, Howard Donofrio, H., and Boles, J. S. (2004). Inter-domain work-family, family–work conflict and police work satisfaction. *Policing: An International Journal of Police Strategies & Management, 27,* 380–395.

Huffman, A. H., Culbertson, S. S., and Barbour, J. (2015). In M. J. Mills (ed.), *Gender and the work-family experience: An intersection of two domains.* New York, NY: Springer.

Ingledew, D. K., Hardy, L., and Cooper, C. L. (1997). Do resources bolster coping and does coping buffer stress? An organizational study with longitudinal aspect and control for negative affectivity. *Journal of Occupational Health Psychology, 2,* 118–133.

Jackson, S. E. and Maslach, C. (1982). After-effects of job-related stress: Families as victims. *Journal of Organizational Behavior, 3*(1), 63–77.

Janzen, B. L., Muhajarine, N., and Kelly, I. W. (2007). Work-family conflict, and psychological distress in men and women among Canadian police officers. *Psychological Reports, 100*(2), 556–562.

Johnson, L. B., Todd, M., and Subramanian, G. (2005). Violence in police families: Work–family spillover. *Journal of Family Violence, 20*(1), 3–12.

Judge, T. A. and Kammeyer-Mueller, J. D. (2012). Job attitudes. *Annual Review of Psychology, 63,* 341–367. doi: 10.1146/annurev-psych-120710-100511.

Kahn, R. L., Wolfe, D. N., Quinn, R. P., Snoek, J. D., and Rosenthal, D. A. (1964). *Organizational stress: Studies in role conflict and ambiguity.* New York, NY: John Wiley & Sons.

Karaffa, K., Openshaw, L., Koch, J., Clark, H., Harr, C., and Stewart, C. (2014). Perceived impact of police work on marital relationships. *The Family Journal, 23*(2), 120–131.

Karasek Jr., R. A. (1979). Job demands, job decision latitude, and mental strain: Implications for job redesign. *Administrative science quarterly, 24,* 285–308.

Kurtz, D. L. (2012). Roll call and the second shift: The influences of gender and family on police stress. *Police Practice and Research, 13,* 71–86.

La Valle, I., Arthur, S., Millward, C., Scott, J., and Clayden, M. (2002). *Happy families? Atypical work and its influence on family life.* Bristol, UK: Policy Press.

Lambert, E. G., Hogan, N. L., and Altheimer, I. (2010). An exploratory examination of the consequences of burnout in terms of life satisfaction, turnover intent, and absenteeism among private correctional staff. *The Prison Journal, 90*(1), 94–114.

Lindsey, D. (2007). Police fatigue. *FBI Law Enforcement Bulletin, 76,* 1–8.

Loo, R. (2004). A typology of burnout types among police managers. *Policing: An International Journal of Police Strategies & Management, 27,* 156–165.

Love, K. G., Vinson, J., Tolsma, J., and Kaufmann, G. (2008). Symptoms of undercover police officers: A comparison of officers currently, formerly, and without undercover experience. *International Journal of Stress Management, 15*(2), 136–152.

Martin, S. E. and Jurik, N. C. (2007). *Doing justice, doing gender: Women in legal and criminal justice occupations.* Thousand Oaks, CA: Sage.

Martinussen, M., Richardsen, A. M., and Burke, R. J. (2007). Job demands, job resources, and burnout among police officers. *Journal of Criminal Justice, 35*(3), 239–249.

Maslach, C. and Jackson, S.E. (1979). Burned-out cops and their families. *Psychology Today, 12,* 58–62.

Maslach, C., Schaufeli, W., and Leiter, M. P. (2001). Job burnout. *Annual Review of Psychology, 52,* 397–422.

Miller, L. (2007). Police families: Stresses, syndromes, and solutions. *The American Journal of Family Therapy, 35*(1), 21–40.

Miller, L. (2008). Stress and resilience in law enforcement training and practice. *International Journal of Emergency Mental Health, 10,* 109–124.

Mumford, E. A., Taylor, B. G., and Kubu, B. (2015). Law enforcement officer safety and wellness. *Police Quarterly, 18*(2), 111–133.

Neidig, P. H., Russell, H. E., and Seng, A. F. (1992). Interspousal aggression in law enforcement families: A preliminary investigation. *Police Stud.: Int'l Rev. Police Dev., 15,* 30.

Nordlicht, S. (1979). Effects of stress on the police officer and family. *New York State Journal of Medicine, 79*(3), 400–401.

Øyane, N. M. F., Pallesen, S., Moen, B. E., Akerstedt, T., and Bjorvatn, B. (2013). Associations between night work and anxiety, depression, insomnia, sleepiness and fatigue in a sample of Norwegian nurses. *PLoS ONE, 8*(8), 1–7.

Perrucci, R., MacDermid, S., King, E., Tang, C., Brimeyer, T., Ramadoss, K., and Swanberg, J. (2007). The significance of shift work: Current status and future directions. *Journal of Family and Economic Issues, 28,* 600–617.

Pinto, J., Dutton, S., Salvanto, A., and Backus, F. (2014, December 10). Michael Brown and Eric Garner: The police, use of force and race. *CBS News*. Retrieved March 25, 2016 from www.cbsnews.com/news/michael-brown-and-eric-garner-the-police-use-of-force-and-race/.

Reiser, M. and Geiger, S. P. (1984). Police officer as victim. *Professional Psychology: Research and Practice*, 15(3), 315.

Rosiello, R. M. and Mills, M. J. (2015). Shiftwork as gendered and its impact on work-family balance. In M. Mills (ed.), *Gender and the work-family experience: An intersection of two domains*. New York, NY: Springer.

Sachau, D. A., Gertz, J., Matsch, M., Palmer, A. J., and Englert, D. (2012). Work–life conflict and organizational support in a military law enforcement agency. *Journal of Police and Criminal Psychology*, 27(1), 63–72.

Schulz, D. M. (2004). *Breaking the Brass Ceiling: Women Police Chiefs and Their Paths To the Top*. Westport, CT: Greenwood Publishing Group.

Secret, M. and Sprang, G. (2001). The effects of family-friendly workplace environments on the work–family stress of employed parents. *Journal of Social Service Research*, 28, 21–41.

Siegrist, J. (1996). Adverse health effects of high-effort/low-reward conditions. *Journal of Occupational Health Psychology*, 1, 27–41.

Somvadee, C. and Morash, M. (2008). Dynamics of sexual harassment for policewomen working alongside men. *Policing: An International Journal of Police Strategies & Management*, 31, 485–498.

Toch, H. (2002). *Stress in policing*. Washington, DC: American Psychological Association.

Weiss, H. M. (2002). Deconstructing job satisfaction. Separating evaluations, beliefs and affective experiences. *Human Resource Management Review*, 12, 173–194.

Wharton, A. S. (1999). The psychosocial consequences of emotional labor. *The Annals of the American Academy of Political and Social Science*, 561, 158–176.

Willis, T. A., O'Connor, D. B., and Smith, L. (2008). Investigating effort–reward imbalance and work–family conflict in relation to morningness–eveningness and shift work. *Work & Stress*, 22(2), 125–137.

Woody, R. H. (2006). Family interventions with law enforcement officers. *American Journal of Family Therapy*, 34(2), 95–103.

World Health Organization (2007). Carcinogenicity of shift-work, painting, and fire-fighting. *The Lancet Oncology*, 8, 1065–1066.

Young, A. T., Fuller, J., and Riley, B. (2008). On-scene mental health counseling provided through police departments. *Journal of Mental Health Counseling*, 30(4), 345–361.

Youngcourt, S. S. and Huffman, A. H. (2005). Family-friendly policies in the police: Implications for work-family conflict. *Applied Psychology in Criminal Justice*, 1(2), 138–162.

Zhang, J., Zhu, Y., Zhan, G., Fenik, P., Panossian, L., Wang, M. M., and Veasey, S. (2014). Extended wakefulness: Compromised metabolics in and degeneration of locus ceruleus neurons. *Journal of Neuroscience*, 34, 4418–4431.

5 Gender issues in policing

Towards a more viable theory for interventions and research

Melchor D. de Guzman

Introduction

Scholars contend that policing is a highly stressful job (Burke, 1993; Morash *et al.*, 2006; Reese, 1986; Robinson, 1981; Selye, 1978; Violanti, 1985). Research has identified several sources of stress as emanating from the nature of the job (Ma *et al.*, 2015; Violanti and Aron, 1993; Wexler and Logan, 1983), the administrative demands of the department (Brown and Campbell, 1990; Spielberger *et al.*, 1981), family and home-work conflict (see Kurtz (2011) for literature review; Burke, 1988; Lonsway, 2007; Miller, 2007; Toch, 2002), including their ethnicity (Morash and Haarr, 1995), and gender (Martin, 1979; Walker, 1985; Rabe-Hemp, 2009). However, there seems to be much more focus on gender in policing due to the implications of this source of stress for a traditionally gendered organizations such as the police (He, *et al.*, 2002; Archbold and Schultz, 2008; Martin, 1980).

Police research seems equivocal that policewomen are the receptors of stress and that, primarily, their gender seems to elicit negative treatments from their co-workers and their workplace environments (He *et al.*, 2005; Patterson, 2003). Except for Balkin (1988), no other research has viewed gender, particularly being female, as a stressor to co-workers, workplace, and community. Although Balkin (1998) was influential in outlining the psycho-social reasons for the antagonistic relationships between men and women in policing, he falls short in presenting a theoretical perspective that explains the aversion of policemen towards policewomen. Shelley *et al.* (2011) state that most inquiries about gender issues in policing remain *atheoretical* and this knowledge gap has not been filled.

This chapter questions the mainstream assumptions about policewomen as mere receptors of stress and suggests that gender-induced stress in policing is multi-directional and/or an interactional phenomenon. The chapter advances the examination of two theories as explanatory models that take into consideration these interactional phenomena and addresses the atheoretical state of the knowledge about gender issues in policing. Mainstream literature regarding gender in policing has been dominated by the feminism, paternalism, and tokenism perspectives. In all of these perspectives, the focus of research considers females as receptors of stress but not as stressors. The proposed theoretical perspectives provide alternative explanations for gender issues in policing. The chapter makes the point that gender issues and their consequential effects on police officers are interactional in nature.

In addition, the chapter argues that gender-related issues are not only rooted within the organization but also emanate from the social order where the organization is culturally situated (Crank, 2003; Crank and Langworthy, 1992).[1] The sources of stress for women in policing, as well as their role and behavioral expectations, could be traced to societal views that are manifested in the relationship dynamics within police organizations (Acker, 1992). Lundman's (1980) theory on policing suggests that the form and character of the police are interwoven with the society where they operate.[2] Hence, the police and their culture will be hard-pressed to rise above the society's cultures where they operate (Caldero and Crank, 2004; Crank, 2003).

This chapter explores the minority threat hypothesis's application and extension to policing. It argues that the theory has potential for explaining the gender issues in policing. The suggested application of the minority threat theory relates to women as presenting a threat to the organizational and social orders that exist in traditionally gendered organizations such as the police. Threats that the female gender poses to social and organizational norms are anomalies that create reciprocal stressful effects for policewomen and policemen simultaneously.

The institutional theory of policing (Crank, 2003) is another potential explanatory theory for gender issues of policing. The theory presents gender (i.e. being a woman) as incompatible with the tradition and culture of the police organization, which is shaped by the institutional environment where it operates (Crank, 2003; Crank and Langworthy, 1992; Katz, 2001). Discussions will center on the twin issues on why "doing gender" (Garcia 2003; Kanter 1977; Rabe-Hemp, 2009) in policing is such a predominant organizational culture (He *et al.*, 2005). The first issue involves the character of policing as being resistant to change (Guyot, 1979; King, 2003) and the constraining effects of its institutional environment (Crank and Langworthy, 1992). The second issue concerns the continuing effort by the police to achieve legitimacy (Bittner, 1970; Klockars, 1985). The image of policing as having the ability to fight crime, coupled with effective accountability measures, has been used as a justification for the establishment of a professional police force in London (Cole *et al.*, 2016; Travis and Langworthy, 2008). This balance of the use of force and accountability has remained a paradox for the police, and it continues to haunt modern US policing (Travis and Langworthy, 2008). The legitimacy of the police in society has been perpetually challenged (Walker, 1977). The inclusion of women in policing has been presented as a solution for this legitimacy dilemma, but has also made policewomen problematic for establishing police legitimacy in society. The institutional environment of the police values masculine qualities such as physical strength, emotional detachment, or aggression among other things (Burke and Mickkelsen, 2005; Garcia, 2003; Lord and Friday, 2003; Martin, 1980).

The implications of these views for interventions and research will be presented. The discussion on intervention outlines practical efforts to reduce the impact of gender on stress. Since stress has always been viewed as a unidirectional phenomenon (women being viewed as the recipients of stress and not the stressors), most interventions have been largely directed towards efforts to eliminate the stressors for policewomen. This chapter highlights approaches that address gender issues in policing in line with the multidirectional perspective. Likewise, future directions for research are presented to better understand gender issues in policing.

The minority threat theory and gender in policing

The minority threat hypothesis is deeply rooted in race studies and has been utilized to explain the use of force by police towards racial minorities. The theory was even used to explain the control tendencies of the state in dealing with the minority population. The theory argues that police tend to use more aggressive force on minorities due to the preconceived notion that they are symbolic assailants (Skolnick, 1994). Holmes, Smith, Freng, & Munoz (2008) suggest that minorities are controlled more aggressively not only because of their actual disproportionate participation in crime commission, but also, more importantly, because of their perceived disruption of the established social order (i.e. the dominance of one race over the other). Hence, the state uses its control agencies, particularly the police, and uses more aggressive means to control the traditional minority population.

Although being female in policing is a minority status—and even as mainstream research on gendered organizations suggests that women are viewed as tokens (Garcia, 2003; Kanter, 1977; Martin, 1980; Rabe-Hemp, 2009)—being a policewoman has not been treated as a source of threat to the existing social and organizational order. Instead, most explanations of female discrimination and tokenism are rooted in theories of paternalism that consider a woman as someone to be protected instead of being a threat. Paternalism has gained a paradigmatic status that has hindered women's status by treating them as minorities. Therefore, women have not been deemed as appropriate and primary foci of the minority threat hypothesis. This adherence to the paternalistic view is a serious theoretical oversight. The theory rests on fallacious assumptions about how society views women and it affirms the very status it tries to denounce. In this regard, it is necessary to explore how the minority threat hypothesis could be considered as viable theory to explain gender issues in policing.

Elements of the minority threat theory

The minority threat hypothesis suggests three critical elements which make it a viable explanation for the differential treatment of minorities. First, the target of force occupies a minority status. Second, the minority presents a threat. In most research testing this theory, threats were conceptualized as committing crimes. Several bodies of research have extended the meaning of threats to perceptions of disorder (Wilson and Kelling, 1982; Caldero and Crank, 2004). Third, the dominant elite in society and its instruments of control are employed on minorities in order to contain the threats they present (Lundman, 1980).[3]

Women as minorities and threats

Minority threat theory could be an explanatory model for why policewomen are treated differently in police organizations. Women in policing are considered as "tokens," who are grudgingly admitted into police departments (Hochstedler *et al.*, 1984; Garcia, 2003; Kanter, 1977; Martin, 1980; Walker, 1985). Therefore, women officers in policing meet the first criterion (i.e. being a minority).

The second criterion consists of policewomen as presenting perceived threats. They are considered as threats to the existing social order and as disruptions to the existing organizational norms and procedures of policing. The inclusion of women in a traditionally gendered organization creates stress both to the minority (i.e. policewomen) and the majority (i.e. policemen) (He *et al.*, 2005). The result is a reciprocal stress that feeds upon the basic instincts of human beings to engage in a flight or fight response. The fight on the part of the women is to advocate for their inclusion and full acceptance into the police organization (Rabe-Hemp, 2009). Because they have to fight for inclusion, they are considered as disruptions and threats to the normal working environment (Walker, 1985).

Women's flight is seen through the avoidance of policing as a profession (Haarr, 2005) or through leaving the police force. Those that eventually become policewomen sometimes have to resort to "doing gender" in order to survive in the organization (West and Zimmerman, 1987). The evidence indicates that there seems to be more flight than fight among women in trying to avoid the stress of being in policing (Haarr, 2005). For example, despite affirmative action, the number of women in policing has not made a steady growth due to struggles and barriers to their inclusion (Cordner and Cordner, 2011; Martin, 2004; Walker, 1985). The latest estimate is that approximately only about12 percent of women make up the composition of local police officers (Reaves, 2015). In Guajardo's (2015) analysis of big-city US police departments, he noted that from 1997 to 2007, female representation in policing has only increased on average by about 2 percent.

The number of policewomen in executive positions is also indicative of the flight response. Although the lower proportion of policewomen in positions of authority has often been considered as indicative of discrimination against women in the workplace (Martin, 1980), there have been research findings that women prefer not to actively seek these promotions for several reasons, but primarily due to their family–work role conflicts (Burke, 1988; 1993; Dodge et al., 2010). Regardless of these motivations, however, the lower proportion of policewomen in command and supervisory positions in police departments is just a statistical reflection of their representation in those departments (Guajardo, 2015). Since policewomen are lower in numbers, it is expected that they should also be disproportionately represented in the upper echelons. Even in large department, only about 7–10 percent of individuals in supervisory and command positions are women (Guajardo, 2015).

Control of women through violence

The third criteria, the violent treatment of policewomen, should be empirically tackled. Recent developments in the conceptualizations of violence support the threat hypothesis with issues of gender in policing. Violence has taken several dimensions aside from its physical form. Psychological and verbal assaults have been legitimately viewed as expressions of violence. Research has documented that policewomen experience harassment (e.g. verbal and sexual), crude jokes, and discrimination, including avoidance by other officers (Balkin, 1988). These actions are now generally accepted as expressions of violence. In turn, these violent actions create psychological stress for those who are subjected to them. Thus, policewomen are victims of violence due to their minority status as women, and their status consequently leads to their being stressed out by the organization.

Police officers who experience higher levels of stress are disproportionately resorting to violence in order to address the source of stress. Therefore, it is not unusual for policemen to treat policewomen with subtle forms of violence in order to alleviate the stress they present to policemen (Franklin, 2005). To date, no research has conceptualized violence towards policewomen in terms of psychological and verbal assault. Instead, these forms of violence are conceptualized either as separate, lighter, or non-violent forms of aggression. The current confinement of the conceptualization of violence to its physical dimension has precluded the use of the minority threat hypothesis as a potential explanation for violence towards women in the workplace. Consequently, a gap in research exists that could explain the perpetuation of gender-related problems in police organizations.

Institutional theory and gender issues in policing

Another theory that might explain the persistence of gender-related problems in policing is the institutional theory of policing. Institutional theory argues that police organizations respond to their environment and navigate through social expectations of the police force (Caldero and Crank, 2004; Crank, 2003; Crank and Langworthy, 1992). Female officers disturb the very principles for which the institution is founded—physicality or the ability to use non-negotiable, coercive force. Community policing should have ushered in a changed perspective on the value of the use of force policing. Community policing values such principles as developing partnerships, problem-solving, and respect for officers, among others (Cordner, 1998). Likewise, community policing attaches lesser premiums to traditional measures of police effectiveness, such as arrest and clearance rates. This shift in emphases for police effectiveness tends to de-emphasize some of the measures that are rooted in masculine qualities of police officers. However, as Olotola (2013) observes, the greatest problem of community policing in the U.S. is the less-than-enthusiastic move towards changing the organization. Policing continues to value masculine characteristics. The organization also continues to relegate community policing to the status of "not a real police job" (Kraska and Cubellis, 1997). In fact, an analysis of the changing paradigm shift from community policing (i.e. a perceived less-than-masculine philosophy) to homeland security policing (i.e. a more masculine philosophy) suggests that police departments are reverting back to their original conception of their role as the distributor of non-negotiable coercive force rather than their role of consensus building and partnership with communities (Kim and de Guzman, 2012).

These empirical facts demonstrate the tendencies for most police departments to revert to their institutional roles, rather than conform their behavior to the formal ethical standards of fairness and equality, by creating myths surrounding their practices (Meyer and Rowan, 1977). Some scholars suggest that police officers subvert the "broken windows theory" (Wilson and Kelling, 1982) by reverting back to their traditional conception of their police roles—"kick ass" or aggressive policing (Innes, 1999; Silverman, 1998). Thus, it has not been surprising that zero-tolerance policing has been touted as community policing when it contains all the characteristics of traditional masculine qualities of policing. It represents the institutional values of masculinity and the paramilitary culture (Kraska, 1996; 2001; Kraska and Kappeler, 1997; Kraska and Cubellis, 1997) being brought back into policing through the back door. Hence, police organizations have not really implemented reforms to conform to the spirit of community policing, but have rather subverted reforms through the manipulation of appearances in order to appear to be conforming to emerging social trends (Manning, 1997)

In King's (2003) analyses about change in police organizations, it is very difficult to implement changes that threaten the reputation of the police organization and its officers such as possessing a command presence and authority. The presence of policewomen challenges those values that are socially attributed as masculine qualities. Policewomen are socially viewed as lacking those masculine attributes and, thereby, become anomalies in police organizations and society in general. Interestingly, Poteyeva and Sun (2009) systematically examined the literature on the views of policemen and policewomen about their roles and values. They found a congruence of views between genders; police roles primarily involve the more masculine role of law enforcement instead of providing a service. Therefore, both genders are indoctrinated to embrace this institutional role and fail to embrace the demand for their role change in a community policing era.

This reluctance to embrace change is founded on the ever-looming problem of police legitimacy. Policing has always struggled with its legitimacy (Bittner, 1970). The acknowledged architect of modern policing, Sir Robert Peel, had to redefine the roles, functions, and administration of the police in order for the organization to become acceptable in society (Travis and Langworthy, 2008). Peel argued for the creation of the police, using as his rationale their potential effectiveness in preventing and controlling crime. Coupled with the assurance of strict control mechanisms, the police force was grudgingly accepted as an experiment in London (Travis and Langworthy, 2008). Recent events continue to highlight the perpetual question about the police in terms of their effectiveness and legitimacy in society (de Guzman *et al.*, 2013; Walker, 1977; Wilson and Kelling, 1982).

Some rhetorical ideas did not help the cause for the acceptance of women in policing and further cemented the institutionalized masculine culture of the police. Foremost among these was the "war on crime" notion. We have been making strides in de-emphasizing the war rhetoric in policing with the community policing revolution. However, the events of 9/11 changed the policing landscape in the U.S. (de Guzman, 2003). Worse, we situated the police as front-liners in the ensuing war on terror. Not only was the government's ability to provide safety questioned, but also the effectiveness of those that provide such safety. The benevolent approach to policing that community policing ushered in was replaced with a more brutish approach seen in the emergence of homeland security policing. These perceptions about safety have again stumped the cause of women in policing. Suddenly, policing became more dangerous again and, no doubt, some women are so daunted by this challenge that they begin to shun policing. Policemen, in turn, begin to doubt the capabilities of women for this new dimension of the crime-fighting situation. Likewise, the cultural notion about policing being a profession for individuals with physical prowess is again reinforced, thereby solidifying the hold of institutional theory in police organizations. In view of the foregoing, institutional theory could become an explanatory model for explaining the perpetuation of masculine qualities in policing and the exacerbation of problems involving gender issues in policing.

The presence of women in policing could be considered as another hurdle to achieving police legitimacy in society. In an era where anti-terrorism has become the central focus of law enforcement, masculine and aggressive qualities are again viewed as the framework for effective anti-terrorism efforts. With counter-terrorism as a backdrop, this gender status of "being feminine" could be a source of stress for both policemen and policewomen. Hence, gender-related problems are expected to be highlighted again in this war on terror.

Elements of institutional theory

Crank (2003, p. 187-188) outlined three elements of institutional theory.

Reflexivity of the social norms

The first element states that "the organization, in its behavior and structure, reflects the values in its institutional environment." This means that organizational norms are conjured to reflect the social norms of their environment (Acker, 1992; West and Zimmerman, 1987). This aspect has not been empirically tested in the U.S., especially with the congruity of departmental norms with social norms of their institutional environment. A direct test of this theoretical proposition was in a study by de Guzman and Kumar (2011) of the changing character of the police, based on the dynamic changes seen in India's political environment. In their study, they found that history has shown that Muslim minorities in India are differentially treated as power elites change from Muslim to Hindu. As enforcers of social norms, the police are often guided by expected social norms (Caldero and Crank, 2004).

Loose coupling of personal and organizational values to social values

Social expectations suggest equality for men and women. However, masculine qualities are desired by society from their police. Police departments are caught in the paradox of promoting equality in society, while reserving the right to offer equality to police officers who possess the desired masculine qualities regardless of gender. This disjunction between gender and social expectations produces stress in police officers. Institutional theory could be used to unravel the degrees and extent of these loose couplings about personal beliefs and organizational policies as the police respond to their institutional environment. The agencies of the criminal justice system are loosely coupled. Therefore, it would not be surprising to find police policies and practices as loosely coupled in relation to gender needs. These loose couplings could precipitate stresses that officers experience in the performance of their function.

Uncritical acceptance of police practices and values

Police practices have taken a long time to evolve (Wilson and Kelling, 1982). Changes in police organizations are hard to implement (Guyot, 1979; King, 2003) due to the tendency for uncritical acceptance of police practices and values. The introduction of women in policing challenges the very core value by which policing has been founded (i.e. the use of able-bodied men in pursuit of criminals). Women in policing would also challenge the deeply ingrained core essence of policing – the distribution of non-negotiable coercive force (Bittner, 1970; Klockars, 1985). Although this core has been challenged by several scholars (see for example, Landau, 1996). Police officers still value the centrality of this core police function. A content analysis of officer perceptions about police roles and values suggests that no significantly different views exist between genders about law enforcement as the primary function that the police force has to perform (Poteyeva and Sun, 2009). This finding suggests that even women are co-opted or indoctrinated to accept the masculine culture of the police. Women are expected to "do gender," as their conformity to gender expectations is viewed by others as accomplishment (West and Zimmerman, 1987)

Institutional theory has been mostly tested on the organizational level. However, in a review of the state of the art of institutional theory in policing, Crank (2003) suggested that it could also be used to explained tendencies at the individual level. The application of the institutional theory of policing in explaining gender issues could shed further light on the theory that gender issues in policing are interactional and multi-directional phenomena.

Implications for interventions

Current efforts to improve gender-related issues in policing involve a two-pronged approach. The first prong involves the provision of infrastructure for equalities or equities in entry and advancement opportunities for women. In this regard, the government relies on affirmative action and other legislation that would make discrimination against and harassment of women illegal and, sometimes, even criminal.

The second prong involves the accommodation of gender-based needs. Under this approach, women are given accommodations to alleviate their work–family role conflicts. These accommodation requirements produce double-edged effects. On the one hand, women are given opportunities to ease the burden of policing work on their other duties. On another hand, these accommodations perpetuate perceptions that women are stressful to have in a police department. Consequently, police departments seem reluctant to provide accommodations, and when forced to comply, they implement minimal compliance (Schulze, 2010).

Between these two approaches, the policy of inclusion seems to be the more effective approach to addressing gender-related issues in policing. Research has shown that increasing the number of a minority in society has led to greater accommodations and has mitigated abuse of minorities (see literature reviews of Holmes *et al.*, 2008). By analogy, having more women in policing will have the same curvilinear effects on reducing the threat and, thereby, increasing their accommodations in the workplace. Thus, the increase of women to a level where they gain strength in numbers will pave the way for more acceptance, greater chances for women to occupy positions of authority, and more opportunities for women to become agents of culture change in policing (Martin, 1980; Martin and Jurik, 1996; Poteyeva and Sun 2009). In effect, the minority threat should first be neutralized through greater representation before the institutionalized culture can be changed. Increasing accommodations before neutralizing effects of minorities presenting danger (i.e. threat) is not going to lessen gender-related problems and stress in the police organization. On the contrary, the reverse solution (accommodation before inclusion) will heighten the threat of women (Walker, 1985), elevate the status of women as tokens (Rabe-Hemp, 2009), and rally policemen to create a masculine culture in the organization (Kraska, 2001).

The greater inclusion of women in policing will also reduce the tensions that women face within the community. The regularity of women in the police department will reduce the perception that they are anomalies in the police organization—that they are a product of forced inclusion that sets aside their competence in doing police work. Their greater number and greater community exposure to performing police work is the major influence in reducing public misconception about the need for masculine hegemony in policing. Hence, women will be viewed by the community as less of a problem, but rather as a solution to the problem of police legitimacy and the different issues that make the police less legitimate in a democratic society (e.g. police abuse and minority discrimination).

Targeting women and their sources of stress is counter-productive. Research has constantly looked for coping mechanisms that tend to work for women. However, women are not the sources of their own stresses; these are a product of their holistic interaction with their fellow officers, the organization, and society. Ignoring the multi-directional effects of gender seems to direct attention to the single recipient of stress but not its effects on other audiences of the police. Current interventions do not necessarily erase the plight of women, but merely exacerbate and highlight the general perception that policewomen bring problems to the organization.

After aggressive inclusion, accommodations for women should be established without repercussions on their organizational status and professional development. Modern management practices demand the matching of personality, skills, and the job. Contingency theorists in policing (e.g. Cordner and Scarborough, 2014) suggest that different types of workers are equally valuable to the organization. Management's ability to match employees to various tasks will maximize efficiency and effectiveness (Travis and Langworthy, 2008).

Injections of women into policing should be followed by accommodations and skillful management. Several policies tend to inject women into the workplace without regard to the existence of infrastructure that should facilitate their entry and stay in the institution. The introduction of women presents the failure of change management that occurred in the profession. Several steps should have been initiated prior to such admission of women into policing. First, there should have been a thorough definition and clarification of police roles in society. Likewise, potential female issues in the workplace should be discussed at the outset. Don't ask-don't tell policies for hiring are not going to alleviate the problem. It has become prohibited to ask about personal circumstances, but it is necessary for that to be a talking point during the hiring process. Expectations about work duties and accommodations should be negotiated at the outset. Van Maanen (1973) states that being a police officer is a mutual choice between the department and the prospective officer. Claims of discrimination happen in the workplace—real or imagined—because of incongruent expectations about work and accommodations. More importantly, this incongruence becomes a source of stress for both men and women in the police force.

Implications for research

Research should focus on interventions for the multi-directional sources and effects of gender in policing. Focusing on threat theory and institutional theory could jump-start the development of a more progressive rather than combative theories about gender— particularly the conflict paradigm or the feminist perspective.

The minority threat theory should, first, start at the exploratory and comparative level. The hypothesis is that women in departments with a greater proportion of women will be perceived as less threatening by policemen and ultimately will be subjected to fewer discriminatory and violent reactions. It would also be of empirical interest to determine the interaction effects of the number of women in positions of authority within the department and the gender issues within the police department. In particular, would departments with women as chiefs of police have significant impacts on the stress levels of police officers (i.e. both men and women) and what implications does this phenomenon have for the prevalence and intensity of gender-related issues in the police department? Wilson (1968) suggested that the chief has a significant impact on the behavior and character of a department. It would be of significant importance to police science to determine the influences of these factors on gender issues.

The next level of research will test the institutional theory of policing. The empirical approach for this line of research would be to investigate qualitatively and longitudinally the change of culture that happens with departments that have increasing numbers of women within the rank and file, and those that have a greater number of policewomen in authority positions. Research should apply the grounded theory approach, as it is establishing the impact of these factors on cultural views about policewomen. It would be interesting to find out whether the prevailing perceptions of society in general are reflected within institutions or not, in particular within police departments. Alternatively, we should be able to investigate whether police organizations are closed or impermeable and intractable in their perceptions about women in policing independent of their institutional environment.

Conclusion

Stress created by gender in policing is not unidirectional (i.e. affecting only females); rather, it is a reciprocal phenomenon (i.e. both males and females are affected). In fact, it is multi-directional. Mainstream research suggests that being female in policing only affects women. This means that women are stressed and the rest are stressors. However, there is evidence to suggest that having women in a department could be a stressor to other policemen, police administration, or society in general. Alternatively, policemen, police administration, or society in general could be stressors for policewomen.

The workplace problem that women introduce in policing is not the perception that they could inflict harm on policemen, or that they could potentially be more harmful to the subjects they come in contact with in the community they police. Research suggests that policemen "fear" that they would be less effective in controlling dangerous situations when partnering with a woman. Paternalistic attitudes and behaviors permeate the psyche of policemen who fear they have a social obligation to protect policewomen. Apprehension about policewomen also includes the perception that policewomen will have difficulty controlling dangerous situations and that they will consequently endanger "blue lives."

Research findings on effectiveness of policewomen suggest that women tend to de-escalate tense situations more effectively and they are less prone to use or abuse force (Rabe-Hemp, 2008). Regardless of the possession of those qualities, the perceived lack of resolve to use force goes against the grain of police business; the application of non-negotiable, coercive force remains the prevailing view of its distinctive characteristic (Bittner, 1970; Klockars, 1985). This view means that although women can indeed contribute to the reduction of tensions that lead to more violence, there is still that question of their ability to use force with decisiveness, especially in split-second situations (Fyfe, 1981) that could spell life or death for an officer. Muir (1977) suggests that given a choice between trusting and dying, police officers would rather be wrong 95 percent of the time than be exposed to the danger of losing their lives. Thus, it is not hard to fathom their apprehension about women in policing. This apprehension about women's inability to be counted upon in the face of dangerous situations (Balkin, 1988), puts policewomen in the spotlight and places an invisible and indelible "?" on their uniforms. Thus, women officers have to constantly prove themselves as "one of the boys," which further highlights the token status they occupy in the organization.

Gender as an issue in policing is not a unique organizational phenomenon, but is reflective of society in general. The aim of this paper is to respond to the observation of Shelley *et al.* (2011), that studies of gender in policing are by and large atheoretical. Although conflict theory and the feminist perspective have often been used, they are inadequate or perhaps inappropriate to use as they seem to neglect the multi-directionality of stress that gender seems to elicit and produce in police organizations. It has been argued that the minority threat theory and the institutional theory are viable explanatory models that overcome assumptions about the unidirectional trajectory of gender. These theories will have practical applications for police and research that remove biases which are commonly found in most research. The knowledge that will be produced will also shed light on gender relationship issues that are evident in policing. The use of these theories will also unravel some of the disincentives for women to enter or stay in policing. Stress coping studies only provide half the picture. The most viable approach to understanding gender issues in policing will be to understand the organizational and cultural dynamics that occur among genders. The use of minority threat theory and institutional theory will pave the way for a more holistic understanding of such problems involving gender.

The United States as an egalitarian society has lagged behind in the integration of women in policing. It has even lagged behind in the promotion of equity and equality among genders in police organizations. It does not help that most police departments do not allow practices that allow women to manifest their femininity, as they are viewed to be unprofessional. If indeed departments have equal treatment of genders, they should not equate femininity with professionalism, as these are neither correlated nor necessary for effective policing. The policies that tend to provide accommodations and preferential treatment of women in recruitment have intensified the views about women as threats to the institutional values of policing. Along with this value bias, police tend to verify their fear that having women in policing is dangerous and ineffective, since they are perceived to have been admitted to the profession not because of their aptitude for policing, but due to the demands of political correctness and diversity.

Notes

1 See Caldero and Crank (2004), Crank (2003), and Crank and Langworthy (1992) for a more complete discussion of the institutional theory in policing. Their arguments suggest that police cannot rise above the society where they operate. They argue that behaviors and values are mediated by space and time, which provide the context for police officers' decisions and reactions.
2 de Guzman and Kumar (2011) unraveled this control of the minorities in society in their empirical tests of the dominant elite's control of minorities in society. They tested Lundman's (1980) model, which stated that the police, as state instruments of control, change their priorities and levels of aggressiveness towards minorities based on the dynamics of majority–minority status changes in society, particularly along political lines.
3 Ibid.

References

Abdollahi, M. K. (2002). Understanding police stress research. *Journal of Forensic Psychology Practice*, 2: 1–24.

Acker, J. (1992). From sex roles to gendered institutions. *Contemporary Sociology*, 21: 565–569.

Amaranto, E., Steinberg, J., Castellano, C., and Mitchell, R. (2003). Police stress interventions. *Brief Treatment and Crisis Intervention*, 3: 47–53.

Archbold, A. C. and Schulz, D. M. (2008). The lingering effects of tokenism on female police officers' promotions aspirations. *Police Quarterly*, 11: 50–73.

Balkin, J. (1988). Why policemen don't like policewomen. *Journal of Police Science and Administration*, 16: 29–38.

Bittner, E. (1970). *The functions of the police in modern society: A review of the background factors, current practices, and possible role models*. Chevy Chase, M.D.: National Institute of Mental Health, Center for Studies of Crime and Delinquency.

Brown, J. A. and Campbell, E. A. (1990). Sources of occupational stress in the police. *Work and Stress*, 4: 305– 318.

Burke, R. J. (1988). Some antecedents of work-family conflict. *Journal of Social Behavior and Personality*, 4: 287–302.

Burke, R. J. (1993). Work–family stress, conflict, coping and burnout in police officers. *Stress Medicine*, 9: 171– 180.

Burke, R. J. and Mikkelsen, A. (2005). Gender issues in policing: Do they matter? *Women in Management Review*, 20: 133–143.

Caldero, M. A. and Crank, J. P. (2004). *Police ethics: A corruption of a noble cause*. Thousand Oaks, CA: Sage.

Cole, G.F., Smith, C.E., and DeJong, C. (2016). *Criminal justice in America (8th edition)*. Boston, MA: Cengage Learning.

Cordner, G. (1998). The Elements of Community Policing. In L. K. Gaines and G. W. Cordner (eds.), *Policing Perspectives: An Anthology* (pp. 137–149). Richmond, TX: Roxbury Publishing Company.

Cordner, G. and Cordner, A. (2011). Stuck on a plateau? Obstacles to recruitment, selection, and retention of women police. *Police Quarterly*, 14: 207–226.

Cordner, G. and Scarborough, K. E. (2014). *Police administration (8th edition)*. Waltham, MA: Anderson Publishing.

Crank, J. P. (2003). Institutional theory of police: A review of the state of the art. *Policing: An International Journal of Police Science & Management*, 26: 186–207.

Crank, J. P. and Langworthy, R. H. (1992). An institutional perspective of policing. *Journal of Criminal Law and Criminology*, 83: 338–363.

de Guzman, M. C. (2003). The changing roles and strategies of the police in time of terror. In J. Victor and J. Naughton (eds.) (pp. 84–94), *Criminal Justice Annual Editions, 03/04* (pp. 84–94), New York: McGraw-Hill.

de Guzman, M. C. and Kumar, S. K. (2011). Extending Lundman's theory of policing: The evidence from the literature focusing on India. *Policing: An International Journal of Police Strategies & Management*, 34: 403–418.

Dodge, M., Valcore, L. and Klinger, D. (2010). Maintaining separate spheres in policing: Women on SWAT teams. *Women & Criminal Justice*, 20: 218–238.

Franklin, C. A. (2005). Male peer support and the police culture: Understanding the resistance and opposition of women in policing. *Women and Criminal Justice*, 16: 1–25.

Fyfe, J. J. (1981). Who shoots? A look at officer race and shooting. *Journal of Police Science and Administration*, 9: 367–382.

Garcia, V. (2003). Difference in the police department: Women, policing, and "doing gender." *Journal of Contemporary Criminal Justice*, 19: 330–344.

Guajardo, S. A. (2015). Women in policing: A longitudinal assessment of female officers in supervisory positions in the New York City Police Department. *Women & Criminal Justice*.

Guyot, D. (1979). Bending granite: Attempts to change the rank structure of American police department. *Journal of Police Science and Administration*, 7: 253–284.

Haarr, R. N. (2005). Factors affecting the decisions of police recruits to "drop out" of police work. *Police Quarterly*, 8: 431–453.

He, N., Zhao, J., and Archbold, C. A. (2002). Gender and police stress: The convergent and divergent impact of work environment, work–family conflict, and stress coping mechanisms of female and male police officers. *Policing: An International Journal of Police Strategies and Management*, 25: 687–708.

He, N., Zhao, J., and Ren, L. (2005). Do race and gender matter in police stress? A preliminary assessment of the interactive effects. *Journal of Criminal Justice*, 33: 535–547.

Hickman, M. J., Fricas, J., Strom, K. J., Pope, M. W. (2011). Mapping police stress. *Police Quarterly*, 14: 227–250.

Hochsteder, E., Regoli, R. M., and Poole, E. D. (1984). Changing of the guard in American cities: A current empirical assessment of integration in twenty municipal police departments. *Criminal Justice Review*, 9: 8–14.

Holmes, M. D., Smith, B. W., Freng, A. B., and Munoz, E. A. (2008). Minority threat, crime control, and police resource allocation in the Southwestern United States. *Crime & Delinquency*, 54, 128–152.

Innes, M. (1999). An iron fist in an iron glove. Zero tolerance policing debate. *Harvard Journal of Criminal Justice*, 38: 397–410.

Kanter, R. M. (1977). Some effects of proportion on group life: Skewed sex ratios and responses to token women. *American Journal of Sociology*, 82: 965–990.

Katz, C. (2001). The establishment of police gang unit: An examination of or organizational and environmental factors. *Criminology*, 39: 37–74.

Kim, B. and Merlo, A. V. (2010). Policing in Korea: Why women choose law enforcement careers. *Journal of Ethnicity in Criminal Justice*, 8: 1–17.

Kim, M. and de Guzman, M. C. (2012). Police paradigm shift after the 9/11: An empirical evidence from the United States municipal police departments. *Criminal Justice Studies: A Critical Journal of Crime, Law and Society*, 25: 323–342.

King, W. R. (2003). Bending granite revisited: The command rank structure of American police organizations. *Policing*, 26: 208–230.

Klockars, C. B. (1985). *The idea of police*. Beverly Hills, C.A.: Sage Publications, Inc.

Kraska, P. B. (1996). Enjoying militarism, Political/personal dilemmas in studying U.S. paramilitary units. *Justice Quarterly*, 13: 405–429.

Kraska, P. B. (2001). *Militarizing the American criminal justice system: The changing roles of the armed forces and the police*. Boston, M.A.: Northwestern University Press.

Kraska, P. B. and Kappeler, V. E. (1997). Militarizing American police: The rise and normalization of paramilitary units. *Social Problems*, 44: 1–17.

Kraska, P. B. and Cubellis, L. J. (1997). Militarizing Mayberry and beyond: Making sense of American paramilitary units. *Justice Quarterly*, 14: 607–629.

Kurtz, D. L. (2011). Roll call and second shift: The influences of gender and family on police stress. *Police Practice and Research: An International Journal*, 13: 71–86.

Landau, T. (1996). Policing and security in four remote aboriginal communities: A challenge to coercive models of police work. *Canadian Journal of Criminology*, January: 1–32.

Lord, V. B. and Friday, P. C. (2003). Choosing a career in police work: A comparative study between applicants for employment with a large police department and public high school students. *Police Practice and Research: An International Journal*, 4: 63–78.

Lonsway, K. (2007). Are we there yet? *Women and Criminal Justice*, 18: 1–18.

Lucas, T., Weidner, N., and Janisse, J. (2012). Where does work stress come from? A generalizability analysis of stress in police officers. *Psychology & Health*, 27: 1426–1477.

Lundman, R. J. (1980). *Police and Policing: An introduction*. New York: Holt, Rinehart, & Winston.

Ma, C. C., Andrew, M. E., Fekedulegn, D., Gu, J. K., Hartley, T. A., Charles, L. E., Violanti, J. M., and Burchfiel, C. M. (2015). Shift work and occupational stress in police officers. *Safety and Health at Work*, 6: 25–29.

Manning, P. K. (1997). *Police work: The social organization of the police*. Prospect Heights, IL: Waveland Press.

Martin, S. E. (1980). *Breaking and entering*. Berkeley, C.A.: University of California Press.

Martin, S. E. (1979). Policewomen and policeWomen: Occupational role dilemmas and choices of female officers. *Journal of Police Science and Administration*, 7: 314–323.

Martin, S. E. (1991). Effectiveness of affirmative action: The case of women in policing. *Justice Quarterly*, 8: 489–504.

Martin, S. E. (1994). Outsider within the station house: The impact of race and gender on Black women police. *Social Problems*, 41: 383–400.

Martin, S. E. (2004). The interactive effects of race and sex on women police officers. In B. R. Price and N. J. Sokoloff (eds.), *The criminal justice system and women offenders, prisoners, victims, and workers (3rd edn)*. New York: McGraw-Hill.

Martin, S. E. and Jurik, N. (1996). *Doing Justice Doing Gender*. Thousand Oaks, C.A.: Sage.

Meyer, J. and Rowan, B. (1977). Institutionalized organizations: Formal structure as myth and ceremony. *American Journal of Sociology*, 82: 340–363.

Miller, L. (2007). Police families: Stresses, syndromes, and solutions. *The American Journal of Family Therapy*, 35: 21–40.

Morash, M. and Haarr, R. (1995). Gender, workplace problems, and stress in policing. *Justice Quarterly*, 12: 113–140.

Morash, M., Haarr, R., and Kwak, D. (2006). Multilevel influences on police stress. *Journal of Contemporary Criminal Justice*, 22: 26–43.

Muir, W. K. (1977). *Police: Streetcorner politicians*. Chicago, I.L.: University of Chicago Press.

Olutola, A. (2013) Community policing: A panacea or a Pandora's Box to tackle the rise of crimes in Nigeria and South Africa. In M. C. de Guzman, A. M. Das, and D. K. Das (eds.), *The evolution of policing: Worldwide innovations and insights,* (pp. 153–172). Boca Raton, F.L.: CRC Press/ Taylor and Francis.

Patterson, G. T. (2003). Examining the effects of coping and social support on work and life stress among police officers. *Journal of Criminal Justice*, 31: 215–226.

Poteyeva, M. and Sun, I. Y. (2009). Gender differences in police officers' attitudes: Assessing current empirical evidence. *Journal of Criminal Justice*, 37: 512–522.

Rabe-Hemp, C. (2008). Female officers and the ethic of care: Does officer gender impact police behaviour? *Journal of Criminal Justice*, 36: 426–434.

Rabe-Hemp, C. (2009). POLICEwomen or policewomen? Doing gender and police work. *Feminist Criminology*, 4: 114–129.

Reaves, B, (2015). *Local Police Departments, 2013: Personnel, Policies, and Practices*. Washington, D.C.: Bureau of Justice Statistics.

Reese, J. T. (1986). Policing the violent society: The American experience. *Stress Medicine*, 2: 233–240.

Robinson, P. (1981). Stress in the police service. *Police Review*, 20: 2254–2259.

Schulze, C. (2010). Institutionalized masculinity in US police departments: How maternity leave policies (or lack thereof) affect women in policing. *Criminal Justice Studies*, 23: 177–193.

Selye, I. (1978). The stress of police work. *Police Stress*, 1: 1–3.

Shelley, T. O., Morabito, M. S., and Tobin-Gurley, J. (2011). Gendered institutions and gender roles: Understanding the experiences of women in policing. *Criminal Justice Studies*, 24: 351–367.

Silverman, E. (1998). Below zero tolerance: The New York experience. In R. Hopkins Burke (ed.), *Zero Tolerance Policy*. Leicester, U.K.: Perpetuity Press.

Skolnick, J. (1994). A sketch of the policeman's working personality. *In Justice without Trial: Law Enforcement in Democratic Society (3rd edn)*, (pp. 41–68). New York: Wiley.

Spielberger, C. D., Westberry, L. G., Grier, K. S., and Greenfield, G. (1981). *The police stress survey: Sources of stress in law enforcement*. Tampa, FL: Human Resources Institute.

Steel, B. S. and Lovrich, N. P. (1987). Equality and efficiency tradeoffs in affirmative action: Real or imagined? The case of women in policing. *Social Science Journal*, 24: 53–70.

Toch, H. (2002). *Stress in policing*. Washington, D.C.: American Psychological Association.

Travis, L. F. and Langworthy, R. H. (2008). *Policing in America: A balance of forces (4th edn)*. Upper Saddle River, NJ: Prentice Hall.

Van Maanen, J. (1973). Observations on the making of policeman. *Human Organization*, 32: 407–418.

Violanti, J. M. (1985). The police stress process. *Journal of Police Science and Administration*, 13: 106–110.

Violanti, J. M. and Aron, F. (1993). Sources of police stressors, job attitudes and psychological distress. *Psychological Reports*, 72: 899–904.

Walker, S. (1977). *A critical history of police reform*. Lexington, M.A.: Lexington Books.

Walker, S. (1985). Racial minority and female employment in policing: The implications of glacial change. *Crime and Delinquency*, 31: 555–572.

West, C. and Zimmerman, D. H. (1987). Doing gender. *Gender and Society*, 1: 125–151.

Wexler, J. G. and Logan, D. D. (1983). Sources of stress among women police officers. *Journal of Police Science and Administration*, 13: 98–105.

Wilson, J. (1968). *Varieties of Police Behavior: The Management of Law and Order in Eight Communities*. Cambridge, M.A.: Harvard University Press.

Wilson, J. Q. and Kelling, G. L. (1982). Broken windows. *The Atlantic Monthly*, March: 29–38.

Yoder, J. D. (1994). Looking beyond numbers: The effects of gender status, job prestige, and occupational gender-typing on tokenism processes. *Social Psychology Quarterly*, 57: 150–159.

6 Policing disasters

A conceptual model and case study of police resilience

John M. Violanti and Douglas Paton

This chapter consists of two sections. Section 1, by John Violanti, describes a case study of resiliency factors among police officers involved in Hurricane Katrina six years post-storm. Section 2, by Douglas Paton, describes (1) developing a model that facilitates learning from experience, (2) anticipating future issues and (3) proactively developing resilience and adaptive capacity in police officers and organizations. Section 2 offers some ideas about how issues identified as contributing to officer resiliency in Section 1 can be incorporated into a comprehensive Critical Incident Stress Management Strategy designed to develop sustained resilience in officers and organizations. The chapter opens with a case study that critically explores the experience of police officers in the context of a major disaster: Hurricane Katrina.

Section 1 Hurricane Katrina and resiliency among police: a case study

Hurricane Katrina made landfall just southeast of New Orleans, LA, on August 29, 2005, resulting in one of the worst natural disasters in U.S. history (DeSalvo *et al.*, 2005; DeSalvo *et al.*, 2006). A series of levee breaks in New Orleans associated with the hurricane led to widespread flooding covering 80 percent of the city—an area of approximately 120 square miles. As a result of the storm, over one million people in the New Orleans metropolitan area were displaced, and all residents of New Orleans proper, an estimated 455,000 people, lived under a mandatory evacuation for 33 days. The police were left with the difficult and often unattainable task of rescue operations, as well as maintaining civil order. The mental strain placed upon these officers was extremely high (West *et al.*, 2006).

Natural disasters of the magnitude of Hurricane Katrina are known to exert significant mental health effects; with post-traumatic stress disorder (PTSD) being the most studied and reported consequence (Galea *et al.*, 2002; Norris *et al.*, 2002; Norris *et al.*, 1999). DeSalvo *et al.* (2006) conducted a web-based survey six months after Hurricane Katrina made landfall and found that the prevalence of PTSD symptoms was 19.2 percent. The prevalence rate of 19.2 percent for symptoms consistent with a diagnosis of PTSD in this population was slightly lower than the 25 percent reported six months after Hurricane Andrew (Burnett *et al.*, 1997).

Despite universal health coverage and the benefits of an employee assistance programs, only 28.5 percent of those with PTSD symptoms had talked to a health professional about the events of Hurricane Katrina or issues encountered since the storm. Observations such as this make it pertinent to ask why this is so. For example, it is important inquire about the extent to which this failure to access mental health services reflects personal beliefs (e.g. a macho culture). It is also necessary to ask whether this phenomenon is influenced by characteristics of the organizational culture of the police agency and whether it facilitates or constrains officer willingness to utilize mental health services (Paton *et al.*, 2009). The need for improved intervention for first responders such as the police was noted by the National Institute for Occupational Safety and Health (NIOSH), based on suggestion in the literature that traumatized individuals are typically resistant to seeking treatment. This is especially true in the police culture (Hodgins *et al.*, 2001; Carlier *et al.*, 1997), and this need is further reinforced by the fact that adverse officer reactions can persist over prolonged periods of time.

A significant burden of PTSD symptoms was present six months following Hurricane Katrina among a large group of adults who had returned to work in New Orleans (DeSalvo, *et al.*, 2006). In additional studies of natural disaster survivors, the one-year prevalence of PTSD has been reported to be as low as 5 percent and as high as 60 percent (Breslau *et al.*, 1998; Canino *et al.*, 1990; Madakasira and O'Brien, 1987; Burnett *et al.*, 1997). PTSD can last from several months to years after a natural disaster, during which time persons experience a reduced quality of life and decreased productivity. It is important to accommodate the fact the persistence of effects long after termination of a specific critical incident (and the fact that regular exposure to critical incidents can lead to cumulative mental health issues) means that officer experience of critical incident and traumatic stress occurs within organizational contexts. The need to consider this issue, and how it can be accommodated in stress management programs, will be picked up in Section 2. Before doing so, it is important to learn more about the mental health causes and consequences officers experience in responding to complex emergencies and disasters.

Police stress and trauma

Law enforcement officers are susceptible to developing PTSD after being involved in a catastrophic, critical incident or after repeated, prolonged exposure to chronic stress (Brown, 2003). PTSD is a psychological disorder that affects approximately 15 percent of all emergency service workers (Kirschman, 1997). Many studies have investigated stress and trauma in law enforcement (Violanti and Paton, 2007; Brough, 2004; Liberman *et al.*, 2002; Maia *et al.*, 2004; Thompson *et al.*; Ward *et al.*, 2006). As many as 87 percent of all emergency service personnel have experienced critical incident stress at least once during their professional service (Ward, *et al.*, 2006). Critical incident stress is characterized as a debilitating syndrome that can seriously jeopardize officers' job performance as well as destroy their personal lives; if left unrecognized and untreated, it can lead to permanent emotional trauma and psychological problems, as well as job suspension, dismissal, or, in severe circumstances, post-traumatic stress disorder (PTSD) and law enforcement suicide (Violanti and Paton, 2007; Kirschman, 1997).

Shortly after the storm, NIOSH initiated a study of the New Orleans Police Department (NOPD) to evaluate the physical and mental health symptoms among personnel involved with hurricane response and recovery (West *et al.*, 2006). Symptoms of PTSD and depression, as well as physical problems, were surveyed. NOPD personnel faced extended working hours, loss of sleep, and austere living conditions. Many of the NOPD district stations and administrative buildings were flooded or damaged during the hurricane, forcing most of the NOPD to operate in temporary facilities (House of Representatives Final Report, 2006; Baum, 2006). Fourteen percent of NOPD personnel reported both depression and PTSD symptoms. Social factors were found to be associated with PTSD and depressive symptoms. Social support from family, friends, supervisors, and co-workers has been shown in repeated studies to attenuate or reduce the effects of psychological stress and depression (Dormann and Zapf, 1999). This discussion highlights a need to go beyond the event itself and include social (co-worker, senior officer, family) context influences on post-trauma outcomes in police officers. This issue will be revisited in Section 2. To develop the latter, it is vital to learn from officers' experiences in large-scale events.

Post-Katrina effects on the police

We conducted several studies on police in the New Orleans geographical area approximately six years after the storm to examine (1) post-Katrina mental health and social impact on officers and the effect of potential protective factors against stress and trauma (McCanlies *et al.*, 2014); (2) the association between increased alcohol use and level of involvement during Hurricane Katrina among officers (Heavey-Cercone, *et al.*, 2015); and (3) the association between stressful life events after the storm and post-traumatic growth in officers (Adjeroh *et al.*, 2014). A brief description of these studies follows.

The primary goal of our first study (McCanlies *et al.*, 2014) was to describe the demographic and psychosocial characteristics among officers from a police department exposed to Hurricane Katrina. In the salutogenic arena, we assessed the impact of certain factors considered protective of psychological stress symptoms. Among these is personal resiliency or the ability to bounce back from adversity, a satisfaction with life and gratitude regardless of circumstances, and growing or becoming a stronger person after the traumatic experience. Pathologically, we looked at storm-related alcohol use and various areas of life changes that were affected by the storm, including health, work, family, and financial matters.

The results of our first study indicated that officers with higher resiliency, life satisfaction, and gratitude experienced fewer PTSD symptoms. Individuals who are able to go beyond the immediate consequences of the trauma and ultimately see how the trauma fits into a broader more abstract view about their sense of self, culture, society, and nature may be more likely to adapt positively to a traumatic event (Christopher, 2004). Christopher (2004) refers to the restructuring of individuals' concept of self, society, and their environment due to trauma as "meta-learning." In contrast, individuals who are unable to form this meta-framework are more likely to develop severe symptoms of PTSD, such as severe and intrusive re-experiencing, extreme avoidance, and hyperarousal (ibid.). In Section 2, the empowerment concept is used to illustrate how this kind of restructuring could be accomplished in comprehensive critical incident stress management strategies.

Resilience has been described as both an innate quality or characteristic that protects an individual from developing PTSD following traumatic events such as disasters, as well as a factor that can be influenced through training or experience resulting in improved psychological outcomes (Bonanno, 2004; Connor and Davidson, 2003; Tedeschi and Kilmer, 2005). With this definition in mind, our expectation in the McCanlies *et al.* (2014) study was that individuals with fewer PTSD symptoms would have higher resiliency scores. Our results reflected this expectation. This finding is consistent with other reports that have found that higher levels of resiliency are associated with fewer PTSD symptoms (Agaibi and Wilson, 2005; Connor *et al.*, 2003). It has been suggested that positive emotions, such as those identified with resiliency including hope, high self-esteem, assertiveness, internal locus of control, and hardiness are associated with less emotional distress following a traumatic event and may protect individuals from negative sequela such as PTSD (Agaibi and Wilson, 2005; Fredrickson *et al.*, 2003).

Expressing gratitude or having a grateful disposition is associated with increased life satisfaction, hope, and happiness (McCullough *et al.*, 2002; McCullough *et al.*, 2004). Individuals who score high on gratitude also tend to score highly in empathy, forgiveness, and agreeableness (McCullough *et al.*, 2002; McCullough *et al.*, 2004). Positive attributes are associated with reduced distress related to PTSD (Agaibi and Wilson, 2005; McCullough *et al.*, 2002). For this reason, we expected that mean PCL-C (PTSD Check-list Civilian) scores would be lower as the gratitude score increased. Research indicates that individuals who experience more gratitude are more satisfied with their lives, happy, and optimistic (McCullough *et al.*, 2002; McCullough *et al.*, 2004). This trait may help an individual who has experienced a trauma recover more quickly or protect them from PTSD.

Satisfaction with life has been found to be associated with lower rates of depression and anxiety (Samaranayake and Fernando, 2011). In our study, officers with high and very high life satisfaction reported the fewest number of PTSD symptoms. However, it is difficult to say, given the cross-sectional nature of this study, whether experiencing PTSD symptoms results in dissatisfaction with life or dissatisfaction with life contributes to PTSD symptoms. In summary, the results of the McCanlies *et al.* (2014) study indicated that resiliency, gratitude, and satisfaction with life might be protective or mitigate symptoms of PTSD in some police officers. These results indicate that clients' strengths are important in helping them address trauma symptoms.

Our research group (Cercone-Heavey *et al.*, 2014) conducted a study to examine the association between increased alcohol use and level of involvement during Hurricane Katrina among law enforcement officers. Officers in the immediate New Orleans area were administered a survey assessing their involvement in Hurricane Katrina and alcohol use (Babor *et al.*, 2001). The primary aim of was to determine whether there was an association between involvement level in Hurricane Katrina and alcohol use among police officers who worked during the storm. The results of this study revealed a significant association between heavy involvement in Hurricane Katrina and higher levels of hazardous alcohol use among the officers, when compared to officers with low or moderate involvement. This has important treatment implications for those with high involvement in disasters, as they may require targeted interventions to overcome the stress of such experiences.

Police work is one example of a "hard-drinking" occupation and shares many risk factors for alcohol abuse, such as stress, isolation, peer influences, preponderance of young males, and group norms (Violanti *et al.*, 2011). Police work stressors include critical incident exposure and the inherent dangers of police work, but also aspects of the work environment, such as administrative, bureaucratic, and organizational components (Liberman *et al.*, 2002). Further, Lindsay and Shelley (2009) suggest that police officers' alcohol use is influenced by a desire to fit in with their peers and the view of alcohol consumption as a social outlet. Thus, it is reasonable to expect these added pressures uniquely affect police officers' experiences during disaster and alcohol use in the post-disaster period.

Previous work suggests that an increase in alcohol consumption in the post-disaster period is an additional negative consequence of disaster exposure. For example, survivors of the Oklahoma City bombing had greater alcohol consumption during the period after the attack (Pfefferbaum and Doughty, 2001). Also, exposure to additional hurricane-related stressors was associated with greater alcohol consumption as well as greater odds of binge drinking in the post-disaster period (Cerda *et al.*, 2011). In addition, the research by Flory, Hankin, Kloos, Cheely, and Turecki (2009) indicates that Hurricane Katrina survivors experienced increased hazardous alcohol use.

There is a dose–response relationship with trauma or disaster exposure and alcohol consumption. Individuals' greater exposure to the World Trade Center disaster was associated with greater alcohol consumption at one and two years after the attacks than those with low levels of exposure; in addition, binge drinking one year after the disaster was also associated with greater exposure to the attacks (Boscarino *et al.*, 2006). In some cases, there appears to be a threshold effect, as those with low or moderate levels of lifetime trauma did not have significant changes in alcohol use, but those with high levels of lifetime trauma did have increased alcohol use after hurricane-related stressors (Cerda *et al.*, 2011).

First responders have higher levels of hazardous alcohol use than is expected in a typical community population (Boxer and Wild, 1993). Nearly two-thirds (64 percent) of a police sample exceeded the recommended daily alcohol consumption, with 17.2 percent engaging in hazardous drinking (defined by the authors as consuming six or more drinks on one occasion, on a weekly or daily basis) (Violanti *et al.*, 2011). This is nearly double the percent of hazardous drinkers in a U.S. national workplace sample that found a rate of 8.8 percent (Larson *et al.*, 2007).

Following Hurricane Katrina, police officers faced many stressors associated with the quality of their personal lives. A number of studies have focused on negative consequences, but few have investigated positive outcomes like post-traumatic growth. Our third study (Adjeroh *et al.*, 2013) examined associations between stressful life events and post-traumatic growth, and whether this relationship was modified by positive factors of satisfaction with life, gratitude, or interpersonal support. Post-traumatic growth was assessed using the post-traumatic growth inventory (Tedeschi and Calhoun, 1996), which measures positive growth following traumatic events. Stressful life events were measured using the Recent Life Changes Questionnaire (RLCQ) (Miller and Rahe, 1997), which includes five sub-factors of stress: health, work, home and family, personal and social, and financial stressors.

Results indicated that the association between stressful life events and post-traumatic growth was statistically significant. After adjustment for age, sex, race, and alcohol intake, the mean post-traumatic growth total score increased across increasing quartiles of stress scores. Among the five sub-factors, only personal and social support were positively associated with post-traumatic growth (adjusted $p = 0.036$). These results indicated that an increasing number of stressful life events are associated with greater post-traumatic growth, particularly among individuals with high levels of satisfaction with life, gratitude, and interpersonal support.

The process of achieving growth in the face of adversities/stress may be a part of personal resources. In essence, people with strong life satisfaction who tend to cope actively might be more optimistic about life, perceive more control over life events, and might be able to thrive in the face of adversity. On the contrary, without strong personal resources, individuals might be pessimistic about life, have a low perception of control and might be vulnerable to the negative effects of stress, which might make it unlikely for them to achieve post-traumatic growth. In summary, stressful life events were associated with post-traumatic growth and this association was particularly strong among officers with high life satisfaction, gratitude, and interpersonal (family, team) support. In the next section, an approach that can be used to capitalize on these understandings is presented as a way of incorporating them into a comprehensive, proactive Critical Incident Stress Management Strategy.

Section 2 A model of resiliency

Consistent with the discussion in Section 1, the literature identifies how police officers experience critical incidents repeatedly over the course of careers that can span decades

(North et al., 2002; Paton, 2005; Paton, Violanti et al., 2009). With little or no warning, officers may find themselves responding to events ranging from domestic disturbances to facing prolonged involvement in complex, evolving natural disasters or acts of terrorism. Involvement in events at the more challenging end of the critical incident spectrum (e.g. terrorist acts and natural disasters) results in officers encountering, over periods of several days or weeks, unpredictable, evolving, and escalating demands that fall well outside the normal pattern of their daily activities or the types of responses they are predominantly trained for (Paton and Violanti, 2007).

For police officers, "critical" incidents create a sense of psychological disequilibrium that represents that period when existing schemata (that guide officers' expectations and actions) lose their capacity to organize experience in meaningful and manageable ways (Dunning, 2003; Paton, 1994). The fact that critical incident experiences can be resolved in positive or negative ways identifies a need to identify those factors that broaden the range of (unpredictable) experiences officers can accommodate and adapt to (Frederickson et al., 2003; Paton, 2006). The goal of this chapter is to provide an evidence base from which to develop this resilient and adaptive capability in police officers and organizations. To do this, it is pertinent to consider officers' "encounters with risk." That is, what they need to be resilient to or adapt to.

What do officers need to be resilient to?

Stress risk arises not only from the unpredictability and suddenness with which officers can find themselves responding to critical incidents, but also from prevailing, transient factors such as health status (e.g. colds), fatigue (e.g. deployed at the end of a shift), and psychological fitness (e.g. occupational stress) (Flin, 1996). The fact that events can occur with little or no warning means that deployment can occur before in-depth intelligence about an event is obtained, at the least for the first party. Officers have to make sense of complex events while coping with death, injury, and suffering, adapt to the scale of events, and plan how to use limited resources. Stress risk is magnified by environmental factors preventing or limiting opportunities for effective action and by the attributions (performance guilt) officers make about such constraints, even when these are beyond their control (e.g. the extent of flooding post-Katrina, limitation on opportunities to protect the public, etc.).

Risk is influenced by officers having to take on higher than usual or higher than expected responsibility and being required to make decisions normally taken by other (or more senior) personnel (often with incomplete, ambiguous information or assumptions). For example, rapid changes in the extent and distribution of flooding might increase the need for officers to make more *ad hoc* decisions. Furthermore, they might have to do so while working under higher than usual physical, environmental, lengthy time, and emotional demands while facing multiple threats (e.g. danger to self, disrupted sewerage systems, exposure to contaminated water, and secondary chemical and biological hazards) and performing body recovery and identification duties. Risk can emanate from a need to function in the face of uncertainty (e.g. regarding the duration of threat or period of involvement). As outlined in Section 1, critical incident stress risk does not end with termination of involvement in a specific event.

Reintegration, the transition back into the "normal" roles and routines of work and family life, introduces risk from managing mental health issues, performance reviews, readjusting to routine work after a highly challenging but professionally rewarding experience, and catching up with any backlog of work. It can also derive from, for example, media scrutiny and socio-legal processes (e.g. public inquiries). This means that the context of experience of, and recovery from, traumatic stress includes the organization and the family (see Section 1). Given the diversity in the post-trauma outcomes (e.g. varying degrees of acute stress/alcohol abuse versus post-traumatic growth outcomes – see Section 1) observed in officers who experienced critical incidents (e.g. Hurricane Katrina), the next step is to identify the protective factors that increase the likelihood of a functional adaptive response. This section will discuss this topic from officer, team, and organizational perspectives.

Critical incident stress and its implications for officer risk and well-being typically focuses on the officers themselves (as stress- and duty-related issues are typically manifest at this level of analysis). Hence the importance of including an officer-focused level of analysis in intervention strategies. These strategies may (occasionally) include team issues (as changes in the status of individual officers readily affect others in highly cohesive police agencies). Intervention and planning does not, however, generally include an organizational level of analysis. This chapter outlines why; it includes all three factors and how they are interrelated in understanding and planning for facilitating officer well-being. It also extends this "ecological" approach to include a role for the family in this process.

Because it exposes officers to institutional histories and enculturates them into organizational and professional ways of thinking (e.g. via selection, socialization, context-relevant training, and management and organizational practices), organizational participation facilitates the development of shared identity, purpose, beliefs, values, goals, and actions (Dunning, 2003; Lissack and Roos, 1999). This shapes the social and organizational context in which critical incident experiences are made sense of and acted on through communication from and with others (e.g. through formal reviews and informal discussions and stories) who have communally shared a negative experience (Dunning, 2003; Lissack and Roos, 1999; Pollock *et al.*, 2003; Paton *et al.*, 2009; Weick and Sutcliffe, 2007). Organization -level intervention thus becomes important. Because programs to facilitate sustained officer well-being need to include officer, team/unit, and organizational factors, planning how this can be achieved calls for a conceptual framework that encompass these factors. One such framework is empowerment. Empowerment is used here to frame how adaptive and well-being outcomes can be understood and how officer-adaptive capacity can be developed and sustained over time and against a backdrop of diverse critical incident experiences.

Empowerment

The utility of empowerment in this context derives from its role in motivating action in conditions of uncertainty. Motivational theories of empowerment argue that if people have sufficient resources (psychological, social, and physical) and the capacity to use them, they can effectively confront environmental challenges (Conger and Konungo, 1988; Spreitzer, 1997). Empowerment is an enabling process that facilitates the development and enactment of competencies necessary to effectively confront unpredictable, challenging circumstances. Conger and Konungo (1988) argue that empowerment facilitates action by removing conditions that foster powerlessness (e.g. organizational hassles) and facilitating practices (e.g. uplifts, self-efficacy information, competencies, etc.) that develop officers' learned resourcefulness (Johnston and Paton, 2003). The potential for empowerment to predict satisfaction following critical incident experience was discussed by Johnston and Paton (2003). This is illustrated in Figure 6.1.

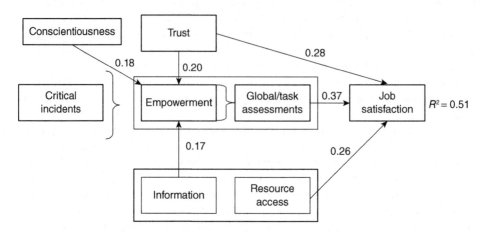

Figure 6.1 Summary of analysis of the relationship between empowerment and satisfaction in medical professionals experiencing critical incidents (adapted from Johnston and Paton, 2003).

Section 1 drew attention to how satisfaction was implicated in the experience of positive critical incident outcomes. The fact that the analysis depicted in Figure 6.1 identified Empowerment as a significant predictor of satisfaction lends support to its importance as a concept with a role to play in comprehensive critical incident stress management.

The inclusion of an interpretive element in empowerment theories helps explain how officers' experience of organizational culture and critical incidents are translated into schema that facilitate their ability to interpret experience in meaningful and manageable ways. Importantly, this extends to anticipating and developing an ability to deal with future challenges (Thomas and Velthouse, 1990). By describing an iterative learning process that is capable of maintaining adaptive capacity in the changing environment of contemporary policing, empowerment theories can accommodate the repetitive nature of police involvement in critical incidents. This outcome reflects the cycle of environmental events, task assessments, and behavior (Figure 6.2) that describes the empowerment process.

Critical incidents, incident assessment and behavior

Critical incidents provide information to officers about both specific, event-related experiences and the conditions they could expect to encounter in future task behavior (Conger and Konungo, 1988). Task knowledge about critical incident experiences can be broadened by information from peers, subordinates, and superiors (e.g. via event reviews, performance appraisals, training, etc.). This feedback process supports the development of the operational schema officers use to anticipate, plan for, interpret, and respond to critical incidents. This is depicted (see Figure 6.2) by the relationship between interpretive styles (schema components) and officers' assessment of their circumstances. These environmental assessments translate into task assessment and global assessment (which collectively influence the sense of coherence).

Thomas and Velthouse (1990) argue that officers' task assessments comprise several components. The first, meaningfulness, describes the level of congruence between the tasks performed and one's values, attitudes, and behaviors (comparable to the "meaningfulness" facet of coherence). Empowered individuals feel a sense of personal significance, purpose, and commitment in their role (Spreitzer, 1997; Thomas and Velthouse, 1990). Meaningfulness could be increased by experiencing uplifts (e.g. receiving recognition and being given responsibility) but being constrained by hassles (e.g. red tape) that shift emphasis from meaningful role performance to meeting administrative expectations (cf. Hart *et al.*, 1993).

The second component, competence, describes officers' beliefs in their ability to perform successfully in their operational role. A direct relationship between levels of competence and the degree of effort and persistence officers invest when facing challenging events results in this component making an important contribution to officers' capacity to adapt to unpredictable, challenging events (Spreitzer, 1997). The third component, choice, reflects officers' beliefs that their behavior is self-determined and is enhanced when organizations delegate responsibility for resource use to officers (ibid.). The final component, impact, reflects officers' belief that they influence important organizational outcomes (ibid.).

While task assessments relate to specific tasks and time periods, global assessments describe a capacity to generalize expectancies and learning across tasks and over time, and to anticipate how to respond if faced with unfamiliar challenges (Thomas and Velthouse, 1990). This aspect of empowerment facilitates officers' ability to learn from current experiences and develop schemata that facilitate future capability.

Both global and task assessments, and thus capacity to adapt, are influenced by officers' interpretive schema (see Figure 6.2). According to Thomas and Velthouse (1990), schema are influenced by the work context, with management practices (see "Interventions" in Figure 6.2) having an important influence on how schema are developed and sustained.

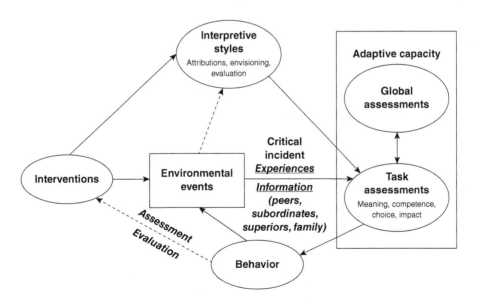

Figure 6.2 The role of empowerment in facilitating sustained resilience and adaptive capacity (adapted from Johnston and Paton, 2003 and Thomas and Velthouse, 1990).

Empowerment schema and resilience

The first schema component concerns attributional beliefs. Empowerment is greater when officers attribute causes for failure to external (i.e. environmental), transient (i.e. factors likely to change over time), and specific (e.g. factors limited to a specific day or event) factors. Feedback processes that differentiate between personal and environmental influences on critical incident outcomes contribute to the development of attributional schema that sustain adaptive capacity (Paton, 1994; Paton and Stephens, 1996). A second schema component, envisioning, refers to the anticipation of future events and outcomes. Officers who anticipate positive rather than negative outcomes experience stronger task and global assessments, and, thus, empowerment. The final schema component, evaluation (Thomas and Velthouse, 1990), describes how officers who adopt less absolutist, more realistic standards experience greater empowerment and adapt more readily to highly threatening circumstances (Paton, 1994; Raphael, 1986).

Person-level factors

Satisfaction with life has been found to be associated with lower rates of depression and anxiety (Samaranayake and Fernando, 2011 – see also Figure 6.1). In Section 1, the role of expressing gratitude or having a grateful disposition in predicting life satisfaction, hope, and happiness (McCullough *et al.*, 2002; McCullough *et al.*, 2004) was identified, as was its ability to influence empathy, forgiveness, and agreeableness, with the latter mediating distress related to PTSD (Agaibi and Wilson, 2005; McCullough *et al.*, 2002). These dispositional characteristics thus need to be accommodated in critical incident stress risk management. Conscientious individuals experience a stronger sense of meaning and competence in their work—particularly during challenging events—demonstrate greater perseverance, and are more committed to team efforts (Hough, 1998; Thomas and Velthouse, 1990). Conscientiousness thus contributes towards sustaining a cohesive team resource when responding to complex events. Similarly, hardiness has a long history as a predictor of resilience. It is strongly influenced by the officer–organization relationship and facilitates learning from experience (Bartone, 2004). However, given that sense-making and coherence are socially constructed (e.g. through socialization, formal reviews, stories shared amongst officers, etc.), a comprehensive model must include the social contexts (teams that are characteristic of protective services work and the organization itself) in which sense-making occurs. An important construct at these levels of analysis is trust.

Trust

Levels of trust are influenced by the organizational culture and the dynamics of interpersonal relationships (Barker and Camarata, 1998; Paton and Stephens, 1996; Siegrist and Cvetkovich, 2000). Trust affects the effectiveness of interpersonal relationships, group processes, and organizational relationships, and is crucial for empowering officers (Kendra and Wachtendorf, 2003). People functioning in trusting, reciprocal relationships feel empowered, are more likely to experience meaning in their work, and are more willing to act cooperatively in high-risk situations (Dirks, 1999; Siegrist and Cvetkovich, 2000). Organizational cultures that value openness and trust facilitate learning and growth and contribute to developing adaptive capacity (Lundberg *et al.*, 2012; Siegrist and Cvetkovich, 2000). While it has not specifically been investigated in protective services agencies, trust may have a bearing on whether or not officers use available mental health services (see Section 1, p. 000). Trust has a significant role to play in sustaining team cohesion (Pollock *et al.*, 2003).

Team cohesion and support

The quality of team dynamics and relationships influences the meaningfulness officers' perceive in their work, and increases levels of social support provided to co-workers (Liden *et al.*, 2000). Members of cohesive work teams are more willing to share their knowledge, contribute to a learning culture, and be available as peer support and communal coping resources (Pollock *et al.*, 2003). Communal coping facilitates officers' collective acceptance of responsibility for problems and the capacity to work cooperatively to resolve problems. Acknowledging and building on effective collaboration during and after the crisis to develop understanding and enhance future preparedness mitigates stress and develops future resilience. How well these lessons can be learned is influenced by managerial behavior.

Interdependence between managers and officers

Senior officers play a pivotal role in developing and sustaining empowering environments (Liden *et al.*, 2000). This reflects their role in translating organizational culture into the day-to-day values and procedures that influence sense-making and the schema officers use to plan for and respond to critical incidents (see Figure 6.2). Supportive, officer-centered leadership practices create an empowering team and operational environment, particularly when they focus on the constructive discussion of response problems and how they can be resolved in future (Paton, 1994; Quinn and Spreitzer, 1997). In this way, senior officer behavior contributes to developing the attributional, envisioning, and evaluative schema (see Figure 6.2) that are instrumental in translating officers' organizational experiences into a sense of coherence. Supportive supervisor behavior facilitates personal growth, enhances general feelings of competence (global assessment), and encourages the development of similar value structures (e.g. via socialization) between officers (Cogliser and Schriesheim, 2000). How managers do this, however, is affected by prevailing organizational procedures and practices.

Organizational issues

The growing likelihood of officer involvement in complex emergencies (e.g. Hurricane Katrina) makes it important that organizations develop autonomous response systems, flexible, consultative leadership, practices that delegate responsibility, and policies to ensure that role and task assignments reflect incident demands (and facilitate an effective, adaptive response) and, given the infrequent nature of disasters, provide the opportunity to learn from experience (Kendra and Wachtendorf, 2003). The development of adaptive capacity requires organizations to confront assumptions derived from a long history of effective response to routine emergency events (which become implicit aspects of cultural beliefs and practices) and accept the need for dedicated disaster response procedures and practices. Organizations need to develop ways of learning and consolidating lessons learned within organizational culture and practices (e.g. training) in ways that facilitate the development of sustained resilience and adaptive capacity. This is encapsulated in the feedback link between "Behavior" and "Intervention" in Figure 6.2.

The effective utilization of this development resource is more likely to be accomplished in an empowering agency.

The capability to learn from experience cannot be taken for granted (Berkes *et al.*, 2003; Mitroff and Anagnos 2001). For example, in autocratic protective services organizations bureaucratic inertia, vested political interests, and centralized power blocks change. Under these circumstances, emergency organizations may underestimate or overlook threats or initiate inadequate actions, reducing their ability to match their capabilities to a changing hazardscape. Organizational cultures that embody these characteristics attempt to render complex emergencies (natural disasters, acts of terrorism, etc.) understandable by making them "fit in" with previous experience. This increases the likelihood that response to future events will be *ad hoc*, with effective response occurring more by chance than by sound planning and good judgment.

To enhance adaptive capacity, organizations must learn from past failures and think "outside the square" (Berkes *et al.*, 2003; Kendra and Wachtendorf, 2003). Organizations must develop a culture appropriate for a contemporary operating environment in which responding to large-scale disasters and complex acts of terrorism will become facts of life in future policing. Recognition of a need for institutional learning thus becomes an important.

According to Berkes *et al.* (2003) this involves, first, ensuring that the memory of prior crises and the lessons learnt, whether positive or negative, are incorporated into institutional memory and accepted as an enduring fact of organizational life. Second, realistic risk estimates should be derived from comprehensive reviews of potential events and realistic audits of competence (e.g. training needs, organizational analyses, etc.) (Jackson *et al.*, 2003). These risk estimates form the basis for future officer and organizational development. Finally, recognition of critical incident risk and the importance of learning from them must be consolidated into a culture that espouses the policies, procedures, practices, and attitudes required to facilitate a capacity for adaptive response to uncertain and unpredictable future events (Berkes *et al.*, 2003; Jackson *et al.*, 2003; Kendra and Wachtendorf, 2003).

The learning process must also expand to include another group that deserves greater representation in critical incident stress management than has hitherto been the case: the family. While it can be easy to appreciate why person, team, organizational, and inter-organizational factors deserve inclusion in a comprehensive model of resilience, the final issue addressed here argues for the inclusion of family in the model.

Family

Figure 6.3 summarizes the analysis of traumatic stress reactions in rescue workers involved in the Estonia disaster. The findings of this study not only provided additional evidence for the role of organizational (culture) on post-trauma outcomes, but also highlighted the significant role that family played in this regard. The analysis identified how psychological debriefing acted as a type of context-relevant training that translated into higher quality social support skills (e.g. increased emotional disclosure, ability to seek and use social support, etc.). This, in turn, enriched the quality of family functioning and facilitated the ability of the family experience to influence the post-trauma outcome (see Figure 6.3). Thus, the family became a resource that contributed towards the mitigation of traumatic stress risk. Similar findings were reported in other studies (Norris *et al.*, 2010; Paton and Kelso, 1991; Shakespeare-Finch *et al.*, 2003; Wraith, 1994).

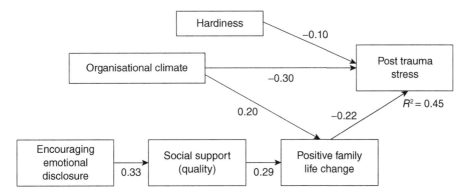

Figure 6.3 Predictors of post-traumatic stress outcomes in Estonia rescue workers (Adapted from Paton *et al.*, 2000)

Norris *et al.* (2010) discussed how family processes (including the dynamics of an intimate relationship, family-level coping strategies and work–family and family–work interfaces) can mediate the relationship between critical incident experience and traumatic stress outcomes. Of particular importance was the finding that higher levels of perceived familial involvement in the employment experience facilitated communication, trust, and availability of resources (at individual, organizational, and family levels) that enhanced coping and adaptation to critical incident consequences. Hence, including the family in critical incident stress management can have direct (e.g. Figure 6.3) and indirect benefits, through its influence on trust and resource access (see Figure 6.1) for post-trauma outcomes.

Conclusions

Individual factors may be effective but resiliency can be enhanced within the social organization of policing. There are specific characteristics that make individuals (and organizations as well) more or less resilient to stress than others (Maddi, 2002; Maddi and Khosaba, 2005; Youseff and Luthans, 2005; Walsh, 2002; Luthar *et al.*, 2000). Taken together, these factors suggest that resilience is not so much a trait as it is an integration process of personal and social processes (Siebert, 2002). The support of the police organization during trauma situations appears to be important in lessening the impact of trauma and stress. While psychological factors such as resilience are generally investigated at the individual level, our results suggest that organizational support also plays a role. Increasing organizational support by the police department was significantly associated with decreasing levels of depressive, PTSD, and psychological symptoms. The police organization defines the context within which officers experience and interpret traumatic incidents and within which future capabilities are nurtured or restricted (Paton, 2006). Officers respond to incidents as members of law enforcement agencies whose organizational culture influences their thoughts and actions and represents the context in which challenging experiences are made sense of (Paton *et al.*, 1999; Weick and Sutcliffe, 2007). As such, the individual and the organization contribute to providing a protective milieu against trauma and stress. This does not, however, negate the need for mental health intervention, particularly for those officers whose disaster experience elicits post-traumatic stress reactions.

Suggestions for intervention

A consideration for reducing trauma and maladaptive behavior among police officers is the use of primary prevention techniques that focus on preparation for traumatic events which have not yet occurred. In other words, primary prevention and preparation for traumatic events such as Hurricane Katrina may alleviate future occurrences of prolonged PTSD, as we have seen in this study. A preliminary study by Arnetz *et al.* (2013) strongly supported the idea that an imagery-based skills training preparatory model improves police performance during a field simulation, and improves mental and physical health and adjustment over two years of police work. Through the use of imagery, Arnetz *et al* (ibid.) demonstrated that exposure, practicing adaptive responses during and after exposure, and frequent practice of learned skills reduced trauma symptoms in police.

Mindfulness-based stress reduction (MBSR) for psychological symptoms is a recent trend that may also be applied in police work. MBSR is a structured, time-limited, group-based intervention in which individuals are taught to pay attention to sensory, cognitive, and emotional experiences occurring in the moment without fixating on the experience or judging any part of it (Kabat-Zinn, 1992). A recent review by Keng *et al.* (2011) concluded that MBSR is an effective treatment strategy for a wide range of psychological conditions including anxiety, depression, stress, rumination, anger, psychological distress, and post-traumatic avoidance symptoms. Although not yet widely applied in policing, mindfulness training has been used in military applications to reduce stress. Stanley *et al.* (2011), in a study of U.S. Marines, found reductions in perceived stress as more time was spent in utilizing mindfulness.

The results of our research can benefit police psychological wellness. We anticipate that findings will provide data to develop a plan on how to increase resilience in police officers and their organizations. Recognition of the fact that stress or trauma can result in positive instead of negative mental health outcomes for police officers means that the police will have at their disposal a utility that they can use to guide the development and maintenance of resilience.

Furthermore, because first responders in general encounter unpredictable and challenging circumstances repeatedly, it is important that resilience programs are designed to identify the resources that facilitate proactive development over time. The components that we discuss in this project are amenable to change through organizational intervention and change strategies.

The mental, behavioral, and social costs of police stress and trauma suggest a substantial need for intervention (Joseph *et al.*, 2010). Losing a police officer to stress problems is costly and can upset the balance of departmental work schedules and coverage. Various levels of stress management may be applied in police work. Establishing a "stress shield" (Paton *et al.*, 2008), which provides a level of integration of organizational and individual resiliency, is part of this process of management. While tertiary and secondary prevention methods are generally considered, such treatment services are underutilized among police, likely due to a police culture that stigmatizes the admission of emotional problems (Joseph *et al.*, 2010). A more effective approach might be to establish a primary stress prevention and resiliency development training protocol for officers. Primary prevention efforts that bolster resilience may be viewed as acceptable to the police culture, because preparation for future events fits that standard police model, does not stigmatize officers, and targets the maintenance of good mental and behavioral health. Future projects that focus on organizational interventions to improve resilience might facilitate our anticipated results in police practice.

The empowerment-based model introduced above can inform the development of primary prevention strategies. All model components, with the exception of the dispositional factors (e.g. conscientiousness, gratitude, and so on, whose influence can be accommodated in selection or assessment procedures), are amenable to change through training, organizational intervention, and change strategies. Guidelines for changing hardiness, peer support, supervisor support, organizational hassles and uplifts, trust, empowerment, and work–family relationships are available (Bartone, 2004; Cogliser and Schriesheim, 2000; Hart *et al.*, 1993; Herriot *et al.*, 1998; Netemeyer *et al.*, 1996; Quinn and Spreitzer, 1997). Organizational change strategies should develop incident management protocols, performance expectations, inter-agency cooperation and, over time, an organizational culture (e.g. emotional disclosure, review and learning practices) that facilitates resilience.

It is also important to recognize and accommodate the family contribution to primary and secondary intervention. This suggests that organizations can benefit from family-friendly policies, support groups, and recovery plans. Police organizations have the capacity to offer the information and training required to facilitate the realization of the benefits that can arise from developing the competencies (e.g. facilitate emotional disclosure, social skills, etc.) of family members as support and recovery resources. Future studies are required to establish the applicability and accuracy of this model of progressive evaluation of historical events to inform resilience training.

References

Adjeroh, L. C., McCanlies, E. C., Andrew, M. E., Burchfiel, C. M. and Violanti, J. M. (2013). Stressful life events and post-traumatic growth among police officers. *Annals of Epidemiology*, 24, 9, 687.

Agaibi, C. E. and Wilson, J. P. (2005). Trauma, PTSD, and resilience: a review of the literature. *Trauma Violence Abuse*, 6, 3, 195–216.

Arnetz, B. B., Arble, E., Backman, L., Lynch, A., and Lublin, A. (2013). Assessment of a prevention program for work-related stress among urban police officers. *International Archives of Occupational Environmental Health*, 8, 1, 79–88. Published online 2012 Feb 25.

Babor, T. F., Higgins-Biddle, J. C., Saunders, J. B., and Monteiro, M. G. (2001). *The alcohol use disorders identification test*. Guidelines for use in primary care, ed. 2. Geneva: World Health Organization.

Barker, R. T. and Camarata, M. R. (1998) The role of communication in creating and maintaining a learning organization: Preconditions, indicators, and disciplines. *The Journal of Business Communication*, 35, 443–467.

Bartone, P. (2004) Increasing resiliency through shared sensemaking: Building hardiness in groups. In D. Paton, J. Violanti, C. Dunning, and L.M. Smith (eds.) *Managing traumatic stress risk: A proactive approach*. Springfield, IL: Charles C. Thomas.

Baum, D. (2006). *Deluged: When Katrina hit, where were the police? The New Yorker*, January 9, 50–63.

Berkes, F., Colding, J. and Folke, C. (2003) *Navigating social-ecological systems: Building resilience for complexity and change*. Cambridge: Cambridge University Press.

Bonanno, G. A. (2004). Loss, trauma, and human resilience: Have we underestimated the human capacity to thrive after extremely aversive events? *American Psychologist*, 59, 20–28.

Boscarino, J., Adams, R. E., and Galea, S. (2006). Alcohol use in New York after the terrorist attacks: A study of the effects of psychological trauma on drinking behavior. *Addictive Behaviors*, 31, 4, 606–621.

Boxer, P. A. and Wild, D. (1993). Psychological distress and alcohol use among fire fighters. *Scandinavian Journal of Work, Environment and Health*, 19, 2, 121–125.

Breslau, N., Kessler, R. C., Chilcoat, H. D., Schultz, L. R., Davis, G. C., and Andreski P. (1998) Trauma and post-traumatic stress disorder in the community: the 1996 Detroit area survey of trauma. *Archives of General Psychiatry*, 55, 626–632.

Brough, P. (2004). Comparing the influence of traumatic and organizational stressors on the psychological health of police, fire, and ambulance officers. *International Journal of Stress Management*, 11, 227–224.

Brown, H. (2003). *The effects of post traumatic stress disorder (PTSD) on the officer and the family,* www.geocities.com/~halbrown/ptsd-family.htm. Accessed November 9, 2013.

Burnett K., Ironson G., Benight C., Winings, C., Greewood, D., Carver, C. S., Cruess, D., Baum, A., and Schneidman, N. (1997). Measurement of perceived disruption during rebuilding following Hurricane Andrew. *Journal of Traumatic Stress*, 10, 673–681.

Canino, G., Bravo, M., and Rubio-Stipec, M. (1990). The impact of disaster on mental health: Prospective and retrospective analyses. *International Journal of Mental Health*, 19, 51–69. *Anxiety Stress and Coping*, 12, 363–396.

Carafano, J. J. (2003) *Preparing responders to respond: The challenges to emergency preparedness in the 21st Century.* Heritage Lectures #812. Washington, DC: The Heritage Foundation.

Carlier I. V., Lamberts R. D., and Gersons B. P. (1997). Risk factors for post-traumatic stress symptomatology in police officers: a prospective analysis. *Journal of Nervous and Mental Disorder*, 185, 498–506.

Cercone, S. A., Homish, G. G., Andrew, M. E., McCanlies, E., Mnatsakanova, A., Violanti, J. M., and Burchfiel, C. M. *Law enforcement officers' involvement level in Hurricane Katrina and alcohol use.* Poster presented at the 142nd Annual Meeting of the American Public Health Association. November, 2014, New Orleans, Louisiana.

Cerda, M., Tracy, M., and Galea, S. (2011). A prospective population based study of changes in alcohol use and binge drinking after a mass traumatic event. *Drug Alcohol Dependence*, 115, 1–8.

Christopher, M. (2004). A broader view of trauma: A biopsychosocial-evolutionary view of the role of the traumatic stress response in the emergence of pathology and/or growth. *Clinical Psychology Review*, 24, 75–98.

Cogliser, C. C. and Schriesheim, C. A. (2000) Exploring work unit context and leader-member exchange: A multi-level perspective. *Journal of Organizational Behaviour*, 21, 487–511.

Conger, J. A. and Konungo, R. (1988). The empowerment process; Integrating theory and process. *Academy of management Review*, 13, 471–482.

Connor, K. M. and Davidson, J. R. (2003). Development of a new resilience scale: The Connor-Davidson Resilience Scale (CD-RISC). *Depression and Anxiety*, 18, 2, 76–82.

Connor, K. M., Davidson, J. R., and Lee, L. C. (2003). Spirituality, resilience, and anger in survivors of violent trauma: aA community survey. *Journal of Traumatic Stress*, 16, 5, 487–494.

DeSalvo, K. B., Muntner, P., and Fox, C. E. (2005). Community-based health care for the city that care forgot. *Journal of Urban health*, 82, 520–523.

DeSalvo, K. B., Hyre, A. D., Ompad, D. C., Menke, A.,Tynes, L. L., and Muntner, P.(2006). symptoms of post-traumatic stress disorder in a New Orleans workforce following Hurricane Katrina. *Journal of Urban Health: Bulletin of the New York Academy of Medicine*, 84, 142–152.

Dirks, K. T. (1999) The effects of interpersonal trust on work group performance. *Journal of Applied Psychology*, 84, 445–455.

Dormann, C. and Zapf, D. (1999). Social support, social stressors at work, and depressive symptoms: Testing for main and moderating effects with structural equations in a three-wave longitudinal study. *Journal of Applied Psychology*, 84, 6, 874–884. http://dx.doi.org/10.1037/0021-9010.84.6.874.

Dunning, C. (2003) Sense of coherence in managing trauma workers. In D. Paton, J. M. Violanti and L. M. Smith (eds.), *Promoting Capabilities to Manage posttraumatic stress: Perspectives on resilience.* Springfield, IL: Charles C. Thomas.

Flin, R. (1996) *Sitting in the hot seat: Leaders and teams for critical incident management.* Chichester: John Wiley & Sons.

Flory, K., Hankin, B. L., Kloos, B., Cheely, C., and Turecki, G. (2009). Alcohol and cigarette use and misuse among Hurricane Katrina survivors: psychosocial risk and protective factors. *Substance Use and Misuse*, 44, 1711–1724.

Fredrickson, B. L., Tugade, M. M., Waugh, C. E., and Larkin, G. R. (2003). What good are positive emotions in crises? A prospective study of resilience and emotions following the terrorist attacks on the United States on September 11th, 2001. *Journal of Personality and Social Psychology*, 84, 2, 365–376.

Galea S., Ahern J., Resnick, H., Kilpatrick, D., Bucuvalas, M., Gold, J., and Vlahov, D. (2002). Psychological sequelae of the September 11 terrorist attacks in New York City. *NEJM*, 346, 982–987.

Hart, P. M., Wearing, A. J., and Headey, B. (1993). Assessing police work experiences: Development of the police daily hassles and uplifts scales. *Journal of Criminal Justice*, 21, 553–572.

Heavey-Cercone, S. Homish, G. G., Andrew, M. E., McCanlies, E., Mnatsakanova, A., Violanti, J. M., and Burchfiel, C. M. (2015). Law enforcment officers involvement in Hurricane Katrina and alcochol use. *Journal of Emergency Mental Health and Human Resilience*, 17, 267–273.

Herriot, P., Hirsh, W., and Reilly, P. (1998). *Trust and transition: Managing today's employment relationship*. Chichester: John Wiley & Sons.

Hodgins, G. A., Creamer, M., and Bell, R. (2001). Risk factors for post-trauma reactions in police officers: A longitudinal study. *Journal of Nervous and Mental Disorder*, 189, 541–547.

Hough, L. M. (1998) Personality at work: Issues and evidence. In M. D. Hakel (ed.). *Beyond multiple choice: Evaluating alternatives to traditional testing for selection* (pp. 131–166). Mahwah, NJ: Lawrence Erlbaum.

House of Representatives (2006). *A failure of initiative. Final report of the Select Bipartisan Committee to investigate the preparation for and response to Hurricane Katrina*. US House of Representatives. Washington, DC: US Government Printing Office.

Hurricane Katrina. Journal of Urban Health: *Bulletin of the New York Academy of Medicine*, 25, 421–439.

Jackson, B. A., Baker, J. C., Ridgely, M. S., Bartis, J. T., and Linn, H. I. (2003) *Protecting emergency responders volume 3: Safety management in disasters and terrorism response*. Cincinatti, OH: National Institute for Occupational Safety and Health.

Johnston, P. and Paton, D. (2003) Environmental resilience: Psychological empowerment in high-risk professions. In D. Paton, J. Violanti, and L. Smith. *Promoting capabilities to manage posttraumatic stress: Perspectives on resilience*. Springfield, IL, Charles C. Thomas.

Joseph, P. N., Violanti, J. M., Donahue, R., Andrew, M. E., Trevisan, M., Burchfiel, C. M., and Dorn, J. (2010). Endothelial function, a biomarker of subclinical cardiovascular disease in urban police officers. *Journal of Occupational and Environmental Medicine*, 52, 1004–1008.

Kabat-Zinn, J., Massion, A. O., Kristeller, J., Peterson, L. G., Fletcher, K., and Pbert, L. (1992). Effectiveness of a meditation-based stress reduction program in the treatment of anxiety disorders. *American Journal of Psychiatry*, 149, 936–943.

Kendra, J. and Wachtendorf, T. (2003) Elements of resilience after the World Trade Center disaster: Reconstituting New York City's emergency operations centre, *Disasters*, 27, 1, 37–53.

Keng, S.-L. Smoski, M. J., and Robins, C. J. (2011). Effect of mindfulness on psyhcological health: A review of empircal studies. *Clinical Psychology Review*, 31, 1041–1056.

Kirschman, E. (1997). *I love a cop: What police families need to know*. New York: Guilford Press.

Larson, S. L., Eyerman, J., Foster, M. S., and Gfroerer, J. C. (2007). *Worker substance use and workplace policies and programs*. Department of Health and Human Services, Substance Abuse and Mental Health Services Administration, Office of Applied Studies.

Liberman, A. M., Best, S. R., Metzler, T. J., Fagan, J. A., Weiss, D. S., and Marmar, C. R. (2002). Routine occupational stress and psychological distress in police. *Policing: An International Journal of Police Strategies & Management*, 25, 421–441.

Liden, R. C., Wayne, S. J., and Sparrow, R. T. (2000) An examination of the mediating role of psychological empowerment on the relations between the job, interpersonal relationships, and work outcomes. *Journal of Applied Psychology*, 85, 407–416.

Lindsay, V. and Shelley, K. (2009). Social and stress-related influences of police officers' alcohol consumption. *Journal of Police and Criminal Psychology*, 24, 87–92.

Lissack, M. and Roos, J. (1999) *The next common sense: Mastering corporate complexity through coherence.* Naperville, IL: Nicholas Brealey Publishing.

Lory, K., Hankin, B. L., Kloos, B., Cheely, C., and Turecki, G. (2009). Alcohol and cigarette use and misuse among Hurricane Katrina survivors: Psychosocial risk and protective factors. *Substance Use and Misuse*, 44, 1711–1724.

Lundberg, J., Törnqvist, E., and Nadjm-Tehrani, S. (2012) Resilience in sensemaking and control of emergency response. *International Journal of Emergency Management*, 8, 99–122.

Luthar, S., Cicchetti, D., and Becher, B.(2000). The construct of resilience: A critical evaluation and guidelines for future work. *Child Development*, 71, 543–562.

Madakasira, S., and O'Brien, K. F. (1987). Acute post-traumatic stress disorder in victims of a natural disaster. *Journal of Nervous and Mental Disorder*, 175, 286–290.

Maddi, S. (2002). The story of hardiness: Twenty years of theorizing, research, and practice. *Consulting Psychology Journal*, 54, 173–185.

Maddi, S. and Khosaba, D. (2005). *Resilience at work: How to succeed no matter what life throws at you.* New York: Amacom.

Maia, D. B., Marmar, C. R., Metzler, T., Nobrega, A., Berger, W., Mendlowicz, M. V., Coutinho, E. S., and Figueira, I. (2007). Post-traumatic stress symptoms in an elite unit of Brazilian police officers: Prevalence and impact on psychosocial functioning and on physical mental health. *Journal of Affective Disorders*, 97, 241–245.

McCanlies, E. C., Mnatsakanova, A., Andrew, M. E., Burchfiel, C. M., and Violanti, J. M. (2014). Positive psychological factors are associated with lower PTSD symptoms among police officers: Post hurricane Katrina. *Stress and Health*, 30, 405414.

McCullough, M. E., Emmons, R. A., and Tsang, J. A. (2002). The grateful disposition: A conceptual and empirical topography. *Journal of Personality and Social Psychology*, 82, 112–127.

McCullough, M. E., Tsang, J. A., and Emmons, R. A. (2004). Gratitude in intermediate affective terrain: Links of grateful moods to individual differences and daily emotional experience. *Journal of Personality and Social Psychology*, 86, 295–309.

Mikkelsen, A. and Burke, R. (2004). Work-family concerns of Norwegian police officers: Antecedents and consequences. *International Journal of Stress Management*, 11, 429–444.

Miller, M. A. and Rahe, R. H. (1997). Life changes scaling for the 1990s. *Journal of Psychomatic Research*, 43, 3, 279–292.

Mitroff, I. I. and Anagnos, G. (2001) *Managing crises before they happen.* New York: Amacom.

Netemeyer, R. G., Boles, J. S., and McMurrian, R. (1996). Development and validation of work–family conflict and family–work conflict scales. *Journal of Applied Psychology*, 81, 400–410.

Norris F. H., Friedman M. J., Watson P. J., Byrne C. M., Diaz E., and Kaniasty K. (2002). 60,000 An empirical review of the empirical literature, 1981–2001, *Psychiatry*, 65, 207–239.

Norris F. H., Perilla J., and Riad J.(1999). Stability and change in stress, resources, and psychological distress following natural disaster: Findings from Hurricane Andrew. *Psychiatry*, 65, 207–239.

Norris, K., Paton, D., and Ayton, J. (2010) Future directions in Antarctic psychology research. *Antarctic Science*, 22, 335–342.

North, C. S., Tivis, L., McMillen, J. C., Pfefferbaum, B., Cox, J., Spitznagel, E. L., Bunch, K., Schorr, J., and Smith, E. M. (2002) Coping, functioning, and adjustment of rescue workers after the Oklahoma City bombing. *Journal of Traumatic Stress*, 15, 171–175.

Paton, D. and Jackson, D. (2002) Developing disaster management capability: An assessment centre approach, *Disaster Prevention and Management*, 11, 115–122.

Paton, D. and Kelso, B. A. (1991) Disaster stress: The impact on the wives and family. *Counselling Psychology Quarterly*, 4, 221–227.

Paton, D. & Stephens, C. (1996) Training and support for emergency responders. In Paton, D. & Violanti, J. (Eds.) *Traumatic Stress in Critical Occupations: Recognition, consequences and treatment.* Springfield, Ill.: Charles C. Thomas.

Paton, D. and Violanti, J. M. (2007) Terrorism stress risk assessment and management. In B. Bonger, L. Beutler, and P Zimbardo (eds.), *Psychology of Terrorism.* San Francisco: Oxford University Press.

Paton, D. (1994) Disaster relief work: An assessment of training effectiveness. *Journal of Traumatic Stress*, 7, 275–288.

Paton, D. (2005) Critical incidents and police officer stress. In H. Copes (ed.), *Policing and Stress*. Upper Saddle River, NJ: Prentice-Hall.

Paton, D. (2006) Post-traumatic growth in emergency professionals. In. L. Calhoun and R. Tedeschi (eds.), *Handbook of post-traumatic growth: Research and practice*. Mahwah, NJ: Lawrence Erlbaum Assoc.

Paton, D., Smith, L. M. Ramsay, R., and Akande, D. (1999) A structural re-assessment of the Impact of Event Scale: The influence of occupational and cultural contexts. In Gist, R. and Lubin, B. (eds.), *Response to disaster*. Philadelphia, PA: Taylor & Francis.

Paton, D., Smith, L. M., Violanti, J., and Eränen, L. (2000). Work-related traumatic stress: Risk, vulnerability and resilience. In D. Paton, J. M. Violanti, and Dunning, C. (eds), *Post-traumatic stress intervention: Challenges, issues and perspectives* (pp. 187–204). Springfield, IL: Charles C. Thomas.

Paton, D., Violanti, J. M., Burke, K., and Gherke, A. (2009). *Traumatic stress in police officers: A career length assessment from recruitment to retirement*. Springfield, IL, Charles C. Thomas.

Paton. D., Violanti, J. M., Johnston, P., Clarke, J., Burjke, K., and Keenan, D. (2008). Stress shield: A model of police resiliency. In L. Territo and J. D. Sewell (eds.), *Stress management in law enforcement, 3rd edition* (pp. 501–522). Durham, NC: Carolina Accademic Press.

Pfefferbaum, B. and Doughty, D. E. (2001). Increased alcohol use in a treatment sample of Oklahoma City bombing victims. *Psychiatry: Interpersonal and Biological Processes*, 64, 296–303.

Pollock, C., Paton, D., Smith, L., and Violanti, J. (2003) Team resilience. In D. Paton, J. Violanti, and L. Smith (eds.), *Promoting capabilities to manage post-traumatic stress: Perspectives on resilience*. Springfield, IL, Charles C. Thomas.

Quinn, R. E. and Spreitzer, G. M. (1997). The road to empowerment: Seven questions every leader should consider. *Organisational Dynamics*, Autumn, 37–49.

Raphael, B. (1986) *When disaster strikes*. London: Hutchinson.

Samaranayake, C. B. and Fernando, A. T. (2011). Satisfaction with life and depression among medical students in Auckland, New Zealand. *The New Zealand Medical Journal*, 124, 12–17.

Shakespeare-Finch, J., Paton, D., and Violanti, J. (2003) The family: Resilience resource and resilience needs. In D. Paton, J. Violanti, and L. Smith (eds.), *Promoting capabilities to manage posttraumatic stress: Perspectives on resilience*. Springfield, IL: Charles C. Thomas.

Siebert A. (2002) How resilience works. Letter to editor. *Harvard Business Review*, July, 121.

Siegrist, M. and Cvetkovich, G. (2000). Perception of hazards: The role of social trust and knowledge. *Risk Analysis*, 20, 713–719.

Spreitzer, G. M. (1997) Toward a common ground in defining empowerment. *Research in Organizational Change and Development*, 10, 31–62.

Stanley, E. A., Schaldach, J. M., Kiyonaga, A., and Jha, A. P. (2011) Mindfulness-based mind fitness training: A case study of a high-stress predeployment military cohort. *Cognitive and Behavioral Practice*, 18, 566–576.

Tedeschi, R. G. and Calhoun, L. G. (1996). The Post-traumatic Growth Inventory: measuring the positive legacy of trauma. *Journal of Traumatic Stress*, 9, 3, 455–471.

Tedeschi, R. G. and Kilmer, R. P. (2005). Assessing strength, resilience, and growth to guide clinical interventions. *Professional Psychology: Research and Practice*, 36, 230–237.

Thomas, K. W. and Velthouse, B. A. (1990). Cognitive elements of empowerment: An "interpretive" model of intrinsic motivation. *Academy of Management Review*, 15, 666–681.

Thompson, B. M., Kirk, A., and Brown, D. (2006). Sources of stress in policewomen: A three-factor model. *International Journal of Stress Management*, 13, 309–328.

Violanti, J. M., Slaven, J. E., Charles, L. E., Burchfiel, C. M., Andrew, M. E., and Homish, G. G. (2011). Police and alcohol use: A descriptive analysis and associations with stress outcomes. *American Journal of Criminal Justice*, 36, 344–356.

Violanti, J. M. and Paton, D. (2007). *Who gets PTSD? Issues of vulnerability*. Springfield, IL: Charles C. Thomas Publishing.

Walsh F. (2002). A family resilience framework: Innovative practice applications. *Family Relations*, 51, 130–139.

Ward, C. L., Lombard, C. J., and Gwebushe, N. (2006). Critical incident exposure in South African emergency services personnel: prevalence and associated mental health issues. *Emerg. Med.*, 23, 226–231.

Weick, K. (2001) *Making sense of the organization*. Maiden, MA: Blackwell Publishing.

Weick, K. E. and Sutcliffe, K. M. (2007). *Managing the Unexpected: Resilient Performance in an Age of Uncertainty (2nd edition)*. San Francisco, CA: Jossey-Bass.

West, C. A., Bernard, B. P., Kitt, M., Mueller, C., Tak, S., Driscoll, R. J., and Hurrell, J. 2006). *NIOSH Health Hazard Evaluation Report 0027–3001*. New Orleans: New Orleans Police Department.

Woods, D. (2006) Essential characteristics of resilience. In E. Hollnagel, D. Woods, and N. Leveson (eds.), *Resilience engineering: Concepts and precepts*. Aldershot: Ashgate.

Wraith, R. (1994) *The impact of major events on children*. In R. Watts and D. J. de la Horne (eds.), www.gpoaccess.gov/katrinareport/mainreport.pdf. Accessed April 3, 2103.

Youssef, C. M. and Luthans, F. (2005). Resiliency development of organizations, leaders and employees: Multi-level theory building for sustained performance. In W. Gardner, B. J. Avolio, and F. O. Walumbwa (eds.), *Authentic leadership theory and practice. Origins, effects, and development*. Oxford: Elsevier.

7 Shots fired

Stresses and strategies in officer-involved shootings

Laurence Miller

The gun

Among all public safety and emergency service workers, the unique and ultimate symbol of the law enforcement officer (LEO) is the gun. No other nonmilitary service group is required to carry a lethal firearm as a standard part of their daily equipment, nor charged to call upon their own discretion and judgment in making split-second decisions to use deadly force in the line of duty. With their unique mandate to utilize coercive physical force against citizens, the police represent the ultimate expression of governmental power in civil society (Klockars, 1996; Miller, 2008a, 2013; White and Klinger, 2012). Although watching any typical TV cop show might convince the viewer that officers regularly pop off multiple rounds without a second thought, in reality an officer's firing of his or her weapon in the line of duty is a profound event that almost always leaves a psychological trace (Bohrer, 2005; Grossman and Christensen, 2007; Miller, 1995, 2006b, 2015e; Nielsen, 1991; Passciak, 2015; Rudofossi, 2007; Solomon and Horn, 1986).

Cops and guns: the facts

Available data indicate that about 600 criminals are killed each year by police officers in the United States. Some of these killings are in self-defense, a few are accidental, and most are to prevent harm to others. By comparison, about 135 officers are killed in the line of duty each year. The sources of stress attached to an *officer-involved shooting* (OIS) are multiple, and include the officer's own psychological reaction to taking a life, the responses of law enforcement peers and the officer's family, rigorous examination by departmental investigators and administrators, potential disciplinary action or change of assignment, possible criminal and civil court action, and unwanted attention and sometimes outright harassment by the media (Baruth, 1986; Bohrer, 2005; Cloherty, 2004; Henry, 2004; Miller, 1995, 2000, 2006c, 2006e, 2009, 2011, 2015a, 2015e; Perrou and Farrell, 2004; Regehr and Bober, 2005; Russell and Beigel, 1990).

In most jurisdictions, the legal test for justification of legitimate use of lethal force by police officers requires that any reasonable person with the training and experience of the involved officer would have perceived a threat to life in the actions taken by the suspect (Blau, 1986, 1994; Blum, 2000; Miller, 2008b, 2015e). The law requires that the level of force used be *objectively reasonable* to control a deadly threat situation (de Carmen, 1994; Meadows and Trostle, 1988; Petrowski, 2002a, 2002b). The FBI provides four categories of such deadly threat: (1) the suspect possesses a weapon or is attempting to gain access to a weapon; (2) the suspect is armed and running to gain the tactical advantage of cover;

(3) a suspect with the capability of inflicting death or serious injury, with or without a weapon, is demonstrating an intention to do so; or (4) the suspect is attempting to escape the vicinity of a violent confrontation in which he or she inflicted or attempted to inflict death or serious injury.

Note that officers are expected to react to the imminent and credible *threat* of violence by the suspect; they are not required to wait until the suspect has committed a violent attack, because by then it would obviously be too late to prevent death or injury to the victim (Klockars, 1996; Petrowski, 2002a). Line-of-duty lethal force actions are most likely to occur in the following situations, in descending order of probability: (1) domestic or other disturbance calls; (2) robbery in progress; (3) burglary in progress; (4) traffic offense; (5) personal dispute and/or accident; and (6) stake-outs and drug busts (Blau, 1994; Russell and Biegel, 1990).

Early surveys from the 1970s and early 1980s cited a high psychological casualty rate among American police officers who killed a suspect in the line of duty, with some studies indicating that 70–95 percent of such officers left law enforcement within five years (Horn, 1991; McMains, 1986a, 1991). By the mid to late 1980s, the larger U.S. law enforcement agencies had cut the loss rate to 3 percent, while smaller departments were still losing about two-thirds of officers involved in a shooting. More recent surveys have showed that, overall, less than 15 percent of officers sampled showed significant post-shooting distress and even fewer left law enforcement as a direct result of the incident (Honig and Roland, 1998; Honig and Sultan, 2004; Miller, 2006b). In fact, some authorities have believed all along that the psychological disability rate from OISs, and from critical incidents in general, has been overestimated (Curran, 2003). Factors accounting for these discrepant findings over time may include increasingly sophisticated research methodology, as well as substantive improvements in the level of administrative and mental health support provided to officers by the larger departments (Zeling, 1986).

Perceptual, cognitive, and behavioral disturbances: the deadly force mindset

Typically, from the moment the 911 call comes in, or the officer encounters a potentially dangerous scenario on patrol, that officer's internal threat radar is engaged. Many use of force encounters, including OISs, escalate gradually, some erupt explosively, but most officers can clearly recall the instant when they decided to draw their weapon and when they decided to fire.

Under emergency life-and-death circumstances, the brain does extraordinary things to allow its owner to survive. However, officers in a deadly force encounter must do more than survive because their job descriptions do not give them the luxury of fleeing. An officer's responsibility is to control the scene, preserve life, and furthermore, to act lawfully in doing so—all in the moments where he or she could be instantly killed (Miller, 2007a). Most officers who have been involved in a deadly force shooting episode have described one or more alterations in perception, thinking, and behavior that occurred during the event (Addis and Stephens, 2008; Alpert *et al.*, 2002; Artwohl, 2002; Artwohl and Christensen, 1997; Bohrer, 2005; Fyfe, 1986, 1988; Geller, 1982; Honig and Lewinski, 2008; Honig and Roland, 1998; Honig and Sultan, 2004; Klinger, 2004, 2006; Miller, 2006b, 2006e, 2015e; Novy, 2012; Ross, 2013; Ross *et al.*, 2012). Most of these can be interpreted as natural adaptive defense mechanisms of a nervous system that is conserving energy and allocating mental resources under extreme cognitive and emotional demand.

Distortions in time perception can take two, seemingly opposite, patterns. Many officers will describe all or some of the events of the shooting episode as having occurred in slow motion ("the guy's gun hand just seemed to float up towards me"). At the same time, the whole episode may seem to have lasted for a much shorter time period than it actually did ("they told me the standoff took ten minutes, but it seemed like just a few seconds to me").

Sensory distortions are common and mostly involve *visual hyperfocus* and *visual exclusion*, i.e. "tunnel vision," in which the officer sharply tunes in to one particular aspect of the visual field, typically, the suspect's gun or weapon—also called "weapon focus"—while blocking out almost everything in the periphery, including, sometimes, the perpetrator's face or the actions of other officers. Some officers describe this as literally looking through a tunnel ("like through a paper towel tube" or "the wrong end of a telescope"), while for others, the experience is more perceptually amorphous and can include focusing on important aspects of the scene ("I saw the guy's crooked teeth when he snarled at me") but blocking out other non-essential items in the same field of vision ("he was smoking? I didn't even see the cigarette in his mouth").

Similarly, *auditory hyperfocus* and *auditory exclusion*, or "tunnel hearing," may occur when the officer's attention is attuned exclusively to a particular set of sounds, most commonly the suspect's voice, while background sounds are muted or excluded, even the shouts of fellow officers or the sound of nearby gunshots, which may perceived as faint pops. On the other hand, some sounds may seem magnified, e.g. the ping of shell casings hitting the sidewalk or a suspect's asthmatic breathing pattern.

Perceptual or behavioral dissociation and/or response automaticity may occur in a variety of forms during the critical event. In rare instances, officers have described feeling as though they were standing outside the scene, observing it "like it was happening to someone else." Probably the most common reaction is just "going on automatic"; this what they have trained for, and that training now kicks in at the critical moment, allowing the officer to carry out whatever actions are necessary, sometimes with a sense of robotic detachment, other times quite deliberately staving off the panic ("I'm not exactly sure how I did it, but I just put the fear on hold") that would otherwise impair an effective tactical response.

A momentary sense of confusion and/or helplessness may transiently occur during the lethal force encounter, but this is probably under-reported due to the potential stigma attached to "folding under pressure." A very small proportion of officers report that they "froze" at some point during the event; however, Artwohl (2002) conceptualizes this supposed immobilization response as actually representing an adaptive *action–reaction gap* in which the officer intuitively hesitates from shooting until the suspect has clearly posed a threat, i.e. a controlled response which actually works in favor of a non-lethal outcome.

Physiological reactions to a critical incident may be immediate or delayed. In general, extreme physiological hyperarousal is typically suppressed until after the emergency is over, at which time the officer may experience the famous *adrenalin dump*: having been able to calmly and competently resolve the deadly threat scenario just a few moments ago, now that the danger has passed, the officer is slammed with a delayed-reaction surge of anxiety which may last for several hours.

Disturbances in memory are commonly reported in shooting incidents, and may involve impaired recall for particular events during the shooting episode or for all or part of the officer's own actions; the latter, in turn, may be associated with the "going-on-automatic" response noted earlier. For example, it is common for officers not to remember how many rounds they fired, frequently underestimating the actual number. More rarely, some aspects of the scene may be recalled with unusual clarity—a "flashbulb memory." Over a third of cases involve not so much a total loss of recall as a distortion of events, to the extent that the officer's account of what happened differs markedly from the report of other observers at the scene.

Research in cognitive psychology (Loftus *et al.*, 1989) has shown that memory is typically selective and reconstructive, and that one's subjective confidence and self-reported clarity of recall may be only weakly related to the factual accuracy of the remembered event. Internal affairs supervisors, grand jurors, and other investigators who are unfamiliar with the cognitive psychology of memory under stress may listen to an officer's spotty recollection of what they think ought to be a vividly memorable event, or they may hear an account by the officer which is discrepant with the testimony of other observers (or with video recordings), and mistakenly conclude that the officer is deliberately distorting facts or covering up events.

Finally, it often unclear to what extent impaired or distorted recall represents a problem with memory per se, and what may relate to perceptual and cognitive factors. That is, if an officer can remember certain elements of an incident but not others, is that because he/she did not process them completely in the first place (tunnel perception) or only selectively recalls certain parts ("tunnel memory") or both? Clearly, this is an important area for further research.

After-effects of an officer-involved shooting

The effects of an OIS do not necessarily end when the shooting stops. For most officers, there will be at least a brief period during which they confront their mortality and cope with the impact and implications of the actions they have carried out.

Stages of post-OIS psychological response

With regard to many officers' post-OIS psychological response, some authorities (Nielsen, 1991; Williams, 1991) have divided the post-shooting reaction into four basic phases, which should be conceptualized flexibly, as not all officers will show this precise pattern in just this precise order; nevertheless, certain elements of this pattern appear to be quite common. The cycle begins with an immediate *impact phase*. For officers who have just shot a suspect during a dangerous confrontation, there may be an initial reaction of relief and even exhilaration at having just survived the encounter. But later, feelings of guilt or self-recrimination may surface, especially where the decision to shoot was less than clear-cut, or where the suspect's actions essentially forced the hand of the officer into using deadly force, such as in botched robberies, domestic disputes, or suicide-by-cop incidents (Kennedy *et al.*, 1998; Lindsay and Dickson, 2004; Miller, 2006f; Mohandie and Meloy, 2000; Pinizzotto *et al.*, 2005). Or the officer may simply be confronting the fact that, however justified the response, he has nevertheless just taken a human life.

During the second *recoil phase*, the officer may seem detached and preoccupied, spacily going through the motions of his job duties, and operating on behavioral autopilot. At the time when all he wants to do is put the event out of his mind, he will typically be barraged with questions from his peers, due to the obvious strong identification factor among officers, each one wondering, "What would I have done under those circumstances?" He may also be sensitive and prickly to even well-meaning congratulations by his peers ("Way to go, supercop—you got the guy"), and especially to accusatory-like interrogation and second-guessing from official investigators or the media ("Officer Jackson, did you really believe you were in fear for your life from a confused teenager?")

As the officer begins to come to terms with the shooting episode, a resolution phase ensues, wherein he assimilates the fact that the use of force action was necessary and justified in the battle for survival that often characterizes law enforcement deadly encounters. Of course, this resolution process may be complicated by ongoing departmental investigations, impending criminal prosecution, or civil litigation (Miller, 2011, 2015a). In addition, even under the best of circumstances, resolution may be partial rather than total, and psychological remnants of the experience may continue to resurface periodically, especially during future times of crisis. But overall, the officer is eventually able to return to work with a reasonable sense of confidence.

In the worst case, sufficient resolution may never occur, and the officer enters into a prolonged post-traumatic phase, which may impede or derail his law enforcement career. One factor in this kind of adverse reaction lies in the emotional disconnect between some officers' expectations of a heroic, armed confrontation (they watched cop shows as kids, too) and the gritty reality of most actual shooting scenarios, which typically involve petty criminals, mentally disordered subjects, domestic violence escalations, or the posturings of young-and-dumb juveniles (Miller, 2006b, 2012, 2015c).

In less severe cases, a period of temporary stress disability allows the officer to seek treatment, to eventually regain his or her emotional and professional bearings, and to ultimately return to the job. Still other officers return to work right away, but continue to perform marginally until their actions are brought to the attention of superiors. In my experience, the vast majority of officers involved in justified deadly force encounters or non-lethal shootings soon return to work without incident. Most of those with more adverse traumatic reactions can eventually get back on the job if provided with the proper psychological intervention and departmental support (Miller, 2006e; see p.122*ff*).

Individual and incident-specific factors in post-OIS response

Although some authors have written about a monolithic "police personality" (Twersky-Glasner, 2005), in actuality officers are not cookie-cutter psychological replicas of one another, and the personalities of individual officers, along with personal experience and departmental enculturation, will influence a given officer's professional activities over his or her career—for good or for ill (Miller, 2003, 2004). This includes his or her response to an OIS. However, certain commonalities in response have emerged from systematic study and clinical experience in this area (Anderson *et al.*, 1995; Blum, 2000; Cohen, 1980; Geller, 1982; Honig and Sultan, 2004; Russell and Beigel, 1990; Williams, 1999). Some of these responses represent general post-traumatic reactions familiar to psychological trauma workers (Bowman, 1997; Gilliland and James, 1993; Greenstone and Leviton, 2001; Miller, 1998, 2008c, 2015f; Regehr and Bober, 2005), while others seem to have a more specific law enforcement line-of-duty shooting focus.

Physical symptoms may include headaches, stomach upset, nausea, weakness and fatigue, muscle tension and twitches, and changes in appetite and sexual functioning. Sleep is typically impaired, with frequent awakenings and sometimes disturbing dreams. Typical post-traumatic psychological reactions of intrusive imagery and flashbacks may occur, along with premonitions, distorted memories, and feelings of déjà vu. Some degree of anxiety and depression is common, sometimes accompanied by panic attacks. There may be unnatural and disorienting feelings of helplessness, fearfulness, and vulnerability, along with self-second-guessing and guilt feelings. Substance abuse may be a risk in those already predisposed.

There may be a pervasive irritability and low frustration tolerance, along with anger and resentment toward the suspect, the department, unsupportive peers and family, or civilians in general. Part of this may be a reaction to the conscious or unconscious sense of vulnerability that the officer experiences after a shooting incident. Sometimes, this is projected outward as a smoldering irritability that makes the officer's every interaction with peers or citizens a grating source of stress and conflict. Combined with an increased hypervigilance and hypersensitivity to threats of all kinds, this reaction pattern may result in over-aggressive policing, leading to abuse-of-force complaints (Miller, 2003, 2004, 2007b, 2011, 2015a; Rostow and Davis, 2004).

Undetected and untreated, this pattern may spiral into a vicious cycle of angry and fearful isolation and withdrawal by the officer, spurring further alienation from potential sources of peer, family, and professional help and support. At the same time, some officers become overly protective of their families, generating an alternating *control-alienation syndrome* (McMains, 1986b, 1991), which is disturbing and disorienting to the family and may add to existing family stresses (Miller, 2007c). All this, combined with emotional lability ("I just get mad or cry at the drop of a hat") and cognitive symptoms of impaired concentration and memory, may lead the officer to fear that he or she is "going crazy."

Apart from the universal reactions and individual personality and history of the officer, certain factors inherent in the line-of-duty shooting incident itself can affect the severity, persistence, and impact of post-shooting symptoms and reactions (Allen, 2004; Anderson *et al.*, 1995; Blau, 1986; Bohrer, 2005; Honig and Sultan, 2004; McMains, 1986a, 1986b).

One obvious factor is the degree of threat to the officer's life, which can operate in two ways. First, the officer who feels that he or she was literally about to die may be traumatized by the extreme fear involved, but may nevertheless feel quite justified and guilt-free in using deadly force on a suspect with clearly murderous intentions. But where the danger was more equivocal, when the suspect's actions are harder to interpret (especially in 20/20 hindsight), there may be less of the fear factor and more second-guessing about what degree of force was actually necessary. Police officers pride themselves in their ability to manage a tense situation and perform under pressure, so they may experience a gnawing sense of doubt and self-recrimination where the situation abruptly got out of control and turned deadly.

For example, at one extreme is the armed bank robber who, having been duly warned and ordered to surrender, brazenly draws down on the officer or puts a gun to a hostage. In such a case, there is likely to be universal agreement that the officer had no choice— indeed, was duty-bound—to fire on the perpetrator in order to save innocent lives. At the other extreme is the obnoxiously inebriated high school punk who is pulled over for a traffic violation, exchanges a few sharp words with the officer, and is shot for refusing to drop an object in his hand that turns out to be a cell phone. A related example is the schizophrenic homeless person who has heretofore been known only as a noisy neighborhood pest, but now is psychotically waving around a hammer or a kitchen knife and is shot while lunging at the officer (Miller, 2006e; 2015e).

A common reaction in ambiguous cases is anger at the suspect himself for forcing the officer to take his life. Inasmuch as anger and guilt are often intertwined, greater anger may be shown toward a relatively more "innocent" suspect who's stupid behavior resulted in a totally unnecessary shooting—e.g. the psychotic street person or the drunk kid with the big mouth— than at a suspect who more clearly "deserves" to get shot, e.g. the armed robber fleeing a bank who fires at the officer first. Much of this anger may smolder below the surface and emerge as general irritability, problems with authority, and family conflicts (Miller, 2004, 2006e, 2007c).

Still another situational factor is the amount of preparation and warning that existed prior to the shooting and the length of time the dangerous incident persisted, which also may have varying effects. On the one hand, officers caught off guard are unlikely to have even a brief interval to think through their decision to shoot and may later perceive themselves, or be perceived by others, as having reacted out of fear, no matter how justified the shooting is later judged to be. At the other extreme, where the shooting followed a prolonged stand-off, with a lot of back-and-forth negotiating and maneuvering, as in hostage-barricade or suicide-by-cop scenarios, the extended period of time the officer spent deliberating over the decision to use deadly force may later take a psychological toll (McMains and Mullins, 1996; Miller, 2005b, 2006f).

All of the above factors relate to two important dimensions: the amount of *control* the officer feels he or she had over the situation and degree of *conflict* that exists over the necessity to take a human life. Generally, the less control and the more conflict the officer has experienced during the event, the more adverse will be the psychological reaction (Miller, 1998, 2006b, 2006e).

Reactions of supervisors and peers

Issues around degrees of control and conflict extend to the post-shooting phase, and will typically involve the amount and kind of attention the officer receives from his/ her administration, peers, the general community, and the media (Blau, 1994; Bohrer, 2005; Henry, 2004; Klein, 1991; Russell and Biegel, 1990; Rynearson, 1988, 1994, 1996; Rynearson and McCreery, 1993; Sewell, 1986; Sprang and McNeil, 1995). While supervisors and administrators are understandably concerned about the public relations aspect of an OIS, most are generally supportive of their involved personnel. However, a department's efforts to appear objective and unbiased to the public and media may at times make it seem that the authorities are coming down especially hard on the officer.

The reactions of the officer's peers may help or harm his/her attempts to cope with the situation. As noted above, at first he/she may receive accolades from his/her fellow officers for surviving, protecting life, and "doing your job." Because of the powerful mutual identification factor, police peers may want to hear all about the event, because, someday, they may be there too and they want to believe that, in the breach, they will do the right thing. Many of these peers also hope that the officer's guts to pull the trigger will "rub off" on them should they encounter a similar situation. However, if the officer fails to regale them with an uplifting narrative of struggle and triumph, and instead reveals the conflict, doubt, and pain he or she is going through, the contagion effect may cause his/her fellow officers to avoid him.

This is because the implied psychological contract of such post-crisis mutual congratulatory rituals seems to involve a kind of blanket immunity against what Solomon and Horn (1986) call the *mark of Cain,* and Henry (2004) describes as the *death taint,* the idea that: "You have now made real for us the life-and-death situation we all fear. So you'd better show us how nobly and heroically you're dealing with this, throw us a positive spin, or all you've done is shove our mortality up in our faces, which frightens us, and so to emotionally insulate and protect ourselves, we'll will shun you or degrade you." This identification factor probably accounts for the creepily uncomfortable post-shooting "attaboys" that are so commonly inflicted on the officer by his colleagues, as they try to conscript him into purveying an inspiring and morale-building narrative, whether he wants to or not. Unfortunately, these reactions may only serve to heighten the officer's anxiety about what he might really do "next time."

We want our societal protectors—police officers, soldiers—to be courageous, but to be human, not robots, and many officers feel genuinely sad at having had to take a human life, even if they objectively recognize that they had no choice in the situation and that the perpetrator's actions warranted deadly force. Human nature being what it is, even those professionals who are trained to kill cannot just automatically shed their familial, religious, and cultural upbringing when they don the uniform. An officer may thus become irritated at his colleagues who want him to play the happy warrior, while they have no clue as to the turmoil he is going through. But the officer is hurting and still needs all the support he can get, so, fearing rejection, he may not want to burst his colleagues' bubble. Painful as putting up this false front may be, it's still better than total isolation (Miller, 2006b, 2006e, 2015b).

Intervention strategies for officer-involved shootings

Officers know that their involvement in an OIS is likely to precipitate a cascade of events that can seriously impact their law enforcement careers. All police agencies take deadly force encounters seriously and have policies in place to deal with them (Hatch and Dickson, 2007; IACP, 2009; Miller, 2006b, 2006e, 2008a, 2009, 2011, 2015e; Petrowski, 2002a, 2002b). Typically, immediately following an OIS, designated personnel will respond to the scene. In smaller departments, this may include the police chief or sheriff; in larger jurisdictions, it is usually the precinct captain or district undersheriff. Other responding personnel typically include paramedics, crime scene investigators, a departmental attorney, and, in some agencies, a mental health clinician (MHC) to assess the officer's psychological status. If the officer does not require medical care, a detailed *walk-through* then occurs, where the involved officer(s) take the investigators step-by-step through the event while it is still fresh in their minds; this is usually video-recorded and may take several hours, especially where the scenario is a complex one and there are multiple officers involved. Following the on-scene investigation, the officer is usually taken home and remains on administrative leave while a departmental investigation of the incident is carried out.

In some departments, the officer may be referred for a *post-critical incident psychological evaluation*, usually within a few days to a week following the incident, in order to assess for any residual adverse psychological reactions. As noted above, normal short-term, post-shooting reactions include heightened tension, impaired sleep, and ruminating and/or dreaming about the incident; these usually abate within a few days. If the shooting is administratively cleared and there are no psychological problems noted, the officer will usually be returned to service within a week or so. If the officer seems to be having an especially hard time coping, stress debriefing or psychological counseling may be recommended. For an otherwise healthy officer, this type of intervention is usually short-term and is typically followed by a second evaluation for return to duty. In high-profile or contested shootings, however, the psychological stress is often far higher and officers may be out of service for prolonged periods of time due to a combination of administrative and mental health concerns (Miller, 2000, 2006a, 2006b, 2007b, 2015a; Rudofossi, 2007; Solomon and Horn, 1986).

Presented here is a composite model protocol for on-scene response to officer-involved shootings culled and amalgamated from a variety of sources (Baruth, 1986; Blau, 1994; IACP, 2009; McMains, 1986a, 1986b, 1991; Miller, 1999b, 2006b, 2006e, 2015b; Williams, 1991). This model can be adapted and modified to the needs of the individual police agency. How this protocol is carried out in practice can make a tremendous difference in the later psychological adjustment of the involved officers and in department-wide morale. More information can be found in Miller (2006e).

On-scene law enforcement response

In the policy-and-procedure planning stages, it should be decided which personnel respond to what types of critical incidents, including OISs. As noted above, responders may include back-up officers, administrative officials, departmental investigators, peer support staff, mental health professionals, the departmental attorney, a media spokesperson or Public Information Officer (PIO), the police chief or division captain, and others. At the time of the shooting, all designated personnel should respond to the scene.

Reassurance for the involved officer should be provided by departmental authorities. This should simply communicate an understanding and appreciation of what the officer has just been through, and the assurance that the department will support him or her as much as possible throughout the process. Especially at this psychologically sensitive stage, the officer should be given the benefit of the doubt and treated with respect by departmental authorities.

The officer should be provided with on-scene access to legal counsel and to a mental health professional. In many jurisdictions officers may refrain from making any statement to authorities at the scene until an attorney is present and/or until they have been assessed as mentally fit to make a statement by a qualified mental health professional. This protects the officer's rights and at the same time makes it difficult to later challenge any on-scene statements on the basis of their having been made under mental duress.

The officer's weapon will almost always be impounded. In the best case, the weapon is turned over in private, and in many instances a replacement weapon is provided or the empty holster removed while the on-scene investigation proceeds. At most shooting scenes, involved personnel will remain at the site for hours in order to carry out the investigation and walk-through. However, no one should hang around the scene longer than necessary and the officer should be released from the scene as quickly as possible and driven home or back to the station by a supervisor or a pair of colleagues, to await further action. When taken home, the peers should accompany the officer to his door and leave only when he has assured them that he is okay.

Of course, when necessary, the officer should be provided with medical care, either at the scene or at a local hospital. The officer's family should be notified of the shooting as soon as possible, even if everybody is still on-scene; family members should not have to hear about it first on their radio, TV, or cell phone, or get a call from neighbor who's seen or heard the story. If the family is out of town, every effort should be made to contact them, preferably through direct contact by a law enforcement agency in that location. Media requests should be handled by the agency's Public Information Officer.

On-scene and follow-up psychological assessment and intervention

Encouragingly, at least one study has found that almost all large departments and over two-thirds of small departments provide some professional mental health support for traumatized officers (McMains, 1986a; 1986b). As part of the on-scene response team, if you are the police psychologist or other licensed mental health clinician (MHC) responder, you have a specific but important role to play (McMains, 1991; McMains and Mullins, 1996).

First, when the call comes in, try find out as much as possible about the nature of the incident. When arriving at the scene, identify the involved officer and try to find a comfortable place to conduct the interview. "On-scene" doesn't necessarily mean standing next to crime scene tape or pacing back and forth in front of news cameras. As long as the officer stays inside the established perimeter and can be found by authorities when needed, he or she is still technically on-scene.

Next, determine the officer's mental status. This may range from extremes of panic, confusion, and disorientation—rare, in my experience—to unnatural calmness and stoic denial ("I'm okay; no problem")—a far more common response. Frequently, emotions will swing back and forth at the scene. As discussed below, validating these reactions as normal stress responses is an important part of on-scene intervention.

For the visibly upset officer, use calming and distraction techniques to bring his or her mental state into a more rational and receptive mode. For the defensive, sealed-over officer, what is often helpful is a one-on-one version of the critical incident stress management procedure known as *defusing*, which follows a basic tripartite structure (Miller, 1999a, 2006b, 2006e; Mitchell and Everly, 1996), as outlined below.

First, ask the officer to tell you what happened. This will typically elicit a stiff, dry, detail-laden rendition of events, as if the officer were testifying before a review board or in court. Listen to the story until you have a good sense of the sequence of events. Next, ask the officer to describe "what was going on in your mind while it was happening." This may yield clues to the officer's cognitive and emotional state. Finally, provide factual information and support regarding any disturbing reactions the officer may be having at the scene. Remember that the goal of on-scene psychological intervention is not to conduct psychotherapy, but rather to allow the officer to loosen up just enough for you to be able to assess his/her mental status, but be able to use temporary mental strengthening techniques (Miller, 2006e, 2008d) to help him "keep it together" until the immediate crisis has resolved.

Following the on-scene evaluation, and while still at the site, the referral can be made for a follow-up evaluation at the psychologist's office, scheduled for several days post-incident. This gives the officer a few days to calm down, and will allow the MHC to get a better perspective on how the officer is coping psychologically after the initial shock of the incident has worn off. If, at this later time, the officer is assessed to be experiencing no unusual signs or symptoms (some degree of residual distress is normal for a few days), release to full duty is usually recommended. Otherwise, a range of recommendations may be made, such as additional time off and/or additional mental health treatment, peer counseling, or other intervention (see below). Ideally, all involved officers in an OIS incident should be mandated to undergo a post-incident psychological "check-up." Note that many departments utilize an on-scene intervention with no mandatory follow-up and other departments do the reverse; a few still have no policy at all on this. Of course, police psychologists should always consult with their departments regarding the protocols for such incidents—ideally, police managers would be involved in developing those protocols in the first place (Miller, 2005a, 2006d, 2006e, 2015c, 2015d).

Psychological treatment of officer-involved shootings

Following the original shooting incident and the follow-up session, some officers may request additional sessions with an MHC, while others may be referred by their supervisors. To preserve objectivity, the MHC who conducts the initial post-OIS evaluation should not be the one to conduct counseling and psychotherapy with the officer. The following recommendations are summarized from a variety of sources (Horn, 1991; McMains, 1986a, 1991; Miller, 2006b, 2006e, 2015b; Wester and Lyubelsky, 2005; Wittrup, 1986; Zeling, 1986), and are directed toward the treating clinician.

Ideally, the intervention should begin as soon after the shooting incident as possible; however, treatment is often delayed as officers may attempt to wait out or tough out adverse reactions on their own, until the need for external help becomes apparent either to the officer himself or (more likely) to peers, supervisors, or family members. In such cases, intervention should be started as quickly as possible when the need surfaces.

In most cases, interventions should be short term and focused on supporting officers through the crisis, as well as returning them to active duty as soon as possible. How narrow or broad are the range issues to be covered will be determined on a case-by-case basis, depending on how the incident has affected the officer, his family, colleagues, and others. But the general guideline is that post-shooting psychological intervention should be focused on resolving the critical incident in question.

Accordingly, a realistically positive atmosphere should prevail during the course of the intervention. Absent clear evidence to the contrary, the assumption should be that the officer acted properly, can successfully manage the current crisis with a little help, and will soon return to active status. Indeed, during particularly contentious investigations, the psychologist's office may be the only place the officer does not feel like a hounded criminal (Miller, 2006e, 2011, 2015a). In this regard, the usual standards of clinician–patient confidentiality must be respected by all parties.

On initial contact with the officer, the MHC's role may replicate the basic intervention stages of a critical incident stress debriefing model (Bohl, 1995; Miller, 1995, 1998, 1999a, 1999b; Mitchell and Everly, 1996), applied, in this case, on an individual level.

First, review the facts of the case with the officer. This allows for a relatively non-emotional narrative of the traumatic event, but in the case of an OIS, it serves a further function. Precisely because of the cognitive and perceptual distortions that commonly occur in these kinds of incidents (see above), what may be particularly disturbing to the officer is the lack of clarity in his own mind as to the actual nature and sequence of events. Just being able to review what is known about the facts of the case in a relatively safe and non-adversarial environment may bring a much-needed dose of mental clarity and sanity to the situation.

In fact, Solomon (1991, 1995) describes one such format for individual debriefing sessions as going over the incident "frame by frame," which allows the officer to verbalize the moment-to-moment thoughts, perceptions, sensory details, feelings, and actions that occurred during the critical incident. This can help the officer become aware of, sort out, and understand what happened. Be sensitive, however, to the pacing and intensity of such recollections, so as not to re-traumatize the officer or force him to "remember" material that may have been incompletely processed in the first place.

Next, review the officer's thoughts and feelings about the shooting incident, but don't expect everything to be sorted out at once. Remember, an OIS represents a special kind of critical incident and it may take more than one attempt for the officer to productively untangle and reveal what's going on in his mind. Give him extra time or extra sessions to express his thoughts and feelings, and be sure to monitor the reaction so as not to encourage unproductive spewing or loss of control. One of the most important things the MHC can do at this stage is to help the officer modulate his or her emotional expression so that it comes as a relief, not as an added stressor.

Provide authoritative and factual information about psychological reactions to a shooting incident. The kinds of cognitive and perceptual distortions that take place during an OIS, the post-traumatic symptoms and disturbances, and the sometimes off-putting and distressing reactions of colleagues and family members, are likely to be quite alien to the officer's ordinary experience, and might be interpreted by him or her as signs of going soft or crazy. Normalize these responses for the officer, and try to give a realistic projection of what will come next. Often, just this kind of authoritative reassurance from a competent and credible mental health professional can mitigate the officer's anxiety considerably.

Finally, provide for follow-up services, which may include additional individual sessions, family therapy, referral to departmental or community support services, possible medication referral, and so on. As with most cases of critical incident psychological intervention with public safety personnel, follow-up psychotherapy for OISs tends to be short-term, although additional services may be sought later for other problems partially related or unrelated to the incident. Indeed, any kind of critical incident may often be the stimulus to explore other troublesome aspects of an officer's life, and the success in resolving this incident in an atmosphere of trust with the MHC may give the officer confidence to pursue other issues in the future (Blau, 1994; Miller, 1998, 2006e).

Peer support programs

As skilled as the MHC may be, however, many public safety personnel will avoid such professionals if not ordered to undergo a mandated examination. This is usually because they have had bad experiences with MHCs in the past, most commonly in the context of contentious pre-employment screenings or fitness for duty evaluations (Max, 2000; Miller, 2007b), or they may simply fear the taint of seeing a clinician who is associated with "going squirrely." To augment or supplement professional mental health services, an increasing number of police departments have instituted *peer support programs* for the psychological aftermath of OISs and other critical incidents (Klein, 1991; McMains, 1991). For these officers, interventions by fellow police members may have more credibility than mental health professionals because the former have "been there" and "know the job." Conversely, some officers may be reluctant to admit weakness in front of a fellow officer, and many of these individuals actually welcome the opportunity to unload on a professional who is not part of the law enforcement fishbowl. The ideal situation, then, is for a given law enforcement agency to have a range of support programs available for its diverse members.

Peer counseling teams typically consist of law enforcement volunteers who have a good performance history with the department, and who have gone through some form of formal training and certification program, which includes a basic understanding of psychological stress syndromes, basic crisis intervention and counseling skills, understanding special problems encountered with officer-involved shootings and other critical incidents, and knowing when and how to refer for professional mental health services when necessary. In this regard, departments who institute peer-counseling programs should be sure to make professional mental health back-up help available if further treatment is indicated.

Always important is the issue of confidentiality. Especially with counselors who are peers and not licensed professionals, officers may fear unwarranted disclosure. This issue cannot be overemphasized because the success of a peer support program will stand or fall based on the confidence officers have in the peer counselors' discretion and competence. Again, this fear of the fishbowl and rumor mill is one of the reasons some officers may actually prefer to talk to an outside clinician. More practically, what happens if the peer-counseled officer admits that he was intoxicated during the shooting, or expresses a clear racist bias that may have contributed to his decision to use deadly force? What does the peer counselor do then? These issues must be carefully worked out in advance for a peer-counselor system to work. A growing trend is for police supervisors, usually in the lieutenant and captain grades, to obtain master's-level counseling degrees and licenses so they can straddle the worlds of law enforcement officer and MHC.

The basic elements of peer counseling are not very different from professional clinical intervention in relatively non-complex cases and include active listening skills, allowing the officer to ventilate and tell his story in a supportive, non-judgmental atmosphere, provision of reassurance and accurate information about stress syndromes, recommendation of strategies for handling symptoms and dealing with other people during the investigation and recovery process, and referral for professional mental health services when issues become more complex (Blau, 1994; Klein, 1991).

Model post-shooting intervention programs

Elsewhere (Miller, 2006e), I have reviewed in detail several post-OIS intervention programs from around the country (Antonovsky and Bernstein, 1986; Milgram and Hobfoll, 1986; Solomon and Mastin, 1999; Somodevilla, 1986) that illustrate the basic elements of peer support and professional intervention for OISs. Here I will summarize the key elements that such successful programs share in common. This model can be used as a template by police psychologists and the law enforcement agencies they serve to design, modify, or adapt their own post-shooting programs and protocols to the needs of their individual agencies:

- *Reasonable respect and compassion:* "We hear what you're going through".
- *Departmental reassurance and validation:* "We may not have all the facts yet, but the leadership is behind you."
- *Information flow:* "Within the limits of departmental policies and procedures, we'll do everything we can to keep you in the loop."
- *Removal from the scene:* "Let's go sit in my patrol unit and go over what happened."
- *Replacement firearm:* "Here's a temporary issue till the investigation is complete."
- *Access to an attorney:* "The departmental attorney is on her way to the scene. For later on, here's how to contact your PBA rep."
- *Family welfare:* "We're going to call your family and let them know you're all right, and that you may have to stay past your shift till we're finished here."
- *Shooting folder:* "This is a private file, separate from your regular jacket, kept by the Captain, so we can accurately collate the facts relevant to this case and communicate only with those on a need-to-know basis."
- *Handling media:* "Our departmental spokesperson (PIO) will be running interference for you during this process and we appreciate your cooperation in honoring our policy of not making any unauthorized statements to the media."
- *Administrative leave:* "Please understand that this is not a disciplinary suspension, but that this kind of administrative leave is part of our departmental policy, both for your own welfare and to give us time to complete our investigation."
- *Psychological services:* "Aside from the standard mandatory post-critical incident psychological follow-up, for any additional mental health care, please feel free to

access our departmental psychologist or any other mental health professional you choose. This is not a requirement or a fitness-for-duty exam, but is for your own well-being, and is confidential."

- *Peer support:* "Would you like to talk to Tony? He's a fellow officer in our peer support program who's been through some critical incidents himself; he knows the drill."
- *Support from the wider law enforcement community and concerned citizens:* [When realistic] "We're getting calls from the deputies over in the next county asking how you're doing. And some of the church members on the block where you took down that crack house have written a nice letter of commendation to the Chief."
- *Reinforcement of professional competence:* [When realistic] "We're not pulling you totally out of service, officer. If you're up to it we still need your help, so for now you're reassigned to communications."
- *Opportunity to learn and grow:* "We're going to make some good out of this by learning how to keep even safer next time."

Overall, successful post-shooting and other post-critical incident programs share the important common elements of: (1) flexible access to peer counselors and/or mental health professionals; (2) the maintenance of an attitude of respect for involved officers, backed up by appropriate actions; and (3) unequivocal support and encouragement of the mental health and peer support program from top levels of the department or agency.

Conclusions

Officer-involved shootings (OISs) need not be the most traumatic critical incidents in policing, but when they are, the reasons are usually due to a mix of incident characteristics, officer response styles, and departmental handling. By providing immediate administrative, legal, psychological, and peer-support services to officers in need, investigators typically find their jobs easier. Even in the unfortunate case of negligence or misconduct, how a department deals with *all* of its members will be watched very carefully by other officers for clues as to how they'll be treated when the time comes for them to fire their weapon in order to fulfill their duty to protect. In the entire process of managing an OIS, police psychologists and other mental health professionals have a vital and indispensable role to play.

References

Addis, N. and Stephens, C. (2008). An evaluation of a police debriefing program: Outcomes for police officers five years after a police shooting. *International Journal of Police Studies and Management, 10,* 361–373.

Allen, S.W. (2004). Dynamics in responding to departmental personnel. In V. Lord (ed.), *Suicide by cop: Inducing officers to shoot* (pp. 245–257). Flushing: Looseleaf Law Publications.

Alpert, G.P., Rivera, J., and Lott, L. (2012). Working toward the truth in officer-involved shootings. *FBI Law Enforcement Bulletin,* May, pp. 1–7.

Alpert, G.P. and Dunham, R. (2004). *Understanding police use of force: Officers, suspects, and reciprocity.* New York: Cambridge University Press.

Anderson, W., Swenson, D., and Clay, D. (1995). *Stress management for law enforcement officers.* Englewood Cliffs: Prentice Hall.

Antonovsky, A. and Bernstein, J. (1986). Pathogenesis and salutogenesis in war and other crises: Who studies the successful coper? In N. Milgram (ed.), *Stress and coping in times of war* (pp. 89–121). New York: Brunner/Mazel.

Artwohl, A. (2002). Perceptual and memory distortion during officer-involved shootings. *FBI Law Enforcement Bulletin*, October, pp. 18–24.

Artwohl, A. and Christensen. L. (1997) *Deadly force encounters: What a cop needs to know to mentally and physically prepare for and win a gunfight.* Boulder, CO: Paladin Press.

Baruth, C. (1986). Pre-critical incident involvement by psychologists. In J.T. Reese and H.A. Goldstein (eds.), *Psychological services for law enforcement* (pp. 413–417). Washington, DC: USGPO.

Blau, T.H. (1986). Deadly force: Psychological factors and objective evaluation: A preliminary effort. In J.T. Reese and H.A. Goldstein (eds.), *Psychological services for law enforcement* (pp. 315–334). Washington, DC: USGPO.

Blau, T.H. (1994). *Psychological services for law enforcement.* New York: Wiley.

Blum, L.N. (2000). *Force under pressure: How cops live and why they die.* New York: Lantern Books.

Bohl, N. (1995). Professionally administered critical incident debriefing for police officers. In M.I. Kunke and E.M. Scrivner (eds.), *Police psychology into the 21st century* (pp. 169–188). Hillsdale: Erlbaum.

Bohrer, S. (2005). After firing the shots, what happens? *FBI Law Enforcement Bulletin*, September, pp. 8–13.

Bowman, M. (1997). *Individual differences in posttraumatic response: Problems with the adversity-distress connection.* Mahwah: Erlbaum.

Cloherty, J.J. (2004). Legal defense of law enforcement officers in police shooting cases. In V. Lord (ed.), *Suicide by cop: Inducing officers to shoot* (pp. 85–150). Flushing: Looseleaf Law Publications.

Cohen, A. (1980). "I've killed that man 10,000 times." *Police*, 3, 4.

Curran, S. (2003). Separating fact from fiction about police stress. *Behavioral Health Management*, 23, 1–2.

del Carmen, R.V. (1994). Criminal and civil liabilities of police officers. In T. Barker and D.L. Carter (eds.), *Police deviance* (3rd ed., pp. 409–430). Cincinnati, OH: Anderson.

Fyfe, J.J. (1986). The split-second syndrome and other determinants of police violence. In A.T. Campbell and J. Gibbs (eds.), *Violent transactions.* New York: Blackwell.

Fyfe, J.J. (1988). Police use of deadly force: Research and reform. *Justice Quarterly*, 5, 165–205.

Geller, W.A. (1982). Deadly force: What we know. *Journal of Police Science and Administration*, 10, 151–177.

Gilliland, B.E. and James, R.K. (1993). *Crisis intervention strategies* (2nd ed.). Pacific Grove: Brooks/Cole.

Greenstone, J.L. and Leviton, S.C. (2001). *Elements of crisis intervention: Crises and how to respond to them.* New York: Wadsworth.

Grossman, D. and Christensen, L.W. (2007). *On combat: The psychology and physiology of deadly conflict in war and peace* (3rd ed.). Mascoutah, IL: Warrior Science Publications.

Hatch, D.E. and Dickson, R. (2007). *Officer-involved shootings and use of force: Practical investigative techniques* (2nd ed.). Boca Raton, FL: CRC Press.

Henry, V.E. (2004). *Death work: Police, trauma, and the psychology of survival.* New York: Oxford University Press.

Honig, A. and Lewinski, W.J. (2008). A survey of the research on human factors related to lethal force encounters: Implications for law enforcement training, tactics, and testimony. *Law Enforcement Executive Forum*, 8, 129–152.

Honig, A.L. and Roland, J.E. (1998). Shots fired: Officer involved. *The Police Chief*, October, 65–70.

Honig, A.L. and Sultan, E. (2004). Reactions and resilience under fire: What an officer can expect. *The Police Chief*, December, 54–60.

Horn, J.M. (1991). Critical incidents for law enforcement officers. In J.T. Reese, J.M. Horn, and C. Dunning (eds.), *Critical incidents in policing* (rev. ed., pp. 143–148). Washington, DC: Federal Bureau of Investigation.

International Association of Chiefs of Police (2009). *Officer-Involved Shooting Guidelines.* Los Angeles: IACP.

Kennedy, D.B., Homant, R.J., and Hupp, R.T. (1998). Suicide by cop. *FBI Law Enforcement Bulletin*, August, 21–27.

Klein, R. (1991). The utilization of police peer counselors in critical incidents. In J.T. Reese, J.M. Horn, and C. Dunning (eds.), *Critical incidents in policing* (pp.159–168). Washington, DC: Federal Bureau of Investigation.

Klinger, D.A. (2004). *Into the kill zone: A cop's eye view of deadly force.* San Francisco: Jossey-Bass.

Klinger, D.A. (2006). Police responses to officer-involved shootings. *National Institute of Justice Journal, 253,* 21–24.

Klockars, C.B. (1996). A theory of excessive force and its control. In W.A. Geller and H. Toch (eds.), *Police violence: Understanding and controlling police abuse of force* (pp. 1–22). New Haven: Yale University Press.

Lindsay, M.S. and Dickson, D. (2004). Negotiating with the suicide-by-cop subject. In V. Lord (ed.), *Suicide by cop: Inducing officers to shoot* (pp. 153–162). Flushing: Looseleaf Law Publications.

Loftus, E.F., Greene, E.L., and Doyle, J.M. (1989). The psychology of eyewitness testimony. In D.C. Raskin (ed.), *Psychological methods in criminal investigations and evidence* (pp. 3–46). New York: Springer.

Max, D.J. (2000). The cop and the therapist. *New York Times Magazine,* December 3, 94–98.

McMains. M.J. (1986a). Post-shooting trauma: Demographics of professional support. In J.T. Reese and H. Goldstein (eds.), *Psychological services for law enforcement* (pp. 361–364). Washington, DC: US Government Printing Office.

McMains. M.J. (1986b). Post-shooting trauma: Principles from combat. In J.T. Reese and H. Goldstein (eds.), *Psychological services for law enforcement* (pp. 365–368). Washington, DC: US Government Printing Office.

McMains, M.J. (1991). The management and treatment of postshooting trauma. In J.T. Horn and C. Dunning (eds.), *Critical incidents in policing* (rev. ed., pp. 191–198). Washington, DC: Federal Bureau of Investigation.

McMains, M.J. and Mullins, W.C. (1996). *Crisis negotiations: Managing critical incidents and situations in law enforcement and corrections.* Cincinnati: Anderson.

Meadows, R.J. and Trostle, L.C. (1988). A study of police misconduct and litigation: Findings and implications. *Journal of Contemporary Criminal Justice, 4,* 77–92.

Milgram, N. and Hobfoll, S. (1986). Generalizations from theory and practice in war-related stress. In N. Milgram (ed.), *Stress and coping in times of war* (pp. 22–41). New York: Brunner/Mazel.

Miller, L. (1995). Tough guys: Psychotherapeutic strategies with law enforcement and emergency services personnel. *Psychotherapy, 32,* 592–600.

Miller, L. (1998). *Shocks to the system: Psychotherapy of traumatic disability syndromes.* New York: Norton.

Miller, L. (1999a). Critical incident stress debriefing: Clinical applications and new directions. *International Journal of Emergency Mental Health, 1,* 253–265.

Miller, L. (1999b). Psychotherapeutic intervention strategies with law enforcement and emergency services personnel. In L. Territo and J.D. Sewell (eds.), *Stress management in law enforcement* (pp. 317–332). Durham: Carolina Academic Press.

Miller, L. (2000). Law enforcement traumatic stress: Clinical syndromes and intervention strategies. *Trauma Response, 6,* 15–20.

Miller, L. (2003). Police personalities: Understanding and managing the problem officer. *The Police Chief,* May, 53–60.

Miller, L. (2004). Good cop – bad cop: Problem officers, law enforcement culture, and strategies for success. *Journal of Police and Criminal Psychology, 19,* 30–48.

Miller, L. (2005a). Command leadership under fire. *Law and Order,* June, 26.

Miller, L. (2005b). Hostage negotiation: Psychological principles and practices. *International Journal of Emergency Mental Health, 7,* 277–298.

Miller, L. (2006a). Critical incident stress debriefing for law enforcement: Practical models and special applications. *International Journal of Emergency Mental Health, 8,* 189–201.

Miller, L. (2006b). Officer-involved shooting: Reaction patterns, response protocols, and psychological intervention strategies. *International Journal of Emergency Mental Health, 8,* 239–254.

Miller, L. (2006c). On the spot: Testifying in court for law enforcement officers. *FBI Law Enforcement Bulletin*, October, 1–6.

Miller, L. (2006d). Psychological principles and practices for superior law enforcement leadership. *The Police Chief*, October, 160–168.

Miller, L. (2006e). *Practical police psychology: Stress management and crisis intervention for law enforcement.* Springfield, IL: Charles C Thomas.

Miller, L. (2006f). Suicide by cop: Causes, reactions, and practical intervention strategies. *International Journal of Emergency Mental Health*, 8, 165–174.

Miller, L. (2007a). Line-of-duty death: Psychological treatment of traumatic bereavement in law enforcement. *International Journal of Emergency Mental Health*, 9, 13–23.

Miller, L. (2007b). The psychological fitness-for-duty evaluation. *FBI Law Enforcement Bulletin*, August, 10–16.

Miller, L. (2007c). Police families: Stresses, syndromes, and solutions. *American Journal of Family Therapy*, 35, 21–40.

Miller, L. (2008a). Military psychology and police psychology: Mutual contributions to crisis intervention and stress management. *International Journal of Emergency Mental Health*, 10, 9–26.

Miller, L. (2008b). When the best force is less force: Anticipating and defusing potential patrol perils. *ILEETA Use of Force Journal*, 8, 7–10.

Miller, L. (2008c). *Counseling crime victims: Practical strategies for mental health professionals.* New York: Springer.

Miller, L. (2008d). *METTLE: Mental toughness training for law enforcement.* Flushing, NY: Looseleaf Law Publications.

Miller, L. (2009). You're it! How to psychologically survive an internal investigation, disciplinary proceeding, or legal action in the police, fire, medical, mental health, legal, or emergency services professions. *International Journal of Emergency Mental Health*, 11, 185–190.

Miller, L. (2011). Cops in trouble: Helping officers cope with investigation, prosecution, or litigation. In J. Kitaeff and K. Cather (eds.), *Handbook of police psychology* (pp. 479–490). New York: Psychology Press.

Miller, L. (2012). *Criminal psychology: Nature, nurture, culture.* Springfield, IL: Charles C Thomas.

Miller, L. (2013). Military and law enforcement psychology: Cross-contributions to extreme stress management. In L.Territo and J.D. Sewell (eds.), *Stress management in law enforcement* (3rd ed., pp. 455–486). Durham, NC: Carolina Academic Press.

Miller, L. (2015a). Police officers in the legal system. In Clevenger, S.M.F., Miller, L., Moore, B.A & Freeman, A. (Eds.). *Behind the badge: A psychological treatment handbook for law enforcement officers* (pp. 171-183). New York: Routledge.

Miller, L. (2015b). Police officer stress: Syndromes and strategies for intervention. In Clevenger, S.M.F., Miller, L., Moore, B.A., and Freeman, A. (eds.), *Behind the badge: A psychological treatment handbook for law enforcement officers* (pp. 202–221). New York: Routledge.

Miller, L. (2015c). Managing mentally ill individuals: Recommendations for police officers. In Clevenger, S.M.F., Miller, L., Moore, B.A. and Freeman, A. (eds.), *Behind the badge: A psychological treatment handbook for law enforcement officers* (pp. 222–238). New York: Routledge.

Miller, L. (2015d). *Stress in policing: Syndromes and strategies.* Presentation to the President's Task Force on 21st Century Policing, Washington, DC, February 23.

Miller, L. (2015e). Why cops kill: The psychology of police deadly force encounters. *Aggression and Violent Behavior*, 22, 97–111.

Miller, L. (2015f). *Posttraumatic stress disorder and forensic psychology: Applications to civil and criminal law.* New York: Springer.

Mitchell, J.T. and Everly, G.S. (1996). *Critical incident stress debriefing: An operations manual for the prevention of traumatic stress among emergency services and disaster workers* (rev. ed.). Ellicott City: Chevron.

Mohandie, K. and Meloy, J.R. (2000). Clinical and forensic indicators of "suicide by cop." *Journal of Forensic Science*, 45, 384–389.

Nielsen, E. (1991). Traumatic incident corps: Lessons learned. In J. Reese, J. Horn, and C. Dunning (eds.), *Critical incidents in policing* (pp. 221–226). Washington, DC: US Government Printing Office.

Novy, M. (2012). Cognitive distortions during law enforcement shooting. *Activitas Nervosa Superior, 54,* 60–66.

Pasciak, A. (2015). *After the smoke clears: Surviving the police shooting – an analysis of the post-officer-involve shooting trauma.* Springfield, IL: Charles C Thomas.

Perrou, B. and Farrell, B. (2004). Officer-involved shootings: Case management and psychosocial investigations. In V. Lord (ed.), *Suicide by cop: Inducing officers to shoot* (pp. 239–242). Flushing: Looseleaf Law Publications.

Petrowski, T.D. (2002a). Use-of-force policies and training: A reasoned approach. Part 1. *FBI Law Enforcement Bulletin,* October, 25–32.

Petrowski, T.D. (2002b). Use-of-force policies and training: A reasoned approach. Part 2. *FBI Law Enforcement Bulletin,* November, 24–32.

Pinizzotto, A.J., Davis, E.F., and Miller, C.E. (2005). Suicide by cop: Defining a devastating dilemma. *FBI Law Enforcement Bulletin,* February, 8–20.

Regehr, C. and Bober, T. (2005). *In the line of Fire: Trauma in the emergency services.* New York: Oxford University Press.

Ross, Darrell L. (2013). Assessing lethal force liability decisions and human factors research. *Law Enforcement Executive Forum, 13,* 85–107.

Ross, Darrell L., Murphy, R.L., and Hazlett, M.H. (2012). Analyzing perceptions and misperceptions of police officers in lethal force virtual simulator scenarios. *Law Enforcement Executive Forum, 12,* 53–73.

Rostow, C.D. and Davis, R.D. (2004). *A handbook for psychological fitness-for-duty evaluations in law enforcement.* New York: Haworth.

Rudofossi, D. (2007). *Working with traumatized police officer-patients: A clinician's guide to complex PTSD syndromes in public safety personnel.* Amityville, NY: Baywood.

Russell, H.E. & Beigel, A. (1990). *Understanding human behavior for effective police work* (3rd ed.). New York: Basic Books.

Rynearson, E.K. (1988). The homicide of a child. In F.M. Ochberg (ed.), *Post-traumatic therapy and victims of violence* (pp. 213–224). New York: Brunner/Mazel.

Rynearson, E.K. (1994). Psychotherapy of bereavement after homicide. *Journal of Psychotherapy Practice and Research, 3,* 341–347.

Rynearson, E.K. (1996). Psychotherapy of bereavement after homicide: Be offensive. *In Session: Psychotherapy in Practice, 2,* 47–57.

Rynearson, E.K. and McCreery, J.M. (1993). Bereavement after homicide: A synergism of trauma and loss. *American Journal of Psychiatry, 150,* 258–261.

Sewell, J.D. (1986). Administrative concerns in law enforcement stress management. In J.T. Reese and H.A. Goldstein (eds.), *Psychological services for law enforcement* (pp. 189–193). Washington, DC: FBI.

Solomon, R.M. (1991). The dynamics of fear in critical incidents: Implications for training and treatment. In J.T. Reese, J.M. Horn, and C. Dunning (eds.), *Critical incidents in policing* (pp. 347–358). Washington, DC: Federal Bureau of Investigation.

Solomon, R.M. (1995). Critical incident stress management in law enforcement. In G.S. Everly (ed.), *Innovations in disaster and trauma psychology: Applications in emergency services and disaster response* (pp. 123–157). Ellicott City: Chevron.

Solomon, R.M. and Horn, (1986). Post-shooting traumatic reactions: A pilot study. In J.T. Reese and H. Goldstein (eds.), *Psychological services for law enforcement* (pp. 383–393). Washington, DC: US Government Printing Office.

Solomon, R.M. and Mastin, P. (1999). The emotional aftermath of the Waco raid: Five years revisited. In J.M. Violanti and D. Paton (eds.), *Police trauma: Psychological aftermath of civilian combat* (pp. 113–123). Springfield, IL: Charles C. Thomas.

Somodevilla, S.A. (1986). Post-shooting trauma: Reactive and proactive treatment. In J.T. Reese and H. Goldstein (eds.), *Psychological Services for Law Enforcement* (pp. 395–398). Washington, DC: US Government Printing Office.

Sprang, G. and McNeil, J. (1995). *The many faces of bereavement: The nature and treatment of natural, traumatic, and stigmatized grief.* New York: Brunner/Mazel.

Twersky-Glasner, A. (2005). Police personality: What is it and why are they like that? *Journal of Police and Criminal Psychology, 20,* 56–67.

Wester, S.R. and Lyubelsky, J. (2005). Supporting the thin blue line: Gender-sensitive therapy with male police officers. *Professional Psychology: Research and Practice, 36,* 51–58.

White, M.D. and Klinger, D. (2012). Contagious fire? An empirical assessment of the problem of multi-shooter, multi-shot deadly force incidents in police work. *Crime and Delinquency, 58,* 196–221.

Williams. M.B. (1999). Impact of duty-related death on officers' children: Concepts of death, trauma reactions, and treatment. In J.M. Violanti and D. Paton (eds.), *Police trauma: Psychological aftermath of civilian combat* (pp. 159–174). Springfield, IL: Charles C. Thomas.

Williams, T. (1991). Counseling disabled law enforcement officers. In J.T. Reese, J.M. Horn and C. Dunning (eds.), *Critical incidents in policing* (pp. 377–386). Washington, DC: Federal Bureau of Investigation.

Wittrup, R.G. (1986). Police shooting – An opportunity for growth or loss of self. In J.T. Reese and H. Goldstein (eds.), *Psychological services for law enforcement* (pp. 405–408). Washington, DC: US Government Printing Office.

Zeling, M. (1986). Research needs in the study of post-shooting trauma. In J.T. Reese and H.A. Goldstein (eds.), *Psychological services for law enforcement* (pp. 409–410). Washington, DC: USGPO.

Part 3

Consequences of stress in policing

8 How police detectives deal with policy alienation in the investigation of human exploitation crimes

Reinforcing or counterbalancing fatalism

Kim Loyens

Introduction

Police detectives investigate several types of law-breaking, such as human trafficking, smuggling of drugs and weapons, and violent crimes. As typical street-level bureaucrats, they directly interact with citizens and have the discretion to not only implement but also shape public policies (Hupe *et al.*, 2015). In performing their daily work, they are not only restricted by laws and procedures, but also by limited resources and time (Lipsky, 1980). This chapter aims to understand what happens when police detectives experience frustration as a result of these restrictions. What if their activities do not lead to law-breaking being discovered and/or stopped? What do they do when feeling powerless towards criminals who exploit legal loopholes? What if they lack legal tools to help the victims they want to protect, or if the laws they have to enforce increase injustice?

The police culture literature partly addresses police officers' experience with such frustrations. Research in this tradition shows that police officers are vulnerable to moral cynicism because of a discrepancy between what they aim to do and what they can realistically accomplish (van Buuren and den Boer, 2008). Cynicism can also result from "the frequent encounters with lawbreakers" (Loyens, 2014: 145–146). Because police detectives often see "the worst side of humanity" and are "exposed to a steady diet of wrongdoing" (Goldstein, 1975: 25), they develop a constant attitude of suspicion that cannot be easily switched off (Reiner, 2000). Combined with their strong moral mission to fight crime and safeguard social order, the police consider themselves to be the "thin blue line" (Chan, 1996). Protecting the public from criminals is central in this moral mission (Crank, 1997), if necessary with illegal means (Reiner, 1992; Loyens, 2014). However, if they perceive citizens to be untrustworthy, for example when victims do not fit their "ideal" victim profile (Christie, 1986), they might even develop cynicism towards general citizens.

The "policy alienation" concept in the implementation literature also covers some of the frustrations of frontline officers mentioned above. Tummers and colleagues (2009) stress that policy alienation consists of two dimensions: being policy powerlessness and policy meaninglessness. The powerlessness dimension refers to "the expectancy or probability held by the individual that his own behaviour cannot determine the occurrence of the outcomes, or reinforcements, he seeks" (Seeman, 1959: 784), while the meaninglessness dimension is linked to "a professional's perception of the contribution the policy makes to a greater purpose" (Tummers *et al.*, 2009: 689). When street-level bureaucrats consider the contribution of the policy they need to implement to the general interest to be limited, then they experience policy meaninglessness. While previous studies in this tradition led to the identification of organizational factors that influence policy alienation

(Tummers *et al.*, 2009) and explanations of how policy alienation impacts change willingness (Tummers, 2011), more research is needed on how street-level bureaucrats cope with the tensions and frustrations that result from policy alienation.

This chapter aims to deepen our understanding of how police detectives deal with policy alienation. It starts from a previously developed exploratory model of how street-level bureaucrats respond to policy meaninglessness in their interaction with human exploitation victims (Loyens, 2015), based on ethnographic research (Loyens, 2012a). This model is further validated using data about police officers interacting with human exploitation suspects and theoretically grounded by means of grid-group cultural theory (Douglas, 1978), which frames such frustrations in terms of fatalism. Hence, this chapter aims to answer the question of how police detectives in human exploitation investigative teams deal with fatalism they experience in the interaction with victims and suspects. The central argument is that some responses to policy alienation reinforce feelings of powerlessness and meaninglessness, which leads to demotivation and apathy that are typical for fatalism. Other responses enable police detectives to stop feeling alienated from the policy they implement, and thus counterbalance the negative emotions policy alienation brings about. The next part describes what is already known about fatalism based on previous police research. Then the preliminary model of police officers coping with policy meaninglessness is introduced and adapted by embedding it in the grid-group cultural theory framework. This adapted model will be empirically validated on the basis of a case study in two Belgian human exploitation investigative teams. The subsequent parts explain the methods used and the empirical findings. In the discussion, hypotheses are formulated about the expected effects of the identified ways of dealing with policy alienation. This chapter concludes with a brief summary of the new model and suggestions for future research.

What is known about fatalism in policing based on previous research

Cynicism as an element of police culture

In classic police culture studies interactions between police officers and law-breakers are presented in a rather negative way. Police officers are said to look at these people with suspicion. An often-heard explanation is their frequent encounters with law-breakers or the "dark side" of society. Therefore, police work is often perceived as "dirty work" in "a jungle" where crime, corruption, and brutality are part of everyday reality (e.g. Westley, 1970; McLaughlin, 2007), and police officers should be constantly aware of potential threats to their safety (Van Maanen, 1974; Skolnick, 1975; Brown, 1981; Crank, 1997). Reiner (1978) explains that police officers develop a "hard skin of bitterness, seeing all social trends in apocalyptic terms with the police as a beleaguered minority to be overrun by the forces of barbarism." Researchers who studied police culture claim that this attitude of suspicion and caution leads to social isolation, because they consider themselves to be part of a special occupational group. They are the "good guys" fighting the "bad guys", which forms the basis for an "us-versus-them" attitude towards criminals (Westley, 1970; Paoline, 2003). Suspicion and scepticism can be highly functional when doing police work, because these attitudes enable officers to be constantly aware of potential threats to their safety (Reiner, 2000; Loyens, 2014). However, they can also lead to extreme forms of cynicism and the perception that dealing with criminals is a game you can only win by bending or breaking the rules (Loyens, 2009). This has also been framed in terms of "noble cause corruption", in which police officers try to catch the "bad guys" by breaking what they perceive as ineffective and unjust rules (Reiner, 1992; Loyens, 2014). Police officers then believe they are allowed to disregard legal procedures if these seem to be ineffective to catch the "bad guys" (Reiner, 1992).

Moral mission and fatalism

Catching the "bad guys" is often inspired by a moral mission that most police officers have in common. Fighting crime and protecting the public from criminals are central elements in detectives' moral mission. They consider themselves to be the "thin blue line" (Chan, 1996) that keeps society safe from criminals and prevents chaos. This moral mission can lead to frustrations when police detectives feel unable to protect citizens from being victimized or to bring those responsible to justice. In other words, frustration results from a perceived discrepancy between what police officers aim to do and what they realistically can accomplish (van Buuren and den Boer, 2008), which relates to policy powerlessness in the policy alienation literature.

There is also evidence that the protective attitude towards citizens, based on police detectives' moral mission, sometimes shifts to cynicism towards these same citizens. The general street-level bureaucracy literature shows that frontline officers—such as police detectives—in their decision-making highly depend on their assessment of clients' trustworthiness. Street-level bureaucrats are, for example, not willing to "go an extra mile" if they feel clients dishonestly work the system (Maynard et al., 2010) or become sceptical when they do not fit the "ideal" victim profile (Christie, 1986). Particularly in human exploitation investigative teams, where detectives often do not have reliable information to check the stories of presumed victims, police detectives have to base their decision on whether or not they think these stories are trustworthy. Moreover, in such investigations, there is a risk that scepticism is particularly high among experienced detectives who habitually hear human exploitation stories (Loyens, 2012a; 2015), as argued in normalization theory (Cohen, 2001: 188–189): "What was once seen as disturbing and anomalous – a sense that things are not as they should be – now becomes normal, even tolerable."

This is further complicated by human exploitation victims using strategies to either exaggerate or downplay their exploitation experience. On the one hand, genuine victims who wish to file a complaint against their traffickers might be tempted to exaggerate what they experienced and its consequences for their personal well-being to make sure authorities will take action (Pitman, 2010). On the other hand, genuine victims who fear retaliation from their traffickers might refuse to tell their full story, giving the impression that they are willing adults who choose to be exploited (Farrell et al., 2015). Previous research in the U.S. shows that police officers sometimes categorize human exploitation victims as offenders, blaming them for lacking a legal permit or voluntarily cooperating with their exploiters (Farrell et al., 2014), even though the latter does not exclude the possibility that these people are exploited (van der Leun and Vervoorn, 2004). Also in Belgium, cases in which undocumented victims of human exploitation do not feel victimized—because their working conditions are better than in their home country—are sometimes not investigated or prosecuted (Debacker and Loyens, 2014), because police detectives and prosecutors doubt whether these victims want or need saving. Such negative perceptions of victims often result in both policy meaninglessness ("victim does not deserve to be saved") and policy powerlessness ("victim cannot be saved if (s)he does not cooperate").

A model of dealing with fatalism in policing

How policy alienation leads to fatalism

Drawing on Seeman's (1959) concept of subjective work alienation, Tummers and colleagues (2009: 686) define policy alienation as the "general cognitive state of psychological disconnection from the policy programme being implemented". Police detectives in human exploitation investigative teams experience policy powerlessness when they lack legal tools to successfully detect and investigate human exploitation. Policy meaninglessness is, for these types of police officers, manifested in the perception that the investigative steps they take do not lead to societal problems being solved, resulting in offenders not being stopped and victims not being saved. This type of policy alienation is also linked to the internal conflicts police detectives experience when, in their perception, activities they perform are beneficial for the police organization (e.g. in terms of organizational accountability, because every arrest of an illegal person "boosts" the numbers), but not for society as a whole or human exploitation victims in particular.

These forms of policy alienation are strongly related to fatalism in grid-group cultural theory. This theory was originally developed in anthropology (Douglas, 1982), but subsequently applied in other research domains (Mars, 1982; Jensen, 1998; Thompson *et al.*, 1990; Hendriks, 1999; Maesschalck, 2004a; Loyens, 2012b; Loyens, 2013). The central hypothesis of the theory is that individuals' behaviour is shaped by characteristics of the organization they are part of, which can be described on the basis of the "grid" and "group" dimensions (Thompson *et al.*, 1990). "Grid" refers to the extent to which an individual's life is bounded by externally imposed rules, prescriptions, and regulations (Douglas, 1982; Thompson *et al.*, 1990). "Group" stands for the incorporation of an individual into a bounded unit of actors or the extent to which individual choice is constrained by group choice (Hood, 1998; Verweij *et al.*, 2006). The combination of the two dimensions leads to four types: hierarchy (high grid, high group), egalitarianism (low grid, high group), individualism (low grid, low group), and fatalism (high grid, low group). In hierarchy, rules prescribe roles and positions. Each individual has its role with accompanying responsibilities (O'Riordan and Jordan, 1999; Breed, 2007; Smullen, 2007). In egalitarianism, group negotiation and aiming for consensus are central (Rayner, 1986; Smullen, 2007). Individual interests are subjected to the welfare of the group (Breed, 2007). Individualism implies a competitive environment where individuals are strategic entrepreneurs and status is derived from personal skills, efforts, and results (Hood, 1998). In fatalism, the central focus of this chapter, individuals are (or feel) highly bound by a system of rules that is beyond their control, that they do not agree with and against which they cannot take collective action, due to a lack of group affiliations (Vaughan, 2002). The fatalistic world is considered a lottery, characterized by unpredictability, where fairness is not to be found and in which there are no possibilities to change it for the better (Verweij *et al.*, 2006).

Reinforcing or counterbalancing fatalism

Grid-group cultural theory adds that each way of organizing has its own built-in weaknesses or blind-spots, and might thus become excessive, when not being counterbalanced by other ways of organizing (Hood, 1998; 6, 2003). In other words, a certain "dose" of all types should be present to avoid fatalism constantly being reinforced, resulting in desperation and isolation (Schwartz, 1991; Hendriks, 2004). Reinforcing and counterbalancing mechanisms regularly shift in an organization, as a result of "surprise" or "the discrepancy

Table 8.1 Four ways of dealing with fatalism and their expected effects

Way of dealing with fatalism	GGCT style	Expected effect
(1) Acquiescence	Fatalism	Reinforcing fatalism
(2) Just do your job	Hierarchical coping	Counterbalancing fatalism
(3) Bond with the victim	Egalitarian coping	Counterbalancing fatalism
(4) Get your share	Individualistic coping	Counterbalancing fatalism

between the expected and the actual" (Thompson *et al.*, 1990: 3). Surprises occur when organization members, in this study police detectives in human exploitation investigative teams, are repeatedly confronted with the limitations or negative side effects of one way of organizing (Jensen, 1998).

This chapter focuses on how police detectives deal with fatalism they experience in their daily work, and whether their responses to fatalism reinforce or counterbalance feelings of policy powerlessness and meaninglessness. The central argument is that when police detectives use a fatalistic coping style, such as resigning themselves to their fate or burying their heads in the sand, fatalism is reinforced, leading to more fatalistic behaviour that in its turn reinforces a fatalistic way of organizing and thus more feelings of powerlessness and meaninglessness. On the other hand, when police detectives are "surprised" because the fatalistic way of organizing does not lead to rule-breaking being stopped or societal problems being addressed, and therefore respond with hierarchical, individualistic, or egalitarian behaviour, they try to counterbalance the excesses of fatalism by bringing in elements of other types of behaviour. While previous research led to the identification of responses to policy alienation, these have not been embedded in a theoretical explanatory model that can explain why certain responses are used in specific situations and what their respective effects are. Table 8.1 shows four ways of dealing with fatalism that were found in a study on how police detectives deal with policy meaninglessness in the interaction with human exploitation victims (Loyens, 2015).[1] These responses to policy alienation will, in this chapter, be embedded in grid-group cultural theory and broadened to policy alienation (including both policy meaninglessness and powerlessness) in police–client interactions (including both victims and suspects of human exploitation).

Methodology

The findings in this chapter result from a comparative ethnographic study in two human exploitation investigative teams of the Belgian federal Police and two field organizations of a Belgian Labour Inspection. In this chapter, only the data of the police organizations will be used. The police officers in this study conduct investigations on human exploitation and trafficking in human beings. They cooperate with a public prosecutor specialized in these matters or with an examining magistrate if special coercive measures are needed, such as a telephone tap, infiltration, systematic observation or arrest. Police officers in these units first discuss the general strategy with the public prosecutor, after which they take the necessary investigative steps. The police do not have the discretion to give a warning or offer perpetrators the chance to rectify the violation.[2] When they encounter illegal workers during inspections, they should arrest them to await the decision of the Public Service of Immigration Affairs.

Data collection in this study was done by using several ethnographic research methods (Hammersley and Atkinson, 1995). Particularly, data were collected in the period 2009–2011 through observation, informal conversation, and in-depth interviewing with 14 police detectives, six supervisors and two public prosecutors.[3] The observations and informal conversations were, on the one hand, aimed at gaining insight into the work context of police detectives in these investigative teams. Particular attention went to analysing how they perceived their job, which factors contributed to policy meaninglessness and powerlessness and how they responded to these forms of policy alienation. For this purpose, the researcher accompanied the respondents in as many different situations as possible (e.g. house searches, interrogations, meetings, and informal meals), during the day and night, on weekdays, and at the weekend. The observations and informal conversations were summarized in detailed reports. In the in-depth interviews, on the other hand, police detectives were asked to think about investigations in which they experienced policy meaninglessness and powerlessness. They were asked to give a detailed narrative of the situation and how they dealt with it. The interviews were recorded and transcribed verbatim. The combination of these qualitative data collection methods resulted in rich data and "thick description" (Geertz, 1973). The data were analysed with the software Nvivo, using topic coding and analytic coding (Richards and Morse, 2007). Because the findings in this chapter result from a case study in a relatively small number of research settings, they are not necessarily representative for how police detectives in general respond to policy alienation. The goal of this qualitative study is therefore not generalization to a wider population, but theory-building by developing hypotheses that can be tested in future research (Smaling, 2003; Yin, 2003).

A Belgian case study on fatalism in human exploitation investigations

This part first explains why police detectives experience fatalism in dealing with victims and suspects of human exploitation. It seems that there exist various sources of policy powerlessness and meaninglessness, such as an ambiguous and seemingly ineffective Immigration Law, lack of victims' cooperation, deprioritization of investigating human exploitation crimes, and suspects exploiting legal loopholes.

Various sources of policy alienation

Policy alienation in the interaction with exploitation victims mainly results from their unwillingness to be saved from their exploiters. According to article 61 of the Belgian Immigration Law of 15 September 2006 and the ministerial circular on the multidisciplinary approach in human exploitation affairs of 26 September 2008, an illegal person who is exploited can be officially recognized as a victim of human exploitation under three conditions: (1) they have to file a complaint with the police against the perpetrators, (2) they have to accept support from a recognized refugee centre, and (3) they have to abandon the network in which they are exploited. Illegal workers or prostitutes in Belgium who comply with these conditions can obtain a permanent residence permit if the information they provide leads to a successful investigation.

However, some victims of human exploitation do not want to comply with these obligations because they do not feel victimized. Although their living and working conditions are below Belgian legal standards, they prefer being exploited in Belgium above returning to their home country where living and working conditions are even worse. These victims argue that in Belgium they at least have shelter and earn some money (albeit below the minimum wage) that they can send to their family who remain in their home country. A police officer in this study explains that victims nowadays are treated much better than they were in the past, which confirms previous empirical research (van der Leun and Vervoorn, 2004) and is obviously a good evolution. The backside of the coin is, however, that victims who are treated well rarely file a complaint against their exploiters, which makes the police feel powerless to detect and dismantle networks of human trafficking. Other reasons for victims not filing a complaint with the police are fear of retaliation, a relationship of dependency with their exploiters, distrust of law enforcement officers, and fear of repatriation (Bales, 2002; Lebov, 2012). When exploited illegal workers do not cooperate with the police, the only legal option police officers have is detaining them and contacting the Public Service of Immigration Affairs, who most likely will order forced deportation to their home country or give them an order to leave Belgium within five days. By not accepting the offer of being officially recognized as an exploitation victim, these victims thus risk secondary victimization by actors within the legal system (Adams, 2011; Rathgeber, 2002). Police officers in this study refer to these policy measures as "dirty" work, in which they (sometimes unwillingly) have a share. A case in point is the arrest of three Romanian prostitutes during an inspection of a brothel. Because these victims did not want to file a complaint against the manager of the brothel or their traffickers, the police officers had no other option than to arrest them and await the decision of the Public Service of Immigration Affairs. This police officer states:

> And I think it's so pathetic, because you know, we do an inspection and the only result is that those girls are put on a plane tomorrow. Tonight they have to sleep in a stinking cell in police zone X. [. . .] Those cells stink like hell. And we have to put the victims in there! [. . .] Then, you pick them up in a van, almost like the Nazis transported the Jews by train. You drop them off at the transit centre and there they have to stay behind barbed wire in order to be deported.

Another source of policy alienation is the vicious circle of repatriation. Police detectives in this study explain that many victims return to Belgium shortly after being repatriated, either on their own initiative or with the help of their traffickers. They then return to the exploitative situation they were "saved" from, until the police apprehend them again. Police detectives feel powerless to stop this vicious circle, which discourages them to keep doing their work in accordance with legal rules and procedures. They might thus be tempted to bend the rules because the formal procedures do not lead to desirable ends.

Also in the interaction with suspects of human exploitation, police detectives experience feelings of powerlessness and meaninglessness. These are partly related to the difficult relation with exploitation victims mentioned above. Unlike crimes such as vandalism, burglary, and murder, human exploitation is difficult to detect (Winterdyk and Reichel, 2010). Victims are often unable to speak up because they are locked up or otherwise controlled by criminals who withhold their legal documents, threaten them or their family, and lure them with money or other kinds of benefits they would no longer enjoy if they talk to the police. Being dependent on witness reports by these victims, police detectives have limited options to stop the criminals if their victims are unable or unwilling to report them. In addition, police detectives in this study perceive the sentences for human exploitation to be extremely low, especially if they are unable to prove that the crime is committed by a criminal organization. Moreover, police detectives in this study state that manpower in human exploitation investigative teams in different Belgian regions has decreased, which makes them believe investigating human exploitation crimes has been deprioritized by policymakers. This can be illustrated by the following quote of a police detective:

> I would like to make the prediction that in two or three years this crime all of a sudden will become a priority. Then it will be a "hot issue" [. . .] because we will have found victims here and there, some dead people in a house or a work place, and then it will become a top priority once more. But by then we will have lost all expertise, because it is being deprioritized now. And then we will have to start all over again, and rebuild what we have been working on since 2004.

Within the context of the current migration crisis in which organized human trafficking plays an important role (Melchior, 2015; Sherwood, 2015), this statement made in 2010 uncovers a fundamental problem in the fight against human exploitation in Belgium.

A final source of policy powerlessness is police detectives' concern that they lack legal tools to successfully detect and investigate human exploitation. They refer to legal loopholes that criminals exploit and laws that are outdated, even before they have been issued as a result of rapid technological developments.

Police officers dealing with fatalism in the investigation of human exploitation

The police detectives in this study deal with these various sources of policy alienation in four different ways. The first response is acquiescence, which reinforces feelings of meaninglessness and powerlessness, because the response itself is characterized by fatalism. The other responses ("just do your job", "get your share" and "bond with the victim") have in common that they are aimed at counterbalancing policy alienation by bringing in elements of non-fatalistic ways of organizing. This part shows how police detectives in this study use these four responses to deal with policy alienation in the interaction with victims and offenders they are confronted with when investigating human exploitation. Table 8.2 gives an overview of these ways of dealing with fatalism and illustrations of how police detectives in this study used them.

Acquiescence

The first way of dealing with policy alienation in this study is acquiescence. When using this response to fatalism, detectives reconcile themselves to the fact that the investigative steps they take only have little impact, which relates to *the skill of powerlessness* (Inauguration by Michel van Eeten, 2010) and the coping style "acceptance" (Skinner *et al.*, 2003). Acquiescence is shown when police detectives stop caring that exploitation victims return to their exploiters shortly after being repatriated or that suspects of human exploitation are released shortly after being arrested. By doing so they try to accept that their actions are ineffective, and convince themselves that they at least offered victims a helping hand and gave suspects the signal that their behaviour is not acceptable. When an investigation is stopped because there is a lack of evidence, detectives in this study often respond by: "You cannot win them all" or "You cannot save them [human exploitation victims] all." An often-heard phrase when another suspect of human exploitation is released too quickly is: "We will see him again in due time." Police detectives explain that this attitude of acquiescence helps them to put things in perspective and to not worry too much about the results of their work. However, when such experiences are piled up, and their powerlessness is constantly confirmed, acquiescence might lead to extreme forms of cynicism, as illustrated in the following quote: "In fact we are garbage collectors; we remove the trash [referring to suspects of crime] from the street."

Just do your job

Police detectives sometimes aim to reduce feelings of powerlessness and meaninglessness by framing their work as "just doing your job". They explain that every agency has its role and responsibilities. Even though their individual actions do not always lead to the aspired results, they should just do their job, and not that of other agencies. They for example do not make the laws, but enforce them. Therefore, as some police detectives explain, if you do not personally agree with legal procedures, you should just comply because you are part of a larger law enforcement system. This response to fatalism is linked to a sense of duty or an inner obligation to having to perform one's role, as is typical in the grid-group cultural theory-type hierarchy.

A police detective explains that in the interaction with victims, just doing your job is sometimes the only thing you can do when you do not agree with policy decisions: "I am not convinced that victims should be put in a police cell like criminals, but the procedure

Table 8.2 Police officers dealing with fatalism in the investigation of human exploitation

Ways of dealing with fatalism	Illustrations
Reinforcing fatalism	
1. Acquiescence (fatalistic response)	• Victims: Not caring about victims returning to their exploiters shortly after being repatriated; "You cannot save them [victims] all." • Suspects: Not caring about suspects of human exploitation being released shortly after being arrested; "You cannot win them all", "We will see him [suspect] again in due time."
Counterbalancing fatalism	
2. Just do your job (hierarchical response)	• Victims: "I am not convinced that victims should be put in a police cell like criminals, but the procedure prescribes it, so I comply"; "If illegal prostitutes refuse to give a statement, then you cannot save them; all you can do is let them be repatriated"; When other agencies are present, there is no room for negotiation. • Suspects: "It is not my role to get them convicted, but to investigate the case."
3. Bond with the victim (egalitarian response)	• Victims: "What I prefer to do is keeping them here, trying to bond with them, hoping that when they see something go wrong in the criminal underworld or themselves experience something they don't like, that they will say 'I will call X'." • Suspects: partnering with victims in the fight against human exploitation, implying the risk of tunnel vision and lack of neutrality.
4. Get your share (individualistic response)	• Victims: "We didn't solve organized crime or round up a gang, but here they say: 'Yes! We are rid of the zero in the administrative arrest list'"; Bend the rules if it leads to better results. • Suspects: Outsmarting the criminals by withholding information.

prescribes it, so I comply." By referring to the procedure, which is part of a legitimate system of rules and laws, individual police detectives do not feel personally responsible for being unable to really help victims. They consider themselves to be only a cog in the system. In addition to the role of policymakers, they also refer to victims' responsibility. They receive help if and only if they cooperate, but if they do not cooperate they have to bear the consequences themselves. A police detectives states: "If illegal prostitutes refuse to give a statement, then you cannot save them; all you can do is let them be repatriated."

Powerlessness to catch and bring to justice known criminals is often dealt with in a similar way. Police officers explain that they are not solely responsible for undesirable outcomes of their investigation, because other agencies are involved as well. The example is given that detectives sometimes suggest to the public prosecutor or examining magistrate that they should allow them to use a certain investigative measure. If they do not agree and the investigation fails, police detectives often do not blame themselves for the failure. Likewise, a detective explains that when their investigation does not lead to a conviction or only to a light punishment, he displaces responsibility by saying: "It is not my role to get them convicted, but to investigate the case."

Bond with the victim

Police detectives sometimes deal with policy alienation by responding in an egalitarian way. "Bonding with the victim" means that detectives consider victims to be partners in catching the bad guys. As explained above, police officers who encounter illegal persons who claim to be exploited but do not want to file a complaint have to arrest them and await the decision of the Public Service of Immigration Affairs. However, by doing so victims are often condemned to return to worse living conditions than they were subjected to in Belgium and the detectives feel powerless to take action against their exploiters. Therefore, police detectives sometimes try a different approach, as explained in the following quote:

> If I enter a brothel and I see three girls who like working there, whose freedom is not restricted, who have come to Belgium on their own free will . . . and they don't want to leave, they feel ok, they feel fine, they do not feel exploited, they live in a good atmosphere [. . .] then arresting them and letting them be repatriated is not useful for me. I don't gain anything from it. If I arrest them, the manager of the brothel will probably not be prosecuted, neither will the pimp, but in the end those girls will be screwed the most. What I prefer to do is keeping them here, trying to bond with them, hoping that when they see something go wrong in the criminal underworld or themselves experience something they don't like, that they will say "I will call X [respondent]."

This way of dealing with policy alienation has implications for interaction with human exploitation suspects. By breaking the rules of the game, detectives seem to take sides, while they should in fact retain their neutrality in investigating crime. Taking sides could lead to the often-discussed "tunnel vision" in which detectives are prejudiced and therefore unable to remain objective (Westmarland, 2005; Findley and Scott, 2006).

Get your share

In the attempt to reduce feelings of powerlessness and meaninglessness, police detectives sometimes get opportunistic, which relates to grid-group cultural theory-type individualism. "Get your share" means that police detectives try to gain something from a situation in which they feel powerless or their role to be meaningless (e.g. because they cannot address victims' needs or catch criminals who are suspected of human exploitation). By trying to get something out of it, they try to compensate for the frustrations those situations bring about. When human exploitation victims are arrested as illegal persons, and thus not treated as genuine victims, some detectives refer to the beneficial effect of the arrest in terms of performance indicators. This is, however, not appreciated by all, as is shown in the following quote:

> What I am averse to is that a colleague here then states: "Oh wow you have got three administrative arrests!" No, we have nothing, Kim. There are two options. One, they come back and continue working in prostitution. Two, they don't come back, but start working in prostitution in X (Eastern Europe country), for a lot less money with nastier men. We didn't solve organized crime or round up a gang, but here they say: "Yes! We are rid of the 'zero' in the administrative arrest list."

Getting your share could also mean that rules are bent to save victims who do not (entirely) comply with the procedure to be officially recognized as a victim of human exploitation (see the three conditions explained above). Then police detectives try to bargain with victims, for example by encouraging them to give any information (officially or off the record) about their exploiters in exchange for not having to leave the network in which they are exploited. Detectives consider it a win–win if the information victims give helps them to catch the bad guys. Interestingly, detectives explain there is no room for negotiation with victims when representatives of other agencies, such as the local police or the Labour Inspection, are present. It seems that in these situations they feel obliged to stick to the official role they have in the law enforcement system (which fits the hierarchical "Just do your job" response). Only in those teams that regularly do joint inspections or investigations do police detectives feel comfortable deviating from official procedures if they think it would be better for their investigation.

Opportunism is also relevant in the interaction with human exploitation suspects. As explained above (p.000), policy alienation in human exploitation investigations is often related to criminals exploiting legal loopholes. Many detectives in this study explain that their response to that is outsmarting the criminals by withholding information, because information is power. One way to do so is separating an investigation about a criminal organization into several smaller case files focused on each individual suspect, who is investigated as part of that criminal organization. When someone in the organization is arrested, and is given the right to read the case file on the basis of which he was arrested, a separate case file will only grant him access to investigative steps that were taken towards him, but not towards other persons in that criminal organization, even though it is part of the same investigation. While one could argue that this strategy harms suspects' rights of defence, police detectives state that not using this strategy would lead to a failure of most investigations of criminal organizations, because arrested suspects are then informed that other persons in their criminal organization are put under surveillance or telephone tap, and will warn them.

In investigations in which police agencies of different countries cooperate in dismantling a criminal organization that commits human exploitation crimes, this splitting strategy is particularly useful. When, for example, police detectives in country A are doing a telephone tap on several members of a criminal organization and hear information about crimes they are planning, they often decide to informally share this information with a police agency in country B that intercepts the suspect by arresting him. The police agency in country B then reports to the police agency in country A that the suspect is arrested. Because the arrest is not made by the police agency in country A, the case file does not need to be opened and the suspect will not find out that his telephone was tapped. The result is that the investigation can be continued as planned because the other members of the criminal organization are not necessarily warned. In other words, splitting an investigation enables the police to conceal information about their investigative steps, by which the police try to stay one step ahead of the criminals.

Withholding information also occurs when suspects are put under surveillance. A detective explains that in some situations police detectives do not report everything they see during observations, because particular events in fact force the police to intervene. By not reporting them, the events seem to not have happened so the investigation can be continued as planned, as shown in the following quote, with the risk of harming victims who are involved:

> [. . .] yes I think sometimes not everything which has been observed is put on paper, and they don't put it in the report because if they do they need to intervene [e.g. to rescue victims involved] and when your investigation is not finished yet you could jeopardize the whole operation by intervening too soon. [. . .] Then they keep it in mind as information that is "nice to know", and they try to launder it later.

Similarly, "paper-trail" evidence of rule-bending is avoided by performing observations during more than five consecutive days without a warrant, even though that is obligatory. A detective explains that this rule can be easily broken by not writing down when the observation period started and starting to write things down when relevant events are observed (even though this happens on the sixth observation day, for example). Some detectives consider this acceptable if it leads to catching criminals.

Discussion

The main goal of this chapter was to further develop an exploratory model of how police officers deal with policy alienation. This was done in a twofold manner. First, the model was empirically validated. While the previous model focused on how police detectives respond to policy alienation in their interaction with human exploitation victims, this chapter has shown that these responses are also relevant in situations where police detectives deal with policy alienation in the interaction with suspects. Second, the model was embedded in the grid-group cultural theory framework, which allows for the formulation of theoretically grounded hypotheses than can be tested in future research. Specifically, the analysis showed that, depending on the situation or the individual, fatalism is dealt with in different ways. Sometimes police detectives respond with behaviour that shows elements of fatalism, as was the case in acquiescence, while the other responses show characteristics of other cultural types. Figure 8.1 shows that, in grid-group cultural theory terms, a fatalistic response to fatalism (response number 1) operates as a reinforcing mechanism because this behaviour can be expected to increase fatalism. Contrarily, when dealing with fatalism otherwise (response numbers 2, 3, and 4) a counterbalancing mechanism is introduced, because individuals want to change the current situation (Thompson *et al.*, 1990).

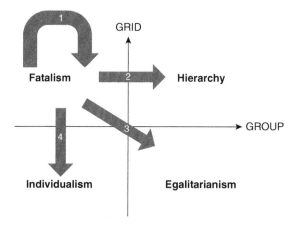

Figure 8.1 Reinforcing and counterbalancing mechanisms when dealing with fatalism.

Conclusion

This chapter aimed to increase the understanding of how police detectives deal with policy powerlessness and meaninglessness, which are two dimensions of policy alienation. Because policy alienation relates to fatalism in grid-group cultural theory, this chapter also aimed to combine insights from the literature on policy alienation and grid-group cultural theory. The case study in this chapter focused on detectives in human exploitation investigative teams. Fatalism is, in this type of police work, manifested in victims unwilling to cooperate with the police, while their statement is often crucial to successfully detect and collect evidence about criminal organizations that commit such crimes. In addition, police detectives state that investigating human exploitation crimes is deprioritized and that still too many legal loopholes exist for criminals to exploit. It is thus clear that police detectives in such teams are constantly faced with sources of policy alienation, making this an interesting case for this study.

Four responses to policy alienation were identified, one of which reinforces powerlessness and meaninglessness (i.e. acquiescence), while the other responses were aimed at regaining control and not being demotivated by policy alienation. In this study, some evidence was found that police detectives were indeed able to reduce feelings of powerlessness and meaninglessness, for example by blaming other agencies for their failures ("Just do your job") or by bending the rules ("Get your share"), while acquiescence in some cases resulted in extreme forms of cynicism that increase policy alienation. Because the data were collected in a specific time period, the long-term effects of these ways of dealing with fatalism, could not be analysed. More systematic longitudinal research is thus necessary to study the long-term effects of the various ways in which police detectives and other street-level bureaucrats deal with policy alienation. More insight is also needed into the respective risks of these responses, such as rule-breaking and tunnel vision, and how these can be avoided.

Notes

1 A fifth way of dealing with policy alienation, emotional habituation, was only relevant in the inspection cases and was therefore omitted in this chapter.

2 Article 40 of the Belgian Law of the Police Function and article 53 of the Belgian Code of Criminal Proceedings.
3 To protect the respondents' identity, neither the judicial district where the organizations are located nor individual characteristics (such as age or years of experience) of the respondents are mentioned. Male and female pronouns are used randomly. The respondents' quotes have been freely translated from Dutch by the researcher.

References

Adams, C. (2011). Re-trafficked victims: How a human rights approach can stop the cycle of re-victimization of sex trafficking victims. *The George Washington International Law Review*, 43, 201–234.

Bales, K. (2002). The social psychology of modern slavery. *Scientific American*, 286, 80–88.

Breed, K. (2007). *Bestuurscultuur en strategie. Een onderzoek naar de cognitieve kaart van topambtenaren*, Sdu uitgevers, Den Haag.

Brown, M. K. (1981). *Working the street: Police discretion and the dilemmas of reform*. New York: Russell Sage Foundation.

Chan, J. (1996). Changing police culture. *British Journal of Criminology*, 36, 109–134.

Christie, N. (1986). The ideal victim. In E. A. Fattah (ed.), *From crime policy to victim policy: Reorienting the justice system* (pp. 17–30). London: MacMillan.

Cohen, S. (2001). *States of denial. Knowing about atrocities and suffering*. Cambridge: Policy Press.

Crank, J. P. (1997). Celebrating agency culture: Engaging a traditional cop's heart in organizational change. In Q. C. Thurman and E. F. McGarrell (eds.), *Community policing in a rural setting* (pp. 49–57). Cincinnati: Anderson Publishing.

Debacker, J. and Loyens, K. (2014). Diversiteit in de opsporing en vervolging van economische uitbuiting. De interpretatieruimte onderzocht in twee kwalitatieve onderzoeksprojecten. *Panopticon: Tijdschrift voor Strafrecht, Criminologie en Forensisch Welzijnswerk*, 35, 8–26.

Douglas, M. (1978). *Cultural bias*. London: Royal Anthropological Institute.

Douglas, M. (1982). *In the active voice*. London: Routledge Kegan & Paul.

Farrell, A., Owens, C., and McDevitt, J. (2014). New laws but few cases: Understanding the challenges to the investigation and prosecution of human trafficking cases. *Crime, Law and Social Change*, 61, 139–168.

Farrell, A., Pfeffer, R., and Bright, K. (2015). Police perceptions of human trafficking. *Journal of Crime and Justice*, (ahead-of-print), DOI: 10.1080/0735648X.2014.995412.

Findley, K. A. and Scott, M. S. (2006). The multiple dimensions of tunnel vision in criminal cases. *Wisconsin Law Review*, 2, 1023.

Geertz, C. (1973). *The interpretation of cultures*. New York: Fontana.

Goldstein, H. (1975). *Police corruption: A perspective on its nature and control*. Washington, DC: Police Foundation.

Hammersley, M. and Atkinson, P. (1995). *Ethnography. Principles in practice*. London: Routledge.

Hendriks, F. (1999). The post-industrialising city: Political perspectives and cultural biases, *GeoJournal*, 47, 425–432.

Hendriks, F. (2004). The poison is the dose: Or how "more egalitarianism" may work in some places but not in all. *Innovation*, 17, 349–361.

Hood, C. (1998). *The art of the state. Culture, rhetoric, and public management*. Oxford: Clarendon Press.

Hupe P., Hill M., and Buffat A. (eds.) (2015). *Understanding street-level bureaucracy*. Bristol: Policy Press.

Jensen, L. (1998). Cultural theory and democratizing functional domains. The case of Danish housing. *Public Administration*, 76, 117–139.

Lebov, K. (2010). Human trafficking in Scotland. *European Journal of Criminology*, 7, 77–93.

Lipsky, M. (1980). *Street level bureaucracy: dilemmas of the individual in public services*. New York: Russell Sage Foundation.

Loyens, K. (2012a). Integrity secured. understanding ethical decision making among street-level bureaucrats in the Belgian labor inspection and federal police. (Doctoral dissertation to obtain the degree of Doctor in Criminology, KU Leuven).

Loyens, K. (2012b). Towards a custom-made whistleblowing policy: Using grid-group cultural theory to match policy measures to different styles of peer reporting. *Journal of Business Ethics* (DOI 10.1007/s10551-012-1344-0).

Loyens, K. (2013). Why police officers and labour inspectors (do not) blow the whistle: A grid group cultural theory perspective, *Policing: an international journal of police strategies and management*, 36, 27–50.

Loyens, K. (2015). Law enforcement and policy alienation: Coping by labour inspectors and federal police officers. In P. Hupe, M. Hill, and A. Buffat (eds.), *Understanding street-level bureaucracy* (pp. 99–114). Bristol: Policy Press.

Loyens, K. and Maesschalck, J. (2014). Police-public interactions: A grid-group cultural theory perspective. *Policing: An International Journal of Police Strategies and Management*, 37, 144–158.

Maesschalck, J. (2004a). Research note: A method for applying cultural theory in the study of organizations. *Innovation: the European Journal of Social Sciences*, 17, 377–386.

Maesschalck, J. (2004b). *Towards a public administration theory on public servant's ethics*. Leuven: Katholieke Universiteit Leuven.

Mars, G. (1982). *Cheats at work. An anthropology of workplace crime*. Aldershot: Ashgate.

Maynard-Moody, S. and Portillo, S. (2010). Street-level bureaucracy theory. In R. F. Durant (ed.), *The Oxford handbook of American bureaucracy*. Oxford: Oxford University Press.

McLaughlin, E. (2007). *The new policing*. London: Sage.

Melchior, J. K. (2015). Who benefits from Syria's refugee crisis: Human smugglers, *National Review*, 26 October 2015. Accessed on 21 March 2016 at: www.nationalreview.com/article/426046/who-benefits-syrias-refugee-crisis-human-smugglers-jillian-kay-melchior.

O'Riordan, T. and Jordan, A. (1999). Institutions, climate change and cultural theory: Towards a common analytical framework. *Global Environmental Change*, 9, 81–93.

Paoline, E. A. I. (2003). Taking stock: Toward a richer understanding of police culture. *Journal of Criminal Justice*, 31, 199–214.

Rathgeber, C. (2002). The victimization of women through human trafficking-an aftermath of war? *European Journal of Crime Criminal Law and Criminal Justice*, 10, 152–163.

Rayner, S. (1986). Management of radiation hazards in hospitals: Plural rationalities in a single institution. *Social Studies of Science*, 16, 573–591.

Reiner, R. (1978). *Blue-coated worker: A sociological study of police unionism*. New York: Cambridge University Press.

Reiner, R. (2000). Cop culture. In R. Reiner (ed.), *The politics of the police* (pp. 85–107). Oxford: Oxford University Press.

Richards, L. and Morse, J. M. (2007). *Read me first for a user's guide to qualitative methods*. Thousand Oaks, CA: Sage.

Schwartz, B. (1991). A pluralistic model of culture. *Contemporary Sociology*, 20, 764–766.

Seeman, M. (1959). On the meaning of alienation. *American Sociological Review*, 24, 783–791.

Sherwood, H. (2015). Unaccompanied young refugees in Europe "at risk from criminal gangs". *The Guardian*, 1 November 2015. Accessed on 21 March 2016 at: www.theguardian.com/world/2015/nov/01/unaccompanied-young-refugees-europe-traffickers.

Skinner, E. A., Edge, K., Altman, J., and Sherwood, H. (2003). Searching for the structure of coping: A review and critique of category systems for classifying ways of coping. *Psychological Bulletin*, 129, 216–269.

Skolnick, J. H. (1975). *Justice without trial: Law enforcement in democratic society*. New York: John Wiley and Sons.

Smaling, A. (2003). Inductive, analogical, and communicative generalization. *International Journal of Qualitative Methods*, 2, 52–67.

Smullen, A. J. (2007). *Translating agency reform. Rhetoric and culture in comparative perspective*. Rotterdam: Erasmus Universiteit Rotterdam.

Thompson, M., Ellis, R., and Wildavsky, A. (1990). *Cultural theory*. Boulder: Westview Press.

Tummers, L. (2011). Explaining the willingness of public professionals to implement new policies: A policy alienation framework. *International Review of Administrative Sciences*, 77, 555–581.

Tummers, L., Bekkers, V., and Steijn, B. (2009). Policy alienation of public professionals. Application in a new public management context. *Public Management Review*, 11, 685–706.

van Buuren, J. and den Boer, M. (2008). State-of-the-art literature review on the ethics research and knowledge among security professionals. security ethics: A thin blue lineInex.

Van der Leun, J. and Vervoorn, L. (2004). Slavernij-achtige uitbuiting in nederland: Een inventariserende literatuurstudie in het kader van de uitbreiding van de strafbaarstelling van mensenhandel Boom.

Van Maanen, J. (1974). Working the street: A developmental view of police behaviour. In H. Jacob (ed.), *The potential for reform of criminal justice* (pp. 83–130). Beverly Hills, CA: Sage.

Vaughan, B. (2002). Cultured punishments: the promise of grid-group theory, *Theoretical Criminology*, 6, 411–431.

Verweij, M., Douglas, M., Ellis, R., Engel, C., Hendriks, F., and Lohmann, S. (2006). Clumsy solutions for a complex world: The case of climate change, *Public Administration*, 84, 817–843.

Westley, W. A. (1970), *Violence and the police: A sociological study of law, custom, and morality*. Cambridge, MA: MIT Press.

Westmarland, L. (2005). Police ethics and integrity: Breaking the blue code of silence. *Policing and Society*, 15, 145–165.

Winterdyk, J. and Reichel, P. (2010). Introduction to special issue: Human trafficking issues and perspectives. *European Journal of Criminology*, 7, 5–10.

Yin, R. K. (2003), *Case study research. Design and methods* (3rd ed.), Thousand Oaks, CA: Sage Publications.

9 Burnout in police work

Sources, consequences, and remedies[1]

Ronald J. Burke

This chapter focuses on the experience of burnout among police officers. It considers the following content.

- What is burnout? Definitions and measures.
- What are potential causes of burnout?
- Why does burnout in police officers matter? Its consequences.
- How prevalent is burnout among police officers?
- Examining process models of burnout—Cherniss, Golembiewski and Leiter.
- Gender differences in police officer burnout.
- Interventions to reduce levels of police officer burnout.

Introduction

There is a vast quantity of research on burnout, which is noteworthy in that it emphasizes negative consequences for individuals and organizations (Burke and Richardsen, 1993). Burnout research has focused on the helping professions, broadly defined. We know a considerable amount about factors contributing to burnout; and knowing the causes of burnout informs potentially helpful intervention efforts.

Burnout is important for several reasons: it may be widespread, related to important individual, organizational and "client" outcomes, and it may be possible to reduce the prevalence and costs of burnout as we come to know more about it.

Maslach and Leiter (1997) note increases in the levels of burnout, which they attribute to changes in managerial philosophy. Employees feel overloaded; they feel that they lack control, receive fewer rewards, unfair treatment, more intense and more complicated work, and value conflicts. Burnout results from the ways that organizations function. Unfortunately burnout has adverse individual and organizational consequences (e.g. stress and health problems, diminished work engagement, etc.).

Definitions and causes of burnout

Burnout has been defined in various ways. The broadest definition (Freudenberger, 1980) equates burnout with stress, associates it with a lengthy list of dissatisfactions and psychological and physical distress, and suggests that it is caused by the single-minded pursuit of success. Narrower definitions have also been proposed. Maslach and Jackson (1981) locate burnout in human service professions, having interpersonal stressors as the cause; frequent exposure to emotionally demanding interpersonal situations results in burnout. Maslach (1982: 20) defines burnout as a syndrome of emotional exhaustion, depersonalization and reduced accomplishment that can occur among individuals who do "people work": It is a response to the chronic emotional strains of dealing extensively with other human beings, particularly when they are troubled or having problems.

Pines and Kafry (1978) define burnout as "a general experience of physical, emotional and attitudinal exhaustion."

Cherniss (1980a, 1980b) interviewed 28 new professionals in four human service fields: mental health, poverty law, public health nursing, and high school teaching. Participants were interviewed several times over a 1–2-year period. His model proposes that work-setting characteristics interact with individuals having particular career orientations, these individuals also having access to extra work demands and supports. This interaction produces particular sources of stress. Individuals cope with these stressors in a variety of ways, including active problem-solving; others cope by displaying the negative attitude change in Cherniss's conceptualization of burnout. Cherniss (1980a) defined burnout as "negative personal changes that occur over time in helping professionals working demanding or frustrating jobs." Burnout, then, is one way of adapting or coping with particular sources of stress.

In a study of a large sample of school teachers ($n = 5,575$) examining the link between burnout and depression, the Maslach burnout Inventory (MBI) and a commonly used measure of depression were administered (Bianchi *et al.*, 2014). Depression was very strongly correlated with emotional exhaustion, and less so with depersonalization and lack of personal accomplishment, suggesting that depressive symptoms are a large element in burnout, and opening up new avenues for the treatment of burnout using clinical treatments for depression.

Causes of burnout include individual factors, "client" factors, and organizational factors. Burke and Richardsen (2001) offered a broad review of burnout and the burnout literature in this regard. Individual characteristics considered as factors in the experience of burnout included sex, age, personality, and career orientations. Organizational and client factors included workload, role conflict and role ambiguity, professional expectations, participation in decision-making levels of social support, and recognition and reward structures. Consequences of burnout included individual-level outcomes such as negative attitude changes, job dissatisfaction, reduced organizational commitment, and organizational level outcomes such as increased absenteeism, turnover, and lowered job performance.

Maslach and Leiter (1997) identify six areas of organization life as causes of burnout: workload, control, rewards, community, fairness, and value conflicts, as well as developing measures of each for organizational assessment.

Burnout develops over time; therefore it is a process (Leiter, 1992). There are two ways to examine burnout as a process. One examines the experience of burnout over time in a longitudinal study. Measures of burnout and its antecedents and consequences are assessed at two points in time. Measures of antecedents at one point in time should predict burnout scores at a later point in time. The second way in which burnout could be examined as a process is based on the idea of phases in the development of burnout within the concept itself by attributing different priorities or levels of importance to various burnout components.

Measures of burnout

At least four measures of burnout have been used in police research (Schaufeli *et al.*, 1993). These include measures created by Maslach and Jackson (1981), Shirom and Melamed

(2006), Cherniss (1980a), and Schaufeli and Van Dierendonck (1993). The Maslach and Jackson measure, the Maslach Burnout Inventory (MBI) assesses three components: emotional exhaustion, depersonalization, and lack of personal accomplishment; the Shirom and Melamed measure assesses three components: physical fatigue, emotional exhaustion, and cognitive weariness; the Cherniss measures assesses six components: reduced work goals, reduced personal responsibility for outcomes, less idealism, emotional detachment, work alienation, and greater self-interest; the Schaufeli and Van Dierendonck measure, a Dutch version of the MBI, assesses two components: emotional exhaustion and personal efficacy.

Models of burnout

The development of burnout is best viewed as a process. In this regard, three process models of burnout have received attention: Cherniss's process model (Cherniss, 1980a, 1980b); Golembiewski's phase model (Golembiewski, 1986; Golembiewski and Munzenrider, 1988); and Leiter's process model (Leiter, 1992). More recently, Gil-Monte *et al.* (1998) entered this area in examining each of these three process models and suggesting a possible fourth model.

A comprehensive model of burnout must include individual and organizational variables representing stressors leading to burnout, personal and organizational consequences of burnout, and potential multi-level interventions to prevent the development of burnout and to reduce burnout levels.

The Cherniss model

The Cherniss model proposes an interaction between work-setting characteristics (e.g. workload, quality of leadership, etc.) and person characteristics (e.g. career orientations, extra work demands and supports, etc.), resulting in the experience of stressors (e.g. lack of collegiality, loss of excitement and fulfillment, etc.) which culminate in burnout (e.g. negative attitude changes such as emotional exhaustion, work alienation, etc.). For Cherniss, burnout is a process that takes place over time and represents one way of adapting to or coping with particular sources of stress. Researchers have provided support for his model in police samples (Burke *et al.*, 1984a; Burke *et al.*, 1984b).

The Golembiewski model

Golembiewski and Munzenrider (1988) suggest phases within the burnout concept itself. They created eight phases of burnout, using high and low dichotomous scores on the three MBI components. Phase I is represented by low scores on the three MBI components. Phase II is represented by a high score on depersonalization and low scores on the other two burnout components. Phase VIII is represented by high scores on all three MBI components. Research support for this phase process model has also been found (Burke *et al.*, 1984a; Burke and Deszca, 1986).

The Leiter model

Leiter's model—based on the MBI—proposes, first, that the three MBI components influence each other over time, and second, that the three MBI components each have unique relationships with personal characteristics and work environment factors.

He places emotional exhaustion in a central role, suggesting that it develops first. Individuals then cope with their feelings of emotional exhaustion by depersonalizing their relationships with co-workers, clients, or the general public, culminating in reduced levels of personal accomplishment. Workplace stressors increase levels of emotional exhaustion, which in turn has effects on a range of work outcomes.

Gil-Monte *et al.* (1998) examined the fit of three previously proposed process models of burnout (Golembiewski, 1986; Leiter and Maslach, 1988; Lee and Ashforth, 1993) using the same dataset. The Golembiewski model proposes that lack of personal accomplishment leads to depersonalization, which in turn leads to emotional exhaustion; the Leiter model proposes that emotional exhaustion leads to depersonalization, which in turn leads to lack of personal accomplishment; the Lee and Ashforth model proposes that emotional exhaustion leads to depersonalization, and that emotional exhaustion also leads to lack of personal accomplishment. Gil-Monte *et al.* (1998) first found that the Golembiewski model did not provide a good fit to their data; the Leiter model provided a good fit to their data; and the Lee and Ashforh model had a low fit to their data. They offered another model possibility that has a reasonable fit to their data: emotional exhaustion leads to depersonalization, and lack of personal accomplishment leads to depersonalization as well.

Types of burnout

Loo (2004) used a cluster analysis of MBI scores to identify burnout types in a sample of 135 male police officers in managerial jobs (sergeant, staff sergeant ranks) in Canada. Three clusters were identified: Laissez-faire managers ($n=15$), well-adjusted managers ($n=74$), and distressed managers ($n=46$). The Laissez-faire managers scored low on all three MBI components; the well-adjusted managers scored high on personal accomplishment and low on both emotional exhaustion and depersonalization; the distressed managers scored high on emotional exhaustion and depersonalization and moderate to high on personal accomplishment. An analysis of these clusters then yielded two MBI functions, one reflecting emotional exhaustion and depersonalization, the other reflecting personal accomplishment. These two functions correctly classified 94 percent of these police managers.

Burnout and emotional dissonance

Bakker and Heuven (2006), in a study of 101 police offices in the Netherlands, found that emotional job demands increased levels of burnout through their effects on emotional dissonance—the need for police officers to show particular feelings to civilians while feeling the opposite. In addition, emotional dissonance was associated with lower levels of job performance (e.g. achieving job expectations) through burnout.

Correlates of burnout phases

We undertook two studies of the phase model of Golembiewski. In the first (Burke *et al.*, 1984b), 426 men and women in police work completed the MBI as well as measures of work-setting characteristics proposed by Cherniss (1980a): a measure of stressful life events—their frequency and how upsetting each was; five sources of stress identified also by Cherniss (e.g. lack of stimulation and fulfillment, etc.); burnout or negative attitude change as outlined by Cherniss (e.g. less idealism, emotional detachment, etc.); two work outcomes (i.e. job satisfaction, intent to quit); two measures of psychological well-being (negative feeling states, psychosomatic symptoms); the impact of the job on some aspects of home and family life (e.g., relationship with one's spouse, family and home life, etc.); a measure of social support; coping through the use of alcohol and drugs; and the use of anger.

Two aspects of the findings were noteworthy. First, about half the sample fell in the two extreme phases (I and VIII). Second, police officers at more advanced or progressive stages indicated less favorable responses in most areas that were considered.

In the second study, Burke and Deszca (1986), using many of the same measures as in the earlier Burke *et al.* (1984b) study, we again examined correlates of the Golembiewski phase model. Data were collected from 833 women and men in police work in Canada. Again, about half the sample fell into the first phase (least burnout) and eighth phase (most advanced burnout). Most of the progressive phases were significantly different (i.e. having higher total MBI scores—22 of 28 paired comparisons—with the overall F being significant ($p<0.001$). On 14 multi-item measures (e.g. job satisfaction, lack of social support, number of stressful life events, use of alcohol and drugs, etc. the overall F was again significant ($p<0.001$), with half the progressive paired comparisons again reaching statistical significance in the expected direction ($p<0.05$), and with more advanced phases indicating less favorable responses.

Relatively few personal demographic characteristics across the eight phases distinguished this phase. Officers at more advanced phases tended to be older, in policing longer, and to be at higher organizational levels. In addition, there were relatively few significant phase differences on eight single items measuring physical health and lifestyle. Again, there was a tendency for officers at more advanced stages of burnout to drink more alcohol, to drink more coffee, to smoke more cigarettes per day, and to participate less in physical exercise.

Career orientations and burnout

Cherniss (1980a) proposed that burnout in the workplace results from the integration of work- setting characteristics and individuals having particular career orientations. He identified four career orientations in his longitudinal interview study of 28 new professionals. These were:

> *Self-investors*: individual is more interested in their personal life outside of work than in their police work. Major source of pleasure comes from family and personal development-off-the-job interests. Not interested in a demanding job or career development.

> *Social Activists*: individual is an idealist and a visionary. Regards policing as a crusade. Not interested in personal status and job security. Wants to contribute towards improving their profession and society at large.

> *Careerist*: individual is interested in recognition, career advancement, prestige, respect, and financial security. Eager to impress those who control the advancement of their careers.

> *Artisans*: individual values independence, freedom, jobs that challenge, jobs that offer new experiences, and skill development. Career and financial success are less important. Wants to perform well according to his/her own standards.

In a study of 426 men and women in police work in Canada, Burke *et al.* (1984b) reported the following: Officers identifying themselves as Social Activists scored higher on the Cherniss burnout measure and on the MBI. Officers identifying themselves as Artisans indicated lower scores on both the Cherniss measure of burnout and the MBI. Thus, in this study, career orientations were only modestly associated with indicators of burnout.

In a second study (Burke *et al.*, 1986), this time involving a larger sample of Canadian women and men in police work, we replicated our earlier investigation. Social Activists reported higher levels of burnout, greater experienced stress, and the least satisfying work setting. Social Activists also indicated poorer individual well-being (more psychosomatic symptoms, more use of alcohol and drugs, smoked more, drank more coffee). Self-investors reported the highest job satisfaction, and the fewest negative impacts of job demands on personal, home, and family life. Careerists and Artisans reported the greatest work satisfaction, lowest levels of burnout, the least stress, and the most satisfying work settings. Interestingly, both the Social Activists and Careerist orientations weakened over time, while the Artisan and Self-investor orientations became stronger over time.

Career stage and burnout

Cannizzo and Liu (1995), in a sample of 212 police officers in the US, examined the relationship of career stage with scores on the MBI. Four career stages were considered: 1–5 years, 6–15 years, 16–25 years and 26 years and above. The highest burnout levels were reported in the 16–25 year career stage, suggesting a curvilinear relationship. Burke and Mikkelsen (2006), in a sample of 466 Norwegian police officers, considered the relationship of five age groups with a range of job demands, work outcomes, work–family concerns, levels of social support, burnout, and both physical and psychological well-being. Officers in the two oldest stages (43–47, 48 years and older) tended to report less favorable standings on some of these outcomes. These two studies suggest the importance of particularly responding to the needs of older officers, and, perhaps, intervening earlier to minimize potential negative outcomes.

Applying the Cherniss model in police samples

We have examined the usefulness of the Cherniss model to understand burnout among police officers. In one study (Burke, 1998) involving 828 women and men in policing in Canada, sources of stress (e.g. chronic stressors, stressful life events, work–family conflict) had significant relationships with burnout assessed by the MBI, controlling for individual demographic and work situation characteristics. However individual coping responses had little effect of levels on burnout after controlling for these three stressors.

In a second set of analyses using the same sample, Burke (1997) found the Cherniss measure of negative attitude change or burnout was positively correlated with work environment stressors, extra–work demands in the form of stressful life events, lack of support, less favorable work outcomes (e.g. less job satisfaction, greater intent to quit), and both poorer lifestyle habits (more consumption of alcohol, and of coffee, and more cigarette smoking, less regular exercise) and ill health (e.g. currently taking medication, more days ill during the previous six months).

Most interventions to reduce burnout target sources that exist in the work environment. These include increasing employee participation in decision-making and problem-solving, improving the quality of supervision, developing a higher level of social support, and making counseling services available.

In a second study (Burke *et al.* (1984a) involving 426 women and men in police work in Canada, the Cherniss model was examined, using many of the same measures used in the earlier Burke (1997) analysis with the addition of a few new measures. Thus, for example, both the Cherniss measure and the MBI were included. As expected, the Cherniss measure of burnout (or negative attitude changes) was significantly correlated with the MBI($r = 0.60$, $p < 0.001$, $n = 426$). Generally similar patterns of results were present with the two indicators of burnout.

First, work-setting characteristics (e.g. workload, lack of autonomy, poor supervision, etc.) were associated with higher levels of burnout. Second, sources of stress (e.g. bureaucratic interferences, problems with citizens, etc.) were positively and significantly associated with burnout levels. Third, stressful work and non-work life events, their number and how upsetting they were, were significantly associated with burnout. Fourth, lack of social support was associated with higher levels of burnout as well. Finally, time spent in one's present job, with one's present force, and in police work (all positively related), were positively associated with higher levels of burnout.

Families as victims

Jackson and Maslach (1982) collected data from 142 police couples in the United States. Officers who scored higher on the MBI were more likely to display anger, spend time off away from their families, be less involved in family matters, and have less satisfying marriages. Interestingly, husbands and wives used different coping strategies.

Coping resources, work–family demands, and burnout

Haines *et al.* (2013), in a study of 289 police officers and civilian staff in Canada, studied the relationship between core self-evaluations (e.g. self esteem, locus of control, emotional stability, etc.) work–family and family–work conflict, and burnout. They found, first, that— controlling for personal and work demographic factors—positive core self-evaluations were related to lower levels of both work–family and family–work conflict; second, the relationship between core self-evaluations and burnout was partially mediated by work–family and family-work conflict; and third, that core self-evaluations moderated the relationship between work–family conflict and burnout, but not between family–work conflict and burnout.

Selected police burnout research findings

A sample of police burnout research is offered to illustrate a range of important findings on sources and effects of burnout.

Mortinussen *et al.* (2007) examined job demands, job resources, burnout, and potential consequences of burnout, in a sample of 223 Norwegian police officers. Burnout levels of police officers were relatively low compared to other occupational groups examined simultaneously. Both job demands (e.g. work conflicts, work–family pressures, etc.) and job resources (e.g. autonomy, social support, etc.) were related to burnout, particularly work–family pressures. Burnout predicted psychosomatic complaints, satisfaction with life, job satisfaction, intent to quit, and organizational commitment.

Van Gelderen *et al.* (2011) undertook three diary studies of Dutch police officers ($n = 25$, 41 and 39 respectively) examining the effects of daily emotional suppression and exhaustion, a key burnout dimension. Across all three studies, officers reporting more emotional disassociation (more suppression of emotions such as anger, sadness, and abhorrence) reported increased levels of exhaustion at the end of work shifts.

Taris *et al.* (2010), in a longitudinal study of 828 Dutch police officers, examined the relationship of both job demands and job control with two dimensions of burnout: emotional exhaustion and professional efficacy. High job demands were related to exhaustion, whereas high job control was related to greater professional efficacy.

Stearns and Moore (1993), in a sample of 290 male and female Royal Canadian Mounted Police officers, examined correlates of the three MBI scales and the total burnout score. Psychological well-being was negatively correlated with scores on emotional exhaustion, depersonalization, and the total score. Burnout was negatively correlated with physical well-being and positively correlated with both cynicism and authoritarianism. Officers spending more time in sports and with hobbies reported significantly lower levels of burnout.

Hall, Dollard, Tuckey, Winefield and Thompson (2010), in a longitudinal study of 257 Australian police officers (with a one-year time lag), found that job demands (emotional demands, time demands, the need for concentration) were associated with higher levels of emotional exhaustion, mediated by work–family conflict, and that job demands were associated with work–family conflict, mediated by emotional exhaustion.

Malach-Pines and Keinan (2006), in a study of 1,182 Israeli police officers during the Palestinian uprising (*Intifadah*), found that job stress was positively correlated with burnout levels, and burnout was correlated with work outcomes such as job dissatisfaction, intent to quit, physical and emotional distress symptoms, and lower perceived job performance levels. In a second study, Malach-Pines and Keinan (2006), in a study of 497 border police, reported that their levels of burnout were very high compared to those of Israeli citizens in general and regular police officers in particular.

Manzoni and Eisner (2006) studied work-related stress, job satisfaction, organizational commitment, and burnout as predictors of the use of force by 422 police officers in Zurich, Switzerland. While all these variables had significant relationships with self-reported use of force, multivariate analyses indicated, however, that those factors had no influence on self-reported use of force. Officers who were themselves victims of force, and those reporting more potential violence and confrontation in their daily routines, indicated greater use of violence.

Backteman-Erlanson, Padyab and Brulin (2013), in a study of 856 Swedish police officers (437 women and 419 men), reported, first, that scores on both emotional exhaustion and depersonalization were higher in their sample than other studies of police officers in Norway and the Netherlands, with males scoring higher than females on depersonalization; second, stress of conscience, high demands and organizational climate were associated with levels of emotional exhaustion, while stress of conscience, decision, and high demands were associated with emotional exhaustion for men; and third, stress of conscience was significantly associated with depersonalization in both males and female officer subsamples. What is meant by "stress of conscience"? Individuals feel stress of conscience when they are prevented from doing "good" because they did not do what they might or should have done if they handled the situation badly. This may result from a lack of time, too much work to do, doing things one knows are wrong, and seeing citizens being treated badly.

Kohan and Mazmanian (2003), in a sample of 199 Canadian police officers, examined the relationship of organizational and operational work experiences—classified into Hassles and Uplifts—with burnout and organizational citizenship behaviors, and with positive and negative affect and both problem-focused and emotion-focused coping as potential moderators and mediators of these relationships. They reported the following:

first, positive and negative work experiences, measured by the Police Daily Hassles (e.g. hard work) and Uplifts (e.g. helping the public) scale were grouped into operational and organizational work experiences. Second, organizational experiences were more strongly related to burnout and organizational citizenship behaviors than were operational work experiences. Third, both problem-focused and emotion-focused coping mediated the work experiences and burnout relationship.

In a study of police officers in Belgium, vanden Broek, De Cuyper and De Witte (2010) examined two types of job demands: job hindrances (e.g. emotional demands, work–family conflict) and job challenges (e.g. cognitive demands, workload), along with job resources, on emotional exhaustion as measured by the MBI and vigor, a component of work engagement. Job hindrances were negatively related to vigor and positively related to exhaustion; job resources were positively related to vigor and negatively related to exhaustion.

Ten Brummelhuis, Bakker and Euwema (2010) collected data from 2,860 police officers, 1,430 employees, and co-worker dyads, in a study of the effects of family to work interference (FWI) on a co-worker's work outcomes. The latter included burnout, work engagement, turnover intentions and sickness absence. They reported that an officer's FWI had a positive relationship with levels of co-worker sickness absence through the cross-over of higher levels of burnout, with officer FWI also being positively related to co-worker turnover intentions through the cross-over of lower levels of work engagement.

Richardsen *et al.* (2006) studied personality (Type A behavior), job demands and job resources, cynicism, and work engagement in a sample of 150 Norwegian police officers. Type A behavior was positively related to both cynicism and work engagement. Job demands and lack of resources were also related to cynicism, with job resources being positively related to work engagement.

Berg *et al.* (2006) examined the association of job stress and physical and mental health in a nationwide sample of 3,272 police officers in Norway. They measured serious operational tasks and work injuries, job pressure and lack of support, subjective health complaints (anxiety and depression), job burnout assessed by the MBI, and suicidal ideation. Job pressures and lack of support were associated with mental and physical health problems.

Burnout and the use of force

Kop *et al.* (1999), in a study of 358 Dutch police officers, found that burnout as measured by the MBI was positively related to attitudes towards the use of violence, and the actual use of violence in their duties. In addition, they reported that organizational stressors (e.g. poor management, reorganization, bureaucracy) were more prevalent than were task-related stressors (e.g. emotionally demanding situations, dealing with unsavory people, danger, use of violence). Interestingly, the sample offered more mentions of positive or rewarding aspects of police work than negative or stressful aspects of police work.

Burke and Mikkelsen (2004), based on a sample of 766 Norwegian police officers, examined the relationship of burnout, assessed by the MBI, and job stress and attitudes towards the use of force and the use of social skills in solving problems. Considering favorable attitudes towards the use of force, single officers, officers working shifts on a regular basis, and officers scoring higher on Cynicism more strongly endorsed the use of force. Moving now to the use of social skills to solve problems, officers working shifts on a regular basis less strongly endorsed the use of social skills to solve problems, and officers reporting higher levels of personal accomplishment (or efficacy) more strongly endorsed the use of social skills. It is suggested that police forces monitor levels of individual burnout as a result.

Finally, Queiros *et al.* (2013), in a sample of 274 male police officers in Porto and Lisbon, Portugal, reported that higher levels of two burnout dimensions (depersonalization and low personal accomplishment) emerged as significant predictors of officer anger and aggression.

Burnout and police suicide and suicide ideation

There is some evidence that suicide levels among police officers are higher than those among women and men in other occupations (Hem *et al.*, 2001; Violanti, 1996). Burke and Mikkelsen (2007), in a study of 766 Norwegian police officers, divided the sample into those indicating no suicidal ideation ($n=495$) and those indicating some suicidal ideation ($n=124$). Officers reporting higher levels of burnout on both exhaustion and cynicism fell in the latter group.

Gender differences in burnout levels among police officers

Given the unique challenges female police officers face in comparison to their male colleagues, one might expect to find women officers reporting higher levels of burnout. Women police officers experience sexual harassment and discrimination from fellow officers and citizens, greater barriers to promotion, more difficulties in combining marriage, family, and careers, and higher levels of job strain (see Archbold and Hassell, 2009; Cordner and Cordner, 2011; Cowan and Bohantin, 2009; Rabe-Hemp, 2007). McCarty (2013) surveyed 171 female and 737 male sergeants in a study of levels of burnout, as well as factors predictive of burnout levels. He found, first, that female sergeants indicated higher levels of emotional exhaustion and lower levels of depersonalization. He then reported that factors predictive of higher levels of burnout were generally similar for females and males, with male and female officers reporting higher levels of dissatisfaction with supervisors and peers and more work–life conflict also indicating increased levels of emotional exhaustion. Work–life conflicts also increased levels of depersonalization for both female and male officers as well.

Prior military experience and burnout

Ivie and Garland (2011) considered the potential role played by prior military experience in the stress–burnout relationship. Their sample contained 231 police officers having a military background and 369 police officers without military experience. Their general hypothesis was that prior military experience would benefit police officers in their responses to stress. They found that negative responses to demanding events increased levels of burnout for all officers in their research, particularly among police officers with no military experience. Use of constructive coping was associated with lower levels of stress in both groups, while use of destructive coping increased levels of stress in both groups as well. They concluded that aspects of military service that created an emotional resilience to negative events reduced stress and burnout.

Some police forces view candidates' having prior military experience as a plus in the recruitment and selection process.

Individual coping versus organizational-level interventions

Coping involves efforts to reduce stresses and strains, including burnout. Individual coping, however, has been shown to have a limited effect in reducing burnout levels (Pines *et al.*, 1981). Some benefits of coping have been noted. Leiter (1991a), in a study of mental health workers, considered both escape coping (avoiding or ignoring difficult situations) and control coping (using strategies to tackle difficulties). Respondents using more control coping indicated less exhaustion, while respondents using more escape coping indicated higher levels of exhaustion. Similar findings were reported by other studies (i.e. Leiter 1991a; Burke, 1998, and Burke *et al.*, 1995), where active coping responses were found to have benefits while negative/avoidance/escape coping responses had none.

Leiter (1991b) and Burke (1998) write that chronic organizationally created sources of stress may be difficult to address using individual coping mechanisms. Along this line, Shinn *et al.* (1984), in a study of 141 human service workers, measured job stressors, coping strategies, and work attitudes. Coping efforts were assessed at three levels: by individuals, by groups of individuals helping one another (social support), and by their employing human service agencies. Only the group level of coping efforts was associated with lower levels of strain. Thus individual coping efforts were less useful than higher-level strategies involving groups of employees or entire units.

These studies indicate that while efforts should be made to initiate both individual- and organizational-level coping efforts, working at the organizational level is likely to yield greater benefits. Organizational-level efforts, however, require more time, resources, and organizational commitment.

Several studies have shown the effectiveness of individual-level interventions in reducing stress and burnout. Bruning and Frew (1986), in a longitudinal study of employees at various levels in a manufacturing organization, evaluated three interventions (cognitive skills training, exercise training, and relaxation/meditation training) as well as using a control group. A number of outcome variables were measured (e.g. self esteem, anxiety, four facets of job satisfaction). These interventions were found to improve these employee attitudes.

Golembiewski and Rountree (1991) evaluated a quality of work–life intervention among senior nursing managers with burnout and work attitudes as outcome measures, and also included a control group. A reduction in burnout phases was observed.

Interventions to reduce burnout and its effects

Reducing burnout through worksite changes, by changing orientations to one's job among newly hired professionals, by education, by improving coping skills, and through training in increasing resilience and reducing stressors likely to be associated with increased burnout have been proposed.

Maslach and Leiter (1997) advocate developing organizational strategies that create management structures and processes that support work engagement and prevent burnout. These efforts start with management and then become organization-wide efforts. Employee input and involvement is vital in identifying and getting commitment to specific organization interventions.

Leiter and Maslach (2005) devote chapters to starting such intervention projects and to each of the six sources of burnout mentioned above, as well as providing assessments of these areas in their appendix.

Here are some examples of their suggestions for each of the six areas.

- *Workload* – reducing workload, developing employee skills, use of support staff
- *Control* – allowing more autonomy, less micro-managing, reviewing tasks
- *Reward* – supervisor training, better assignments, acknowledging accomplishments
- *Community* – more and better communication, build community identity and spirit, increase support
- *Fairness* – increase respect, reduce incivility, clarify procedures, increase transparency
- *Values* – change the organization's values, add meaning to employee's work.

Most of the proposed burnout interventions were targeted at reducing burnout at its source by changing the work environment of workers (Richardsen and Burke, 1995). Thus Cherniss (1980a) discussed staff development and counseling initiatives, increasing worker involvement and participation in decision-making (Schwab *et al.*, 1986), having supervisors clarify work goals (Maslach and Jackson, 1984; Schwab *et al.*, 1986), and increasing levels of workplace social support (Schwab *et al.*, 1986).

Some examples of burnout interventions

Reducing burnout by worksite changes

Golembiewski *et al.* (1987) undertook an organizational development project with a 31-member human resource unit from a single organization. They assessed levels of burnout as well as various aspects of their work environment, collecting data over a two-year period and administering a survey at five points in time. The group scored high on burnout, work pressures, and turnover. The intervention involved data collection, feedback, and action planning. Levels of burnout dropped immediately following the intervention but increased at the one-year point as a result of a major reorganization. Group cohesiveness and reductions in turnover improved over the time period.

Reducing burnout through training

Schaufeli (1995) evaluated a burnout workshop for community nurses ($n=64$). The workshop included relaxation training, didactic and cognitive stress management, interpersonal skills training, and the development of a more realistic professional role. Nurses' levels of emotional exhaustion, strain, and somatic complaints were reduced. Nurses' negative attitudes towards their patients did not change however.

Reducing burnout through changing orientations of new employees

Falconer and Hornick (1983), working with the Children's Aid Society of Toronto, designed a new program to deal with early career burnout of frontline social workers in childcare. First, new employees were hired as a group. The group was kept together for at least the first six months of employment. Caseload was reduced at the start and gradually increased to 60 percent of the normal caseload after six months. Their supervisor's role now emphasized education, an improved training program (1–2 days of training every two weeks, increased social support within the group, and attempts to address stressors found to be associated with burnout. Qualitative data suggested that the program was successful in meeting its objectives, with supervisors believing this group achieved a level of skill in six months compared to previously achieving this level after 12 months.

Burnout interventions following from the Cherniss, Maslach and Leiter models

The main focus of interventions in the Cherniss model will be on addressing workplace factors. These include providing a lengthy orientation and training program for new hires. This could include weekly in-service training, external training sessions, the observation of more experienced colleagues, close supervision, and adding more work responsibility as the individual becomes more experienced and skilled. Increasing the support of colleagues will also reduce stress. Intervention early in one's career is particularly valuable, since, as burnout develops, it is more efficient to tackle it early.

The Golembiewski phase model is less helpful in identifying useful interventions, since individuals are likely to follow different paths in the development of burnout, in moving from Phase I to Phase VIII. Perhaps a traditional organizational development intervention involving problem identification, data collection, dialogue with relevant participants and soliciting their feedback, involving relevant police officers in problem-solving, then undertaking action planning to introduce relevant changes would be more effective (Golelmbiewski, 1981; Golembiewski *et al.*, 1983).

The Leiter model emphasizes the gap or conflict between individual aspirations and organizational limitations and barriers. Thus organizations need to empower staff as well as being more responsive to the goals and aspirations of employees. Then, both individuals and organizational-level interventions make sense. Priority should be given to identifying and reducing sources of stress that directly increase emotional exhaustion. These might include realigning workloads, increasing variety and meaning in one's job, and increasing one's sense of competence through training and utilization of ones' skills. Increasing autonomy through participative decision-making, and training supervisors to provide higher levels of support and encouragement, would also be useful here as well.

Each of the three process models identifies a range of intervention targets, with some similarities evident between them (see Richardsen and Burke, 1995, for a detailed listing of these). A sample of possible intervention targets in each of the three models would include the following:

* *Cherniss* – orientation practices, workload management, increasing autonomy, leadership training, increasing opportunities of formal and informal staff contact;
* *Golembiewski* – undertake an organizational development intervention involving data collection, feedback, creating problem-solving groups that identify key issues and generate potential solutions. Such initiatives would likely address some of the issues targeted by both Cherniss and Leiter;
* *Leiter* – workload, job redesign, skills training, supervisor and co-worker support.

1   *Recruitment and selection.* Use of realistic job previews, so that applicants have a deeper understanding of the nature and demands of police work; use of personality tests to eliminate applicants that might have a hard time performing well; and use of intensive training of newcomers to appropriately socialize their attitudes and behaviors.

2   *Counseling interventions.* Offer trauma counseling in case of heightened levels of stress (child rape, spouse abuse, using a weapon, death of a citizen in an accident, etc.). Offer an employee assistance program help to address officer alcohol and drug use, work–family distress, and family problems.

3   *Training interventions*. Sessions dealing with job stressors and effective coping, and management development to improve the quality of supervision and leadership.

4   *Work–family interventions*. These include spouse/partner support groups, couples workshops, work–family content in training sessions, and the use of peer counseling.

5   *Individual initiatives*. Use of active coping (e.g. problem-solving, talking with others, anticipating demands) as opposed to passive coping (e.g. use of alcohol and drugs, doing nothing, avoiding the problems, etc.). Kroes and Hurrell (1975) found that 25 percent of police offices used alcohol as a stress reducer. Burke (1997), in a study of police officers, found that the use of active coping led to more positive outcomes (e.g. greater job satisfaction) whereas greater use of passive coping was associated with higher levels of psychological distress.

Note

1   Preparation of this chapter was supported in part by York University. Cobi Wolpin helped to identify relevant literature. Carla D'Agostino assisted in the preparation of the manuscript.

References

Archbold, C. A. and Hassell, K. D. (2009) Paying a marriage tax: An examination of the barriers to the promotion of female police officers. *Policing: An International Journal of Police Strategies and Management*, 32, 56–74.

Backteman-Erlanson, S., Padyab, M., and Brulin, D. (2013) Prevalence of burnout and associations with psychosocial work environment, physical strain, and stress of conscience among Swedish female and male police personnel. *Police Practice and Research*, 14, 491–505.

Bakker, A. B. and Heuven, E. (2006) Emotional dissonance, burnout, and in-role performance among nurses and police officers. *International Journal of Stress Management*, 13, 423–440.

Berg, A. M., Hem, E., Lau, B., and Ekeberg, O. (2006) An exploration of job stress and health in the Norwegian police service: A cross-sectional study. *Journal of Occupational Medicine and Toxicology*, 1, 26–29.

Bianchi, R., Schonfeld, S., and Laurent, E. (2014) Is burnout a depressive disorder? A reexamination with special focus on atypical depression. *International Journal of Stress Management*, 21, 307–324.

Bruning, N. S. and Frew, D. R. (1986) Can stress intervention strategies improve self-esteem, manifest anxiety, and job satisfaction? A longitudinal field experiment. *Journal of Health and Human Services Administration*, 9, 110–124.

Burke, R. J. (1997) Toward an understanding of psychological burnout among police officers. *International Journal of Stress management*, 4, 13–27.

Burke, R. J. (1998) Work and non-work stressors and well-being among police officers: The role of coping. *Anxiety, Stress and Coping*, 10, 1–18.

Burke, R. J. and Deszca, E. (1986) Correlates of psychological burnout among police officers. *Human Relations*, 39, 487–502.

Burke, R. J. and Richardsen, A. M. (1993) Psychological burnout in organizations. In R. T. Golembiewski (ed.), *Handbook of organizational behavior*. New York: Marcel Dekker. pp. 327–364.

Burke, R. J. and Richardsen, A. M. (2001) Psychological burnout in organizations: Research and intervention. In R. T. Golembiewski (ed.), *Handbook of organizational behavior*, 2nd ed. New York: Marcel Dekker, pp. 327–364.

Burke, R. J. and Mikkelsen, A. (2004) Burnout, job stress and attitudes towards the use of force by Norwegian police officers. *Policing: An International Journal of Police Strategies and Management*, 28, 269–278.

Burke, R. J. and Mikkelsen, A. (2006) Police offices over career stages: satisfaction and well-being. *European Journal of Psychology*, 2, 47–63.

Burke, R. J. and Mikkelsen, A. (2007) Suicidal ideation among police officers in Norway. *Policing: An International Journal of Police Strategies and Management*, 30, 228–236.

Burke, R. J., Shearer, J., and Deszca, E. (1984a) Correlates of burnout phases among police officers. *Group and Organization Studies*, 9, 451–466.

Burke, R. J., Shearer, J., and Deszca, E. (1984b) Burnout among men and women in police work: An examination of the Cherniss model. *Journal of Health and Human Resources Administration*, 7, 62–88.

Burke, R. J., Deszca, E., and Shearer, J. (1984c) Career orientations and burnout in police officers. *Canadian Journal of Administrative Sciences*, 1, 179–194.

Burke, R. J., Deszca, G., and Shearer, J. (1986) Career orientations, satisfactions and health among police officers: Some consequences of person-job misfit. *Psychological Reports*, 62, 639–649.

Burke, R. J., Greenglass, E. R., and Konarski, R. (1995) Coping, work demands and psychological burnout among teachers. *Journal of Health and Human Services Administration*, 18, 90–103.

Cannizzo, T. A. and Liu, P. (1995) The relationship between levels of perceived burnout and career stage among sworn police officers. *Police Studies*, 18, 53–68.

Cherniss, C. (1980a) *Professional burnout in human service organizations*. New York: Praeger.

Cherniss, C. (1980b) *Staff burnout: Job stress in the human services*. Beverly Hills, CA: Sage.

Cordner, G. and Cordner, A. (2011) Stuck on a plateau? Obstacles in the recruitment, selection, and retention of women police. *Police Quarterly*, 14, 207–226.

Cowan, R. L., and Bohantin, J. E. (2009) Pregnancy and motherhood on the thin blue line: Female police officers' perspectives on motherhood in a highly masculinized work environment. *Women and Language*, 32, 22–30.

Falconer, N. E. and Hornick, J. P. (1983) *Attack on burnout: The importance of early training*. Toronto: Children's aid Society of Metropolitan Toronto.

Freudenberger, H. J. (1980) *Burnout: The high cost of high achievement*. Garden City, NY: Anchor Press.

Gil-Monte, P. B., Peiro, J. M., and Valcarcel, P. (1998) A model of burnout process development: An alternative from appraisal models of stress. *Comport a Mento Organizacional e Gestao*, 4, 165–179.

Golembiewski, R. T. (1981) Organization development (OD) interventions: Limiting burnout through changes in interaction, structures, and policies. In W. S. Paine (ed.), *Proceedings of the First National Conference on Burnout. Philadelphia*, pp. 265–312.

Golembiewski, R. T. (1986) The epidemiology of progressive burnout: A primer. *Journal of Health and Human Resources*, 9, 16–37.

Golembiewski, R. T. and Munzenrider, R. (1988) *Phases of burnout: Development in concepts and applications*. New York: Praeger.

Golembiewski, R. and Rowntree, B. (1991) Releasing human potential for collaboration: A social intervention targeting supervisory relationships and stress. *Public Administration Quarterly*, 15, 32–45.

Golembiewski, R. T., Munzentrider, R., and Carter, D. (1983) Phases of progressive burnout and their work site covariants: Critical issues in OD research and praxis. *Journal of Applied Behavioral Science*, 19, 461–481.

Golembiewski, R. T., Hilles, R., and Daly, R. (1987) Some effects of multiple OD interventions on burnout and work site features. *Journal of Applied Behavioral Science*, 23, 295–313.

Haines, V., Harvey, S., Durand, P., and Marchand, A. (2013) Core-self evaluations, work–family conflict, and burnout. *Journal of Marriage and Family*, 75, 778–793.

Hall, G. B., Dollard, M. F., Tuckey, M. R., Winefield, A. H., and Thompson, B. M. I. (2010) Job demands, work–family conflict, and emotional exhaustion in police officers: A longitudinal test of competing theories. *Journal of Occupational and Organizational Psychology*, 83, 237–250.

Hem, E., Berg, A. M., and Ekeberg, O. (2001) Suicide in police: A critical review. *Suicide and Life Threatening Behavior*, 31, 224–231.

Ivie, D. and Garland, B. (2011) Stress and burnout in policing: Does military experience matter? *Policing: An International Journal of Police Strategies and Management*, 34, 49–66.

Jackson, S.E., and Maslach, C. (1982) After-effects of job-related stress: Families as victims. *Journal of Organizational Behavior*, 3, 63–77.

Kohan, A. and Mazmanian, D. (2003) Police work, burnout, and pro-organizational behavior. *Criminal Justice and Behavior*, 30, 559–583.

Kop, N., Euwema, M., and Schaufeli, W. B. (1999) Burnout, job stress and violent behavior among Dutch police officers. *Work and Stress*, 13, 326–340.

Kroes, W. and Hurrell, J. (1975) *Job stress and the police officer*. Washington, DC: Department of Health, Education and Welfare.

Lee, R. T. and Ashforth, B. E. (1993) a longitudinal study of burnout among supervisors and managers: Comparisons between the Leiter and Maslach (1988) and GolembiewskI et al. (1986) models. *Organizational Behavior and Human Decision Processes*, 54, 369–398.

Leiter, M. P. (1991a) Coping patterns as predictors of burnout: The function of control and escapist coping. *Journal of Organizational Behavior*, 12, 123–144.

Leiter, M. P. (1991b) The dream denied: Professional burnout and the constraints of human service organizations. *Canadian Psychology*, 32, 547–555.

Leiter, M. P. (1992) Burnout as a developmental process: Consideration of models. In W. B. Schaufeli, C. Maslach, and T. Marek (eds.), *Professional burnout: Recent developments in theory and research*. Washington, DC: Taylor and Francis, pp. 237–250.

Leiter, M. P. and Maslach, C. (1988) The impact of interpersonal environment on burnout and organizational commitment. *Journal of Organizational Behavior*, 9, 297–308.

Leiter, M. P. and Maslach, C. (2005) *Banishing burnout: Six strategies for improving your relationship with work*. San Francisco: Jossey-Bass.

Loo, R. (2004) A typology of burnout types among police managers. *Policing: An International Journal of Police Strategies and Management*, 27, 156–165.

Malach-Pines, A. and Keinan, G. (2006) Stress and burnout in Israeli border police. *International Journal of Stress Management*, 13, 519–540.

Manzoni, P. and Eisner, M. (2006) Violence between the police and the public Influences of work-related stress, job satisfaction, burnout, and situational factors. *Criminal Justice and Behavior*, 33, 613–645.

Maslach, C. (1982) *Burnout: The cost of caring*. Englewood Cliffs: Prentice-Hall.

Maslach, C. and Jackson, S. E. (1981) Measurement of experienced burnout. *Journal of Occupational Behavior*, 2, 99–113.

Maslach, C. and Jackson, S. E. (1984) Patterns of burnout among a national sample of public contact workers. *Journal of Health and Human Resources Administration*, 7, 189–212.

Maslach, C. and Leiter, M. P. (1997) *The truth about burnout: How organizations cause personal stress and what to do about it*. San Francisco: Jossey-Bass.

McCarty, W. P. (2013) Gender differences in burnout among municipal police sergeants. *Policing: An International Journal of Police Strategies and Management*, 36, 803–818.

Mortinussen, M. Richardsen, A. M., and Burke, R. J. (2007) Job demands, job resources, and burnout among police officers. *Journal of Criminal Justice*, 34, 397–409.

Pines, A. M. and Kafry, D. (1978) Occupational tedium in the social services. *Social Work*, 23, 499–507.

Pines, A. M., Aronson, E., and Kafry, D. (1981) *Burnout: From tedium to personal growth*. New York: Free Press.

Queiros, C., Kaiseler, M., and DaSilova, A. L. (2013) Burnout as a predictor of aggressivity among police officers. *European Journal of Police Studies*, 1, 110–135.

Rabe-Hemp, C. (2007) Survival in an "all boys club": Policewomen and their fight for acceptance. *Policing: an International Journal of Police Strategies and Management*, 31, 251–270.

Richardsen, A. M. and Burke, R. J. (1995) Models of burnout: Implications for intervention. *International Journal of Stress Management*, 2, 31–43.

Richardsen, A. M., Burke, R. J., and Martinussen, M. (2006) Work and health outcomes among police officers: The mediating role of cynicism and engagement. *International Journal of Stress Management*, 13, 555–579.

Schaufeli, W. B. (1995) The evaluation of burnout workshop for community nurses. *Journal of Health and Human Services Administration*, 18, 11–30.

Schaufeli, W. B. and Van Dierendonck, D. (1993) The construct validity of two burnout measures. *Journal of Organizational Behavior*, 14, 631–647.

Schaufeli, W. B., Enzman, D., and Girault, N. (1993) Measures of burnout: A review. In W. B. Schaufeli, C. Maslach, and T. Marek (eds.), *Professional burnout: Recent developments in theory and research*. London: Taylor and Francis, pp. 199–215.

Schwab, R. L., Jackson, S. E., and Schuler, R. S. (1986) Educator burnout: Sources and consequences. *Educational Research Quarterly*, 10, 15–30.

Shinn, M., Rosario, M., March, H., and Chestnut, D. E. (1984) Coping with job stress and burnout in the human services. *Journal of Personality and Social Psychology*, 46, 864–876.

Shirom, A. and Melamed, S. (2006) A comparison of the construct validity of two burnout measures among two groups of professionals. *International Journal of Stress Management*, 13, 176–200.

Stearns, G. M. and Moore, R. J. (1993) The physical and psychological correlates of job burnout in the Royal Canadian Mounted Police. *Canadian Journal of Criminology*, 35, 127–148.

Taris, T. W., Kompier, M. A. J., Geurts, S. A. E., Houtman, I. L. D., and van den Heeuvel, F. F. M. (2010) Professional efficacy, exhaustion, and work characteristics among police officers: A longitudinal test of the learning-related predictions of the demand-control mode. *Journal of Occupational and Organizational Psychology*, 83, 455–474.

Ten Brummelhuis, L. L., Bakekr, A. B., and Euwema, M. C. (2010) Is family-to-work interference related to co-workers work outcomes? *Journal of Vocational Behavior*, 77, 461–469.

Vanden Broek, A., De Cuyper, N., and DeWitte, H. (2010) Not all job demands are equal: Differentiating job hindrances and job challenges in the Job Demands-resources model. *European Journal of Work and Organizational Psychology*, 39, 735–759.

Van Gelderen, B. R., Bakker, A. B., Konijn, E. A., and Demerouti, E. (2011) Daily suppression of discrete emotions during the work of police service workers and criminal investigation officers. *Anxiety, Stress, and Coping*, 24, 515–537.

Violanti, J. (1996) *Police suicide: Epidemic in blue*. Springfileld, IL: Charles Thomas.

10 Preventing officer–involved domestic violence

Leadership challenges and opportunities

Karen Oehme and Stephanie Grace Prost

The grievous harm inflicted by domestic violence is exacerbated when committed by the very officers charged with preventing this crime. In addition to causing the suffering of victims and families, the crime also reverberates through the law enforcement agency, the community, and the profession, all of which are negatively affected. Officers who choose to use violence and threats against intimate partners should be held responsible for their actions. Certain risk factors for officer-involved domestic violence (OIDV), however, have recently gained the attention of researchers, the media, and the public. These include job-related strain, stress, post-traumatic stress, and substance abuse. A renewed focus on these factors may provide leadership with a timely opportunity to work to prevent domestic violence within the ranks, hold perpetrators accountable, and increase the professionalism and public legitimacy of law enforcement agencies. Such efforts present both challenges and opportunities that, if embraced by leadership, can save lives and livelihoods.

Domestic violence, also called domestic abuse or intimate partner violence, is defined by local law and federal authorities. Therefore, the crime's definition varies by jurisdiction. Generally, however, the crime describes the violent, coercive control that perpetrators use against their spouses or intimate partners. Such control includes physical violence, threats, intimidation, emotional abuse, isolation, and a variety of other tactics that are used to assert power over an intimate partner. The International Association of Chiefs of Police (IACP) defines domestic violence as an act or pattern of violence perpetrated by an individual against a family or household member not done in the defense of self or others, and includes specific acts such as bodily injury or threat of bodily injury, sexual abuse or assault, physical restraint, property crime directed against the victim, stalking, strangulation, violation of a court order of protection, and death threats or death (IACP, 2003). For the general public, the Centers for Disease Control and Prevention (CDC) state that a substantial proportion of the U.S. population has suffered from such violence, with both women and men being victimized (CDC, 2011). The CDC notes that women, in particular, are most heavily affected, with about one in three women experiencing violence, sexual assault, and stalking during their lifetimes (CDC, 2011). The IACP has developed tools for agencies to address both domestic violence perpetrated by civilians (see www.theiacp.org/MPDomesticViolence) and by police officers ("Model Policy," IACP, 2003). The IACP (1999) states that domestic violence among officers exists at "some serious level and deserves careful attention." Research attempting to determine incidence of domestic violence among officers has yet to reveal the exact prevalence of the crime. Regardless of prevalence, agencies have been strongly encouraged to take active steps to prevent OIDV.

The extent of the crime

Beyond knowing that some officers do commit domestic violence, researchers have been unable to ascertain precise rates (Ammons, 2005; Johnson *et al.* 2005; Lonsway, 2006). Some previous studies have posited that rates of OIDV are markedly higher than rates of civilian domestic violence (Garvey, 2015). For instance, one study found that more than 40 percent of responding officers self-reported engaging in violent behaviors towards their partners or children (Johnson, 1991). A later study queried both officers and their wives regarding violent behavior, and found that between 37 and 41 percent of respondent relationships involved some form of intimate partner violence over the preceding year (Neiding *et al.*, 1992). High-profile investigations have revealed similar findings. An investigation scandal involving the Los Angeles Police Department (LAPD) exposed 227 cases of violence by officers toward intimate partners and family members from 1990 to 1997. In that examination, the United States Office of the Inspector General found that the LAPD regularly failed to investigate domestic violence complaints against its officers (Los Angeles Board of Police Commissioners, 1997). Not long after this revelation, Crystal Judson was murdered by her husband, David Brame, in a shopping center parking lot in the presence of their two children. The crime was particularly shocking, as Brame was the police chief of the Tacoma Police Department in Washington State (*New York Times*, 2003).

Most recently, researchers examined published newspaper articles in an attempt to provide updated and comprehensive statistics regarding OIDV (Stinson & Liederbach, 2012). Authors identified 324 arrests for police related to a criminal offense of OIDV across 226 agencies. Males constituted 96 percent of the alleged perpetrators and 43 (13.3 percent) of these arrests were for individuals in a supervisory role. The researchers indicated that the failure to integrate local, state, and federal databases often results in ineffective recording, tracking, and verification of domestic violence committed by officers, further obscuring accurate estimates of OIDV (Stinson & Liederbach, 2012).

Importantly, not all research has revealed a strong relationship between law enforcement officers and domestic violence. One study found that police officer profiles were distinct from those of non-police batterers, indicating that personality characteristics were dissimilar between the two groups (Aamodt *et al.*, 1998). Another study explored violence committed by law enforcement officers towards intimate partners, and results revealed markedly lower self-reported perpetration rates (9 percent) than those previously noted (Lonsway, 2006). Despite the lack of specific data, and because of officers' role as crime fighters in the community, agencies must seek to prevent any domestic violence committed by officers against their intimate partners. These agency efforts to prevent OIDV, in turn, require accurate and timely reporting. It is this lack of reporting that stands as an additional barrier to victim safety.

Lack of reporting

Like the larger "dark-figure" of violent crime, researchers have long noted that *all* domestic violence is under-reported (Gracia, 2004); thus, reported cases of domestic violence represent only a small portion of the problem. Reasons for lack of reporting include, but are not limited to, the victim's fear of retaliation; the family wish to keep their "dirty laundry" under wraps (Johnson *et al.*, 2005); the law enforcement "Code of Silence"; and the desire of the agency to project to the community an image of credible support for domestic violence victims.

Several studies have purported that the lack of reporting of domestic violence generally is related to family fears of reprisal or concerns regarding privacy (Felson *et al.*, 2002; Felson & Paré, 2005). Victims may justifiably worry that contacting authorities will further anger the perpetrator, who is then likely to retaliate (Felson *et al.*, 2002). Victims may also feel embarrassed and believe that the incident is a "private" or "family matter." Some scholars have contended that this may result from the victim's perception that domestic violence is not a crime (Felson *et al.*, 2002) or the fact that victims lack confidence in the criminal justice system (Felson & Paré, 2005). Research has also revealed that victims are often blamed for their own victimization by outsiders who do not understand the complex web of tactics (e.g., physical injury, stalking, threats to take the children, isolation from friends and family) and pressures (financial, familial, religious) that keep victims in violent relationships (Policastro, 2012). Such damaging dynamics prolong many victim–perpetrator relationships and result in limited reporting.

Much of the lack of research related specifically to law enforcement officers and domestic violence, including low rates of reporting, is attributed to the "blue wall." This wall is understood as the invisible barrier purported to exist between law enforcement and the civilian world. Often called a "Code of Silence," the phenomenon reinforces officer reluctance to inform on other officers, even if they suspect serious wrongdoing (Ammons, 2005; Johnson *et al.*, 2005; Rothwell & Baldwin, 2007). This unwritten Code creates an expectation that officers will turn a "blind eye" to misconduct, even to the point of committing perjury to protect their colleagues (Johnson *et al.*, 2005; Rothwell & Baldwin, 2007). In fact, a recent poll indicated that 65 percent of respondents felt police did a "fair" or "poor" job of holding fellow officers accountable for misconduct (Chumley, 2014). Protocols associated with rank-and-file misconduct, where supervisors are often held responsible for subordinate wrongdoing (Rothwell & Baldwin, 2007) may also reflect the Code as agency leaders may desire to keep officer misconduct under wraps to preserve both their own reputation and that of the agency.

Officers' refusal to report suspected violence and an agency's purposeful, ineffectual investigation of allegations of OIDV would further expand and reinforce the power and control of the perpetrator. These compounding problems, in turn, increase victim danger by reducing the likelihood that the victim will call for help. Placing agency loyalty over integrity undermines public safety and can reduce civilian confidence in both law enforcement and, more broadly, the criminal justice system (Rothwell & Baldwin, 2007). Law enforcement officers and supervisors also fear what they consider to be a "contemptuous media, and relentless scrutiny when they err," predicating the necessity for a close-knit, supportive community (Rothwell & Baldwin, 2007, p. 610) which may reinforce the Code and further reduce public support. Police work is contingent upon citizen confidence and trust and without these, agencies risk ineffective and dysfunctional practice (Baker, 2010). Agency supervisors may perceive their actions as assuring a collective well-being or as a desire to insulate the public (Rothwell & Baldwin, 2007) when dismissing or obscuring cases of OIDV. However, silence and purposeful ignorance of the crime within the agency assures the maintenance of dangerous, and sometimes lethal, OIDV.

The impact on victims

Regardless of precise data on the extent of the crime and reasons for reduced reporting, researchers and victim advocates acknowledge that victims of OIDV face enormous obstacles to achieving safety. Like their civilian counterparts, victims of OIDV often face disbelief, blame, and shame from others when they disclose their victimization (Beck *et al.*, 2011; Witte *et al.*, 2006). Civilian victims of domestic violence, and those affected by OIDV, face serious physical and mental health problems as well (Campbell, 2002). These consequences include injuries such as bruises (Berrios & Grady, 1991), contusions (Lee *et al.*, 2001), broken teeth (Turkel, 2007), fractured bones (Berrios & Grady, 1991), head injuries (Kenney, 2006), chronic pain (Campbell, 2002), gastrointestinal and cardiovascular problems, and sexually-transmitted diseases. Female victims of IPV (intimate partner violence) often also face gynecological problems, including vaginal bleeding, unwanted pregnancies, and difficult deliveries as a result of forced sex. (American Medical Association, 1992). Mental health sequelae may include post-traumatic stress, anxiety, depression, and suicidal tendencies (Campbell, 2002).

Victims of violence perpetrated by officers, however, face additional barriers to escaping violence when compared to their civilian counterparts (Ammons, 2005). Officers are proficient in the use of weaponry, effective interrogation and investigation skills, and are intensely aware of how to navigate the criminal justice system (Ammons, 2005; Johnson *et al.*, 2005; Stinson & Liederbach, 2012; Wetendorf, 2007). Officers who batter are also capable of inflicting physical harm in ways that reduce the risk of visibility by targeting easily concealable areas of the body (Ammons, 2005). Further, civilian victims are often told to use the local domestic violence shelter, but officers know where those shelters are located (Wetendorf, 2015). Civilians are told to seek safety, but OIDV victims can be tracked and stalked by their abusers due to their proficiency with electronic surveillance and multiple kinds of records (Garvey, 2015). These skills help create a formidable abuser. Additional concerns arise due to the recent increased militarization of law enforcement (Baker, 2011; Chumley, 2014). Use of military-style tactics and access to enhanced weaponry have been criticized as fostering a "militaristic mind-set," which casts the roles of the military and police too closely (Baker, 2011). The clear line meant to exist between the police and military is fading (Baker, 2011), and it is possible that these blurred boundaries may impact victims of OIDV, as well.

Risk factors of officer-involved domestic violence

The fact remains that while some officers use violence to control intimate partners, importantly, many do not perpetrate violence against their partners. This issue has lead researchers to examine the risk factors associated with OIDV. Theoretical frameworks offered as risk factors for OIDV include different "spillover" effects of job-related dynamics, including general strain (Gibson *et al.*, 2001), post-traumatic stress (Kopel & Friedman, 1997) and PTSD, and authoritarianism (i.e. power and control; Johnson, 1991; Johnson *et al.*, 2005). Factors including mental health problems (e.g., depression) and substance abuse (e.g., alcohol) have been proposed as associated risks for domestic violence as well. Researchers agree that these and other factors require further investigation, as the inquiry regarding OIDV remains relatively unexplored (Stinson & Liederbach, 2012).

General strain

Little debate exists regarding the difficulty, danger, and stressors associated with police work (Johnson, 1991; Lennings, 1997; Storch & Panzarella, 1996; Swatt *et al.*, 2007). In fact, researchers have indicated that sources of police stress are both "on the street," involving crime patrol and investigation, and behind the desk, with departmental politics and top-down management practices (Liberman *et al.*, 2002; Toch, 2002; Violanti & Aron, 1993). It is no wonder, then, that police work is associated with negative affective states (Gibson *et al.*, 2001). Perceived strain may be actual or imagined and may be a result of achievement failure, the removal of positive stimuli, or the presentation of negative stimuli. Strain results in negative states (e.g., anxiety, depression, anger, and violence) that foster a desire to manage—or cope with—the strain. Coping can be adaptive (positive) or maladaptive (negative) in nature.

Findings regarding general strain theory (GST) support the relationship between strain and negative affect in police officers, with some studies having examined strain and officer-involved domestic violence. Researchers examined the relationships among strain, negative affect, and subsequent domestic violence in a sample of 1,104 Maryland police officers (Gibson *et al.*, 2001). Domestic violence was defined as the officers having "gotten out of control and been physical with (e.g., pushing, shoving, grabbing)" their partners, children, or pets. Of the 596 responding officers, 7.4 percent indicated having been physical with their partners, 8.1 percent indicated having been physical with their children, and 11.6 percent indicated having been physical with their pets. In total, nearly 18 percent of responding officers self-reported having committed a domestic violence act. Results indicated that strain emerged as a predictor of domestic violence perpetration. A later examination of the relationship between GST and negative affect revealed that strain had a significant, positive relationship with anxiety, depression, and anger (Swatt *et al.*, 2007). In fact, the relationship between officer strain and subsequent anxiety and depression was higher than any other factor. Researchers have purported that stressors may manifest as strain, and later burnout, without proper intervention (Golembiewski & Kim, 1990). Researchers found that high levels of professional burnout in officers were related to strain and that many wives reported aggressive behavior in their officer spouses (Maslach & Jackson, 1979).

Post-traumatic stress

Traumatic stress theory, or post-traumatic stress theory, indicates that when a person is exposed to violence or the threat of injury or death, he or she undergoes a two-state response: (1) intrusion and (2) avoidance. Intrusion is best understood as the unwanted reliving or remembering of a past traumatic experience. Avoidance is defined as the attempt to prevent intrusive thoughts. Both primary and secondary traumatic experiences may impact the likelihood of developing PTSD-like signs and symptoms (e.g., hyper-vigilance, sleep disturbances)—for some individuals, symptoms are even exacerbated by media coverage (Kay *et al.*, 2010). Police often face great danger and risk in the course of their jobs (Johnson, 1991); this danger and professional risk of injury or death makes post-traumatic stress particularly applicable to law enforcement officers. Upon examin-ing post-traumatic responses in a sample of police officers, one study found that nearly half (47 percent) of responding officers involved in a serious shooting incident met the diagnostic criteria for PTSD (Gersons, 1989). More recently, approximately 18 percent of responding officers taking an online training course reported PTSD signs and symptoms predicating a clinical diagnosis (Oehme *et al.*, 2012).

Some studies have shown that PTSD emerges as a consistent predictor of male-perpetrated intimate partner violence (IPV) in the parallel literature involving military vet-erans. Researchers found that PTSD symptomology was directly associated with IPV in a sample of military veterans (Orcutt *et al.*, 2005). A later investigation revealed that violence in a perpetrator's family of origin was exacerbated by PTSD and made manifest as later domestic violence (Taft *et al.*, 2008). Though law enforcement officers are not all veterans, they are considered to be para-militarized, due to the increased acquisition of military-style tactics and equipment previously noted (Baker, 2011; Chumley, 2014; Edwards, 2006). Thus, the parallel literature concerning the military may have application when exploring the links between PTSD and domestic violence for law enforcement officers.

The consequences of PTSD for many people are also highly problematic. Violanti (2004) noted that elevated PTSD scores were associated with nearly six times the risk of having suicidal thoughts and more than twice the likelihood of using substances in a sample of police officers. Results of an additional study indicated that officers with PTSD were four times more likely to self-report using physical violence against an intimate partner (Oehme *et al.*, 2012). These are important considerations for agency administrators, from both a risk and wellness perspective.

Authoritarian spillover and privilege

In addition to PTSD, professional spillover is a risk factor for OIDV (Johnson *et al.*, 2005). Spillover in this context is best understood as the phenomenon whereby the necessary and often conditioned thoughts and behaviors of effective police work are used by the officer in his home and intimate relationships. Specialized police tactics and training such as surveillance of suspects, interrogation techniques, knowledge and use of weapons, and "command presence" may penetrate officers' personal lives (Johnson *et al.*, 2005). Effective police work is contingent on the appropriate application of both power and control (Johnson *et al.*, 2005)—however, the most commonly cited factors at the core of domestic violence are the perpetrator's power and control over the victim (Yllö, 2005). It becomes clear that the inappropriate application of these core thoughts and behaviors may bleed from professional to personal spheres and place families of law enforcement officers at risk.

Some researchers, especially feminist theorists, note that throughout history society has been heavily influenced by male dominance and male power and privilege over women. Domestic violence, under this model, does not result from strain or stress, but as a manifestation of the larger societal problem of women having less power than men in the cultural hierarchy, which results in male privilege to use violence (Babcock *et al.*, 1993; Schumacher *et al.*, 2001). It is critical to note, however, that not all men commit violence against their partners—even in patriarchal cultures. Further, not all police officers trained to embrace power and control in their professional roles use these skills on family members.

In their study of married couples, researchers found that male partners in domestically violent marriages who reported less power in the relationship were more likely to commit violence against their female partners (Babcock *et al.*, 1993). The authors suggest that violent behaviors may be a result of male perception of inferiority. A later examination of gender role stressors and subsequent self-reported aggression and violence found that men's fear of emotions and masculine gender role stress were a significant predictor of relationship violence (Jakupcak, 2003). The author noted that this result may reflect male efforts to reassert dominance over female partners (Jakupcak, 2003). Evidence from a meta-analysis of factors related to domestic violence found similar results. Traditional sex-role ideology had a moderate, significant effect on male-perpetrated violence (Stith *et al.*, 2004). These studies illustrate that gendered power differentials may be at least one important root of IPV. The tempering of rigid gender roles could also have profound implications for victims of OIDV and may serve as an area for targeted intervention.

Mental health

Police officers in the United States are exposed to violence and shooting incidents at a much higher rate than the civilian population (Lennings, 1997). Police work and subsequent exposure and job stressors are associated with mental health concerns (Violanti (2014). Many of these stressors faced by law enforcement may increase the risk of illness and early death when compared to many other social service professions. In one sample of 119 police officers, childhood trauma, low self-worth, and perceived work stressors predicted depressive symptoms even when controlling for PTSD symptomology and baseline depression (Violanti, 2014). It is understandable, therefore, that police service is associated with various deleterious mental health effects, including anxiety (Storch & Panzarella, 1996), depression (Wang et al., 2010), and alcohol use (Stinson & Liederbach, 2012)—many of which can be linked to domestic violence.

Depression

Depression is an important concern for law enforcement officers and may be rooted in many factors. Using the Center for Epidemiological Studies Depression Scale (CES-D), researchers found that both organizational stress and inherent stressors associated with police work were related to psychological distress in a sample of police officers (Violanti & Aron, 1993). Both stressors and exposure to trauma are common predictors of depression in police and efforts to provide officers techniques to manage stress are essential to reducing the risk of depression. In one sample of police officers, over 77 percent of participants reported depressive symptoms one year post-academy, with symptoms most often related to sleep quality, energy, and fatigue (Wang et al., 2010).

Results of a systematic review indicated that depression was an important risk factor for male-to-female partner physical abuse, though quantitative effect sizes were not calculated (Schumacher et al., 2001). A more recent study found a large effect of perpetrator depression in the prediction of domestic violence across 14 studies and over 2,700 perpetrators (Stith et al., 2004). Interestingly, depression on the part of female victims was also strongly related to domestic violence (Stith et al., 2004).

Despite these consistent findings, little examination of depression and OIDV has taken place. One such study examined the relationships among a variety of factors, including occupational stress and depression, and domestic violence (Gibson et al., 2001). The researchers found that depression emerged as a predictor of subsequent officer-involved domestic violence (Gibson et al. 2001). Further, officers who were more depressed were significantly more likely to report self-perpetrated domestic violence than their less-depressed counterparts. Findings suggest that depression in police officers may manifest as an important risk factor for OIDV, just as in civilian families.

Alcohol use

Alcohol use has been linked to violence generally, and to domestic violence perpetration specifically, in civilian populations. Alcohol consumption is a known contributor to interpersonal violence (Collins & Messerschmidt, 1993). The researchers further noted that there is increased confidence in scientists' ability to identify a causal relationship between alcohol use and domestic violence due to the availability of large, generalizable national data (Collins & Messerschmidt, 1993). Alcohol use emerged as a moderately strong effect in the prediction of domestic violence in a later meta-analysis across 22 studies and over 14,500 participants (Stith *et al.*, 2004). A more recent meta-analytic review illustrates similar findings, with as much as a moderate effect emerging regarding the relationship between alcohol use and male-to-female partner abuse, with the drinking category of abuse/dependence demonstrating the largest effect (Foran & O'Leary, 2008). Similar, though smaller, effects were found with female-to-male partner abuse (Foran & O'Leary, 2008).

For decades, research has suggested that many officers abuse alcohol, though the rationale for use varies (Copes, 2005; Johnson *et al.*, 2005; Kohan & O'Connor, 2002; Swatt *et al.*, 2007). Some researchers indicate that alcohol use stems from a need to cope with job stress (Johnson *et al.*, 2005; Russel & Beigel, 1990; Swatt *et al.*, 2007). Other researchers contend that alcohol use is normative in police culture (Johnson, 1991; Johnson *et al.*, 2005). Using the Alcohol Use Disorders Identification Test (AUDIT), a recent study found that 15 percent of responding officers self-reported hazardous drinking levels (score 8–15), while an additional 8.2 percent of officers indicated levels that illustrated dependency (score 20–40; Oehme *et al.*, 2012).

Even without subsequent domestic violence, officers who abuse alcohol on and off duty risk many negative physical, family, and career consequences. An analysis of arrests for off-duty officers throughout the United States revealed over 2,100 cases involving arrests of sworn officers representing all 50 states throughout a three-year period (Stinson *et al.*, 2012). Though not mutually exclusive, the majority of offenses were categorized as "violent" (*n* = 1,059). Statutory rape accounted for 81 offenses, simple assault for 277 offenses, and 236 offenses were for aggravated assault. Alcohol was often found to be implicated in officer offenses, including aggravated assault (*n* = 37), simple assault (*n* = 30), and harassment or intimidation (*n* = 320; Stinson *et al.*, 2012). In addition to arrests, police officers with problematic alcohol use face ineffective police work, poorly functioning intimate relationships (Johnson *et al.*, 2005), maladaptive coping (Violanti *et al.*, 1983), and physiological effects such as liver disease or suicide (Swatt *et al.*, 2007; Violanti, 2004).

It is important to note, however, that a direct causal link between substance or alcohol use and OIDV has yet to be found (Johnson *et al.*, 2005; Stinson *et al.*, 2012). Indeed, many officers drink alcohol without using domestic violence. Still, the IACP includes alcohol among the warning signs of possible OIDV (IACP, 1999). This warning, alongside the aforementioned consequences, warrants agency efforts to prevent alcohol abuse.

Lack of employee assistance program usage

Individual risk factors including strain, stress, and poor mental health may well continue if they go unaddressed (Chapin *et al.*, 2008). This may also be the case when officers decline to use existing agency resources created to help them manage their work-related problems. One study found that only 22 percent of responding officers utilized the Employee Assistance Program (EAP) at the agency, despite all participants being aware of the program and nearly 71 percent of participants having reviewed or seen the EAP policy (Asen & Colon, 1995). A more recent exploration with law enforcement officers and EAPs again revealed that a minority of respondents, 16.2 percent, reported accessing their agency's EAP, although 56.4 percent reported knowing enough about their EAP and how to access it. Over a third of participants reported being unlikely to access their EAPs for issues related to domestic violence; 43.5 percent reported being undecided; and only 23.1 percent said they were likely to access their EAPs (Donnelly *et al.*, 2015).

Although a variety of theoretical frameworks have been posited as explanations for domestic violence generally, and OIDV specifically, and many factors have been identified as risk factors for the perpetration of OIDV, domestic violence is not a unitary phenomenon (Johnson, 2006). It is likely, therefore, that the interaction of individual- and agency-level factors plays a role in the manifestation of IPV perpetrated by members of law enforcement.

Opportunities for leadership

Every law enforcement agency has its own unique culture and environment of unwritten rules and norms, values and beliefs (Chemerinsky, 2001). Agency culture is tightly oriented to a chain of command, and it is the Chief, supervisors, and administrators who must act to address the problem of officer-involved domestic violence. High-ranking supervisors, most notably the Chief, are largely responsible for establishing the agency's culture (Patton, 1993). The crucial first step in any agency's work to prevent officer-involved domestic violence begins with a Chief who prioritizes the issues of prevention, wellness, and accountability. When the Chief prioritizes wellness, supervisors will subsequently model attitudes and behaviors that influence their subordinates (Engel, 2000; Johnson, 2015).

New officers also look up to more experienced and veteran officers to mold their own attitudes and behaviors (Robinson, 2000). New officers similarly look to supervisors when forming their own professional identity. As a result, senior leaders in law enforcement are called upon to demonstrate and reward ethical behavior, as well as to establish the value of ethics within the organization by using clear and explicit guidelines for practice. The Chief and supervisors must both set the stage for agency culture by embodying a reputation of character and integrity and ensuring that those officers who remain unable to demonstrate professional standards are removed from service (Baker, 2010). Supervisors must also be aware of stress levels within the unit (Chapin *et al.*, 2008). Enhanced supervisor awareness can help to foster a "supportive and therapeutic" environment for police officers, and, with targeted intervention, appropriately address traumatic exposure and operational stress (Chapin *et al.*, 2008). Baker (2010) further notes that leadership ought to complete self-assessments in an effort to examine their own strengths and limitations. These examinations are key to instituting change and, therefore, reducing OIDV.

Despite the awareness of the organizational structure and its impact on officers' learned behaviors, no research has examined supervisor beliefs regarding OIDV and the subsequent translation to line officers. However, it is clear that leadership has the potential to prioritize prevention and accountability and thereby shift the culture. A natural first step in that process is for leadership to speak openly about the agency's goals, and then to set clear agency expectations and policies regarding prevention and intervention. The IACP model policy, for instance, can be redrafted to reflect local laws (IACP, 2003). The initial IACP policy, established in 1999 and revised in 2003, provides a comprehensive, zero-tolerance approach to domestic violence within police departments. The four main components of the policy are prevention and training, early warning and intervention, incident response protocols, victim safety and protection, and post-incident administrative and criminal decisions. Several states quickly adapted the 2003 IACP model policy. For instance, the Washington Association of Sheriffs and Police Chiefs (2004) policy details agency, supervisor, and employee actions in the event of alleged OIDV, as well as incident protocols. North Dakota (2005) collaborated with several partners including the state Attorney General's Office, the North Dakota Department of Health, and the Minot

State University when developing its policy. Once a state adopts a model policy, all local agencies have a roadmap to follow.

Unfortunately, many agencies may have missed this important opportunity created by the IACP. Lonsway (2006) examined the prevalence and provisions of OIDV policies and found that fewer than 30 percent indicated that such a policy was in place. Moreover, many statewide policies that do exist are related to domestic violence generally, and do not contain specific content related to OIDV (Oehme & Martin, 2011).

Since then, several additional states have implemented additional policies. The model policy for the state of New Jersey (2009) aims to provide a uniform policy for managing incidents of OIDV and includes protocols related to pre-hire screening and investigation, post-conditional employment, continuing education and training, and intervention strategies. Florida's model policy on OIDV (2010) involves partnerships with several community support agencies (Law Enforcement Families Partnership [LEFP]); Institute for Family Violence Studies at the Florida State University) not unlike those in North Dakota. Many states continue to embed OIDV-specific policies within civilian protocols. For example, Texas and Ohio merely provide the IACP policy as an addendum to the civilian protocol. Currently, Hawaii legislators are proposing H.B. 456 related to OIDV (Hawaii, 2015). Gaps in the national patchwork of laws ignore the crucial responsibility to prevent and respond to the distinct and dangerous dynamics of domestic violence.

Training

A statewide policy is a significant first step, but its value only emerges when implemented at the local level. Indeed, agencies may have appropriate policies in place; however, practices may stand in stark contrast to what these policies dictate (Lonsway, 2006). Once a policy regarding OIDV has been put in place, the entire agency must be trained on its implementation. In addition, leadership should offer initial and ongoing training regarding the dynamics of officer-involved domestic violence using local experts and victim advocates who are knowledgeable about domestic violence. Training should emphasize the need for early, pre-hiring screenings of warning signs and risk factors as well as the need to screen current officers. Training must also underscore the obligation to report a colleague's domestic violence as being equally important as responding swiftly to a crime in progress in the community. One resource to start this process is the free National Prevention Toolkit on Officer-Involved Domestic Violence, funded by the Verizon Foundation and Florida State University, which is available at nationaltoolkit.csw.fsu. edu. The online training provides two free modules, one for rank and file officers, and one for supervisors and administrative staff, and is an important resource in the prevention of OIDV across the country.

New emphasis on wellness

Other proposed solutions and targeted interventions should be undertaken by the agency and the community. These interventions are best understood as two closely related approaches: risk management and wellness.

The recent heightened interest in the promotion of positive mental health and well-being (Wahlbeck, 2015) creates an opportunity for leaders and agencies to focus on law enforcement families. For decades, researchers have argued that such focus should stand as a national priority (Johnson, 1991). Emphasizing health over "strength" can help agencies sidestep fiscal dangers in an era of reduced funding; in fact, good health represents a sound investment for law enforcement (Violanti, 2014). When an agency manages the mental and physical health of its police workforce, the investment translates to a reduced fiscal burden for costs, such as disability and premature retirement. Fiscal responsibility also extends to civil cases—lawsuits alleging officer-involved domestic violence are costly consequences for agencies and the communities that fund them.

Whether they are chosen for their risk management potential or as a tool to enhance wellness, there are many agency-level interventions available to proactive Chiefs. Agency supervisors can provide support to their officers via training and enhanced resources such as EAPs, police psychologists, and referrals to non-agency community resources (such as medical professionals) who can speak on issues such as the effect of alcohol abuse, alternatives for stress reduction, and local avenues for healthcare and counseling. Another important component of agency intervention is reaching out to family members to provide information and resources about domestic violence. Local certified domestic violence centers can help provide such information. Departmental training courses are helpful for educating officers about domestic violence and can help bring health and wellness issues to the forefront. Inviting local mental health professionals or physicians from community medical centers or universities to discuss issues such as managing job stress, anxiety, depression, and substance abuse can be an important step in ensuring that law enforcement officers know that the agency emphasizes wellness and the provision of resources to officers. A department representative should be tasked with creating these ongoing training opportunities. Inviting the local domestic violence center and a survivor of domestic violence to training courses can also help officers better understand the realities and dynamics of domestic violence. Brief questionnaires that officers can take privately at home to assess their own attitudes about violence, controlling behavior toward intimate partners, and mental health issues, are available on the National Toolkit training. Just as with the self-assessments recommended by Baker (2010), these tools can help officers to think about what assistance they may need to get and stay healthy. Fliers and handouts are also available to help officers consider how ethical principles become ethical actions at home. These can be circulated to remind officers to find non-violent resolutions to family problems, acknowledge that couples can share power at home regardless of gender, and provide suggestions such as considering their own friendships and whether they should avoid certain people who are disrespectful to their own families.

Finally, community responses to OIDV are also critical. Communities must work closely with police when problem-solving, and community members must help to guide police behavior (Baker, 2010). Collaboration between law enforcement agencies and local domestic violence experts is essential to enhancing an understanding of each other, building trust, and increasing opportunities for cross-training and education. Communities and city managers also hold responsibility for electing law enforcement leadership (i.e., the Chief). A powerful coalition may manifest itself as city managers and leadership work together to meet community challenges (Baker, 2010). City administrators formulate the vision for the agency's future and must prioritize the prevention of, and response to, officer-involved domestic violence. This prioritization assures the wellness of both officers and their families. With supportive city management, a motivated Chief, and active and engaged supervisors, the message of prevention and intervention can be incorporated throughout agency culture. Leadership is indeed the agency's best opportunity to help law enforcement officers and their families.

References

Aamodt, M. G., Brewster, J. A., and Raynes, B. L. (2000). Is the "Police Personality" Predisposed to Domestic Violence? In Domestic violence by police officers: A compilation of papers submitted to the Domestic Violence by Police Officers Conference at the FBI Academy, Quantico, VA (3, p. 15). U.S. Dept. of Justice, Federal Bureau of Investigation, Behavioral Science Unit.

Advocates for Human Rights. (2009). Officer-involved domestic violence. Retrieved on March 21, 2016 from www.stopvaw.org/officer-involved_domestic_violence.

American Medical Association. (1992). Diagnostic and treatment guidelines on domestic violence. National Center on Domestic and Sexual Violence, 1–21. Retrieved on March 21, 2016 from www.ncdsv.org/images/AMA_Diag&TreatGuideDV_3-1992.pdf.

Ammons, J. (2005). Batterers with badges: Officer-involved domestic violence. *Women Lawyers Journal J.*, *90*, 28–39.

Asen, J. and Colon, I. (1995). Acceptance and use of police department employee assistance programs. *Employee Assistance Quarterly*, *11*, 45–54.

Babcock, J. C., Waltz, J., Jacobson, N. S., and Gottman, J. M. (1993). Power and violence: The relation between communication patterns, power discrepancies, and domestic violence. *Journal of Consulting and Clinical Psychology*, *61*, 40–50.

Baker, A. (2011). When the police go military. *The New York Times*, December 3. Retrieved on March 21, 2016 from: www.nytimes.com/2011/12/04/sunday-review/have-american-police-become-militarized.html?_r=0.

Baker, T. E. (2010). *Effective police leadership: Moving beyond management*. Flushing, NY: Looseleaf Law Publications.

Beck, J. G., McNiff, J., Clapp, J. D., Olsen, S. A., Avery, M. L., and Hagewood, J. H. (2011). Exploring negative emotion in women experiencing intimate partner violence: Shame, guilt, and PTSD. *Behavior Therapy*, *42*(4), 740–750.

Bell, K. M. and Orcutt, H. K. (2009). Posttraumatic stress disorder and male-perpetrated intimate partner violence. *Journal of the American Medical Association*, *302*, 562–564.

Berrios D. C. and Grady, D. (1991). Domestic violence: Risk factors and outcomes. *Western Journal of Medicine*, *155*, 133–135.

Blumenstein, L., Fridell, L., and Jones, S. (2012). The link between traditional police sub-culture and police intimate partner violence. *Policing: An International Journal of Police Strategies & Management*, *35*, 147–164.

Campbell, J. C. (2002). Health consequences of intimate partner violence. *The Lancet*, *359*, 1331–1336.

Centers for Disease Control and Prevention. (2011). *National intimate partner and sexual violence survey: 2010 Summary Report, United States, 2011.* Retrieved on March 21, 2016 from www.cdc.gov/violenceprevention/pdf/nisvs_executive_summary-a.pdf.

Chapin, M., Brannen, S. J., Singer, M. I., and Walker, M. (2008). Training police leadership to recognize and address operational stress. *Police Quarterly*, *11*, 338–352.

Chemerinsky, E. (2001). An independent analysis of the Los Angeles Police Department's Board of Inquiry Report on the Rampart Scandal, *Loyola of Los Angeles Law Review*, *34*, 545–656. Retrieved on March 21, 2016 from http://digitalcommons.lmu.edu/cgi/viewcontent.cgi?article=2262&context=llr).

Chumley, C. K. (2014, August 26). Public trust in police low, criticism of militarization rises: Poll. *The Washington Times*. Retrieved on March 21, 2016 from: www.washingtontimes.com/news/2014/aug/26/public-trust-police-low-poll-finds/.

Collins, J. J., and Messerschmidt, P. M. (1993). Epidemiology of alcohol-related violence. *Alcohol Health & Research World*, *17*, 93–100.

Copes, H. (ed.). (2005). *Policing and stress*. Upper Saddle River, NJ: Prentice Hall.

Diane Wetendorf, Inc. (2015). *Domestic violence shelters*. Retrieved on March 21, 2016 from www.abuseofpower.info/Vict_Shelters.htm.

Donnelly, E., Valentine, C., and Oehme, K. (2015). Law enforcement officers and employee assistance programs. *Policing: An International Journal of Police Strategies & Management, 38*, 206–220.

Edwards, J. B. (2006). Law enforcement officers involved in domestic violence as batterers: An integrative treatment model. *Journal of Couple & Relationship Therapy, 5*, 27–50.

Engel, R. S. (2000). The effects of supervisory styles on patrol officer behavior. *Police Quarterly, 3*, 262–293.

Erwin, M. J., Gershon, R. R., Tiburzi, M., and Lin, S. (2005). Reports of intimate partner violence made against police officers. *Journal of Family Violence, 20*, 13–19.

Federal Bureau of Investigation. (2014). *Crime in the United States, 2013.* Retrieved on March 21 from www.fbi.gov/news/stories/2014/november/crime-statistics-for-2013-released/crime-statistics-for-2013-released.

Felson, R. B. and Paré, P. P. (2005). The reporting of domestic violence and sexual assault by non-strangers to the police. *Journal of Marriage and Family, 67*, 597–610. Retrieved on March 21, 2016 from www.jstor.org/stable/3600191.

Felson, R. B., Messner, S. F., Hoskin, A. W., and Deane, G. (2002). Reasons for reporting and not reporting domestic violence to the police. *Criminology, 40*, 617–648.

Florida's Model Policy on Officer-Involved Domestic Violence. (2010). Retrieved on March 21, 2016 from www.dcf.state.fl.us/programs/domesticviolence/publications/docs/FloridaModelPolicyonOfficerDV2010.pdf.

Foran, H. M. and O'Leary, K. D. (2008). Alcohol and intimate partner violence: A meta-analytic review. *Clinical Psychology Review, 28*, 1222–1234.

Garvey, T. M. (2015). The highly trained batterer: Prevention, investigation, and prosecution of officer-involved domestic violence. *Strategies, 2015*, 1–12.

Gersons, B. P. (1989). Patterns of PTSD among police officers following shooting incidents: A two-dimensional model and treatment implications. *Journal of Traumatic Stress, 2*, 247–257.

Gibson, C. L., Swatt, M. L., and Jolicoeur, J. R. (2001). Assessing the generality of general strain theory: The relationship among occupational stress experienced by male police officers and domestic forms of violence. *Journal of Crime and Justice, 24*, 29–57.

Golembiewski, R. T. and Kim, B. S. (1990). Burnout in police work: Stressors, strain, and the phase model. *Police Studies: International Review of Police Development, 13*, 74–80.

Gracia, E. (2004). Unreported cases of domestic violence against women: Towards an epidemiology of social silence, tolerance, and inhibition. *Journal of Epidemiology & Community Health, 58*, 536–537.

Hawaii House Bill 456. (2015). *County Police Departments; Police Officers; Citizen Complaints; Officer-involved Domestic Violence.* Retrieved on 21 March, 2016 from www.capitol.hawaii.gov/session2015/bills/HB456_.HTM.

International Association of Chiefs of Police (IACP). (1999). *Police officer domestic violence: Concepts and issues paper.* Retrieved on March 21, 2016 from www.ncjrs.gov/pdffiles1/nij/grants/181409.pdf.

International Association of Chiefs of Police (IACP). (2003). *Domestic violence by police officers model policy.* Retrieved on 21 March, 2016 from www.theiacp.org/MPDomesticViolencebyPO.

Jakupcak, M. (2003). Masculine gender role stress and men's fear of emotions as predictors of self-reported aggression and violence. *Violence and Victims, 18*, 533–541.

Johnson, L. B. (1991). *On the front lines: Police stress and family well-being. Hearing before the Select Committee on Children, Youth, and Families, House of Representatives: 102 Congress First Session May 20 (pp. 32–48).* Washington, DC: US Government Printing Office.

Johnson, L. B., Todd, M., and Subramanian, G. (2005). Violence in police families: Work–family spillover. *Journal of Family Violence, 20*, 3–12.

Johnson, M. P. (2006). Conflict and control. Gender symmetry and asymmetry in domestic violence. *Violence Against Women, 12*, 1003–1008.

Johnson, R. R. (2015). Leading by example: Supervisor modeling and officer-initiated activities. *Police Quarterly, 18*, 223–243.

Kay, L., Reilly, R. C., Connolly, K., and Cohen, S. (2010). Help or harm? Symbolic violence, secondary trauma and the impact of press coverage on a community. *Journalism Practice, 4*, 421–438.

Kenney, J. P. (2006). Domestic violence: A complex health care issue for dentistry today. *Forensic Science International*, 158: S121–S125.

Kohan, A. and O'Connor, B. P. (2002). Police officer job satisfaction in relation to mood, well-being, and alcohol consumption. *The Journal of Psychology*, *136*, 307–318.

Kopel, H. and Friedman, M. (1997). Posttraumatic symptoms in South African police exposed to violence. *Journal of Traumatic Stress*, *10*, 307–317.

Lee, B. T., Dierks, E. J., Ueeck, B. A., Homer, L. D., and Potter, B. F. (2001).Maxillofacial injuries associated with domestic violence. *Journal of Oral Maxillofacial Surgery*, *59*: 1277–1283.

Lennings, C. J. (1997). Police and occupationally related violence: A review. *Policing: An International Journal of Police Strategies & Management*, *20*, 555–566.

Liberman, A. M., Best, S. R., Metzler, T. J., Fagan, J. A., Weiss, D. S., and Marmar, C. R. (2002). Routine occupational stress and psychological distress in police. *Policing: An International Journal of Police Strategies & Management*, *25*, 421–441.

Lonsway, K. A. (2006). Policies on police officer domestic violence: Prevalence and specific provisions within large police agencies. *Police Quarterly*, *9*, 397–422.

Los Angeles Board of Police Commissioners (1997). *Domestic violence in the Los Angeles Police Department: How well does the Los Angeles Police Department police its own?* Report of the Domestic Violence Task Force, Office of Inspector General. Los Angeles, CA.

Martin, S. E. and Jurik, N. C. (2007). *Doing justice, doing gender: Women in legal and criminal justice occupations* (2nd ed.). Thousand Oaks, CA: Sage.

Maslach, C. and Jackson, S. E. (1979). Burned-out cops and their families. *Psychology Today*, *12*, 59–62.

Meyer, E., Hone-McMahan, K., and McKnight, K. (1999). Few lose jobs. *Akron Beacon Journal*, December 5, p. A1.

National Toolkit for the Prevention of Officer-Involved Domestic Violence. (2015). Unpublished statistics for 2014. Florida State University: Florida Institute for Family Violence Studies.

Neidig, P. H., Russell, H. E. and Seng, A. F. (1992). Interspousal aggression in law enforcement families: A preliminary investigation. *Police Studies: The International Review of Police Development*, *15*, 30–38.

Newman, D. W. and Rucker-Reed, M. L. (2004). Police stress, state-trait anxiety, and stressors among US Marshals. *Journal of Criminal Justice*, *32*, 631–641.

North Dakota Model Law Enforcement Involved Domestic Violence Policy. (2005). Retrieved on March 21, 2016 from www.ag.nd.gov/bci/NDModelOfficerInvolvedDomesticViolencePolicy.pdf.

Office of the Attorney General of New Jersey (2009). *Departmental policy for handling of domestic violence incidents involving law enforcement officers*. Retrieved on March 21, 2016 from www.nj.gov/lps/dcj/agguide/DV-Model-Policy-Final-12-11-09.pdf.

Oehme, K. and Martin, A. (2011). A practical plan for prevention and intervention: Florida's new Model Policy on officer-involved domestic violence. *Criminal Justice Studies*, *24*, 395–408.

Oehme, K., Donnelly, E., and Martin A. (2012). Alcohol abuse, PTSD, and officer-committed domestic violence. *Policing: A Journal of Policy and Practice.6*, 418–430.

Oehme, K., Siebert, D. C., Siebert, C. F., Stern, N., Valentine, C., and Donnelly, E. (2011). Protecting lives, careers, and public confidence: Florida's efforts to prevent officer-involved domestic violence. *Family Court Review*, *49*, 84–106.

Oehme, K., Stern, N., and Mennicke, A. (2015). A deficiency in addressing campus sexual assault: The lack of women law enforcement officers. *Harvard Journal of Law and Gender*, *38*, 712. Retrieved on March 21, 2016 from http://papers.ssrn.com/sol3/papers.cfm?abstract_id=2523935.

Orcutt, H. K., King, L. A., and King, D. W. (2003). Male-perpetrated violence among Vietnam veteran couples: Relationships with veteran's early life characteristics, trauma history, and PTSD symptomatology. *Journal of Traumatic Stress*, *16*, 381–390.

Patton, A. L. (1993). The endless cycle of abuse: Why 42 U.S.C. § 1983 is ineffective in deterring police brutality. *Hastings Law Journal*, *44*, 780.

Policastro, C. and Payne, B. K. K. (2012). The blameworthy victim: Domestic violence myths and the criminalization of victimhood. *Journal of Aggression, Maltreatment & Trauma*, *22*, 329–347. Retrieved on March 21, 2016 from www.tandfonline.com/doi/full/10.1080/10926771.2013.775985.

Robinson, A. L. (2000). The effect of a domestic violence policy change on police officers' schemata. *Criminal Justice and Behavior, 27*, 600–624.

Rothwell, G. R. and Baldwin, J. R. (2007). Whistle-blowing and the code of silence in police agencies. *Crime & Delinquency, 53*, 605–632.

Russell, H. E. and Beigel, A. (1990). *Understanding human behavior for effective police work* (3rd ed.). New York, NY: Basic Books.

Schumacher, J. A., Feldbau-Kohn, S., Slep, A. M. S., and Heyman, R. E. (2001). Risk factors for male-to-female partner physical abuse. *Aggression and Violent Behavior, 6*, 281–352.

Stinson, P. M. and Liederbach, J. (2012). Fox in the henhouse: A study of police officers arrested for crimes associated with domestic and/or family violence. *Criminal Justice Policy Review, 24*, 601–625.

Stinson, P. M., Liederbach, J., and Freiburger, T. L. (2012). Off-duty and under arrest: A study of crimes perpetuated by off-duty police. *Criminal Justice Policy Review, 23*, 139–163.

Stith, S. M., Smith, D. B., Penn, C. E., Ward, D. B., and Tritt, D. (2004). Intimate partner physical abuse perpetration and victimization risk factors: A meta-analytic review. *Aggression and Violent Behavior, 10*, 65–98.

Storch, J. E. and Panzarella, R. (1996). Police stress: State-trait anxiety in relation to occupational and personal stressors. *Journal of Criminal Justice, 24*, 99–107.

Swatt, M. L., Gibson, C. L., and Piquero, N. L. (2007). Exploring the utility of general strain theory in explaining problematic alcohol consumption by police officers. *Journal of Criminal Justice, 35*, 596–611. doi: 10.1016/j.jcrimjus.2007.09.005.

Taft, C. T., Schumm, J. A., Marshall, A. D., Panuzio, J., and Holtzworth-Munroe, A. (2008). Family-of-origin maltreatment, posttraumatic stress disorder symptoms, social information processing deficits, and relationship abuse perpetration. *Journal of Abnormal Psychology, 117*, 637–646.

The New York Times (2003) Tacoma police chief shoots wife before killing himself, authorities say, April 28. Retrieved on March 21, 2016 from www.nytimes.com/2003/04/28/us/tacoma-police-chief-shoots-wife-before-killing-himself-authorities-say.html.

Toch, H. (2002). *Stress in policing.* Washington, DC: American Psychological Association.

Turkel A. (2007). "And then he choked me": Understanding, investigating, and prosecuting strangulation cases. *American Prosecutors Research Institute, 2*, 1–4.

Valentine, C., Oehme, K., and Martin, A. (2012). Correctional officers and domestic violence: Experiences and attitudes. *Journal of Family Violence, 27*, 531–545.

Violanti, J. M. (2004). Predictors of police suicide ideation. *Suicide and Life-Threatening Behavior, 34*, 277–283.

Violanti, J. M. (2014). *Dying for the job: Police work exposure and health.* Springfield, IL: Charles C. Thomas.

Violanti, J. M. and Aron, F. (1993). Sources of police stressors, job attitudes, and psychological distress. *Psychological Reports, 72*, 899–904.

Violanti, J., Marshall, J., and Howe, B. (1983). Police occupational demands, psychological distress and the coping function of alcohol. *Journal of Occupational and Environmental Medicine, 25*, 455–458.

Wahlbeck, K. (2015). Public mental health: The time is ripe for translation of evidence into practice. *World Psychiatry, 14*, 36–42. Retrieved on March 21, 2016 from http://onlinelibrary.wiley.com/doi/10.1002/wps.20178/pdf.

Wang, Z., Inslicht, S. S., Metzler, T. J., Henn-Haase, C., McCaslin, S. E., Tong, H., and Marmar, C. R. (2010). A prospective study of predictors of depression symptoms in police. *Psychiatry Research, 175*, 211–216.

Washington Association of Sheriffs and Police Chiefs (WASPC). (2004). *Officer involved domestic violence.* Retrieved on 21 March, 2016 from www.waspc.org/assets/ProfessionalServices/modelpolicies/waspc_model_policy-oidv-final.pdf.

Weaver, T. L., Sanders, C. K., Campbell, C. L., and Schnabel, M. (2008). Development and preliminary psychometric evaluation of the Domestic Violence–Related Financial Issues Scale (DV-FI). *Journal of Interpersonal Violence, 24*, 569–585.

Weisheit, R. A., Falcone, D. N., and Wells, L. E. (2005). *Crime and policing in rural and small-town America*. Long Grove, IL: Waveland Press.

Wetendorf, D. (2007). Representing victims of police-perpetrated domestic violence. *Family Law Forum, 16*, 14–23.

Witte, T. H., Schroeder, D. A., and Lohr, J. M. (2006). Blame for intimate partner violence: An attributional analysis. *Journal of Social and Clinical Psychology, 25*, 647–667.

Yllo, K. A. (2005). Through a feminist lens. In Loseke, D. R., Gelles, R. J., and Cavanaugh, M. M. (eds.), *Current controversies in family violence* (pp. 19-34). Thousand Oaks, CA: Sage.

Part 4

Reducing levels of police misconduct

11 Prediction and intervention to prevent police misconduct

Robert E. Worden and Sarah J. McLean

Introduction

The misuse of police authority and other misconduct is by many measures concentrated disproportionately among a fairly small fraction of officers. Perhaps the best-known example is the group of 44 "problem officers" in the Los Angeles Police Department (LAPD) who were featured in the Christopher Commission report 20-plus years ago (Independent Commission on the Los Angeles Police Department, 1991: 36–37), but we have seen in other agencies that indicators of what might be misconduct follow a similarly skewed distribution across sworn personnel. We should be circumspect in the inferences that we draw from these data, since, as we will discuss below, they are ambiguous as measures of misconduct. But the 80–20 rule appears to have wide applicability, and so it is quite plausible that a large fraction of police misconduct stems from a small fraction of officers. Efforts to identify and intervene with this small set of officers would therefore seem to hold a lot of promise for preventing misconduct.

Intervention turns first on predictions of future behavior.[1] Intervention makes sense only insofar as an agency anticipates that an officer's future performance is likely to be problematic. Policing in the U.S. and Australia has accumulated some experience with such prediction and intervention through administrative mechanisms that are widely known as early identification (or early warning) systems, which are intended to identify officers who are exhibiting signs of problematic behavior and intervene with counseling, retraining, or other interventions as appropriate. The experience has not generated a commensurate volume of systematic evidence on the accuracy of the predictions or the effectiveness of the interventions, however; to the contrary, the evidence is, on the whole, weak and fragmentary.

In this chapter, we build on this small body of research on police early intervention (EI) systems, on the larger body of research on police misconduct, and on other research as it is relevant. We discuss some of the forms that police misconduct takes, and the potential heterogeneity even within categories of misconduct. We discuss some notable challenges that are confronted in efforts to predict who among an agency's sworn personnel are at high risk of misconduct, and describe efforts that have been made to make such predictions in the context of EI systems. Then we review what is known about the forms that preventive interventions take and about their effectiveness. We conclude with some observations about the further development of prediction and intervention to prevent misconduct.

Predicting misconduct

We discuss several forms of police misconduct: the use of excessive force; illegal searches; and discourtesy. We first review extant evidence on the frequency with which each of these forms of behavior occur, and evidence on the characteristics of officers who engage in these behaviors with greater frequency. Then we discuss several considerations that arise in efforts to predict the risk of these behaviors.

Varieties of misconduct

Misconduct is, so far as we know, an infrequent or even rare event relative to the large volume of police–citizen contacts. Consider the use of force. Police use physical force in a very small fraction of their interactions with the public. A recent analysis of four administrations of the Police–Public Contact Survey (Hyland *et al.*, 2015) estimated that 44 million people in the U.S. had a contact with the police each year between 2002 and 2011, and only 1.6 percent reported that the police threatened or used force; less than 1 percent reported the use of physical force—a push or grab, hit or kick, the use of pepper spray, or pointing a firearm. Even when the denominator is limited to encounters with suspected offenders, as it can be when studies make use of in-person observations of police, the use of physical force is not common (Friedrich, 1980; Worden, 1995), and the force that police use is predominantly at the low end of the force spectrum (Bayley and Garofalo, 1989; Klinger, 1995; Terrill, 2005).

Moreover, the misuse of force is still less frequent. In about three-quarters of the police contacts in which police used physical force, the force was excessive in citizens' judgments (Hyland, *et al.*, 2015: 6), though we should not take citizens' assessments at face value. From estimates based on independent observation in the 1960s and 1970s, it appears that the force that police used was excessive about one-third of the time, or in 1.3 to 1.8 percent of encounters with suspects (Friedrich, 1980; Worden, 1995). A finer-grained analysis of citizen resistance and police force based on observations in Indianapolis and St. Petersburg in the 1990s showed that police "jumped" a generic force continuum in 20 to 25 percent of their encounters with suspects (Terrill, 2005); the same analysis also showed that police were more likely to use lesser rather than greater force than that justified by the resistance of the citizens with whom they interact (also see Alpert and Dunham, 1997), and the upward departures from the continuum were of "minimal" magnitude.

Officers' authority to conduct searches is also subject to abuse. Using systematic social observations in one city in the early 1990s, coupled with legal experts' judgments about the propriety of observed searches, Jon Gould and Stephen Mastrofski (2004) examined the frequency with which officers conducted discretionary searches (beyond "plain view") and how often the searches were unconstitutional (based on a matrix of Fourth Amendment court rulings). They found that searches were fairly infrequent—about one every ten hours in the field. Nearly one-third of the searches were assessed as unconstitutional, though Gould and Mastrofski note that they found "only two or three instances that would reach the level of egregiousness required for civil liability" (2004: 334). The context was a city with strong political support for the police department's priority on fighting the war on drugs, and searches for drugs were four times as likely to be unconstitutional, so we might therefore be guarded in extrapolating these findings to other sites and other times.

Mastrofski *et al.* (2002) analyzed police disrespect toward citizens, which encompassed "name calling, derogatory statements about the citizen or the citizen's family, belittling remarks, slurs, cursing, ignoring the citizen's questions (except in an emergency), using a loud voice or interrupting the citizen (except in an emergency), obscene gestures, or spitting" (2002: 529–530).[2] Examining observational data collected in Indianapolis and St. Petersburg, they found that the officer was disrespectful to the citizen in 9 percent of the police–suspect encounters. Further, they found that in more than half of these instances, the officer responded in kind to disrespect by the citizen; only 4 percent of the respectful citizens were subjected to "unprovoked" disrespect by police. Moreover, officers did *not* respond in kind to displays of disrespect by citizens *two-thirds* of the time. Officers in these cities more often than not maintained a professional (i.e. civil) demeanor, even in the face of citizens' discourtesy.

Two studies have examined through observation the procedural justice with which police treat citizens, and inasmuch as discourtesy is a form of procedural injustice, these studies also shed some light on police discourtesy. Jonathan-Zamir *et al.* (2015) completed a small-scale observational study whose purpose was to develop and validate an instrument with which the procedural justice of police behavior could be measured. Conducting observations in a small suburban city, they formed a scale of "dignity" that reflects degrees of respect, from disrespectful to businesslike (neither disrespectful nor respectful), briefly respectful, intermittently respectful, and dominantly respectful. Police were disrespectful in 5 percent of the police–citizen interactions, business-like in 30 percent, and displayed varying degrees of respect in the remainder. Worden and McLean (2014) completed "armchair observations"—coding police–citizen encounters from audio and video recordings through in-car cameras—in a small city in upstate New York, with the purpose of measuring officers' overt procedural justice. Their quality of treatment subscale for procedural injustice captured occasions

> when officers greet or leave citizens in an insulting way (with name-calling, for example), when officers' "manner" is hostile, when the officer makes derogatory remarks or is otherwise disrespectful to the citizen, and when officers are patronizing, sarcastic, or angry toward citizens.
>
> (Worden and McLean, 2014: 7–9)

Less than 10 percent of the observed encounters had subscale scores of 1 or more.

If prediction is hampered by the low frequency of misconduct, it is further complicated insofar as acts or even patterns of misconduct comprise a heterogeneous class of phenomena, and they may have different etiologies. Consider again the use of force. The 44 problem officers highlighted in the report of the Christopher Commission appeared to be prone to the use of force. They had each accumulated at least six (and an average of nearly eight) complaints of excessive force or improper tactics in a five-year period (1986–1990), in addition to complaints with other allegations (about six each, on average). On the face of it, these officers were "problem officers," even though the Commission did not take systematic account of the officers' assignments, which might have frequently exposed them to situations in which the use of force might be necessary.[3]

But among officers who are prone to the use of physical force, we can find various dynamics. James Fyfe (1989) distinguishes officers who engage in wanton brutality from those who simply lack the appropriate preparation to properly handle the situations that they confront as police officers. Officers might misjudge when force is required or how much force is required, even while they make a good-faith effort to use their authority appropriately. Sometimes, their misjudgments stem from a lack of adequate training and preparation; at other times, their judgments might be affected by the emotional intensity of the situation, the level of illumination, or other factors. But officers might instead use force maliciously, even when no force at all is required—e.g. when the person against whom force is used is not resisting the officer's direction, and may even be securely in police custody. These are not misjudgments, but rather instances of calculated brutality prompted by malevolence or corruption.

Ellen Scrivner draws additional distinctions, finding through her survey of police psychologists five distinct profiles of officers who use excessive force: officers whose job-related experiences——e.g., traumatic incidents such as police shootings—put the officers at risk for abusing force; young and inexperienced officers who were also "highly impressionable and impulsive"; officers who develop inappropriate patrol styles; officers with personal problems; and officers with personality disorders that placed them at chronic risk. The last group is the smallest of the groups that Scrivner identified, and it resembles Fyfe's brutal officers:

> These officers have pervasive and enduring personality traits (in contrast to characteristics acquired on the job) that are manifested in antisocial, narcissistic, paranoid, or abusive tendencies. These conditions interfere with judgment and interactions with others, particularly when officers perceive challenges or threats to their authority. Such officers generally lack empathy for others. These characteristics, which tend to persist through life but may be intensified by police work, may not be apparent at pre-employment screening. Individuals who exhibit these personality patterns generally do not learn from experience or accept responsibility for their behavior, so they are at greater risk for repeated citizen complaints (Scrivner, 1994: 3).

This group also resembles the violence-prone officers that Hans Toch (1995) describes, who over-react to disrespect.

Gould and Mastrofski analyzed the distribution of unconstitutional searches across individual officers, finding a concentration not unlike that in citizen complaints and the use of force: 14 percent of the sampled officers were responsible for 60 percent of the encounters with illegal searches (2004: 344). They went on to describe this small group of officers:

> Perhaps surprisingly, none appeared to be angry, cynical, or the composite of a disillusioned officer with an axe to grind. That is, none fit the classic portrait of the officer predisposed to cut legal corners . . . but for their proclivity to search illegally, these patrolmen might be considered model officers. They were "Dudley Do-Rights" who did wrong, but in the war-against-drugs context, their unconstitutional searches were viewed as normal and necessary, virtually unchallenged by the police hierarchy, the courts, or the public.
>
> (Gould and Mastrofski, 2004: 345)[4]

They leave open—but could not empirically test—the possibility that some or much of the search-related misconduct was due to officers' lack of knowledge about legal requirements. Other studies have shown that many officers do not have a good working knowledge of the legal rules that govern warrantless searches and seizures (Heffernan and Lovely, 1991; Memory and Smith, 1988).

Discourtesy is a far more common form of misconduct than the use of excessive force, but the evidence on the well-springs of discourtesy by police is very thin. We might suppose that violence-prone officers are also discourtesy-prone, but it is only a supposition. Moreover, we could reasonably hypothesize that some officers frequently cross the line of courtesy even though they respect the line of proper force. If the perpetration of misconduct is a slippery slope, as some forms of police corruption might be (Sherman, 1974), with lesser acts of misbehavior and moral adjustment leading to more serious acts of misconduct, then discourtesy might be a precursor to brutality. But the evidence is so limited that we are left with only speculation. Mastrofski, *et al.* (2002: 536–537) estimated the effects of officers' characteristics—their race, sex, length of service, education, and training in mediation—on their disrespect toward citizens, and found null relationships. Mastrofski *et al.* (2015) estimated the effects of both situational and officer variables on a scale of procedural justice (including but not limited to "dignity"), and they found that neither officers' race nor sex bore any relationship to this behavior.

On the whole, then, extant research shows that these forms of misconduct by police are relatively infrequent—relative, that is, to the large number of police–citizen contacts. We have surmised from commission and journalistic accounts that the officers who are prone to misconduct are a small fraction of all officers, comprising the tail of a skewed distribution of counts of misconduct, like the 44 problem officers identified in the Christopher Commission report. But we also can see from research findings that the individual dynamics that underlie a pattern of misconduct may vary, and the heterogeneity of misconduct surely complicates both prediction and intervention.

Prediction

The prediction of misconduct would be facilitated by a theory of misconduct, that is, by a set of propositions that together explain misconduct, the independent variables in which are predictors of misconduct. Sadly, there is no theory of misconduct. The literature on police includes a number of propositions about the use of force (Garner *et al.*, 2002; Terrill, 2005; Terrill and Mastrofski, 2002; Worden, 1995), though most of those concern the influence of situational factors that are largely (if not entirely) beyond the control of police organizations. The same can be said about illegal searches and discourtesy.

We should pause here to emphasize that the prediction in question is not of individual incidents of misconduct—e.g. specific occasions of excessive force or unconstitutional searches—but rather of officers at high risk of misconduct. Rare events are devilishly difficult to predict. Considering one kind of rare event—school shootings—Edward Mulvey and Elizabeth Cauffman (2001: 798) observe that "there are severe restrictions on the ability of any predictive strategy (even if reasonably accurate) to identify true positives for a low base-rate behavior without also identifying a large number of false positives" (also see Hart *et al.*, 1993). Even for problem officers, individual acts of misconduct are almost surely contingent on features of situations that evoke, facilitate, or inhibit misconduct. It may well be useful to understand those contingencies when intervening with officers, as with Toch's violence-prone officers, whose use of excessive force was triggered by challenges to their authority—a situational contingency. But the predictions on which we focus here are of individual officers' temporally aggregated misconduct, e.g. excessive force in an immediately future period of time. These predictions are risk assessments. They are not easy predictions to make, but they are certainly more tractable than predictions of behavior in individual incidents. Assessment of adult offenders' risk of violence has enjoyed moderate predictive success, though it is based on a much larger and stronger evidence base (see, for example, Campbell *et al.*, 2009; Yang *et al.*, 2010) than that on police misconduct.

Any prediction is subject to errors of one type or another: false positives and false negatives. False negatives—in this instance, officers who are assessed as lower risk but whose performance later proves to be problematic—are a major concern for obvious reasons: they are missed opportunities to prevent misconduct for the benefit of both officers and citizens. False positives—officers who are assessed as high risk but whose performance would be satisfactory in the absence of intervention—are also consequential, for they demand resources and entail opportunity costs, at a minimum, and their treatment as high risk might also erode the legitimacy of the system, not only in their eyes but also the eyes of their peers and supervisors.

Arguably the best predictor of future behavior is past behavior, and, by that logic, the best predictor of future misconduct is past misconduct. That—past misconduct, or at least "risk-related" outputs (Bobb *et al.*, 2009)—is what police EI systems capture. But the limitations of these predictive mechanisms should be recognized as we learn from experience with EI systems. Two limitations stand out: the ambiguity of the behavioral indicators; and the duration over which behaviors are assessed.

First, the indicators of past behavior are all deeply flawed as metrics of misconduct. Let us consider two such indicators on which EI systems have most heavily relied: citizen complaints and use of force reports (but similar observations could be made of the other indicators, such as officer-involved shootings). Citizen complaints are subject to both under-reporting and misreporting. Most citizens who have a contact with police and believe that the police acted improperly do not report the misconduct to authorities, and an even smaller fraction file formal complaints. Worden and Becker (2015) analyzed three different sets of survey data on people who had a contact with the police, finding that among those who believed that the police acted improperly, only 5 to 7 percent reportedly filed complaints. Even if the more serious forms of misconduct are more likely to be reported, then a large fraction of misconduct is not captured in police records. At the same time, complainants are not infrequently mistaken (or deceptive) in alleging misconduct by police, such that substantial fractions of complaint investigations result in exoneration—that is, the accused officer is determined to have engaged in the alleged conduct, but it was within policy or—in "unfounding" the allegation—the alleged behavior did not occur. Consequently, citizen complaints understate the incidence of police misconduct overall, and they understate or overstate individual officers' misconduct as under-reporting and misreporting is distributed across officers in a way that is largely unpatterned, and mainly a function of the volume of officers' citizen contacts. Thus counts of citizen complaints rise and fall with officers' levels of citizen contact and especially enforcement activity (Brandl *et al.*, 2001; Lersch, 2002), but higher counts—which seldom exceed three in a year—for individual officers do not reliably signify a pattern of genuine misconduct.

The use of force is probably subject to less under-reporting by officers than complaints by citizens, particularly in departments that exercise oversight, but of course police are authorized to use physical force as necessary in performing legitimate police functions, and, as we discussed above, the force that they use is seldom greater—and is often less—than the force commensurate with citizen resistance. Like citizen complaints, then, counts of officers' uses of force correlate with their levels of enforcement activity (Lersch *et al.*, 2006), and higher counts are not necessarily indicative of misconduct or even of an inability to interact successfully with citizens. This will be true especially in police departments that have low thresholds for the level of force that is subject to reporting, where recorded uses of force will reflect largely the stochastic nature of citizen resistance as well as officers' success in managing police–citizen interactions.

It is sometimes said that where there's smoke, there's fire, and that the smoke of citizen complaints (even unfounded or exonerated complaints) and uses of force should be treated as a visible signal of the flames of misconduct. But we think that an equally credible metaphor can be invoked: that like an internal combustion engine, police work generates exhaust—uses of force, citizen complaints—when it is performed properly and even skillfully. Distinguishing the smoke of misconduct from the exhaust of routine police work based on the kind of information captured in police records is difficult to do.

At a minimum, greater effort should be made to take assignments and activity into account in making predictions. Most contemporary EI systems use a "time-and-numbers" approach to identifying officers who may have performance problems; for each behavioral indicator, a time period—say, 12 months—and a numerical threshold—say, three—is specified, and an officer whose count reaches or exceeds the threshold is selected or "flagged" by the system. The predictive model that underlies a time-and-numbers system is simple but crude, neglecting entirely the differing nature of individual officers' assignments and thus their exposure to situations that are more or less likely to necessitate the use of force or to yield citizen complaints. A few departments, such as Pittsburgh's (Davis, *et al.*, 2002), use peer comparisons, which has the potential to adjust for officers' exposure to risk, though it is surely difficult to define the peer groups for patrol officers properly, since exposure varies both spatially, across beats (even within precincts or districts) and temporally, across shifts or platoons. A few departments, such as LAPD (Office of the Inspector General, 2014), specify ratios of risk-related outputs (e.g. uses of force) to activity indicators (e.g. arrests), which might better take account of variation in exposure. But most systems use some variation on the time-and-numbers approach (Worden *et al.*, 2015).

The second limitation of the predictions made in contemporary EI systems is their narrow focus on *immediately* past behavior, i.e. the previous year or even the previous three months. Even if the indicators contained less "noise" as measures of police misconduct, we would be well advised not to discard information that may (and probably does) have some predictive value. Given the random elements that are intrinsic parts of the indicators, we might hope that over a longer period of time, they would cancel one another out. Just as criminal histories, including offenders' age at first arrest, have predictive value in assessing the risk of future offending, so might officers' histories have value in predicting their future performance.

Time-and-numbers predictions are thus liable to generate a large number of false positives. We find some empirical support for this proposition in the reported experiences of agencies that, in effect, treat EI system indicators as screens, with supervisory review as a further test of performance problems. For example, over a nearly three-year period beginning in 2009, Denver police officers reached "review limits"—three citizen complaints or uses of force in a quarter, five in six months, six citizen complaints or seven uses of force in a year—232 times (see Osher, 2011). They were reviewed by a board that includes managers, supervisors, officers, union officials, and a citizen. The board's review of these cases resulted in informal notification of the officer's commander 84 times, and a notification of both the officer and the officer's commander that required an informal response 28 times; in two cases the board required a formal plan for remediation. In 118 of the 232 cases, the board determined that no action was warranted.

For another example, the LAPD's EI system automatically generates "action items" when officers reach a threshold. Supervisors are required to determine whether corrective action is appropriate and, if so, what that action should be; supervisors' recommendations are subject to review through the chain-of-command. The Office of the Inspector General for the Los Angeles Police Commission (2014) performed a review of the EI system, including an analysis of action items generated during a four-month period, from November of 2012 through February of 2013. Of the 748 action items generated, the dispositions of 70 percent were "no action": "no pattern of behavior posing potential risk was identified."

These outcomes could be construed as reflecting a cultural tolerance for misconduct, as officers' immediate supervisors might be expected to give the benefits of any doubt to the officers, and we cannot categorically reject the possibility that some of what appear to be false positives were in fact true positives. But review by a board would involve a different—and we think a less forgiving—set of dynamics, and so it seems quite plausible that a large fraction of the occasions on which officers reach these time-and-numbers thresholds do not represent emergent patterns of misconduct that call for intervention.

False negatives are also likely, though they can be difficult to confirm as false negatives even in retrospect. The review of LAPD's EI system by the Office of the Inspector General (2014) noted that of 40 officers whose employment with LAPD was involuntarily terminated between 2011 and 2013, 17 had been the subject of only one EI system action item in the preceding five years and an additional 13 had generated no action item at all. The report concluded from this examination that the system "generally provided no advance 'warning' prior to the event that resulted in each officer's termination" (2014: 3). But termination might stem from behavior—such as a failed drug test—that an EI system is not designed to forecast, and so it should not be treated as a criterion against which to measure the success of its predictions.

Consider also the example of the Chicago police officer who in November of 2015 was charged with murder in the shooting of a knife-wielding African-American teen. Over a 14-year career, this officer accumulated at least 17 complaints prior to the fatal shooting; ten complaints alleged excessive force, and other allegations included improper searches and racial slurs (Kaplan, 2015), none of which was sustained. He was, therefore, among the 10 percent of the police force that generated 30 percent of the complaints. Chicago's Behavioral Intervention System, which was established in March of 2005, provides for the placement of officers in the system based on a number of different performance indicators over a 12-month period (Chicago Police Department, 2015). For example, placement may be initiated based on two or more sustained complaints, or three not-sustained excessive force complaints, in a 12-month period. Unfounded and exonerated complaints are not counted. Since as an accused person he is presumed innocent, we should not jump to the conclusion that the officer is a problem officer and thus a false negative in Chicago's system, and the available data do not include the dates of the incidents giving rise to the allegations. But as an officer who accumulated a large number of complaints, his case offers some insights into how such an officer can be overlooked for intervention: spaced out over a span of time much greater than 12 months, even recurring misconduct can elude identification as a pattern.

Thomas Bazley *et al.* (2009) analyzed a large south-eastern police department's experience with an EIS. They found that, for the calendar year 2000, the frequency and intensity of use of force reports were predictive of which officers were selected by the department's EIS. However, officers who used *lower* levels of force to handle higher levels of suspect resistance were *more* likely to be identified by the EIS. Among the officers who tended to use *more* force than called for relative to suspect resistance, *none* were identified by the EIS. Simple predictive mechanisms can produce poor results—in the form of both false positives and false negatives.

We believe that there is considerable potential to improve prediction, not only by taking better advantage of the information at the disposal of police departments, such that the predictions are based on more than three to 12 months' of performance data, but also by incorporating into the predictive models identified correlates of behavioral indicators that might be considered risk factors. The body of empirical evidence is not voluminous, but it has found associations between misconduct in various forms—e.g. complaints, substantiated rule violations, and disciplinary sanctions up to and including involuntary separation—and features of officers' backgrounds, such as pre-employment arrests, and discipline or dismissals by previous employers (including the military). In addition, misconduct is inversely associated with officers' length of service; the likelihood of complaints (Harris, 2009) and "career-ending" misconduct (Fyfe and Kane, 2005) decline over the course of an officer's career, making less-experienced officers greater risks for misconduct. These risk factors could be incorporated into predictive models, and we suspect that they would substantially improve the accuracy of the predictions that are made. (See Worden *et al.* [2014] for further discussion.)

Efforts to manage the risk of police misconduct through interventions with high-risk officers turn first on the success of predictions, or assessments of risk. Police agencies need to intervene with officers who are at risk and need intervention, and they correspondingly need to not intervene with officers who do not need it. Having identified officers at high risk of further misconduct, police agencies must determine how to intervene and then deliver the intervention. To those matters we turn next.

Intervention

Police departments have been widely seen as "punishment-centered bureaucracies," and for the most part, preventive, non-disciplinary interventions have emerged in the context of EI systems. Thus our discussion of intervention relies heavily on practices associated with EI systems, the associated challenges, and their effectiveness. Several kinds of intervention are suitable for use in an EIS (Lersch *et al.*, 2006; Walker, 2003), with the focus not on punishment but on correcting and changing the behavior of the individual officers who have exhibited problematic performance (Walker, Alpert, and Kenney, 2000). The types of interventions made available are, for the most part, similar across agencies of different sizes and types (Worden *et al.*, 2015). Selected officers are subjected to an intervention that normally consists of counseling or retraining. Additionally, the department may continue to monitor officers' performance afterwards to ensure correction of problem behaviors.

Just as approaches to predicting police misconduct are varied, with much remaining to be learned regarding the accuracy of the predictions, the interventions applied to officers are varied, and the intended and unintended consequences of interventions are not well understood. Only a few outcome evaluations have been conducted. Walker *et al.*. (2000) conducted evaluations of EI systems in three agencies: the Miami-Dade Police Department (MDPD); the Minneapolis Police Department (MPD); and the New Orleans Police Department (NOPD). Bobb *et al.*. (2009) assessed the Personnel Performance Index of the Los Angeles Sheriff's Department (LASD). Macintyre *et al.* (2008) examined the operation of the Victoria, Australia Police EI system. Worden *et al.* (2013) evaluated the effects of the EI system of an anonymous agency in the north-eastern U.S.

All of those evaluations have reported changes of the expected nature in officers' performance: declines in complaints (Macintyre *et al.*, 2008; Walker *et al.*, 2000; Worden *et al.*, 2013), use of force (Walker *et al.* 2000), secondary arrests (Worden *et al.*, 2013), and "risk-related" incidents (Bobb *et al.*, 2009). However, their review of then-previous research led Worden and his colleagues to opine that:

> the strength of the current research on EI system interventions is . . . no greater than a 3 on the 5-point Maryland Scientific Methods Scale (see Sherman and Gottfredson, 1997), with methodology that is rigorous in some respects and weak in others.
>
> (2013: 411)

(For detailed critiques of the evaluations, excepting their own, see Worden *et al.*, 2013.) And the one evaluation that provided for a genuine control group found that the changes in treated officers' performance were no greater than those of the matched controls. It also detected evidence of an unintended impact: officers subject to intervention subsequently made fewer arrests, especially proactive arrests, suggesting that the intervention deterred them from engaging the public.

We examine intervention from the stage of diagnosis—determining the nature of the issues that give rise to officers' performance problems—and selection of an intervention, to the delivery of the intervention, and post-intervention monitoring. We consider the dominant forms of intervention in EI systems: supervisory counseling; counseling by others; and training. We also consider an innovative intervention that was developed outside of an EI system.

Diagnosis

In most departments, though initial identification is mechanical, turning on numerical counts, discretion is exercised in a second-stage review of the officers who reach thresholds (Walker *et al.*, 2000; Worden *et al.*, 2015). Among these agencies, immediate supervisors are most commonly responsible for reviewing officer performance and arriving at a judgment of whether and, if so, what kind of intervention is needed. But in some agencies, internal affairs/professional standards are solely responsible for conducting the second-stage review, and other arrangements for second-stage review can also be found. In the Los Angeles Sheriff's Department, for example, a committee determines whether intervention is appropriate. The same is true in the Victoria (Australia) Police. There, the Research and Risk Unit (RRU) is responsible for monitoring complaint patterns and trends to detect both location-level and individual-level patterns of misconduct (Macintyre *et al.*, 2008). When a pattern of misconduct is identified at either level, the RRU prepares a profile.

Regardless of who conducts further inquiry into the behavior of officers who exceed a threshold, the depth of the investigation and the time frame over which an officer's behavior is examined is surely important for identifying patterns of genuine misconduct and diagnosing the issues giving rise to the behaviors. We know that the same behavior or "problem" may be driven by different underlying issues (Scrivner, 1994) and we might suppose that the same intervention would not have positive effects for all officers exhibiting the same "problem." Effective intervention will turn on understanding the causes associated with the exhibited behaviors which would, in turn, strengthen the ability to fit appropriate interventions to problem behaviors. Just as a more thorough understanding of the risk factors associated with problem behavior would improve predictive accuracy so, too, would it improve the ability to tailor interventions to problems.

Although the mechanisms underlying problem behaviors remain somewhat unclear, there are "clusters" in the types of performance issues that are manifested and in factors that give rise to them (cf. Scrivner, 1994). This can provide insight into the range of intervention options that agencies ought to make available. We take as a positive example Victoria's RRU, which taps a host of data sources and analyzes a variety of indicators (e.g. the member's complaint history, use of force incidents, performance appraisals, and incidents of assaults against the member) as a means to diagnose performance and to inform its *recommendation* for an intervention plan (Macintyre *et al.*, 2008). The intervention plan is ultimately formed by a committee in consultation with the individual member. These plans typically include training, counseling, and reassignment.

Contemporary EI systems include a variety of interventions, many of which do not presume that "one size fits all." The Pittsburgh Police Bureau's Performance Assessment Review System (PARS), for example, allows for a wide range of options with interventions ranging from informal counseling, retraining, and referrals to psychological therapy (Davis *et al.*, 2002, 2005). This range, which need not be infinite in order to respond appropriately to the circumstances that underlie officers' misconduct, must go beyond a training module in communication skills (as valuable as that could be for officers with communication skill deficits).

Well-trained supervisors are central to—or the "lynchpin" of—an effective EI system (Walker and Milligan, 2005). They are often charged with conducting their own investigation into officers whose behavior generates a system notification. The depth and breadth of the review they conduct has real implications for whether an officer will be subject to an intervention and for the form that intervention will take, which will be shaped by not only departmental policy regarding interventions available but also, in many cases, on supervisors' skill in selecting from among those interventions those that are most appropriate for addressing the underlying causes of problematic behavior. We know that supervisors will vary in the extent to which they are competent at both "diagnosing" a problem and fitting an appropriate strategy to deter and/or change an officer's behavior. While responsibility for selecting appropriate interventions often falls to front-line supervisors, input from others within or outside the chain of command is beneficial (Walker and Milligan, 2006).

Supervisory counseling

Front-line supervisors who identify and address personal and professional issues exhibited by subordinates early on play a preventative role by assisting subordinates in correcting their behavior before it escalates to the level of a formal EI system alert. Once the formal EI system "kicks in," front-line supervisors emerge as key figures in the decision to intervene, the delivery of the intervention, and post-intervention monitoring in many contemporary EI systems (Walker and Milligan, 2005; Worden *et al.*, 2015).

Based on Walker and colleagues' survey of 571 police agencies in 1998–1999, we know that officers' immediate supervisors were commonly responsible for counseling officers (62 percent), although other personnel were charged with such duties (45 percent). More recently, Worden and his colleagues' national survey findings indicate that the large majority of EI systems (89 percent) provide for counseling by one's immediate supervisor.[5] At the time of Walker *et al.*'s study, Miami-Dade's EIS provided for informal counseling by a supervisor and, at the supervisor's discretion, referrals to employee assistance programs inside or outside the department. The Minneapolis EIS intervention consisted of informal counseling between an officer and his or her immediate supervisor, with no post-intervention monitoring.

Front-line supervisors can affect some types of behavior, but not all supervisors are created equal, and their impact on behavior will be attenuated or amplified by supervisors' own orientations and styles (Engel, 2001; 2002). Supervisors should be actively engaged in developing their subordinates' skills and judgment, and Muir (1977) explains why such supervisory coaching can be instrumental in their subordinates' professional growth and moral renewal. But such forms of supervision have not been normal in law enforcement (Brown, 1981; Engel, 2001, 2002; Van Maanen, 1983); the potential impact of supervision probably remains unfulfilled in many cases. As Brown observed, "the pressures for loyalty and solidarity are refracted throughout the police bureaucracy" (1981: 90), with norms that prohibit second-guessing and micro-management.

Yet in many cases, effective EI system functioning will turn to a large extent on training, support and accountability for front-line supervisors. Walker *et al.* (2000: 2.32) caution:

> because intervention counseling sessions are by design informal and off-the-record, there is no way of documenting the content of the intervention. It is entirely possible that the counseling session contains no substantive content related to the goals of the EW [early warning] system. Potentially even worse, it is possible that the content delivered undermines the goals of the EW system . . . even where substantive content is delivered that is consistent with program goals, there are questions about consistency across supervisors. It is entirely possible that some supervisors deliver threats about possible future discipline while others make an effort to help the officers they counsel.

Counseling by others

Counseling need not be the exclusive responsibility of officers' immediate supervisors. Walker *et al.* (2000) reported that other personnel counseled subject officers in 45 percent of agencies' EI systems, and Worden *et al.* (2015) found that 84 percent of agencies operating an EI system provided for counseling by someone other than (or in addition to) immediate supervisors. In LASD, the intervention consists of mentoring and monitoring by three supervisors (Bobb *et al.*, 2009). Referral to professional counseling provided by an agency psychologist or through contract with external providers is common in many systems. Tapping into counseling provided through employee assistance programs widens the scope of counseling services and the ability to address the range of personal, professional, or family issues that may affect performance issues (Walker *et al.*, 2000). Moreover, evidence-based approaches of professional counseling can successfully address common mental health disorders like depression, post-traumatic stress disorders, or substance use disorders (Ramchand *et al.*, 2011). Unfortunately, among those in law enforcement, there exists distrust and a stigma associated with accessing counseling services, including EAP providers, for fear the information will not be kept confidential or that accessing care could harm their career path (Fox *et al.*, 2012; Tucker, 2015; Walker *et al.*, 2000).

Training

Walker *et al.* (2000) reported that group training classes conducted with selected officers were common in EI systems. In New Orleans, for example, the intervention is a four-day training session, attended by as many as 21 or as few as six officers (Walker *et al.*, 2000: 4.54). The training includes several components, such as stress and conflict management, complaint avoidance, verbal judo, and sensitivity training. In an unidentified agency in the north-eastern U.S., the intervention consisted of an Officer–Civilian Interaction School, a four-day group training course designed to enhance officers' communication and interaction skills in police–citizen encounters (Worden *et al.*, 2013). The group training approach may appeal to agencies insofar as it seems administratively straightforward. The course need only be repeated on a periodic basis, it is easy to track officers' compliance in attending, it limits the number of individuals in the agency responsible for intervention, and it offers the benefit of economy of scale. Walker (2003) highlights a number of drawbacks to the group training approach, however. These include the concern that the stock subject matter of the course may not address the particular problem facing individual officers, the time lag between when an officer is identified and when the intervention course is held, and the bonding dynamic that can ensue when "bad boys" are brought together.

Agencies' EI systems also include training as an intervention in a form that provides the opportunity to tailor the training to the individual's particular needs. Consistent with Walker's findings, (re)training remains a common intervention. Today's EI systems include training in a host of topics, from review of departmental policies, defensive driving tactics, weapons care, to human relations, verbal judo, and stress awareness (Worden *et al.*, 2015). For many training topics that are de rigueur for new hires, we would suppose the intervention represents retraining (e.g. defensive driving or weapons care), while others expose officers to new skills.

Peer review

One remarkable intervention that was devised and implemented outside of an early intervention system was the Violence Prevention Unit of the Oakland Police Department in 1969 (Toch and Grant, 1991; Toch *et al.*, 1975). The intervention was applied to officers by their peers, a panel drawn from among officers who themselves had histories of violence and officers nominated as good cops by their supervisors. The officers with whom the panel intervened were those who had conflicts with citizens at a rate—0.37 per month— that far exceeded that of other officers (0.1 per month, on average). Each intervention was preceded by the panel's review of documents (e.g. arrest reports) and interviews with the officer's supervisors and co-workers, out of which hypotheses were formed about the officer's role in the violent incidents. Then the panel would meet with the officer, with whom they reviewed the chronology of selected incidents, identified commonalities and patterns, and considered how alternative courses of police action might produce less violent outcomes. The rate of these officers' conflicts with citizens subsequently dropped by more than half, to 0.16 per month, while that of others dropped slightly, to 0.08 per month.

In addition to these numerical results, we would note that the subject officers were willing to reflect self-critically on their role in conflicts with citizens, fulfilling Toch and Grant's hopes for officers' honest assessment of the data, and their "uninhibited exploration of intervention options yielded a departure from familiar responses" (1991: 246). Commenting on these findings, Jerome Skolnick and James Fyfe observe that "officers' historic unwillingness to comment critically upon their colleagues' work is rooted in the fact that they almost invariably are asked to do so only in interrogation rooms and in other proceedings designed to find and punish culprits" (1993: 249). Instead, they go on to say, the Oakland project "harnessed officers' skills and experience in intervening in citizens' problems and applied them to the problems of the people closest to them: their police peers" (1993: 250). We would hope that the lessons of this undertaking are not lost on those who further develop interventions to prevent misconduct.

Post-intervention monitoring

The majority of agencies that have an EI system report that it includes post-intervention monitoring of officers' performance after initial intervention. Walker and his colleagues (2000) found that follow-up monitoring after intervention was conducted by 90 percent of responding agencies, although the duration varied (i.e. 40 percent monitored for 12 months, 47 percent monitored for 36 months). They reported that Miami-Dade's EIS post-intervention monitoring expectations were informal and also fell to the immediate supervisor. The Minneapolis EIS provided for no post-intervention monitoring. The NOPD included post-intervention monitoring, with supervisors expected to complete evaluations of the selected officers who were under their supervision for six months.

More recent estimates indicate that two-thirds of EI systems provide for post-intervention monitoring, and, consistent with earlier findings, there is wide variation in the duration of post-intervention monitoring, from one month to two years (Worden et al., 2015). The largest agencies (1,000 or more sworn) are less likely than agencies with fewer sworn to provide for post-intervention monitoring. Among those agencies that require post-intervention monitoring, most (78 percent) require a written report as part of the follow-up process. An immediate supervisor is most often responsible for completing the written report (in 66 percent of the agencies requiring written follow-up). Monitoring is important to determine whether or not interventions are being delivered, being delivered in the most appropriate manner possible, and achieving the desired goals.

Prevention

Stephens observes that in police departments, normally "the focus of discipline is predominantly punishment, not behavior change" (2011: 6). In somewhat more colorful terms, Hunt (n.d.) observes that "the underlying philosophy behind law enforcement discipline has long been the traditional 'burn 'em to learn 'em' concept." Thus the continued evolution of preventive interventions in police agencies is to be lauded, but contemporary EI systems remain in an early stage of development, and we might hope that they will facilitate the further development of preventive approaches and mechanisms. Sanctions are appropriate in some instances, to be sure. But if for many officers the misconduct in which they engage is a matter of under-preparation for the job—developing a better repertoire of tactics for the management of police-citizen encounters, or better understanding about the restrictions on police searches—then counseling or (re)training would appear to be suitable interventions.

Conclusions

The prediction of police misconduct risk poses a number of difficulties, from its low base-rate and heterogeneity to the inability to isolate most misconduct from proper police work. Officers who are at high risk for misconduct are, fortunately, few in number; unfortunately, they are not readily identifiable, and their patterns of misconduct are not all the same, nor do they spring from the same set of traits or conditions. We cannot say, based on empirical evidence, how well police agencies currently do in predicting the risk for misconduct, but we think that there is good reason to believe that the predictions yield many false positives and too many false negatives. But we also believe that improvements are feasible, even as we await the accumulation of more and better research findings about patterns of police misconduct (see Worden et al., 2014). Moreover, predictions need not turn on only actuarial assessments of risk. While initial identification of signs of problematic behavior is typically mechanical, there is an important human element introduced into the determination of whether and, if so, what kind of intervention is needed.

"Early" intervention is intendedly non-disciplinary and remedial. Just as recognizing true patterns of misconduct remains challenging so, too, does diagnosing the issues that give rise to problem behavior. Front-line supervisors often bear the burden of responsibility for this, which is intuitively sensible since it would seem that they are in the best position to understand the forces shaping the quality of subordinates' performance. Supervisors thus emerge as key actors in preventive intervention, and effective intervention will turn to a large extent on how supervisors play their roles, and how their agencies prepare and support them.

Measuring the effects of interventions is also challenging. The behaviors that interventions address are not easily measured, nor do we know if the targeted behavior would have "corrected" itself without intervention. Most outcome evaluations to date have been limited by fairly weak designs. Therefore, we do not yet know if interventions "work." We know little about their intended and unintended consequences. We take as a premise that it is unlikely, and understandably so, that the "gold standard" of randomized controlled trials would be embraced by police administrators in the context of police misconduct. Even the more rigorous quasi-experimental designs are vulnerable to threats to internal validity.

As daunting as these challenges may be, it is imperative that practitioners and researchers persevere in meeting them, for police misconduct has pernicious effects on individual citizens and officers, on police organizations and their relationships to communities, and society at large.

Notes

1 Walker observes that early identification systems "do not attempt to predict officer performance based on background characteristics of officers or other factors, rather they indicate that current performance levels ... warrant improvement" (2003: 4). But prediction inheres in the rationale for intervention, and, as we explain below, the focus on "current performance levels" impairs the capacity of such systems to intervene with officers whose future performance would most benefit from intervention.
2 Nearly 90 percent of the police disrespect "involved at least one act of commission (a statement or gesture) as opposed to one of omission (ignoring a query)."
3 The Commission asserted that

> misconduct is not established merely by the fact that an officer has many use of force reports, repeated personnel complaints, or even several shootings. It may be argued that active officers assigned to high-crime areas or specialized duties will appropriately use force more often, and may generate more complaints against them, than the "average" officer. Yet, there are many "productive" officers in high-crime areas who do not accumulate complaints, shootings, or use of force reports in relatively large numbers. The extreme concentration of these data cannot be explained solely by officer assignments or arrest rates.
>
> (Independent Commission, 1991: 38)

4 Eugene Paoline and William Terrill (2005) found that officers whose occupational attitudes conform more closely to the tenets of the traditional police culture are more likely to conduct searches during traffic stops, but they did not differentiate among legal and illegal searches.
5 The results of these two surveys cannot be compared directly due to differences in their sampling strategies.

References

Alpert, Geoffrey P. and Roger G. Dunham, 1997. *The Force Factor: Measuring Police Use of Force Relative to Suspect Resistance* (Washington: Police Executive Research Forum).

Bayley, David H. and James Garofalo, 1989. "The Management of Violence by Police Patrol Officers," *Criminology* 27: 1–25.

Bazley, Thomas D., Thomas Mieczkowski, and Kim Michelle Lersch, 2009. "Early Intervention Program Criteria: Evaluating Officer Use of Force," *Justice Quarterly* 26: 107–124.

Brandl, Steven G., Meghan S. Stroshine, and James Frank, 2001. "Who Are the Complaint-Prone Officers? An Examination of the Relationship between Police Officers' Attributes, Arrest Activity, Assignment, and Citizens' Complaints about Excessive Force," *Journal of Criminal Justice* 29: 521–529.

Brown, Michael K., 1981. *Working the Street: Police Discretion and the Dilemmas of Reform* (New York: Russell Sage).

Bobb, Merrick J., Matthew Barge, Yael Mazar, Camelia Naguib, and Tim Shugrue, 2009. *Los Angeles County Sheriff's Department: 27th semiannual report,* Police Assessment Resource Center, Los Angeles.

Campbell, Mary Ann, Sheila French, and Paul Gendreau, 2009. "The Prediction of Violence in Adult Offenders: A Meta-Analytic Comparison of Instruments and Methods of Assessment," *Criminal Justice and Behavior* 36: 567–590.

Chicago Police Department, 2015. Behavioral Intervention System, Employee Resource E06-05. http://directives.chicagopolice.org/lt2015/data/a7a57be2-1292279e-2c512-9237-2a79f1 bb0e30bb7a.html, accessed January 22, 2014.

Davis, Robert C., Christopher W. Ortiz, Nicole J. Henderson, Joel Miller, and Michelle K. Massie, 2002. *Turning Necessity into Virtue: Pittsburgh's Experience with a Federal Consent Decree* (New York: Vera Institute of Justice).

Davis, Robert C., Nicole J. Henderson, Janet Mandelstam, Christopher W. Ortiz, and Joel Miller, 2005. *Federal Intervention in Local Policing: Pittsburgh's Experience with a Consent Decree* (Washington: Office of Community Oriented Policing Services).

Engel, Robin, 2002. "Patrol Officer Supervision in the Community Policing Era," *Journal of Criminal Justice* 30: 51–64.

Engel, Robin S., 2001. "Supervisory Styles of Patrol Sergeants and Lieutenants," *Journal of Criminal Justice* 29: 341–355.

Fox, Justin, Mayur M. Desai, Karissa Britten, Georgina Lucas, Renee Luneau, and Marjorie S. Rosenthal, 2012. "Mental-Health Conditions, Barriers to Care, and Productivity Loss Among Officers in An Urban Police Department," *Connecticut Medicine* 76: 525–531.

Friedrich, Robert J., 1980. "Police Use of Force: Individuals, Situations, and Organizations," *Annals of the American Academy of Political and Social Science* 452: 82–97.

Fyfe, James J., 1989. "The Split-Second Syndrome and Other Determinants of Police Violence," in Roger G. Dunham and Geoffrey P. Alpert (eds.), *Critical Issues in Policing: Contemporary Readings* (Prospect Heights, IL: Waveland).

Fyfe, James J. and Robert Kane, 2005. *Bad Cops: A Study of Career-Ending Misconduct among New York City Police Officers*, Report to the National Institute of Justice (New York: John Jay College of Criminal Justice).

Garner, Joel H., Christopher D. Maxwell, and Cedrick Heraux, 2002. "Characteristics Associated with the Prevalence and Severity of Force Used by the Police," *Justice Quarterly* 19: 705–746.

Gould, Jon B. and Stephen Mastrofski, 2004. "Suspect Searches: Assessing Police Behavior Under the U.S. Constitution," *Criminology & Public Policy* 3: 315–361.

Harris, Christopher, 2009. "Exploring the Relationship between Experience and Problem Behaviors: A Longitudinal Analysis of Officers from a Large Cohort," *Police Quarterly* 12: 192–213.

Hart, Stephen D., Christopher D. Webster, and Robert J. Menzies, 1993. "A Note on Portraying the Accuracy of Violence Predictions," *Law and Human Behavior* 17: 695–700.

Heffernan, William C. and Richard W. Lovely, 1991. "Evaluating the Fourth Amendment Exclusionary Rule: The Problem of Police Compliance with the Law," *University of Michigan Journal of Law* 24: 311–369.

Hunt, Ted, n.d. "Education, Not Punishment, Creates a Better System," *American Police Beat*, www.apbweb.com/policy-updates-news-menu-25/1093-education-not-punishment-creates-a-better-system.html, accessed January 22, 2014.

Hyland, Shelley, Lynn Langton, and Elizabeth Davis, 2015. *Police Use of Nonfatal Force, 2002-2011*. Special Report. Washington: Bureau of Justice Statistics.

Independent Commission on the Los Angeles Police Department, 1991. *Report of the Independent Commission on the Los Angeles Police Department* (Los Angeles: Author).

Jonathan-Zamir, Tal, Stephen D. Mastrofski, and Shomron Moyal, 2015. "Measuring Procedural Justice in Police–Citizen Encounters." *Justice Quarterly* 32: 845–871.

Kaplan, Sarah, 2015. "Chicago Police Officer Charged in Deadly Shooting Has a History of Misconduct Complaints," *The Washington Post*, November 25, www.washingtonpost.com/news/morning-mix/wp/2015/11/25/chicago-cop-charged-in-deadly-shooting-has-a-history-of-misconduct-complaints/?tid=sm_tw, accessed January 22, 2014.

Klinger, David A., 1995. "The Micro-Structure of Nonlethal Force: Baseline Data from an Observational Study," *Criminal Justice Review* 20: 169–186.

Lersch, Kim Michelle, 2002. "Are Citizen Complaints Just Another Measure of Officer Productivity? An analysis of citizen complaints and officer activity measures," *Police Practice and Research* 3: 135–147.

Lersch, Kim Michelle, Thomas Bazley, and Thomas Mieczkowski, 2006. "Early Intervention Programs: An Effective Police Accountability Tool, or Punishment of the Productive?" *Policing* 29: 58–76.

Mastrofski, Stephen D., Michael D. Reisig, and John D. McCluskey, 2002. "Police Disrespect toward the Public: An Encounter-Based Analysis." *Criminology* 40: 519–551.

Mastrofski, Stephen D., Tal Jonathan-Zamir, Tal, Shomron Moyal, and James J. Willis, 2015. "Predicting Procedural Justice in Police-Citizen Encounters," *Criminal Justice and Behavior* 43: 119–139.

Macintyre, Stuart, Tim Prenzler, and Jackie Chapman, 2008. "Early Intervention to Reduce Complaints: An Australian Victoria Police Initiative," *International Journal of Police Science and Management* 10: 238–250.

Memory, John Madison and Barbara Smith, 1988. *Line Police Officer Knowledge of Search and Seizure Law: Results of an Exploratory Multi-City Test*. Columbia, SC: Authors.

Muir, William Ker, Jr., 1977. *The Police: Streetcorner Politicians* (Chicago: University of Chicago Press).

Mulvey, Edward P. and Elizabeth Cauffman, 2001. "The Inherent Limits of Predicting School Violence," *American Psychologist* 56: 797–802.

Office of the Inspector General for the Los Angeles Police Commission, 2014. *Review of the Department's Early Warning System*. Los Angeles: Author.

Osher, Christopher N., 2011. "Out of 232 Red Flags on Denver Officers, Two Led to Formal Remediation," *The Denver Post*, November 11.

Paoline, Eugene A., III, and William Terrill, 2005. "The Impact of Police Culture on Traffic Stop Searches: An Analysis of Attitudes and Behavior." *Policing: An International Journal of Police Strategies and Management* 28: 455–472.

Ramchand, Rajeev, Beth A. Griffin, Marika Suttorp, Katherine M. Harris, and Andrew Morral, 2011. "Using a Cross-Study Design to Assess the Efficacy of Motivational Enhancement Therapy-Cognitive Behavioral Therapy 5 (MET/CBT5) in Treating Adolescents with Cannabis-Related Disorders." *Journal of Studies on Alcohol and Drugs* 72: 380–389.

Scrivner, Ellen M., 1994. *Controlling Police Use of Excessive Force: The Role of the Police Psychologist* (Washington, DC: National Institute of Justice, Research in Brief).

Sherman, Lawrence W., 1974. "Becoming Bent: Moral Careers of Corrupt Policemen," in Lawrence W. Sherman (ed.), *Police Corruption: A Sociological Perspective* (Garden City, NY: Anchor).

Sherman, Lawrence W. and Denise Gottfredson, 1997 "Appendix: Methodology for this Report," in Lawrence W. Sherman, Denise Gottfredson, Doris MacKenzie, John Eck, Peter Reuter, and Shawn Bushway, *Preventing Crime: What Works, What Doesn't, What's Promising* (College Park, MD: University of Maryland).

Skolnick, Jerome H., and James J. Fyfe, 1993. *Above the Law: Police and the Excessive Use of Force* (New York: Free Press).

Stephens, Darrell W., 2011. *Police Discipline: A Case for Change* (Washington, DC: National Institute of Justice).

Terrill, William, 2005. "Police Use of Force: A Transactional Approach," *Justice Quarterly* 22: 107–138.

Terrill, William and Stephen D. Mastrofski, 2002. "Situational and Officer-Based Determinants of Police Coercion," *Justice Quarterly* 19: 215–248.

Toch, Hans, 1995. "The Violence-Prone Police Officer," in William A. Geller and Hans Toch (eds.), *And Justice for All: Understanding and Controlling Police Abuse of Force* (Washington: Police Executive Research Forum).

Toch, Hans, and J. Douglas Grant, 1991. *Police as Problem Solvers* (New York: Plenum).

Toch, Hans, J. Douglas Grant, and Raymond T. Galvin, 1975. *Agents of Change: A Study in Police Reform* (New York: John Wiley & Sons).

Tucker, Jane M., 2015. "Police Officers Willingness to Use Stress Intervention Services: The Role of Perceived Organizational Support (POS), Confidentiality and Stigma," *International Journal of Emergency Mental Health and Human Resilience*, 17: 304–314.

Van Maanen, John, 1983. "The Boss: First-Line Supervision in an American Police Agency," in Maurice Punch (ed.), *Control in the Police Organization* (Cambridge: MIT Press).

Walker, Samuel, 2003. *Early Intervention Systems for Law Enforcement Agencies: A Planning and Management Guide* (Washington, DC: Office of Community Oriented Policing Services).

Walker, Samuel and Stacy Osnick Milligan, 2005. *Supervision and Intervention within Early Intervention Systems: A Guide for Law Enforcement Chief Executives* (Washington, DC: Police Executive Research Forum).

Walker, Samuel and Stacy Osnick-Milligan, 2006. *Strategies for Intervening with Officers through Early Intervention Systems: A Guide for Front-Line Supervisors* (Washington, DC: Police Executive Research Forum).

Walker, Samuel, Geoffrey P. Alpert, and Dennis J. Kenney, 2000. *Responding to the Problem Police Officer: A National Study of Early Warning Systems*, Report to the National Institute of Justice (Washington, DC: National Institute of Justice).

Worden, Robert E., 1995. "The 'Causes' of Police Brutality: Theory and Evidence on Police Use of Force," in William A. Geller and Hans Toch (eds.), *And Justice for All: Understanding and Controlling Police Abuse of Force* (Washington, DC: Police Executive Research Forum).

Worden, Robert E. and Sarah J. McLean, 2014. *Assessing Police Performance in Citizen Encounters: Police Legitimacy and Management Accountability*, Report to the National Institute of Justice (Albany, NY: John F. Finn Institute for Public Safety, Inc.).

Worden, Robert E. and Kelly J. Becker, 2015. "Tip of an Iceberg: Citizen Complaints and Citizen Dissatisfaction with the Police," presented at the Annual Meeting of the American Society of Criminology.

Worden, Robert E., Christopher J. Harris, and Sarah J. McLean, 2014. "Risk Assessment and Risk Management in Policing," *Policing: An International Journal of Police Strategies & Management* 37: 239–258.

Worden, Robert E., Sarah J. McLean, Eugene A. Paoline, III, and Julie Krupa, 2015. *Features of Contemporary Early Intervention Systems: The State of the Art* (Albany, NY: John F. Finn Institute for Public Safety, Inc.).

Worden, Robert E., MoonSun, Kim, Christopher J. Harris, Mary Anne Pratte, Shelagh Dorn, and Shelley S. Hyland, 2013. "Intervention with Problem Officers: An Outcome Evaluation of an EIS Intervention," *Criminal Justice and Behavior* 40 (April): 410–438.

Yang, Min, Stephen C. Wong, and Jeremy Coid, 2010. "The Efficacy of Violence Prediction: A Meta-Analytic Comparison of Nine Risk Assessment Tools," *Psychological Bulletin* 136: 740–767.

12 Early intervention systems and the prevention of police misconduct

Christopher J. Harris

Introduction

Early intervention (EI) systems are often touted as an effective means to increase account-ability amongst US police departments. Indeed, EI systems have been endorsed as a best practice by the US Department of Justice (2001) and recommended by the International Association of Chiefs of Police (IACP) as a means of controlling corruption and increas-ing integrity (International Association of Chiefs of Police [IACP], 1989). These systems have also received coverage in professional police publications and academic journals as a means for law enforcement agencies to reduce their overall volume of police mis-conduct (Hughes and Andre, 2007; Schultz, 2012; Walker, 2005), and have even been proposed as a means of dealing with racial bias in police traffic stops (Walker, 2001). In addition, police agencies seeking accreditation through the Commission on Accreditation for Law Enforcement Agencies (CALEA) must now have a written policy detailing their Personnel Early Warning System (see CALEA Standard 35.1.15, 1999), and EI systems are often required as part of consent decrees between the Department of Justice and police departments who been accused of engaging in a "pattern or practice" which deprives individuals of their constitutional rights (Ross and Parke, 2009). Yet at a time when police are increasingly encouraged to be evidence-based in their adoption of policies and practices, it is curious that EI systems have been so widely endorsed when the research base for their effectiveness is small, and with many other proposed benefits currently unanswered. What follows is a brief review of the emergence of EI systems and their history, followed by what we know about the contemporary functioning and effective-ness of these systems. As we shall see, the research literature that forms the basis of our knowledge on EI systems is not large and generally suffers from significant limitations. Finally, promising avenues in which to improve the current functioning of EI systems are explored, with directions for future research.

The emergence of EI systems

EI systems are behavioral management devices designed to scan potential indicators of problematic police behavior (e.g. citizen complaints), flag officers who meet or exceed some designated threshold on those indicators (e.g. three citizen complaints in 12 months), intervene with officers when deemed necessary, and follow up with those officers who receive intervention to ensure success. Such systems emerged largely due to consistent findings that a small number of officers in any given police agency account for a dispro-portionate amount of misconduct. While such a notion has been around since the 1970s (see Goldstein, 1977: 171), it gained significant traction when reported by the Christopher Commission, whose investigation of the Los Angeles Police Department (LAPD) following the Rodney King incident found a set of 44 "problem officers" who were disproportionately involved in incidents in which force was used or allegedly misused (Independent Commission on the Los Angeles Police Department, 1991). These problem officers each had six or more citizen complaints of excessive force or improper tactics in the five-year period between 1986 and 1990. When compared to other members of their department, these 44 officers represented less than one-half of one percent of all officers, but accounted for more than 15 percent of allegations of excessive force or improper tactics (a 30:1 degree of disproportion) (Adams, 1999). Yet the Commission lamented in its report that while these officers were readily identifiable in department records, such data were not employed in performance evaluations, nor were there any steps taken to remedy these officers' performance problems. As a solution, the Commission recommended that supervisors be regularly provided with use of force information, look for "early warning" signs of developing problems, and have officers receive counseling or training as necessary (Independent Commission on the Los Angeles Police Department, 1991: 62).

Other investigations and academic research have revealed similar patterns in other police departments as well, with small numbers of officers accounting for a disproportionate amount of personnel complaints and uses of force (Walker and Bumphus, 1992). Using a similar process to the Christopher Commission, the Kolts Commission investigating the Los Angeles County Sherriff's Department (LASD) found that 62 deputies were responsible for nearly 500 complaint investigations relating to use of force/harassment (Kolts, 1992). Seventeen of these deputies had been involved in 22 civil suits against the department, resulting in settlements or damages awarded in the sum of $3.2 million and leading the Commission to conclude that the LASD had failed to properly deal with these deputies who exhibited identifiable patterns of excessive force. Journalistic examinations of records in both Kansas City and Boston Police Departments found similar patterns as well: in the former, 2 percent of officers accounted for half of all citizen complaints, while in the latter, 11 percent of officers accounted for 61.5 percent of all complaints (Walker, 2003). Subsequent empirical examinations by police scholars also confirm similar findings in other agencies (Brandl *et al.*, 2001; Harris, 2010; Lersch and Mieczkowski, 1996; Terrill and McCluskey, 2002; Walker *et al.*, 2000).

As such, EI systems are predicated on the notion that problem officers can be readily identified in police department data, and so intervening in the careers of police officers who appear to have frequent and recurring performance problems could go a long way in reducing the overall volume of police misconduct. These system are "early" in the sense that they attempt to intervene in the careers of officers before their performance problems become a more serious liability (Walker *et al.*, 2000), and thus focus on the prevention of misconduct rather than its identification.

Since EI systems attempt to correct performance problems, they are not intended to be part of an agency's formal disciplinary process. While officers could be disciplined for particular actions that led them to be identified by the system, EI system interventions are not usually documented in an officer's personnel file (Walker, 2003). This is a significant and welcomed departure from traditional police discipline, which departments have historically used to deal with problem officers, and is often characterized as punishment orientated, reactive, and concerned with only the most egregious acts (Westley, 1970). Insofar as EI systems seek to correct performance problems before they become more serious, it makes sense to seek to change officer behavior constructively through mentoring, counseling, retraining, and the like instead of relying on formal punishment, which may potentially *increase* the likelihood of future misconduct (see Harris and Worden, 2014).

The earliest EI systems were developed in the 1970s and were *ad hoc* and experimental. The early adopters included the Oakland, New York City, and Kansas City Police Departments, but all were short lived and little documentation remains of their existence (Walker, Alpert, & Kenney, 2000).[1] The Miami and Miami-Dade Police Departments were amongst the first to develop more permanent EI systems in the late 1970s and early 1980s, and Miami's system in particular has evolved into a comprehensive model for the monitoring of police behavior.[2] Nearly two decades after the emergence of these systems, a survey by Walker and his colleagues in 1998 found that 27 percent of local police agencies serving populations of 50,000 or more had some version of an EI system at the time, and an additional 12 percent were planning such systems (Walker *et al.*, 2000). In the 2007 Law Enforcement Management and Administrative Statistics (LEMAS) survey, 39 percent (344 of 883) reported to be using such a system (Worden *et al.*, 2015). Given that the LEMAS survey was deployed nearly a decade ago, it is likely that the percentage of agencies that have adopted or are planning EI systems has increased, particularly for large police departments ("An Early Intervention System," 2010).

With the increasing adoption of EI systems over the years has also come an evolution of the concept itself. Such systems began with a singular focus on identifying and intervening with problem officers, but have broadened to incorporate principles from risk management and personnel management more generally. For example, both the Pittsburgh and Phoenix Police Departments run comprehensive EI systems that employ a large number of performance indicators and can therefore address a wide range of issues beyond police misconduct (Bobb, 2003). Moreover, EI system goals have broadened to not only involve change in individual officers, but also for supervisors—by providing them with data on officers' performance and changing the expectations of their supervisory role, and police departments as a whole—by contributing to a greater culture of accountability and possibly improving community relations (Walker, 2003).

The current landscape of EI systems

Despite existing for several decades, EI systems are still very much in their infancy. Yet, amongst the agencies that employ this technology, there is a range of variation in terms of their scope and operation. General commonalities exist to be sure, but it is difficult to make sweeping claims about the nature of EI systems among US police departments.

To date, the only national survey of EI system functioning was conducted by Walker and his colleagues (2000) and includes data from 362 municipal and county police departments and 209 Sheriff's departments serving populations of 50,000 people or more. The most recent information concerning EI systems comes from a survey by Worden *et al.* (2015). Here, the researchers reached out to all 334 agencies that indicated they employed an EI system in the 2007 LEMAS survey, and inquired further about the nature of their system's operation. Of the agencies contacted, 80 percent ($N=243$) responded. Of the agencies whose systems were examined, 64 percent had fewer than 500 sworn officers; 18 percent had a sworn force ofbetween 500 and 999; and the remaining 18 percent had a force of 1,000 or more. Most of agencies (73 percent) were municipal police departments, followed by 50 sheriffs' offices and 15 state police agencies (Worden *et al.*, 2015). The information from both the Walker *et al.* and the Worden *et al.* survey is employed to describe the components of EI systems across the US

EI systems are comprised of four key components: (1) The indicators of potential misconduct employed; (2) the thresholds used for identifying officers with problematic performance; (3) the interventions used to address the performance problems of officers identified by the system; and (4) post-intervention monitoring. The current functioning of each component is considered in turn below.

The performance indicator component consists of the officer activities that are recorded and monitored by a department's EI system database. The performance indicators employed by police departments range considerably, depending on their size and scope. Some departments collect a narrow range of indicators and are generally characterized as *performance problem systems* (Walker, 2005). For example, the Minneapolis Police Department used only citizen complaints as their performance indicator. By contrast, other departments are more comprehensive and collect a wide range of indicators. The Oakland Police Department's consent decree with the Department of Justice lists 20 indicators mandated as part of the EI system, which includes typical indicators such as citizen complaints and use of force reports, but also includes sick leave usage and resisting arrest charges filed by the officer. These systems are generally characterized as comprehensive *personnel assessment systems*. The Walker *et al.* (2000) survey found that while eight EI systems relied only on citizen complaint data, most others use a variety of indicators in addition to complaints, which include use of force incidents, high-speed pursuits, and involvement in civil litigation. Worden *et al.*'s (2015) survey of agencies found that the most common indicators of EI systems were citizen and internal complaints, non-lethal force, vehicle damage/accidents, and internal investigations. Forty-four percent of agencies used all five of these indicators, while 46 percent of agencies used ten or more indicators. No agency used a single indicator.

Currently no consensus exists regarding the types or number of indicators to be employed by EI systems beyond the repeated advice that such systems should not rely on only one indicator, particularly citizen complaints, due to the ambiguity of available misconduct indicators (more on this below). The IACP report on police integrity and corruption control recommends that departments collect data on seven different performance categories: (1) firearms discharges, (2) excessive force incidents, (3) motor vehicle damage, (4) loss of departmental equipment, (5) injury on duty, (6) excessive use of sick leave, and (7) all personnel complaints (IACP, 1989). Schultz (2012) identifies 18 categories of performance data, which include, in addition to the IACP recommendations, such factors as discretionary arrests, inability to work with co-workers, and being the subject of a criminal investigation or restraining order. Of course, there is a trade-off between the numbers of indicators employed, allowing departments to monitor a greater range of officer performance, and the administrative demands such systems impose in terms of ensuring timely access to performance measures and a more complex level of data analysis.

The second component of EI systems is the selection criteria by which officers are flagged by the system for possible intervention. As with the indicators themselves, there is currently no consensus on where to set the selection criteria, and so administrators are left to use their intuition and professional expertise. The national survey conducted by Walker *et al.* (2000) demonstrated that most agencies flag officers if they meet or exceed three of a given indicator in twelve months (e.g. three citizen complaints in a year). Similar results were found in the Worden *et al.* (2015) survey, with few agencies considering a time frame of more than 12 months, and the vast majority using either an officer's previous six or 12 month performance period. The thresholds during those time periods varied somewhat, however. Eight agencies set their threshold for three complaints in three months, while 51 agencies set theirs for three complaints in 12 months. This variation in thresholds represents a trade-off: the lower the threshold, the more likely it is that officers will be selected by the system.

Some systems however vary the selection criteria according to the indicator. For example, the Miami-Dade EI system flags officers who have two or more citizen complaints or three or more use of force incidents in any quarterly reporting period (Walker, 2005). To my knowledge, no EI systems combine indicators to form performance indices that could then be used to flag officers, although certainly such combinations are feasible and might better triangulate officers in need of intervention (Worden and Harris, 2015).

Instead of department-wide thresholds, two other selection criteria have been suggested: peer officer averages and performance indicator ratios (Walker, 2003). In the former, EI systems compare an officer's performance indicators to his/her similarly situated peers, such as those working the same shift, area type, or unit. This has the benefit of comparing officers who share similar occupational environments since, for example, one might reasonably expect officers who work in high-crime areas to generate more citizen complaints or use of force reports when compared to officers who work in low-crime areas, regardless of their proclivity for misconduct. In the second case, performance data is analyzed in terms of their ratios. As such, an EI system could examine the ratios of use of force reports to arrests. An officer using force in an unusually large proportion of his/her number of arrests might suggest a performance issue requiring intervention regardless of the overall volume of arrests. While seemingly advantageous when compared to department-wide thresholds, only a handful of agencies are currently experimenting with these alternative means of selecting officers for intervention.

In addition to variation in system indicators and thresholds, how officers are selected can differ across departments. In some EI systems, once flagged, officers are automatically referred for intervention. There is growing concern, though, that such automation fails to take into account the nature and context of the indicators that triggered the flag in the first place. More sophisticated EI systems treat identification and selection as a two-stage process, such that officers who are flagged by the system (which typically employ department-wide thresholds) are then reviewed by supervisors to determine if a given officer does indeed require intervention, or if some other explanation exists as to why the officer was flagged by the system. The survey conducted by Worden *et al.* (2015) found that two-thirds of agencies provide for a two-stage process, and this was typically conducted by the officer's immediate supervisor (49 percent of agencies) or by internal affairs/professional standards personnel (21 percent of agencies).

As an example, the LASD's EI system employs the two-stage approach. Once an officer is flagged, a performance review committee solicits input from the officer's Captain about whether a performance review is necessary. Then, taking into account the Captain's input, sergeants from the agency's Risk Management Bureau prepare a more detailed report if necessary. Between 1996 and 2002, a total of 1,213 officers were flagged by the EI system, but only 19 percent were placed under formal performance review (Walker, 2003). Currently there is no research on the how supervisors make their decisions about whether or not an officer selected by an EI system is actually in need of an intervention, although the percent of officers flagged and then determined to need intervention does say something about how supervisors may regard the EI system's ability to identify potentially problematic officers.

The third component of EI systems is the intervention itself. Ideally interventions should be tailored to the underlying issue which is causing the officer to manifest performance problems, although some agencies have employed group interventions.

The CALEA standard for EI systems states that departments should have a menu of remedial actions for officers selected for intervention. According to both the national survey by Walker *et al.* (2000) and the survey by Worden *et al.* (2015), the most often-used forms of intervention are some form of counseling or retraining for selected officers. The officer's immediate supervisor typically carries out the counseling, while retraining is usually handled by the department's training unit. It is interesting to note that while the indicators employed and thresholds used by EI systems across the country vary quite extensively, the range of interventions options is fairly limited and is much more consistent across police departments. To date there is little discussion of what to do when an officer fails to improve his/her performance after being the subject of one (or possibly) more interventions.

The final component of EI systems is post-intervention monitoring, which involves efforts by the department to monitor the performance of an officer selected for intervention to determine whether or not the intervention was successful in improving his/her performance. The scope and nature of follow up amongst EI systems varies considerably. Some systems employ a formal review of an officer's performance by immediate supervisors for several months following an intervention, while others have no formal commitment and instead rely on informal review (Walker, 2003). Most of the formal reporting is done by the officer's immediate supervisor (Worden *et al*, 2015).

The effectiveness of EI systems

Despite the best-practice label of EI systems, there have only been a handful of studies that directly assess EI system interventions. While most have found a positive effect of such interventions, the scientific rigor of these studies has generally been low. To date, only six agencies' EI systems have been evaluated (Bobb *et al.*, 2009; Macintyre, *et al.*, 2008; Walker, *et al.*, 2000; Worden *et al.*, 2013). With the exception of Worden *et al.* (2013), these studies report positive findings about the effects of EI systems' interventions, despite differences in the systems' components and the nature and content of the interventions. Yet the studies that report positive findings all rest on weak research designs. Most are fairly simple; they employ only the group of officers subject to intervention and examine pre- and post-intervention outcomes (and the range of these outcomes is limited). They do not provide a control group, or when they do, the control group differs in key respects and there are no adjustments made to account for those differences. Thus, they are vulnerable to several threats to internal validity, including maturation, history, and regression to the mean (Worden *et al.*, 2013).

The one study that does not find positive effects of EI system interventions was based on a stronger design, providing for a control group matched on sex, race, academy class, and pre-intervention complaints to those officers who received intervention. Based on a panel analysis, the authors find that the EI system intervention had no effects on rates of personnel complaints, uses of force, or secondary arrests (Worden *et al.* 2012). Perhaps more importantly, the authors find that officers who were subject to EI system intervention made fewer arrests (particularly proactive arrests) after the intervention (and compared to the matched controls), indicating that the intervention had the unintended effect of deterring selected officers from being proactive. Thus, to the extent that research does find fewer performance issues in the period following an EI system intervention, that benefit might be due to officer engaging in less police work overall, which is certainly not the intent of such systems.

There is currently little research on the other intended goals of EI systems, particularly their effects on increasing accountability for supervisors or the organization as a whole. Some EI systems do contain mechanisms by which to hold supervisors accountable. For example, the San Jose Police Department has initiated a Supervisors Intervention Program, whereby supervisors are flagged in the system when an officer under their command receives three or more citizen complaints in a six-month period. That supervisor is then required to meet with his/her immediate superior, the head of the Professional Standards office, or the Assistant Chief (Walker, 2003). While this relies on only a single indicator, it is perhaps the first EI system to include a means to formally evaluate the performance of supervisors. By contrast, the Pittsburgh Police Department requires supervisors to access the EI system daily to review officers under their command, and supervisors are encouraged to intervene even before officers are flagged by the system (Walker, 2003). Whether either of these systems actually increases the accountability of supervisors remains an open question, but an evaluation of the Pittsburgh EI system notes that the system has made sweeping changes as to how supervisors conduct their job (Davis *et al.*, 2005).

A single study has been conducted examining supervisors' perceptions of the EI system in their respective departments, although the response rate for this study was rather low (26 percent) and the sample size quite small ($N=54$). The questions were largely open-ended, but supervisors frequently reported positive experiences with their EI system. Sixty-four percent of respondents reported positive assessments of their EI system, and about half reported that the system had a positive effect on the quality of police work in their agencies. Sixty-five percent also reported that the system had a positive effect on management and supervision within the department. In terms of difficulties, most respondents reported problems with the EI system, with the most common being implementation issues surrounding a lack of communication about the nature of the system and a lack of follow-through by responsible officials (Walker, 2003).

As for the impact of EI systems on agencies, no formal evaluations have been undertaken. There are no studies which assess whether EI systems increase the accountability of police agencies, and such research would be difficult, as it is likely that these systems would be adopted in conjunction with other important changes in an overall effort to increase accountability (e.g. changes in complaint procedures or use of force reporting), and so teasing out the individual effect of an EI system would be daunting. There is also no research on whether or not EI system adoption improves police–community relations.

In addition to our limited knowledge about the outcomes of EI system intervention on either individual officers, supervisors, or the department at large, there is neither research nor professional consensus offering guidance about EI system structure, nor are there any "best practices" for identifying officers with performance problems. No matter how configured, the validity of the predictions upon which EI system selection criteria are currently based (that is, that officers who exceed some threshold will continue to be problematic without intervention) have not been thoroughly examined by research, and there are reasons to be skeptical of such predictions (see also Worden and McLean, this volume). First, police misconduct is something that occurs infrequently and is difficult to predict with a high level of accuracy, and this may be further hampered because EI systems only consider a narrow range of an officer's career (e.g. the previous quarter or year) (Harris, 2012). Second, the indicators of misconduct employed by EI systems are, at best, ambiguous. For example, most EI systems employ citizen complaints and use of force reports as an indicator of potentially problematic performance. Yet research demonstrates that officers who make more arrests also tend to use force more frequently, and are also more frequently the subjects of citizen complaints (Brandl *et al.*, 2001; Hassell and Archbold, 2010; Lersch, 2002; Lersch *et al.* 2006), which seems to suggest that these potential indicators of misconduct are correlated to some degree with productivity. We also know that neither every citizen complaint nor every use of force report signifies misconduct. Complaints can be filed based on misunderstanding, calculations of legal advantage, or malice (Lersch, 2002), and of course many uses of force by police are necessary, lawful, and often reflect restraint (Terrill, 2005). Third, since most police agencies employ department-wide thresholds for EI system selection, they fail to take into account important factors such as the nature of officers' shifts or assignments. Having a two-stage identification and selection process could potentially mitigate this problem, but we know nothing about how supervisors decide whether or not officers are in need of intervention once flagged by an EI system. As well, research has yet to shed much light on EI system selection criteria, and no research has been undertaken to determine whether peer officer averages or performance indicator ratios are any better at identifying officers in need of intervention when compared to department-wide criteria.

To date, only a single study has assessed the predictive accuracy of EI system selection criteria. Worden *et al.* (2003) tested the predictive accuracy of conventional EI system selection criteria using retrospective, longitudinal data on multiple performance indicators for more than 7,000 officers from one large US police agency. Simulating the application of various selection criteria and assessing their predictive performance against composite, two-year indices of later problem behavior, they found that the customary EI system criteria (e.g. three complaints in 12 months) generated what appeared to be a large proportion of false positives (that is, officers who were flagged by the system, but did not engage in future misconduct), as well as false negatives (that is, officers who did engage in future misconduct, but were not selected by the established criteria). Adjusting selection thresholds up or down served to strike different balances between false positives and false negatives, of course, but each of the conventional thresholds generated large numbers of errors.

Adding to these difficulties, there are reasons to suspect that EI systems which employ inaccurate selection criteria may be needlessly costly. Some research has shown that police officers decrease their misconduct over time, even for officers who exhibit high rates of citizen complaints and for whom no intervention (beyond routine supervision) has been applied (Harris 2009; 2010). This suggests that younger, more inexperienced officers may be more likely to be selected by EI systems for intervention, though they may not need it (Bazley *et al.*, 2009). While some error is inevitable, if EI systems too often select officers for intervention who in fact do not require it, several negative effects can occur (Worden *et al.*, 2014). First, resources are wasted when interventions are applied to personnel who do not need them. Second, officers subject to an EI system intervention may suffer an informal stigma in their selection, and so the officers who are inaccurately selected carry the burden of such a stigma unnecessarily. Third, and perhaps most importantly, a moderate to high rate of inaccurate selection is likely to reduce the legitimacy of an EI system in the eyes of line officers and the immediate supervisors who are responsible for them. If officers see peers or subordinates who, in their estimation, are solid performers and who are nevertheless selected for intervention, then they are likely to see the system as broken. This can be further exacerbated when the recommendations of front-line supervisors go unheeded or are overruled by others (Walker *et al.*, 2003). This type of characterization by front-line officers and their immediate supervisors would adversely affect the potential of such a system for organizational reform. In short, EI system selection criteria need to rest on firm ground so that we may be confident that officers who are most at-risk for future misconduct are properly selected and, to date, it does not.

It is also important to note that these limitations apply to those EI systems that are up and running, and are carefully monitored by administrators to ensure proper functioning. Some agencies have experienced considerable difficulty in planning, implementing, or maintaining their EI system (Walker, 2005). While such systems have not been vigorously resisted by police officer unions, lessons from departments which have planned and put EI systems into place demonstrate that they are complex administrative devices which take considerable monitoring to ensure that they are functioning properly. For example, the LAPD's implementation of its EI system, which was recommended by the Christopher Commission following the high-profile incident involving Rodney King, floundered for well over a decade. In a 1996, report to the LA Police Commission, Bobb reported that the EI system was not operational and that what was planned was weak and inadequate (Walker, 2005). A subsequent investigation of the LAPD following the Rampart scandal in 1999 found that the $175,000 federal grant awarded the department to help improve their EI system had not been used, and the resulting pattern and practice suit which followed the scandal directed the department to implement its EI system. Walker (2005) noted that by mid-2004, the system was still not operational, and so in over two decades since the Rodney King incident and enormous public scrutiny, the LAPD still did not have a functioning EI system. It appears that now, however, under the LAPD's federal consent decree, the system was operational as of mid-2007 and is being evaluated by researchers (Uchida *et al.*, 2014).

Even when implemented, EI systems can prove difficult to sustain. The Boston Police Department is a cautionary tale, as it appears that the EI system in that agency faltered between 2000 and 2004 and stopped in 2005 (Mason and Mashberg, 2013). Part of the difficulty appears to be that supervisors needed to pull together potential misconduct indicators from several different databases in a piecemeal fashion, instead of having all of the information stored in a single system. The agency also twice switched the software it employed to track complaints against officers in a three-year period. When Commissioner Ed Davis learned that the department's EI system was not functioning in 2008, he ordered a review of the system and the program was reinstated. Ninety four officers were retroactively selected for intervention. Such a case speaks to the difficulties agencies might experience over time when trying to maintain an EI system.

Given the above review, there are many questions related to EI systems that remain. In fact, Walker (2007) published a report on key questions related to police accountability, and many of the questions he posed in that report on EI systems remain. These include whether EI systems can improve officer performance, hold supervisors accountable, and improve the overall accountability of agencies. In terms of EI system functioning, questions still remain about what indicators and thresholds work best at identifying officers with performance problems (if any) and whether certain types of interventions works better for certain types of problems.

EI systems version 2.0

Given the reasons for skepticism outlined above, what can we do to improve EI systems going forward? One could certainly argue that having an EI system in place is better than relying solely on police disciplinary systems to change officer behavior. Traditionally, police discipline has been viewed as harsh, unfair, and uneven in many agencies (Harris *et al.*, 2015), and this has certainly been less true of EI systems (although supervisors do see a lack of follow- through after selection, see Walker, 2003). One could also argue that having police supervisors examine the performance data of their line officers, look- ing for signs of trouble so that these officers can be counseled or retrained, is far better than reassigning them or "dumping" them on minority neighborhoods, as was done in the past (US Commission on Civil Rights, 1981). While conceding these arguments, one must acknowledge that EI systems are in an early stage of development, even in 2015. Even Walker (2001), who is a leading researcher and a proponent of EI systems, states that such systems, "should be regarded as a *promising but not fully proven* technique for reducing officer misconduct" (ibid.: 84).

In a recent article, Worden *et al.* (2014) argued that while we know little about the prediction of police misconduct, there are some key principles developed from the field of assessing offenders for their risk of recidivism in corrections which might benefit efforts to assess and manage officers' risk of future misconduct. Most important of these, risk assessments in corrections are *actuarial* rather than *clinical*. That is, risk assessments of offenders are accomplished by examining risk factors that demonstrate an established association with recidivism. These factors are measured via risk assessment instruments that typically combine risk factors into an index to produce a risk score, such that higher scores indicate higher risk. While not designed to be determinative of future offending, these instruments do place offenders into low-, medium-, and high-risk categories so that limited resources can be directed at those deemed as medium and high risk. The most sophisticated of these instruments even allows risk scores to vary over time as offenders' life circumstances change. Such risk assessment instruments have been repeat- edly shown to perform better than clinical judgments in predicting future recidivism. In policing, while EI systems use specific indicators and thresholds to assess officers' likeli- hood for future performance problems, these indicators and thresholds are not based upon empirically established risk factors. Instead, these indicators are currently chosen based on intuitive professional judgments, and as such EI system selection criteria are more similar to the judgment of clinicians than based upon established factors associated with misconduct.

Yet as Worden *et al* (2014) note, there are findings in the police misconduct litera- ture on factors which place officers at increased risk of misconduct, as well as factors that mitigate against it (which are termed *protective factors*), which EI systems might incorporate to better predict an officer's risk for future misconduct. For example, pre- service factors such as a history of arrests, and/or of disciplinary actions or termination at previous jobs have been shown to place officers at increased risk of misconduct, and could be incorporated into risk assessments of officers. Length of service is an empiri- cally established protective factor that could also be used, since research demonstrates that officers are most at-risk for misconduct early in their careers (Harris, 2009). As such, Worden *et al.* (2014: 24) suggest that, for police organizations, developing a risk assess- ment instrument that includes histories of risk-related outputs such as personnel com- plaints, length of service, pre-service arrests, and/or employment discipline/termination might form a viable instrument that is feasible and economical. In addition, the authors suggest that EI systems only capitalize on a limited time frame to identify at-risk officers, and discard historical information (e.g. activities that occurred more than three or 12 months ago) that may be of some (or possibly much) predictive value, such as officers' histories of complaints, uses of force, etc. Such factors could easily be incorporated into officer risk assessment.

Conclusion

While EI systems have been highly regarded as a means of enhancing the performance of police officers, and is indeed being adopted by (and sometimes imposed on) police departments throughout the country, there are reasons to be skeptical of the advocated benefits of these systems. The successful operation of EI systems rests on their capacity to accurately identify officers at high risk for future misconduct from those who are not, as well as to successfully intervene with those officers once identified. The evidence base for the effectiveness of EI system interventions is thin; so far there has been only one study that has assessed the predictive validity of current EI system selection criteria, and this work casts doubt that future police misconduct can be predicted with any degree of accuracy. Based on this overall assessment, there is much room for improvement. There are some promising avenues by which EI systems might be improved, but of course more research is necessary to evaluate the validity of these suggestions. Some of this research, such as determining if historical information can enhance the prediction of future misconduct, can be done fairly quickly. Other work, such as how to combine risk and protective factors into some kind of risk assessment instrument to more accurately predict officers' risk for future misconduct, will take much longer. In order to explore these important issues, we need to know much more about the cross sectional and longitudinal patterns of potential indicators of police misconduct, how these indicators associate with each other, and how these also associate with police activity—particularly arrests and other signs of proactive police work. Of course to do so, police departments will have to grant access to scholars or in-house researchers to such data and allow for the dissemination of findings. These are important issues that can be successfully addressed only with collaboration between police scholars and practitioners. If these partnerships are successful, they could constitute a tremendous contribution to the proper functioning of EI systems and to police risk management more generally in the future.

Notes

1 It is interesting to note that at the time of this writing, both Kansas City and New York are currently devising new EI systems.
2 The Miami system has not been without its problems however (see Walker, 2005: 129–130).

References

Adams, K. (1999). What we know about police use of force. In *Use of Force by Police: Overview of National and Local Data*. Washington, DC: National Institute of Justice.

"An Early Intervention system fits agencies of all sizes." *Law Enforcement Technology, 37*, 75–77.

Bazley, T. D., Mieczkowski, T., and Lersch, K. M. (2009). Early intervention program criteria: Evaluating officer use of force. *Justice Quarterly, 26*, 107–124.

Bobb, M. (2003). *Los Angeles County Sheriff's Department: 16th Semiannual Report*. Los Angeles, CA: Police Assessment Resource Center.

Bobb, M. J., Barge, M., Mazar, Y., Naguib, C., and Shugrue, T. (2009). *Los Angeles County Sheriff's Department: 27th Semiannual Report*. Los Angeles, CA: Police Assessment Resource Center.

Brandl, Steven G., Stroshine, M. S., and Frank, J. (2001). Who are the complaint-prone officers? An examination of the relationship between police officers' attributes, arrest activity, assignment, and citizens' complaints about excessive force. *Journal of Criminal Justice, 29*, 21–529.

Commission on Accreditation for Law Enforcement Agencies (1999). Standards for *Law Enforcement Agencies*. 4th ed. Fairfax, VA: CALEA.

Davis, R. C., Henderson, N. J., and Ortiz, C. W. (2005). *Can Federal Intervention Bring Lasting Change in Local Policing? The Pittsburgh Consent Decree.* New York, NY: Vera Institute of Justice.

Goldstein, H. (1977). *Policing a Free Society.* Cambridge, MA: Ballinger.

Harris, C. J. (2009). Exploring the relationship between experience and problem behaviors: A longitudinal analysis of officers from a large cohort. *Police Quarterly, 12,* 192–213.

Harris, C. J. (2010). Problem Officers? An analysis of problem behavior patterns from a large cohort. *Journal of Criminal Justice, 38,* 216–225.

Harris, C. J. (2012). The residual career patterns of police misconduct. *Journal of Criminal Justice, 40,* 323–332.

Harris, C., Chierus, K., and Edson, T. (2015). The prevalence and content of police discipline matrices. *Policing: An International Journal of Police Strategies and Management, 38,* 788–804.

Harris, C. and Worden, R. E. (2014). The effect of sanctions on police misconduct. *Crime & Delinquency, 60,* 1258–1288.

Hassell, K. and Archbold, C. (2010). Widening the scope on complaints of police misconduct. *Policing, 33,* 473–489.

Hughes, F. and Andre, L. B. (2007). Problem officer variables and early warning system. *Police Chief Magazine, 74.* Retrieved on March 21, 2016 from www.policechiefmagazine.org/magazine/index.cfm?article_id=1313&fuseaction=display&issue_id=102007.

Independent Commission on the Los Angeles Police Department (1991). *Report of the Independent Commission on the Los Angeles Police Department.* Los Angeles: Independent Commission on the Los Angeles Police Department.

International Association of Chiefs of Police (1989). *Building Integrity and Reducing Drug Corruption in Police Departments.* Retrieved on March 21, 2016 from www.ncjrs.gov/pdffiles1/Digitization/120652NCJRS.pdf.

Kolts, J. G. and staff (1992). *The Los Angeles County Sheriff's Department.* Retrieved on March 21, 2016 from www.clearinghouse.net/chDocs/public/PN-CA-0001-0023.pdf.

Lersch, K. M. (2002). Are citizen complaints just another measure of officer productivity? An analysis of citizen complaints and officer activity measures. *Police Practice and Research, 3,* 135–147.

Lersch, K. M., Bazley, T. and Mieczkowski, T. (2006). Early intervention programs: An effective police accountability tool, or punishment of the productive? *Policing, 29,* 58–76.

Lersch, K. M. and Mieczkowski, T. (1996). Who are the problem-prone officers? An analysis of citizen complaints. *American Journal of Police, 15,* 23–44.

Macintyre, S., Prenzler, T., and Chapman, T. (2008). Early intervention to reduce complaints: An Australian Victoria police initiative. *International Journal of Police Science and Management, 10,* 238–250.

Mason, E. and Mashberg, T. (2013, January 15). The Boston Police Department may be paying the price for letting a program to help troubled cops lapse. *Commonwealth Magazine.* Retrieved on March 21, 2016 from http://commonwealthmagazine.org/criminal-justice/003-policemisconduct/.

Ross, D. L. and Parke, P. A. (2009). Policing by consent decree: an analysis of 42 USC. § 14141 and the new model for police accountability. *Police Practice & Research, 2,* 199–208.

Schultz, P. (2012). Personnel Early Warning systems for small law enforcement agencies. *Law & Order, 60,* 48–51.

Terrill, W. (2005). Police use of force: A transactional approach. *Justice Quarterly, 22,* 107–138.

Terrill, W. and McClusky, J. D. (2002). Citizen complaints and problem officers: Examining officer behavior. *Journal of Criminal Justice, 30,* 143–155.

U. S. Commission on Civil Rights (1981). *Who is Guarding the Guardians?* Washington DC: The United States Commission on Civil Rights.

Uchida, C. D., Swatt, M. L., Solomon, S. E., and Mastrofski, S. D. (2014). *Evaluating the LAPD TEAMS II Early Intervention System: Methods and Measures.* Paper presented at the American Society of Criminology, San Francisco, CA.

US Department of Justice (2001). *Principles for Promoting Police Integrity.* Washington, DC: Department of Justice.

Walker, S. (2001). Searching for the denominator: Problems with police traffic stop data and an early warning system solution. *Justice Research and Policy*, *3*, 63–95.

Walker, S. (2003). *Early Intervention Systems for Law Enforcement Agencies: A Planning and Management Guide*. Washington, DC: Office of Community Orientated Policing Services.

Walker, S. (2005). *The New World of Police Accountability*. California: Sage Publications.

Walker, S. (2007). *Police Accountability: Current Issues and Research Needs*. Washington, DC: US Department of Justice.

Walker, S. and Bumphus, V. W. (1992). The effectiveness of civilian review: Observations on recent trends and new issues regarding the civilian review of the police. *American Journal of Police*, *11*, 1–26.

Walker, S., Geoffrey A. P., and Kenney, D. J. (2000). *Responding to the Problem Police Officer: A National Study of Early Warning Systems*. Washington, DC: National Institute of Justice.

Westley, W. (1970). *Violence and the Police: A Sociological Study of Law, Custom, and Morality*. Cambridge, MA: MIT Press.

Worden, R. E., Harris, C. J., and McLean, S. J. (2014). Risk assessment and risk management in policing. *Policing: An International Journal of Police Strategies and Management*, 37, 239–258.

Worden, R. E. and Harris, C. J. (2015). *Problem Officers and Problem Behaviors: Cross-sectional and Longitudinal Patters of Police Misconduct*. Paper presented at the American Society of Criminology, Washington, DC.

Worden, R. E., Kim, M., Harris, C., McGreevy, M., Catlin, S., and Schlief, S. (2013). Intervention with problem officers. An impact evaluation of one agency's EIS. *Criminal Justice & Behavior*, 40, 409–437.

Worden, R. E., McLean, S. J., Paoline, E., and Krupa, J. (2015). *Features of Contemporary Early Intervention Systems: The State of the Art*. Albany, NY: The John F. Finn Institute for Public Safety, Inc.

Worden, R. E., McGreevy, M., Catlin-Dorn, S., Harris, C., and Schlief, S. (2003). *Problem Officers, Problem Behavior, and Early Warning Systems*. Paper presented at the Academy of Criminal Justice Sciences, Boston, MA.

13 Reducing police misconduct

Kimberly D. Hassell

Introduction

Understanding the causes of, and the mechanisms for, curbing police misconduct is important for many reasons. First, police misconduct costs taxpayers a great deal of money. Schwartz (2014), in her recent national study on police indemnification, found that city governments paid approximately 99.98 percent of the monies that plaintiffs recovered in civil suits alleging civil rights violations by law enforcement. For the 81 police departments that participated in her study, local governments spent $730 million between 2006 and 2011 on police misconduct. Reports regarding payouts from individual agencies suggest that Schwartz's figure is understated (Balko, *The Washington Post*, 2014). Second, citizens have a constitutional right to due process and equal protection under the law; police officers are charged with executing laws in a constitutional manner (18 U.S.C. §§ 241, 242). When police engage in misconduct that violates the Constitution, the result is legal cynicism, which contributes to growing dissatisfaction with local and national government (Kirk and Matsuda, 2011). Third, and related to the second point, police misconduct erodes public confidence in police and police legitimacy (Harris and Worden, 2014; Ivkovic, 2009). This erosion has a criminogenic effect (Harris and Worden, 2014; National Research Council, 2004; Tyler, 2004). People obey the law when they believe the police, as agents of government, are legitimate; legitimacy is largely impacted by perceptions of procedural fairness. That is, police legitimacy hinges on the public belief that police are procedurally fair in all their actions (Mazerolle *et al.*, 2014; Tyler, 2004). In short, police misconduct erodes the legitimacy of government, which has a criminogenic effect, and costs local governments large sums of money—money that could be spent more wisely on helping to eradicate the social and structural causes of crime.

Police misconduct generally refers to procedural violations of departmental rules and regulations, violations of state and federal law, and constitutional civil rights violations (The Cato Institute's National Police Misconduct Reporting Project). As the Cato Institute's National Police Misconduct Reporting Project makes clear, police misconduct is complex in nature, scope, and consequence (See also Ivkovic, 2009). This complexity requires agencies to employ adaptive and varied prescriptive approaches to reduce police misconduct. This chapter focuses on the most prominent approaches for reducing police misconduct.

Approaches for reducing police misconduct

Most of our knowledge on police misconduct is derived from empirical studies that rely on citizens' complaints of misconduct as a proxy for actual misconduct. While complaints are not the most reliable proxy of actual misconduct (Brandl *et al.*, 2001; Hassell and Archbold, 2010; Kane and White, 2009), the research has provided some clear implications for curbing police misconduct. The most established approaches for reducing police misconduct can be found at multiple levels and stages: (1) recruitment, hiring, and retention, (2) effective policies and procedures, (3) training, (4) fair supervision, (5) administrative oversight, (6) organizational culture, and (7) national priorities. A "one or another" approach will not curb police misconduct; all aspects must be addressed in order to effectively reduce problematic police behavior (Walker and McDonald, 2009). These approaches are interrelated, but are presented and explained separately below.

Recruitment, hiring, and retention

An abundance of research outlines that certain types of officers are more likely to engage in police misconduct (Brandl *et al.*, 2001; Hassell and Archbold, 2010; Lersch, 1998; Lersch and Mieczkowski, 1996, 2000; McElvain and Kposowa, 2004; National Center for Women and Policing, 2002; Pate and Fridell, 1993; Steffensmeier, 1979; Van Wormer, 1981; Wagner, 1980). Research has documented that female officers are less likely than male officers to be the subject of citizen complaints (Brandl, et al., 2001; Hassell and Archbold, 2010; Lersch, 1998; Lersch and Mieczkowski, 1996, 2000; Melvain and Kposowa, 2004; National Center for Women and Policing, 2002; Pate and Fridell, 1993; Steffensmeier, 1979; Van Wormer, 1981; Wagner, 1980), and that male officers are more likely to receive multiple complaints within short periods of time (Lersch and Mieczkowski, 2000).

Some studies have found that racial/ethnic officers, when compared to white officers, are more likely to have complaints for misconduct filed against them (Lersch and Mieczkowski, 1996, 2000) while other research has found no difference (Brandl *et al.*, 2001; McElain and Kposowa, 2004; Wagner, 1980). There is consistent research demonstrating that younger officers are more likely to generate complaints than older officers (Brandl *et al.*, 2001; Cao and Huang, 2000; Lersch and Mieczkowski, 1996; McElvain and Kposowa, 2004, Wagner, 1980). Accordingly, officers with less experience also seem to be named more often in complaints of police misconduct (Brandl *et al.*, 2001; Cao and Huang, 2000; Lersch and Mieczkowski, 1996, 2000; McElvain and Kposowa, 2004).

Research is mixed regarding education; some studies indicate that the more educated an officer, the less likely he/she is to engage in misconduct (Kappeler *et al.*, 1992; Sanderson, 1977; Wilson, 1999). Officers with more aggressive personalities (Brandl *et al.*, 2001; Lersch, 2002; Worden, 1989) and low self-control (Donner and Jennings, 2014) generate a greater number of complaints. Finally, officers who are hired with criminal records and past employment problems are more likely to engage in career-ending misconduct (Ivkovic, 2009; Kane and White, 2009). Consequently, police administrators should be diligent in the recruitment, hiring, and retention of qualified police officers (Ivkovic, 2009; Kane and White, 2009; Mollen Commission, 1994; PERF, 2015; USDOJ, 2001).

The effectiveness of a police agency is contingent upon selection of the most appropriate and qualified officers (Palmiotto, 2001; PERF, 2015; USDOJ, 2001). The U.S. Department of Justice (2001) in *Principles for Promoting Police Integrity* explicitly recommends that police agencies develop a continuous recruitment plan to attract a diverse candidate pool (e.g. women, LGBT candidates, and racial/ethnic minorities) and make readily available to all segments of the community recruitment literature, applications, and examination procedures that stress the agency's commitment to community service. Police agencies should, therefore, recruit candidates at high schools, local colleges and universities, in central city communities (using connections with community-based practitioners and organizations), at special interest groups/clubs like local Boys and Girls Clubs to attract young adults and LGBT organizations, and conferences (Wilson, 2004). Police agencies should also enlist the support of the media, including internet media, marketing their commitment to community service and collaborative problem-solving to attract compatible candidates (Pearsall and Kohlhepp, 2000; Wilson, 2004). Finally, police agencies should build employee referral networks, utilizing their own officers to recruit qualified candidates (Wilson, 2004).

Police agencies should have strong hiring standards and be diligent in their screening and selection processes (Palmiotto, 2001). The typical hiring process generally consists of several stages, including a written test, polygraph test, federal fingerprint assessment, criminal records check, background investigation, psychological testing, drug screening, physical/medical examination, physical agility test, and oral interview board (Palmiotto, 2001). Use of these procedures has largely remained unchanged since the 1970s (Wilson, 2004). Procedures should be updated to include composite examinations that measure cognitive abilities and personality traits, with an emphasis on social and communication skills/competencies and problem-solving abilities (USDOJ, 2001). Further, because of the time-intensive and costly nature of the selection process, police administrators are not always ardent in following through with rigorous screening before making hiring decisions (Mollen Commission, 1994; Palmiotto, 2001). This lack of follow-through has had disastrous effects for many police departments, including New York City, Los Angeles, and Washington, D.C. (Palmiotto, 2001), all agencies requiring U.S. Department of Justice intervention (PERF, 2013). Police agencies must invest the necessary resources (time and fiscal) to conduct thorough screening processes of potential candidates (Palmiotto, 2001; USDOJ, 2001; Wilson, 2004). Only the most capable applicants should be chosen to represent the agency as sworn officers.

To ensure retention of qualified officers, police agencies should be as competitive as possible with respect to salary, fringe benefits, educational incentives, and training opportunities to promote career growth (Wilson and Grammich, 2009). Police agencies should mandate a collegial, harassment-free workplace climate by having clear policies regarding harassment, mandatory periodic anti-harassment training for all officers, and a zero-tolerance approach to investigating harassment complaints (USDOJ, 2001). Police administrators should practice procedural fairness in assignment and promotional decisions (USDOJ, 2001) and supervisors should be fair, courteous and respectful in demeanor and interaction (Wilson and Grammich, 2009).

To reduce police misconduct, police agencies must focus efforts on recruiting, hiring and retaining high-quality persons (PERF, 2015; USDOJ, 2001). They must use varied and proven approaches to recruit a diverse pool of applicants (Pearsall and Kohlhepp, 2000; Wilson, 2004). Police agencies must conduct a thorough and detailed screening and selection process (Mollen Commission, 1994; Palmiotto, 2001; PERF, 2013), and must be competitive with respect to salary, fringe benefits, educational incentives, and training opportunities to promote career growth and to encourage retention (Wilson and Grammich, 2009). Police administrators must be procedurally fair in their decision-making, courteous and respectful in interactions with officers, and should promote an organizational climate of acceptance and tolerance (Wilson and Grammich, 2009; USDOJ, 2001).

Effective policies and procedures

An organization without policies and procedures is an organization without a legitimate structure for control. An organization without policies and procedures is also an organization without a formal and public statement of values or a functional groundwork for training (Walker and Archbold, 2014). Police policies and procedures convey expectations for appropriate on-the-job conduct and decision-making, provide officers with essential guidance on handling situational encounters, extend a structure upon which to exact compliance and restraint, and provide formal mechanisms for transparency to promote public accountability (Davis, 1975; President's Task Force, 2015).

Police agencies should have clear policies and procedures for the use of force (lethal and non-lethal), vehicle pursuits, positional asphyxia, pepper spray (*Oleoresin Capsicum*), the deployment of canines, administrative reviews of shootings, use of force reporting systems, interactions with persons with disabilities, high-speed pursuits, complaint and misconduct investigations, monitoring resisting arrest charges, searches and seizures, public information and feedback, non-discrimination policies, conduct of police stops, traffic stop data collection, pedestrian stop reporting, foot pursuits, in-car cameras, body-worn cameras, bias-free policing, de-escalation, and harassment prevention (USDOJ, 2001; Walker and Archbold, 2014). It is not enough, however, to *have* written policies and procedures; the policies and procedures must also be managed and enforced properly and consistently (Walker and Macdonald, 2009). As Walker and Macdonald (2009: 484) make clear, the "new consensus of opinion" maintains that patterns of police misconduct are the result of insufficient management policies and practices, including written policies to govern police conduct.

Police agencies must also address the development of informal policies and procedures, which are cultural byproducts of ongoing interpretations and practice and have significant impacts on police officer behavior. In many police agencies, the informal culture is one of self-protection; that is, the message that "your most important job is to get home safely to your family at the end of your shift" is stressed internally by supervisors and peers during roll calls and emphasizes the dangerousness and potentially life-threatening nature of the work (Wexler, 2015: 4). The self-protection model also emphasizes a "war" mentality, leading officers to expect physical resistance.

The "21-foot rule" is another byproduct of a self-protection model. The 21-foot rule was created in a 1983 magazine article and later incorporated in a police training video by an organization called Calibre Press (Wexler, 2015). The rule describes the distance an officer must maintain from a suspect armed with a knife (or a similar object that could be used as a weapon) in order to allow the officer enough time to draw and discharge a firearm (Wexler, 2015). In many agencies, the 21-foot rule has become part of the informal policies and procedures regarding force. A breach of the 21-foot rule essentially creates a "kill zone" (Wexler, 2015: 5). Given the nature of policing and the need for quick decision-making, officers following the self-protection model act first and think later, resulting in officer-involved shootings in encounters that may have been resolved through careful negotiation.

According to Chuck Wexler (2015), Executive Director of the Police Executive Research Forum (PERF), police chiefs are recognizing that use-of-force policies (formal and informal) that lead officers to think only of their own personal safety and that of their comrades can ultimately preclude them from engaging, negotiating, de-escalating, and minimizing harm. Use-of-force policies (formal and informal) should accentuate the sanctity of all human life and stress the fact that officers should use force only as a last resort (Wexler, 2015).

To reduce police misconduct, police agencies must have clear written policies and procedures, and these policies and procedures must be enforced and managed with due diligence. Officers should also understand through socialization and supervisory reinforcement that all lives matter and that disengagement, critical thinking, and de-escalation should be routine in all potentially volatile encounters (USDOJ, 2001; Walker and Archbold, 2014; Wexler, 2015). Officers should think first, and act later.

Training

New recruits are inculcated with the nuts and bolts of policing through mandatory completion of training at their agency's authorized training academy. At the academy, new recruits are taught the mechanics of policing, introduced to policies and procedures, and begin the socialization process whereby they are introduced to the occupational culture (PERF, 2015). It is their introduction to the world of policing.

Although there is state-level variation in training standards, recruits typically spend four to six months in the academy. Entry-level training is primarily task-oriented, with officers receiving training in policies and procedures on patrol operations, criminal investigations, the use of firearms, and the use of force (Bradford and Pynes, 1999; Haarr, 2001; PERF, 2013). Recruits receive minimal entry-level training in cognitive and decision-making competencies (Bradford and Pynes, 1999). Bradford and Pynes (1999) found in their study of 22 state training academies that less than 3 percent of basic training academy time is spent on developing analytical skills, such as how to engage and reason with a diverse array of persons and use communication skills to manage problematic situations. These are the skills necessary for community engagement, collaborative problem-solving and de-escalation of potentially volatile encounters. It is not surprising, then, that the Police Executive Research Forum (2015: 4) recently concluded that "the training currently provided to new recruits and experienced officers in most departments is inadequate."

Upon graduating from the academy, recruits begin field training. Field training is designed to fill the gap between what is taught in the academy and what actually occurs on the street (Haarr, 2001). During field training, new officers are assigned to a more experienced, qualified Field Training Officer for a specified period of time. Upon completion of field training, the new officer is evaluated and either passes or fails.

Field training indoctrinates the new officer into the organizational culture, or "the way things are done around here." Field training is where new officers learn how to interact with their constituents and the typical manner in which to manage the daily demands of their work (Haarr, 2001). It is common knowledge that field training officers instruct recruits "to forget everything you just learned in the academy. I will teach you how policing is really done." Indeed, Haarr (2001) found that the field training process in Phoenix changed recruits attitudes and actually had a negative impact on their outlooks related to community engagement and problem solving. Haarr (2001: 428) concludes that:

> once the police recruit leaves the training academy and enters into the field-training process in their [sic] respective police agency, organizational environment factors, including the informal culture of a police agency, become more powerful forces in shaping police recruits' attitudes and skills related to community policing, traditional policing, problem-solving policing, and police-public relations.

Gains made in the academy, therefore, can be diminished depending on the Field Training Officer, other officers' attitudes, and the organizational cultures (Haar, 2001).

Officers continue training throughout their policing careers. Police officers are required to complete a number of mandatory and voluntary in-service training hours per year. In light of the copious public examples of the detrimental effects of police use-of-force incidents, many agencies are requiring officers to complete crisis intervention, cultural competency, and "re-engineered" use-of-force and de-escalation training (President's Task Force, 2015; PERF, 2015).

Crisis intervention training seeks to teach officers how to recognize and interact with persons with mental illness and other debilitating conditions. Training is typically collaborative, involving both policing and mental health practitioners, as well as individuals with mental health problems (Oliva and Compton, 2008; President's Task Force, 2015). Cultural competency and responsiveness training is designed to ensure that officers recognize the unique needs and characteristics of racial/ethnic minority communities (President's Task Force, 2015). There is no greater need in contemporary policing than to regain public trust and confidence from members of racial/ethnic groups, particularly those residing in inner-city communities who frequently interact with police due to the volume and nature of crime in their communities (President's Task Force, 2015). De-escalation tactics training is designed to teach officers the skills needed to negotiate compliance in potentially explosive encounters to minimize use-of-force incidents that have deleterious effects on police–community relations (PERF, 2015). As Wexler (2015: 3, emphasis as in original) makes clear:

> As we look back at the most controversial police shooting incidents, we sometimes find that while the shooting may be legally justified, there were missed opportunities to ratchet down the encounter, to slow things down, to call in additional resources, in the minutes *before* the shooting occurred.

Publicly *perceived* police abuse is as detrimental to police legitimacy as *actual* police abuse (Tyler, 2002). To reduce police misconduct, agencies should overhaul their training programs (academy, field training, and in-service) to devote more time to cognitive development, community-building and social interaction techniques, and problem-solving skills (Bradford and Pynes, 1999; Haarr, 2001; President's Task Force, 2015). Mirroring police agencies' policies and procedures, training should stress the sanctity of life and the use of force only as a last resort (PERF, 2015). Officers should be instructed in de-escalation tactics to defuse potentially volatile situations through effective communication strategies and careful negotiation (PERF, 2015). Field Training Officers should be carefully selected and receive specialized training to develop the skills and outlook needed to reinforce what recruits learn during academy training (Haarr, 2001). Crisis intervention training should be a part of basic recruit and in-service training, and cultural competency and responsiveness training should be mandatory for all officers (President's Task Force, 2015). Finally, police training academies should partner with academic institutions to develop curricula on evidence-based practices, and for research assistance in evaluating the efficacy of their training programs (President's Task Force, 2015).

Fair supervision

In the past, police organizations have relied on the law as the mechanism for legitimacy by perpetuating the myth of full enforcement (Davis, 1969; Hassell, 2006). That is, traditional police organizations asserted the image of full enforcement of the law as a means of maintaining legitimacy, avoiding criticism for disparate treatment of citizens, and shielding themselves from external review (Davis, 1969; Skolnick, 1966; Goldstein, 1977; Hassell, 2006). In actuality, the hallmark of policing is discretion. Police officers are not only authorized to use non-negotiable coercive force (Bittner, 1975), but they have considerable decision-making authority regarding situational outcomes (National Research Council, 2004).

There is a unique structural dynamic to policing as well; those positioned on the lowest rung of the organizational hierarchy in policing undoubtedly possess the greatest amount of discretion and decision-making capability within the organization (Wilson, 1968). These officers have the most direct contact with the public and operate with almost unbridled decision-making authority; their actions, temperament and decisions impact police legitimacy more than any other member of the organization (Tyler, 2002). These officers are also the least experienced, and oftentimes, the least educated persons within the organization (National Research Council, 2004), which is why quality training is vital. Within this context lies perhaps the most startling reality in the realm of policing: most of what patrol officers do during their frequent interactions with the public are done out of earshot and eyesight of their supervisors.

The impact of police supervision on shaping officer behavior is not as straightforward as one might expect, and most agree that supervising patrol officers is challenging and, oftentimes, overwhelming (Engel, 2001). Research on police supervision has uncovered wide variation in supervisory styles (Cohen, 1980; Engel, 2001; Reuss-Ianni, 1983). Some researchers have found that police supervisory styles vary due to the dialectical nature of their job: first-line supervisors must manage affairs with upper command while also managing relationships with subordinates. Managing the inherent conflict in middle-management positions causes patrol supervisors to define their roles differently, resulting in varying adaptations of their supervision (Engel, 2001; Reuss-Ianni, 1983; Trojanowicz, 1980; VanMaanen, 1983). Others have developed typologies of police supervisors, arguing that morality, individual values and ideals, the contextual nature of precinct assignments, and organizational cultures produce variation in supervisory styles (Engel, 2001; Hassell, 2007; Muir, 1977).

Several researchers have tested the influence of supervisory styles on police officer behavior and practice, but these studies have produced mixed results (Brown, 1988; Engel, 2001; Engel and Worden, 2003; Muir, 1977; Trojanowicz, 1980; Van Maanen, 1983; Wilson, 1968). Even with the variation in supervisory styles, ultimately, the research shows no clear pattern regarding a supervisor's ability to control and influence officer behavior. Given the context and nature of street-level policing, Engel and Worden (2003:138) conclude that, "the effects of supervision are generally small in magnitude." Despite their inability to directly influence police officer behavior due to the nature of patrol, the manner in which supervisors conduct themselves during interactions with their subordinates, and how they make decisions, can impact officer work performance.

Recent research has begun to uncover the role of supervision and organizational justice in shaping officer misconduct (Lind and Tyler, 1988; Wolfe and Piquero, 2011). There are three primary components to organizational justice: distributive, procedural, and interactional (Wolfe and Piquero, 2011). Distributive justice concerns the perceived fairness of outcomes; procedural justice emphasizes the importance of the process by which those outcomes are achieved; and interactional justice stresses the magnitude of supervisory respect, honesty, and courtesy during interpersonal communication and conduct (Cohen-Charash and Spector, 2001; Wolfe and Piquero, 2011). Research has found that organizational justice is related to work performance and productivity, organizational commitment, and workplace deviance (Cohen-Charash and Spector, 2001; Wolfe and Piquero, 2011). Wolfe and Piquero (2011), in their study of police misconduct in the Philadelphia Police Department, confirmed that organizational justice is related to several modes of police misconduct (the filing of citizen complaints, the instigation of IAD investigations, and the imposition of formal disciplinary charges).

The implications of the research on supervision and organizational justice are clear: to reduce police misconduct, supervisors need to be fair in process and outcome, respectful, and treat their officers politely and courteously (Bueermann, 2012; Wolfe and Piquero, 2011). As Jim Bueermann (2012: 19–20), former police practitioner and president of the Police Foundation, states in his discussion of the guiding principles of policing, "At an organizational level, the manner in which police officers feel they are treated by the leadership of the department creates a sense of internal police legitimacy and frames officer–citizen interactions." How police officers are treated within their organization directly impacts how they treat their constituents outside the organization.

Administrative oversight

Officers who are aggressive, make more arrests, and issue more citations are more likely to receive a greater number of citizen complaints (Brandl *et al.*, 2001; Hassell and Archbold, 2009; Lersch, 2002). Research clearly indicates that citizen complaint data underestimate the actual incidence of misconduct (Ivkovic, 2009; Kane and White, 2009). Research also demonstrates that a small number of officers are disproportionately responsible for generating problematic police behavior (USDOJ, 2001; Walker and Archbold, 2014). Consequently, internal monitoring through administrative oversight is fundamental for reducing police misconduct (Goldstein, 1977).

The most commonly recommended mechanism for providing administrative oversight is early intervention systems (Hassell and Archbold, 2009; Walker and Macdonald, 2009; USDOJ, 2001). In fact, Walker and Archbold (2014:137) claim that early intervention systems "are now recognized as the most powerful police accountability tool." Early warning systems filter police performance data into a computerized repository and allows agency leaders to compare the activity of officers assigned to similar shifts and geographic areas (Hassell and Archbold, 2009). In theory, the activity levels of all officers who work in similar areas with corresponding shifts should be comparable. Vigilant monitoring of early intervention systems provides an opportunity for administrators to uncover problematic patterns that can be addressed and corrected prior to the eruption of more serious police misconduct (IACP, 2006). Further, early intervention systems hold potential for identifying a host of problems, and not just at the individual officer level (IACP, 1989; Walker and Archbold, 2014).

Samuel Walker, a leading expert on police accountability, devotes an entire chapter in his book, *The New World of Police Accountability* (2014) to early intervention systems. As Walker explains, early intervention systems are designed to be proactive in nature and aimed at corrective action rather than discipline. This is a data-driven approach for identifying the underlying and proximate causes of problematic behavioral issues before the issues become consequential and harmful. The data analyzed involve multiple performance indicators, such as officer activities (i.e. arrests, peer complaints, field observation cards, traffic citations, use of force incidents, on-duty traffic accidents and vehicle pursuits, etc.) and personnel information (sick leave usage, on-the-job injuries, assignment and rank history, etc.) officially recorded by police agencies (Walker and

Archbold, 2014). The data analysis allows for the identification and selection of officers in need of intervention.

Identifying and selecting the officers who are in need of intervention is a complex process requiring administrative agreement regarding the appropriate threshold (Walker and Archbold, 2014). That is, how many performance indicators over what period of time denote a problematic pattern? While there is no consensus, experts do agree that administrators should not rely strictly on quantitative data, but should also assess qualitative data (Walker and Archbold, 2014). For example, perhaps an officer is working on a special project that would inflate his arrest numbers, producing an early intervention "hit." In this instance, the quantitative data (arrest numbers) are contextualized by the qualitative data (special project justification). Analysis for proper identification and selection is labor intensive but, if done properly, can provide opportunities for intervention before a pattern results in misconduct and/or a major critical incident.

Interventions can range from counseling and retraining, to other more formal actions (Walker and Archbold, 2014). Although there is variation, typically an officer's immediate supervisor discusses the need and purpose of the chosen intervention(s). This requires that sergeants have the appropriate skill set as well as a commitment to the processes and goals of early intervention systems. Following intervention, selected officers are monitored for a specified period of time to ensure that the intervention successfully eradicated the underlying and proximate causes of the problematic behavior (Walker and Archbold, 2014).

There has been scant research regarding the effectiveness of early intervention systems. Walker *et al.* (2001) studied early intervention systems in three police departments —Miami, Minneapolis and New Orleans—and found significant reductions in use of force and citizen complaints among officers following intervention. They also found that administrators in all three departments successfully identified and selected officers for intervention. Worden and colleagues (2013) conducted a longitudinal assessment of a Northeast police department's early intervention system and cautiously concluded that officer conduct (measured as complaints, uses of force, and arrests) improved over the course of a decade as a result of Officer–Civilian Interaction School classes (the intervention).

Due to the complexity of policing and variability in the internal and external environment in which police agencies operate, it is extremely difficult to methodologically isolate the impact of early intervention systems. The little research conducted, coupled with anecdotal evidence, suggests that early intervention systems can transform police organizations by allowing for the identification of problem officers and larger organizational patterns (Walker and Archbold, 2014). Early intervention systems also hold promise for promoting an atmosphere of accountability within the organizational culture.

Organizational cultures

There is a growing body of research that links organizational culture and police misconduct (Armacost, 2004; Cao and Huang, 2000; Lundman, 1980); that is, there is something about the organization that creates and condones police misconduct. According to Schein (1985: 9), organizational culture is,

> A pattern of basic assumptions – invented, discovered, or developed by a group as it learns to cope with its problems of external adaptation and internal integration – that has worked well enough to be considered valid and, therefore, to be taught to new members as the correct way to perceive, think, and feel in relation to those processes.

Further, there is a behavioral aspect to organizational culture; culture is the product of interactions between employees and supervisors/managers that convey expectations of levels of performance (Thompson and Luthans, 1990). From a compilation of behavior–consequence transactions (being rewarded or punished for individual and group-related actions), organizational members learn the full spectrum of the "way things are done around here," which becomes the cognitive interpretation of the culture for that individual (Hassell, 2006; Herbert, 1998; Thomas and Luthans, 1990). While a thorough overview of police organizational culture extends beyond the parameters of this chapter, policing research clearly establishes that culture is a major component affecting performance and behavior (Bittner, 1975; Crank, 1998; Haarr, 2001; Hassell, 2006; Klinger, 1997; Paoline, 2003; Westley, 1970).

Major critical incidents can destroy the reputation of a police department. In these cases, police departments typically claim that rogue officers engaged in isolated acts of misconduct; doing so allows the police organization to absolve and distance itself from the misconduct (Armacost, 2004; Kaplan, 2009; Mollen Commission, 1994). Research indicates, however, that police organizational cultures shape individual officer behavior, and, in policing, supervisors and administrators often condone and encourage policing in the "gray area" (Armacost, 2004; Kaplan, 2009; Klinger, 1997; Herbert, 1998). Being in the gray area allows officers to operate unchecked until they draw public attention, at which point administrators claim "rotten apples" and dissociate themselves from the "rogue cops." Essentially, officers are thrown under the bus for the sake of the organization.

Independent investigations of police agencies underscore the role of culture in creating and sustaining an environment that condones incidents and patterns of police misconduct (Armacost, 2004; Kaplan, 2009; USDOJ, 2015). First, Kaplan's (2009) overview of the LAPD's Rampart Scandal in the late 1990s provides an excellent illustration of the effects of organizational culture on the perpetration of police misconduct. The Rampart Scandal originated with the arrest of LAPD Officer David Mack in 1997 for bank robbery. Suspicions regarding additional misconduct arose during interviews with two of Mack's LAPD colleagues. Following investigation and the subsequent arrest of LAPD Officer Rafael Perez, Perez agreed to plead guilty and offered testimony regarding patterns of police corruption and widespread due process abuses against civilians (Kaplan, 2009). According to Perez, many officers in Rampart's Community Resources Against Street Hoodlums (CRASH) Unit regularly manufactured probable cause to arrest citizens, beat citizens, planted evidence to obtain arrests and justify officer-involved shootings, and lied under oath (Kaplan, 2009). Perez repeatedly remarked about the culture within Rampart (officers "being in the loop") that supported a widespread willingness by at least 70 officers to participate in and/or condone misconduct. According to Kaplan's (2009: 64, emphasis added) review of the Rampart Scandal: " . . . this practice was so deeply embedded in CRASH *culture* that new officers were trained to hide misconduct from superiors."

Second, Armacost's (2004) overview of the Christopher Commission's findings following the Rodney King incident in Los Angeles in 1991 also highlights the powerful role of organizational culture in shaping police misconduct:

> In sum, the Commission's investigation revealed an organizational *culture* characterized by: formal and informal norms that favored a confrontational, hard-nosed style of policing; an evaluation and promotion system that had the functional effect of rewarding illegal uses of force through nonenforcement of stated management policies; and a work environment that tolerated (and even encouraged) violent and discriminatory

language and attitudes that may have contributed to violent and discriminatory conduct. All of this leads to a picture of a police department in which, regardless of formal policies, the informal message that the department conveyed was that confrontational, aggressive policing would be rewarded, even if it resulted in repeated incidents of violence that gave rise to citizen complaints and lawsuits (emphasis added).

Finally, the USDOJ, in its 2015 report regarding the investigation of the Ferguson Police Department (FPD) following the shooting of Michael Brown and the subsequent civil unrest that ensued following the prosecutor's decision not to charge the officer involved, also emphasized the role of culture in police misconduct:

> This *culture* within FPD influences officer activities in all areas of policing, beyond just ticketing. Officers expect and demand compliance even when they lack legal authority. They are inclined to interpret the exercise of free-speech rights as unlawful disobedience, innocent movements as physical threats, indications of mental or physical illness as belligerence. Police supervisors and leadership do too little to ensure that officers act in accordance with law and policy, and rarely respond meaningfully to civilian complaints of officer misconduct. The result is a pattern of stops without reasonable suspicion and arrests without probable cause in violation of the Fourth Amendment; infringement on free expression, as well as retaliation for protected expression, in violation of the First Amendment; and excessive force in violation of the Fourth Amendment (emphasis added).

The President's Task Force on 21st Century Policing, comprised of national policing experts (practitioners and academics), recognizes the need for cultural transformation in reducing police misconduct. The Task Force (2015: 11) made many recommendations in its 116 page report, but the prevailing theme is the absolute necessity of changing the occupational (nature of policing in the United States) and organizational cultures of police agencies:

> Law enforcement *culture* should embrace a guardian—rather than a warrior—mindset to build trust and legitimacy both within agencies and with the public. Toward that end, law enforcement agencies should adopt procedural justice as the guiding principle for internal and external policies and practices to guide their interactions with rank and file officers and with the citizens they serve. Law enforcement agencies should also establish a *culture* of transparency and accountability to build public trust and legitimacy. This is critical to ensuring decision making is understood and in accord with stated policy (emphasis added).

While changing a police organization's culture is difficult, it can be done (Couper, 2014).
David Couper (2014: 159), Chief of Police for the Madison Police Department from 1972–1993, succinctly details the necessary changes police administrators must embrace and promote in order to transform their organization's culture:

> Changing police isn't just about changing a few things, but everything: hiring, training, leadership, solving problems, community-orientation, and evaluation. It is about changing the very nature of the police function itself and the multiple ways that will have to be put in place to raise the intellectual capacity of police, curtail their

excessive force, drive out the vestiges of corruption and racism, and implement a new *culture* of courtesy, customer focus, and restraint in using physical force. They will also have to learn how to properly handle protesting people not only singularly but in large crowds and develop ongoing formal relationships with academic institutions (emphasis added).

While early intervention systems (Walker and Archbold, 2014) and police body-mounted cameras, the most recent panacea for police misconduct, (Jennings *et al.*, 2015), *if implemented and monitored properly*, can promote an atmosphere of accountability within the police organization, cultural transformation requires a complete overhaul of the organization. Unfortunately, many police chiefs are either unable or unwilling to make the necessary changes (Mayo, 2012). It should not be surprising, consequently, that the U.S. Department of Justice has found more than 20 police agencies guilty of patterns and practices of civil rights abuses (Mayo, 2012; Walker, 2015).

National priorities

The criminal justice system in the United States is decentralized. While some debate the actual number of police agencies in the United States, there is consensus that there are at least 18,000, with most at the local level. Consequently, police agencies and the localized nature of policing vary tremendously. As we have outlined, police chiefs and administrators must make major changes if they are to effectively eradicate police misconduct. Most of the responsibility for doing so, due to the decentralized nature of criminal justice in the United States, lies at the local level, *but not all*. Only when national priorities change will policing become more equitable, effective, and ethical.

The "War on Crime," declared by President Johnson in 1965, established fighting crime as a national priority. The passing of the Law Enforcement Assistance Act in that same year entrenched the federal government's influence and authority in local police operations through the appropriation of federal dollars to state and local police agencies. President Johnson proudly declared that 1965 would become known as "the year when this country began a thorough, intelligent, and effective war against crime" (Hinton, 2015). The war analogy has been extended. President Nixon declared "War on Drugs" in 1971, making drugs "public enemy #1" and establishing the federal Drug Enforcement Administration (DEA) in 1973. President George W. Bush declared "War on Terror" in 2001 following the 9/11 attacks in the United States, and created the federal Department of Homeland Security in 2002.

The major consequence of declaring war on crime, drugs, and terror—intentional or unintended—has been the militarization of police who wage "war" against the poor and racial/ethnic minorities living in communities characterized by concentrated disadvantage, social disorganization, and, of course, crime and disorder (national priorities created these problems as well):

When any soldiers go to war, they must have enemies. When cops go to war against crime, their enemies are found in inner cities and among our minority populations. There, in a country as foreign to most officers as Vietnam was to GIs, cops have trouble distinguishing the good guys from the bad. (Skolnick and Fyfe, 1993: 116; See also Kaplan, 2009: 74)

The result has been an uptick in perceptions of police misconduct, the continued deterioration of police legitimacy, and persistent crime and disorder problems in inner-city areas (Kaplan, 2009). In the end, the "War on Crime," "War on Drugs," and "War on Terror" have been waged disproportionately against racial/ethnic minorities and Muslims (ACLU, 2014; Chambliss, 1994; Kaplan, 2009; President's Task Force, 2015; Tonry, 1996; Walker *et al.*, 2012), have produced a mass incarceration epidemic (Alexander, 2012; Tonry, 1996), contributed to the decline of inner-city communities (Tonry, 1996), amplified the militarization of police (Skolnick and Fyfe, 1993), politicized public safety (Chambliss, 1994; Kaplan, 2009), transformed neighborhoods into war zones (ACLU, 2014), and resulted in the tolerance, and in some agencies the tacit encouragement, of police misconduct (Chambliss, 1994; Kaplan, 2009). In war, the ends justify the means.

To reduce police misconduct, our nation must change its national priorities (Kaplan, 2009). The policing paradigm needs to shift in actual practice and not just verbal acknowledgement away from the "war" mentality to that of a community-based, collaborative problem-solving model (Bullock *et al.*, 2012; Goldstein, 1979; Hassell and Lovell, 2014; Stephens, 2012). Police, community-based practitioners, and residents must work collaboratively to address the proximate and underlying causes of disorder and crime; doing so promotes equity, procedural fairness, police legitimacy, and effective crime reduction (Bullock, *et al.*, 2012; Engel and Eck, 2015; Goldstein, 1979). And even though there have been federal initiatives geared toward community building for decades (e.g. Weed and Seed, Byrne Criminal Justice Innovation Grants, etc.), a Community Oriented Policing Services Office within the United States Department of Justice since 1994, and billions of dollars spent in promoting "community policing," our national priorities have not been dramatically altered, and the media continue to broadcast the cycle of police brutality, due process violations, and illegitimacy that continues in many communities within the United States.

Conclusion

Misconduct by police creates pressing social and legal issues with serious consequences. As detailed above, police misconduct erodes the legitimacy of police and government, has a criminogenic effect, and costs local governments large sums of money that otherwise could be used to address the social and structural causes of crime and disorder. Identifying successful strategies for reducing misconduct is the first step in controlling problematic police behavior. Based on a thorough review of research and practice, this chapter presented the most prominent approaches for reducing police misconduct.

Clearly, police misconduct is complex in nature, scope, and consequence. As such, there is no single solution for controlling problematic police behavior. Dealing with police misconduct requires strong leadership and administrative commitment. Police agencies must invest the time, resources, and energy necessary to promote Walker's ideal for a new world of police accountability. Change is difficult, but not impossible.

References

Alexander, M. (2012). *The New Jim Crow: Mass Incarceration in the Age of Colorblindness*. New York, NY: The New Press.

American Civil Liberties Union (2014). War comes home: The excessive militarization of American policing. *American Civil Liberties Union* (June).

Armacost, B.E. (2004). Organizational culture and police misconduct. *The George Washington Law Review*, 72, 453–546.

Balko, J. (10/1/14). U.S. cities pay out millions to settle police lawsuits. *The Washington Post*, www.washingtonpost.com/news/the-watch/wp/2014/10/01/u-s-cities-pay-out-millions-to-settle-police-lawsuits/. Accessed April 11, 2016.

Bittner, E. (1975). *The Functions of the Police in Modern Society*. New York: Academic Press.

Bradford, D and J.E. Pynes (1999). Police academy training: Why hasn't it kept up with practice? *Police Quarterly*, 2, 283–301.

Brandl, S.G., M.S. Stroshine, and J. Frank (2001). Who are the complaint-prone officers? An examination of the relationship between police officers' attributes, arrest activity, assignment, and citizens' complaints about excessive force. *Journal of Criminal Justice*, 29: 521–529.

Brown, M.K. (1988). *Working the Street: Police Discretion and the Dilemmas of Reform*. New York: Russell Sage Foundation.

Bueermann, J. (2012). Preparing the police for an uncertain future: Four guiding principles (pp. 17–21) in *American Policing in 2022: Essays on the Future of a Profession*, D.R. McCullough and D.L. Spence (eds.). Washington, DC: COPS Office, USDOJ.

Bullock, K., R. Erol, and N. Tilley (2012). *Problem-Oriented Policing and Partnerships: Implementing an Evidence-based Approach to Crime Reduction*. New York, NY: Routledge Publishing.

Cao, L. and B. Huang (2000). Determinants of citizen complaints against police abuse of power. *Journal of Criminal Justice*, 28, 213.

Chambliss, W.J. (1994). Policing the ghetto underclass: The politics of law and law enforcement. *Social Problems*, 41, 177–194.

Cohen, B. (1980). Leadership styles of commanders in the New York City Police Department. *Journal of Police Science and Administration*, 8, 125–138.

Cohen-Charash, Y. and P.E. Spector (2001). The role of justice in organizations: A meta-analysis. *Organizational Behavior and Human Decision Processes*, 86, 278–321.

Couper, D. (2014). *Arrested Development: A Veteran Police Chief Sounds About Protest, Racism, Corruption and the Seven Steps Necessary to Improve Our Nation's Police*. Self-published.

Crank, J.P. (1998). *Understanding Police Culture*. Cincinnati, Ohio: Anderson Publishing Company.

Davis, K.C. (1969). *Discretionary Justice: A Preliminary Inquiry*. Urbana, IL: University of Illinois.

Davis, K.C. (1975). *Police Discretion*. St. Pail, MN: West.

Donner, C. and Jennings, W. (2014). Low self-control and police deviance: Applying Gottfredson and Hirschi's general theory to officer misconduct. *Police Quarterly* September, 17, 203–225.

Engel, R.S. (2001). Supervisory styles of patrol sergeants and lieutenants. *Journal of Criminal Justice*, 29, 341–355.

Engel, R.S. and R.E. Worden (2003). Police officers' attitudes, behavior, and supervisory influences: An analysis of problem solving. *Criminology*, 41, 131–166.

Engel, R.S. and J.E. Eck (2015). Effectiveness vs. equity in policing: Is a tradeoff inevitable? *Ideas in American Policing*, 18. Washington, DC: Police Foundation.

Goldstein, H. (1977). *Policing a Free Society*. Cambridge, MA: Ballinger.

Goldstein, H. (1979). Improving police: A problem-oriented approach. *Crime and Delinquency*, 25, 236–258.

Haarr, R.N. (2001). The making of a community policing officer: The impact of basic training and occupational socialization on police recruits. *Police Quarterly*, 4, 402–433.

Harris, C. and R. Worden (2014). The effects of sanctions on police misconduct. *Crime & Delinquency*, 60, 1258–1288.

Hassell, K.D. (2006). *Police Organizational Cultures and Patrol Practices*. New York: LFB Scholarly Publishing.

Hassell, K. D. (2007) Cross-Precinct Analysis of Patrol Supervision: A View from the Inside. *Law Enforcement Executive Forum*, 7, 33–50.

Hassell, K.D. and C.A. Archbold (2010). Widening the scope on complaints of police misconduct. *Policing: An International Journal of Police Strategies & Management*, 33, 473–489.

Hassell, K.D. and R.D. Lovell (2014). Fidelity of Implementation: Important Considerations for Policing Scholars. *Policing and Society: An International Journal of Research and Policy*, 1–17.

Herbert, S. (1998). Police subculture reconsidered. *Criminology*, 36, 343–369.

Hinton, E. (2015). Why we should reconsider the war on crime. *Time Magazine* (March 20, 2015), http://time.com/3746059/war-on-crime-history/. Accessed March 21, 2016.

International Association of Chiefs of Police (1989). *Building Integrity and Reducing Drug Corruption in Police Departments*. Arlington, VA: IACP.

International Association of Chiefs of Police (2006). *Protecting Civil Rights: A Leadership Guide for State, Local and Trial Law Enforcement*. Washington, DC: IACP.

Ivkovic, S.K. (2009). Rotten apples, rotten branches and rotten orchards: A cautionary tale of police misconduct. *Criminology and Public Policy*, 8, 777–785.

Jennings, W.G., M.D. Lynch, and L.A. Fridell (2015). Evaluating the impact of police officer body-worn (BWCs) on response-to-resistance and serious external complaints: Evidence from the Orlando police department (OPD) experience utilizing a randomized controlled experiment. *Journal of Criminal Justice*, 43, 480–486.

Kane, R.J. (2002). The social ecology of police misconduct. *Criminology*, 40, 867–896.

Kane, R.J. and M.D. White (2009). Bad cops: A study of career-ending misconduct among New York City police officers. *Criminology & Public Policy*, 8, 737–769.

Kaplan, P.J. (2009). Looking through the gaps: A critical approach to the LAPD's rampart scandal. *Social Justice*, 36, 61–81.

Kappeler, V.E., A.D. Sapp, and D.L. Carter (1992). Police officer higher education, citizen complaints and departmental rule violations. *American Journal of Police*, 11, 37–54.

Kirk, D.S. and M. Matsuda (2011). Legal cynicism, collective efficacy and the ecology of arrest. *Criminology*, 49, 443–472.

Klinger, D.A. (1997). Negotiating order in patrol work: An ecological theory of police response to deviance. *Criminology*, 35, 277–306.

Lersch, K.M. (1998). Exploring gender differences in citizen allegations of misconduct: An analysis of a municipal police department. *Women & Criminal Justice*, 9, 69–79.

Lersch, K.M. (2002). Are citizen complaints just another measure of officer productivity? An analysis of citizen complaints and officer activity measures. *Police, Practice and Research*, 3, 135–147.

Lersch, K.M. and T. Mieczkowski (1996). Who are the problem prone officers? An analysis of citizen complaints. *American Journal of Police*, 15, 23–44.

Lersch, K. and Mieczkowski, T. (2000). An examination of the convergence and divergence of internal and external allegations of misconduct filed against police officers. *Policing: An International Journal of Police Strategies & Management*, 23, 54–68.

Lersch, K.M. and L.L. Kunzman (2001). Misconduct allegations and higher education in a Southern Sheriff's department. *American Journal of Criminal Justice*, 25, 161–172.

Lind, E.A. and T.R. Tyler (1988). *The Social Psychology of Procedural Justice*. New York: Plenum Press.

Lundman, R. (1980). *Police and Policing - An Introduction*. New York, NY: Holt, Rinehart and Winston.

Mayo, L.A. (2012). Moving beyond the myths and misdirection impeding community policing success (pp. 33–36) in *American Policing in 2022: Essays on the Future of a Profession*, D.R. McCullough and D.L. Spence (eds.). Washington, DC: COPS Office, USDOJ.

McElvain, J., and A. Kposowa. (2004). Police officer characteristics and internal affairs investigations for use of force allegations. *Journal of Criminal Justice*, 32, 265–279.

McElvain, K.M. and T. Mieczkowski (2004). Police officer characteristics and internal affairs investigations for use of force allegations. *Journal of Criminal Justice*, 32: 265–279.

Mollen Commission (1994). *New York City Commission to Investigate Allegations of Police Corruption and the Anti-corruption Procedures of the Police Department*. New York: Mollen Commission.

Muir, W.K. (1977). *Police: Street Corner Politicians*. Chicago, IL: University of Chicago Press.

National Center for Women and Policing (2002). *Men, Women, and Police Use of Excessive Force: A Tale of Two Genders*. Beverly Hills, CA: The National Center for Women and Policing.

National Research Council (2004). *Fairness and Effectiveness in Policing: The Evidence*. Washington, DC: National Research Council of the National Academies.

Oliva, J.R. and M.T. Compton (2008). A statewide crisis intervention team initiative: Evolution of the Georgia CIT Program. *Journal of the American Academy of Psychiatry and the Law*, 36, 38–46.

Palmiotto, M. (2001). Can police recruiting control police misconduct? (pp. 344–354) in *Police Misconduct: A Reader for the 21st Century*. New Jersey: Prentice Hall.

Paoline, E.A. (2003). Taking stock: Toward a richer understanding of police culture. *Journal of Criminal Justice*, 31, 199–214.

Pate, A.M. and L.A. Fridell (1993). Police Use of Force: Official Reports, Citizen Complaints and Legal Consequences. Washington, DC: Police Foundation.

Pearsall, A.A. and K. Kohlhepp (2000). Strategies to Improve Recruitment. *The Police Chief* 77 (April): 128–130.

Police Executive Research Forum (2013). *Civil Rights Investigations of Local Police: Lessons Learned*. Critical Issues in Policing Series. Washington, DC: PERF.

Police Executive Research Forum (2015). *Re-engineering Training on Police Use of Force*, Critical Issues in Policing Series. Washington, DC: PERF.

President's Task Force on 21st Century Policing. 2015. *Final Report of the President's Task Force on 21st Century Policing*. Washington, DC: Office of Community Oriented Policing Services.

Reuss-Ianni, E. (1983). *Two Cultures of Policing: Street Cops and Management Cops*. New Brunswick, NJ: Transaction Publishers.

Sanderson, L.W. (1977). Police officers: The relationship of college education to job performance. *The Police Chief*, 44, 62–63.

Schein, E.H. (1985). *Organizational Culture and Leadership: A Dynamic View*. San Francisco, CA: Jossey-Bass.

Schwartz, J (2010). Myths and mechanics of deterrence: The role of lawsuits in law enforcement decision making. *UCLA Law Review*, 57 (April), 1023–1094.

Skolnick, J. (1966). *Justice Without Trial*. New York: Wiley & Sons.

Skolnick, J.H. and J.J. Fyfe (1993). *Above the Law: Police and the Excessive Use of Force*. New York: The Free Press.

Smith, B.W. and M.D. Holmes (2003). Community accountability, minority threat, and police brutality: An examination of civil rights criminal complaints. *Criminology*, 41, 1035–1064.

Steffensmeier, D.J. (1979). Sex role orientation and attitudes toward female police. *Police Studies*, 2, 39–42.

Stephens, D.W. (2012). Focusing on what we can control (pp. 53–57) in *American Policing in 2022: Essays on the Future of a Profession*, D.R. McCullough and D.L. Spence (eds.). Washington, DC: COPS Office, USDOJ.

Terrill, W. and J. McCluskey (2002). Citizen complaints and problem officers: Examining officer behavior. *Journal of Criminal Justice*, 30, 143–155.

Terrill, W. and S.D. Mastrofski (2002). Situational and officer-based determinants of police coercion. *Justice Quarterly*, 19, 215–248.

The Cato Institute's National Police Misconduct Reporting Project (n.d.) http://www.policemisconduct.net/. Accessed April 11, 2016.

Thompson, K.R. and F. Luthans (1990). Organizational culture: A behavioral perspective (pp. 319–344) in B. Schneider (ed). Organizational Climate and Culture. San Francisco, CA: Jossey-Bass.

Tonry, M. (1996). *Malign Neglect*. New York, NY: Oxford University Press.

Trojanowicz, R. C. (1980). *The Environment of the First-Line Police Supervisor*. Englewood Cliffs, NJ: Prentice Hall.

Tyler, T.R. (1990). *Why People Obey the Law*. New Haven, CT: Yale University Press.

Tyler, T.R. (2001). Public trust and confidence in legal authorities: What do majority and minority group members want from the law and legal institutions? *Behavioral Sciences and the Law* 19, 215–235.

Tyler, T. (2002). A national survey for monitoring police legitimacy. *Justice Research and Policy*. 4, 71–86.

Tyler, T. R. (2004). Enhancing police legitimacy. *Annals of the American Academy of Political and Social Science*, 593, 84–99.

United States Code (n.d.), Title 18—Crimes and criminal procedure, part 1—crimes chapter 13—civil rights, § 241. Conspiracy against rights; § 242. Deprivation of rights under color of law.

United States Department of Justice (2001). *Principles for Promoting Police Integrity*. Washington, DC: USDOJ.

United States Department of Justice (2015). *Investigation of the Ferguson Police Department. Civil Rights Division*. Washington, DC: USDOJ.

Van Maanen, J. (1983). The boss: First-line supervision in an American police agency (pp. 275-317) in M. Punch (ed.), *Control in the police organization*, M. Punch (ed.). Cambridge, MA: MIT Press.

Van Wormer, K. (1981). Are males suited to police patrol work? *Police Studies*, 3, 41–44.

Wagner, A. (1980). Citizen complaints against the police—the complainant. *Journal of Police Science and Administration*, 8, 247–252.

Walker, S. (2015). When policing goes wrong. *The Crime Report* (November 25, 2015): www.thecrimereport.org/news/inside-criminal-justice/2015-11-when-policing-goes-wrong. Accessed March 21, 2016.

Walker, S. and M. Macdonald (2009). An alternative remedy for police misconduct: A model state pattern or practice statute. *George Mason University Civil Rights Law Review*, 19, 479–552.

Walker, S. and C.A. Archbold (2014). *The New World of Police Accountability*, 2nd Ed., Los Angeles, CA: Sage Publications.

Walker, S., G.P. Alpert, and D.J. Kenney (2001). *Early Warning Systems: Responding to the Problem Officer*. Washington, DC: National Institute of Justice.

Walker, S., C. Spohn, and M. DeLone (2012). *The Color of Justice*, 5th Ed. Belmont, CA: Wadsworth Publishing.

Westley, W.A. (1953). Violence and the police. *American Journal of Sociology*, 59: 34–41.

Westley, W. A. (1970). *Violence and the Police*. Cambridge, MA: MIT Press.

Wexler, C. (2015). Summary: What you will find in this report (pp. 3–10) in *Re-engineering Training on Police Use of Force, Police Executive Research Forum Report*. Washington, D.C.: PERF.

Wilson, H. (1999). Post-secondary education of the police officer and its effect on the frequency of citizen's complaints. *Journal of California Law Enforcement*, 33, 3–10.

Wilson, J.M. (2004). Strategies for police recruitment: A review of trends, contemporary issues, and existing approaches. *Law Enforcement Executive Form*, 14, 78–97.

Wilson, J.M. and C.A. Grammich (2009). *Police Recruitment and Retention in the Contemporary Urban Environment: A National Discussion of Personnel Experiences and Promising Practices from the Frontlines*. Arlington, VA: Rand Corporation.

Wilson, J.Q. (1968). *Varieties of Police Behavior*. Cambridge, MA: Harvard University Press.

Wolfe, S.E. and A.R. Piquero (2011). Organizational justice and police misconduct. *Criminal Justice and Behavior*, 38, 332–353.

Worden, R.E. (1989). Situational and attitudinal explanations of police behavior: A theoretical reappraisal and empirical assessment. *Law and Society Review*, 23, 667–711.

Worden, R.E., M. Kim, C.J. Harris, M.A. Pratte, S.E. Dorn, and S.S. Hyland (2013). Intervention with problem officers: An outcome evaluation of an EIS Intervention. *Criminal Justice and Behavior*, 40, 409–437.

Part 5

Coping interventions to address stress in policing

14 Coping with stress in law enforcement

Mark H. Anshel

It is well known that members of law enforcement experience an array of stressful events, both short term—called acute stressors—and long term—called chronic stressors. Sample sources of stress in this area of work include poor work–life balance (i.e. "all work, no play"), negative relationships with supervisors, higher-level administrators, or colleagues, lack of supervisory support, racism—perceived or real, sexism (i.e. sexual harassment), frustration with the court (legal) system, exposure to physical violence, physical confrontation with offenders or suspects, excessive work hours, physical discomfort and pain, and poor family relationships. Some of these stressors can be controlled and some cannot. The controllability of a stressful source is important because that has implications for the manner in which officers and other members of law enforcement respond to these stressors, a process called coping.

Perhaps not surprisingly, the consequences of experiencing stress in law enforcement, especially in the absence of effective coping skills, include relatively high rates of divorce and suicide, poor health, low energy, and ineffective job performance (Anshel, 2000; Aumiller and Corey, 2007; Rybicki and Nutter, 2002). It is ironic, yet somewhat surprising to outside observers and researchers, that some of the most intense and frequent sources of stress are *internal*, that is, from inside the department or unit, generated by a toxic work environment (Anshel *et al.*, 2013). Hart *et al.* (1995) found, for example, that "police organizations are the main source of psychological distress among police officers" (p. 150). Perhaps not surprisingly, police personnel report markedly reduced passion for their job, leading to chronic stress, burnout, and quitting the law enforcement profession due to the effects of prolonged and unpleasant behavioral patterns (Slate *et al.*, 2007). Another group of members in the law enforcement community that has received limited attention by researchers and mental health professionals related to stress and coping is emergency dispatchers.

Emergency dispatchers (EDs) often experience both chronic and acute forms of stress, at times very intense, that can lead to burnout, poor job performance, and quitting the job (Anshel *et al.*, 2010; Jenkins, 1997). EDs, who are not sworn members of law enforcement, are integrated into the processes of police operations. Similar to other members of law enforcement, EDs experience enormous stress in both chronic and acute forms, sleep deprivation, occasional poor relationships with co-workers and supervisors, disrespect by law enforcement officers, and verbal abuse by 911 callers (Kirmeyer, 1988; Shepherd and Hodgkinson, 1990). Perhaps it is not surprising, then, that EDs tend to lead a sedentary lifestyle and engage in unhealthy habits, such as smoking, overeating of high fat foods, and sleep deprivation. Often, the results are lack of weight control and poor general health. They may experience low life satisfaction at rates very similar to their police counterparts

(Anshel *et al.*, 2013). The primary agent of recovery from job-related stress that allows members of law enforcement to perform their job at the highest level is coping.

Thus, the purposes of this chapter are: (1) to describe the coping process in response to acute and chronic stress that is generally accepted by scholars and researchers, with particular implications for members of law enforcement (e.g. police officers, detectives, administrators, administrative assistants, emergency dispatchers), and (2) to provide a framework for effective (adaptive) and *ineffective* (maladaptive) responses to stressful events using an approach and avoidance coping framework. Outcomes from effective coping will also be discussed, emphasizing favorable changes in emotion, cognition, job performance, and quality of life. Understanding the coping process in law enforcement is especially important for applying effective coping interventions.

The coping process

Coping is typically defined as the ability to manage stressful feelings and to deal with the unpleasant events from which those feelings originate (Lazarus, 1999). Coping is a multidimensional process. It consists of a vast array of thoughts, emotions, and actions that are often executed in a very rapid, sometimes parallel, manner, and are influenced by various personal and situational factors. The failure to cope effectively with acute stress often leads to reduced performance quality and, eventually, mental fatigue, burnout, and leaving the stressful situation (e.g., quitting, retiring). It is surprising, then, that research on coping with acute stress in law enforcement remains understudied. Coping is a *conscious* process, consisting of psychological and physical efforts to improve one's resourcefulness or reducing external demands in dealing with stressful events (Krohne, 1993; Lazarus, 1999).

Examples of building internal resources include increased self-confidence, reinterpreting the situation, also called reappraisal, increased perceptions of self-control, or optimism. Examples of reducing external demands include managing the environment, avoiding the source of stress, or seeking information about the stressor. While researchers often agree that coping is a conscious attempt at reducing or managing stress, some coping strategies are initiated with minimal cognition (Anshel & Sutarso, 2007), and may appear to be performed automatically.

Coping strategies versus coping styles

There is a clear distinction in the literature between coping *strategies* and a related concept called coping *styles*. Coping strategies reflect a person's use of specific cognitive or behavioral techniques that assist the person to build personal resources or manipulate environmental demands that promote stress reduction or management (Lazarus and Folkman, 1984). Coping strategies are changeable and form the focus of coping interventions, also called stress management.

Coping *styles*, on the other hand, reflect a person's disposition to use certain types, or categories, of coping strategies; usually the type of coping strategies the individual prefers may be predicted from his or her style (Anshel *et al.*, 2010). Coping style is not a personality trait that reflects long-term stability and is often established early in life. It is a disposition and, therefore, predictable. Coping styles, unlike coping strategies, are a person's usual manner of using certain types/categories of coping strategies, such as approach and avoidance. Coping style remains susceptible to change through learning and experience (Anshel *et al.*, 2010).

Another misunderstood area in the coping process is the assumption that coping necessarily reflects a person's effective/adaptive use of a technique that manages stress. This is untrue; coping can be ineffective/maladaptive. One can cope—and one often does—improperly, sometimes resulting in more, rather than less, stress. It is crucial to differentiate between proper (i.e. adaptive, or effective) and improper use (i.e. maladaptive, or ineffective) of coping strategies in law enforcement. Table 14.1 provides sample coping strategies categorized as approach and avoidance in adaptive and maladaptive forms.

Adaptive coping

Adaptive coping "refers to processes employed to manage environmental demands" (Zeidner and Saklofske (2006, p. 506). While most people perceive the term—and the process of—coping as synonymous with "effective" responses to stress, this is not true. Coping can be, and often is, maladaptive (ineffective). Whether a coping technique is effective or ineffective is often a function of the desired outcome. Adaptive (effective) coping should lead to a safe, legal, and permanent resolution of the problem, with no additional conflict, while maintaining a positive emotional state. Other forms of adaptive coping include discussing the problem, avoiding the stressor, exercise, prayer, meditation, psychological distancing, and various forms of distraction. See Table 14.1 for a list of common coping strategies categorized as effective and ineffective.

Maladaptive coping

Maladaptive (ineffective) responses to stress may exacerbate the effects of stress on a person's emotions, thoughts, and behaviors. Maladaptive (ineffective) coping consists of strategies that may contribute to the person's stress intensity, lead to undesirable

Table 14.1 Adaptive and maladaptive coping strategies categorized as approach and avoidance and sub-categorized as cognitive and behavior sub-dimensions in response to acute stress

Approach-behavior coping	*Approach-cognitive coping*
Confronting, threatening, arguing, information-seeking, social support, explaining, friendly non-verbal/verbal affirmation, verbal acknowledgment, discussing, catastrophizing, speaking to a mentor or supervisor, receiving counseling, soliciting opinions from others.	Covert rehearsal, planning, analyzing, self-talk re-analyzing, justifying, psyching-up, prayer (if related to coping with the stress), self-statements, logic/reason.
Avoidance-behavior coping	*Avoidance-cognitive coping*
Walking away, social engineering (avoiding a certain location), exercise, reading, watching television, listening to music, attending church, ingesting an alcoholic beverage, recreational activity, engaging in sexual behavior, playing or watching sports, reading, target shooting.	Discounting, psychological distancing, labeling, empathy, thought-stopping, ignoring, self-talk, mental imagery, progressive relaxation, focusing on the next task, prayer (if focusing on the Lord and not on the stressor).
Examples of ineffective/maladaptive approach and avoidance coping	
Excessive alcohol, smoking, mind-altering drugs, emotional eating, prolonged anger and hostility, car speeding, thoughts of self-destructive actions, negative self-talk, rumination (repeating self-blame), resignation (helplessness/hopelessness), exhibiting bad mood toward others, excessive exercise.	

emotions and poorer performance outcomes, and, perhaps, result in reduced job satisfaction and general physical and mental well-being. According to Zeidner and Saklofske (1996), examples of ineffective coping strategies that have implications in law enforcement include the excessive use of alcohol, tobacco, sudden explosive anger, hallucinogenic (mind-altering) drugs, impatience, anger, and verbal or physical confrontation. In their study of EDs, Anshel et al. (2010) found that the over-use of approach coping led to excessive stress (e.g. persistent negative thoughts about difficult colleagues, unpleasant or ineffective unit policies, an ineffective supervisor, general low job satisfaction). Thus, what may be effective coping in one situation or under one condition may be ineffective in other situations and conditions.

There is ample evidence that coping with stress in law enforcement is often maladaptive (Anshel, 2000; Anshel et al., 1997; Hart et al., 1995). Hart et al. (ibid.) contend that the goal of programs intended to improve coping skills in law enforcement, including for EDs, should not be to eliminate stress, but rather to help the individual better manage it, thereby reducing its unpleasant effect on job performance and mental, emotional, and physical well-being. The results of poor coping in law enforcement include relatively high rates of divorce, thoughts of or actual suicide, negative mood state, chronic anxiety, depression, ineffective communication with others, hallucinogenic drugs, alcohol or tobacco, uncontrolled anger, seeking revenge, mental disengagement—even thoughts of quitting—and actually leaving the profession, sometimes through retirement, and poor performance (Rybicki and Nutter, 2002). Thus, it is apparent that detecting and attempting to change poor coping skills is especially important with EDs.

An angry or hostile response to a stressor might seem "appropriate" and even expected at times, depending on the situation. There are, however, clear disadvantages to using the "wrong" coping strategy. Ineffective (maladaptive) coping with acute forms of stress might result in reduced concentration, higher state anxiety, weight gain through overeating, boredom, lack of physical activity, and, perhaps, the formation of chronic stress or burnout. None of these responses would be considered an effective outcome.

Maladaptive coping may consist of strategies that may actually increase stress or increase stress intensity (e.g. fighting, arguing), are illegal (e.g. ingesting illegal drugs), may lead to undesirable performance outcomes (e.g. unnecessary belligerent behavior toward a suspect), or result in negative emotion (e.g. anger, anxiety, depression). Maladaptive coping consists of strategies that may contribute to the person's stress intensity, lead to undesirable emotions and poorer performance outcomes, and, perhaps, result in reduced job satisfaction and general physical and mental well-being (Zeidner and Saklofske, 1996). Maladaptive coping responses may exacerbate the effects of stress on an employee's emotions, thoughts, and behaviors.

Zeidner and Saklofske (1996) warn against prejudging particular coping strategies as adaptive or maladaptive. Rather, they contend, "the concern must be for whom and under what circumstances a particular coping mode has adaptive consequences rather than the wholesale categorization of coping as adaptive versus maladaptive" (pp. 506–507). Thus, the authors contend that, "coping strategies should not be prejudged as adaptive or maladaptive. Rather, the concern must be for whom and under what circumstances a particular coping mode has adaptive consequences." (pp. 506–507). It is important, therefore, that the "cure" is not worse than the "disease," in other words, that the coping strategy does not cause additional stress and other problems for law enforcement. Coping with stress is a function of immediate external conditions, risk, and the safety of individuals affected by those conditions. This is especially the case in law enforcement (Hart et al., 1995).

Coping is a conscious (not automatic) process

Another area of confusion is whether automated responses to stress constitute coping. Some authors (e.g. Compas *et al.*, 1997) contend that coping begins with conscious and effortful attempts to manage stress. However, with repeated practice, the coping strategy becomes automated. The question becomes: When coping reaches the automated stage, is it still coping? Not necessarily. Compas *et al.* contend that, "some responses to stress that initially require effortful control may become automatic as a result of over learning and thus are no longer considered coping" (p. 109).

A model for coping with stress in law enforcement

Researchers, theorists, and practitioners are in general agreement with the primary components and sequences of the coping process with respect to responding to either acute or chronic stress across most performance domains. A coping model is presented here that reflects the sequence and interaction between coping structures (i.e. "boxes") and processes (i.e. "arrows") with particular relevance to stress in law enforcement (see Anshel *et al.*, 2001, for a full description of this process).

The coping process in this chapter consists of four stages, with implications for law enforcement at each stage: (1) detecting a stimulus or experiencing an event or situation, (2) cognitive appraisal of each stressor, (3) the decision to cope versus not using a coping strategy, and (4) the use of either approach or avoidance coping strategies, each with cognitive and behavioral sub-dimensions.

Detecting a stimulus or experiencing an event or situation

As noted by Lazarus (1999), the coping process begins with the athlete's detection of an external stimulus or experiencing an event or situation which enters into the information processing system (i.e. perception, memory storage or retrieval, decision-making, responding). Coping is a conscious, not automatic, process. If the stimulus or event is ignored or not processed, then the athlete is unable to appraise (interpret) it, and coping is not required. Thus, the athlete's self-awareness of incoming data is necessary prior to interpreting and categorizing this input as meaningful and worthy of subsequent information processing. If a person filters out stimuli or information categorized as irrelevant or unnecessary, the lack of detection of a stressor results in no need to cope because no stress has been recognized. The labeling of a stimulus, event, or condition to determine the need for coping is called *cognitive appraisal.*

Cognitive appraisals

The concept of appraisal has been conceptually defined differently among researchers. Cognitive appraisal is defined as an individual's subjective assessment of whether or not a particular experience is perceived as stressful, to then determine his/her coping response based on that assessment (Gottlieb, 1997). Appraisals can be non-stressful (e.g. positive, benign) or stressful. Typically, researchers have sub-categorized stress appraisals as positive (e.g. challenging) or negative (e.g. harmful, threatening, involving a sense of loss). Only a stressful appraisal requires coping; a benign, harmless, or positive appraisal requires no coping due to the absence of perceived stress.

Harm/loss appraisals, which may be preferred under conditions of low controllability (Dewe, 1992), reflect perceived stress or damage that has already occurred. Examples include making a physical or mental error, exposure to unpleasant input from others, being injured, or receiving pain. As Gignac and Gottlieb (1997) contend, "people subjectively assess whether their endeavors help them achieve some degree of success in meeting their coping goals within a specific stressful context" (p. 246). Given the importance of appraisal in determining one's selection and application of coping strategies, research on the appraisal process in law enforcement is surprisingly rare. Along these lines is an apparent absence of research on evidence of a person's appraisal style in response to perceived stress. Do we have a tendency to make certain types of appraisals following a stressful encounter? Is our appraisal of events while on duty dispositional and predictable? Future research is needed to make this determination.

A threat appraisal is a function of the person's state anxiety about how the situation might turn out (McCrae, 1992). It consists of expectations of possible future harm or danger, often accompanied by unpleasant self-statements such as "What if . . . " or "I hope . . . ." Examples include uncertainty about the potentially harmful effect of experiencing an injury or being exposed to a potentially noxious situation. Sometimes threat appraisals are irrational, based on the person's thoughts about worse-case scenarios (e.g. "What if my driving speed results in a car accident?" "What if I am faced with a weapon? Do I fire first?") Threat is probably the most common stress appraisal in law enforcement (Anshel, 2011). Police examples include investigating a domestic complaint, patrolling in an area known for drug-related violence, or being threatened by a suspect.

One advantage of a threat appraisal is that people can make appropriate psychological and behavioral adjustments and increase readiness before the stressor becomes more serious or is more damaging. Perceived threat also allows law enforcement employees to raise their personal resources in meeting future demands, such as using positive self-talk, psyching-up, or avoiding additional exposure to the threatening condition. Threat appraisals, per se, are not deleterious to performance success. According to Gignac and Gottleib (1997), however, the failure to use positive personal resources to meet and overcome threatening stressful events, such as confidence, arousal, positive expectancies, high self-esteem, optimism, and improving self-control, may exacerbate the stressor's effect on the individual's emotional state, perhaps creating additional anxiety. This condition may have a deleterious influence on work performance.

A *challenge* appraisal reflects the person's determination to confront and overcome the stressful situation. In perceiving a stressful event as challenging, law enforcement officers understand that their job is inherently stressful at any given moment, and that effective job performance is contingent on the ability to overcome any obstacle in order to achieve a desirable outcome (Peacock and Wong, 1990). Challenge appraisals often increase perceived control of the stressful event.

Another form of cognitive appraisal is *perceived control*, or controllability. A stressful event that is perceived by the person as *highly controllable* could suggest the use of approach coping, as opposed to avoidance coping. Sample approach coping strategies include confronting the stressor, gaining and reacting to information, or reflecting on the stressor and planning an immediate response. Stressful events that possess *low-control* properties (e.g. the judicial system, the negative emotions of a work colleague) might induce avoidance coping. Examples include discounting the situation; that is, not taking it seriously or considering the source of the stress source, or quickly moving forward and attending to the next task at hand. Thus, high and low control is a form of cognitive appraisal that is especially important in law enforcement.

In one rare related study, Kirmeyer (1988) observed the work demands, cognitive appraisals (i.e. perceived work stress and overload), and coping strategies of 72 dispatchers throughout one work shift. EDs who were categorized as having Type A behavior patterns had lower thresholds of appraising demands such as overloading and taking coping actions than dispatchers designated as having Type B behaviors. Interruption is an uncontrollable and unpredictable stressor among EDs, resulting in information overload and cognitive fatigue. Interruption was particularly disruptive to EDs who scored high on Type A, as compared to those who scored high on Type B. Kirmeyer speculates that Type As might work harder than Type Bs due, in part, to their higher level of "job involvement and hard-driving competitiveness" (ibid. p. 627). Apparently, Type A behavior may be a mediating variable in experiencing job-related stress in law enforcement, and among dispatchers, in particular.

The decision to cope or not cope

The next stage of the coping process is the person's decision to apply a coping strategy or to simply not cope. Coping consists of learned skills that are consciously applied to specific situations that a person has interpreted as stressful and, usually, unpleasant. If, however, the person has not learned the proper coping response following a certain type of stressor, let's say psychological distancing in response to the drug-induced, hostile speech of a suspect, than the officer may not cope at all. The cost of not coping will likely increase the level and lengthened period of perceived stress.

Researchers and practitioners agree that the main objective of coping is not to prioritize one coping style and to eliminate the other. Rather, the objective of effective coping is to use approach and avoidance coping selectively, based on various situational characteristics. Approach and avoidance coping *styles*, however, are dispositional and reflect the individual's preference for using certain types (categories) of coping *strategies*. Coping effectiveness is an important outcome of selecting and properly using both types of coping. Often, however, the law enforcement officer will decide not to cope; either making a conscious decision not to deal with the stressful situation or doing so due to the lack of coping skills (Anshel *et al.*, 2010, 2013; Krohne, 1993). Failure to cope in response to stressful situations or to use improper coping strategies is a particular problem in law enforcement, whose training rarely includes learning coping skills.

Although several coping frameworks have been studied and published, the literature reflects one framework that has been applied effectively with respect to coping with stress in law enforcement and other areas of physical performance, approach and avoidance (Anshel et al., 2010; Anshel and Sutarso, 2007; Krohne, 1993).

Approach coping

A popular conceptual framework to identify categories of coping is approach and avoidance (Anshel, 2000; Anshel *et al.*, 2010; Krohne, 1993). *Approach* coping, also referred to as attention, sensitization, monitoring, engagement, or vigilance, consists of the thoughts or actions of a person following an event perceived as stressful with the intention of reducing or managing the unpleasant experience (Anshel, 2001). To Roth and Cohen (1986), an approach coping strategy is characterized by cognitive and emotional activity that is oriented toward the threat. Along these lines, Krohne refers to approach (vigilance) coping "as those strategies which are characterized by intensified intake and processing of threatening information" (1993, p. 21).

Use of *approach* coping strategies usually focuses on the person's thoughts or behaviors following stressful appraisals of an event for the purpose of reducing or managing the stressful event (Anshel, 2000). Krohne (1993, p. 21) refers to approach coping, what he calls vigilance, "as those strategies which are characterized by intensified intake and processing of threatening information." Examples of approach coping include seeking information, obtaining knowledge, verbal confrontation, planning a strategy, monitoring actions, venting emotions, and visualization. For Anshel (2000), an approach coping strategy in law enforcement reflects the person's conscious attempt to confront the threat, either directly (e.g. physical actions that help resolve the situation) or indirectly (e.g. thoughts of confrontation or planning direct action).

Approach-behavioral

Approach coping can consist of the person's actions or thoughts. Examples of effective approach-behavioral coping strategies include "I confronted/faced the problem," "I discussed the problem with another person," and "I investigated the source/cause of the stressor." Ineffective approach-behavioral coping might include fighting, reprimanding, or arguing with a work subordinate, knowingly breaking a rule or performing an illegal act, and driving recklessly or over the speed limit.

Approach-cognitive

This form of coping reflects the person's use of thoughts or emotions that promote coping with stress. Effective forms of approach–cognitive coping include reflecting, analyzing, or praying if the prayer focuses on ways to overcome a stressful situation. Ineffective forms of approach–cognitive coping consist of self-defeating thoughts, heightened negative emotions, rumination (sometimes consisting of self-blame), doubts or regret about one's actions, and self-talk that distracts the person from attending to the next task at hand.

Avoidance coping

Avoidance coping consists of physically removing oneself from a perceived threat (e.g. exercising, walking away), filtering out or ignoring information, discounting the relevance or meaningfulness of potentially stressful input (i.e. not taking it seriously), or psychologically distancing oneself from the stressor (Anshel, 2001; Krohne, 1993; Roth and Cohen, 1986). This form of coping is also referred to as desensitization, distraction, repression, blunting, non-vigilance, passive, or disengagement coping. Perhaps not surprisingly, approach rather than avoidance coping is used most often in law enforcement (Anshel, 2011). Avoidance coping, however, is likely underused in law enforcement and helps explain the high rate of stress and poor coping skills in this profession (Anshel, ibid.).

There is relatively close proximity and frequent verbal interaction among law enforcement members who work the same shift. Emergency dispatchers, for instance, may take 15-minute rest (and smoking) breaks every 90 minutes. Given the stressful and relentless nature of this work over the eight-hour shift, it is not surprising that negative emotions emerge: work quality is continuously judged by colleagues and the opportunity to rest and recover is rare, or non-existent. The demands of normal dispatcher work in this setting include a variety of stressors that the ED has little control over: (1) absent co-workers (resulting in being short-staffed), (2) experiencing insults and hostility from emotionally distraught callers, (3) exposure to threats of violence and suicide, and (4) actual suicide and other forms of violent behavior from callers, all of which are combined with a relatively low salary. In this context, effective coping skills, in general, and avoidance coping, in particular, are needed to maintain job satisfaction, good health, and effective performance.

Avoidance-behavioral

This form of coping consists of literally "walking away" or removing oneself from the stressful environment or condition. When drivers purposely avoid a certain road or part of town during rush hour to either avoid heavy traffic or increase the speed of reaching their destination, they are managing stress through avoidance-behavioral coping. Sample items that reflect avoidance-behavioral coping are "I did something else to get my mind off the situation."

Avoidance-cognitive

This category of coping skills refers to limited processing of information, filtering out unwanted, uninformative, or stressful information that has increased stressed levels; what Krohne (1993, p. 3) calls "turning attention away from threatening cues". Coping techniques include psychological distancing (i.e. analyzing or perceiving the stressor objectively), discounting (i.e. reducing the importance of or not taking the stressor seriously), and attentional refocusing (i.e. concentrating on the next task at hand). See Bramson (1981) for a description of these avoidance–cognitive coping techniques. Sample items of avoidance coping style include "I did not take the person/situation seriously"; "Don't pay attention to that person; he's had too much to drink"; and "the Captain is unfair reprimanding me; the situation could not be helped."

There is a paucity of research examining the effectiveness of coping interventions on perceived stress among members of law enforcement, in general, and emergency dispatchers, in particular. The close working stations and ongoing interactions between the public and police officers, detectives, and especially EDs throughout an eight-hour shift create sources of stress that are unique, continuous, and intense in the law enforcement community. The unique job characteristics of EDs virtually mandate mastery of avoidance coping, although evidence is lacking that members of law enforcement use this important coping technique.

As Anshel (2000), Anshel and Sutarso (2007), Krohne (1993), and Suls and Fletcher (1985) claim, responding to stressful events is preferred in low-control situations that require the performer's persistent vigilance, intense cognitive processing, and rapid and accurate decision-making. Responding to emergencies should allocate attention to the task at hand with as few distractions as possible. This is especially true if the stressor is unrelated to resolving the unpleasant situation, such as the caustic remarks of a work colleague or an abusive person.

Taken together, the type of coping skills employed is a function of several characteristics about the situation and the individual's preferences, or style. As Snyder and Dinoff (1999, p. 5) correctly contend, "the effectiveness of the coping strategy rests on its ability to reduce immediate distress, as well as to contribute to more long-term outcomes such as psychological well-being." The use of coping strategies, therefore, is a learned skill expressed in a conscious manner and used selectively under various conditions.

Coping effectiveness

As indicated earlier, the coping process does not infer coping effectiveness. An operational definition of effective coping, however, is a function of the situation such as type(s) of stressor(s), type of measurement of the dependent (outcome) variable, and selected personal and situational characteristics. Zeidner and Saklofske (2006) list eight criteria for assessing the effectiveness of coping outcomes. These are worth noting when determining their proper use in various situations related to law enforcement, each followed by a practical example. Either approach or avoidance coping strategies may be used for each outcome.

1 *Resolution of the conflict or stressful situation.* The officer now has control over the suspect's actions or the ED has maintained emotional control in response to an angry caller and can obtain the needed information to dispatch an officer.
2 *Reduction of physiological or biochemical reactions.* The supervisor's arousal is reduced so that he or she can respond to the subordinate's misconduct in a professional manner.
3 *Reduction of psychological distress.* Emotional distress and state anxiety are controlled and managed. The officer takes a deep breath and uses avoidance coping when arresting a belligerent suspect.
4 *Normative social functioning.* The event is interpreted/appraised realistically (e.g. stressful, non-stressful, challenging, threatening) and the person's response is socially acceptable (i.e. professional, rational, measured, non-belligerent).
5 *Return to pre-stress activities.* The dispatcher resumes her job by attending to the next phone call or interacting with the field officer or with her supervisor at a level of stress at or below the stressful event.
6 *Well-being of self and others affected by the situation.* This criterion includes work colleagues, supervisors, friends, neighbors, and family members. Due to adaptive coping methods all individuals in the stressful environment are more relaxed and under emotional control.
7 *Maintaining positive self-esteem.* In most cases of stress, negative self-esteem reflects poor adjustment and ineffective coping. An effective reaction to stress occurs if the stressed person returns to or maintains a positive mood state and feels good about his or her reaction to the stressful situation.
8 *Perceived effectiveness.* This criterion involves the person's acknowledgement that their coping strategy or reaction to stress was helpful in some way. This reaction would be further validated if their self-reported perceptions were followed by "desirable" behaviors that reinforce an effective reaction to stress. An example is an officer who was upset by the actions of a suspect but calmly wishes the suspect good luck or wishes them a desirable outcome when experiencing the justice system.

Examples of effective coping include dealing directly and professionally with the problem through discussion, avoiding the stressor, exercise, prayer, meditation, psychological distancing, and various forms of distraction. Poor coping skills, addressed in the Disconnected Values Model (Anshel, 2008), carry costs to the officer's mental and physical well-being. These include reduced fitness, weight gain, low energy, persistent higher stress and anxiety, hypertension, heart disease, low attention span, distraction from the task at hand, job burnout, and leaving the law enforcement profession.

There is a paucity of research examining the effectiveness of coping interventions on perceived stress among police officers. The close working stations and ongoing interactions among police officers, especially when dealing with the public during an eight-hour shift, create an array of continuous sources of stress. The responsibilities of police officers on duty and the need for remaining vigilant during a typical eight-hour shift virtually mandate approach coping (Anshel, 2000). Responding to emergencies, for instance, should allocate attentional focusing to the task at hand with as few distractions as possible. This is especially true if an event or experience that the officer perceives as stressful (e.g. disparaging remarks or gestures from others) is unrelated to resolving the situation. There are times, however, when avoidance coping is not only more effective, but even potentially life saving. An example would be when an officer is exposed to unpleasant stimuli (e.g. a negative non-verbal cue; use of profanity) but does not know its source, particularly in a high-crime location. If the officer (or anyone else) is not in harm's way and there is no apparent dangerous situation that requires monitoring by law enforcement, it may be best to ignore the transgression and move on (Anshel, 2000, 2011).

Coping interventions

Before describing interventions to help manage or reduce stress among members of law enforcement, it is important to understand the difference between interventions, treatments, and strategies. An *intervention* is a global concept that includes all types of strategies, treatments, and mental skills programs intended to improve performance outcomes. It is also defined as a process by which a researcher or practitioner attempts to influence the thoughts, emotions, or performance quality of the client or patient. Interventions include one or more strategies—cognitive or behavioral—that are intended to change some predetermined outcome.

A *treatment* is a specific procedure, or action, that is intended to elicit a predictable outcome. An intervention consists of a series of treatments, or a program, that is performed over a longer period of time and may consist of several forms of treatment. Thus, an intervention would require a person to learn and apply multiple treatments.

Strategies, which are often categorized as cognitive or behavioral, are self-initiated, conscious processes designed to enhance a specific outcome or achieve a goal. A *cognitive strategy* is the conscious use of a mental technique intended to alter the person's thoughts (e.g. a mental image that improves confidence), emotions (e.g. increasing a person's arousal level by engaging in "psyching up"), or performance. A *behavioral strategy* is a person's observable actions that seek to alter thoughts, emotions, or performance. Examples include the use of music to increase arousal or endurance, goal setting, avoiding a certain person or situation, called social engineering, and light exercise to reduce stress. See Anshel (2014) for a discussion on each of these concepts.

Coping skills in law enforcement

The proper use of coping strategies should lead to a safe, legal, and permanent resolution of the problem, with no additional conflict, while maintaining a positive emotional state (Zeidner and Saklofske, 1996). As indicated earlier, coping is a skill and, like any skill, must be learned and practiced in order to properly reduce external demands (e.g. removal of the stressor, altering the situation) and/or build internal resources (e.g. confidence, hardiness, mental toughness, anticipation). Each of these factors explains or predicts the level of effectiveness in using a particular coping strategy. As indicated earlier, Table 14.1 categorizes approach and avoidance coping skills, including cognitive and behavioral sub-dimensions.

Exercise and wellness programs

Obesity is ubiquitous in law enforcement in general, and among emergency dispatchers in particular (Hoffman and Collingwood, 2005). The result of this unhealthy physical condition is low physical energy and poor general health, often leading to a shortened professional career (Dunn *et al.*, 1998). In their study of 67 male and female police officers employed in a moderate- sized police department in the southeastern U.S., Anshel and Kang (2008) found that the vast majority of these officers (86 percent) were diagnosed as obese immediately prior to the study. As Wyllie (2011) asserts, a high-quality fitness routine in law enforcement can help prevent injuries that have unnecessarily forced many police officers into medically retired status.

Aumiller *et al.* (2007) recommend the institution of wellness programs aimed at reducing stress and promoting good physical and mental health for police officers. McCarty *et al.* (2007) found similar needs for wellness programs in law enforcement for both male and female police officers. Anshel *et al.* (2010) examined the combination of coping skills and participation in a wellness program on perceived stress and physical energy among police emergency dispatchers. They found that combining exercise—receiving coaching and instruction from a personal trainer once per week over ten weeks—resulted in significantly lower perceived stress than another (control) group of dispatchers who did not experience the fitness program. Pre- and post-intervention fitness tests indicated significantly improved cardiovascular and strength fitness as a function of the ten-week program, providing corroboration for the benefits of exercise on lower perceived stress levels.

One popular explanation of the benefits of various forms of physical activity—including exercise—on reduced stress and anxiety, and improved overall mental health is the *distraction, or time-out, hypothesis* (Bahrke and Morgan, 1978). The authors contend in this hypothesis that anxiety-reducing effects of exercise (and other forms of physical activity such as competitive sports and recreational activities) are due to the distraction from one's normal routine. The person is focusing on the physical and mental demands of the activity, thereby reducing thoughts and emotions unrelated to the present situation. Exercise, then, serves as a distractor or "time-out" from regular behaviors that might be stressful. This is particularly the case when exercise is experienced at the end of a person's work shift, in which the possible unpleasant events previously experienced are at least temporarily "forgotten" and replaced by more pleasant actions and thoughts.

Guidelines for conducting exercise and wellness programs

Approximately 30–50 percent of individuals who begin a formal exercise program will drop out within six months (Buckworth & Dishman, 2002). The most common reasons for dropping out of an exercise program include failure to meet expectations, lack of enjoyment, injury, and lack of time. Adherence to an exercise regimen is more likely if health professionals help clients and patients follow a few important guidelines, including the following. While there are several reasons for this high dropout rate, researchers in the area of exercise psychology have suggested guidelines for assisting exercise novices to adhere to their respective exercise program.

Have realistic expectations and goals, and be patient. One primary reason for dropping out of exercise programs is that the person was not getting fitter or losing weight in accordance with their expectations. If a person has lived a sedentary lifestyle it will take several weeks to obtain a detectable improved fitness level, especially related to cardiovascular fitness. Patience—likely a minimum of 6–8 weeks—is needed to reach the goals of improved fitness and/or reduced body weight.

Schedule your exercise session. Time management skills are needed to initiate and maintain any new habit, especially related to regular exercise. Researchers have found that building new habits into our schedule requires planning and scheduling (Anshel, 2008).

Receive exercise instruction and coaching. Exercise is a science. Improvement may not occur unless exercises are conducted properly. Receiving instruction from a certified trainer is a good investment in the long-term adherence of an exercise habit. Proper exercise technique is more likely to result in obtaining the desirable outcomes.

Engage in types of exercise or other forms of physical activity that are considered enjoyable. Exercise enjoyment is a difficult goal. Physical exertion in a state of low fitness is very uncomfortable for a lot of people. Novices should be encouraged to engage in exercises they prefer and find appealing; at least in the early stages of a new exercise program. For example, a person may want to build muscular strength, but not want to improve cardiovascular fitness, at least initially.

Detect improvement in performance outcomes. People are often driven by numbers; we have a strong need to achieve and using changes in test data and improved performance outcomes are among the more common and easy ways to obtain sources of achievement. Comparing scores obtained before the exercise program (i.e. pre-test scores) with scores gathered after a certain period of time, let's say after exercising for at least ten weeks (i.e. post-test scores), will likely lead to the perception of improved outcomes and increased exercise motivation.

Do not focus exclusively on body weight. The scale does not always tell the truth, especially after clients begin an exercise program. It fails to disclose how much of their weight is fat and how much is muscle. Because muscle weighs more than fat, and muscle is gained through exercise, an individual's body weight may or may not change. But their fitness has improved dramatically and they are much healthier.

Obtain and maintain social support. The extent to which an individual receives various forms of support from others, either directly as a co-exerciser or indirectly through verbal messages of approval and motivation, is referred to as social support (Anshel, 2006). Hoffman and Collingwood (2005) found similar patterns among law enforcement supervisors who offered positive messages for improved fitness to subordinates. Anshel and Kang (2007a, 2007b) found that wellness programs resulted in significantly improved fitness, changes in dietary habits, and high exercise adherence rates if participants in their ten-week wellness program interacted intermittently with fitness and nutrition coaches during the program. Developing desirable, permanent changes in health behavior, therefore, is more likely if individuals in law enforcement receive coaching and/or exercise with others.

Link your fitness habits to your values. One of the most powerful methods to improve a person's exercise motivation is help the exerciser to develop healthy habits that are related to their deepest values (see Anshel, 2008, 2013).

The Disconnected Values Model (DVM): a coping intervention for law enforcement

The DVM is predicated on two postulates, often missing from existing health behavior change intervention research. The first postulate is that a person's decision to initiate a behavior pattern reflects his or her deepest values and beliefs. Values are a person's core beliefs about what they consider to be very important to their health, happiness, and quality of life (Rokeach, 1973). An individual's ability to link their healthy habits to their values increases their desire to perform activities that are categorized as very relevant to meeting personal goals (Anshel, 2013).

The second DVM postulate is that understanding the short-term costs and long-term consequences of unhealthy habits should increase a person's incentive to adopt healthier routines and be consistent with their values. The goal is to overcome the disconnects between a person's unhealthy habits and their values. The challenge for most individuals is to consistently hold themselves accountable to living a values-based life. Thus, an individual whose values include, for instance, health, family, faith, and performance excellence in law enforcement should be self-motivated to regularly engage in at least some behavior patterns that reflect these values. Deeply held values fuel the energy to favorably influence health behavior—particularly in law enforcement, whose commitment to excellence is of paramount importance to job satisfaction and performance quality (Anshel *et al.*, 2010).

Establishing a disconnect

At the heart of the DVM is to identify an inconsistency between a person's values and his or her unhealthy, often self-destructive, habits (Anshel, 2013). The person is asked,

> To what extent are your values consistent with your actions? If you value your health, for instance, do you have habits that are not good for you, and therefore, inconsistent

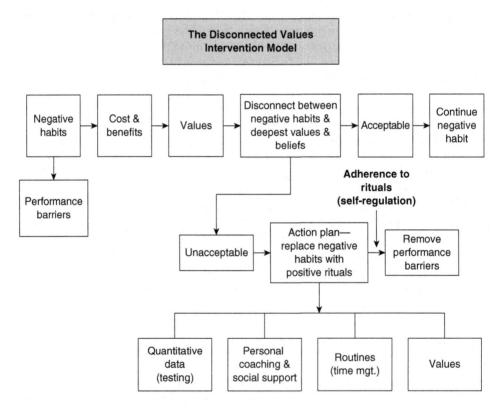

Figure 14.1 The Disconnected Values Model

with your values? What about your family? Is family among your values? If you lead a sedentary lifestyle, you are overweight, avoid vigorous physical activity, have poor nutrition, have trouble sleeping, and feel stressed, and yet, you consider health to be among your deepest values, to what extent are your unhealthy lifestyle consistent with your actions? Do you detect a, inconsistency, or "disconnect," between the value you place on good health and your unhealthy behavioral patterns?

(Anshel, 2016)

Acceptability of the disconnect. If officers acknowledge that their negative habits are inconsistent with their deepest values and beliefs about what is really important to them, the follow-up question must be asked:

> Given the *short-term costs*, such as weight gain, high stress, low job satisfaction, and poor relationships with work colleagues and family members, and *long-term consequences* of your negative habit(s), such as heart disease, cancer, unhappiness, poor quality of life, burnout, quitting your job in law enforcement, is the disconnect between your unhealthy habits and your values of health, family, faith, and job performance acceptable to you?

If the disconnect *is* acceptable—and for many individuals who feel that changing the negative habit is either undesirable or beyond their control—then no change in the officer's actions or behavior patterns will likely occur. It is necessary, therefore, to identify another disconnect between at least one unhealthy habit and their values. Only when an acknowledged disconnect is *unacceptable* to the individual will there likely be a commitment to change behavior and replace the unhealthy habit with at least one healthier routine. If a disconnect is viewed as unacceptable, the individual should be ready to develop and carry out an action plan.

Developing an action plan

This segment of the model—and of a person's lifestyle—is often neglected, yet forms one of the most important aspects of using the DVM effectively. The decision to initiate an exercise program is followed by the development of a detailed action plan. The plan consists of using time management skills in creating a schedule for initiating and maintaining the new exercise ritual. For starting an exercise program, for example, this might include determining the location of the exercise venue, scheduling one or more sessions with an exercise (fitness) coach, determining the type and schedule of exercise, planning the exercise schedule (i.e. days of the week, time of day for exercise), planning exercise tests to establish a baseline of fitness and other health indicators, and the availability of social support (e.g. exercising with a friend, exercising as a group or class), and perhaps obtaining nutritional coaching, as well to establish proper eating patterns; it is suggested that only qualified individuals, such as a registered dietician, be consulted for this information.

Finally, either the orientation coach or fitness coach and the client will work together to develop a 24-hour self-regulation action plan consisting of new routines that are built into the individual's workday and days off. The scheduled activities, connected to the client's values, will include pre-sleep rituals (e.g. no excessive food or alcohol intake within two hours before bedtime), activity that induces positive emotion and positive communication with family members), sleep (e.g. times for lights out and waking), specified times for exercise, water intake (i.e. hydration), meals, snacks, recovery breaks, connecting with family members and significant others, and other rituals linked to each dimension and the client's values.

In summary, the work demands of members of law enforcement create "the perfect storm" of factors that contribute to being overweight, highly stressed, and generally unhealthy. The work routine combines overeating, both in frequency and volume of food intake per sitting (i.e. relatively high fat and low fiber), remaining sedentary over a long period of time, selected individuals working in a dimly lit, enclosed environment that often excludes daylight or fresh air, constant monitoring by colleagues and supervisors, and chronic exposure to negative input from work colleagues, the media, and members of the public creating a toxic work environment. The excessive rate of alcohol, tobacco, and drug use—both legal pharmacological agents and illegal mind-altering drugs—only exacerbates the unhealthy work environment (Hoffman and Collingwood, 2005). Members of law enforcement need to receive instruction on the proper use of coping skills to the extent that they receive opportunities for target practice and other in-service training requirements. The lives and mental well-being of our law enforcement personnel are at stake.

References

Anshel, M. H. (2000). A conceptual model and implications for coping with stressful events in police work. *Criminal Justice and Behavior: An International Journal, 27*, 375–400.

Anshel, M. H. (2001). Qualitative validation of a model for coping with acute stress in sport. *Journal of Sport Behavior, 24*, 223–246.

Anshel, M. H. (2006). *Applied exercise psychology: A practitioner's guide to improving client health and fitness.* New York: Springer Publishing Company.

Anshel, M. H. (2008). The Disconnected Values Model: Intervention strategies for health behavior change. *Journal of Clinical Sport Psychology, 2*, 357–380.

Anshel, M. H. (2011). The Disconnected Values Model: A brief intervention for improving healthy Habits and coping with stress in law enforcement. In J. Kitaeff (ed.), *Handbook of police psychology* (pp. 525–540). New York: Routledge Psychology Press.

Anshel, M. H. (2013). A cognitive-behavioral approach for promoting exercise behavior: The Disconnected Values Model. *Journal of Sport Behavior, 36*, 107–129.

Anshel, M. H. (2014): *Applied health fitness psychology.* Champaign, IL: Human Kinetics.

Anshel, M. H. (2016). *Intervention strategies for changing health behavior: Applying the Disconnected Values Model.* New York: Routledge.

Anshel, M. H. and Sutarso, T. (2007). Relationships between sources of acute stress and athletes' coping style in competitive sport as a function of gender. *Psychology of Sport and Exercise, 8*, 1–24.

Anshel, M. H. and Kang, M. (2007a). Effect of an intervention on replacing negative habits with positive routines for improving full engagement at work: A test of the Disconnected Values Model. *Journal of Consulting Psychology: Practice and Research, 59*, 110–125.

Anshel, M. H. and Kang, M. (2007b). An outcome-based action study on changes in fitness, blood lipids, and exercise adherence based on the Disconnected Values Model. *Behavioral Medicine, 33*, 85–98.

Anshel, M. H. and Kang, M. (2008). Effectiveness of motivational interviewing on changes in fitness, blood lipids, and exercise adherence among police officers. *Journal of Correctional Health Care, 14*, 48–62.

Anshel, M. H., Robertson, M., and Caputi, P. (1997). Sources of acute stress and their appraisals and reappraisals among Australian police as a function of previous experience. *Journal of Occupational and Organizational Psychology, 70*, 337–356.

Anshel, M. H., Kang, M., and Meisner, M. (2010). Developing the approach-avoidance framework for identifying coping style in sport. *Scandinavian Journal of Psychology, 51*, 341–349.

Anshel, M. H., Umscheid, D., and Brinthaupt, T. (2013). Effect of a combined coping skills and wellness program on perceived stress and physical energy among police emergency dispatchers: An exploratory study. *Journal of Police and Criminal Psychology, 28*, 1–14.

Anshel, M. H., Kim, K. W., Kim, B. H., Chang, K. J., and Eom, H. J. (2001). A model for coping with stressful events in sport: Theory, application, and future directions. *International Journal of Sport Psychology, 32*, 43–75.

Aumiller, G., Corey, D., Allen, S. Brewster, J., Cuttler, M., Gupton, H., and Honig, A. (2007). Defining the field of police psychology: Core domains and proficiencies. *Journal of Police and Criminal Psychology, 22*, 65–76.

Bahrke, M. S. and Morgan, W. P. (1978). Anxiety reduction following exercise and meditation. *Cognitive Therapy and Research, 4*, 323–333.

Bramson, R. M. (1981). *Coping with difficult people*. Garden City, NY: Doubleday.

Buckworth, J. and Dishman, R. K. (2002). *Exercise psychology*. Champaign, IL: Human Kinetics.

Compas, B. E., Connor, J., Osowiecki, D., and Welch, A. (1997). Effortful and involuntary responses to stress. In B. H. Gottlieb (ed.), *Coping with chronic stress* (pp. 105–130). New York: Plenum.

Dewe, P. (1992). The appraisal process: Exploring the role of meaning, importance, control and coping in work stress. *Anxiety, Stress, and Coping, 5*, 95–109.

Dunn, A. L., Andersen, R. E., and Jakicic, J. M. (1998). Lifestyle physical activity interventions. History, short- and long-term effects, and recommendations. *American Journal of Preventive Medicine, 15*, 398–412.

Gignac, M. A. M. and Gottlieb, B. H. (1997). Changes in coping with chronic stress: The role of caregivers' appraisals of coping efficacy. In B. H. Gottlieb (ed.), *Coping with chronic stress* (pp. 245–268). New York: Plenum Press.

Gottlieb, B. H. (1997). Conceptual and measurement issues in the study of coping with chronic stress. In B. H. Gottlieb (ed.), *Coping with chronic stress* (pp. 3–42). New York: Plenum.

Hart, P. M., Wearing, A. J., and Headey, B. (1995). Police stress and well-being: Integrating personality, coping and daily work experiences. *Journal of Occupational and Organizational Psychology, 68*, 133–156.

Hoffman, R. and Collingwood, T. R. (2005). *Fit for duty: The police officer's guide to total fitness* (2nd ed.). Champaign, IL: Human Kinetics.

Jenkins, S. R. (1997). Coping and social support among emergency dispatchers: Hurricane Andrew. *Journal of Social Behavior and Personality, 12*, 201–216.

Kirmeyer, S. L. (1988). Coping with competing demands: Interruption and the Type A pattern. *Journal of Applied Psychology, 73*, 621–629.

Krohne, H. W. (1993). Vigilance and cognitive avoidance as concepts in coping research. In H. W. Krohne (ed.), *Attention and avoidance* (pp. 19–50). Seattle, WA: Hogrefe & Huber.

Lazarus, R. S. (1999). *Stress and emotion: A new synthesis*. New York: Springer Publishing Company.

Lazarus, R. S. and Folkman, S. (1984). *Stress, appraisal, and coping*. New York: Springer.

McCarty, W. P., Zhao, J., and Garland, B. E. (2007). Occupational stress and burnout between male and female police officers: Are there any gender differences? *Policing: An International Journal of Police Strategies & Management, 30*, 672–691.

McCrae, R. R. (1992). Situational determinants of coping. In B. N. Carpenter (ed.), *Personal coping: Theory, research, and application*. Westport, CT: Praeger.

Peacock, E. J. and Wong, P. T. P. (1990). The stress appraisal measure (SAM): A multidimensional approach to cognitive appraisal. *Stress Medicine, 6*, 227–236.

Rokeach, M. (1973). *The nature of human values*. New York: Free Press.

Roth, S. and Cohen, L. J. (1986). Approach, avoidance, and coping with stress. *American Psychologist, 41*, 813–819.

Rybicki, D. and Nutter, R. (2002). Employment-related psychological evaluations: Risk management concerns and current practices. *Journal of Police Criminal Psychology, 17*, 8–31.

Shepherd, M. and Hodgkinson, P. E. (1990). The hidden victims of disaster: Helper stress. *Stress Medicine, 6*, 29–35.

Slate, R. N., Johnson, W. W., and Colbert, S. S. (2007). Police stress: A structural model. *Journal of Police and Criminal Psychology, 22*, 102–112.

Snyder, C. R. and Dinoff, B. L. (1999). Coping: Where have you been? In C. R. Snyder (ed.), *Coping: The psychology of what words* (pp. 3–19). New York: Oxford University Press.

Suls, J. and Fletcher, B. (1985). The relative efficacy of avoidant and nonavoidant coping strategies: A meta-analysis. *Health Psychology, 4*, 249–288.

Wyllie, D. (2011). Implementing a tactical fitness program. *Police One.Com News*, October 27.

Zeidner, M. and Saklofske, D. (1996). Adaptive and maladaptive coping. In M. Zeidner and N. S. Endler (eds.), *Handbook of coping: Theory, research, applications* (pp. 505–531). New York: Wiley.

15 The impact of resilience training on officers' wellness and performance

Rollin McCraty and Michael Nila

In early December 2015, a police commander and nearly 30-year veteran of a medium-sized police agency in a major metropolitan city suffered a massive and fatal heart attack. He had just turned 50 and was a leading candidate to fill a vacant police chief position. By all appearances he was healthy, hearty, vibrant and youthful. That is the tragic ending of an almost 30-year career.

His service, career and sudden death were honored with a cop's funeral, with public accolades and much talk of his sacrifice—but was it preventable?

Prologue

Research suggests that police work is among the most stressful occupations in the world and officers typically suffer a variety of physiological, psychological, and behavioral effects and symptoms. Officers operating under severe or chronic stress may well be at greater risk of error, accidents, and over-reactions that can compromise their performance, jeopardize public safety, and pose significant liability costs to the organization. This chapter discusses the nature and degree of physiological activation typically experienced by officers on the job, and the positive impact the Blue Courage and Resilience Advantage performance enhancement-training programs have on police officers. Results have shown that the resilience-building training improves officers' capacity to recognize and self-regulate their responses to stressors in both work and personal contexts. Officers experience improved ability to self-regulate in high-stress contexts and have overall reductions in stress, negative emotions, and depression, as well as increased peacefulness and vitality. Improvements in family relationships, more effective communication and cooperation within work teams, and enhanced work performance have also been found.

Introduction

The prologue to this chapter reflects an all too common ending to a police career. In fact of the 116 officers in the U.S. lost in the line of duty from January through November of 2015, 17 died from heart attacks and another eight from duty-related illnesses. Some of those officers were in their twenties, with most in their thirties and forties—all young and appearing to be healthy men and women.

One of the authors of this chapter (Nila), a retired police commander from Aurora, Illinois, started his career in policing in 1970, retiring in 1999. In the police academy at that time, the instructors spoke of the chronic stress that characterizes policing. A couple years into his career Nila was taught by Dr. Mike Roberts of the San Jose Police

Department about "Officer Survival", not "tactical survival", which is about surviving the physical, mental, and emotional challenges of policing. Back in the 1970s, Dr. Roberts was speaking of early deaths, suicides, chronic illness, divorces, alcoholism, and cynicism that too often pervade our profession. It was a lesson and warning of what would likely come to be if officers did not learn preventative steps to thwart what loomed in their future. Just a few years later, Nila met a neuroscientist who suggested that humans often live in one of two worlds: impoverished or enriched. He described an "impoverished environment" as one devoid of the necessary nutrients of life and equated it to being a prisoner of war who is denied the physical, mental, emotional, and spiritual nutrients required for health and wellness. He also suggested that policing had every characteristic of an impoverished environment—100 percent of them! No surprise that in a March 14, 2014 article in *The Atlantic Magazine*, Erika Hayasaki described a life in policing as being: "medically and psychologically ruinous."

He also described what happens to the brain when subjected to chronic exposure to an impoverished environment. The brain begins to shrink in size, the neurons and connections that allow the different parts of our brain to work in synergy are reduced, and what we have spent a lifetime learning can be diminished or lost while our ability to learn new things is hindered.

He went on to describe an environment he called an "enriched environment." This can be described as the prisoner being released from captivity who now gets all the necessary nutrients for health and wellness. Almost magically the degenerative process begins to reverse itself. The brain begins to grow in size, and new connections are made, memory is restored and learning capacity is enhanced. Today we have a much better understanding of these processes and new terms have emerged such as neurogenesis, and neuroplasticity, which describe the brain's ability to learn and heal itself when in a positive, healthy, and "enriched" environment.

These and other lessons and experiences led Cmdr. Nila to develop an education process for police officers and first responders called Blue Courage (bluecourage.com). Blue Courage was created to enhance the "capacity" of public safety personnel to not only survive in their careers, but to thrive while effectively and healthily responding to the impoverished world of policing. In essence, he and his team set out to learn how to teach officers to create their own enriched environment. In this quest, they discovered the research that had been conducted by the HeartMath Research Center and HeartMath's Resilience Advantage training program, which became the cornerstone of the self-regulation component of the Blue Courage Program. As such, Blue Courage instructors have become HeartMath Certified Trainers in the science and practices to improve the health, well-being, and performance of police officers.

While Blue Courage is relatively new to the law enforcement profession, it has spread quickly to large and small police agencies across the U.S. gaining interest internationally as well. In 2015, NYPD trained over 20,000 officers in the fundamentals of Blue Courage and is now integrating it into the basic academy. The Federal Law Enforcement Training Center (FLETC), which trains all federal law enforcement officers and puts 60,000 officers/agents a year through training, is adopting Blue Courage and integrating it into its own programs. Within the space of two years, Blue Courage has been taught in over 30 states and reached over 600 organizations. Agencies of note embracing Blue Courage include: the U.S. Secret Service, NYPD, San Francisco and Los Angeles County Sheriff's Departments, Maricopa County Sheriff's Office, Atlanta, and Chicago, and it is being taught and integrated into police academies nationwide. In fact, several states are working towards immersion of Blue Courage on a state-wide basis, with Washington and Ohio creating a model for that immersion. Blue Courage has been embraced and supported by the U.S. Department of Justice Bureau of Justice Assistance, which provides federal funding to support and advance Blue Courage.

The experience of stress in police work

Police work can indeed be an extremely stressful occupation, and officers typically suffer a variety of physiological, psychological, and behavioral stress effects, causing them to be exposed to stress outside the range of usual human experience.[1, 2] The subjective experience of stress in police officers is unique and varies widely based on a number of individual factors and the context in which it occurs.

Most would agree that failures of self-regulation are central to the vast majority of health, organizational, and societal problems that plague modern societies.[3] This is also true in law enforcement, as an officer often has to deal with citizens who lack basic self-regulation skills or who have mental health issues. Some officers themselves have not developed the necessary self-regulation skills to effectively maintain their composure in highly complex and stressful situations. It is also the lack of effective mental and emotional self-regulation that often underlies chronic stress, anxiety and overwhelm that lead to errors in judgment. For some, the lack of self-regulatory capacity is due to a lack of proper training and skill acquisition, for others it can be due to a past trauma or destabilization in the neural systems that affect one's ability to self-regulate.

One of the important research outcomes at the HeartMath Institute was the identification of a specific physiological state called coherence and then the introduction of the physiological coherence model, which draws on dynamic systems theory.[4] The optimal, coherence state is associated with enhanced self-regulation, cognitive functioning, and emotional stability that, with practice, can be self-initiated at will, even in highly stressful situations.[5–9] The model emphasizes the importance of healthy physiological variability, feedback, inhibition and reciprocal interactions among a hierarchy of nested neural systems that underlie a complex psychophysiological system for maintaining stability and adaptability to complex changing environments and social demands such as those encountered in law enforcement.[8] The practice of the "in the moment" skills that shift the physiology into the coherence state has been associated with sustained resilience and increased ability for self-regulation.[10, 11]

The need for effective self-regulation skills

The operational duties of police work by their nature may at any time place officers in life-threatening situations in which the decisions they make can mean the difference between life or death for both themselves and others. In addition to the intensity of the acute stress experienced in the moment, the feelings that officers carry with them after such emotionally charged incidents represent a more enduring source of stress for many police officers.[12, 13] Constant exposure to society's interpersonal violence, negative or confrontational interactions with individuals, a sense of personal endangerment, fear of revenge from criminals, and subservience to an ambivalent watchful public produce negative emotional repercussions that can affect police officers on a chronic basis.[2, 13–17]

In addition to the operational stressors inherent in police work, numerous studies have shown that factors related to organizational structure and climate can be an even greater source of stress for the police officer.[2, 18–21] Shift schedules that disrupt normal sleep patterns and social life, authoritarian management styles, poor interpersonal relationships with supervisors, interdepartmental politics, lack of adequate planning and resources, lack of promotion and transfer opportunities, excessive paperwork, lack of autonomy in performing duties and lack of recognition for work accomplishments are among the organizational stressors faced by members of the police force.[13, 18, 19, 22–24]

At the psychological level, the daily stressors of police work may result in chronic negative emotions such as anger, anxiety, or depression, which can eventually lead to psychological burnout or emotional exhaustion.[2, 16, 24–27] Post-traumatic stress disorder (PTSD) can also be a consequence of the exposure to extremely stressful incidents such as violence or major disasters encountered by police officers.[2, 28–30] The high rates of alcohol use among police are one reflection of unmanaged emotional stress.[28, 31–34] Other research has confirmed that the mortality rate from suicide is nearly three times higher in police than in other municipal employees.[35] Finally, the repercussions of unmanaged stress in police clearly extends to officers' families, where it is reflected in poor relationships with spouses and children and the notably high rates of marital disruption and divorce known to exist within this profession.[12, 36–38]

The inability to effectively manage stress has its most dangerous consequences in the line of duty. Police work often places officers in situations where reaction speed, coordination, and the capacity to make rapid decisions and accurate judgments under pressure is critical, and inefficient mental and emotional responses to stress can significantly impair these abilities.[12, 39] In the extreme, stress can cause officers to lose balance and composure to the degree that they employ inappropriate or excessive force in dealing with subjects. [40, 41] Recent years have seen the wide publicization of incidents of police brutality and homicides committed by individual officers throughout the U.S. Errors made in the line of duty can have grievous consequences not only on the officers and the particular suspects they encounter, but also on the public's perception of an entire department and even the entire profession. The consequences of these incidents can include automobile accidents, injury, death, lawsuits, loss of credibility, and even community-wide riots in reaction to an officer's behavior.

Unfortunately, the stress experienced by police is not well understood by those outside law enforcement. It has instead been suggested that police work is a professional environment that encourages emotional detachment from others as well as from individuals' own feelings.[12, 32, 42, 43] While police receive ample training in the theoretical knowledge and technical skills required to take effective action in an emergency situation, most receive little if any training in the self-management skills needed to help them quickly prepare for challenges or regain psychological and physiological equilibrium after a stressful event. Similarly, they are generally not provided with tools to help them manage the emotions they may process internally long after involvement in a traumatic incident. The unusually stringent demands for self-control, and ability to maintain composure, which are typically compounded by the unavailability of effective strategies for self-regulation in the heat of the moment, can become an added stressor in their own right for police.[12, 25, 40]

Without effective self-regulation and energy management skills, the various acute and chronic stressors of police work impose a significant burden on physical and psychological health, leading to numerous adverse physiological, emotional, and behavioral outcomes.[2, 22, 24, 25, 34, 37] Following acutely stressful incidents encountered in the line of duty, bodily systems must recover from an extreme degree of physiological arousal. Over time, repeated physiological responses to stressors and challenges can lead to the chronic activation or dysregulation of the autonomic nervous system. In the long term, this physiological strain can reset the officer's physiological baseline, which can harm health, and increase stress-related illnesses known to exist in the police profession.[2, 24, 32, 34] Research has shown that police officers are over twice as likely as people in other occupations to develop cardiovascular disease.[2, 34, 44] Police also die at a higher rate from cancer than the general population.[35] The cumulative, harmful physiological and psychological effects of stress may also cause work performance to deteriorate, leading to reduced engagement, efficiency, and motivation in performing job duties, poor morale, excessive absenteeism, and premature retirement. One study conducted in the UK found that over one million police working days were lost annually through sickness-related absence (an average rate of 11 days per officer) and that approximately 25 percent of these absences could be attributed specifically to stress.[22]

It is clear that practical resilience-building and stress management techniques are needed not only to help officers remain more balanced during and after the acute stressors of their jobs, but also to take action to better manage and seek real solutions to the chronic stressors related to organizational and family issues. [12, 45]

Resilience training

In order to help police officers, military members, and other first responders better deal with day-to-day stressors and challenges, the HeartMath Institute developed a training program called the Resilience Advantage™. This program provides a set of research-based, self-regulation techniques that can be used in the heat of the moment, when effective self-regulation is typically needed the most. The goal of the Resilience Advantage program is for officers to learn to build and sustain their resilience and diminish the symptoms of operational stress, thereby significantly reducing the development of more serious and long-lasting stress injuries.[5] To be effective, program implementation must be done in a manner that addresses such critical issues as leadership support and modeling, stigmatization, scalability, program sustainability and needs of family members.

The objectives of the Resilience Advantage program are:

1   leveraging officers' ability to think clearly under pressure and discern appropriate solutions to problems
2   increasing officers' ability to maintain situational awareness
3   diminishing officers' physical symptoms of operational stress such as sleep disturbance and fatigue
4   improving officers' reaction times and coordination
5   increasing officers' personal resilience and stress tolerance
6   enhancing officers' ability to more quickly find their "center," gain new perspectives, and counter ineffective and maladaptive thoughts, feelings, and behaviors
7   enhancing intelligent utilization of energy and ability to recoup energy more quickly

To achieve these objectives, the program teaches self-regulation skills[46] that are practical, easy to learn and employ, and that allow officers to more intelligently "take charge" of their mental, emotional, and physical systems. The skills are self-empowering and adaptable in multiple contexts, cost-effective, replicable, and can improve job performance and effectiveness. When properly utilized, the self-regulation skills lead to a measurable shift in physiological functioning to an optimal state called physiological coherence.[4, 47] The program also uses technology (emWave®) to help achieve physiological coherence.

With practice of the skills learned, one is able to shift into a more coherent physiological state before, during, and after challenging or adverse situations, which optimizes mental clarity and emotional stability. Using these skills can lead to profound short- and long-term changes in perception, physiology, mental clarity, and emotional balance. Additionally, these coherence-building skills offer a wide range of benefits, including increased emotional awareness, resilience, vitality, overall well-being, cognitive flexibility, and enhanced problem-solving, as well as countering such conditions as hyperarousal, sleep disturbance, anxiety, anger, depression, and relational conflicts.[5–8, 10, 48, 49]

> On July 17, 2014, New York police officers attempted to arrest Eric Garner for selling untaxed, loose cigarettes. After the use of force, seven-minutes passed before the ambulance arrived. None of the officers recognized that Garner had stopped breathing and he was pronounced dead one-hour later. Even though a $5.9 million dollar settlement was paid to Garner's spouse, hundreds of protests and riots occurred throughout the United States and the policing profession as a whole was badly tarnished. What would have happened if responding officers had been trained in the self-regulation program outlined in this chapter during this stressful encounter? What if one of the officers sounded like this officer:
>
> "Last week I was in a situation in which a person squared off on me and started reaching in his jacket. I went to my breath and activated coherence and never felt anything but calm. As I noticed the sirens of my backup arriving, I realized my heart was beating slowly. Every other time that has happened, I basically screamed for backup and it took me a whole day to calm down. When my Captain got there, he said he thought I was kidding when I put out the call because I sounded so calm on the radio. He asked what I'd been doing differently. This stuff is for real."
>
> (A San Diego police officer)

Why coherence?

Complex living systems, including human beings, are composed of numerous dynamic, interconnected networks of biological structures and processes. Coherence implies order, structure, harmony, and alignment within and amongst the body's various systems. Coherence always implies correlations, connectedness, consistency, and efficient energy utilization. We refer to people's speech or thoughts as coherent if the words fit together well, and incoherent if they are uttering meaningless nonsense or presenting ideas that make no sense as a whole. Coherence, then, refers to wholeness and global order, where the whole is greater than the sum of its individual parts. Thus, the HeartMath Institute introduced the term *physiological coherence* to describe the degree of order, harmony, and stability in the various rhythmic activities within living systems over any given time period.[50]

Many contemporary scientists believe that it is the underlying state of our physiological processes that determines the quality and stability of the feelings and emotions we experience. The feelings we label as "positive" actually reflect body states in which "the regulation of life processes become efficient, or even optimal, free-flowing and easy."[51] For the brain and nervous system to function, the neural activity, which encodes information, must be stable and coordinated and the various centers within the brain must be able to dynamically synchronize their activity in order for information to be smoothly processed and perceived.

A harmonious order signifies a globally coherent system, whose efficient or optimal function is directly related to the ease and flow in life processes. By contrast, an erratic, discordant pattern of activity denotes an incoherent system whose function reflects stress and inefficient utilization of energy in life processes. Interestingly, we have found that positive emotions such as appreciation and courage, as opposed to negative emotions such as anxiety, anger, and fear, are reflected in a heart rhythm pattern that is more coherent (see Figure 15.1).[4, 52] The coherent state has been correlated with a general sense of well-being, and improvements in cognitive, social and physical performance.[4, 9, 10] There is abundant evidence that emotions alter the activity of the body's physiological systems, and that beyond their pleasant subjective feeling, heart-felt positive emotions and attitudes provide a number of benefits that enhance physiological, psychological, and social functioning.[53–55] As coherence tends to naturally emerge with the activation of regenerative emotions such as appreciation, compassion, and courage, it suggests that such feelings increase the coherence and harmony in internal systems.[49]

The power of emotions

Everyone experiences a wide range of emotions every day. Some emotions deplete energy, while some renew energy as they are the primary drivers of our physiological systems. Emotions determine one's level of engagement in life's events, what motivates us and what we care about. Most police officers do their jobs because they care about their community and the safety and well-being of the citizens they serve; and because they have the courage to willingly go into harm's way to protect and to serve. Police officers are often defined by the values of courage, dignity and honor, which can provide a source of energy that enables them to meet the demands of the moment.

On the other hand, policing is often described as a cynical profession framed by negative emotions—in fact some police officers describe cynicism as "policing's new corruption." From an energy perspective, energy draining emotions are costly and inefficient. They drain our energy reserves and also affect people around us. An officer's capacity to maintain composure is determined by his/her ability to self-regulate emotions and stop energy leaks. "Taking charge" of one's emotional system is about the intelligent regulation of emotional energy for maintaining tactical stability, clarity, and safety for oneself and others.

Coherence and resilience

Coherence and resilience are closely related. The HeartMath Institute defines resilience as the capacity to prepare for, recover from, and adapt in the face of stress, adversity, trauma, or tragedy. Resilience is not just about bouncing back and recovering after challenging situations, but is especially important for preventing stress build-up and wasted time and energy. If an officer has a full charge they are in a "ready" state and have the energy to deal with whatever comes their way. Constant energy expenditures without the balance of adequate rest and recovery lead to burnout errors, diminished performance and health challenges. The most basic way the body restores its energy is through rest and sleep. Sleep disruption and fatigue are strong risk factors for developing more serious stress injuries such as PTSD.[56–60]

Resilience is related to an individual's energy resource and self-regulatory capacity across four domains: physical, emotional, mental, and spiritual. Physical resilience is reflected in physical flexibility, endurance, and strength, while emotional resilience is

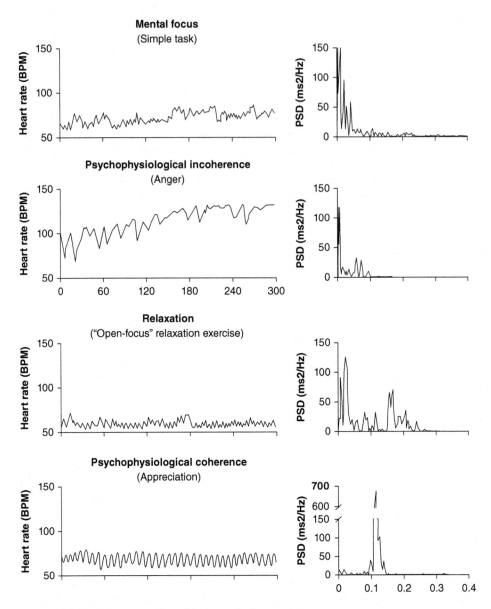

Figure 15.1 Emotions are reflected in heart rhythm patterns.

Note

The left-hand graphs are heart rate tachograms which show beat-to-beat changes in heart rate. To the right are the heart rate variability power spectral density (PSD) plots of the tachograms at left. The examples depicted are typical of the characteristic aspects of the more general patterns observed for each state. *Mental Focus* is characterized by reduced HRV. Activity in all three frequency bands of the HRV power spectrum is present. Anger is an example of *Psychophysiological Incoherence*, characterized by a lower frequency, more disordered heart rhythm pattern and increasing mean heart rate. As can be seen in the corresponding power spectrum to the right, the rhythm during anger is primarily in the very low frequency region, which is associated with sympathetic nervous system activity. *Relaxation* results in a higher frequency and lower amplitude rhythm, indicating reduced autonomic outflow. In this case, increased power in the high frequency region of the power spectrum is observed, reflecting increased parasympathetic activity (the relaxation response).

(continued)

Figure 15.1 (continued)

Psychophysiological Coherence, which is associated with sustained positive emotions (in this example, apprecia-tion), results in a highly ordered, sine-wave-like heart rhythm pattern. As can be seen in the corresponding power spectrum, this psychophysiological mode is associated with a large, narrow peak in the low frequency region, centered around 0.1 Hz. Note the scale difference in the amplitude of the spectral peak during the coherence mode. This indicates system-wide resonance, increased synchronization between the sympathetic and parasympathetic branches of the nervous system, and entrainment between the heart rhythm pattern, res-piration, and blood pressure rhythms. The coherence mode is also associated with increased parasympathetic activity, thus encompassing a key element of the relaxation response, yet it is physiologically distinct from relaxation because the system is oscillating at its resonant frequency and there is increased harmony and syn-chronization in nervous system and heart–brain dynamics.

reflected in one's emotional flexibility, ability to self-regulate emotions, and the quality of relationships. Mental resilience is reflected in attention span, mental flexibility, an opti-mistic world view and ability to integrate multiple points of view. Spiritual resilience is typically associated with one's commitment to core values, intuition, and tolerance of oth-ers' values and beliefs. When we are in a coherent state, the increased physiological effi-ciency and alignment of the mental and emotional systems accumulates resilience (energy) across all four energetic domains. Having a high level of resilience is important for not only recouping after challenging situations, but for preventing unnecessary stress reactions (frustration, impatience, anxiety) that deplete our physical and psychological resources.

Therefore, coherence is fundamental to self-regulation and resilience, optimal func-tioning, and being at one's best. When an officer is coherent, his/her systems are working together, and he/she is better able to "take charge" of themselves and maintain compo-sure in the face of challenge. One can think of "resilience capacity" as the amount of energy that can be stored in a battery.

Given the demands of modern policing on public safety professionals, building and sustaining resilience is more vital than ever and it is this "whole person wellness" emphasis that both Blue Courage and HeartMath's Resilience Advantage program are focused upon.

Establishing a new baseline

In order to understand how increased physiological coherence facilitates self-regulation and helps reset the regulatory systems, it is helpful to learn how emotions reflect complex internal body states[51, 61] that become "set points" in the neural architecture, which act as a baseline reference.[62]

Emotional information is carried by various internal rhythms in the form of low-frequency oscillations produced by these systems. As the brain monitors these inputs, neural patterns are established in nested feedback loops in the neural architecture. These inputs from the body lead to an unconscious form of memory which functions as a baseline against which we assess all current sensory input.[63] In other words, we establish physiological and behavioral set points or default patterns that, once established, the brain and nervous system strive to maintain. Although more complex, this is analogous to set-ting the temperature to a specific setting on a thermostat that the heating system works to maintain. It is important to note that the default patterns that are established are adaptive and while appropriate in one context, may not be healthy or optimal in another.

Once a stable pattern is formed and established, all sensory input to the brain from both the internal and external sensory systems is compared to the reference patterns and programs. When the current inputs match the baseline pattern, the brain recognizes them as familiar, which we experience as comfortable and safe. It is important to note that this same process occurs even if the reference pattern is one that is associated with anxiety, chaos, confusion, overwhelm, etc. It becomes comfortable because it is familiar and becomes the natural emotional and behavioral default.

In order to maintain stability and feelings of safety and comfort, we must be able to maintain a match between our current experience or "reality" and one of our previously established neural programs.[64] When we encounter a new experience or challenge, there can be a mismatch between the input patterns of the new experience and the lack of a familiar reference. Depending on the degree of mismatch, it requires either an internal adjustment (self-regulation) or an outward behavioral action to re-establish a match and feeling of comfort. When a mismatch is detected from either external or internal sensory systems, a change in activity in the central and autonomic nervous systems is produced. If the stimulus or event is recurrent, the brain eventually adapts and we habituate by updating the internal reference. For example, people who live in a noisy city adapt to the ambient noise and eventually tune it out. Subsequent to this adaptation, it is only when they take a trip to the quiet countryside that the actual lack of noise seems strange and is quite noticeable. The mismatch between the familiar noisy background and the quiet setting leads to an arousal reaction that gets our attention. It is this departure from the familiar that gives rise to a signaling function that creates the experience of an emotion, alerting us to the current state of the mismatch.

In addition to the monitoring and control processes for regulation "in the here-and-now," there are also appraisal processes that determine the degree of consistency or inconsistency between a current situation and the projected future. Appraisals of future outcomes can be broadly divided into optimistic and pessimistic.[63] Appraisals that project an inability to successfully deal with a situation may result in feelings of fear and anxiety or overwhelm. In keeping with the recent research on attentional bias,[65] this appraisal might not be accurate, as it could be the result of hypersensitivity to cues that resemble past traumatic experiences in the current situation. Alternately, an inaccurate appraisal can be due to an instability in the neural systems due to stress, or a lack of experience or insight of how to effectively deal with the projected future situation.[63] Despite the lack of accuracy of the appraisal, the familiarity of the input can be sufficient to elicit a pessimistic response. This means we can easily get "stuck" in unhealthy emotional and behavioral patterns and that lasting improvements in emotional experience or behaviors cannot be sustained in the absence of establishing a new set point for the baseline. If behavior change or improved affective states are desired, it is critical to focus on strategies that help to establish a new internal reference. As we successfully navigate new situations or challenges, the positive experience updates our internal reference. In essence, we mature through this process as we learn to more effectively self-regulate our emotions and deal with new situations and challenges. It is through this process that we are able to develop a new, healthier internal baseline reference against which we match inputs so that our assessments of benign inputs are more accurate and result in a feeling of safety and comfort rather than threat and anxiety.

Self-regulation and stability

Ultimately, when we achieve control through the process of self-regulation, it results in feelings of satisfaction and gratification. In contrast, failure to effectively self-regulate and regain control often results in feelings of frustration, impatience, anxiety, overwhelm, hopelessness, or depression.

If the neural systems that maintain the baseline reference patterns are unstable, unsettled emotions and atypical reactions are likely to be experienced. These neural systems can be destabilized by trauma, stress, anxiety or chemical stimulants, to name only a few possibilities. Therefore, it is clear that responding in healthy and effective ways to ongoing inner and outer demands and circumstances, such as daily life situations, depends to a great extent on the synchronization, sensitivity, and stability of our physiological systems.[4, 47]

In the context of self-regulation and ability to maintain composure in highly emotionally charged situations, it is important to note that the heart's rhythmic patterns and the patterns of afferent neurological signals change to a more ordered and stable form when one uses the heart-focused self-regulation techniques. Regular practice of these techniques, which include a shift of attentional focus to the center of the chest (heart area) accompanied by the conscious self-induction of a calm or positive emotional state, reinforces the association (pattern match) between a more coherent rhythm and a calm or positive emotion. Positive feelings then more naturally initiate an increase in cardiac coherence. Increased coherence initiated through heart-focused breathing tends to facilitate the felt experience of a positive emotion. Thus, practice facilitates the *repatterning process*.

This is important in situations where there is exposure to truly high-risk environments or if a past trauma has occurred. The patterns developed at that time no longer serve the individual in current safe environments. As regulatory capacity is increased and new reference patterns are established, which the system then strives to maintain, it becomes much easier for people to maintain stability and self-directed control during daily activities—even during more challenging situations. Without a shift in the underlying baseline, it is exceedingly difficult to sustain behavioral change, placing people at risk of living their lives through the automatic filters of past familiar experience.[8]

Implications for police officers

The above discussion has important implications for police officers in how they interact with citizens and especially in situations where they have to make split-second decisions about the use of force. The matching process discussed above is automatic and dominant over the "rational" neural systems and our baselines determine the default behavior. In order to improve officers' appropriate response and even survival in a force-on-force confrontation, appropriate training should provide coached repetition under realistic stress to verify the achievement of an appropriate baseline and emotional control.

Pro-social behaviors

As human beings, we are not limited to fight, flight, or freezing behavioral responses. We can self-regulate and initiate pro-social behaviors when we encounter stressors. We have a set of neural structures called the social engagement system which act as a braking function and allow for self-regulation and ability to calm ourselves and inhibit sympathetic outflow to the heart and body.[66]

The health of this system sets the limits or boundaries for the range of one's emotional expression, quality of communication, and the ability to self-regulate emotions and behaviors.[67] The sympathetic nervous system in concert with the endocrine system, responds to threats to our safety and quality communication and pro-social behaviors can only be effectively engaged when these defensive circuits are inhibited. The challenge for police officers is that when they perceive that they are threatened, the prefrontal cortex can be taken "offline" and with prolonged exposure to stressful environments, reduced prefrontal activity can lead to hypervigilance, defensiveness, and social isolation.[68]

The sustained practice of self-regulation skills that increase physiological coherence through a "bottom-up" process maintain a more healthy physiological baseline and allow for more accurate assessments and perceptions and capacity for inhibition of the defense response.

Research questions

The use of interventions utilizing the self-regulation techniques and HRV coherence feedback technology (emWave) to reduce stress has significantly improved key markers of health and wellness. These include: immune function,[69, 70] ANS (autonomic nervous system) function, and balance,[50, 71] and significant reductions in stress hormones.[72] Several studies with police officers have found that their capacity to recognize and self-regulate their responses to stressors in both work and personal contexts was significantly improved after leaning the HeartMath self-regulation skills. A study of California correctional officers with high workplace stress found reductions in total cholesterol, glucose, and both systolic and diastolic blood pressure (BP), as well as significant reductions in overall stress,

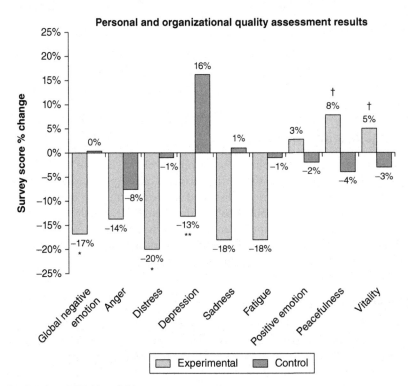

† *p* 0.1, *p* < 0.05, **p* < 0.01

Figure 15.2 Improvements in stress and emotional well-being.

Note

Compares the differences between the average pre- and post-training scores for each variable as measured by the Personal and Organizational Quality Assessment. Compared to the control group, participants trained in the Resilience Advantage program exhibited significant reductions in distress, depression, and global negative emotion, and increases in peacefulness and vitality. The global negative emotion score is the overall average of the individual scores for the anger, distress, depression, and sadness constructs. Note that the control group experienced a marked rise in depression over the same time period. †*p*<0.1, *p*<0.05, **p*<0 .01.

anger, fatigue, and hostility with projected savings in annual healthcare costs of $1,179 per employee.[73] Another workplace study of employees with a clinical diagnosis of hypertension showed significant reductions in (BP) and a wide range of stress measures.[74]

One study explored the nature and degree of physiological activation typically experienced by officers on the job and the effects of HeartMath's Resilience Advantage training program on a group of police officers from Santa Clara County, California.[5] Areas assessed included vitality, emotional well-being, stress coping and interpersonal skills, work performance, workplace effectiveness and climate, family relationships, and physiological recalibration following acute stressors. Physiological measurements were obtained to determine the real-time cardiovascular effects of acutely stressful situations encountered in highly realistic simulated police calls used in police training, and to identify officers at increased risk of future health challenges. The results showed that the resilience-building training improved officers' capacity to recognize and self-regulate their responses to stressors in both work and personal contexts. Officers experienced significant reductions in stress, negative emotions, and depression, compared to a control group, and increases in peacefulness and vitality, compared to the control group. (see Figures 15.2 and 15.3). Improvements in family relationships, more effective communication and cooperation within work teams, and enhanced work performance were also noted.

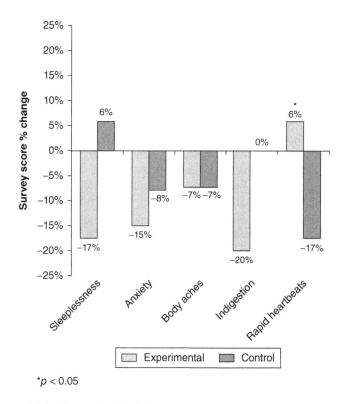

Figure 15.3 Changes in physical stress symptoms.

Note

Shows the changes in five physical symptoms of stress for all participants at the start of the study and 16 weeks later (four weeks after completion of the training).

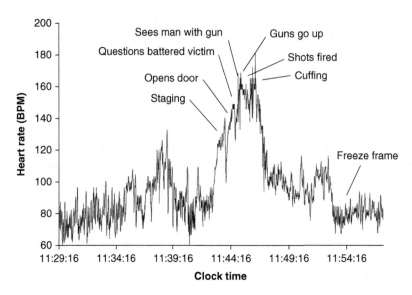

Figure 15.4 This graph provides a typical example of the ability of an officer from the experimental group to shift and reset after the domestic violence scenario. Note that when the scenario ends, the officer's heart rate initially falls, but remains elevated in a range above the normal baseline When this officer used the Freeze Frame Technique, there was an immediate, further reduction in the heart rate back to baseline. In pre-training scenarios it took on average, 1 hour and 5 minutes before returning to baseline values.

Enhanced work performance in the trained group was also noted, as well as improvements in strained family relationships and communication difficulties at work, two principal and well-recognized sources of stress in the policing profession. The majority of participating officers felt that application of the HeartMath skills increased their calmness, clarity, and focus during the scenarios and facilitated a more rapid and full recovery, both physiologically and psychologically, following the acute stress (see Figure 15.4). These findings underscore the importance and potential long-term health implications of providing effective self-management interventions to individuals in high-stress professions such as law enforcement. The integration of such interventions in police training may enable officers to perform their jobs with greater effectiveness, preserve and enhance their physical and emotional health, and ultimately provide better protection to the citizens they serve.

Key benefits of the Resilience Advantage Training for police officers

- increased awareness and self-management of stress reactions
- greater confidence, balance and clarity under acute stress
- quicker physiological and psychological recalibration following acute stress
- improved work performance
- reduced competition, improved communication, and greater cooperation within work teams

- reduced distress, anger, sadness, and fatigue
- reduced sleeplessness and physical stress symptoms
- increased peacefulness and vitality
- improved listening and relationships with family.

Another study was conducted with ten male and four female police officers and two dispatchers with the San Diego Police Department. It included self-regulation skills training comprising an introductory two-hour training session, and four one-hour telephone mentoring sessions by experienced HeartMath mentors spread over a four-week period. In addition, the officers were issued with an iPad app called Stress Resilience Training System (SRTS), which includes training modules on stress and its effects, HRV coherence biofeedback, a series of HeartMath self-regulation techniques and HRV-controlled games.

Outcome measures were the Personal and Organizational Quality Assessment (POQA) survey, the mentors' reports of their observations and records of participants' comments from the mentoring sessions. The POQA results were overwhelmingly positive: All four main scales showed improvement, including emotional vitality, up 25 percent ($p=0.05$), and physical stress, up 24 percent ($p=0.01$). Eight of the nine subscales showed improvement, with the stress subscale improving approximately 40 percent ($p=0.06$). Participant responses were also uniformly positive and enthusiastic. Individual participants praised the program and related improvements in both on-the-job performance and personal and familial situations.[75]

Other studies have indicated that heart rhythm coherence is clearly associated with significant improvements in cognitive performance.[4, 10, 76] Significant outcomes have been observed in discrimination and reaction-time experiments and more complex domains of cognitive function, including memory and academic performance.[4, 77] One study found that being in a state of coherence for five minutes prior to a discrimination task produced significant improvements in performance. It also showed the carry over effect of being in the coherence mode on subsequent cognitive performance as well as a significant correlation between participants heart rhythm coherence and performance.[4]

A study conducted in the United Kingdom found that regular practice of the coherence-shifting techniques to self-regulate stress enhanced a broad range of cognitive functions, including long-term memory, which also correlated with improvements in participants' coherence measures. In another study conducted at the Veterans Administration facility in Columbia South Carolina, with soldiers who had recently returned from Iraq and were diagnosed with PTSD, a relatively short period of coherence biofeedback training resulted in significant improvements in cognitive functions, especially in the ability to self-regulate and inhibit negative responses, which again correlated with coherence measures.[10] Another recent study with pilots engaging in flight simulator tasks found an association between both self-report and expert ratings on task load and task performance and heart rhythm measures.[78] Thus, the coherence mode promotes a calm, emotionally balanced, yet alert and responsive state that is conducive to cognitive and task performance, including problem-solving, decision-making, and activities requiring perceptual acuity, attentional focus, coordination, and discrimination.

In several large-scale implementations of the Resilience Advantage program in military contexts with deploying troops, a number of important factors that impact the success of the programs' ability to increase resilience and achieve the intended benefits have been learned. The first is that leadership support is critical for success. It is important that leadership is trained separately before the lower ranks and that those leaders openly model and support the program. Second, it is best to conduct resilience training early in the training cycle. We found that participants are much more likely to use the skills and HRV coherence technologies (emWaves) on the job when they have learned and used them during training cycles. The third important factor is the family. Often, one of the biggest sources of stress comes from issues occurring at home. This has been addressed through workshops specifically for families and a phone-based Personal Resilience Mentoring Program.

However, the most important factor is the implementation of a robust sustainability component following the initial training. Capt. Laraway, the Navy's Operation Stress Control Officer at that time said,

> I cannot overstate how valuable the ongoing mentoring of these groups has been. I had the opportunity to visit with our Sailors in Afghanistan last fall and the leadership told me that the program is clearly helping the Sailors that use it and they had a number of compelling examples. A common theme was improved sleep, and ability to sustain their composure in high stress interactions with the detainees.[79]

No matter how effective the tools and technologies may be, their potential to increase resilience and performance and reduce symptoms of operational stress cannot be realized if they are not utilized on a regular basis. As with any new skill, it takes practice and repetition before they become automatic responses, especially in challenging situations. In our experience, the most effective approach to facilitate the ongoing use and grounding of the skills is by providing participants with ongoing support from a Leader/Mentor. The primary objective of the mentoring component is to provide the team or unit leaders with the necessary knowledge and tactics to effectively lead personnel in sustaining and expanding the use of self-regulation and healthy energy management skills. The intent is for squad leaders to have the primary mentoring role, but the program includes what we call a "chain of support", where all levels of the leadership are being mentored and supported. Other important elements of the Resilience Advantage program that have been implemented in numerous military contexts to more effectively sustain the use of the resilience skills are: (1) pocket flip-books; (2) follow-up lessons; (3) weekly emails; and (4) HeartMath books on anger and stress management.

Police training can greatly benefit from taking into account modern knowledge in psychophysiology to better provide officers with the capability to keep the highest possible degree of emotional and situational control. In addition, it is also clear that an officers' performance in highly stressful or violent situations is affected by many factors beyond the moment of contact between the officer and the citizen. What was the officer's emotional state? How much sleep did they have prior to the shift, and how long had they been awake? What similar past experiences has the officer encountered? What was happening in the officer's personal life? All are factors that will impact on the officer's state at the moment of decision and action.

Conclusions

The numerous and severe effects of stress in the police profession clearly point to the need for effective resilience-building and stress regulation strategies.

The effects of stress on police officers not only have a detrimental effect on performance, but also on their quality of life and the quality of their interactions with the public. How can a police officer in an uncertain and stressful environment consistently treat members of the public with empathy, dignity, and respect in the furtherance of service, justice, and fundamental fairness? Here is another example of what is often possible:

> Cops are going to tell you that they aren't practicing resilience, but they are. The other day, we made a high profile, felony stop on a stolen vehicle in the Double Rock Housing Projects. About 50 people came out of their homes and tried to start a riot. One woman ran up to a plainclothes officer, got in his face, and called him a "mother★★&^^%" and every other name she could think of. The officer interjected, "Excuse me. I need to activate resilience!" The officer took three steps back, maintained a bladed stance for officer safety, and took a breath. The woman expected a fight and when she didn't get one, she turned and quietly walked away.
>
> (A San Francisco police officer)

In order to enhance our officers' capacity to operate in a coherent state in spite of the conditions around them, and to enhance the capacity of police officers to be good human beings in spite of all that they have seen on the job, there must be a cultural transformation in the hearts and minds of all police officers toward stress resilience and away from the belief that suicide, depression, alcoholism, divorce, and an "us vs. them" mentality is "just the cost of police work."

The accelerated rise of stress and unrest in today's societies is likely to mean an increasing workload for police in the future. The need for officers to maintain their resilience through these challenging times will likely generate an increased emphasis on training in self-regulation for those employed in law enforcement. The integration in police training of programs providing officers with practical and effective self-management skills has enormous potential to result in more comprehensive training for officers in skills enabling them to perform their jobs with greater effectiveness and ultimately provide better protection to the citizens whom they serve.

References

1 Anshel, M., *A conceptual model and implications for coping wtih stressful events in police work.* Criminal Justice and Behavior, 2000. **27**(3): pp. 375–400.

2 Vyas, M.V., et al., *Shift work and vascular events: Systematic review and meta-analysis.* Bmj, 2012. **345**.

3 Baumeister, R.F. and J.J. Exline, *Virtue, personality, and social relations: Self-control as the moral muscle.* J Pers, 1999. **67**(6): pp. 1165–94.

4 McCraty, R., M. Atkinson, D. Tomasino, and R. T. Bradley, *The coherent heart: Heart–brain interactions, psychophysiological coherence, and the emergence of system-wide order.* Integral Review, 2009. **5**(2): pp. 10–115.

5 McCraty, R. and M. Atkinson, *Resilence training program reduces physiological and psychological stress in police officers.* Global Advances in Health and Medicine, 2012. **1**(5): pp. 44–66.

6 McCraty, R., M. Atkinson, L. Lipsenthal, and L. Arguelles, *New hope for correctional officers: An innovative program for reducing stress and health risks.* Appl Psychophysiol Biofeedback, 2009. **34**(4): pp. 251–72.

7 McCraty, R., M. Atkinson, and D. Tomasino, *Impact of a workplace stress reduction program on blood pressure and emotional health in hypertensive employees.* J Altern Complement Med, 2003. **9**(3): pp. 355–69.

8 McCraty, R. and M. Zayas, *Cardiac coherence, self-regulation, autonomic stability, and psychosocial well-being.* Frontiers in Psychology, 2014. **5**(September): pp. 1–13.

9 Bradley, R.T., R. McCratey, M. Atkinson, D. Tomasino, A. Daugherty and L. Arguelles, *Emotion self-regulation, psychophysiological coherence, and test anxiety: Results from an experiment using electrophysiological measures.* Appl Psychophysiol Biofeedback, 2010. **35**(4): pp. 261–83.

10 Ginsberg, J.P., M.E. Berry, and D.A. Powell, *Cardiac coherence and PTSD in combat veterans.* Alternative Therapies in Health and Medicine, 2010. **16**(4): pp. 52–60.

11 Pipe, T.B., V.L. Buchda, S. Launder, B. Hudak, L. Hulvey, K.E. Karns, and D. Pendergast, *Building personal and professional resources of resilience and agility in the healthcare workplace.* Stress and Health, 2012. **28**(1): pp. 11–22.

12 Waters, J.A. and W. Ussery, *Police stress: History, contributing factors, symptoms, and interventions.* Policing: An International Journal of Police Strategies & Management, 2007. **30**(2).

13 Zimmerman, F.H., *Cardiovascular disease and risk factors in law enforcement personnel: A comprehensive review.* Cardiol Rev, 2012. **20**(4): pp. 159–66.

14 Arnetz, B., A. Arble, L. Backman, A. Lynch, and A. Lublin, *Assessment of a prevention program for work-related stress among urban police officers.* Int Arch Occup Environ Health, 2013. pp. 1–10.

15 Burke, R.J., *Stressful events, work–family conflict, coping, psychological burnout, and well-being among police officers.* Psychol Rep, 1994. **75**(2): pp. 787–800.

16 Gaines, J. and J. Jermier, *Emotional exhaustion in a high stress organization.* Academy of Management Journal, 1983. **26**(4): pp. 567–586.

17 Sewell, J., *Police stress.* FBI Law Enforcement Bulletin, Federal Bureau of Investigation, 935 Pennsylvania Avenue, N.W., Washington, D.C. 20535-0001., 1981. **April**: pp. 7–11.

18 Dollard, M.F., M.R. Tuckey, and C. Dormann, *Psychosocial safety climate moderates the job demand-resource interaction in predicting workgroup distress.* Accid Anal Prev, 2012. **45**: pp. 694–704.

19 Cooper, C.L., M.J. Davidson, and P. Robinson, *Stress in the police service.* Journal of Occupational Medicine, 1982. **24**(1): pp. 30–6.

20 Kirkcaldy, B., C.L. Cooper, and P. Ruffalo, *Work stress and health in a sample of U.S. police.* Psychol Rep, 1995. **76**(2): pp. 700–2.

21 Violanti, J.M. and F. Aron, *Sources of police stressors, job attitudes, and psychological distress.* Psychol Rep, 1993. **72**(3 Pt 1): pp. 899–904.

22 Brown, J. and E. Campbell, *Stress and Policing: Sources and Strategies*, 1994, Chichester: John Wiley & Sons.

23 Stotland, E. and M. Pendleton, *Workload, stress, and strain among police officers.* Behav Med, 1989. **15**(1): pp. 5–17.

24 Kales, S.N., A.J. Tsismenakis, C. Zhang, and E.S. Soteriades, *Blood pressure in firefighters, police officers, and other emergency responders.* Am J Hypertens, 2009. **22**(1): pp. 11–20.

25 Burke, R.J., *Stressful events, work–family conflict, coping, psychological burnout, and well-being among police officers.* Psychol Rep, 1994. **75**(2): pp. 787–800.

26 Cannizzo, T. and P. Liu, *The relationship between levels of perceived burnout and career stage among sworn police officers.* Police Studies, 1995. **18**(3/4): pp. 53–67.

27 Dollard, M.F., M.R. Tuckey, and C. Dormann, *Psychosocial safety climate moderates the job demand-resource interaction in predicting workgroup distress.* Accid Anal Prev, 2012. **45**: pp. 694–704.

28 Austin-Ketch, T.L., J. Violanti, D. Fekedulegn, M.E. Andrew, C.M. Burchfield, and T.A. Hartley, *Addictions and the criminal justice system, what happens on the other side? Post-traumatic stress symptoms and cortisol measures in a police cohort.* J Addict Nurs, 2012. **23**(1): pp. 22–9.

29 Carlier, I.V., R.D. Lamberts, and B.P. Gersons, *Risk factors for posttraumatic stress symptomatology in police officers: a prospective analysis.* J Nerv Ment Dis, 1997. **185**(8): pp. 498–506.

30 McCafferty, F.L., G.D. Domingo, and E.A. McCafferty, *Posttraumatic stress disorder in the police officer: Paradigm of occupational stress.* South Med J, 1990. **83**(5): pp. 543–7.

31 Blaauw, E., R. Vermunt, and A. Kerkhof, *Deaths and medical attention in police custody.* Med Law, 1997. **16**(3): pp. 593–606.

32 Sewell, J., *Police stress.* FBI Law Enforcement Bulletin, 1981. **April**: pp. 7–11.

33 Anderson, A.S., R. Litzenberger, and D. Plecas, *Physical evidence of police officer stress.* Policing: An International Journal of Police Strategies & Management 2002. **25**(2): ppp. 399–420.

34 Zimmerman, F.H.M.D., *Cardiovascular Disease and Risk Factors in Law Enforcement Personnel: A Comprehensive Review.* Cardiology in Review July/August, 2012. **20**(4): pp. 159–66.

35 Vena, J.E., J.M. Violanti, J. Marshall, and R.C. Fiedler, *Mortality of a municipal worker cohort: III. Police officers.* Am J Ind Med, 1986. **10**(4): pp. 383–97.

36 Jackson, S. and C. Malasch, *After-effects of job-related stress: Families as victims.* Journal of Occupational Behavior, 1982. **3**: pp. 63–77.

37 Sewell, J., *The development of a critical life events scale for law enforcement.* Journal of Police Science and Administration, 1983. **11**(1): pp. 109–16.

38 Territo, L. and H. Vetter, *Stress and police personnel.* Journal of Police Science and Administration, 1981. **9**: pp. 195–208.

39 Arnsten, A., *The biology of being frazzled.* Science, 1998. **280**: pp. 1711–12.

40 Moore, L. and J. Donohue, *The patrol officer: Special problems/special cures.* Police Chief, 1976. **45**(Nov.): p. 42.

41 Rajaratnam, Sw, L.K. Barger, and S.W. Lockley, *Sleep disorders, health, and safety in police officers.* JAMA: The Journal of the American Medical Association, 2011. **306**(23): pp. 2567–78.

42 Blackmore, J., *Are police allowed to have problems of their own?* Police Magazine, 1978. **1**(3): pp. 47–55.

43 Coman, G. and B. Evans, *Stressors facing Australian police in the 1990s.* Police Studies, 1991. **14**(4): pp. 153–65.

44 Franke, W.D., S.A. Collins, and P.N. Hinz, *Cardiovascular disease morbidity in an Iowa law enforcement cohort, compared with the general Iowa population.* J Occup Environ Med, 1998. **40**(5): pp. 441–4.

45 Collins, P.A. and A.C.C. Gibbs, *Stress in police officers: A study of the origins, prevalence and severity of stress-related symptoms within a county police force.* Occup Med (Lond), 2003. **53**(4): pp. 256–64.

46 Childre, D. and H. Martin, *The HeartMath Solution* 1999, San Francisco: HarperSanFrancisco.

47 McCraty, R., and D. Childre, *Coherence: Bridging personal, social and global health.* Alternative Therapies in Health and Medicine, 2010. **16**(4): pp. 10–24.

48 McCraty, R., B. Barrios-Choplin, D. Rozman, M. Atkinson, and A.D. Watkins, *The impact of a new emotional self-management program on stress, emotions, heart rate variability, DHEA and cortisol.* Integr Physiol Behav Sci, 1998. **33**(2): pp. 151–70.

49 McCraty, R. and D. Tomasino, *Emotional stress, positive emotions, and psychophysiological coherence*, in *Stress in Health and Disease*, B.B. Arnetz and R. Ekman, Editors. 2006, Wiley-VCH: Weinheim, Germany. pp. 342–65.

50 Tiller, W.A., R. McCraty, and M. Atkinson, *Cardiac coherence: A new, noninvasive measure of autonomic nervous system order.* Alternative Therapies in Health and Medicine, 1996. **2**(1): pp. 52–65.

51 Damasio, A., *Looking for Spinoza: Joy, Sorrow, and the Feeling Brain* 2003, Orlando: Harcourt.

52 McCraty, R., M. Atkinson, W.A. Tiller, G. Reisn, and A.D. Watkins, *The effects of emotions on short-term power spectrum analysis of heart rate variability.* Am J Cardiol, 1995. **76**(14): pp. 1089–93.

53 Fredrickson, B.L., *Positive emotions*, in *Handbook of Positive Psychology*, C.R. Snyder and S.J. Lopez, Editors. 2002, Oxford University Press: New York. p. 120-134.

54 Isen, A.M., *Positive affect*, in *Handbook of Cognition and Emotion*, T. Dalgleish and M. Power, Editors. 1999, John Wiley & Sons: New York. pp. 522–39.

55 Wichers, M.C., I. Myin-Germeys, N. Jacobs, F. Peeters, G. Kenis, C. Derom, R. Vlietinck, P. Delespaul, and J. van Os, *Evidence that moment-to-moment variation in positive emotions buffer genetic risk for depression: A momentary assessment twin study.* Acta Psychiatr Scand, 2007. **115**(6): p. 451-7.

56 Belenky, G., N.J. Wesensten, D.R. Thorne, M.L. Thomas, H.C. Singh, D.P. Redmond, M.B. Russo, and T.J. Balkin, *Patterns of performance degradation and restoration during sleep restriction and subsequent recovery: A sleep dose-response study.* J Sleep Res, 2003. **12**(1): pp. 1–12.

57 Chua, E.C., W.Q. Tan, S.C. Yeo, P. Lau, I. Lee, I.H. Mien, K. Puvanendran, and J.J. Gooley, *Heart rate variability can be used to estimate sleepiness-related decrements in psychomotor vigilance during total sleep deprivation.* Sleep, 2012. **35**(3): pp. 325–34.

58 Eriksen, C.A. and G. Kecklund, *Sleep, sleepiness and health complaints in police officers: The effects of a flexible shift system.* Ind Health, 2007. **45**(2): p. 279–88.

59 Lamond, N., J. Dorrian, G.D. Roach, K. McCulloch, A.L. Holmes, H.J. Burgess, A. Fletcher, and D. Dawson, *The impact of a week of simulated night work on sleep, circadian phase, and performance.* Occup Environ Med, 2003. **60**(11): p. e13.

60 Neylan, T.C., T.J. Metzler, C. Henn-Hasse, Y. Blank, C. Tarasovsky, S.E. McCaslin, M. Lenoci, and C.R. Marmar, *Prior night sleep duration is associated with psychomotor vigilance in a healthy sample of police academy recruits.* Chronobiol Int, 2010. **27**(7): pp. 1493–508.

61 Cameron, O.G., *Visceral Sensory Neuroscience: Interception* 2002, New York: Oxford University Press.

62 Pribram, K.H. and F.T. Melges, *Psychophysiological basis of emotion,* in *Handbook of Clinical Neurology,* P.J. Vinken and G.W. Bruyn, Editors. 1969, North-Holland Publishing Company: Amsterdam. p. 316–341.

63 Pribram, K.H., *Feelings as monitors,* in *Feelings and Emotions,* M.B. Arnold, Editor 1970, New York: Academic Press, pp. 41–53.

64 Miller, G.A., E.H. Galanter, and K.H. Pribram, *Plans and the Structure of Behavior* 1960, New York: Henry Holt & Co.

65 Olatunji, B.O., et al., *Heightened attentional capture by threat in veterans with PTSD.* J Abnorm Psychol, 2013. **122**(2): pp. 397–405.

66 Porges, S.W., J.A. Doussard-Roosevelt, and A.K. Maiti, *Vagal tone and the physiological regulation of emotion,* in *Emotion Regulation: Behavioral and Biological Considerations. Monographs of the Society for Research in Child Development,* N.A. Fox, Editor 1994. pp. 167–86, 250–83.

67 Porges, S.W., *The polyvagal perspective.* Biol Psychol, 2007. **74**(2): pp. 116–43.

68 Thayer, J.F., A.L. Hansen, E. Saus-Rose, and B.H. Johnsen, *Heart rate variability, prefrontal neural function, and cognitive performance: The neurovisceral integration perspective on self-regulation, adaptation, and health.* Ann Behav Med, 2009. **37**(2): pp. 141–53.

69 Rein, G., M. Atkinson, and R. McCraty, *The physiological and psychological effects of compassion and anger.* Journal of Advancement in Medicine, 1995. **8**(2): pp. 87–105.

70 McCraty, R., M. Atkinson, G. Rein, and A.D. Watkins, *Music enhances the effect of positive emotional states on salivary IgA.* Stress Medicine, 1996. **12**(3): pp. 167–75.

71 McCraty, R., M. Atkinson, W.A. Tiller, G. Rein, and A.D. Watkins, *The effects of emotions on short-term power spectrum analysis of heart rate variability.* American Journal of Cardiology, 1995. **76**(14): pp. 1089–93.

72 McCraty, R., M. Atkinson, D. Tomasino, and W.A. Tiller, *The electricity of touch: Detection and measurement of cardiac energy exchange between people,* in *Brain and Values: Is a Biological Science of Values Possible,* K.H. Pribram, Editor 1998, Mahwah, NJ: Lawrence Erlbaum Associates, Publishers, pp. 359–79.

73 McCraty, R., M. Atkinson, L. Lipsenthal, and L. Arguelles, *New Hope for Correctional Officers: An Innovative Program for Reducing Stress and Health Risks.* Appl Psych and Biofeedback in press.

74 McCraty, R., M. Atkinson, and D. Tomasino, *Impact of a workplace stress reduction program on blood pressure and emotional health in hypertensive employees.* Journal of Alternative and Complementary Medicine, 2003. **9**(3): pp. 355–69.

75 Weltman, G., J. Lamon, E. Freedy, and D. Chartrand, *Police department personnel stress resilience training: An institutional case study.* Global Advances in Health and Medicne, 2014. **3**(2): pp. 72–9.

76 Lloyd, A., D. Brett, and K. Wesnes, *Coherence training improves cognitive functions and behavior in children with ADHD.* Alternative Therapies in Health and Medicine, 2010. **16**(4): pp. 34–42.

77 Bradley, R.T., R. McCraty, M. Atkinson, and D. Tomasino, *Emotion Self-Regulation, Psychophysiological Coherence, and Test Anxiety: Results from an Experiment Using Electrophysiological Measures.* Association for Applied Psychophysiology and Biofeedback, in press.

78 Lehrer, P., M. Karavidas, S.E. Lu, E. Vaschillo, B. Vaschillo, and A. Cheng, *Cardiac data increase association between self-report and both expert ratings of task load and task performance in flight simulator tasks: An exploratory study.* International Journal of Psychophysiology, 2010. **76**(2): pp. 80–7.

79 Laraway, C.L. and R. McCraty, *A New Perspective on Self-Regulation and Resilience: Lessons Learned from Detainee Operations Sailors,* in *Naval Center for Combat and Operatinal Stress Control Conference 2011* 2011: San Diego.

16 The components of stress management interventions for law enforcement personnel

George T. Patterson

Introduction

This chapter examines the components of stress management interventions that were included in two systematic reviews. One systematic review included studies that provided psychosocial interventions to prevent psychological disorders among law enforcement personnel, whereas the second review examined stress management interventions. The interventions and accompanying components, when reported by study authors, form the basis of recommendations for developing, implementing, and evaluating law enforcement stress management interventions.

Previous chapters have examined the sources of stress among law enforcement personnel as well as stress outcomes. With the purpose of reducing the negative effects of stress, law enforcement organizations provide numerous types of stress management interventions. These interventions assist police officers and recruits with managing organizational, field, and personal stressors. Multiple components and techniques are often included in a single intervention.

Interventions established as evidence-based practices have the most potential to reduce the negative effects of stress. Richardson and Rothstein (2008) conducted a systematic review to examine stress management intervention outcomes. Study populations included teachers, nurses, factory workers, and maintenance personnel. The authors found that studies primarily measured psychological outcomes. Organizational and physiological outcomes were measured less often.

Meta-analysis results revealed larger effect sizes for cognitive-behavioral stress management interventions than relaxation, organizational, multimodal, or alternative interventions. When additional intervention components were included in the cognitive-behavioral intervention smaller effects were found.

In their review that included only studies investigating the effects of secondary prevention interventions such as support groups and stress management training for health workers, van Wyk and Pillay-Van Wyk (2010) examined stress reduction. Primary and tertiary prevention interventions were not included in the review. Wyk and Pillay-Van Wyk asserted that the studies were low quality and, consequently, insufficient evidence was found to support the efficacy of secondary prevention interventions.

Another systematic review included only studies having a precondition that study participants had traumatic stress symptomatology prior to participating in the intervention (tertiary prevention interventions). Any psychological intervention was also included. Trauma-focused cognitive-behavioral therapy, EMDR (Eye Movement Desensitization and Reprocessing) and stress management interventions were found to be more effective for ameliorating symptomatology than supportive or psychodynamic therapy (Bisson and Andrew, 2009). However, Webster (2013) synthesized 103 studies in a meta-analysis and found that more social support was associated with lower perceptions of stress among law enforcement personnel. Webster concluded that the implications for stress management interventions are that the type of social support is irrelevant. It is more important that some form of social support is provided.

In sum, numerous factors contribute to the mixed findings demonstrating the efficacy of stress management interventions. These factors include the wide range of stressors that workers experience, numerous types of stress management interventions given, intervention outcomes measured across studies, diverse worker populations, and varied intervention goals.

Purpose of this chapter

The purpose of this chapter is to examine the components of stress management interventions that were identified in two systematic reviews. The premise of this chapter is based on Coulson's (1987: 14) argument that: "a careful comparison of the various stress training models and further refinement by compatible grouping of similar variables, would allow for a more manageable model for the teaching of basic stress control methodology." The present work compares the stress management interventions that were investigated in studies utilizing control or comparison groups; identifies intervention components; and then groups the components based on frequency of occurrence. The intervention components, when reported by the study authors, such as intervention duration, site, trainer qualifications, and citations identifying the theoretical framework are used to provide recommendations for developing, implementing, and evaluating stress management interventions for law enforcement personnel.

The first systematic review included ten studies that examined psychosocial interventions provided to prevent psychological disorders among law enforcement personnel or to decrease the negative psychological outcomes resulting from stress (Peñalba *et al.*, 2009). Peñalba *et al.* did not conduct a meta-analysis, asserting that the study populations, interventions, and outcomes were too varied and that many of the studies did not report data that could be synthesized in a meta-analysis.

The second systematic review included 12 studies that examined the efficacy of stress management interventions for law enforcement personnel (Patterson *et al.*, 2014).

Meta-analysis results showed a small effect among stress-related physiological outcomes. The effect was not statistically significant but it was clinically significant. Thus the evidence is insufficient to support the efficacy of stress management interventions provided to reduce the negative physiological outcomes, although the clinically significant effect is promising.

Similarly, a small negative effect was found among stress management intervention behavioral outcomes. The effect was not statistically significant but clinically significant. These results are also promising. The small effects found among psychological outcomes were not statistically significant and suggest that the stress management interventions do not have an effect on the psychological outcomes that were measured in the studies.

Clinical intervention model

Wide-ranging interventions that provide skills and techniques from education, to exercise, to cognitive behavioral modalities have been described in the law enforcement stress and coping literature. In general, law enforcement agencies provide stress management interventions using one of two approaches. The first approach is the clinical intervention model. This model provides psychological and other clinical interventions such as counseling. The Employee Assistance Program (EAP) is an example of the clinical intervention model that has been implemented within law enforcement organizations. This model is the most established form of stress management intervention within law enforcement organizations (Stinchcomb, 2004).

Individual coping model

The second approach is the individual coping model. This model emphasizes stress management training by providing interventions as varied as exercise, diet and/or biofeedback. The goal of these interventions is to improve officer's abilities to manage negative stress outcomes (Stinchcomb, 2004).

Primary, secondary, and tertiary stress prevention interventions

Three categories of stress prevention interventions have been described (Hurrell and Murphy, 1996). First, the goals of primary prevention interventions are to reduce environmental work conditions that cause stress. Management policies and procedures and the structure of law enforcement organizations contribute to stress (Ayres and Flanagan, 1990; Stinchcomb, 2004).

Waters and Ussery (2007) suggested that primary prevention interventions developed to reduce stress among law enforcement personnel should consist of examining shiftwork, providing training that is consistent with law enforcement functions, and conducting constructive performance evaluations. Similarly, Burke and Mikkelsen (2006) propose that interventions developed to address organizational stress should consist of developing job roles that are consistent with law enforcement functions, providing law enforcement personnel with greater participation in decisions about their job assignments, and providing management training to supervisory officers.

Giving law enforcement personnel recognition and appreciation for good police work is offered as an additional intervention that law enforcement organizations can consider in order to reduce stress (Daniello, 2011). These interventions are different from those provided to address other types of stressors because the major focus of the intervention is the source of the stress—the law enforcement organization. Moreover, Hurrell and Murphy (1996) assert that primary stress interventions require the use of outcome measures such as absenteeism, worker turnover, and worker performance to assess the efficacy of the primary interventions.

Primary prevention interventions are often not feasible in work settings due to limited resources (van Wyk and Pillay-Van Wyk, 2010). These interventions are more expensive than the other two types of prevention interventions and require organizational change.

Second, the goals of secondary prevention interventions are to change employees' responses to stress. The majority of interventions provided to workers are secondary interventions, with fewer primary interventions provided (Richardson & Rothstein 2008). Providing stress management interventions to employees is an example. Examples include biofeedback, self-help groups, meditation, muscle relaxation techniques, exercise, diet, and improving communication skills, among others (Waters and Ussery, 2007), and training to improve coping skills, stress education, and peer mentoring (Burke and Mikkelsen, 2006).

Third, tertiary prevention interventions are provided to employees who have stress symptoms before participating in an intervention. Stress management interventions can be either secondary or tertiary in nature (Bisson and Andrew, 2009). For example, law enforcement organizations often provide an employee assistance program (EAP). Murphy (1988) noted that tertiary prevention interventions are most commonly provided by organizations, followed by secondary prevention interventions and then primary prevention interventions. However, stress prevention interventions should focus on both the organizational environment and the well-being of employees (Hart and Cooper, 2001). The focus of this chapter is secondary and tertiary stress prevention interventions. These are the types of interventions that were included in the two systemic reviews.

Types of law enforcement stress interventions

Law enforcement personnel employed in organizations that sanction counseling interventions report lower levels of stress, fewer counseling needs, and more favorable attitudes toward participating in counseling (Carlan and Nored, 2008). Furthermore, the name of the stress management intervention influences officer's attitudes toward the intervention as well as their participation. Consequently, identifying a suitable name for the intervention is critical although little information is available to determine which name is the most beneficial (Finn and Tomz, 1997).

Blau (1994) acknowledged numerous types of stress management interventions for law enforcement personnel. These include: critical incident counseling, individual and family counseling, brief counseling, inoculation training, relaxation training, health and wellness, support and referral. Miller (2006) recommended interventions to assist officers with managing stress outcomes that result while responding to emergencies and critical situations. These interventions are: controlling arousal, relaxation techniques, controlling attention, effective imagery, visuo–motor behavior rehearsal, positive affirmations, thought stopping, cognitive restructuring, task-relevant instructional self-talk, mental conditioning and psychological survival training, controlling the scene, and officer survival training.

Finally, Anderson et al. (1995) identified spot checking and scanning, deep breathing, progressive muscle relaxation, exercise, building and anchoring, thought stopping, constructive self-talk, cognitive rehearsal and desensitization, autogenic training, imagery, meditation, peer counseling, family meetings, and stress inoculation (comprised of 14 components such as time management, sleep, nutrition, relaxation, exercise, and recreation).

Exposure to stressors varies based on the type of police agency, location, officer's work assignment, and rank, among other demographic characteristics. There is a need for effective stress management interventions that address organizational, field-work, and personal stressors. To address these varied stressors, a variety of interventions are needed and a single intervention may not address such stressors.

Indeed, implementing effective stress management interventions in law enforcement organizations can be a complex endeavor. Recognizing the lack of empirical support for critical incident stress debriefing (CISD) for law enforcement personnel, Newbold et al. (2008) provide a detailed account of problems that transpired in the Federal Bureau of Investigation (FBI) associated with providing CISD to FBI agents. Concerns that were raised about the efficacy of CISD were not supported and a request for program evaluation activities was not encouraged. The FBI EAP administration strongly supported the use of CISD. Although a working group was established and recommended that only effective stress management interventions be implemented, CISD continued to be supported in the documents. Newbold *et al.* concluded that stress management interventions for law enforcement personnel require policy modifications in EAP contracts and health insurance plans.

Stress management interventions identified in two systematic reviews

Brief Eclectic Psychotherapy (BEP)

Gersons *et al.* (2000) describe Brief Eclectic Psychotherapy (BEP), which consisted of 60- minute sessions that were held once a week over a 16-week period for a total of 16 intervention hours. Individual psychotherapy sessions were provided by clinical psychologists with expertise in providing BEP to police officers experiencing trauma. The study required that police officers be clinically diagnosed with post-traumatic stress disorder (PTSD) prior to receiving the intervention. The goal of the intervention was to reduce PTSD symptoms. A citation is provided to obtain a copy of the manualized treatment protocol from the first author. BEP includes five components:

Psychoeducation

Psychoeducation is provided during the first session to police officers, whose significant others were also invited to participate. During this component, the treatment approach is described and participants are informed that the treatment will reawaken the intense emotional reactions that initially accompanied the traumatic event.

Imaginary guidance

This component consists of muscle relaxation provided over four or five sessions. It also involves reliving, activating memories, and emotional outbursts. Imaginal exposure lasts for 20 to 30 minutes

Mementos and writing assignments

These components are used from the second session until treatment completion. Mementos and writing assignments are used to evoke emotional trauma. Officers are instructed to write a letter to an individual who was associated with the traumatic event. The letter is written at home each day for approximately 30 minutes throughout the treatment period.

Domain of meaning or integration

These techniques are taught after six weeks of treatment has been completed. The techniques help police officers to recognize the changes in their worldview following the traumatic event and to begin to accept the change.

Farewell ritual

This is the final treatment component. Officers perform a ritual with their significant others involving burning, burying, or throwing into water the mementos letter that was written. The ritual also allows officers to share their emotional responses to the traumatic event for the last time.

Writing assignment

Ireland *et al.* (2007) identified a writing assignment intervention in which officers were instructed to write about any emotional responses associated with work or non-work situations, and to describe the actions they would take in response to their emotions. The goal of the intervention was to reduce psychological distress. The intervention required writing for four successive shifts for 15 minutes during each shift. The total duration of the intervention was 60 minutes. The writings are private and not shared with anyone including the trainer. A citation is provided for the intervention.

Stress inoculation training

Digliani (1994) reported the use of a stress inoculation training (SIT) program that utilized a cognitive-behavioral approach. The goal of the intervention was to reduce officers' perceptions of stress, anxiety, anger, self-efficacy, and to increase coping skills. SIT was provided in five, two-hour sessions over a seven-week period for a total of ten hours of intervention. A citation is provided and the SIT training protocol are reported in an appendix that outlines each of the five sessions. Digliani identified three major intervention components:

Conceptualization

This component involved establishing a relationship with SIT participants, providing a transactional model of stress and coping, and confidentiality issues. A homework worksheet was included in an appendix.

Skill acquisition and rehearsal

Relaxation was included in the SIT. A relaxation exercise was provided that involved breathing, progressive muscle relaxation, physiological awareness, imaging, cognitions, and awareness.

Application and follow-through

This final component included review of homework, imagery rehearsal, modeling, and role-play.

Stress management

Ackerley (1986) described the development of a physiological and psychological stress management program. The program was provided during a six-week period; it comprised four hours each week, for a total of 24 intervention hours. The five goals of the program were to (1) provide stress education, (2) increase the officer's ability to recognize work and personal stressors, (3) increase the officer's ability to improve their diet and utilize techniques such as exercise, communication skills, and relaxation, among others, (4) increase coping skills, and (5) create a support system within the law enforcement organization. An outline of the program components, including a summary of the content of the six sessions, is provided in an appendix. The intervention consists of five components. A citation is provided for each of the following components:

Relaxation

Relaxation was offered over a four-session period using progressive muscle relaxation tapes.

Exercise

After the second session, which emphasized the role of exercise, physical exercise was included in four of the six sessions. A period of time was also provided for showering.

Diet and nutrition

The importance of diet and nutrition were included. After the role of diet was given in lecture format, officers were assigned homework in which they focused on the importance of diet and developed a diet plan.

Thought intervention techniques

Thought intervention techniques are based on the rational emotive model. These techniques include thought processing, sleeping patterns, and biological cycles, which were presented in a lecture format in the fourth of six sessions. Officers were then assigned homework to continue their work on thought identification and modification, and their sleeping and biological patterns.

Communication skills

The communication skills training is based on assertiveness training techniques. These techniques are provided in a lecture format that include communication and assertions, followed by an assertion exercise.

Stress reduction program

Coulson (1987) developed a four-session model for teaching stress awareness. The four sessions lasted two and a half hours, for a total intervention time of ten hours. The goal of the program was to teach officers about stress awareness and techniques to manage stress. The program was individualized, and based on demographic characteristics such as age, gender, marital status, and years of police experience. An outline is provided that describes the content for each session. Coulson's three-step teaching process includes three components:

Assessment

Requires the completion of a stress survey to assess stressors. The survey is included in an appendix.

Stress management information

This component includes information about psychological and physiological stress outcomes, and information about law enforcement stress issues such as community factors and managing off-duty stress.

Didactic interchange

A didactic interchange with police officers is provided that reviews the stressors officers identified in the stress survey.

Circuit weight training program

Norvell and Belles (1993) described a 16-week circuit weight training program that was provided three times a week for 20 minutes, using 12 circuit machines. The total intervention lasted 16 hours. The goal of the intervention was to improve psychological, physical, and job outcomes among officers. The exercise sessions were monitored by a trainer although no weight training instruction was provided beyond the first training session. Police officers were instructed about the number of repetitions to use, when to increase the amount of weight, and to document] the amount of weight lifted during each session. No citations were provided that described the theoretical framework for the intervention.

Instructional and aerobic conditioning program

Short *et al.* (1984) explain an instructional and aerobic conditioning program offered to police officers with a precondition for program participation that police officers be 20 percent or more overweight. The goal of the intervention was to increase psychological well-being after participating in the program. Police officers were instructed to discontinue additional physical activity and maintain levels of activity that were performed prior to the intervention. Citations are provided for the theoretical framework and the aerobic conditioning goals. The program consists of two components:

Aerobic conditioning program

The aerobic conditioning program included supervised walking and jogging. Target heart rates were established at 80 percent of an officer's maximum rate. The program was provided in three sessions each week over an eight-week period. Each session lasted approximately 45 minutes for a total of approximately 18 hours of aerobic conditioning.

Instruction

The instruction component consisted of nutritional, dietary, and exercise education. Weekly 90-minute sessions were provided over an eight-week period for a total of 12 hours of instruction.

HeartMath Stress and Emotional Self-Management Program

McCraty *et al.* (1999) examined the effects of the HeartMath Stress and Emotional Self-Management Program. The goals of the intervention were to "provide practical techniques designed to reduce stress in the moment, improve physiological and emotional balance, increase mental clarity and enhance performance and quality of life" (ibid., p. 1).

The program was developed for utilization by police officers with the goal of reducing stress reactions as they occur during a stress situation, thereby improving job performance. Consequently, as part of the intervention, police officers participated in role-play scenarios developed to arouse stress reactions and assess job performance.

Training occurred at a law enforcement organization. Three sessions were provided during a one- month period that lasted 4–6 hours each for a total of 12–18 hours of intervention. Numerous components of the intervention are not reported, although descriptions are reported for a few of the program components. Each of the following components is unique to the HeartMath Stress and Emotional Self-Management Program and includes:

Freeze frame

This component emphasizes developing skills to reduce stress reactions that can be utilized while responding to a stressful situation. The technique can be implemented in less than 60 seconds.

Heart lock-in

Heart lock-in is a technique used to stimulate positive emotions and requires that officers concentrate on their heart. This component includes listening to music to help reduce stress reactions.

Coherent communication

This component emphasizes the development of improved communication skills.

Brief interventions

Richmond *et al.* (1999) discuss brief interventions that were provided as part of a health assessment and promotion program conducted within a law enforcement organization. The goal of the intervention is to reduce the use of alcohol, smoking, and stress symptomatology. The intervention was comprised of three brief interventions that offered brief advice and self-help materials focusing on either alcohol use, smoking, or stress. Before participating in the brief interventions police officers were required to complete an assessment instrument to determine levels of alcohol use, smoking, and stress.

If an officer required more than one intervention, an intervention for alcohol use was provided first, followed by smoking and, lastly, stress symptoms. The following time frames illustrate the duration of the brief interventions—alcohol use (approximately 15 minutes), smoking (five to ten minutes), and stress symptoms (five to ten minutes) for a total intervention of approximately 25 to 35 minutes if officers required all three brief interventions. Citations are provided for the assessment instruments and brief interventions.

Visuo-motor behavior rehearsal (VMBR)

Shipley and Baranski (2002) reported a visuo-motor behavior rehearsal (VMBR) that was adapted for use in law enforcement. VMBR was provided to recruits during week 14 of their 16- week academy training. The purpose of the intervention was to reduce acute stress symptoms and improve job performance. A stressful role-play shooting scenario was included to assess recruits' job performance after completion of VMBR. Two components are described:

Progressive relaxation

This component consisted of a breathing exercise followed by a muscle relaxation exercise that lasted approximately ten minutes. A citation was provided.

Imagery/mental rehearsal

This component emphasized the identification of positive-self statements and mental imagery of acquired skills, which lasted approximately 20 minutes. The total duration of VMBR is not reported.

Wellness counseling

Tanigoshi *et al.* (2008) outline the application of five, one-hour individual counseling sessions offered by counselors holding doctorate degrees. The counselors were trained in VMBR prior to providing the intervention. The sessions were provided every other week throughout the course of 10–15 weeks for a total of five hours of intervention.

The majority of sessions focused on helping police officers to develop cognitive-behavioral intervention treatment plans and goals. The goal of the intervention was improve wellness among police officers. A standardized instrument was administered at the start of the intervention to assess levels of wellness. This instrument was subsequently used to identify several areas of wellness that officers pinpointed for improvement.

The indivisible self model of wellness

This component focused on defining wellness, examining the relationship between wellness and health, and developing an individualized wellness plan. Officers' wellness plans included several areas of wellness that officers identified as needing improvement.

Eye Movement Desensitization and Reprossing (EMDR)

Wilson *et al.* (2001) depict the use of Eye Movement Desensitization and Reprocessing (EMDR) that was provided to police officers by six licensed mental health professionals—four psychologists and two social workers in the professional's office. Police officers were encouraged to participate in the study jointly with their significant others. The EMDR intervention consisted of three, two-hour EMDR sessions for a total of six hours. A clinical interview was first conducted prior to officers participating in EMDR. The interviews enabled each officer and their significant other to identify stressors.

There are eight components to EMDR: client history and treatment planning, preparation, assessment, desensitization (this is the component where eye movements are provided), installation, body scan, closure, and re-evaluation. A summary of these components is not provided, although a citation was provided.

Social skill training

Aremu (2006) reported the use of Social Skills Training (SST) to improve interpersonal relationships among police officers. The intervention was not described as a stress management intervention. Although a citation is provided that describes the SST theoretical framework, information about the length of the training and trainer qualifications is not provided. The training is provided in eight sessions that focus on social skills, role-playing and practising the skills.

Problem-solving skills training

Aremu (2006) also reported the use of Problem-Solving Skills Training (PST) to improve interpersonal relationships among police officers. Similar to SST, the intervention was not described as a stress management intervention. Officers who received PST were part of a second experimental group used in the study. A citation is provided for PST. Information concerning the length of the training and trainer qualifications is not provided. PST was also provided in eight sessions that focused on improving policing, developing solutions for improving policing, and techniques for implementing the solutions.

Mental imaging training

Backman and Arnetz (1997) describe the use of mental imaging training provided to recruits at a training academy. The training instructors were police officers who had received training in mental imaging prior to providing the training. Mental imaging training consisted of two-hour sessions provided throughout a ten-week period for a total of 20 hours of training. A citation is provided for the physical and mental relaxation cassette tapes. The training included the following three components:

Theory

This component focused on stress theory and stress outcomes.

Physical and mental relaxation

After practicing physical relaxation, mental relaxation was practised as homework, using cassette tapes.

Learning activities

Learning activities were taught that emphasized managing problems, triggers, self-image, concentration, and environment.

Group counseling

Doctor *et al.* (1994) explain the use of group counseling sessions provided at a central police station. The sessions followed an unstructured format. The goal of the sessions was to provide a confidential environment for police officers where they could openly and safely share their feelings related to stress. Prior to participating in the sessions, police officers completed a stress situation questionnaire. The questionnaire results were used to stimulate discussion during the counseling sessions. Twelve group counseling sessions, facilitated by a psychiatric mental health professional and lasting one hour each were held over a 12-week period for a total of 12 hours of intervention. A citation is not provided for the intervention.

Stress management training

McNulty *et al.* (1984) report some of the details of stress management training sessions that were provided weekly during the last ten weeks of recruit academy training. Training occurred at the academy comprised of sessions lasting one and a half hours for a total of 15 hours. The intervention was provided in small groups that focused on physical and cognitive techniques for managing stress. Recruits were instructed to practice these techniques for homework. No other information is provided for the intervention.

Stress prevention program

O'Neill *et al.* (1982) discussed the use of a stress prevention program. A citation was provided although no further details of the intervention were reported. The intervention consisted of three components (each component was given to a separate group of officers):

Physical fitness modality

The goal of the physical fitness modality was to improve physical fitness as a method for reducing stress. This component was provided as a "low-cost" (ibid., p. 391) intervention that included exercise, consultation, and a newsletter, focusing on nutrition and stress prevention, that was distributed each week.

Psychological modality

The police officers participating in this modality were first stratified based on job characteristics such as rank, then assigned to stress education support groups. The groups included audio-visual materials, and emphasized education and practice of techniques. Groups were held for a period of one and a half hours each session although the total number of intervention hours is not reported.

Psychophysical modality

This modality combined both the physical fitness and psychological modalities.

Professional modality

This modality involved a training program based on participating in continuing education programs. Officers participating in this modality were considered to be a placebo group.

Stress management program

Sarason focused on nutrition and stress prevention (1979) describe a Stress Management Program designed with the goal of increasing awareness of cognitive and physiological reactions among recruits that result from responding to situations involving anger and threat. The intervention was intended to help recruits understand how their reactions affected their job performance.

A citation is provided for the intervention and a description of the stress management program is available from the study authors. The intervention included role-play, modeling, and awareness of reactions to stress during role-play. The intervention was provided over a period of six sessions lasting two hours each for a total of 12 hours.

Components of the intervention included individuals self-monitoring their cognitive and physiological reactions, progressive muscle relaxation, and the acquisition of positive self-statements. These components are not described in detail.

Recommendations

Among the 22 studies included in the two systematic reviews, there were duplicate studies such that five studies were included in both reviews. A total of 19 interventions were identified in the two systematic reviews. There were 12 distinct interventions identified by Patterson *et al.* (2014), and seven distinct interventions identified by Peñalba *et al.* (2009). Of these interventions, five were included in both reviews. As the summary of interventions has shown, some authors reported more detailed descriptions of the interventions.

Among the 19 interventions, 42 intervention components were identified although a description was not provided for all of the intervention components. Some interventions, such as a writing intervention, did not include any supplementary components, whereas other interventions were comprised of multiple components. Seven interventions were described that did not include any identified components. EMDR comprised most of the intervention components, having eight separate and distinct components. This was followed by BEP and a stress management intervention (Ackerley, 1986), each of which comprised of five components. The most frequently reported intervention components that were provided in order of frequency were: (1) mental or physical relaxation, (2) communication skills, and (3) diet and nutrition, and exercise.

Among the 19 identified interventions, more than half of the interventions (approximately 53 percent) used the phrases stress, psychotherapy, or counseling in the naming of the intervention. Approximately 37 percent of the interventions referred to stress in the intervention names, followed by references to psychotherapy or counseling (approximately 16 percent) in the name. Highly specialized interventions such as VMBR and EMDR were named only one time each.

The goals of the interventions also varied among the studies. Several of the interventions had preconditions for participating in the intervention, and a few utilized stressful role-play scenarios, such as a shooting situation, that were used to stimulate negative stress reactions that were subsequently associated with job performance assessed during the role-play.

Although insufficient evidence exists to support the effectiveness of stress management interventions provided to law enforcement personnel, based on the information reported in the studies included in the two systematic reviews several recommendations are proposed. These recommendations include:

1   *Sufficient time should be provided during the intervention for law enforcement personnel to learn and practice new techniques.* It is imperative to have realistic expectations about the types of stress management techniques that can be taught, learned, and practiced during the intervention. Patterson *et al.* (2014) reported that among the studies included in their meta-analysis, the time period ranged from 30 minutes to 24 hours over a one- to 16-week period. The average time frame of the interventions was 10.95 hours (*SD*=7.33).

2   *Information that is disseminated about intervention outcomes should include complete outcome data.* It is also imperative that study authors and law enforcement organizations conducting

outcome evaluations report complete outcome data. Peñalba *et al.* (2009) observed the problem of missing data describing intervention outcomes. Webster (2013) observed similar problems among studies that investigated perceptions of stress among law enforcement personnel. A large amount of missing data, low-quality methodology, and inconsistent measurement approaches and outcomes were noted among the studies,

3   *Trainer qualifications and experience with the intervention should be included in disseminated reports and trainers should have training and experience in providing the intervention.* Interventions provided by qualified and experienced trainers are essential and should be included in reports. Particularly given that the majority of law enforcement organizations in the U.S. will rely on external trainers to provide stress management interventions (Finn and Tomz, 1997). Blau (1994) emphasized the importance of a trainer's experience and training. In most of the studies included in the two systematic reviews, the trainer's qualifications and prior experience providing the intervention were not reported. Among the studies that did report trainers' experience, most trainers received training prior to facilitating the intervention.

4   *More training materials are needed that can be replicated.* Training materials such as newsletters, handouts, referral lists, and intervention manuals that include training resources should be available.

5   *Interventions and intervention outcomes should be related to specific types of law enforcement stressors.* Different outcome measures are required based on the goals and type of intervention provided. As Hurrell and Murphy (1996) suggested, primary stress interventions require the use of outcome measures that examine factors such as absenteeism, turnover, and job performance to assess intervention efficacy. Equally as important, the use of reliable and valid outcome measures are necessary to assess whether the intervention goals have been achieved.

6   *Theoretical frameworks that guide the intervention should be reported in disseminated documents and interventions should be grounded in theory.* Most of the studies included a citation for the prior work establishing the theoretical framework for the intervention. Given that theory guides research and practice interventions, it is essential that interventions be grounded in theoretical frameworks.

7   *Intervention goals should be determined prior to providing the intervention, articulated with intervention participants, and reported in disseminated intervention descriptions.* This practice can assist law enforcement organizations in selecting appropriate interventions, and law enforcement personnel with acquiring a better understanding of the intervention.

8   *Establish the most appropriate site(s) for the intervention.* More evidence is needed that establishes the preferences held by law enforcement personnel regarding the most appropriate site for the intervention. Recruits may have less flexibility regarding where the intervention is offered. The site of the intervention could possibly affect participation due to travel time, off-duty status and concerns about not participating in job-related activities while off duty. The majority of studies did not report the intervention site. When the intervention sites were reported, a law enforcement organization or the off-site office of the facilitator were the described intervention locations.

Conclusion

This examination of stress management interventions, identified in two systematic reviews, has shown that the interventions were varied and many were comprised of multiple components. It is noteworthy that all of the interventions were investigated together with a comparison group (either using random assignment or quasi-experimental designs). A need exists for manualized, evidence-based stress management interventions for law enforcement personnel. It is also important to have a directory of these interventions. A well-developed directory can be used to guide law enforcement organizations in the selection of interventions and target them to specific stressors. However, more rigorous, randomized controlled trials are necessary to investigate the efficacy of such interventions.

References

**Ackerley, D.G. (1986). *The effects of a stress management program on police personnel.* Dissertation Abstract International. Order No. 8716685.

Anderson, W., Swenson, D., and Clay, D. (1995). *Stress management for law enforcement officers.* Englewood Cliffs, NJ: Prentice Hall.

*Aremu, O.A. (2006). The effect of two psychological intervention programmes on the improvement of interpersonal relationships of police officers in Osogbo, Nigeria. *Criminal Justice Studies,* 19, 139–152.

Ayres, R.M. and Flanagan, G.S. (1990). *Preventing law enforcement stress: The organization's role.* M.B. Ayres (ed.). Alexandria, VA: National Sheriffs' Association.

*Backman, L. and Arnetz, B.B. (1997). Psychophysiological effects of mental imaging training for police trainees. *Stress Medicine, 13,* 43–48.

Bisson, J. and Andrew, M. (2009). *Psychological treatment of post-traumatic stress disorder (PTSD).* Cochrane Database of Systematic Reviews, 3.

Blau, T.H. (1994). *Psychological services for law enforcement.* New York: John Wiley & Sons, Inc.

Burke, R.J. and Mikkelsen, A. (2006). Burnout among Norwegian police officers: Potential antecedants and consequences. *International Journal of Stress Management, 13,* 64–83.

Carlan, P.E. and Nored, L.S. (2008). An examination of officer stress: Should police departments implement mandatory counseling? *Journal of Police and Criminal Psychology, 23,* 8–15.

**Coulson, J.E. (1987). *The effectiveness of a stress reduction program for police officers.* Dissertation Abstract International. Order No. 8713941.

Daniello, R.J. (2011). *Police officer stress awareness and management. A handbook for practitioners.* Lanham, MD: Hamilton Books.

**Digliani, J.A. (1994). *Stress inoculation training: The police.* Dissertation Abstract International. Order No. 9524023.

*Doctor, R.S., Curtis, D., and Isaacs, G. (1994). Psychiatric morbidity in policemen and the effect of brief psychotherapeutic intervention. *Stress Medicine, 10,* 151–157.

Finn, P. and Tomz, J. E. (1997). *Developing a law enforcement stress program for officers and their families.* Washington, DC: US Department of Justice, Office of Justice Programs, National Institute of Justice.

**Gersons, B.P.R., Carlier, I.V.E., Lamberts, R.D., and van der Kolk, B.A. (2000). Randomized clinical trial of brief eclectic psychotherapy for police officers with post-traumatic stress disorder. *International Society for Traumatic Stress Studies, 13,* 333–347.

Hart, P.M. and Cooper, C.L. (2001). Occupational stress: Toward a more integrated framework. In N.R. Anderson, D.S. Ones, H.K. Sinangil, and C. Viswesvarian (eds.), *Handbook of industrial, work and organizational psychology* (vol. 2, pp. 93–144). London: Sage.

Hurrell, J.J. and Murphy, L.R. (1996). Occupational stress intervention. *American Journal of Industrial Medicine, 29,* 338–341.

**Ireland, M., Malouff, J.M., and Byrne, B. (2007). The efficacy of written emotional expression in the reduction of psychological distress in police officers. *International Journal of Police Science & Management, 9,* 303–311.

**McCraty, R., Tomasino, D., Atkinson, M., and Sundram, J. (1999). *Impact of the HeartMath self-management skills program physiological and psychological stress in police officers.* Boulder Creek, CA: HeartMath Research Center, Publication No. 99–075.

*McNulty, S., Jefferys, D., Singer, G., and Singer, L. (1984). Use of hormone analysis in the assessment of the efficacy of stress management training in police recruits. *Journal of Police Science and Administration, 12,* 130–132.

Miller, L. (2006). *Practical police psychology: Stress management and crisis intervention for law enforcement.* Springfield, IL: Charles C. Thomas.

Murphy, L.R. (1988). Workplace interventions for stress reduction and prevention. In C.L. Cooper and R. Payne (eds.), *Causes, coping and consequences of stress at work* (pp. 301–339). New York: Wiley.

Newbold, K.M., Lohr, J.M., and Gist, R. (2008). Apprehend without warrant: Issues of evidentiary warrant for critical incident services and related trauma interventions in a federal law enforcement agency. *Criminal Justice and Behavior, 35,* 1337–1353.

***Norvell, N., & Belles, D. (1993). Psychological and physical benefits of circuit weight training in law enforcement personnel. *Journal of Consulting and Clinical Psychology, 61,* 520–527.

*O'Neill, M.W., Hanewicz, B.W., Fransway, L.M., and Cassidy-Riske, C. (1982). Stress inoculation training and job performance. *Journal of Police Science and Administration, 10,* 388–397.

Patterson, G. T., Chung, I.W., and Swan, P.G. (2014). Stress management interventions for police officers and recruits: A meta-analysis. *Journal of Experimental Criminology, 10,* 487–513.

Peñalba, V., McGuire, H., and Leite, J.R. (2009). *Psychosocial interventions for prevention of psychosocial disorders in law enforcement officers.* The Cochrane Library, Issue 4. Retrieved on March 21, 2016 from www.thecochranelibrary.com.

Richardson, K.M. and Rothstein, H.R. (2008). Effects of occupational stress management intervention programs: A meta-analysis. *Journal of Occupational Health Psychology, 13,* 69–93.

**Richmond, R.L., Kehoe, L., Hailstone, S., Wodak, A., and Uebel-Yan, M. (1999). Quantitative and qualitative evaluations of brief interventions to change excessive during, smoking and stress in the police force. *Addiction, 94,* 1509–1521.

*Sarason, I.G., Johnson, J.H., Berberich, J.P., and Siegel, J.M. (1979). Helping police officers to cope with stress: A cognitive-behavioral approach. *American Journal of Community Psychology, 7,* 593–603.

***Shipley, P. and Baranski, J.V. (2002). Police officer performance under stress: A pilot study on the effects of visuo-motor behavior rehearsal. *International Journal of Stress Management, 9,* 71–80.

***Short, M.A., DiCarlo, S., Steffee, W.P., and Pavlou, K. (1984). Effects of physical conditioning on self-concept of adult obese males. *Physical Therapy, 62,* 194–198.

Stinchcomb, J.B. (2004). Searching for stress in all the wrong places: Combating chronic organizational stressors in policing. *Police Practice and Research, 5,* 259–277.

**Tanigoshi, H., Kontos, A.P., and Remley, T.P. (2008). The effectiveness of individual wellness counseling on the wellness of law enforcement officers. *Journal of Counseling & Development, 86,* 64–74.

van Wyk B.E. and Pillay-Van Wyk, V. (2010). *Preventive staff-support interventions for health workers.* The Cochrane Library, Issue 3. Retrieved on March 21, 2016 from www.thecochranelibrary.com.

Waters, J.A. and Ussery, W. (2007). Police stress: History, contributing factors, symptoms, and interventions. *Policing: An International Journal of Police Strategies & Management, 30,* 169–188.

Webster, J.H. (2013). Police officer perceptions of occupational stress: The state of the art. *Policing: An International Journal of Police Strategies & Management, 36,* 636–652.

***Wilson, S.A., Tinker, R.H., Becker, L.A., and Logan, C.R. (2001). Stress management with law enforcement personnel: A controlled outcome study of EMDR versus a traditional stress management program. *International Journal of Stress Management, 8,* 179–200.

★ Studies included in the Peñalba *et al.* (2009) systematic review.
★★ Studies included in the Patterson *et al.* (2014) systematic review.
★★★ Studies included in the Peñalba *et al.* and Patterson *et al.* systematic review.

Part 6

Cultural-level interventions to address stress in policing

17 Effective leadership in policing

Michael J. Kyle and Joseph A. Schafer

Leadership is a nebulous concept that is most often understood as a characteristic or quality of an individual or a collective of individuals that manages an organization. It is often framed solely in a positive light and as a false dichotomy—one is or is not a leader. However, bad leaders abound in every segment of society. Corporate, government, religious, public, and private organizations alike, both present and past, are replete with bad leaders (Kellerman, 2004), and policing is no exception. Research indicates that the stressors officers receive or perceive from their administration have a greater impact on job satisfaction than the dangers and hostility they face on the street (Crank, 1998; Kroes et al., 1974; Martelli et al., 1989; Shane, 2010; Stinchcomb, 2004). Bad leadership includes a range of behaviors, both acts of commission and omission, incompetence, apathy, egocentrism, and maliciousness, among others. Naturally bad leadership produces stress for subordinates. While the focus of this chapter is effective leadership as an intervention to reduce police officer stress, it is first necessary to define bad leadership in order to gain an understanding of what effective leadership looks like, as well as address bad leadership as a significant source of police officer stress. With the latter established, the chapter proceeds to define and describe effective leadership and how the effective police leader might play a role in the reduction of officer stress.

Ineffective and toxic leadership

What has thus far been referred to as bad leadership can be broken down into two categories: ineffective and toxic. While a toxic leader is by extension also an ineffective leader, the reverse does not necessarily hold. A police executive might be inept as an administrator and thus ineffective, but not toxic. Nevertheless, each is a form of bad leadership with the potential to cause stress for the leader's subordinates. The concept of toxic leadership received its name from Marcia L. Whicker (1996, p. 11), who described toxic leaders as "maladjusted, malcontent, often malevolent, even malicious. They succeed by tearing others down. They glory in turf protection, fighting and controlling rather than uplifting followers." The subject of toxic leadership has increasingly appeared in the literature concerning private sector business and industry, and more recently in regard to the armed forces. Although the topic has received very little attention in the policing context, the research regarding military leadership is closely related to the pervasive paramilitary structure and culture of policing (cf. Cowper, 2000). According to Colonel George E. Reed (2004), three key elements of the toxic leader syndrome are:

1   an apparent lack of concern for the well-being of subordinates
2   a personality or interpersonal technique that negatively affects organizational climate
3   a conviction by subordinates that the leader is motivated primarily by self-interest.

However, toxic leadership should not be confused with people who are simply difficult to get along with. According to Marco Tavanti (2011, p. 129):

> On one hand, a decisive, demanding, and sometimes verbally abusive leader may not be "toxic" to subordinates and the organizational unit. On the other hand, even charming and cheerful leaders may be toxic; it is the systemic discouraging effects that often indicate toxic dynamics. Toxic leaders might be highly competent and effective in their jobs, but they contribute to an unhealthy climate among their peers and subordinates with consequences far beyond the morale of a few victims.

One study involving a survey of military personnel measured toxic leadership with eight items, such as "My leader publicly belittles subordinates," and "My leader expresses anger at subordinates for unknown reasons" (Gallus *et al.*, 2013, p. 593). The results of this research indicate a "trickle-down" effect of abusive leadership that promotes incivility among unit members (Gallus *et al.*, 2013). Thus toxic leadership may breed more toxic leadership. This is especially concerning for policing, where promotion from within the ranks is traditional, creating fertile ground for the advancement of toxic leaders due to the standard selection process for advancement.

Promotion to supervisory and command ranks in policing, not unlike the military, is most often based on one's mastery of their current responsibilities, testing of their knowledge regarding bureaucratic rules and regulations, and past proficiency and conduct evaluations (Schafer, 2013b). While these criteria may indicate that an employee is exemplary in their current position, they provide little insight in terms of an individual's leadership capacity. A popular axiom that exemplifies this phenomenon is the "Peter Principle" (Peter and Hull, 1969), which asserts that one is promoted to increasingly more responsible positions to a point that the demands of a given assignment exceed one's skills and abilities. According to the Peter Principle, some incompetent leadership can be anticipated. Similar to the military, the combination of the trickle-down effect with the tradition of promotion from within and the selection criteria for advancement make toxic leadership problematic for policing. One may best grasp exactly what constitutes ineffective and/or toxic leadership in policing and its stress- producing effects through an examination of the remarks of officers on the subject.

One aspect of a study conducted at the FBI National Academy in Quantico, Virginia, consisted of an open-ended survey instrument administered to 304 participants, which asked them to describe traits and habits of ineffective leaders (Schafer, 2010). The FBI National Academy is a residential ten-week professional development course for mid-level police managers who are selected from law enforcement agencies across the US, as well as internationally. The sample was drawn from three sessions between October 2006 and April 2007 and represented a variety of agency types and sizes. Some of the responses illustrate the concepts set forth above. Four examples of participant descriptions of ineffective leader characteristics are as follows:

> quick temper, judgmental, lazy, inability to follow through, lack of focus, poor communication/interpersonal skills, moody, negative thinkers, lack of ability to delegate,

lack of confidence in others, micromanagers. These are all things that make people poor leaders. Most of these, they would like to overcome, but are either unable, or don't know how.

Dishonesty, lack of candor, lack of empathy, selfishness. They fail to inspire, fail to lead by example, and fail to work hard to solve long-term problems, and fail to empower subordinates to solve the short term problems. Failure to recognize good, hard work.

Among the traits I have witnessed in those described: selfishness, unwilling-ness to make tough decisions, failure to delegate responsibilities, making decisions while angry/upset, failure to trust others. Most of those I am describing failed to use resources around them, namely the experiences and minds of those around them.

Usually inconsistent and do not possess the characteristics of self-discipline needed to become an effective leader. Where many fail is by not taking a balanced approach to their role; either too authoritarian or fail to transition into the role and try to remain "one of the guys."

(see Schafer, 2013b; original emphasis)

The preceding remarks bring to light two additional elements of ineffective leadership that are of importance. The first is common to the traditional authoritative management style consistent with the paramilitary structure of policing. Perhaps Harry Levinson (1973) best articulates how this management approach is stress producing and counterproduc-tive in his book *The Great Jackass Fallacy*. According to Levinson (1973), the notion that employees lack motivation and require "carrot and stick" management to accom-plish even the most basic tasks, not to mention larger organizational goals, is misplaced. However, the management approach often utilized in policing relies heavily on the stick (threat of punishment), with no carrot in sight. Second, is what police scholar John Crank (1998) refers to as "bullshit." Although a euphemism for this term might be considered more appropriate, the abrasiveness clearly conveys the meaning of the concept and the sentiments of police personnel. "Bullshit" refers to the endless number of policies and procedures produced by agency administrators in an attempt to define and control any facet of conduct, discretion, or procedure deemed problematic. Crank's (1998) research indicates that police officers find "bullshit" more stressful than the physical dangers or hostilities they face on the street.

In sum, the ineffective leader fails to create a productive working environment in which subordinates are motivated, demonstrate initiative, find their work rewarding, and are professionally developed to their fullest potential. What is more, toxic leaders fail in all of the aforementioned ways, while also producing a milieu that can consist of incivility, mistrust, lack of respect, harassment, indignity, and hostility. In either case, bad leadership produces significant stress for subordinate personnel through uncertainty, lack of support, fear, and unnecessary hassles, as well as neglect of numerous other sources of stress presented in other chapters of this volume. With a clear picture of what constitutes ineffective and toxic leadership, the task of conceptualizing effective leader-ship is simplified.

Effective leadership

Effective leadership consists of several different dimensions including the traits and habits of the leader, the espousing of ethical principles, and the willingness to take responsibility for the welfare of his or her charges. Honesty and integrity are vital. Good listening, communication, and interpersonal skills are essential. Effective leaders must lead by example, empower their subordinates and appropriately delegate tasks, promote innovation and growth, and, perhaps most importantly, establish and maintain trust and fairness. Lastly, the effective leader must take appropriate action. As part of the last item, and crucial in regard to effective leadership as an intervention, effective leaders address stress and the consequences of stress in the professional and private lives of their personnel. Just as FBI National Academy participants identified the characteristics of ineffective leaders, the respondents to the survey who were asked to identify the traits and habits of effective leaders indicated these qualities and actions as most important (Schafer, 2013b).

Honesty and integrity

Honesty and integrity were considered two of the most important qualities of an effective leader by the majority of respondents. Recurrent themes in their remarks included that it is crucial an effective leader can be trusted; that they carry out their duties with honor and transparency. Honesty and integrity are not only important to garner the respect of subordinates (McCall and Lombardo, 1983), but research indicates that setting such an example is paramount in the shaping of subordinate officers' attitudes and, in turn, the honesty and integrity of the agency as a whole (Weisburd *et al.*, 2000).

Listening, communication, and interpersonal skills

Good listening and communication skills, both verbal and written, are another attribute the participants identified as essential for an effective leader. Listening in this context is more than just allowing subordinates to speak or "vent," but considering their perspectives and integrating that knowledge into the decision-making process when appropriate. Candid communication is of the upmost importance for effective leadership. Police leaders often issue new policy and procedure or changes to existing orders with little or no explanation as to the purpose (Enter, 2006). This lack of communication likely contributes to the "bullshit" perspective and associated stress (Crank, 1998). Therefore, clear and candid communication is critical to a leader's efficacy. In addition, an effective leader will consider their audience when choosing modes of communication. For instance, younger officers prefer communications via technology while older officers would likely prefer face-to-face communication (Schafer, 2013b).

Interpersonal skills refer to the ability to engage people and demonstrate care, compassion, and respect for others. Effective leaders are attuned to their subordinates' needs, problems, and concerns. The notion of servant leadership speaks directly to the necessity of interpersonal skills for leadership efficacy (Greenleaf, 2002). At the heart of the servant leadership perspective is that the leader places the needs of his or her subordinates above his or her own. The effective leader cares for his or her charges. This trait and habit is central to how and why effective leadership serves as an intervention for police officer stress, which shall be discussed in greater detail in a later section (see p. 301).

Leadership by example

Remarks of National Academy respondents such as "[leading] from the front; don't direct from the rear," and leadership by example means "[supervisors] are the first through the door," illustrate this concept. Leadership by example, simply put, refers to demonstrating the behavior and level of performance one wishes one's subordinates to emulate. Although the responsibilities of executives and command-level personnel in larger agencies usually do not allow for interaction in the field, it is important to demonstrate the work ethic and professionalism expected of line personnel. For the front-line supervisor, leadership by example means engaging in enforcement activities and working alongside subordinates (Engel, 2001).

Delegation and empowerment

An executive from a large municipal agency who was a FBI National Academy participant and survey respondent provided a remark that exemplifies the importance of delegation and empowerment in effective leadership:

> Effective leadership involves getting goals accomplished with the resources you have in an efficient manner and in a way that everyone involved has ownership and accountability for the issues and also share in the success of the mission. Effective leaders encourage participation and risk taking and are willing to let subordinates make mistakes.
>
> (see Schafer, 2013b)

The opposite of delegation and empowerment is micromanagement, which is a characteristic of an ineffective leader. The link to leadership efficacy is twofold. First, assigning tasks and providing autonomy to others serves the function of freeing the leader to attend to their leadership role. Second, delegation and empowerment have positive effects on subordinate personnel in terms of morale and commitment (Noblett *et al.*, 2009; Skogan and Hartnett, 1997).

Promote innovation and growth

Although policing has historically been resistant to change (Greene *et al.*, 1994), respondents indicated that effective leadership required attention to changes in the environment and innovation as necessary. Considering the increasing pace at which change is occurring, particularly in terms of technology, it comes as no surprise that innovation is considered essential for effective leadership. In addition, respondents recognized that effective leaders must attend to personal growth through continuing education and training to facilitate and enhance organizational growth and innovation. For example, one respondent remarked "[effective leaders] look at ways for self-improvement, continuing education/training [and] keeping up with advances in the field."

Take appropriate action

It may seem odd to indicate a leader must take action, but studies of police personnel suggest that ineffective leaders either take the wrong actions or fail to act when decisions are needed (Schafer, 2010). Taking action was ranked as highly important for effective leadership by FBI National Academy participants/respondents. A captain of a medium sized municipal agency remarked:

The single most important trait that makes an effective leader is the ability and will-ingness to accept responsibility and to act on it, while not being intimidated into inaction through fear. Too many weak leaders avoid responsibility and avoid issues that they know they should address, but are too timid to do so.

(see Schafer, 2013b)

There is more to this statement than initially meets the eye. Law enforcement leaders are in a precarious position between serving at the pleasure of a political body and attempt-ing to meet the needs and expectations of both police personnel and the public. Effective leadership requires that a leader take action when it is clearly called for, and the leader must do so with integrity. The effective leader does what is right regardless of the backlash he or she might receive. In some situations it might even mean he or she faces dismissal. Nonetheless, the effective leader takes appropriate action.

Establish and maintain trust and fairness

The establishment and maintenance of trust and fairness overlaps most of the other traits and habits mentioned thus far, and are arguably the most important elements of effective leadership. Trust is ranked as being absolutely crucial for the efficacy of a leader and trust was identified earlier as the outcome of honesty and integrity. However, the effective leader must not only be trustworthy, but trust his or her subordinates as well. A lack of trust of one's subordinates leads to micromanagement and, arguably, is a mark of toxic leadership. A subordinate's trust in, respect for, and willingness to follow a given leader is likely made or broken by their perception of whether the leader treats all of his or her charges fairly.

Organizational justice

A theoretical perspective that is particularly instructive in this discussion is that of organi-zational justice, which incorporates several previously mentioned elements of effective leadership. This construct considers how individuals view issues of fairness, trust, com-munication, and integrity within their organizational settings (Greenberg and Colquitt, 2005). It is predicated on the notion that an individual's perception of fairness in their work environment is related to job satisfaction, organizational commitment, evaluation of authority, organizational citizenship behavior, and job performance (Colquitt *et al.*, 2001). In other words, how employees are treated within the workplace has an influence on a variety of organizational and personnel outputs and outcomes.

The organizational justice perspective was initially unidimensional and concerned only with distributive justice, which refers to equity in the distribution of resources, rewards, or other outcomes (Colquitt, 2001). The consistency of salaries among similarly quali-fied and positioned individuals within an agency is one example. Later, the dimensions of procedural, interpersonal, and informational justice were added. These additional dimen-sions represent a shift from an outcome focus to a process focus. This notion of procedural justice, first conceived of by John W. Thibaut and Laurens Walker (1975) as an issue of "process control," was applied to the organizational context by Gerald S. Leventhal (1980). Procedural justice in the organizational context refers to fairness in internal processes such as promotional selection, disciplinary actions, and policy and procedure making. It can be viewed as an individual's ability to have a voice in the decision-making process (Colquitt 2001; Colquitt *et al.* 2001).

The last two dimensions of the organizational justice construct: interpersonal and informational justice were introduced by Robert J. Bies and Joseph S. Moag in 1986. These two dimensions, collectively referred to as interactional justice, are concerned with the treatment individuals receive from their superiors, candid communication, and the dissemination of adequate information to evaluate decisions made by leaders (Colquitt *et al.*, 2001). Interpersonal justice also includes subordinate individuals' perceptions regarding their supervisor's interest in their well-being and professional development.

While research is scant in terms of application of the organizational justice theoretical framework to law enforcement agencies, the body of literature is growing. What has been published in other fields indicates that organizational justice is strongly linked with employee perceptions of many of the aforementioned leadership traits and habits (see Cohen-Charash and Spector, 2001), and stress (see Judge and Colquitt, 2004). In terms of the literature that specifically addresses organizational justice in the policing context, only a handful of studies have been published in refereed journals. These studies have examined organizational justice within police agencies with regard to officer well-being (Srivastava, 2009), officer willingness to assist citizens, quality of services rendered, internal and external transparency, and external procedural justice (Beckley, 2014; Myhill and Bradford, 2013; Schafer, 2013a), officer's job satisfaction, level of organizational commitment and stress (Crow *et al.*, 2012; Noblett *et al.*, 2009), officer misconduct (Wolfe and Piquero, 2011), and officer compliance with policy and procedure (Haas *et al.*, 2015). In each of these studies, perceptions of organizational justice were found to be a significant predictor of the measured outcome. Thus, the importance of fairness for effective leadership cannot be understated.

Leadership responsibilities/stress management interventions

While all of the traits and habits of effective leadership contribute to stress reduction for subordinates, effective leaders also address stress and the consequences of stress in the professional and private lives of their personnel. As demonstrated, ineffective and/or toxic leadership generates much stress for officers. However, as detailed throughout the other chapters of this volume, there are many sources of stress other than bad leadership, some generated by the organization and some generated externally. In either case effective leadership requires action when interventions to reduce, eliminate, or otherwise address sources of stress are possible. The effective leader begins by creating a healthy organizational environment.

According to Richard M. Ayres and George S. Flanagan (1990), police leaders do not typically address the root causes of the majority of stress faced by officers, namely organizational factors. Instead, they address the symptoms under a medical model, which views individual officers as vulnerable to stress and in need of training to prevent negative impacts, or treatment should they suffer negative effects. Rather than the medical model's individual approach to addressing police officer stress, an organizational health model, Ayres and Flanagan (1990) assert, is more productive. In this model "emphasis is shifted from the person-centered stress management and stress intervention programs of the psychologists to the organization-centered strategies of management" (Ayres and Flanagan, 1990, p. 6). The underlying principles are twofold. First, an "unhealthy workplace" is the cause of most officer stress and the latter is but a symptom; and second, the preferable stress management approach is to identify stressors in the work environment and eliminate them wherever and whenever possible to create a healthy organizational environment (Ayres and Flanagan, 1990).

There are several organizational sources of stressors that effective leaders can address under this model; however, this is not to say that individual treatment is not warranted when it is needed. Monitoring for stress-related issues and addressing officer exposure to critical incidents will be addressed later, but effective leaders can prevent many stress-related issues by developing and maintaining a healthy work environment. Some specific areas that can be addressed include authoritarian management, administration support, supervision, communications and officer input, work schedules, redundant/excessive paperwork, internal investigations and discipline, performance evaluations, wages and resources, promotion systems, and race and gender issues (Ayres and Flanagan, 1990; Stinchcomb, 2004).

Authoritarian management and administration support

Authoritarian management practices are pervasive in policing and are largely based on the previously mentioned "jackass fallacy" and a punishment orientation. Under this management approach officers are thought to be unmotivated and seeking ways to circumvent rules and regulations, and policies and procedures. The threat of punishment is thought to be necessary to obtain compliance and performance. Moreover, the authoritarian management style assumes that an officer is guilty until proven innocent in any type of possible rule, regulation, policy, or procedure violation (Violanti, 1988). Administration support is an overlapping issue. A lack of administration support can be the source of significant stress for an officer. This occurs when administrators "arm chair quarterback" (analyze over a period of time) split-second decisions made by officers under stressful conditions, then pick apart their actions, but offer no constructive criticism. Or, a much worse scenario, when an officer is involved in a high-profile incident such as an officer-involved shooting and they lack their administration's support, perhaps to avoid a public relations issue. A lack of administrative support can cause stress not only for the officers who are subjected to it, but across the agency. The effective leader can reduce or eliminate these sources of stress by implementing a more participatory style of management and ensuring administration support except when improper (i.e. clear criminal or serious conduct violation).

Supervision

Inept or apathetic supervisors are a significant stress-producing problem that effective leaders must address. Eisenberg (1975) offers what perhaps remains the best description of this issue:

> Styles of supervision vary tremendously, some providing a haven for the nurturance of psychological stress, while others tend to prohibit its manifestation or at least provide a vehicle available to the police officer for coping with stress. The supervisor who always "goes by the book," is never available on a complicated or delicate street situation, is overly demanding, tends not to back up a subordinate when conditions justify such support, or who fails to attend to subordinates' personal needs represents a supervisor who can substantially contribute to the psychological stress of his subordinates. The importance of the supervisor in the life of the patrol officer cannot be underestimated.

As mentioned earlier, aptitude for one's current position does not equate to leadership ability in future positions or ranks. The supervisor described above may have been an excellent patrol officer, but did not possess leadership traits, habits, or skills. The effective leader must ensure that candidates for promotion are properly vetted, carefully selected, and receive quality training. Excellent leadership at the first-line supervisory level not only significantly reduces stress, but also enhances monitoring of personnel and the possibility of early detection of officers experiencing stress-related problems.

Communications and officer input

As indicated earlier, organizational justice requires two-way communication throughout the ranks. On the one hand employee perceptions of procedural justice are heavily influenced by whether or not one has a "voice" in the organizational decision-making process. Perceptions of informational justice, on the other hand, are based on individuals receiving candid communication and sufficient information from their superiors to evaluate decisions made by leaders. Effective leaders facilitate two-way communication. For example, a police chief who is considering the implementation of body-worn cameras at his or her agency clearly communicates the reasoning for adopting the devices, conducts a field trial, elicits feedback from officers regarding functioning of the equipment, logistics, and any other problems or concerns they might have, and then elicits input from officers regarding the development of relevant policy and procedure. Such two-way communication following the organizational justice framework is likely to produce officer buy-in and compliance with innovations.

Work schedules and redundant/excessive paperwork

Shift work is a significant source of stress for officers. Rotating shifts, compressed work weeks, overtime, call outs, and court appearances increase that stress, often leading to sleep issues, fatigue, decreased quality of life and family issues, and myriad health issues, and these negative impacts can create more stress (Vila, 2006). Although law enforcement executives are limited by budget constraints and staffing needs, effective leaders address scheduling to minimize these sources of stress such as considering research regarding ideal shift length (see Amendola *et al.*, 2011). Effective leaders craft creative scheduling solutions to accommodate such additional duty commitments as court appearances, especially when these occur in the midst of a work week for night shift officers.

A related issue, as it commonly leads to overtime, is excessive paperwork. The nature of police work requires careful documentation; however, as new and more complex laws are passed, case law evolves, new innovations are adopted and new policies and procedures emerge to address liability concerns, documentation requirements increase. It is not uncommon to find several redundant forms or data collection systems in any given police agency. For instance, many agencies require officers to complete daily activity logs and report all activity to dispatch via radio or mobile data terminal. The effective leader seeks to both reduce officer stress and increase efficiency by eliminating this kind of redundancy in paperwork.

Internal investigations and discipline, performance evaluations, wages and resources, and promotion systems

These elements of an agency are considered alongside one another because in regard to each of them, an employee is concerned with fairness. Under the organizational justice theoretical framework the disciplinary process, performance evaluations, wages and resources, and promotion systems all have both procedural and distributive justice considerations. In terms of procedural justice, the effective leader establishes and maintains objective, fair, and consistent procedure for internal investigations and discipline, performance evaluations, selection for promotion, and distribution of resources such as patrol vehicle assignment. In terms of distributive justice the effective leader must ensure that discipline, evaluation and promotion criteria, wages/raises, and resource distributions are equitable.

Race and gender

In order to achieve organizational health, a leader must address race and gender issues. Research has produced evidence that racial minority and female officers suffer higher rates of stress than their white male counterparts, due most often to perceived, if not actual, discriminatory organizational dynamics (Violanti and Aron, 1995). The effective leader demands equitable treatment of all officers and establishes a zero-tolerance policy for any type of discriminatory practice or behavior. Effective leaders mold the agency's culture to conform to these principles.

Promoting positive coping methods

In addition to all of the aforementioned ways in which the effective police leader creates a healthy workplace, they must also promote positive, healthy coping methods. According to Katherine W. Ellison (2004), nutrition, physical fitness, (regular exercise), and rest and relaxation are all important positive coping methods. The effective police leader encourages and promotes these types of positive coping methods within their agency. Police leaders can do this by providing training regarding these and other positive coping methods for their personnel, providing workout equipment or fitness center memberships, and ensuring personnel receive sufficient time off and vacations.

Monitoring personnel

While creating a healthy work environment and promoting positive methods for coping are extremely important to reduce stress and by extension the negative cumulative effects of stress stemming from organizational factors, the effective leader must also monitor personnel for stress-related issues and address officer exposure to critical incidents to prevent serious negative impacts. The consequences of prolonged stress and/or stress from exposure to critical incidents are well documented elsewhere in this volume and can include alcohol and drug abuse, serious health issues, burnout, and even suicide. Therefore, the importance of police leaders recognizing signs of stress and coping difficulties in their subordinates cannot be understated.

First, the effective leader equips his or her command staff and supervisors to be able to identify personnel having stress-related difficulties. One such training program was based on the U.S. Army's methods of identifying stress in military personnel. These techniques were taught to Cleveland Police Department supervisors to enable them to monitor their charges and identify warning signs of stress-related problems (Chapin *et al.*, 2008). Second, the effective leader endeavors to change the traditional police culture that attaches stigma to seeking help for stress- related issues, a phenomenon supported by empirical research (Karaffa and Koch, 2015; Tucker, 2015). If effective leadership is to successfully intervene in police officer stress, the stigma attached to seeking mental health services must be dealt with.

Research results support a potential solution to the stigma problem. Studies indicate that officers who believe that their agency supports officer use of mental health services, and they themselves feel supported by their agency, are more likely to use such services (Carlan and Nored, 2008; Tucker, 2015). However, due to the pervasiveness of the stigma attached to seeking help from mental health services, it has been suggested that agencies make periodic counseling mandatory for all officers, "a procedural tactic that that camouflages counseling need while concurrently treating the source of officer stress" (Carlan and Nored, 2008, p. 8). Another option the effective police leader should consider is an employee assistance program, or EAP, which also might be an effective way to overcome the stigma problem.

EAPs are intervention programs designed to provide employees with assistance resolving personal problems such as marital and/or family issues, financial problems, drug and/or alcohol abuse, etc. Besides connecting employees with appropriate counseling services, EAPs may also offer other services like medical advice hotlines and legal assistance. EAPs are usually funded completely by the agency and made available to the officer's spouse/partner and family as well. Confidentiality is generally assured to those who avail themselves of EAP services, which may allow these types of programs to overcome the aforementioned stigma barrier.

Critical incidents

Due to the nature of policing, even if stress-generating organizational factors are addressed, healthy coping methods are encouraged, and chronic stress is identified and treated, some officers will be exposed to critical incidents. According to Raymond B. Flannery *et al.* (2000, p.119):

> Critical incidents are sudden, unexpected, often life-threatening time-limited events that may overwhelm an individual's capacity to respond adaptively. Frequently, extreme critical incident stressors may result in personal crises, traumatic stress, and even Posttraumatic Stress Disorder (PTSD).

Officers who are exposed to critical incidents, such as an officer involved shooting, may "suffer psychological/emotional trauma associated with a critical incident (CI), and this response is referred to as critical incident stress (CIS). If unrecognized or untreated, CIS can lead to long-term disability, termed post-traumatic stress disorder (PTSD)" (Oster and Doyle, 2000, p. 339). The standard mental health protocol for critical incident exposure is critical incident stress management (CISM). According to Everly *et al.* (2000, p. 23):

> Critical incident stress management (CISM) comprises a range of crisis intervention services that usually include precrisis training, individual crisis counseling, group debriefing, and postincident referral for primary and secondary victims. CISM is utilized to address the aftermath of violent acts, and has evolved from earlier crisis intervention and group psychological debriefing procedures.

Due to the seriousness of the potential effects, the effective police leader provides immediate treatment for officers exposed to critical incidents.

Conclusion

This chapter has related how an ineffective leader fails to create a productive working environment in which subordinates are motivated, demonstrate initiative, find their work rewarding, and are professionally developed to their fullest potential. Toxic leaders fail in may of these ways, plus they produce a milieu of incivility, lack of respect, harm, and indignity for employees. The chapter demonstrated that both toxic leadership and ineffective leadership produce significant stress for subordinate personnel. This stress is related to uncertainty, lack of support, fear, and unnecessary hassles as well as neglect of numerous other sources of stress presented in other chapters of this volume.

Effective leadership, on the other hand, was shown to consist of traits and habits, ethical principles, and taking responsibility for the welfare of employees. Honesty and integrity, good listening, communication, and interpersonal skills were identified as essential traits, and leadership by example, empowerment of subordinates and delegation of tasks, promotion of innovation and growth, the development and maintenance of trust and fairness, and the willingness to take action were identified as the essential habits of the effective leader. There are, however, other challenges to maintaining effective leadership. The effective leader must pay attention to the evolution of policing and rapid changes that result in the emergence of new stressors in order to care for his or her charges.

While there are pragmatic reasons that a police leader would want to employ the principles of effective leadership presented here, such as to increase employee job satisfaction and decrease turn over, ultimately effective leadership leads to the provision of the highest quality police services to citizens possible. In addition, police officers and their families make great sacrifices in service of their communities and the police leader takes on responsibility for these men and women. They deserve effective leadership.

References

Amendola, K.L., Weisburd, D., Hamilton, E., Jones, G., Slipka, M., Heitmann, A., and Tarkghen, E. (2011). *The impact of shift length in policing on performance, health, quality of life, sleep, fatigue, and extra-duty employment.* Washington, DC: Police Foundation.

Ayres, R.M. and Flanagan, G.S. (1990). *Preventing law enforcement stress: The organization's role.* Washington, DC: Bureau of Justice Assistance.

Beckley, A. (2014). Organisational justice: Is the police service ready for it? *Journal of Policing, Intelligence and Counter Terrorism, 9*(2), 176–190.

Bies, R.J. and Moag, J.S. (1986). Interactional justice: Communication criteria of fairness. *Research on negotiation in organizations, 1*(1), 43–55.

Carlan, P.E. and Nored, L.S. (2008). An examination of officer stress: Should police departments implement mandatory counseling? *Journal of Police and Criminal Psychology, 23*(1), 8–15.

Chapin, M., Brannen, S.J., Singer, M.I., and Walker, M. (2008). Training police leadership to recognize and address operational stress. *Police Quarterly, 11*(3), 338–352.

Cohen-Charash, Y. and Spector, P.E. (2001). The role of justice in organizations: A meta-analysis. *Organizational behavior and human decision processes, 86*(2), 278–321.

Colquitt, J.A. (2001). On the dimensionality of organizational justice: A construct validation of a measure. *Journal of Applied Psychology, 86*(3), 386–400.

Colquitt, J.A., Conlon, D.E., Wesson, M.J., Porter, C., and Ng, K.Y. (2001). Justice at the millennium: A meta-analytic review of 25 years of organizational justice research. *Journal of Applied Psychology, 86*(3), 425–445.

Cowper, T.J. (2000). The myth of the "military model" of leadership in law enforcement. *Police Quarterly, 3*, 228–246.

Crank, J.P. (1998). *Understanding Police Culture*. Cincinnati, OH: Anderson Publishing Co.

Crow, M.S., Lee, C.B., and Joo, J.J. (2012). Organisational justice and organizational commitment among South Korean police officers: An investigation of job satisfaction as a mediator. *Policing: An International Journal of Police Strategies & Management, 35*(2), 402–423.

Eisenberg, T. (1975). Job stress and the police officer: Identifying stress reduction techniques. In Kroes, W.H. and Hurrell, J.J. (eds.). *Job stress and the police officer: Identifying stress reduction techniques*, (pp. 26–34). Washington, DC: US Government Printing Office.

Ellison, K.W. (2004). *Stress and the police officer*. Springfield, IL: Charles C. Thomas Publisher.

Engel, R.S. (2001). Supervisory styles of patrol sergeants and lieutenants. *Journal of Criminal Justice, 29*(4), 341–355.

Enter, J.E. (2006). *Challenging the law enforcement organization: Proactive leadership strategies*. Dacula, GA: Narrow Road Press.

Everly Jr., G.S., Flannery Jr., R.B., and Mitchell, J.T. (2000). Critical incident stress management (CISM): A review of the literature. *Aggression and Violent Behavior, 5*(1), 23–40.

Everly Jr., G.S., Flannery Jr., R.B., and Eyler, V.A. (2002). Critical incident stress management (CISM): A statistical review of the literature. *Psychiatric Quarterly, 73*(3), 171–182.

Flannery, R.B. and Everly, G.S. (2000). Crisis intervention: A review. *International Journal of Emergency Mental Health, 2*(2), 119–126.

Gallus, J.A., Walsh, B.M., van Driel, M., Gouge, M.C., and Antolic, E. (2013). Intolerable cruelty: A multilevel examination of the impact of toxic leadership on US military units and service members. *Military Psychology, 25*(6), 588–601.

Greenberg, J. and Colquitt, J.A. (eds.). (2005). *Handbook of organizational justice*. New York: Erlbaum Associates, Inc.

Greene, J.R., Bergman, W.T., and McLaughlin, E.J. (1994). Implementing community policing: Cultural and structural change in police organizations. In D.P. Rosenbaum (ed.), *The challenge of community policing: Testing the promises*, (pp. 92–109). Thousand Oaks, CA: Sage.

Greenleaf, R.K. (2002). *Servant leadership: A journey into the nature of legitimate power and greatness, 25th anniversary edition*. New York: Paulist Press.

Haas, N.E., Van Craen, M., Skogan, W.G., and Fleitas, D.M. (2015). Explaining officer compliance: The importance of procedural justice and trust inside a police organization. *Criminology and Criminal Justice, 15*(4) 442–463.

Judge, T.A. and Colquitt, J.A. (2004). Organizational justice and stress: The mediating role of work–family conflict. *Journal of Applied Psychology, 89*(3), 395.

Karaffa, K.M. and Koch, J.M. (2015). Stigma, pluralistic ignorance, and attitudes toward seeking mental health services among police officers. *Criminal Justice and Behavior*, November 9.

Kellerman, B. (2004). Leadership: Warts and all. *Harvard Business Review, 82*(1), 40–45.

Kroes, W.H., Margolis, B.L., and Hurrell, J.J. Jr. (1974). Job stress in policemen. *Journal of Police Science and Administration, 2*(2), 145–155.

Leventhal, G.S. (1980). What should be done with equity theory? In K. Gergen (ed.), *Social exchange: Advances in theory and research*, (pp. 27–55). New York: Springer.

Levinson, H. (1973). *The great jackass fallacy*. Boston, Division of Research, Graduate School of Business Administration, Harvard University.

McCall, M.W. and Lombardo, M.M. (1983). *Off the track: Why and how successful executives get derailed*. Greensboro, NC: Center for Creative Leadership.

Martelli, T.A., Waters, L.K., and Martelli, J. (1989). The police stress survey: Reliability and relation to job satisfaction and organizational commitment. *Psychological Reports, 64*(1), 267–273.

Myhill, A. and Bradford, B. (2013). Overcoming cop culture? Organisational justice and police officers' attitudes toward the public. *Policing: An International Journal of Police Strategies & Management, 36*(2), 338–356.

Noblet, A., Rodwell, J. and Allisey, A. (2009). Job stress in the law enforcement sector: Comparing the linear, non-linear and interaction effects of working conditions. *Stress and health, 25*(1), 111–120.

Oster, N. S. and Doyle, C. J. (2000). Critical incident stress and challenges for the emergency workplace. *Emergency medicine clinics of North America, 18*(2), 339–353.

Peter, L.J. and Hull, R. (1969). *The Peter principle*. New York: William Morrow.

Reed, G.E. (2004). Toxic leadership. *Military Review, 84*(4), 67–71.

Reiser, M. (1974) Some organizational stresses on policemen. *Journal of Police Science and Administration, 2*(2), 156–159.

Schafer, J.A. (2010). The ineffective police leader: Acts of commission and omission. *Journal of Criminal Justice, 38*(4), 737–746.

Schafer, J.A. (2013a). The role of trust and transparency in the pursuit of procedural and organizational justice. *Journal of Policing, Intelligence and Counter Terrorism, 8*(2), 131–143.

Schafer, J.A. (2013b). *Effective leadership in policing: Successful traits and habits*. Durham, NC: Carolina Academic Press.

Shane, J.M. (2010). Organizational stressors and police performance. *Journal of Criminal Justice, 38*(4), 807–818.

Skogan, W.G. and Hartnett, S.M. (1997). *Community policing, Chicago style*. New York: Oxford University Press.

Srivastava, S. (2009). Explorations in police organisation: An Indian context. *International Journal of Police Science & Management, 11*(3), 255–273.

Stinchcomb, J.B. (2004). Searching for stress in all the wrong places: Combating chronic organizational stressors in policing. *Police Practice and Research, 5*(3), 259–277.

Tavanti, M. (2011). Managing toxic leaders: Dysfunctional patterns in organizational leadership and how to deal with them. *Human Resource Management, 2011*, 127–136.

Thibaut, J.W. and Walker, L. (1975). *Procedural justice: A psychological analysis*. Hillside, NJ: L. Erlbaum Associates.

Tucker, J.M. (2015). Police officer willingness to use stress intervention services: The role of perceived organizational support (POS), confidentiality and stigma. *International Journal of Emergency Mental Health and Human Resilience, 17*(1), 304–314.

Vila, B. (2006). Impact of long work hours on police officers and the communities they serve. *American journal of industrial medicine, 49*(11), 972–980.

Violanti, J.M. (1988). Operationalizing police stress management: A model. *Police Psychology: Operational Assistance*. Washington, DC: Department of Justice, pp. 423–435.

Violanti, J.M. and Aron, F. (1995). Police stressors: Variations in perception among police personnel. *Journal of Criminal Justice, 23*(3), 287–294.

Weisburd, D., Greenspan, R., Hamilton, E.E., Williams, H., and Bryant, K.A. (2000). *Police attitudes toward the abuse of authority: Findings from a national study*. Washington, DC: National Institute of Justice.

Whicker, M.L. (1996). *Toxic leaders: When organizations go bad*. New York: Doubleday.

Wolfe, S.E. and Piquero, A.R. (2011). Organizational justice and police misconduct. *Criminal Justice and Behavior, 38*(4), 332–353.

18 The potential benefits of police culture and support and work outcomes among police officers

Amanda Biggs and Paula Brough

Introduction

Police culture has long been of interest to researchers, in recognition of its pervasive influence on policing effectiveness. Police culture has been defined as "a set of values, attitudes, and norms that are widely shared among officers, who find in the culture a way to cope with the strains of their working environment" (Paoline *et al.*, 2000, p. 575). Recurring characteristics of police culture have been observed, including a crime-fighter orientation, exaggerated sense of mission, masculine ethos, suspicion, cynicism, isolation, and solidarity. These aspects of culture have often been maligned, due to their potential to undermine police reforms and perpetuate misconduct. The overwhelming focus on the "dark-side" of police culture has been criticised, however, for failing to adequately recognise adaptive outcomes, such as effective teamwork and knowledge sharing. Nonetheless, an ongoing challenge for police services is to promote the adaptive functions of police culture, while attenuating the adverse aspects of culture. Recent police-specific research has suggested that many of the adverse outcomes of culture might be mitigated by enhancing psychosocial safety and support within police organisations. This chapter will provide an overview of research on police culture and its potential disadvantages and advantages. Furthermore, an overview of research on psychosocial safety climate and supportive work cultures, conducted within policing organisations, will be presented.

Organisational and occupational culture

Police culture is conceptualised as an occupational *and* organisational phenomenon, reflecting the shared values and practices of front-line police officers that transcend organisational boundaries (i.e. occupational culture) as well as those shared by employees embedded within a single organisation (i.e. organisational culture; Manning, 2007; Van Maanen and Barley, 1984). Both perspectives are relevant, as police culture is strongly influenced by the stressors and challenges unique to police officers in addition to those arising from the organisational contexts in which they work (Chataway, 2014; Paoline, 2003).

Organisational culture refers to values and beliefs shared by organisational members, and their influence on daily practices (Bajdo and Dickson, 2001; Hofstede *et al.*, 1990). The shared basic assumptions of a group originate from organisational leaders and emerge as organisational members interact with one another and adapt to external demands; these values and practices are subsequently transmitted to new employees through formal training and informal socialisation processes as the correct way to appraise the stressors and challenges of working in the organisation (Schein, 2010). Most conceptualisations of organisational culture emphasise its multifaceted nature; the presence of tangible and intangible components; its socially constructed and shared nature; and its resistance to change (Chataway, 2014).

Although organisational culture plays a pivotal role in shaping the values and practices of police officers, police culture cannot purely be conceptualised as an organisational phenomenon. Police possess their own cultural identity, shaped by the stressors and challenges they experience, which transcends the organisational and socio-political context in which they work (Christensen and Crank, 2001). *Occupational culture* is a variant of organisational culture (Glomseth et al., 2007), and refers to the taken-for-granted knowledge, values, and practices associated with a particular occupational role (Farkas and Manning, 1997). Occupational culture differs from organisational culture, as it is shared by members of a single occupational group; is not limited by organisational boundaries; and originates from, and is maintained by, front-line employees, rather than organisational leaders (Brough et al., 2016; Chataway, 2014; Paoline, 2003; Van Maanen and Barley, 1984).

Police culture: overarching themes and subcultural variations

Policing is a high-stress occupation, with officers exposed to organisational stressors, external pressures, and routine and traumatic stressors arising from the unique operational requirements of the job itself (i.e. occupational stressors), the organisational environment (i.e. organisational stressors), and the broader socio-political context (Brough and Biggs, 2010; Brough et al., 2016). Police culture is believed to emerge from officers' common experiences of these stressors, which informs the way in which they approach their work (Campeau, 2015; Cosgrove, 2015). Researchers have generally studied police culture from two perspectives: (1) examining overarching cultural themes encompassing all police officers and (2) examining subcultural variations within the broader police culture (Campeau, 2015; Paoline, 2004).

Early research striving to capture overarching cultural themes emphasised the loyalty and camaraderie amongst officers in response to the dangers and isolation inherent within the policing role (Campeau, 2015). The concept of police culture has since been expanded to "encompass a complex system of values and attitudes that define the normative social world of police" (Campeau, 2015, p. 671). Although numerous characteristics of police culture have been identified, some recurring themes have emerged:

- A clear *sense of mission*, reflecting the "feeling that policing is not just a job but a way of life with a worthwhile purpose" and emphasising officers' pride in their unique role in "safeguarding social order" (Cosgrove, 2015; Loftus, 2010; Reiner, 2000, p. 89).
- A *crime-fighter, action orientation*, in which crime-oriented tasks, containing elements of action and excitement, are preferred over administrative and community-oriented tasks (Reiner, 2000; Terrill et al., 2003). Loftus (2010, p. 5) noted that despite officers actually spending very little time on tasks "which had a distinctly criminal element," crime-fighting was still regarded as the core police mission.
- A *masculine ethos*, in which greater value is placed on stereotypically masculine coping strategies and approaches to policing (Cosgrove, 2015; Loftus, 2010; Reiner, 2000). Loftus (2010, p. 7), for example, observed that "powerful undercurrents of masculinity encourage an aura of toughness" and celebrate dominating and aggressive behaviours as a means for maintaining control and respect.

- *Cynical and pessimistic* attitudes formed in response to the challenges of day-to-day policing, directed at members of the public; the criminal justice system's perceived leniency on crime; and organisational leaders, policies, and procedures that inhibit efficient police work (Bradford and Quinton, 2014; Loftus, 2010). These attitudes develop when officers' sense of mission (e.g. upholding social order) is challenged by their exposure to the darker side of humanity and they witness the degradation of the social morals they strive to uphold (Reiner, 2000).
- A heightened and pervasive sense of *suspicion,* developed as "police need to develop fine-grained cognitive maps of the social world, so they can readily predict and handle the behaviour of a wide range of others" (Reiner, 2000, p. 91).
- *Isolation* from members of the public and senior management, resulting in strong camaraderie and defensive *solidarity* amongst fellow officers (Cosgrove, 2015; Loftus, 2010; Reiner, 2000; Terrill *et al.*, 2003) An "us-versus-society" mentality arises dually from characteristics of police work that alienate police from society and reinforce bonds amongst fellow officers, such as the threat of danger; fear or hostility from the public; suspicion and cynicism; possession of coercive authority; and performance of shift work (Brough *et al.*, 2016; Chataway, 2014; Reiner, 2000). An "us-versus-senior management" mentality arises in response to perceived scrutiny or punitive work environments, resulting in solidarity amongst colleagues who conceal one another's misdemeanours to avoid punishment (Paoline *et al.*, 2000; Reiner, 2000).
- *Prejudicial and informal work attitudes* (e.g. joking culture; Brough *et al.*, 2016; Cosgrove, 2015; Reiner, 2000).

Despite the pervasiveness of these core features, police culture is seldom viewed as monolithic or unchangeable (Reiner, 2000; Terrill *et al.*, 2003). Subcultural variations may occur as a function of the national, local, and organisational context; varying police ranks and functions within a department; and the characteristics and styles of individual police officers (Chataway, 2014; Reiner, 2000; Worden, 1995). This is evidenced by research demonstrating intergroup conflict between officers performing different roles or shifts within a department (e.g. Loftus, 2010) and variations in officers' attitudes towards elements of police culture (e.g. Paoline *et al.*, 2000). Researchers have also developed typologies, emphasising differences in core attitudes between groups of police officers. Worden (1995), for example, identified five police officer types, including *Professionals, Tough-cops, Clean-beat crime-fighters, Problem-solvers,* and *Avoiders.* Terrill *et al.* (2003) identified three clusters of police officers that upheld traditional cultural values, two clusters that moderately upheld traditional values, and two clusters that rejected traditional values. Their research also demonstrated that the clusters of police officers whose attitudes aligned more closely with traditional cultural values were more likely to use coercive force. Finally, Paoline (2004) identified seven distinguishable groups of officers they labelled *Lay lows, Old-pros, Traditionalists, Organizational street cops, Dirty Harry enforcers, Peacekeepers,* and *Law enforcers.* The existence of subcultural variations challenges the notion of a monolithic culture, showing that officers do not uniformly embody the values of the dominant culture, react to stressors or challenges in culturally prescribed ways, are consistently loyal to fellow officers, or are passively socialised within the culture (Cosgrove, 2015; Paoline, 2004; Terrill *et al.*, 2003).

Limitations of each of these approaches have been noted. Attempts to delineate the unique dimensions of police culture typically lack a strong theoretical basis, failing to acknowledge and explain the socially embedded nature of the construct (Campeau, 2015). It has also been observed that police culture dimensions identified in classic studies are perpetuated in the literature, serving as a "collective imprint" in observations of police culture, "diverting attention from new directions and emerging trends" (Campeau, 2015, p. 671). Similarly, typographies often strive to align officers with a predefined, stereotyped classification derived from a small number of police attitudes, revealing little about actual between-group behavioural differences (Bradford and Quinton, 2014; Campeau, 2015; Paoline, 2004; Terrill et al., 2003). Furthermore, key conceptualisations consider culture to be inherently static, failing to account for the complexity and fluidity of officers' attitudes and behaviours (Bradford and Quinton, 2014; Campeau, 2015; Cosgrove, 2015). One explanation is that police literature has predominantly drawn on conceptualisations of culture as an internalised set of values that motivate attitudes and behaviour, rather than a contemporary understanding of culture as a resourceful tool on which people draw to make sense of their day-to-day work situations (Campeau, 2015). Two additional limitations – that conceptualisations of police culture have generally relied on classic, potentially outdated, ethnographies and the overwhelming focus on negative police culture attributes – will be discussed in greater depth.

Durability of police culture in light of police reform

Characteristics of police culture are relatively enduring and resistant to change, given their evolution from a longstanding history of emotionally intense shared experiences and high degrees of group cohesion (Brough et al., 2016). However, there has been some speculation that cultural attitudes are likely to have shifted or weakened over time, given the significant amount of reform experienced by police services (Paoline *et al.*, 2000). These reforms include transitions to community-based policing models; recruitment strategies aiming to increase diversity; externally driven performance expectations and austerity measures; and enhanced scrutiny from the government, media, and public regarding police misconduct (Brough *et al.*, 2016; Loftus, 2010; Paoline *et al.*, 2000). Many of the key police culture studies precede these reforms and several studies have been conducted to determine whether these reforms have weakened previously documented cultural themes or resulted in the emergence of new themes (Campeau, 2015; Chataway, 2014; Loftus, 2010; Paoline, 2004).

Loftus (2010) demonstrated the enduring nature of traditional cultural themes in an ethnographic study of an English police force. The centrality of an exaggerated sense of mission and action-orientation was identified, with fighting crime still being viewed as the core police mission. A masculine ethos valuing action and dominating behaviour was another prevailing theme, with participants idealising aggression and confrontational approaches to policing and displaying domineering behaviours in their interactions with members of the public (Loftus, 2010). Furthermore, cynicism and pessimism towards the general public, the criminal justice system, organisational leaders, and victims of crime; suspicion; isolation; and solidarity remained key features of the police culture, as police officers acknowledged they were still aware of their alienation from organisational outsiders. Loftus (2010) also observed that the solidarity between officers was partially reinforced through officers' actions to routinely cover up the (minor) deviant actions of their colleagues. Loftus (2010, p. 15) argued that while the officers were not "culturally homogenous", the strength of the shared assumptions, values, and practices outweighed any subgroup conflicts.

A recent Australian study aimed to identify core features of police culture, in addition to assessing how the culture within the organisation had changed (Chataway, 2014). Five key themes were identified:

1   The "police family" theme reflected the strong camaraderie existing between officers as a result of their shared identity and experiences. Subthemes included *trust, loyalty, and protection* amongst colleagues; *support* for fellow officers; and *acceptance* within the police family.

2   The "us-versus-them" theme reflected the officers' isolation from the general public and perception that civilians hold negative attitudes towards the police, due to their authority, negative media portrayals, and instances of police misconduct. An additional subtheme reflected the division between front-line officers and senior managers, related to a perceived lack of support from senior managers and a punitive work environment, which focused on monitoring and punishing misdemeanours while failing to reward good performance.

3   The "masculinity" theme referenced the presence of *masculine interactions,* such as teasing and playing pranks; a *law enforcement mission,* in which enforcing the law and keeping the community safe were viewed as being the core police mission; and stereotypically masculine coping styles and negative perceptions of emotions and psychological illness.

4   The "control" theme reflected cultural attitudes borne from the organisation's hierarchical structure, including perceptions of a strong focus on compliance with procedures, promoting a positive image of the organisation, accountability and scrutiny of behaviour, and punishing procedural violations.

5   Subcultural differences were identified by most participants in the study, and occurred across job roles, ranks, and stations, challenging the traditional notion of a monolithic police culture.

Perceptions of how the police culture has changed were also addressed, and included a reduction in social rituals such as informal social gatherings; increased scrutiny, exacerbating the "cover your ass" element of culture; less respect for ranks; and reduced negative stigma associated with psychological illness (Chataway, 2014). Despite some changes, these studies do point to the enduring nature of police culture. It has been suggested that themes identified in earlier research remain relevant, as the fundamental policing role has not substantially changed; several traditional cultural attitudes are just as pertinent to contemporary policing models incorporating community-based policing (e.g. a sense of mission); and reforms may have had a limited impact on culture, as some have not been implemented as intended or conflict with one another (e.g. community-oriented policing goals are somewhat inconsistent with an emphasis on achieving results; Loftus, 2010). Furthermore, some of the reforms may have intensified, rather than attenuated, traditional elements of culture: the increased scrutiny noted by researchers most likely exacerbates cultural attitudes of isolation, solidarity, and us-versus-them (Campeau, 2015; Chataway, 2014; Terrill *et al.*, 2003).

Advantageous and adverse effects of police culture

Police culture influences numerous outcomes relating to the performance and well-being of employees, and the organisation's capacity to strategically and successfully achieve its objectives. Discussions of these outcomes have generally emphasised the "dark side" of police culture. For instance, resistance to police reforms has been attributed to police culture, as required modifications to policing services are thought to conflict with prevailing cultural norms (Barton, 2004; Brough *et al.*, 2016; Loftus, 2010). However, research identifying variations in adherence to traditional police culture attitudes also suggests that culture may not be as significant a barrier to reform as originally reported, as there are sub-groups of officers who do support the changes (e.g. community-based policing; Paoline et al., 2000). Furthermore, while cultural resistance to change has often been held respon-sible for reform failures, some researchers have pointed to the reforms themselves as being poorly implemented, or conflicting with concurrent changes (Loftus, 2010).

Police culture is also considered to negatively influence police officers' behaviour and interactions with the public and minority groups (Loftus, 2010). Terrill et al. (2003), for example, found that police officers who more closely embodied traditional police culture attitudes were more likely to use coercion in their daily encounters with the public, even after controlling for a range of demographic and situational variables. In particular, offic-ers who either subscribed to traditional views of police culture or held mixed views were statistically more likely to use coercion than officers who rejected traditional police culture attitudes. Related to this, aspects of police culture may perpetuate harassment, bullying, and the exclusion of employees based on their gender or minority group status (Brough et al., 2016). For example, the existence of a joking culture, where playing pranks and telling inappropriate jokes are acceptable forms of coping and socialisation, can easily perpet-uate bullying if an officer is deemed unable "take it like a man" (McKay, 2013; Salin, 2003).

Aspects of traditional police culture, such as the masculine ethos and value placed on dominant and authoritative behaviours, may deter officers from complaining about stress and bullying or revealing emotional distress and psychological illness. This stems from apprehension that violating normative expectations that one needs to be tough in order to be an effective police officer will result in punitive reactions, stigmatisation, and the belief that the distressed employee is weak and incapable of performing their job tasks effectively (Tuckey et al., 2012). This fear may result in prolonged stressor exposure that unnecessarily exacerbates strain if the stressed employee suppresses negative emotions and fails to seek support, or if colleagues distance themselves from the distressed employee to avoid associated stigma (Winwood et al., 2009). A recent qualitative study indicated that officers were more likely to manage stress and psychological issues alone, or draw on dark humour as a coping mechanism, due to negative perceptions of emotional distress, the common belief that psychological illness is a sign of weakness, and to avoid repercussions for their careers (e.g. missed promotion opportunities; Chataway, 2014).

Facets of culture, such as secrecy and protective solidarity, have also been associated with police misconduct (Brough et al., 2016; Prenzler, 2002). Although protective solidarity and unethical behaviour occur in many occupations, instances of police misconduct have cap-tured the attention of the public to a greater extent, inspiring reforms to increase transpar-ency and ethical practice within police organisations (Prenzler, 2002; Prenzler and Ransley, 2002). Recent qualitative studies have noted an increased focus on scrutiny and account-ability, which participants believe contributes to a lack of support from management and a punitive culture, whereby officers are closely monitored and disciplined for procedural vio-lations but seldom recognised for good performance (Chataway, 2014). Although increased scrutiny and accountability is intended to ensure that misconduct is exposed and effectively managed, it may also encourage the concealment of misconduct by officers seeking to protect themselves and their colleagues from punishment within punitive cultures, further reinforcing secrecy, solidarity, and the "cover-your-ass aspects" of culture (Chan, 2007; Chataway, 2014; Loftus, 2010; Prenzler, 2002; Terrill et al., 2003).

Researchers have called for a more balanced approach to studying police culture, which acknowledges its positive and negative aspects (Chan, 1996; Paoline, 2003; Waddington, 1999). One major criticism of police culture research is that many of the labels used to describe characteristics of police culture are not neutral in tone or effect, but "draw attention to simplify and condemn the negative beliefs, attitudes, and practices of police" (Bradford and Quinton, 2014, p. 1029). Despite the overwhelming focus on the dark side of police culture, positive outcomes have been noted. For example, police culture provides an outlet for coping with the stressors and challenges of the job (Brough *et al.*, 2016; Terrill *et al.*, 2003); a means of socialisation, in which police officers learn the "craft" of being a police officer, as well as how to interact with one another, their leaders, and members of the public (Chataway, 2014); enhances officers' capacity to control crime, protect public safety, and protect fellow officers (Shockey-Eckles, 2011); and facilitates knowledge sharing and performance in police investigations (Glomseth *et al.*, 2007)) In addition, a recent Australian study (Chataway, 2014) found that some of the more negative aspects of culture are changing in a more positive direction, such as participants' observations of less negative stigma surrounding the admittance of stress and psychological illness.

Supportive and psychologically safe work cultures

Reflecting the focus on the dark side of police culture, strategies to promote cultural transformation have typically strived to attenuate the negative aspects of that culture. For instance, policies and procedures have been implemented to ensure that inappropriate behaviours and misconduct are exposed and dealt with, rather than concealed. However, the increased scrutiny and accountability is perceived to have reinforced the punitive culture, which may in fact sustain or exacerbate the very aspects of culture these measures were aiming to eliminate (e.g. defensive solidarity and cover-your-ass culture). Recent research conducted in police services has suggested that adopting an approach focusing on building positive, supportive, and psychologically safe work cultures is likely to reinforce strategies to transform police culture, without reinforcing the negative aspects of culture.

Building positive, supportive, and psychologically safe cultures is also expected to facilitate stress management and bullying prevention. Policing is regarded as a high-stress occupation, and while the fundamental police officer role, along with its associated stressors and dangers, has remained relatively unchanged, the unprecedented transformations impacting police organisations have intensified officers' exposure to stress. For example, austerity measures and restructuring enacted in response to economic downturn, technological advances, and the changing nature of crime (e.g. cybercrime and terrorism) alter the way police services operate, increase uncertainty and competition for resources, and reduce job security and promotion opportunities, all of which enhance stress (Brough *et al.*, 2016). Exposure to unprecedented change, and the heightened risk of exposure to psychological injury experienced by police officers, is often exacerbated by aspects of the culture that undermine the availability of support.

While police research has established the vital role of social support from supervisors and colleagues (e.g. Brough and Frame, 2004), these proximal forms of support have a limited impact unless the wider organisational culture is also viewed as supportive. Supportive work cultures facilitate socio-emotional, informational, and instrumental support amongst co-workers; promote the belief that the organisation genuinely cares about employees' well-being and values their contributions; provide the tangible and psychological resources necessary for police officers to perform effectively; and facilitate clear communication and consultation between leaders and employees (Boateng, 2014; Tuckey *et al.*, 2009). Building positive and supportive work cultures is also likely to capitalise on the positive facets of police culture, while attenuating the negative aspects of police culture. Constructs related to the supportiveness of a work culture studied in police research have included *perceived organisational support*, the *psychosocial safety climate*, and *work culture support*. These constructs will be discussed in greater depth, followed by a discussion of their beneficial effects and strategies for promoting positive and supportive cultures in police organisations.

Perceived organisational support

Perceived organisational support (POS) reflects employees' global beliefs that their organisation values and rewards their contributions and cares about their well-being (Eisenberger *et al.*, 1986; Eisenberger *et al.*, 2002; Rhoades *et al.*, 2001). POS is primarily shaped by organisational policies, procedures, leadership behaviours, and organisational decisions that communicate concern for employee well-being (Armeli *et al.*, 1998). For example, a meta-analysis of over 70 studies identified three broad categories of organisational precursors of POS: fairness, supervisor support, organisational rewards and favourable job conditions (e.g. job security, and role stressors; Rhoades and Eisenberger, 2002).

POS has been linked to favourable individual and organisational outcomes, including job satisfaction, positive mood, affective commitment, performance, and extra-role behaviours, as well as reduced withdrawal behaviours and strain (Rhoades and Eisenberger, 2002). In police-specific research, POS was significantly associated with police officers' perceived effectiveness in a sample of Ghanaian police officers (Boateng, 2014), while both POS and supervisor support predicted higher levels of self-determined motivation and engagement in a series of studies conducted with French police officers (Gillet *et al.*, 2013). Finally, Armeli *et al.* (1998) found that POS was associated with police patrol officer performance (measured as arrests for driving under the influence of alcohol or drugs and issuing speeding citations) for officers who reported a high level of need for esteem, affiliation, emotional support, and approval.

Psychosocial safety climate

Psychosocial safety climate (PSC), reflecting shared beliefs about the extent to which the organisation is committed to promoting employee well-being and preventing stress, has also been studied in police-specific research (Dollard *et al.*, 2012). Unlike POS, PSC is a multifaceted construct comprising four theoretical components: (1) managerial support of employees' well-being (*management support and commitment*); (2) managerial prioritisation of psychological well-being (*management priority*); (3) organisational communication with employees about psychological health–related issues (*organisation communication*); and (4) organisational participation and consultation with different stakeholder groups at all organisational levels, reinforcing joint responsibility for well-being (*organisation participation*; Idris *et al.*, 2012).

PSC is primarily cultivated by senior managers, and acts as an upstream organisational resource, which shapes the proximal job conditions (e.g. demands, autonomy, supervisor support, colleague support) that influence employee psychological health outcomes (Dollard and Bakker, 2010). Research has demonstrated that PSC is an important factor protecting the well-being of police officers. Within a sample of South Australian police officers, positive perceptions of PSC were associated with lower workplace bullying. Furthermore, PSC buffered the adverse associations between workplace bullying at Time 1 and Time 2, and between workplace bullying and post-traumatic stress symptoms

(Bond *et al.*, 2010). In a study of Australian police officers, emotional resources only buffered the adverse impact of emotional demands on distress when high levels of PSC existed within the workgroup (Dollard *et al.*, 2012). Finally, the results of a qualitative study of police officers demonstrated that a major driver of post-traumatic and erosive psychological injuries was a poor PSC, in which socialisation processes that encourage emotional stoicism and insufficient concern over the psychological well-being of officers prevail (Tuckey *et al.*, 2012). Collectively, these studies illustrate the juxtaposition confronting officers who work in a high-stress context, in which the culture discourages displays of emotional distress and support-seeking behaviours.

Perceived work culture support

Finally, perceived work culture support is defined as an organisational resource reflecting "employees' perceptions that the organization's work culture is concerned with their well-being, is committed to continuous improvement (i.e., positive changes in work culture), and facilitates a positive and supportive work environment consistent with the organization's espoused philosophy" (Biggs *et al.*, 2014c, p. 237). The construct was developed via qualitative research that indicated support for police officers, both during times of critical incidents and in response to daily hassles; alignment of organisational practices with the police organisation's documented commitment to facilitating a positive and supportive workplace; and evidence of a commitment to continual positive change were key attributes of positive and supportive police cultures (Gracia, 2007).

Research conducted with police services has demonstrated the positive effects of perceived work culture support. Biggs *et al.* (2014c) conducted a longitudinal study with a sample of 1,196 police employees, which demonstrated that perceived work culture support predicted increased supervisor support, colleague support, and work engagement over time-lags of 12, 18, and 30 months. In another study, conducted with a sample of 1,623 police officers, work culture support was associated with higher levels of intrinsic job satisfaction and engagement, and lower levels of turnover intentions and psychological strain (Biggs *et al.*, 2014b). A study on bullying, conducted with 1,198 police employees, also demonstrated that work culture support measured at Time 1 predicted lower levels of bullying as well as greater confidence in the organisation's capacity to respond fairly and appropriately to bullying complaints assessed 18 months later (Time 2). Furthermore, perceived confidence in the organisation's capacity to respond fairly and appropriately to bullying complaints (Time 2) was a stronger predictor of work culture support measured 12 months later (Time 3) than the actual experience of bullying (Biggs and Brough, 2014). These studies indicate that a supportive police work culture, in which positive interpersonal relationships are encouraged and conflict and bullying are discouraged, is likely to enhance social resources and motivate employees to be psychologically attached to their job role and experience positive affective perceptions of their job.

Building supportive and psychologically safe police cultures

Although conceptually distinct, each of the constructs discussed above reflects perceptions that well-being is an organisational priority, in which employees feel valued and supported, resulting in positive individual and organisational outcomes. In addition to these benefits, cultivating positive, supportive, and psychologically safe police cultures is likely to address some of the negative aspects of police culture and support the implementation of police reforms. For instance, fairness and trust are established within positive and supportive work cultures, resulting in employees being less motivated to disengage or conceal misdemeanours to avoid punishment, minimising the us–versus–them management mentality or punitive nature of police culture (Boateng, 2014). This point is illustrated in research by Biggs and Brough (2014), which indicated that the existence of a supportive work culture was strongly related to confidence in the organisation's capacity to respond fairly and appropriately to formal bullying complaints.

Stress tends to be lower in positive and supportive work cultures, as work is designed and managed to ensure that employees possess the psychological and tangible resources needed to manage job demands (Bond et al., 2010). Several studies have demonstrated the resource-generating capacity of work environments that are perceived as being highly supportive. Biggs *et al.* (2014c), for instance, found that work culture support predicted supervisor support and colleague support reported by police employees, 12, 18, and 30 months later. Similarly, Dick (2011) demonstrated that a supportive work culture influenced perceived managerial support, which in turn effect organisational commitment reported by police officers.

Fostering positive and supportive police cultures is also likely to reduce bullying and harassment, as interpersonal conflicts are resolved more swiftly; clearer communication exists; leaders and employees are jointly committed to policies protecting employees' well-being; and leaders are more willing to take corrective action to ensure that bullying is neither tolerated nor rewarded (e.g. Bond *et al.*, 2010; Tuckey *et al.*, 2009). In such environments, employees develop expectancies of penalties for perpetuating psychologically damaging behaviours (Bond *et al.*, 2010; Hall *et al.*, 2010).

A positive and supportive work culture is also likely to mitigate aspects of police culture that perpetuate stigma associated with stress and bullying. As emotional control and toughness are desired attributes of police officers, the expression of psychological distress and support-seeking behaviours may be interpreted as a sign of weakness or incapacity to perform effectively (Tuckey *et al.*, 2012). Fear of such stigma may result in prolonged exposure to stress and bullying, which unnecessarily exacerbates strain if the stressed employee suppresses negative emotions and fails to seek support in a timely manner (Winwood *et al.*, 2009). A positive and supportive culture, in contrast, enables employees to voice concerns and seek support for stress and bullying, without exposing them to punitive responses, stigma, and further isolation (e.g. Bond *et al.*, 2010; Tuckey *et al.*, 2009).

Any attempts to build a supportive and psychologically safe police culture should include employees at multiple organisational levels, recognising that police culture is dually shaped by senior leaders and front-line employees (Brough *et al.*, 2016). Strategies include conducting ongoing risk assessment and monitoring to identify organisational issues and inform the development and evaluation of policy. Furthermore, it may be necessary to develop policies that prioritise employee well-being; these should be developed in consultation with multiple organisational stakeholders to ensure they meet the needs of the organisation and to gain employee buy-in. Education and training for employees at all levels to increase awareness of organisational policies, establish joint responsibility for maintaining a positive and supportive workplace, and reduce stigma surrounding support seeking and emotional distress may also be useful strategies (Salin, 2008).

Importantly, building a positive and supportive culture requires the involvement and commitment of senior leaders to ensure that policies and procedures are enacted in a manner that consistently communicates the importance of employee well-being (Dollard and Bakker, 2010). The critical role of senior leaders in shaping organisational culture is well-established. Berson *et al.* (2008), for instance, demonstrated alignment between leaders' self-reported values and employees' perceptions of the organisational culture. Specifically, self-directive leader values were positively associated with innovative culture; benevolent leader values were positively associated with supportive work culture; and security leader values were positively associated with the perception of a highly bureaucratic work culture, and were negatively associated with innovative cultures. Cultivating positive and supportive police cultures is, therefore, likely to be challenging as police organisations tend to be hierarchically and bureaucratically structured, with prevailing cultural norms being perpetuated by senior leaders who have progressed through the ranks. The provision of training and support for leaders, and increasing the diversity of leadership teams, may assist in transforming police culture (Brough *et al.*, 2016). For example, research by Biggs *et al.* (2014a) has demonstrated that perceptions of the supportiveness of the work culture, strategic alignment, work engagement, and job satisfaction improved over time for police employees whose supervisors completed a leadership development programme.

Conclusion

The pervasive effect of police culture on policing effectiveness has been well documented, although much of the discourse has focused on its negative effects. In particular, police culture has been blamed for perpetuating stress, bullying, misconduct, and resistance to reforms. Recent police-specific research has suggested that strategies aiming to build positive, supportive, and psychologically safe police cultures may counteract facets of traditional police culture that perpetuate negative outcomes. Further research is of course required, but studies conducted to date have demonstrated the beneficial effect of supportive police cultures on a range of individual and organisational outcomes.

References

Armeli, S., Eisenberger, R., Fasolo, P., and Lynch, P. (1998). Perceived organizational support and police performance: The moderating influence of socioemotional needs. *Journal of Applied Psychology*, *83*(2), 288–297.

Bajdo, L. M. and Dickson, M. W. (2001). Perceptions of organizational culture and women's advancement in organizations: A cross-cultural examination. *Sex Roles*, *45*(5/6), 399–414.

Barton, H. (2004). Cultural reformation: A case for intervention within the police service. *International Journal of Human Resources Development and Management*, *42*(2), 191–199.

Berson, Y., Oreg, S., and Dvir, T. (2008). CEO values, organizational culture and firm outcomes. *Journal of Organizational Behavior*, *29*(5), 615–633.

Biggs, A. and Brough, P. (2014, July). *Bullying and harassment in "tough" work cultures*. Paper presented at the 28th International Congress of Applied Psychology, Paris, France.

Biggs, A., Brough, P., and Barbour, J. P. (2014a). Enhancing work-related attitudes and work engagement: A quasi-experimental study of the impact of a leadership development intervention. *International Journal of Stress Management*, *21*(1), 43–68.

Biggs, A., Brough, P., and Barbour, J. P. (2014b). Exposure to extraorganizational stressors: Impact on mental health and organizational perceptions for police officers. *International Journal of Stress Management*, *21*(3), 255–282.

Biggs, A., Brough, P., and Barbour, J. P. (2014c). Relationships of individual and organizational support with engagement: Examining various types of causality in a three-wave study. *Work & Stress*, *28*(3), 236–254.

Boateng, F. D. (2014). Perceived organizational support and police officer effectiveness: Testing the organizational support theory in Ghana. *International Criminal Justice Review*, *24*(2), 134–150.

Bond, S. A., Tuckey, M. R., and Dollard, M. F. (2010). Psychosocial safety climate, workplace bullying, and symptoms of posttraumatic stress. *Organization Development Journal*, *28*(1), 37–56.

Bradford, B. and Quinton, P. (2014). Self-legitimacy, police culture and support for democratic policing in an English constabulary. *British Journal of Criminology*, *54*(6), 1023–1046.

Brough, P. and Biggs, A. (2010). Occupational stress in police and prison staff. In J. Brown and E. Campbell (eds.), *The Cambridge handbook of forensic psychology* (pp. 707–718). Cambridge, UK: Cambridge University Press.

Brough, P., Brown, J., and Biggs, A. (2016). *Improving criminal justice workplaces: Translating theory and research into evidence-based practice*. Oxon: Routledge.

Brough, P. and Frame, R. (2004). Predicting police job satisfaction and turnover intentions: The role of social support and police organisational variables. *New Zealand Journal of Psychology*, *33*(1), 8–16.

Campeau, H. (2015). "Police Culture" at work: Making sense of police oversight. *British Journal of Criminology*, *55*(4), 669–687.

Chan, J. (1996). Changing police culture. *British Journal of Criminology*, *36*(1), 109–134.

Chan, J. (2007). Police stress and occupational culture. In M. O'Neill, M. Marks, and A. Singh (eds.), *Police occupational culture: New debates and directions* (pp. 129–151). Oxford: Elsevier.

Chataway, S. (2014). *Change or continuity? A mixed methods investigation of contemporary police culture.* Doctoral Thesis, Griffith University, Brisbane, Australia.

Christensen, W. and Crank, J. P. (2001). Police work and culture in a nonurban setting: An ethnographic analysis. *Police Quarterly*, *4*(1), 69–98.

Cosgrove, F. M. (2015). "I wannabe a copper": The engagement of Police Community Support Officers with the dominant police occupational culture. *Criminology and Criminal Justice*, *15*(5) 119–138.

Dick, G. P. M. (2011). The influence of managerial and job variables on organizational commitment in the police. *Public Administration*, *89*(2), 557–576.

Dollard, M. F. and Bakker, A. B. (2010). Psychosocial safety climate as a precursor to conducive work environments, psychological health problems, and employee engagement. *Journal of Occupational and Organizational Psychology*, *83*(3), 579–599.

Dollard, M. F., Opie, T., Lenthall, S., Wakerman, J., Knight, S., Dunn, S., and MacLeod, M. (2012). Psychosocial safety climate as an antecedent of work characteristics and psychological strain: A multilevel model. *Work & Stress*, *26*(4), 385–404.

Dollard, M. F., Tuckey, M. R., and Dormann, C. (2012). Psychosocial safety climate moderates the job demand–resource interaction in predicting workgroup distress. *Accident Analysis and Prevention*, *45*, 694–704.

Eisenberger, R., Huntington, R., Hutchinson, S., and Sowa, D. (1986). Perceived organizational support. *Journal of Applied Psychology*, *71*(3), 500–507.

Eisenberger, R., Stinglhamber, F., Vandenberghe, C., Sucharski, I. L., and Rhoades, L. (2002). Perceived supervisor support: Contributions to perceived organizational support and employee retention. *Journal of Applied Psychology*, *87*(3), 565–573.

Farkas, M. and Manning, P. K. (1997). The occupational culture of corrections and police officers. *Journal of Crime and Justice*, *20*(2), 51–68.

Gillet, N., Huart, I., Colombat, P., and Fouquereau, E. (2013). Perceived organizational support, motivation, and engagement among police officers. *Professional Psychology: Research and Practice*, *44*(1), 46–55.

Glomseth, R., Gottschalk, P., and Solli-Saether, H. (2007). Occupational culture as determinant of knowledge sharing and performance in police investigations. *International Journal of the Sociology of Law*, *35*, 96–107.

Gracia, N. J. (2007). *Police leadership, culture and well-being: Implementing positive workplace change.* Unpublished honours thesis, Griffith University, Brisbane, Queensland, Australia.

Hall, G. B., Dollard, M. F., and Coward, J. (2010). Psychosocial safety climate: Development of the PSC-12. *International Journal of Stress Management, 17*(4), 353–383.

Hofstede, G., Neuijen, B., Ohayv, D. D., and Sanders, G. (1990). Measuring organizational cultures: A qualitative and quantitative study across twenty cases. *Administrative Science Quarterly, 35*(2), 286–316.

Idris, M. A., Dollard, M. F., Coward, J., and Dormann, C. (2012). Psychosocial safety climate: Conceptual distinctiveness and effect on job demands and worker psychological health. *Safety Science, 50*(1), 19–28.

Loftus, B. (2010). Police occupational culture: Classic themes, altered times. *Policing and Society, 20*(1), 1–20.

Manning, P. K. (2007). A dialectic of organisational and occupational culture. In M. O'Neill, M. Marks, and A. Singh (eds.), *Police occupational culture* (vol. 8, pp. 47–83): Emerald Group Publishing. Retrieved from http://dx.doi.org/10.1016/S1521-6136(07)08002-5.

McKay, R. B. (2013). Confronting workplace bullying: Agency and structure in the Royal Canadian Mounted Police. *Administration & Society, 46*, 548–572.

Paoline, E. A. (2004). Shedding light on police culture: An examination of officers' occupational attitudes. *Police Quarterly, 7*(2), 205–236.

Paoline, E. A. (2003). Taking stock: Toward a richer understanding of police culture. *Journal of Criminal Justice, 31*(3), 199–214.

Paoline, E. A., Myers, S. M., and Worden, R. E. (2000). Police culture, individualism, and community policing: Evidence from two police departments. *Justice Quarterly, 17*(3), 575–605.

Prenzler, T. (2002). Corruption and reform: Global trends and theoretical perspectives. In T. Prenzler and J. Ransley (eds.), *Police reform: Building integrity* (pp. 3–23). Sydney, Australia: Hawkins Press.

Prenzler, T. and Ransley, J. (2002). *Police reform: Building integrity*. Sydney, Australia: Hawkins Press.

Reiner, R. (2000). *The politics of the police*. (3rd ed.). New York: Oxford University Press.

Rhoades, L. and Eisenberger, R. (2002). Perceived organizational support: A review of the literature. *Journal of Applied Psychology, 87*(4), 698–714.

Rhoades, L., Eisenberger, R., and Armeli, S. (2001). Affective commitment to the organization: The contribution of perceived organizational support. *Journal of Applied Psychology, 86*(5), 825–836.

Salin, D. (2003). Ways of explaining workplace bullying: A review of enabling, motivating and precipitating structures and processes in the work environment. *Human Relations, 56*(10), 1213–1232.

Salin, D. (2008). The prevention of workplace bullying as a question of human resource management: Measures adopted and underlying organizational factors. *Scandinavian Journal of Management, 24*(3), 221–231.

Schein, E. H. (2010). *Organizational culture and leadership*. (4th ed.). San Francisco, CA: Jossey-Bass.

Shockey-Eckles, M. L. (2011). Police culture and the perpetuation of the officer shuffle: The paradox of life behind "the blue wall". *Humanity & Society, 35*(3), 290–309.

Terrill, W., Paoline, E. A., and Manning, P. K. (2003). Police culture and coercion. *Criminology, 41*(4), 1003–1034.

Tuckey, M. R., Dollard, M. F., Hosking, P. J., and Winefield, A. H. (2009). Workplace bullying: The role of psychosocial work environment factors. *International Journal of Stress Management, 16*(3), 215–232.

Tuckey, M. R., Winwood, P. C., and Dollard, M. F. (2012). Psychosocial culture and pathways to psychological injury within policing. *Police Practice and Research, 13*(3), 224–240.

Van Maanen, J. and Barley, S. R. (1984). Occupational communities: Culture and control in organizations. In B. M. Staw and L. L. Cummins (eds.), *Research in organizational behaviour*. (vol. 6, pp. 287–365). Greenwich, CT: JAI Press.

Waddington, P. A. J. (1999). Police (canteen) sub-culture: An appreciation. *British Journal of Criminology, 39*(2), 287–309.

Winwood, P. C., Tuckey, M. R., Peters, R., and Dollard, M. F. (2009). Identification and measurement of work-related psychological injury: Piloting the psychological injury risk indicator among frontline police. *Journal of Occupational and Environmental Medicine, 51*(9), 1057–1065.

Worden, R. E. (1995). Police officers' belief systems: A framework for analysis. *American Journal of Police, 14*(1), 49–81.

19 Providing support to police officers

Perspectives on peer assistance and work-related stress

Briana Barocas and Danielle Emery

Introduction

Policing is by its very nature a violent, high-stress job that can challenge and traumatize those trained to do this work. Confronted with a multiplicity of daily work-related stressors, the capacity of police officers to maintain their emotional balance and equilibrium and act in a professional manner is an arduous task. Work perceived as lacking in flexibility and control, coupled with intense physical and psychological demands, places considerable strain on the stress tolerance of individuals (Ganster and Rosen, 2013; Grosch and Sauter, 2005; Hurrell and Aristeguieta, 2005; Quick *et al.*, 1997; Sauter and Murphy, 1995). Furthermore, exposure to critical incidents and traumatic stress, inherent in police work, heightens the potential for work strain. Multiple exposures to trauma also contribute towards a greater risk of developing psychological problems such as post-traumatic stress disorder (PTSD) and depression (Perez *et al.*, 2010; Stephens *et al.*, 1999). Police work also has the potential to reactivate unresolved issues and symptoms associated with earlier job-related traumas (Wilczak, 2002; Violanti, 2004). Unrelenting high levels of work stress have been linked to adverse individual and organizational consequences (Brown and Cambell, 1994; Collins and Gibbs, 2003; Ganster and Rosen, 2013). These negative outcomes have been reported in the research literature linking police stress with problem drinking, marital discord, divorce, violence, cardiovascular disease, and even suicide (Miller, 2015; Coughlin, 2011; Violanti *et al.*, 2011).

The empirical evidence establishing the relationship between police work stress and its adverse consequences has been well documented (Miller, 2015; Patterson *et al.*). Yet, despite the growing realization of the occupational hazards and stress-related problems associated with police work, studies have shown that police officers are reluctant to seek help or assistance for work-related stress (Paton, 1997; Wester *et al.*, 2010; Woody, 2005;). According to Collins and Gibbs (2003), problems endemic to police work continue to escalate at an alarming rate in a profession that is a 24-hour, 365-days-a-year activity. Nevertheless, within the context of a paramilitary organization, self-disclosure and help seeking by police officers is seen as incongruous with their self-concept and professional identity, putting them at greater risk for developing psychological, behavioral, and physical problems. The hierarchical structure and organizational culture of the police force continues to view help seeking as a sign of weakness and personal deficiency, rather than as strength and a positive attribute. Despite this prevalent attitude, a growing body of literature has called attention to improved ways of buffering the deleterious effects of police stress through peer support (Anshel *et al.*, 2012; Morris *et al.*, 1999).

Intervention programs and services

A variety of programs and services have been adapted by police organizations to address stress (Tucker, 2015). Such programs are designed to promote employee well-being, enhance job performance, improve organizational efficiency, and foster a healthy work–family balance (Grauwiler *et al.*, 2008). While there are a variety of intervention programs and services for police officers, this chapter focuses on two established police peer support programs and does not specifically address peer-led intervention models such as Critical Incident Stress Management (CISM).

Peer support

Social support in the workplace is significant in moderating the impact of stress on well-being (House, 1981). Social support can buffer the stress of work demands and help alleviate the impact of work exhaustion. It has also been found to prevent negative long-term physical and psychological health consequences following a traumatic event (Norris and Kaniasty, 1996; Norris and Stevens, 2007; Stephens and Long, 2000; Creamer *et al.*, 2012). An understanding of social support is important in examining peer support programs in workplace settings.

As a workplace assistance initiative, police peer support programs provide first-line assistance and basic crisis intervention services to fellow officers. Such programs rely on carefully selected, highly trained paraprofessionals, who are drawn from within the organizations they serve (Robinson and Murdoch, 2003). These programs offer immediate and ongoing peer support to mitigate cumulative day-to-day work stress as well as traumatic stress. Peer support programs attempt to reduce the potential negative consequences of this high-risk occupation such as substance abuse, domestic violence, depression, illness, or more serious psychological disorders (Chamberlin, 2000; Dowling *et al.*, 2006; Levenson and Dwyer, 2003; Robinson and Murdoch, 2003).

Peer support programs have been promoted as a reliable method for addressing police stress (Finn and Tomz, 1997; Finn and Tomz, 1998; Grauwiler *et al.*, 2008). Many officers believe that only fellow officers can fully comprehend the challenges and daily work stressors they encounter on the front lines (Graf, 1986). The trust they have in their fellow officers to watch their backs in dangerous situations makes peer counseling all the more appropriate as a support service. Previous studies report that officers who believed they had a strong peer support program in place found their jobs less stressful (LaRocco *et al.*, 1980; Graf, 1986).

Police work exposes officers to multiple traumas over the course of their careers. Therefore, in providing assistance, it is important to identify what training and psychological interventions, including peer support, are most effective in facilitating optimal work performance within this high-risk occupation.

Previous research

Previous research studies on police and workplace assistance have focused on awareness and utilization of EAP (employee assistance program) services (Asen and Colon, 1995); awareness and utilization of peer support services (Goldstein, 2005); social support from supervisors and peers (Stephens and Long, 2000); workplace stress and perceived support (Berg *et al.*, 2005); and a review of law enforcement stress and stress programs, including peer support (Finn and Tomz, 1997). However, the empirical research on police peer support programs remains limited (Creamer *et al.*, 2012; Grauwiler *et al.*, 2008).

Public Safety Trauma Response study

The Public Safety Trauma Response (PSTR) project examined the two peer support programs available to New York City Police Department (NYPD) officers to address work-related stress and trauma: the Early Intervention Unit (EIU) (now known as the Employee Assistance Unit (EAU)) and the Police Organization Providing Peer Assistance (POPPA). Specifically, the study examined police attitudes and beliefs about help seeking for work-related and other stress, awareness and utilization of the peer programs and how police officers manage day-to-day work stress, exposure to critical incidents, and traumatic stress. The primary goal was to examine strategies that promote the ongoing health and well-being of police officers in an effort to reduce stress-related adverse outcomes. The PSTR project was funded by the Department of Homeland Security (DHS) and awarded to New York University's Center for Catastrophe Preparedness and Response (CCPR) after September 11, 2001.

The NYPD is the largest public safety agency in the United States and one of the largest police departments in the world (Falkenrath, 2006). It has a staff of over 49,000 people, including approximately 34,500 uniformed members, and provides law enforcement services to over eight million residents in the five boroughs of New York City (United States Department of Justice, 2015). NYPD activities range from community relations to counter-terrorism.

Although both programs offer peer support to the NYPD, EIU was a program internal to the NYPD and POPPA is a program that is external. At the time of this project, EIU was located at NYPD headquarters and was part of the Employee Management Division. It was staffed by trained uniformed police officers and civilians who worked as peer counselors.[1] Sources of referral to EIU included: self, co-workers, supervisors, union representatives, fraternal organizations, family members, and friends. Officers could also be mandated to EIU by supervisors. Services provided by EIU included: short-term counseling, referrals, and education and support groups (i.e. domestic violence and bereavement/loss). When this project was conducted, the peer counselors were available weekdays from 6:00 a.m. until 2:00 a.m. In emergency cases during non-business hours EIU staff were contacted and would respond promptly.

POPPA is an independent not-for-profit organization working collaboratively with the NYPD and operates out of office space in downtown Manhattan. It is staffed by trained, active and retired uniformed police officers (who volunteer their time as peer support officers) and mental health professionals. POPPA has recruited and trained volunteers from all ranks as peer support officers (PSOs) (see http://poppanewyork.org). There is currently a volunteer network of 200 PSOs. POPPA accepts voluntary self-referrals only. Furthermore, POPPA is not permitted to work with officers who are involved in any form of internal NYPD investigation or other disciplinary action. In addition to the PSOs, POPPA trains and coordinates a panel of mental health professionals who provide ongoing mental health services. Over 100 mental health professionals are part of the POPPA clinician network. Services provided by POPPA include: crisis-intervention and referral to POPPA clinicians, psychopharmacology and, in critical cases, an immediate escort to a psychiatric emergency room. PSOs staff a 24-hour, 7-day-a-week helpline and provide face-to-face crisis intervention services.

The study

The data for this study are derived from interviews and focus groups conducted with users and non-users of the peer support programs and the peer providers from EIU and POPPA. Data collection occurred between July 2005 and January 2006. In-depth, semi-structured individual interviews were conducted with officers who have and have not used EIU and/or POPPA.[2] In-depth, semi-structured, individual interviews were conducted with the EIU peer counselors. Focus groups were conducted with the volunteer Peer Support Officers (PSOs) from POPPA. Separate interview and focus group guides were developed for each group and all included similar content. Questions focused on stress management; attitudes and beliefs about help seeking and mental health services; awareness and utilization of the available peer programs; and views on peer support and the peer programs. The peer provider interviews and focus groups also included questions about training and supervision as well as the nature of service provision.

The sample for this qualitative study consisted of 39 officers who had or had not used one of the two available peer programs (14 users and 25 non-users) and 33 officers who were peer providers (nine EIU peer counselors and 24 POPPA PSOs). The majority of those who participated in the study were in the rank of either Police Officer or Detective, while only one third held the status of Supervisor in the department. An inductive approach was employed for the data analysis, which identified themes and patterns across interviews and focus groups.

Findings

The findings that are presented here represent the recurring patterns that occurred across interview and focus group transcripts. The important areas that emerged from the interviews and focus groups are the characteristics of police officers, the significance of police culture and the nature of police work in New York City, and the related stressors. These areas are discussed in more detail below and provide the context for the characteristics of the individual, the structure and demands of the work, and the capacity of the individual to cope with daily work stressors and to seek help within the culture of the police department. Additionally, this must all be viewed in the context that when this study was conducted, the NYPD top administration was very supportive of the peer programs. Understanding of this context is also key to facilitating utilization and providing support services to police officers. These key areas and contexts are incorporated into a discussion of the attitudes and beliefs about help seeking and the need for peer support programs.

Police work and stress

Characteristics of police officers

There are certain key characteristics and values of police officers that emerged in this study. Participants detailed the characteristics of police officers, in general, noting that they have a strong professional identification, are ambitious, self-reliant, hard working and career minded, view themselves as helpers, are family and community oriented, and value respect and appreciation. What emerged as an overall finding was a genuine desire on the part of officers to help people.

> Everyone in our field has this hero mentality, we want to help, we want to get out there and just do things, we take on the burdens of everyone else. And paying attention to the little details. Sometimes it's not what you say, it's just the fact that you're there, helping, showing support for someone. Sometimes you don't have all

the answers and being in my field, this field, my personality, so to speak. I want to have all the answers. I want to go out there and give advice. But it's really not about that all the time. Sometimes it's just being there for the person at their time of need.

(EIU peer counselor)

Police culture and nature of police work

Participants outlined the significance of the police culture and the paramilitary structure which limits autonomy and interpersonal relationships between supervisors and subordinates. Officers discussed the lack of reward, recognition, and acknowledgement from within the department (including supervisors), describing it as "a thankless job." In an occupation where there is no room for error, participants stressed the focus on scrutiny and the punitive nature of the job. Officers described working within a culture where gossip and rumors create a sense of suspicion and mistrust in the workplace. They also emphasized the negative community attitudes toward police that they frequently encounter. They noted the unpredictable nature of the work in terms of both the lack of control over one's work schedule and the nature of the police response to situations where they never know what to expect. Participants acknowledged the changing nature of policing in New York City, in particular, the ongoing threat of terrorism, and the issue of low manpower. One might also expect that due to recent events and the national debate surrounding race relations and police practices, these observations remain relevant today.

The police department nowadays, because of traditional responsibilities and the threat of terrorism, is at times definitely spread thin. We've got to do more with less. That's a given in today post-9-11 world.

(EIU peer counselor)

you could be a hero one day, and the next day you could be treated like a child because your shoes aren't polished.

(Police officer—non-user of the peer programs)

Participants acknowledged that being a police officer is one of the most stressful jobs and that police are expected to be able to handle the stress. Many aspects of the nature of police work and the organizational culture were described as stressors that officers confront and are challenged by. Additionally, participants noted several other related occupational stressors, including: unpredictable hours, an intermittent work pace (which ranges from boredom to terror), financial stress, and exposure to critical incidents. The events of 9/11 were seen as a particularly stressful time, which lingers in the back of officers' minds. Sources of stress range from the micro to the macro and have an impact that reaches beyond the workplace to affect family and community.

Stressors of police work

Among the emerging themes in this study was the radiating impact of police work and stress, and how it pervades both personal and family life. Officers talked about stress related to relationships, finances, and traumatic stress.

I mean, if you've seen something happen tragically to someone, you're an eyewitness to an atrocity, to man's inhumanity to man, how are you going to sit there and share that with your loved one at home?

(POPPA peer support officer)

I mean, finances are a big thing, too. People come to us living from check to check. They got a couple kids, they got a house, they got a mortgage, and the money, we get lots and lots of money on this job [over time], but it's hard, living in this environment it's very expensive and New York is a very expensive city.

(EIU peer counselor)

Especially after 9/11. It was very bad. The nightmares, I had nightmares for a year, and my wife kept telling me, "Why don't you go see a doctor, maybe it's something that they could fix." You're exposed to body parts and we worked the morgue for eight months. . . . It was just the nightmares and it was hard.

(Police officer—non-user of the peer programs)

Police work has an effect on officers' control over their lives as well as an ongoing impact on their interpersonal relationships, family functioning, and family relationships. The nature of the work, in particular, the lack of control over the work schedule and unpredictable hours, can prevent an officer from being able to spend time with his/her family. The shift work, scheduling issues and subsequent unavailability to spend time with family, along with financial stress, were all noted as affecting family relations.

Participants in this study noted the desire to police to keep work and family separate. Officers want to protect their families from their experiences at work (e.g. exposure to critical incidents and other traumas), so they are silent at home about work. In order to protect their family members, participants talked about shutting down, leaving work in the locker, and keeping it close to the vest. Both the schedule and not talking to family about work can cut off an officer from his or her natural support system.

You work long hours and you never know if you will be able to spend time with the family. Sometimes work does interfere. I work nights. When you're working at night, sleeping during the day. When do you have time for anyone else?

(Police officer—non-user of the peer programs)

Attitudes and beliefs about help seeking

Given the characteristics of police officers, the nature and culture of police work, and the stressors of the job, a number of attitudes and beliefs about help seeking emerged as themes in this study and have a profound influence on officers' willingness to seek help. Ultimately, these attitudes and beliefs were identified as significant barriers to help seeking through formal sources of support.

Help seeking is a sign of weakness

The need for help and help seeking were viewed as a sign of weakness. Participants discussed the expectations that officers should be able to handle the stress, and, therefore, should not need to seek assistance. There is a fear of shame, humiliation, and ridicule associated with being seen as weak. The tendency is to pathologize the process of help seeking; stigmatizing it rather than viewing it as an appropriate and necessary course of action. The concern is that they will be viewed as ineffective police officers and as incapable of carrying out the responsibilities of their job. Help seeking is seen as incongruous with the image and role expectation of police officers, where self-reliance is highly valued.

> It's the nature of being a cop. We fix it ourselves, or ignore it. But tell somebody else about it? Oh no. That's not a good idea.
>
> (EIU peer counselor)

> throughout the years there's been a whole big stigma if you go and seek counseling, you're crazy, you're weak, you're not a good person, you're not a good cop.
>
> (EIU peer counselor)

> Cops are afraid. First they're afraid of being embarrassed if somebody finds out they're weak.
>
> (Police officer—user of POPPA)

> they're afraid. They're fearful. They're guarded. See the job really discourages cops from going to them because it ends up in ridicule in the police officer's eyes. Ridicule and then embarrassment because I come to you for help and then you go and say, "You know what? You're not able to do your job." And if I'm not able to do my job, and that's all I have; it's what I'm holding on to, then you just killed me.
>
> (Police officer—non-user of the peer support programs)

> Some are willing to seek help, some are not. I think the big thing may be being labeled, like if you say I'm stressed or this or that, someone may look at you like it's too much, maybe [you] can't handle it. So I think the stigma may keep a lot of people from seeking help.
>
> (Police officer—non-user of the peer support programs)

From the interview data, it appears that help seeking has a detrimental effect on how officers view themselves. There is a strong need to preserve and maintain their professional image, even at the expense of personal suffering and distress. For some, help seeking is tantamount to being a bad cop, someone not worthy of wearing a badge. Also, the prevalence of negative attitudes towards seeking help and utilizing services among police officers contributes to the fear of them being seen as impaired and incapable of doing their job.

Help seeking is a threat to an officer's career

Police officers have a strong professional identification that is at odds with help-seeking behaviors. They do not seek help due to the fear of adverse consequences to their career (i.e. fear of losing their weapon, no longer being a cop and thus losing their identity— their livelihood). Officers want to avoid the ridicule and humiliation of having their guns taken away from them. Officers expressed fears that help seeking would be a mark against them and jeopardize career advancement. The perceived consequences of help seeking (e.g. being given modified duty) are seen as exacerbating the problem or making a bad situation even worse. Police avoid seeking help through the department since it is too threatening to their career. Officers want to avoid the stigma associated with help seeking, as it will follow them throughout their career. Some officers even expressed reluctance to use their health insurance when seeking outside support, for fear that if this got out their careers would be damaged.

> Oh, you don't do that. You don't go to the job. You don't tell them anything. They're going to take your firearms, it will ruin your career, it will ruin your chance of promotion.
>
> (Police officer—non-user of the peer support programs)

As noted by some respondents, the indelible and enduring impact of being stigmatized serves as a very powerful deterrent to help seeking,

> And when you get stigmatized in this job, it's like almost any job. It follows you through every place you sit there and go, through the lifetime of your career.
>
> (POPPA peer support officer)

> Other members of the department put the stigma to their name that they wigged out or they can't function or they're crazy or you know. Who's going to want to work with you? Members feel like to go back to the command they're going to go, and they know that you came here for help, no one's going to work with you.
>
> (EIU peer counselor)

The fear of being stripped of power and authority and losing their professional identity by having their shields and weapons taken away, along with the ensuing humiliation, was noted by several respondents:

> when you take someone's weapons, it's like being stripped, you know, it's part of your identity. . . . And other officers can be cruel, in terms of jokes, sick sense of humor, here's a rubber gun squad, here's a rubber gun. It's funny to everybody else, it's not funny to the person who's affected.
>
> (EIU peer counselor)

> I guess because you're not seen as a cop anymore. You're seen more as a civilian. You kind of get that prestige taken away because you wear a uniform, but what does that represent without your shield, without your firearm.
>
> (Police officer—non-user of the peer support programs)

> And I'm not going to go to an organization that could possibly take away the one thing that means the most to me.
>
> (Police officer—non-user of the peer support programs)

These pervasive attitudes reflect the deeply entrenched belief that help seeking has the potential to undermine the career paths of police officers and result is serious professional and personal damage. With officers viewing the department as a "rumor mill," help seeking is regarded as dangerous to their careers and something to be avoided.

The biggest concern members of the service have regarding any type of counseling services is how much the job is going to become in one's personal life. Taking advantage of one of these services is considered to be a guaranteed way of losing one's gun and shield which would be like taking golf clubs away from Tiger Woods.

> (Police officer—user of EIU)

Attitudes and beliefs about an officer's role and responsibilities in the workplace have an overwhelming influence on their willingness to seek help. Ultimately these attitudes and beliefs were identified as key obstacles to formal help seeking. The predominant attitude among police participants in this study was that the role of an officer is to provide help—not to ask for or need help. Officers are trained to believe in their capacity to solve any problem that is thrown their way. Should an officer need help or evidence any stress in reaction to their work, they are likely to be perceived of as weak and are potentially ostracized.

> Because we're in a position where we do the helping, we don't ask for help. We're out in the street and we're told and we're trained that you are in charge out there. Something goes wrong, you take control, don't let anybody else take control over you.
>
> (EIU peer counselor)

Officers need to be willing to help themselves

Several participants openly acknowledge that if officers need help they should get it. They believe it is important to seek help before problems escalate and become life threatening. They also recognize that is takes courage and strength to seek help and overcome the barriers of resistance inherent in the police department.

> My philosophy is if you need it, you need it. You need to go get help because the law enforcement business can be stressful, it definitely could.
>
> (Police officer—non-user of the peer support programs)

> Well, the attitudes are always leery about coming out and saying that they have these situations because . . . they don't want to be labeled as someone who has mental problems or titled as someone who wigged out. . . . Only someone who's really comfortable with themselves, they would come and ask for help.
>
> (EIU peer counselor)

> people think that going to get help for yourself is a sign of weakness but in reality, it's a sign of strength.
>
> (POPPA peer support officer)

> you can have the best program, but it really comes down to the individual. If they're going to admit to themselves, "Listen I have a problem, and I have to seek help" you can have the best programs and if the individual is just not willing to help himself or herself first, you can have the best program in the world, and it's just not going to matter. So it comes down to the individual.
>
> (Police officer—non-user of the peer support programs)

While there is a predominant expectation that police must be self-reliant and self-sufficient, there is also the stated belief that they should avail themselves of help when necessary. While suicide was not specifically addressed in interview and focus group questions, most participants raised the problem and threat of suicide among the ranks. They felt strongly that police stress, combined with the stigma attached to help seeking, has resulted in some police suicides. However, they also viewed the risk of becoming suicidal (in response to police stress) as the primary reason to seek help through formal support. One participant noted the following in an interview conducted the same week that a NYPD Captain committed suicide:

> You don't have the courage. This is what kills me. This captain had enough courage to blow himself away. Do you know how much courage that takes? It's just a moment's courage. But it takes a lot to take your gun out and put it to your head. But didn't have enough courage to go and pick up a phone to call these people and see if they could help him or prescribe something or just get medical help or whatever. The courage it takes to kill yourself with your weapon is greater, I believe, than the courage it takes to pick up the phone. But in his twisted mind he could blow himself away. He could do that, no problem, but he can't pick up the phone. It's messed up.
>
> (Police officer—non-user of the peer support programs)

Participants acknowledged the difficulty in reconciling the need for help while maintaining the traditional macho image of police officers and believed that this contributed to many in-service tragedies. Moreover, peer providers noted that providing assistance to someone who is not willing to help themselves can be extremely difficult.

> When a person's not willing to help themselves. Where you can guide them or direct them but they won't take the steps to help themselves, that's very difficult. Because you can't help someone who's not willing to be helped. That's very difficult.
>
> (EIU peer counselor)

9/11 made help seeking acceptable

Participants acknowledge that the magnitude of the events of 9/11 had an impact on officers' attitudes and beliefs about help seeking. There is an acknowledgement that the time period around 9/11 was seen as particularly stressful, culminating in a change in attitudes and beliefs regarding help seeking. Suddenly, with the devastating loss of numerous police officers and other first responders, as well as civilians, it became acceptable and appropriate for NYPD officers to seek help during this post-disaster period. A catastrophic event had brought about an attitudinal shift. The expectations of how officers should handle a highly stressful situation changed; 9/11 was both a threat as well as an opportunity for change, a change that was not feasible under normal circumstances. It took an unfortunate tragedy to neutralize the powerful resistance to help seeking among police officers. This is reflected in the sentiments expressed by several participants:

> I think more people have gotten help because that was very traumatic. To see people jumping, not one but hundreds of them just jumping. We're all human. It affected all

of us. But I think more people went for help . . . because there was so much that we were exposed to, and we don't have the option of retreating. We have to go towards the problem.

(Police officer—non-user of the peer support programs)

It became such a catastrophic event that so many people needed to get something out or needed to get something off their chest that the attitude needed to change because people needed to go and speak to somebody or needed to go and work through something one way or another.

(Police officer—non-user of the peer support programs)

For people who want to talk about 9/11, the experiences, people they lost, I think that's something that won't be ridiculed, that won't be looked down upon. However, anything after that . . . like your family, having not to do with September 11th, still keep it to yourself, or job related stress keep it to yourself, except for that day. I think everything to do with that day is always seen as acceptable.

(Police officer—non-user of the peer support programs)

You know, people who you would be very surprised who prior to 9/11 would have never done anything like that. I think it woke a lot of people up to realize that sometimes you can't go it alone. You've got to reach out. It's not going to be the end of your career if you do. Because that's the biggest fear that you're going to be disgraced and shut away somewhere. It's still there but not as much.

(EIU peer counselor)

Well, it's just like the stereotype. You're supposed to be macho. You're supposed to go and handle all that stuff and you shouldn't need to. But I think that was more the generation before us. I think a lot of people realize that—like after 9/11, which by the way was very stressful—I think they realized. They're a lot more accepted. People realized, you know, if you heard of somebody that was going to one of these organizations in the past, they might be ostracized or people would worry about working with. And I don't think you have as much of that anymore.

(Police officer—user of EIU)

Many participants felt that 9/11 had an impact (at least temporarily) on some officers' and the department's views on help seeking, while others felt that over time old attitudes and beliefs were resurfacing. Ironically, when the massive psychological trauma of 9/11 hit, traditional coping mechanisms were shattered and defenses were lowered. The psychological fallout from 9/11 was ubiquitous and seeking help had become destigmatized and was even encouraged. In fact, in November of 2001, the NYPD mandated that employees, including uniformed members, attend mental health counseling sessions. This program, with funding from the Police Foundation, was started in partnership with Columbia University and provided individual, group, and family assistance. A similar approach, utilized in Oklahoma City, served as a model for this program (Jones, 2001).

Police acknowledge that 9/11 had an influence on help seeking. There was a recognition that officers needed to be willing to help themselves (and that it takes courage) and among EIU peer counselors that it can be challenging to work with an officer who does not voluntarily seek out assistance. The need for various assistance options was acknowledged. Finally, participants discussed the strong preference amongst officers for seeking assistance outside the department.

Stress management strategies

Officers discussed the need to be strategic in how they manage their stress. Participants outlined some of the more common strategies that officers employ: separating work and home, keeping stress to oneself, using humor, and using informal sources of social support.

There is a desire to keep work and family separate and to not allow work to spill over into family life. Officers described how they compartmentalize work and family by leaving work at work and not taking it home. They establish boundaries between work and home, which they believe are essential to maintain.

Officers described the informal sources of social support that they utilized to cope. Participants underscored the importance of informal sources of social support (particularly, family members and friends) as critical to their day-to-day occupational functioning.

> I have a network of friends who I can talk to—in and outside of the department. That helps me to get through my stressors.
>
> > (Police officer—non-user of the peer support programs)

The partners who came in for the individual interview together described how they support one another.

> R2: one thing about this job is that if you have certain problems, everybody knows about it. You don't want that. That's why it's always good to have somebody you work with that you can talk to. You keep it there with your partner.
>
> R1: We say that it stays inside the car.
>
> > (Police officers—non-users of the peer support programs)

The peer support programs build on this natural support that exists for officers in the workplace. Participants detailed the impact that these stressors have on officers' personal and professional lives.

Barriers to service utilization

The location of services, privacy, and confidentiality are critical to accessing and utilizing any assistance and support services to address stress, including peer-based programs. Officers expressed the desire for true confidentiality and privacy and the need for trust. There was a strong preference for outside assistance, which was seen as key to maintaining confidentiality and privacy. Skepticism and cynicism amongst officers was also discussed, with a number of participants describing a culture of suspicion and doubt. Some officers were even suspicious about participating in the study interview.

> I've used the POPPA service, and the preference for that was that, at least from my understanding, it was outside the police department. You always take a chance; you don't know. Like, I'm taking a chance being here [in this interview]. But the goal to me to reduce my stress was that important that I needed to speak to someone because

I was probably at the end of my rope in that certain instance, and I don't mean like suicide or anything like that, but I just didn't know anywhere else to turn.

(Police officer—user of POPPA)

Peer providers from both EIU and POPPA discussed the ways in which they assure officers of confidentiality. Peer providers commented on the fact that they do not take notes as a way of maintaining confidentiality. However, for EIU cases that are a "line organization referral" (LOR), in which an officer is referred officially, or for those who are in the monitoring program, there will be a folder on that individual. They also mentioned the limits of confidentiality and the practice of informing officers of those limits upfront. Providers acknowledged the perception amongst officers that there is a lack of confidentiality in department-based services.

The need for peer support

Participants in this study believe that there is a need for a range of options of services for officers needing assistance (wanting to seek help), including the peer programs. They stressed the need for services that are external and separate from the department to ensure confidentiality. They also stressed options for service provision based on an officer's preference for one-on-one or group services. Officers believe that having choices is a good thing, as different options will work for different people, although, as noted above, they also acknowledge that officers need to be willing to help themselves. As on officer noted, "Police won't admit that they need help." Furthermore, several officers stressed the need for services for both officers as well as family members. Officers also acknowledge the need for assistance after an event like 9/11. Finally, as one officer acknowledged, "Not every officer in the department needs help."

I personally think that if they stop you from going down the wrong way, then I definitely think you've got to have them. You have to have them. There are just too many people.

(Police officer—non-user of the peer support programs)

But they both [EIU and POPPA] do a phenomenal job and they are both very much needed in the police department. Because some people feel very comfortable going outside the job, and that's when POPPA is most useful. And some people don't mind coming to Early Intervention, so they have a choice, so I think that's a good thing.

(Police officer—non-user of the peer support programs)

You know, sometimes I think they can be very valuable. Because I just think that in this day and in age that we're in, in the way that things are, sometimes people need someone to speak to. Sometimes you don't know which direction to go to to get something out that you're holding inside. Now, as it's getting better and better and people might be more apt to use it, I think it will be very valuable.

(Police officer—non-user of the peer support programs)

frankly speaking, most cops will go to POPPA because it's outside the police department. Confidentiality . . . and quite frankly, I don't blame them. But at the same time, you will have officers who get in trouble. And it might be that they get in trouble that's disciplinary related, i.e., the person's late a lot. But you never know, if you look deeper, there might be something else that's underlying that problem. So, I think the more resources you have, the better . . . there are options that are open to them.

(EIU peer counselor)

Have the programs available for us because I'm sure, if not twice, at least once, you'll need it. You turn on the news, there's still talks of terrorist attacks happening. They say that they're not finished with us. You have the train bombing in Madrid, and you have all these attacks in Israel, London, so you never know. You never know when some day someone might be too stressed out, but if the program is not there or any program is not there for us to turn to, there's no telling what may happen.

(Police officer—non-user of the peer support programs)

From these narratives, there is a growing recognition of the need for and value of support services for police officers; however, the underlying fears of using internal resources like the Early Intervention Unit persists. Participants viewed the EIU as too threatening, and the perceived lack of confidentiality, gossip, and stigma was offered as a justification to avoid utilizing this program.

There is a strong conviction that peer support programs can prevent individuals from becoming derailed in their job performance. Officers appear to display a preference for seeking assistance outside the department, such as going to POPPA, a service rendered outside the job. When the boundaries between help seeking and work are more clearly demarcated, officers are obviously more comfortable in seeking assistance. Nevertheless, concerns about trust and fears of breaching confidentiality were also voiced by those participants who were receptive to using POPPA.

A number of participants mentioned support from the top administrators for the peer support programs.

I've seen over the past few years, especially with this police commissioner, pushing the POPPA program, the Early Intervention Unit . . . years ago we never had that.

(Police officer—non-user of the peer support programs)

NYPD officers have a web of support programs that work together to ensure that officers get the help they need as soon as they need it, and the peer support programs are a large part of that web.

Significance of shared experience and understanding

Peers were seen as significant in providing both informal and formal support, since officers have shared experience and understanding. This shared experience and understanding gives peers credibility. Peers can also make officers feel more comfortable with seeking services and make help seeking more acceptable, since they share a common language. Furthermore, the shared experience and understanding creates an important bond and a sense of trust.

And I think that right away gave me some belief, some trust in them because at one time or another they were police officers, in terms of sitting in a patrol car or standing on a foot post or having to meet a quota for some activity, so they know exactly what I was talking about.

(Police officer—user of POPPA)

In the grand scheme of things, you just don't want to be left out in the cold. You want to know that someone understands, that someone is in your corner.

(Police officer—user of EIU)

The street experience gives me more credibility because you know, in my experience, there've been people who have either master's degree, MSW, CSW, and a lot of times, different officers, male and female, they feel a lot of times, unless you've walked in our shoes, you don't really know what we go through, you know . . . being able to have that credibility that hey I know what its like to be shot at. I know what its like to run in a dark alley, heart beating, and say oh my god, why am I here? Where's my back-up? So, you know.

(EIU peer counselor)

We know what it's like to have to juggle the job, the family, the illnesses, the upset and try to keep it all going in various respects. Again, it just makes us that much stronger that much of a better resource for people.

(EIU peer counselor)

The shared experience and understanding of police culture and the nature of police work was seen as being one of the most important requirements for a peer provider to have.

I would say one of the most important things is experience, experience on the job. Experience where he's been there, done that, he's been around, experienced. It doesn't hurt to have some kind of background, educational background. I think the number one thing is he needs experience. That's the number one factor.

(Police officer—non-user of the peer support programs)

Peers make helping seeking for officers more acceptable since there is this shared understanding.

I think by using peers it's making it more acceptable to guys who hate the job or think the job wouldn't understand them or think there would be repercussions, but by making it a peer thing, it's great. It makes people a lot more comfortable with seeking the services.

(Police officer—user of EIU)

So the thing is that we're trying to sit there and break that wall that yes, you can ask for help and there are people that you can sit there and trust and who know exactly what you feel and what you sit there and you think because we all were rookies at one time. We all went to the Academy, we all sit there and did the first 2 years and let's face it, after the first 5 years, you get a pretty good handle on this job. You know what police work is like. And now the whole thing is that we've been there and we can help them along.

(POPPA peer support officer)

Role of peers

Participants in the study described peer providers as facilitators, gatekeepers, and bridges; they described peers as normalizing help seeking and linking officers to services. The peer providers noted that they do not provide long-term counseling and some pointed out the importance for peer providers to be aware of the limits of their training. They also acknowledged the importance of training in giving peer providers the helping skills they need to handle the range of issues they confront.

> As a peer . . . you are actually at the bridge between a police officer and the clinician, getting the help that they need. You can only go to one part of the bridge.
>
> (POPPA peer support officer)

> I think the main thing we're effective with is information and additional resources because a lot of times people are like, wow I didn't realize you had access to all these services. One of the biggest services I think we do is being that bridge from police work to the outside world, whether it's outside counseling, the American Cancer Society, being that bridge. To kind of say, it's legit, its legitimate, it's ok.
>
> (EIU peer counselor)

> We're basically triage here. We hear what the problem is; plug them into the right resource to have that work done. They're not coming to me to fix them.
>
> (EIU peer counselor)

> Our objective or our goal is just to kind of get you what you need. . . . We're like the quarterback, we hand you the ball off and you take the ball, you tell me this is what you got, and this is where it's got to go. So we're middle men.
>
> (POPPA peer support officer)

> We don't do long-term counseling. I think the biggest thing that we do is basically vent. You know, on our literature, sometimes you need someone to talk to. So I think that's the biggest thing we do. The biggest thing, you know, I remember as an acronym LAR: Listen, Assess, Refer, you know. And you've got to know the limits of your training.
>
> (EIU peer counselor)

> Let them know that you're here to help them and that your main focus is to make referrals out to where he can get professional counseling for him or her or whatever it is, family members, and that everything is kept confidential.
>
> (EIU peer counselor)

> Training is always important. Number one, you can't do this without the proper training.
>
> (POPPA peer support officer)

In addition to training, participants noted the need for peer providers to have some time on the job to have credibility in their role as a peer:

> I think they should have a few years, just for credibility. I mean, I would think a veteran of 15, 20 years, wouldn't feel, what do you have to offer me, kid?
>
> (POPPA peer support officer)

Outreach

The peer providers discussed the outreach initiatives that they were involved in, including police academy training and going out to roll calls. They noted that awareness can increase with the passage of time. Outreach was seen as an ongoing effort that can lead to increased awareness and acceptance. However, due to the size and structure of the department, ongoing outreach can be challenging. It may not be possible to reach everyone (e.g. officers in specialized units). Furthermore, even if they reach officers they are not necessarily on an officer's radar, as there are competing demands and other things going on. For example, if an officer is preoccupied with counter-terrorism training, the peer programs that are available to him/her may not even register (unless they need them).

> The more they know about us, I think the more comfortable they feel with us.
>
> (POPPA peer support officer)

> And it's evolving every day and it's wonderful because we're more recognized and we're more accepted.
>
> (POPPA peer support officer)

Recognition

There was recognition that officers need to take stress seriously and to be cognizant about how they manage their stress.

> I would say it's something that's taken a little more seriously, as far as stress, because some cops end up killing themselves, or the drink, or they take it home and it turns into a domestic or family problem. So that's a little bit more serious actually. It's very easy to get into trouble as far as getting into an argument with your spouse—your wife, your husband—it's very easy to get into trouble. Like, your neighbors will hear something, and they call the cops. Next thing you know they take your gun and shield away. So they always tell us if you're going to argue with your wife, don't do it. Go outside, take a walk. The stress thing, they take it a lot more serious.
>
> (Police officer—non-user of the peer support programs)

Several participants noted that it takes courage for officers to seek help.

> We realize that it takes a tremendous amount of strength and courage for someone to pick up the phone and actually ask for help and be a member of the service. We recognize that and we realize that what we do from that point on can make a big effect on their career and stuff like that and their life.
>
> (POPPA peer support officer)

> I just always try to leave my groups, when we talk, with this thinking that people think that going to get help for yourself is a sign of weakness but in reality, it's a sign of strength. You know, if you can reaffirm that with them and they actually kind of think about that for a second, they can relate to that. And it just puts a different twist on it.
>
> (POPPA peer support officer)

Finally, some officers who were supervisors discussed the importance of recognizing when one of their officers needs assistance and encouraging them to get help. In describing referring one of his commands to EIU, one supervisor stated:

> Well, the person who I had asked to go there was somebody who was really losing touch. He was blowing up at everybody; he wasn't staying at home with his wife anymore. He was in bad shape, and that's what I thought it was for, somebody who was really at the end of his rope and about to have a real problem. That's what I would have thought it was for.
>
> (Police officer—user of EIU)

Conclusion

Although the data presented here was collected between 2005 and 2006, the findings are applicable to current police work. The study highlights the growing recognition of the need for support services to help ameliorate the psychological and physiological problems associated with the stress of police work and the significance of peer support. While anecdotally participants in this study believed that peer support can be an effective intervention, more research is needed that evaluates effectiveness. Components of an effective peer support program include: trained peers, confidentiality, privacy, and a network of clinicians who have experience working with police. Key elements of an effective peer support approach include a menu of options for officers, with an internal and external program that facilitates choice and utilization.

Confidentiality, privacy, and location are key to encouraging officers to get help early and may offset the effects of day-to-day and traumatic stress. Continuing outreach efforts to help educate officers about normal reactions to police stress is key. Using internal and external peer programs to accomplish those outreach efforts can help address police stress. Beginning in the academy, outreach and education are paramount for the duration of an officer's career, regardless of rank. Police officers are smart, resourceful, and multi-talented, and thus, have the greatest chance of ending stigma among fellow officers regarding help seeking. Police officers can and should play a significant role, formally or informally, in raising the awareness of police stress and promoting the importance of help-seeking.

It should not take a catastrophic event like 9/11 to destigmatize help seeking among police officers. This attitude is something that has to be built into police culture early on, and across ranks, on a day-to-day basis.

Given that the focus of this study was police peer support within a large, urban police department, certain findings may have limited transferability/generalizability to other police department settings. However, the findings are in line with the key recommendations of the peer support guidelines in high-risk organizations developed by an international consensus using the Delphi method (Creamer *et al.* 2012). Most notable is the selection of peer support providers and the training that they receive, the involvement of mental health professionals, and the role of peer support providers. A key aspect of the two peer support programs available to NYPD officers is their ability to respond to critical incidents as well as being part of routine officer health and welfare. Furthermore, EIU provided an important structure for addressing police officers needs in the workplace. POPPA provides an important safety net for police officers who might otherwise not seek help in the workplace. Programs like EIU (now EAU) and POPPA can help to alleviate stressful reactions and symptoms among police officers, and equip them with the necessary tools to maintain a healthy professional and personal identity.

Notes

1 While EIU is staffed by and serves both uniform and civilian members of the NYPD, this study focused on the uniform members only.
2 While the majority of these interviews were with individual officers, on three occasions, interviews were conducted with groups of officers who scheduled interviews back-to-back and who came in together and wanted to be interviewed together—one group was comprised of three friends from the same unit of which two were partners, another group was two friends who work together, and the third group was two partners.

References

Anshel, M., Umscheid, D., and Brinthaupt, T. (2012). Effect of a combined coping skills and wellness program on perceived stress and physical energy among police emergency dispatchers: An exploratory study. *Journal of Police and Criminal Psychology*, *28*(1), 1–14.

Asen, J. and Colon, I. (1995). Acceptance and use of police department employee assistance programs. *Employee Assistance Quarterly*, *11*(1), 45–54.

Berg, A., Hem, E., Lau, B., Haseth, K., and Ekeberg, O. (2005) Stress in the Norwegian police service. *Occupational Medicine*, *55*(2), 113–120.

Brown, J. M. and Campbell, E. A. (1994). *Stress and Policing, Sources and Strategies*. New York: John Wiley and Sons, Ltd.

Chamberlin, J. (2000). Cops trust cops, even one with a PhD. *Monitor on Psychology*, *31*(1), 74–76.

Collins, P. A. and Gibbs, A. C. C. (2003). Stress in police officers: A study of the origins, prevalence and severity of stress-related symptoms within a county police force. *Occupational Medicine*, *53*(4), 256–264.

Coughlin, S. S. (2011). Post-traumatic stress disorder and cardiovascular disease. *Open Cardiovascular Medicine Journal*, 5, 164–170.

Creamer, M. C., Varker, T., Bisson, J., Darte, K., Greenberg, N., Lau, W., Moreton, G., O'Donnell, M., Richardson, D., Ruzek, J., Watson, P. and Forbes, D. (2012). Guidelines for peer support in high-risk organizations: An international consensus study using the Delphi method. *Journal of Traumatic Stress*, *25*(2), 134–141.

Dowling, F. G., Moynihan, G., Genet, B., and Lewis, J. (2006). A peer-based assistance program for officers with the New York City police department: Report on the effects of September 11, 2001. *American Journal of Psychiatry*, *163*(1), 151–153.

Falkenrath, R. (September 12, 2006). Prepared statement of testimony before the committee on homeland security and governmental affairs United States Senate. *United States Senate Hearing on Homeland Security: The Next Five Years*. Retrieved November 1, 2015 from www.fbi.gov/about-us/cjis/ucr/crime-in-the-u.s/2014/crime-in-the-u.s.-2014/tables/table-78/table-78-by-state/Table_78_Full_time_Law_Enforcement_Employees_New_York_by_Cities_2014.xls; www.investigativeproject.org/documents/testimony/259.pdf.

Finn, P. and Tomz, J. E. (1997). *Developing a law enforcement stress program for officers and their families*. Washington, DC: US Department of Justice, Office of Justice Programs, National Institute of Justice.

Finn, P. and Tomz, J. (1998). Using peer supporters to help address law enforcement. *FBI Law Enforcement Bulletin*, *67*(5), 10–18.

Ganster, D. and Rosen, C. (2013). Work stress and employee health: A multidisciplinary review. *Journal of Management*, *39*(5), 1085–1122.

Goldstein, D. B. (2005). A comparison of utilization of peer support services and perceived stigma within the Vermont state police. *The Forensic Examiner*, *14*(3), 44–48.

Graf, F. (1986). The relationship between social support and occupational stress among police officers. *Journal of Police Science and Administration, 14*(3), 178–186.

Grauwiler, P., Barocas, B., and Mills, L. G. (2008). Police peer support programs: Current knowledge and practice. *International Journal of Emergency Mental Health, 10*(1), 27–38.

Grosch, J. and Sauter, S. (2005). Psychologic stressor and work organization. In L. Rosenstock, M. Cullen, C. Brodkin and C. Redlich (eds.), *Textbook of clinical occupational and environmental medicine, second edition* (pp. 931–942). Philadelphia, PA: Elsevier Saunder.

House, J. S. (1981). *Work stress and social support.* Reading, MA: Addison-Wesley.

Hurrell, J. J. and Aristeguieta, C. (2005). Occupational stress. In B. Levy, D. Wegman, S. Baron and R. Sokas (eds.), *Occupational and environmental health: Recognizing and preventing disease and injury* (5th ed., pp. 382–396). Philadelphia, PA: Lippincott Williams & Wilkins.

Jones, R. L. (2001). A nation challenged: The New York police. *The New York Times* (November 30) Retrieved August 15, 2007, from http://query.nytimes.com/gst/fullpage.html?sec=health&res=9 401E4DD123DF933A05752C1A9679C8B63.

LaRocco, J. M., House, J. W. and French, J. R. P., Jr. (1980). Social support, occupational stress, and health. *Journal of Health and Social Behavior, 21*(3), 202–218.

Levenson, R. L. and Dwyer, L. A. (2003). Peer support in law enforcement: Past, present, and future. *International Journal of Emergency Mental Health, 5*(3), 147–152.

Miller, L. (2015). Police officer stress: Syndromes and strategies for intervention. In S. M. M. Clevenger, L. Miller, B. A. Moore, and A. Freeman (eds.). *Behind the badge: A psychological treatment handbook for law enforcement officers* (pp. 202–221). New York: Routledge.

Morris, A., Shinn, M., and Dumont, K. (1999). Contextual factors affecting the organizational commitment of diverse police officers: A levels of analysis perspective. *American Journal of Community Psychology, 27*(1), 74–105.

Norris, F. H. and Kaniasty, K. (1996). Received and perceived social support in times of stress: A test of the social support deterioration deterrence model. *Journal of Personality and Social Psychology, 71*(3), 498–511.

Norris, F. H. and Stevens, S. P. (2007). Community resilience and the principles of mass trauma intervention. *Psychiatry: Interpersonal and Biological Processes, 70*(4), 320–328.

Paton, D. (1997). Post-event support for disaster workers: Integrating recovery resources and the recovery environment. *Disaster Prevention and Management, 6*(1), 43–49.

Patterson, G., Chung, I., and Swan, P. (2014). Stress management interventions for police officers and recruits: A meta-analysis. *Journal of Experimental Criminology, 10*(4), 487–513.

Perez, L., Jones, J., Englert, D., and Sachau, D. (2010). Secondary traumatic stress and burnout among law enforcement investigators exposed to disturbing media images. *Journal of Police and Criminal Psychology, 25*(2), 113–124.

Quick, J. C., Quick, J. D., Nelson, D. L., and Hurrell, J. J. (1997). *Preventive stress management in organizations.* Washington, DC: American Psychological Association.

Robinson, R. and Murdoch, P. (2003). *Establishing and maintaining peer support programs in the workplace* (3rd ed.). Elliot City, MD: Chevron Publishing Corporation.

Sauter, S. L. and Murphy, L. R. (1995). *Organizational risk factors for job stress.* Paper presented at the American Psychological Association, Washington, DC.

Stephens, C. and Long, N. (2000). Communication with police supervisors and peers as a buffer of work-related traumatic stress. *Journal of Organizational Behavior, 21*, 407–424.

Stephens, C., Long, N., and Flett, R. (1999). Vulnerability to psychological disorder: Previous trauma in police recruits. In J. M. Violanti and D. Paton (eds.). *Police trauma: Psychological aftermath of civilian combat* (pp. 65–77). Springfield, IL: Charles C. Thomas Publisher.

Tucker, J. M. (2015). Police officer willingness to use stress intervention services: The role of perceived organizational support (POS), confidentiality and stigma. *International Journal of Emergency Mental Health and Human Resilience, 17*(1), 304–314.

United States Department of Justice, Federal Bureau of Investigation. (September 2015). *Crime in the United States, 2014.* Retrieved November 1, 2015 from www.fbi.gov/about-us/cjis/ucr/

crime-in-the-u.s/2014/crime-in-the-u.s.-2014/tables/table-78/table-78-by-state/Table_78_
Full_time_Law_Enforcement_Employees_New_York_by_Cities_2014.xls.

Violanti, J. M. (2004). Predictors of police suicide ideation. *Suicide and Life-Threatening Behavior,* *34*(3), 277–283.

Violanti, J., Slaven, J., Charles, L., Burchfiel, C., Andrew, M., and Homish, G. (2011). Police and alcohol Use: A descriptive analysis and associations with stress outcomes. *American Journal of Criminal Justice, 36*(4), 344–356.

Wester, S., Arndt, D., Sedivy, S., and Arndt, L. (2010). Male police officers and stigma associated with counseling: The role of anticipated risks, anticipated benefits and gender role conflict. *Psychology of Men and Masculinity, 11*(4), 286–302.

Wilczak, C. (2002). Three perspectives on trauma from New York City police officers. *Division 17 Newsletter of the American Psychological Association, 3,* 13–15.

Woody, R. H. (2005). The police culture: Research implications for psychological services. *Professional Psychology: Research and Practice,* 36, 525–529.

20 Workplace mental health

Development of an integrated intervention strategy for an Australian policing organisation

Kathryn M. Page, Amanda Allisey,
Irina Tchernitskaia, Andrew J. Noblet,
Anthony D. LaMontagne, Nicola Reavley,
Allison J. Milner, and Angela Martin

Mental health problems in the working population

Mental health problems account for 24 per cent of total years lost due to disability and are the third largest cause of the overall disease burden in Australia (Begg *et al.*, 2007; Mathers *et al.*, 1999). The majority of these mental health problems occur in working-age Australians, with one in five Australians aged 25–64 years experiencing an anxiety, affective, or substance use disorder (AIHW, 2010).

Past studies across a number of countries have demonstrated that stressful working conditions, such as the combination of high job demands and low job control (job strain), have detrimental impacts on mental health (Bonde, 2008; LaMontagne *et al.*, 2010; Stansfeld and Candy, 2006). In Australia, previous research has estimated a job strain-population attributable risk for depression of 13 per cent among working males and 17 per cent among working females (LaMontagne *et al.*, 2008) and an associated cost burden of $730 million per year nationally (LaMontagne *et al.*, 2010). This is only a fraction of the total depression-related workplace costs, which we have estimated at $12.6 billion per annum (LaMontagne *et al.*, 2010) but likely underestimates the job stressor-attributable burden of mental health problems, as other job stressors (e.g. bullying, job insecurity) and other mental health problems associated with job stressors (e.g. anxiety, burnout) have not been accounted for (LaMontagne *et al.*, 2010).

In parallel to the growing recognition of and responses to job stress, interventions to promote mental health and mental health literacy in the workplace are gaining acceptability as a means to prevent, screen, and effectively manage depression, anxiety, and other mental health problems among employees in various industrialised democracies (Jorm, 2012; LaMontagne *et al.*, 2014; Martin *et al.*, 2009; Sanderson and Andrews, 2006). A prominent Australian example of this is *beyondblue's* National Workplace Programme, which aims to raise awareness of depression and anxiety as treatable illnesses, to improve help-seeking behaviours, to reduce stigmatising attitudes, and to develop confidence and skills in providing help to people who might be experiencing a mental illness.

Another Australian example is Mental Health First Aid (MHFA), which has been developed by Professor Tony Jorm and others. MHFA seeks to improve mental health literacy by developing knowledge and skills on how to recognise common mental disorders and provide 'First Aid' support until professional help can be obtained, increasing understanding about the causes of mental disorders, improving knowledge of the most effective treatments, and reducing stigma (Kitchener and Jorm, 2004, 2006). There is evidence of effectiveness of MHFA from various studies (Kitchener and Jorm, 2006), including randomised-controlled trials (Kitchener and Jorm, 2004) and cluster randomised-controlled trials (Jorm *et al.*, 2010). In addition to improvements in mental health literacy, there is also some evidence of improvements in mental health among MHFA trainees (Kitchener and Jorm, 2004).

These programmes address some aspects of mental health literacy, but not all; to date, they have tended to emphasise the secondary and tertiary levels, with less emphasis on primary prevention. In the workplace setting, primary prevention should include reduction of work-related risks to mental health, as well as the enhancement of mental health-promoting aspects of work. Job stress prevention features prominently here, and is relevant in all work contexts (Noblet and LaMontagne, 2006).

Where job stress interventions have tended to focus on the primary and secondary intervention levels, mental health literacy interventions have tended to focus on the secondary and tertiary levels, and the two have tended to operate independently (LaMontagne *et al.*, 2014). A fully integrated approach would bring these together to encompass primary, secondary, and tertiary intervention. There is growing recognition among employers of the value of such integrated or comprehensive approaches, which to some extent are practiced in Europe (Barry and Jenkins, 2007) but rarely in Australia (LaMontagne *et al.*, 2014). This stems from growing recognition of the need to fulfill occupational health and safety obligations with respect to psychological as well as physical health, as well as growing awareness of the impact of common mental disorders (work-related or otherwise) on productivity at work (e.g. sickness absence, presenteeism) (LaMontagne *et al.*, 2010; Martin, Sanderson *et al.*, 2009; Sanderson and Andrews, 2006).

Accordingly, we define *workplace mental health literacy* as the knowledge, beliefs, and skills that aid in the prevention of mental illness in the workplace, and the recognition, treatment, rehabilitation, and return to work of working people affected by mental illness. This includes consideration of working conditions and their influence on mental health, as well as addressing mental illness among working people regardless of cause.

Stress and mental health problems in the police sector

In this chapter, we describe the development of a workplace mental health literacy intervention for use in the policing sector. The intervention is currently being used in a cluster randomised-controlled trial[1] in Victoria Police.

While all occupations are potentially exposed to job stressors, some occupations are more exposed than others. Research in the Australian context (Noblet *et al.*, 2009) as well as internationally (Johnson *et al.*, 2005) has identified police work as being particularly stressful. High levels of job stressors in police have been linked to burnout, work–family conflict, (Hall *et al.*, 2010), depression, partner violence (Gershon *et al.*, 2009), psychological distress (Noblet *et al.*, 2009;), and suicide (Loo, 2003). Like other occupations, high job demands (e.g. time pressures and work overload), low supervisor or collegial support (Collins and Gibbs, 2003; LaMontagne *et al.*, 2012; Noblet *et al.*, 2009), and low levels of control (i.e. latitude in deciding how to do one's work) have been found to be significant sources of stress in police work (Collins and Gibbs, 2003; Noblet *et al.*, 2009). It is also necessary to consider that stress-induced mental and physical health outcomes in police may also be linked to their greater exposure to violence and distressing events (Penalba and Leite, 2006; Waters and William, 2007). However, evidence to date suggests that organisational sources of job stress such as excessive job demands, lack of control, and low levels of social support are better predictors of police distress (Brown and Campbell, 1990; Kop and Euwema, 2001; Kop *et al.*, 1999) than operational factors, such as exposure to violence and trauma.

There have been a number of job stress intervention studies in the police sector (Amaranto *et al.*, 2003; Patterson *et al.*, 2012). However, these have tended to focus on improving individual responses to stressors (secondary intervention, such as developing officer coping strategies), rather than addressing stressors (primary intervention, such as improving decision-making processes). Given that many of the stressors experienced by police stem from both individual and organisational sources, it is appropriate to address intervention efforts at both of these levels. This is further supported by the findings of systematic reviews of job stress intervention studies, which indicate that the most effective interventions combine secondary worker-directed (e.g. coping and time management skills) with primary work-directed intervention (e.g. moderation of demands, improved supervisory support) (Bambra *et al.*, 2009; LaMontagne *et al.*, 2007).

Recognizing the need to better address job stress and mental health in their workforce, Victoria Police, a partner in this project as well as the intervention site, was keen to develop and implement a comprehensive workplace mental health literacy program. Victoria Police is one of the largest employers in Victoria (approximately 15,500 employees), and has one of the highest job stress-related claims burdens in the workers compensation system thus making it a well-suited intervention site.

Workplace prevention of mental health problems: guidelines for organisations

The first phase of the project involved developing guidelines for organisations wishing to implement a strategy for workplace prevention of mental health problems, encompassing mental health problems that may be caused by work, and also those that may become apparent in the working environment. The resulting guidelines have been disseminated and are available at https://mhfa.com.au/cms/guidelines#mhfaprevent.[2]

The guidelines were developed on the basis of those items with the highest level of endorsement from the Delphi panels engaged for that project, and consist of ten broad areas of focus. These included:

1   have a mental health and well-being strategy
2   foster a work environment that supports and encourages mental health
3   balance job demands with job control
4   appropriately reward employees' efforts
5   create a fair workplace
6   provide workplace supports
7   manage staff effectively during times of organisational or role change
8   develop leadership and management skills
9   provide mental health education to employees.

The guidelines may be used to facilitate the development of an integrated workplace mental health literacy intervention strategy. However, organisations wishing to implement the guidelines are likely to need assistance in tailoring the guidelines to their particular organisational contexts.

An integrated approach to workplace mental health literacy: intervention strategy

This chapter provides the details of an integrated workplace mental health promotion programme for an Australian policing organisation. The strategy touches on all ten elements of the Workplace Prevention of Mental Health Problem Guidelines for Organisations. The strategy draws on two prior studies we have conducted at Victoria Police – the VicHealth-funded Creating Healthy Workplace stress prevention pilot and a WorkSafe-funded study to identify police members' mental health literacy needs.

Intervention design

Figure 20.1 provides an overview of the integrated intervention strategy for promoting workplace mental health at Victoria Police.

As shown, the purpose of the integrated intervention strategy is to improve:

1 psychosocial working conditions (supervisor support, job control, and workload), and
2 mental health literacy (proximal outcomes).

This, in turn, will reduce perceived stress at work (operationalised and measured as job tension), improve mental health (operationalised and measured as increased job satisfaction and reduced psychological distress), and work productivity and performance (operationalised and measured by Victoria Police data on sickness absence and work output).

The intervention will engage all ranks and levels within participating police stations in a range of activities. Together, the intervention activities address both primary and secondary prevention of mental health problems in a work context.

- The main *primary prevention* activities include engaging senior sergeant and sergeants in (a) 360-degree leadership assessment (focusing on stress prevention leadership competencies and (b) leadership skill development workshops. Workshops will focus on fostering a work environment that supports and encourages mental health; balancing job demands with job control; appropriately rewarding employees' efforts; creating a fair workplace; providing workplace supports, and managing staff effectively during times of organisational or role change; appropriately managing mental health-related under-performance; and educating staff around mental health.
- The main *secondary prevention* activities include providing other ranks (all members below the rank of sergeant in a station and non-sworn members) with training that focuses on how to manage workload effectively, cope effectively with stress, resilience and some aspects of mental health literacy.

We will also meet regularly with existing peer support officers at each intervention station. The purpose of this will be to ensure that peer support officers fully understand the project and are prepared to engage in meaningful peer-to-peer dialogue around mental health.

Intervention delivery

To optimise feasibility and effectiveness, the program will be implemented on a station-by-station basis (see Figure 20.2).

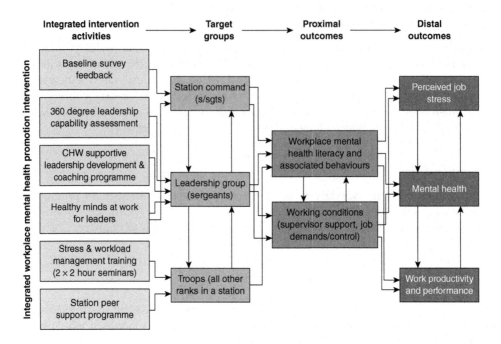

Figure 20.1 Integrated intervention logic Creating Healthy Workplaces: Stage 2.

Note

CHW Stage 2 refers to the integrated program, as funded by the NHMRC partnership project grant

Step 1	The program will commence with a station survey.
Step 2	Station command will complete be a 360-degree leadership assessment and engage in a 90-minute feedback and development session with a psychologist. The session will help station command to explore the links between their leadership style, station culture and employee well-being outcomes measured by the baseline survey). The desired outcome is for senior sergeants to recognise what they can do to prevent workplace mental health problems at a station level as well as to be highly engaged in the intervention activities at their station. The session will also ensure that station command is prepared to support their station through the intervention (and beyond).
Step 3–4	Sergeants will commence the 360-degree tool and engage in a 90-minute feedback and development planning session with a psychologist.
Step 5	Senior sergeants and sergeants will attend CHW workshop 1 (Leading for Well-being), which will be delivered by Deakin University staff. The workshop will build leaders' supportive management skills (e.g. providing effective feedback, providing support, having effective conversations, effectively developing members, etc.).
Step 6–7	Sergeants will receive the first two of four individual leadership-coaching sessions with a trained coach.[3] The coaching sessions will focus on building rapport, fine tuning leadership development goals (e.g. ensuring that there are SMART goals and that the goals align with overarching programme goals), and then completing a series of structured activities that focus on

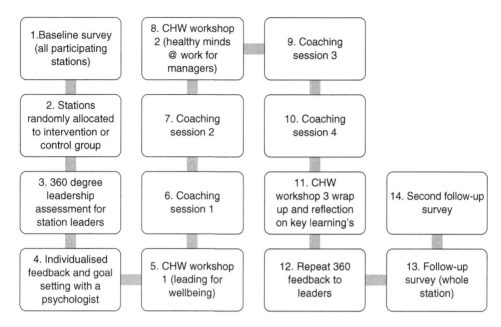

CHW = Creating Healthy Workplaces

Figure 20.2 Integrated intervention delivery strategy.

Note

CHW=creating healthy workplaces

	members (e.g. the skill/will model) and checking in on any actions taken since workshop 1.
Step 8	Senior sergeants and sergeants will attend CHW workshop 2 (Healthy Minds@Work for managers), which will be delivered by the Police Psychology Unit at Victoria Police. The workshop will continue to build leaders' supportive management skills, focusing, in particular, on how to manage mental health in the workplace (e.g. appropriately managing mental health-related under-performance and addressing suspected mental health concerns in the workplace, taking action to support members with a suspected mental health problem). Peer support officers will also be encouraged to attend this session.
Step 9–10	Sergeants will receive their third and fourth individual leadership-coaching sessions with their Peer Coach. Sessions will focus on any welfare-related conversations that have taken place since workshop 2, as well as follow up on progress towards their leadership goals.
Step 11	Senior sergeants and sergeants will engage in a half-day, wrap-up workshop focusing on key learnings that took place and progress made towards their goals. Sergeants will discuss how they can work together as a team to continue progress made towards programme goals and set 1–3 team goals (to be followed up and supported by the senior sergeants moving forward).
Step 12	The 360-degree assessment may be re-administered for those who request it.

Step 13–14   Two follow-up, station-level surveys will be implemented to assess change
              to baseline levels.

Other activities

Other ranks (all those below sergeant rank) will participate in a two-hour Healthy Minds@
Work foundation workshop. This workshop will address mental health and stress-related
stigma and provide tools for managing stress at work.

Junior members (those with less than five years service, including probationary
constables) will benefit from the more supportive leadership approach taken by their
'corro' ('correspondence') sergeant (formal supervision), more feedback, development and coaching from other senior members in the station (informal supervision),
and a greater number of supportive conversations with peer support officers. We
believe this whole of station, systems approach to improving workplace mental health
literacy will be more effective and sustainable than implementing individual-level
intervention activities (e.g. training for members) as is the status quo within Victoria
Police at present.

Feasibility, sustainability, and capacity building

Our approach has been designed with feasibility and sustainability in mind and with a
conscious effort to pass knowledge gained through the project on to those who could be
responsible for delivering the programme internally in the future.

Drawing on existing expertise and internal knowledge and resources

Our approach integrates our work with existing Victoria Police programmes. This will
ensure that our work adds unique value to the organisation, whilst still ensuring that the
approach is feasible and sustainable. Our long-term aim is for Victoria Police to have the
capacity, knowledge and resourcing to roll the programme out across the whole of the
organisation after the research project concludes.

Our strategy involves partnering closely with members of Victoria Police – namely,
the Welfare Services (peer support) and the Police Psychology Unit to roll out various
aspects of the intervention (i.e. The Healthy Minds@Work programme for managers and
for other rank members). These programmes were developed by Victoria Police and are
a new addition to their mental health strategy.

Building new capability

We ran a 'Coach-the-Peer Coach' training programme within Victoria Police alongside
the CHW programme. This programme involves us directly developing selected Victoria
Police staff members to play the role of 'coach' in delivery of the programme. Special care
has been taken to select members who have the right combination of factors needed to be
a Peer Coach (e.g. 'psychological mindedness', supportive, warm, other focused). These
members were hand selected by Welfare Services (the peer support coordinators) who
have direct knowledge of the members. All Peer Coaches are sworn members (sergeant
rank or above) who have already been trained (and served for an extensive period) as peer
support officers within the organisation.

Selected members were emailed directly by the head of the peer support programme and invited to attend a full day Coach-the-Coach workshop.

It was expected that members who attended the workshop would be able to perform the following actions by the end of the workshop:

1   explain the purpose of the Creating Healthy Workplaces (CHW) project to others
2   recognise the role that Peer Coaches will play in the CHW project
3   identify key differences between coaching and other styles
4   describe how coaching can be applied to develop supportive, healthy leaders and, in turn, reduce job stress and increase well-being in a policing context
5   identify several practical coaching tools and when, where, and how to use them
6   effectively apply various coaching skills as part of a structured (and unstructured) coaching process.

Thirty-two participants attended the workshop (approximately 16 sworn members and 16 members of the police psychology unit, police welfare, or peer support).

Communication strategy

A critical element of the programme is to secure high levels of support, commitment, and buy-in from all levels of the station and, in particular, senior members. Members will be more likely to 'buy-in' to the programme if they hear about the value of the programme from other members. As such, we will 'sell' the programme to each intervention station by tapping into 'champions' from previous CHW intervention sites. Champions from each new site will then help us to on board subsequent sites.

It will also be important to demonstrate to junior and other members that the programme is truly integrated – that is, that we are attempting to simultaneously improve their working conditions as well as how they handle stress and mental health issues. There are a number of elements to the full programme, and all members need to know that there are things being done in parallel (that they don't necessarily see), as well as what they are directly participating in.

Consultation with Victoria Police

We completed two pilot projects as part of our preparation for the current project. This involved: (1) piloting the leadership development and coaching aspects of the program; (2) assessing member mental health literacy needs; and (3) conducting a series of subject-matter expert interviews to ensure that the intervention logic was relevant and feasible.

Job stress prevention strategies in a policing environment: key learnings from the Creating Healthy Workplaces project

We implemented a pilot study in Victoria Police that looked at work-based strategies for preventing stress, funded by the Victorian Health Promotion Foundation (VicHealth).

Whilst a full review of this project is beyond the scope of this chapter, a summary is provided in Figures 20.3 and 20.4 respectively. This includes our programme logic, including prioritised stressors, stress prevention strategies, and desired outcomes, as well as the intervention process.

As described here, the aim of the CHW stress prevention pilot was to improve supervisor support and job control through a coaching-based leadership programme for sergeants. The programme was designed and implemented using participatory action research (PAR) principles. The programme addressed both work/organisational-level strategies (sergeant leadership coaching and the implementation of a new workload management system) with worker/individual-level (workload management training) activities. A novel feature of the programme was its coaching style of delivery to enable effective and sustained behaviour change. The model included:

- leadership assessment and feedback
- three, full-day workshops (start, middle and end of programme), and
- four individual leadership coaching sessions.

The individual coaching sessions were carried out by a member of our team who is a practicing organisational psychologist, in partnership with senior police members as 'trainee' coaches. The latter was included to allow for organisational capacity building.

Feedback from station command and external coaches was positive. Sergeants demonstrated the desired behaviour changes, including providing more regular and constructive feedback and putting a greater emphasis on developing junior members. Senior staff members have observed and reported high levels of commitment from the sergeants and a noticeable improvement in station morale. A comprehensive evaluation of the programme is currently underway.

In line with a PAR model, a number of programme improvements were made to the CHW programme in response to participant feedback. This resulted in high levels of engagement and buy-in from the group and a more effective delivery mode. Participants were particularly positive about the coaching-based methodology and flexible implementation style of the programme.

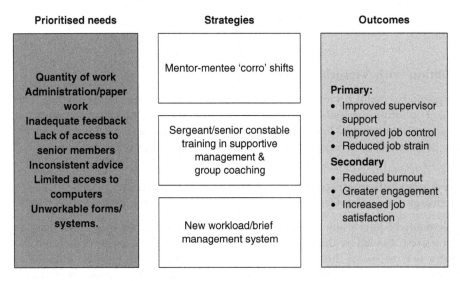

Figure 20.3 Creating health Workplaces Stress Prevention plot (funded by VicHealth): Program Logic.

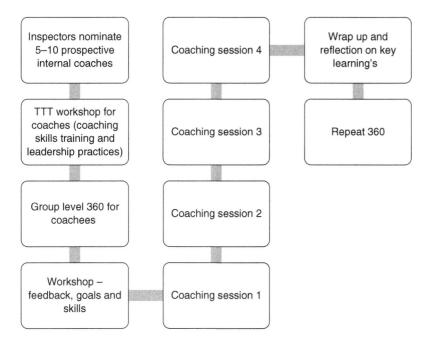

Figure 20.4 Creating health Workplaces Stress Prevention plot (funded by VicHealth): Intervention process.

Changes made to the programme

On the basis of feedback from participants themselves, junior members with the intervention station, and members of the delivery team, several changes were made to the programme:

1 Participating sergeants will receive an individualised 360-feedback session on their leadership style. The feedback will be provided by an organisational psychologist and will occur prior to the leadership development workshop. This will help sergeants to understand their strengths and development areas.

2 Each sergeant will receive and sign a coaching agreement prior to the first coaching session, which outlines our responsibilities to them and what their responsibilities are in the programme. This will help to hold leaders to greater account for behaviour change.

3 Each sergeant will draw on their 360-degree assessment feedback to form individual leadership goals and a leadership developmental action plan. Each sergeant will provide a current performance rating for each goal (a score out of ten). Their senior sergeant will also rate the sergeant's current performance against each leadership goal. This will help ensure that the senior sergeant understands and supports sergeant goal achievement.

4 Senior sergeants will attend the leadership workshop with their sergeant group (supporting point 3) to ensure that they understand the focus of the programme and can support the development of their sergeants.

5   The workshop material will remain largely the same. Minor changes are:

  a   Inclusion of an exercise in which each sergeant will share their feedback with their peers. We will then set up a buddy system (peer to peer) to ensure that peers give each other feedback more regularly and support each other. Buddies will be chosen on the basis of strengths and gaps where possible, so peers can learn from each other's strengths.

  b   Include group discussion on: What should good performance look in the station?' (i.e. ensure that performance expectations are aligned and promoted consistently). What do we want to be known for as a leadership group? What do we, as a leadership group, commit to doing to enable high performance and well-being of our station?

6   Only one coach will coach each sergeant. The coach will be a senior uniformed police member (senior sergeants or above), or a registered psychologist or member of the research team who has attended the Coach- the-Coach programme. Coaches will receive ongoing supervisor and support from an experienced coaching psychologist.

Identifying police member's mental health literacy needs

A complementary study was conducted to identify strategies for improving police member's mental health literacy. Five junior (probationary and confirmed and senior constables) and 13 senior (sergeant level and above) uniformed members were recruited to participate in semi-structured interviews. The interviews focused on mental health literacy, mental health needs, and strategies to address workplace mental health in Victoria Police. The interviews were recorded and transcribed. A qualitative thematic analysis was undertaken to identify key themes. The findings were combined with previous knowledge and understanding of Victoria Police as a work setting and incorporated into recommendations for an integrated approach. These key themes, findings, and recommendations were then presented to seven subject-matter experts (SMEs) for validation and feedback. Feedback from the SMEs on the feasibility and relevance of the recommendations was then incorporated into the proposed integrated approach.

Overall, it was found that senior members had better mental health literacy (knowledge, beliefs, and skills that help prevent workplace mental health problems and understanding of what to do for people affected by mental illness) than junior members. There was a significant level of stigma associated with mental health issues in a policing context, and inconsistent experiences of mental health first aid training. Most police members learned skills associated with helping people with mental health problems through life experience, rather than through formal training. Interviewees only felt comfortable approaching a small selection of their leaders to discuss mental health issues. Members preferred training via case studies, role play and other mediums, rather than online. Lastly, interviews identified the meaningfulness of their work and camaraderie with their work colleagues as positive and well-being-promoting aspects of their work with Victoria Police.

Consultation with subject matter experts

We consulted with seven subject-matter experts (SMEs) to test whether our intervention protocol is relevant, practical, and feasible for Victoria Police. SMEs were chosen on the basis of their expertise or relevant experience with one or more aspect of the intervention protocol. The seven experts included:

- a senior sergeant with an interest in staff welfare and peer support
- a senior occupational health and safety member
- a representative of the police psychology unit
- two inspectors with a significant staff welfare portfolio
- a senior peer support manager.
- an inspector with expertise in Sergeant and Senior Sergeant leadership training.

The SMEs confirmed and validated the results regarding mental health literacy within Victoria Police, including the suggestions made by members for how to address mental health literacy gaps in this context (e.g. role play and face-to-face contact rather than online training). They also offered constructive feedback and advice that enabled the intervention strategy to be refined and finalised in preparation for implementation in the upcoming NHMRC partnership project. In particular, the SMEs endorsed the integrated, station-by-station approach; the use and integration of both new and existing resources; and the coaching-based delivery method. They reiterated the importance of engaging early with station leadership and applying a consultative relationship management approach.

Conclusion

Whilst it is well recognised that improving workplace mental health is a critical organisational issue, approaches to date have tended to differ in focus. Job stress interventions have tended to focus on the primary and secondary intervention levels, whereas mental health literacy interventions have tended to focus on the secondary and tertiary levels, and the two have tended to operate independently (LaMontagne *et al.*, 2014). A fully integrated approach, such as that described here, brings these together to encompass primary, secondary, and tertiary interventions. The current chapter builds on previous work on workplace mental health interventions to detail an integrated approach to workplace mental health literacy in the policing sector. We reported on the results of a recent qualitative interview study at Victoria Police to identify mental health needs and integrated these findings with what we currently know about implementing job stress prevention strategies in this context. The resulting intervention takes a systems approach, specifying activities that can be implemented at the station, leadership, and individual level to simultaneously prevent job stress and promote mental health.

The intervention strategy will be implemented within Victoria Police using a randomised-controlled trial as part of our NHMRC partnership project, with the long- term aim of improving workplace mental health in this setting.

Acknowledgements

We continue to be grateful for the extensive support of Victoria Police. Particular thanks to Craig van Dugteren, Graham Wilson, and Dr Alexandra West, the Police Psychology Unit and the Peer Support Unit. The Victorian Health Promotion Foundation (VicHealth) funded a key component of the integrated approach to workplace mental health literacy (Creating Healthy Workplaces: Stress Prevention Pilot, 2011–2014). This project forms part of a larger National Health and Medical Research Council (NHMRC) Partnership Project with Victoria Police, WorkSafe and VicHealth (APP#1055333).

Notes

1 NHMRC partnership project with Victoria Police, WorkSafe and VicHealth (2013–2015), led by CIA LaMontagne and others.
2 Coaches will be sworn Victoria Police members (sergeant rank and above), a registered psychologist, or a member of Faculty who has completed our Coach-the-Peer-Coach training programme.
3 This study will form part of a companion paper.

References

AIHW. (2010). *Australia's health 2010. Cat. no. AUS 122.* Canberra: Australian Institute of Health and Welfare.

Amaranto, E., Steinberg, J., Castellano, C., and Mitchell, R. (2003). Police Stress Interventions *Brief Treatment and Crisis Intervention, 3*(1), 47–54.

Bambra, C., Gibson, M., Sowden, A. J., Wright, K., Whitehead, M., and Petticrew, M. (2009). Working for health? Evidence from systematic reviews on the effects on health and health inequalities of organisational changes to the psychosocial work environment. *Prev Med, 48*(5), 454–461.

Barry, M. M. and Jenkins, R. (2007). Promotion mental health in the workplace. In M. M. Barry and R. Jenkins (eds.), *Implementing mental health promotion* (pp. 215–253). Philadelphia: Churchill Livingston.

Begg, S., Vos, T., Barker, B., Stevenson, C., Stanley, L., and Lopez, A. D. (2007). *The burden of disease and injury in Australia 2003.*

Bonde, J. P. (2008). Psychosocial factors at work and risk of depression: A systematic review of the epidemiological evidence. *Occup Environ Med, 65*(7), 438–445.

Brown, J. M. and Campbell, E. A. (1990). Sources of occupational stress in the police. *Work Stress, 4*(4), 305–318.

Collins, P. A. and Gibbs, A. C. C. (2003). Stress in police officers: A study of the origins, prevalence and severity of stress-related symptoms within a county police force. *Occupational Medicine, 53*(4), 256–264.

Gershon, R. R. M., Barocas, B., Canton, A. N., Xianbin Li, and Vlahov, D. (2009). Mental, physical, and behavioral outcomes associated with perceived work stress in police officers. *Criminal Justice and Behavior, 36*(3), 275–289.

Hall, G. B., Dollard, M. F., Tuckey, M. R., Winefield, A. H., and Thompson, B. M. (2010). Job demands, work–family conflict, and emotional exhaustion in police officers: A longitudinal test of competing theories. *Journal of Occupational and Organizational Psychology, 83*(1), 237–250.

Johnson, S., Cooper, C., Cartwright, S., Donald, I., Taylor, P., and Millet, C. (2005). The experience of work-related stress across occupations. *Journal of managerial psychology, 20*(2), 178–187.

Jorm, A. F. (2012). Mental health literacy: Empowering the community to take action for better mental health. *American Psychologist, 67*(3), 231–243.

Jorm, A. F., Kitchener, B. A., Sawyer, M. G., Scales, H., and Cvetkovski, S. (2010). Mental health first aid training for high school teachers: A cluster randomized trial. *BMC Psychiatry, 10*(51), 2–12.

Kitchener, B. A. and Jorm, A. F. (2004). Mental health first aid training in a workplace setting: A randomized controlled trial [ISRCTN13249129]. *BMC Psychiatry, 4*(1), 23.

Kitchener, B. A. and Jorm, A. F. (2006). Mental health first aid training: Review of evaluation studies. *Australian New Zealand Journal of Psychiatry, 40*(1), 6–8.

Kop, N. and Euwema, M. (2001). Occupational stress and the use of force by Dutch police. *Criminal Justice and Behavior, 28*(5), 631–652.

Kop, N., Euwema, M., and Schaufeli, W. (1999). Burnout, job stress and violent behaviour among Dutch police officers. *Work & Stress, 13*(4), 326–340.

LaMontagne, A. D., Keegel, T., Shann, C., & DeSouza, R. (2014) An integrated approach to workplace mental health: An Australian feasibility study. International Journal of Mental Health Promotion, 16, 205-215.

LaMontagne, A. D., Keegel, T., Louie, A. M., and Ostry, A. (2010). Job stress as a preventable upstream determinant of common mental disorders: A review for practitioners and policy-makers. *Advances in Mental Health*, 9(1), 17–35.

LaMontagne, A. D., Keegel, T., Louie, A. M., Ostry, A., and Landsbergis, P. A. (2007). A systematic review of the job stress intervention evaluation literature: 1990–2005. *International Journal of Occupational & Environmental Health*, 13(3), 268–280.

LaMontagne, A. D., Keegel, T., Vallance, D. A., Ostry, A., and Wolfe, R. (2008). Job strain–attributable depression in a sample of working Australians: Assessing the contribution to health inequalities. *BMC Public Health*, 27(8), 181–190.

LaMontagne, A. D., Noblet, A. J., and Landsbergis, P. A. (2012). Intervention development and implementation: Understanding and addressing barriers to organizational-level interventions. In C. Biron, M. Karanika-Murray, and C. L. Cooper (eds.), *Improving Organizational Interventions for Stress and Well-Being: Addressing Process and Context* (pp. 21–38). London: Routledge/Psychology Press.

LaMontagne, A. D., Sanderson, K., and Cocker, F. (2010). *Estimating the economic benefits of eliminating job strain as a risk factor for depression.* Retrieved on 20 November 2015. from www.vichealth.vic.gov.au/jobstrain.

Loo, R. (2003). A meta-analysis of police suicide rates: Findings and issues. *Suicide and Life-Threatening Behavior*, 33(3), 313–325.

Martin, A., Sanderson, K., and Cocker, F. (2009). Meta-analysis of the effects of health promotion intervention in the workplace on depression and anxiety symptoms. *Scand J Work Environ Health*, 35(1), 7–18.

Martin, A., Sanderson, K., Scott, J., and Brough, P. (2009). Promoting mental health in small–medium enterprises: An evaluation of the "Business in Mind" program. *BMC Public Health*, 9(1), 239–247.

Mathers, C., Vos, T., and Stevenson, C. (1999). *The burden of disease and injury in Australia.* Canberra: AIHW.

Noblet, A. and LaMontagne, A. D. (2006). The role of workplace health promotion in addressing job stress. *Health Promot Int*, 21(4), 346–353.

Noblet, A., Rodwell, J., and Allisey, A. F. (2009). Job stress in the law enforcement sector: Comparing the linear, non-linear and interaction effects of working conditions. *Stress and Health*, 25, 111–120.

Noblet, A. J., Rodwell, J. J., and Allisey, A. F. (2009). Police stress: The role of the psychological contract and perceptions of fairness. *Policing: An International Journal of Police Strategies & Management*, 32(4), 613–630.

Patterson, G. T., Chung, I. W., and Swan, P. G. (2012). The effects of stress management interventions among police officers and recruits. *Campbell Systematic Reviews*, 7, 1–53.

Penalba, V. and Leite, J. R. (2006). Psychosocial interventions for prevention of psychological disorders in law enforcement officers (Protocol). *Cochrane Database of Systematic Reviews*, 1, No: CD005601.

Sanderson, K. and Andrews, G. (2006). Common mental disorders in the workforce: Recent findings from descriptive and social epidemiology. *Canadian Journal of Psychiatry*, 51(2), 63–75.

Stansfeld, S. A. and Candy, B. (2006). Psychosocial work environment and mental health – a meta-analytic review. *Scandinavian Journal of Work Environment and Health*, 32(6), 443–462.

Waters, J. A. and William, U. (2007). Police stress: History, contributing factors, symptoms, and interventions. *Policing: An International Journal of Police Strategies & Management*, 30(2), 169–188.

Index

Printed in the United States
by Baker & Taylor Publisher Services